Windows® XP
Power Tools

Jim Boyce

SYBEX

San Francisco · London

Associate Publisher: Joel Fugazzatto

Acquisitions and Developmental Editor: Ellen L. Dendy

Editors: Pete Gaughan, Pat Coleman

Production Editor: Erica Yee

Technical Editor: Michael L. Williams

Graphic Illustrator: Jeff Wilson, Happenstance Type-O-Rama

Electronic Publishing Specialist: Maureen Forys, Happenstance Type-O-Rama

Proofreaders: Laurie O'Connell, Dave Nash, Yariv Rabinovitch, Nancy Riddiough, Abigail Sawyer

Indexer: Ted Laux

CD Coordinator: Dan Mummert

CD Technician: Kevin Ly

Cover Design: Richard Miller, Calyx Design

Cover Illustration: Richard Miller, Calyx Design

Library of Congress Card Number: 2002103168

ISBN: 0-7821-4067-X

For Bud, who always fights the good fight.

Acknowledgments

This was my first book for Sybex, but it was definitely a great experience, thanks to the hard work of everyone involved. I'd first like to thank Jordan Gold and Joel Fugazzatto for the opportunity to do this book for Sybex. Ellen Dendy did a great job of bringing the project on line and putting together all of the pieces of the puzzle, and I really appreciate her efforts in helping with the CD content.

Many thanks also to Pete Gaughan, Pat Coleman, and Erica Yee, who did a superb job of fine-tuning the book's content. Great editors make a good book even better. A special thanks to Michael Williams, who did a very thorough review and suggested several excellent additions.

I also want to thank all of the folks who had a hand in developing the book design and laying out the finished product. They work behind the scenes but are not forgotten!

Finally, I offer a special thanks to Guy Hart-Davis, Kate Chase, and Brian Culp for their contributions to the book's content. It's always a pleasure to work with such talented co-authors!

Contents at a Glance

Contents

Introduction

Windows XP builds on the many core changes in Windows 2000, adding several very useful features and simplifying (in most cases, anyway) the Windows environment. Features like Remote Desktop extend the functionality of the operating system, while numerous other changes make it easier to use. Other new features add core capabilities such as CD recording, eliminating the need for some third-party applications.

Windows XP Professional is targeted primarily at business users; Windows XP Home Edition is targeted at home users but can be a useful and less expensive alternative for small offices that don't need some of the more advanced features offered by Professional.

Whichever edition you choose, *Windows XP Power Tools* will help you make the most of your new Windows operating system. This book focuses on the techniques and tricks that will let you implement advanced features and bend Windows XP to your will. I also cover many of the excellent third-party applications that extend or enhance Windows XP's features. The *Windows XP Power Tools CD* contains more than 40 of these applications and scripts.

Who Is This Book For?

Windows XP Power Tools is geared to the intermediate to advanced user who is comfortable using Windows and wants to know how to make every day tasks easier to accomplish and how to implement many of Windows XP's advanced features. For example, *Windows XP Power Tools* not only explains how to host a website under Windows XP Professional, but also how to run CGI applications on the computer, serve up files with FTP, and create a site that submits information using e-mail. Most of the topics in the book are appropriate for both home and business users.

To get the most from this book, you should be comfortable using a computer and be familiar with general Windows concepts such as using applications, working with folders and windows, and using the mouse. You don't need to have a degree in computer science or even know how your computer works behind the scenes. In every case I'll tell you how to quickly and easily implement the features discussed in the book.

What Does This Book Cover?

Windows XP Power Tools is divided into nine parts that cover specific groups of tasks. Part I, "Windows XP Overview, Installation, and Startup," covers a variety of topics related to installation and setup. It starts with an overview of the new features in Windows XP, then covers several methods and options for performing stand-alone and distributed installations. If you're looking for tips on using more than one operating system, you'll find pointers and techniques in Part I, as well as some very useful third-party applications that make it much easier to support multiple operating systems. Part I ends with a look at the many ways you can control Windows XP startup and shutdown.

Part II, "Running and Customizing Windows XP," offers advice on ways to improve your day-to-day work experience in XP. It includes chapters that cover customizing the XP interface, shortcuts for working in Windows, tips for printing, useful command-line tools, and how to use and customize the new Windows XP help system.

Part III, "Managing the System and Applications," will help you with the many setup, configuration, and management tasks you'll face on a regular basis. Chapters in Part III cover application installation and tuning, adding and removing Windows XP components, using management consoles, auditing and performance monitoring, and how to manage disk space with quotas.

Part IV, "Hardware," is the place to go for tips and tools that will help you install, configure, and manage hardware. These chapters offer tips on how the Registry works and how to perform some nifty tricks in the Registry, how to install and manage hardware and drivers, and how to choose and manage a file system.

In Part V, "Communications and Networking," you'll find lots of useful tips and tools for configuring and maximizing Internet and network connections, optimizing TCP/IP, troubleshooting and monitoring network connections, and turning your computer into a server for incoming connections. Part V also covers ways to use Windows XP remotely, such as Remote Desktop and third-party utilities such as VNC and pcAnywhere.

If you use the Internet or bundled communications applications such as Outlook Express (and I'm sure you do), turn to Part VI, "Internet Applications and Services," for tips on how to optimize the Internet apps included with Windows XP. Part VI also explains how to make the most of Internet Information Services (IIS) for hosting web and FTP sites, and how to set up a Telnet server. Throughout each chapter, I point out useful third-party tools that extend Windows XP's capabilities.

Part VII, "Managing Users," does much more than just explain how to create and manage user accounts and groups. You'll find extensive discussion of group and local policies, with lots of advice on techniques and policies you can use to apply restrictions and effectively manage users' data for easy recoverability and network roaming.

Part VIII, "Backup and Disaster Recovery," is one section I hope you never have to use, but which sooner or later you're bound to need. It covers the methods in Windows XP that you can use to back up and restore a system.

I round out the book with Part IX, "Security," which covers many of the security-related features in Windows XP. Part IX explains how to manage certificates, encrypt files for security, and set up a secure connection between computers with IPSec. The final chapter covers virtual private networking (VPN) solutions.

I've included four bonus chapters on the companion CD. One discusses the many security configuration tools included with Windows XP. The others are in the area of automating your computing environment; these chapters cover batch programming, using command history and Doskey, and scheduling applications.

And finally, I've made some additional content available on the Sybex website. These web bonus chapters cover the Indexing Service, the SMTP service, and desktop conferencing and chat applications. You can access these bonus chapters by going to www.sybex.com and calling up the *Windows XP Power Tools* page.

Conventions Used in This Book

The following icons indicate helpful tips and warnings. They're flagged to get your attention, and are usually worth reading for that very reason!

TIP   Tips include time-saving information to help you make your PHP scripting easier, faster, and more effective.

SEE ALSO   See Alsos direct you to other parts of the book for more information or related topics.

NOTE   Notes go into more detail on related topics or provide extra resources you can refer to.

WARNING   Warnings flag potential trouble spots (or potential sources of trouble, anyway). Ignore them at your own risk!

The CD icon in the margin is your signal that the companion CD-ROM includes a copy of the software mentioned in the text. For more information about what's available there, see the What's On The CD sheet next to the CD insert.

The book also uses some text conventions to make it more readable. Any code elements—filenames, paths, code lines from configuration files, URLs, and more—are shown in this font. And anything that you should actually, literally type is shown **in bold font**.

How to Contact the Author

I always welcome comments, suggestions, and tips from my readers. I invite you to visit my website at www.boyce.ws, where you'll find lots of additional tips, sample chapters from other books, and of course, contact information.

PART I

Windows XP Overview, Installation, and Startup

CHAPTER 1

What's New in Windows XP?

Windows XP suffers somewhat from a dual personality. In some ways it is a significant release, but in others it is more a maintenance release of Windows 2000. For that reason, Windows 2000 users will not see major changes other than the interface, although there are numerous changes under the hood that improve Windows' performance and functionality.

For Windows 9*x*, Me, and NT users, Windows XP is a significant change. Not only is the interface considerably different, but the underlying core operating system is completely changed, with several core features either new or improved. The biggest transition is for users migrating from Windows 9*x* and Me to Windows XP—the additional security features, file system options, and management features in XP make it a distinct shift.

This chapter explores the new and changed features in Windows XP. In addition to an exhaustive feature list, I've included sections that will help users of specific Windows platforms get up to speed quickly on Windows XP's features and function.

Major Differences between Home Edition and Professional

Windows XP is available in two versions: Home Edition and Professional. Many of the features are the same from one to the other, and both have the same look and feel. Because it is targeted at business users, Professional includes features not really necessary for home users, such as added security, centralized administration, and remote access. The following sections provide a brief overview of the features included in the Professional version that are not available in Home Edition.

Access Control

When sharing a folder under all Windows operating systems, including Windows XP, you can specify *share permissions* that control the level of access that users have to the folder across the network. For example, you might grant users the ability to read the contents of a folder but not to write to it. Both Professional and Home Edition offer the ability to share folders and set share permissions to control access.

Windows XP Professional adds the ability to apply *access control lists*, or ACLs, to a folder. An ACL is a set of specific access permissions for a folder granted to specific users or groups. For example, you might grant one group of users the ability to read the contents of a folder and grant another group full control over the contents, including the ability to modify and delete items. Figure 1.1 shows the Security tab of a folder's properties, which you use to configure permissions on the folder.

FIGURE 1.1:

Use the Security tab to specify permissions for a folder.

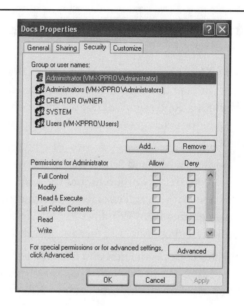

TIP   You can apply permissions on a folder or file only on NTFS volumes. FAT volumes support sharing permissions but do not allow you to assign permissions for folders or files.

Permissions you set through ACLs apply for both local and network access. For example, if you don't have permission to read a folder, you will be unable to read the folder even if you log on locally to that computer.

SEE ALSO   For more information on setting sharing security, see Chapter 25.

Centralized Administration

Windows XP Professional systems can function as stand-alone computers, as members of a workgroup, or in a domain served by Windows NT Server, 2000 Server, or .NET Server domain controllers. Windows XP Home Edition computers can function as stand-alone computers or as members of a workgroup but do not support domain membership. Domains provide several centralized administrative features, with *centralized security* being one of the most important of those features. Centralized security refers to the ability to control access to resources on multiple systems across the network with a single set of user credentials (account and password.)

Domains also provide other important capabilities, including the abilities to remotely manage systems and to enforce restrictions and other system properties through group policy.

SEE ALSO   For more information on group policies, see Chapter 42.

Encrypting File System

Encrypting File System (EFS) is a core component of Windows XP Professional that is not available in Home Edition. EFS allows users to encrypt folders and files to prevent others from being able to read those files. EFS can be an important tool for protecting data on systems that are susceptible to compromise, such as notebook computers that could be lost or stolen. EFS is also useful for protecting data on removable media.

SEE ALSO   For a detailed discussion of EFS, see Chapter 49.

It's easy to encrypt a folder or file in Windows XP: You simply select a check box in the folder's or file's properties as shown in Figure 1.2. Windows XP takes care of the encryption and decryption process automatically. However, you should implement an EFS recovery policy, as explained in detail in Chapter 51, to ensure your ability to recover encrypted files if the encryption certificate becomes corrupted or is lost.

FIGURE 1.2:
You can easily encrypt a folder or file through a single check box in its properties.

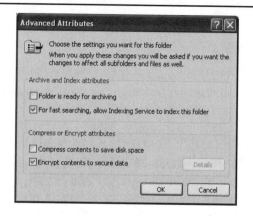

Group and Local Policies

Group policy is another feature supported by Windows XP Professional that is not supported by Windows XP Home Edition. Group and local policies allow a broad range of properties and restrictions to be applied to Windows XP for a specific computer or user. For example, an administrator can use group policy to redirect a user's My Documents folder to a network server, so that the folder is always available regardless of the user's logon location and can be easily backed up.

Group policy has much broader implications than just managing a user's data, however. It provides a means for *change control*, which is the ability to regulate the changes that users can make to their systems and Windows environment. Group policy is also the mechanism through which technologies such as Remote Installation Services (RIS) and IntelliMirror allow administrators to automatically deploy operating systems and applications to computers across the enterprise.

NOTE   Group policies rely on Windows 2000 or .NET domain controllers and domain membership. You can apply local policies to Windows XP Professional computers in a domain, workgroup, or stand-alone configuration.

SEE ALSO   For a complete discussion of group and local policies and their implications, see Chapter 42.

Multilingual User Interface Add-On

Windows XP is currently available in 24 localized versions in addition to English. Localization provides menus, dialog boxes, and other elements in a specific language. The Multilingual User Interface Pack is an add-on for Windows XP Professional that allows administrators to switch the user interface elements such as menus, dialog boxes, and Help files into a different language. For more information on this add-on, see www.microsoft.com/WINDOWSXP/pro/techinfo/planning/multilingual/default.asp

Offline Files

Windows XP Professional includes a feature called Offline Files, which allows users to continue to work with network resources even when those resources are unavailable or they are disconnected from the network. For example, assume a server in your network provides access to a set of common documents that you need to use on a regular basis. Most of the time you're in the office and connected to the network, which means the documents are available from the server. Occasionally, however, you need to use your notebook while out of the office and still work with those documents. With offline folders, Windows XP creates a local copy of the offline resource on your computer and allows you to work with the resource there rather than from its network location. XP makes the transition between online and offline use transparent to the user and provides the mechanism to automatically synchronize changes when the network resource again becomes available.

> **TIP** You can't use offline files on a system that has Fast User Switching enabled. Configure Fast User Switching through the option "Change the way users log on or off" in the User Accounts object in the Control Panel.

You enable Offline Files for a particular folder through the Offline Files tab of the folder's properties (see Figure 1.3).

FIGURE 1.3:

Enable Offline Files through the Folder Options dialog box.

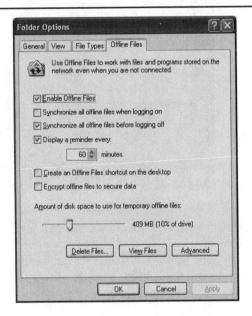

Remote Desktop

Remote Desktop allows you to work with a Windows XP Professional computer from a remote location. For example, you might use Remote Desktop to connect from your home computer to your office computer, in order to access files, printers, or other resources, working with your office PC as if you were physically in the office. You can also use the client portion of Remote Desktop to connect to a Windows 2000 or .NET Terminal Server.

Windows XP Home Edition includes the client portion of Remote Desktop, enabling you to connect to a Windows XP Professional computer that is configured to allow access to Remote Desktop users (Figure 1.4), or to a Terminal Server. You can't connect to a Windows XP Home Edition computer through Remote Desktop—Home Edition doesn't include the server-side components of Remote Desktop.

FIGURE 1.4:
Use Remote Desktop
to connect to and use
a system remotely.

TIP   A handful of third-party applications, such as pcAnywhere and Unicenter Remote Control, provide capabilities similar to Remote Desktop for remote access and control. These third-party apps typically provide expanded functionality, such as the ability to allow the local user to continue working while the remote session is active.

SEE ALSO   For more information on Remote Desktop and its alternatives, see Chapter 31.

Remote Installation Services

Windows XP Professional includes support for Remote Installation Services (RIS), which allows Windows 2000 and XP to be installed on a computer remotely. In a typical RIS deployment, the computer boots from a PXE-compliant network adapter, which allows it to submit a request to a RIS server for service. (PXE stands for Preboot Execution Environment, an open industry standard that allows the system to boot directly from a PXE-compliant network card to initiate an operating system installation or repair.) The RIS server provides the client computer with OS installation options based on the computer's membership in Active Directory. After the user selects the OS options to install, RIS installs the operating system across the network. A system that does not include a PXE-compliant network adapter can use a special boot disk created by RIS to allow it to communicate with available RIS servers at boot.

TIP   RIS relies on the Active Directory and therefore requires domain membership. Windows XP Home Edition systems do not support RIS.

RIS is primarily a server-side feature requiring either Windows 2000 Server or .NET Server, and must be configured and managed by a system administrator. For that reason, RIS is not covered except in passing in this book.

SEE ALSO   For a detailed discussion of RIS, see *Mastering Windows 2000 Server* by Mark Minasi (Sybex, 2002).

Roaming User Profiles

A *user profile* is a collection of folders and data that make up the majority of a user's working environment. A user's profile includes the My Documents folder, Start menu, Desktop, and other folders. On stand-alone computers and in many network installations, the user profile resides on the local computer. The disadvantage to this is that when you log on from another computer, you don't receive the same desktop settings, documents, or other environment settings as when you log on from your primary workstation. A *roaming* profile overcomes that disadvantage by storing your profile on a network server and copying it to the current logon location. This means that you have the same Desktop, documents, and settings regardless of where you log on—in other words, your working environment follows you around the network.

Folder Redirection Complements Roaming Profiles

As explained in Chapter 44, you can redirect folders from the default profile location to a network server. For example, you might redirect My Documents to a folder on the server. When the user logs on and opens the My Documents folder, he sees the files stored in his folder on the network server, rather than the My Documents folder that would otherwise be stored on his local computer. Redirecting folders in this way helps ensure that the user's documents are always available regardless of logon location. In some ways this might seem to be exactly what roaming profiles achieve. However, folder redirection and roaming profiles are different.

If a user had a roaming profile without folder redirection, the folder would be copied from the server where the profile is stored to the user's local computer at logon. With folder redirection, the folder remains on the server, and the user's computer is redirected to the server when she opens the folder. Folder redirection therefore complements roaming profiles and reduces the amount of data that must be copied across the network during logon.

Scalable Processor Support

Windows XP Home Edition supports a single processor. Windows XP Professional supports up to two processors to provide better performance.

Software Installation and Maintenance

Windows 2000 introduced a featured called IntelliMirror, which is an umbrella term for a selection of technologies. Windows XP Professional also includes support for IntelliMirror. One of the major purposes for IntelliMirror is to allow applications to be installed, updated, and managed automatically. When a user logs on, group policy and Active Directory membership determine which applications should be installed on the user's computer and which should be made available as an option. Applications that are *assigned* through IntelliMirror appear as if they are already installed on the user's computer. Attempting to start the application causes it to be installed automatically across the network. Applications that are *published* through IntelliMirror are available for installation but not installed automatically. Instead, the user can add these applications through the Add Or Remove Programs object in Control Panel.

Most aspects of IntelliMirror are primarily server-side features and are configured and managed at the server level. For that reason, software installation and maintenance are covered only in passing in this book.

SEE ALSO   For more information on IntelliMirror and automated application deployment, see *Windows 2000 Group Policy, Profiles, and IntelliMirror* by Jeremy Moskowitz and *Windows 2000 Automated Deployment and Remote Administration* by Christa Anderson (both Sybex, 2001).

Major Differences for Windows 9x and Me Users

Everyone who switches to Windows XP from another Windows platform will see the obvious differences in the interface. Users who switch from Windows 9x and Windows Me will see certain core differences in Windows XP.

Security

The primary difference is in security. Windows XP builds on the Windows NT security model, which requires an existing user account in order to log on to the system. You can log on with a local account or, in the case of Windows XP Professional, a domain account. Windows 9x and Me systems, by contrast, allow you to bypass logon and access the system by simply pressing Esc when prompted to log on. Or, you can enter a new account name and password at logon to create a new user profile. Both pose a potential security risk, as anyone can gain local access to a Windows 9x or Me computer.

During a new installation, Windows XP creates an Administrator account (which appears on Home Edition systems as Owner) that gives you full control over the computer, including the ability to add other local accounts as needed. During an upgrade from Windows 9x or Me, Windows XP converts any existing user profiles on the computer to local accounts, in addition to creating the Administrator account. (Windows XP does not assign passwords by default to accounts, which means anyone can log on to a computer by simply selecting the desired account from the logon dialog. You can configure Windows to require passwords, if desired.)

SEE ALSO   For more information on managing user accounts, see Chapter 41.

Requiring an account to log on is an important step in protecting a system but by no means offers high security. For example, you might share your computer with another user. It's possible for that user to log on to your computer and view your documents and other data unless you protect those resources. The NTFS file system and access control lists (ACLs) are the mechanism by which you provide that protection. Windows 9x and Me systems provide support for FAT file systems but not NTFS. Unlike FAT (including variations such as FAT16 and FAT32), NTFS gives you the ability to set permissions on a per-folder and per-file basis to specify the level of access that a particular group or user has to a specific item.

SEE ALSO   For a detailed discussion of NTFS, see Chapter 25.

Multiuser Support and Remote Desktop Connection

Another important difference between Windows XP and 9x/Me is in XP's multiuser support. On 9x/Me systems, only one user can log on at a time. Both Windows XP Professional and Home Edition include a new feature called Fast User Switching, which allows a user's session to be disconnected without shutting down applications or closing documents. This allows another user to work on the computer without requiring that the first user close all applications and documents and log off. In addition, Windows XP Professional allows others to connect to the computer remotely using Remote Desktop. A Remote Desktop connection is treated like a fast user switch: the current local user, if any, is disconnected to allow the remote user to connect. Windows XP prompts the local user whether to allow or deny the connection.

NOTE   Terminal Services, available in Windows server platforms such as Windows 2000 Server and Windows .NET Server, allows multiple concurrent connections. Multiple users can have sessions open at one time on a Terminal Services server.

SEE ALSO   For information on fast user switching, see Chapter 41. For detailed information on configuring and using Remote Desktop, see Chapter 31.

Support for Group Policies

The other primary difference from 9*x*/Me systems in Windows XP Professional is support for group policies, which were introduced in Windows 2000. Group policies allow change control and other configuration to be applied to a system automatically based on computer and/or user membership in Active Directory domains, providing a means for administrators to centrally manage systems and users. As a Windows XP Professional user, you won't deal directly with group policies in most cases but will simply see their effects in such things as automatic application installation and restrictions on the changes you can make to your computer. However, you can configure many properties through local policies (Figure 1.5).

FIGURE 1.5:

You can configure many policies locally as well as at the site, domain, or OU level.

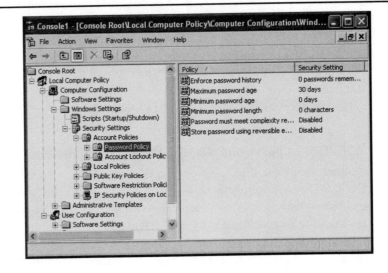

SEE ALSO   For a detailed discussion of group and local policies, see Chapter 42.

There are numerous other differences between 9*x*/Me systems and Windows XP, including changes in accessory applications such as Internet Explorer, Paint, and Fax. However, the features I've discussed are the primary core differences that will have the most impact on how you work in Windows.

Major Differences for Windows NT and 2000 Users

Most Windows NT and Windows 2000 users are familiar with user accounts and with security features such as NTFS permissions. If you are migrating from either of these platforms to Windows XP, you'll find that the user interface and wealth of new accessory applications and capabilities are the most striking differences. Remote Desktop, discussed earlier in this chapter, is a good example of a Windows XP feature not available in Windows NT or 2000. Under the hood, however, Windows XP is very similar to both platforms because they all share a common code base.

The primary core difference that Windows NT users will see is a vast improvement in hardware support. For example, Windows XP supports USB and other technologies not supported by Windows NT (Figure 1.6). This feature alone can make it worthwhile to upgrade from Windows NT.

FIGURE 1.6:

Windows XP provides Plug and Play support and expanded support for new technologies.

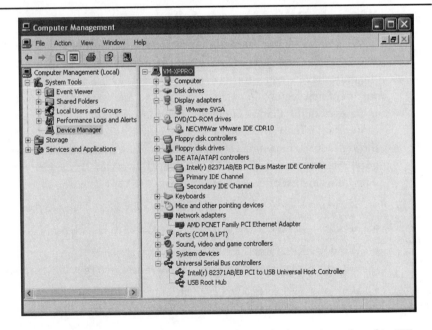

Another major change for Windows NT users is NTFS 5, which was introduced in Windows 2000 and carries over to Windows XP. One of main changes in NTFS 5 is the introduction of *junction points*. You can think of a junction point as a sort of flag in the file system that directs Windows XP to pass off processing to a file system driver other than the NTFS driver. An example of a feature made possible by junction points is the Encrypting File System (EFS). As the NTFS driver is reading a file and comes to a junction point indicating the file is encrypted, it passes the process to the EFS subsystem to process. Volume mount points are another example. This feature allows you to mount a volume into an empty NTFS folder on another volume. To the local system and to users across the network, the mounted volume appears as a folder under the host volume.

TIP   When you install Windows XP on a Windows NT system, Setup converts existing NTFS volumes to NTFS 5.

Just as they are for 9x/Me users, group policies and the features they make possible (explained in the previous section) are another core difference for Windows NT users. System policies in Windows NT offer some of the functionality of group policies, but with considerably less flexibility and power.

Where to Go for More Details

The features discussed throughout this chapter are some of the core features in Windows XP that are either new or improved over previous Windows platforms. These are by no means the only changes and improvements, however. There are significant interface changes, a wealth of new features for remote access and management, improved recoverability, additional system installation and update options, firewalls and other security features, and much more. Rather than cover all these changes in this one chapter, I've opted to describe them throughout the remainder of the book to put them in context. However, there are several good references available to help you get an overview of the new features in Windows XP. The following list offers several sources:

- *Mastering Windows XP Home Edition* by Guy Hart-Davis (Sybex, 2001)
- *Mastering Windows XP Professional* by Mark Minasi (Sybex, 2001)
- Windows XP Home Edition evaluation web page:
  www.microsoft.com/windowsxp/home/evaluation/features.asp
- Windows XP Professional evaluation web page:
  www.microsoft.com/windowsxp/pro/evaluation/features.asp

CHAPTER 2

Stand-Alone Installations

There isn't much to the actual installation process for Windows XP—in most cases you pop in the CD, answer a few easy questions, and sit back for half an hour or so while Setup installs and configures the operating system. Usually, the whole process completes without a hitch. This is true for both clean installs and upgrades.

Getting to the point where you insert that CD is the trick, however. You need to consider several issues before you even obtain a copy of Windows XP, much less install it. Do you have enough disk space? What applications will be compatible and which will cause problems? Should you clone your existing operating system so you can revert to it quickly if Windows XP doesn't live up to your expectations? Not least of all, what is Windows Product Activation and how is it going to affect you?

This chapter answers these questions, and others. I won't cover the actual installation process except in passing, because there really isn't much to it. Instead, I'll focus on your upgrade options, getting your system ready for Windows XP, and what to expect after it's installed. You'll also find several tips on ways to improve and simplify the installation process, as well as update the system.

Understanding Upgrade Options

Upgrading a system gives you a handful of key advantages over installing a clean copy of the operating system. First and perhaps foremost, you don't have to reinstall all of your applications. This can save you a lot of time in the installation process. Performing an upgrade also reduces—to some degree at least—the chance that you might lose data during the process. For example, assume you decide to format your hard disk and install a clean copy of Windows XP, then reinstall all of your applications. You need to back up all of your documents and other data before the installation, and then restore it afterwards. Can you be sure you've backed up all the right information? Are you sure you can restore it where it needs to be? How easy will it be to import the data from the backup location?

While you should certainly back up your crucial documents and other data before performing an upgrade to Windows XP, it's less likely that a problem will occur during the upgrade that will adversely affect that data. There's a better chance that you will *introduce* a problem while trying to backup and restore your data. So, performing an upgrade rather than a clean install is not only a lot less work, it's also somewhat safer.

You can upgrade most versions of Windows to Windows XP. Table 2.1 shows the upgrade path for all versions.

TABLE 2.1: Windows XP Upgrade Options

Existing OS	Windows XP Home Edition	Windows XP Professional
Windows 3.1	No	No
Windows 95	No	No
Windows 98	Yes	Yes
Windows 98 SE	Yes	Yes
Windows Me	Yes	Yes
Windows NT 3.51	No	No
Windows NT Workstation 4.0	No	Yes
Windows 2000 Professional	No	Yes
Windows XP Home Edition	N/A	Yes
Windows XP Professional	No	N/A
All server platforms	No	No
All evaluation versions	No	No

As the table indicates, you can't upgrade Windows 3.1, Windows NT 3.51, or Windows 95 systems to Windows XP. Instead, you'll need to perform a clean installation on these systems. Even so, there are still some steps you can take on these systems to simplify the migration to Windows XP. See the section "Migrating Applications Manually," later in this chapter, for details.

You'll also note from Table 2.1 that you can't upgrade any evaluation or server platform to Windows XP. For example, you can't upgrade Windows NT Server 4.0 to Windows XP Professional. This isn't generally a drawback, however, because it's unlikely you'll want to replace a server operating system with a workstation version. Also, note that you can upgrade from Windows XP Home Edition to Windows XP Professional. So, if you install Home Edition today and later decide you need the features in Professional, you have an easy migration path.

Analyzing and Prepping the System

There are several steps you should perform before you install Windows XP on a system. This section explains the steps you should take and what tools are available to help you prepare your system(s) for Windows XP.

SEE ALSO   This chapter is targeted at single, local Windows XP installations. See Chapter 3 for tips on installing Windows XP across the network and on multiple systems.

Using Upgrade Advisor

Microsoft has developed a tool called Upgrade Advisor that will help you determine if your system is ready for Windows XP. Inexplicably, Microsoft failed to include Upgrade Advisor on the Windows XP CD. That's too bad, because although you can download the file from Microsoft's website, it's nearly 50 MB in size. Putting it on the CD would have saved a lot of time. If you want to download the tool, point your browser to

    www.microsoft.com/windowsxp/pro/howtobuy/upgrading/advisor.asp

After you download UpgAdv.exe, double-click the file to install Upgrade Advisor. The application runs automatically when the installation is complete. Before you move through the advisor to check your system, first connect to the Internet. This enables Upgrade Advisor to download updates to check for hardware and software compatibility. If you can't connect to the Internet for some reason, you can still run Upgrade Advisor, but the data it provides will not be as current as possible.

TIP   Running Upgrade Advisor is a good idea even if you decide not to install Windows XP on a particular system, because Upgrade Advisor can point you to potential problems on your existing OS.

Upgrade Advisor (Figure 2.1) first gives you some background information on application and hardware compatibility. Then, it analyzes your system and provides a report listing any potential problems, as shown in Figure 2.2. You can click each item in the report to obtain more information about the issue and how to resolve it.

TIP   Click Save As when Upgrade Advisor displays its report and save the report to a text file that you can review later.

Using the information provided in Upgrade Advisor's report, start obtaining software patches, device drivers, or other updates that need to be applied to your system prior to installing Windows XP.

FIGURE 2.1:

Upgrade Advisor offers general information about hardware and software compatibility.

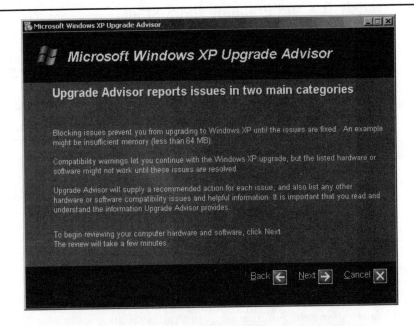

FIGURE 2.2:

Upgrade Advisor presents a report of any potential upgrade problems.

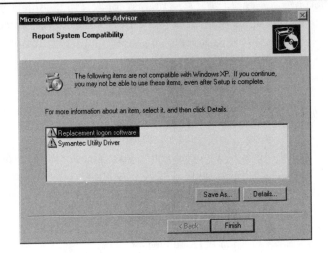

Backing Up Your Data

Although it's unlikely that any of your data will be corrupted or lost during an upgrade, you should still back up your critical documents, message store, and any other data you can't afford to lose. In the case of a new installation—such as migrating from an older PC to a newer one—you'll probably need to perform a backup of your data so you can move it to the new system.

Backup Options

Before you use your current operating system's Backup program to back up your data, make sure you'll be able to read the data in Windows XP. Like Backup in Windows 2000, Windows XP supports backing up to a file, tape, or removable media. The Windows 9*x* version of Backup also can back up to a file, but not in a format supported by Windows XP. So, backup files that you create in Windows 9*x* or Me can't be read by the XP version of Backup. This means you won't be able to recover these files from Windows XP if the originals are lost or corrupted.

Restoring tape backup sets created with a different version of Backup is also very iffy. In most cases, you'll be able to restore a backup set if Windows XP supports the tape drive, but only if the tape set was created without software compression. The compression algorithm used in Windows 9*x*/Me Backup is different in the Windows XP version.

One alternative is to back up your files to a removable disk, second local hard disk, network share, or CD-R/CD-RW. Just copy the files rather than backing them up with the Backup utility. Then simply drag them back to the appropriate locations after you install Windows XP.

Another alternative is to run the original backup utility under Windows XP. You'll need to set compatibility options on the program to do so. First, copy the Backup program and its support files from the original system to a media that you can read on the Windows XP system after installation. For example, the Windows 9*x* and Me versions are located in `\Program Files\Accessories\Backup`. Copy the entire folder to the Windows XP system.

Next, set the path to include the Backup program's support files. In the case of the Windows 9*x*/Me versions, this is the `\Backup\System` folder. Right-click My Computer, choose Properties, and click the Advanced tab. Click Environment Variables to open the dialog box shown in Figure 2.3.

Click Path in the System Variables list and click Edit. In the Edit System Variable dialog box (Figure 2.4), append a semicolon and the additional path string, and then click OK. Close all the dialog boxes.

Next, configure the program's compatibility settings. On the Windows XP system, open the folder containing the Backup program, right-click the executable file (such as `Msbackup.exe`), and choose Properties. Click the Compatibility tab, select Run This Program In Compatibility Mode For, and then select the source operating system from the drop-down list. Click OK, then launch the program and perform the restore operation.

FIGURE 2.3:

Modify environment
variables with the
Environment Variables
dialog box.

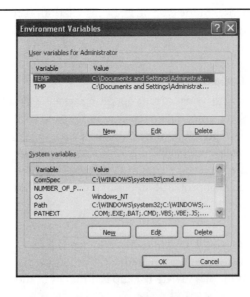

FIGURE 2.4:

Append the additional
path string to the
existing path variable.

TIP   At this point, you can see that it would be much simpler to copy the files to a CD, second
hard disk, or network share, rather than hassle with getting the older version of Backup to
run under Windows XP. Use one of these options, if possible, to save time.

What to Back Up

Now that you have some options for backing up your data on the current system, what
should you back up?

Documents   This includes the documents in My Documents as well as any other data files
(drawings, databases, checkbook, etc.) that you have created and stored on the system.
Make it a habit to keep all of your documents under My Documents, if possible, to make it
easier for you to back up or move your documents whenever it becomes necessary.

TIP   Use My Documents as the root folder for your documents and create other subfolders in
My Documents to contain specific types of documents. For example, I keep my checkbook
in \My Documents\Personal.

Outlook Express folders   The collection of files that hold the data for Outlook Express is called the *store*. You can find the location of the Outlook Express (OE) store this way: Open Outlook Express and choose Tools ➤ Options. Click the Maintenance tab and click Store Folder. The resulting Store Location dialog box shows the path to your OE folders. If others share your computer, make sure to back up their OE folders as well. If your version of Outlook Express doesn't offer the Maintenance tab in the Options, search the system for the folder containing the file `Folders.dbx` or `Inbox.dbx` and back up the entire contents of the folder.

SEE ALSO   For more information on moving your Outlook Express message store from one computer to another, see Chapter 36.

Outlook local store(s)   If you use Outlook and have a set of personal folders (these are kept in a PST file), you should back that up as well. If using Outlook 2002 with multiple accounts, keep in mind that you're probably using multiple PST files, even though you might not be aware of it. Outlook uses PSTs to store Hotmail and certain other accounts separate from your personal folders. Check your Outlook profile for the names and locations of your PST files. Also back up your offline store (OST file) if using an Exchange Server account.

Windows Address Book   This address book stores contacts for Outlook Express and other applications that can tap into it (such as your fax program.) Your address book has the name *user*`.wab`, where *user* is your logon name. Look in the `\Application Data\ Microsoft\Address Book` folder of your current profile folder for this file.

TIP   Your OS system folder (i.e. `\Windows`) *is* your "profile folder" if individual profiles are turned off in Windows 9x.

Preparing the System

Before you begin installing Windows XP, you should take a few preparatory steps. First, if upgrading your existing OS, take the time to review your hard disk(s) and delete any old documents or other files you no longer need. Use the Add Or Remove Programs object in Control Panel to uninstall any programs you no longer use or which you will not use after upgrading to Windows XP. This will make additional space available for Windows XP.

TIP   If you're performing a clean install and don't need to retain any of your existing files, or you've backed them up, consider reformatting the disk to start from a truly clean system. Just make sure you can restore your files afterward!

After clearing out the hard disk, consider defragmenting the drive. This will ensure the most possible contiguous disk space on the drive and will improve performance. All versions of Windows except Windows NT include a disk optimizer, and you can obtain third-party tools such as Diskeeper for Windows NT.

SEE ALSO   For more information on Diskeeper, check out the Diskeeper website at `www.diskeeper` `.com/coverpage.asp`.

The final step in preparing to install Windows XP is to make sure your hardware is ready for it. Run Upgrade Advisor if you haven't already done so, to check for potential hardware or driver problems. Check the Windows XP Hardware Compatibility List to make sure your hardware is compatible with Windows XP. You'll find the HCL at `www.microsoft.com/hcl`. If you still have questions about driver compatibility for a specific item, check the manufacturer's website for Windows XP compatibility information and upgraded drivers.

Tips for Running Setup

As I mentioned previously, this chapter doesn't cover Setup itself. Rather, I focus on things you can do before and after Setup to simplify the installation process and improve performance. In this section, I offer some tips on using Setup in specific situations.

Installing on a Blank System

The Windows XP CD is bootable, enabling your computer to boot from the CD to run Setup and install Windows XP. This eliminates the need for a boot disk with CD-ROM drivers or for formatting the hard disk beforehand. In order to boot from a CD, your computer must support that feature and have the CD configured as one of the boot options in the BIOS. Boot the system and enter the BIOS configuration program (the method for doing so varies from one computer to another.) Then check your BIOS for a setting that specifies the boot order and make sure to include the CD in the list. The CD need not be the first boot device. If your system boots from a SCSI CD-ROM, you might also need to configure the BIOS to boot from SCSI before IDE. Check with your system's manufacturer or system documentation if you're not sure how to configure these settings.

Creating Boot Disks

If you can't get your system to boot from the CD, you can create a boot disk set that will allow the system to boot, see the CD-ROM drive, and start the installation process. The tool required to create the boot disk set isn't included with Windows XP, but you can download it from Microsoft's website. The download for Windows XP Professional is located at

www.microsoft.com/downloads/release.asp?ReleaseID=33291

You'll find the files for the Home Edition at

www.microsoft.com/downloads/release.asp?ReleaseID=33290

Download the appropriate executable file and run it. The utility prompts you to provide six blank, formatted, high-density diskettes. After the utility finishes copying the files to the disks, insert Disk 1 in the computer on which you want to install Windows XP and reboot. The system will boot from the floppy, load the necessary CD-ROM driver(s), and start Setup.

After you create the boot disk set, insert Disk 1 in the computer's floppy drive and restart the computer. The text-based portion of Setup will run from the floppies and allow you to format the hard disk and specify other options to begin the installation process from the CD.

Understanding Setup Switches

As I explained earlier, in most cases—whether upgrade or clean install—you'll simply insert the CD, boot the system, and let Setup install Windows XP for you with little or no interaction. In some cases, however, you might need to exercise more control over how Setup performs the installation. There are several switches you can use if you start Setup from a command prompt. These switches control the actions that Setup performs and the way in which it installs Windows XP.

There are two Setup programs, both located in the i386 folder of the Windows XP CD. You can run Winnt.exe on 16-bit operating systems such as DOS, Windows 3.1, or Windows for Workgroups 3.11. You can run Winnt32.exe on 32-bit operating systems such as Windows 9x, Me, NT, and 2000.

Why a 16-bit version of Setup if none of those operating systems allow you to upgrade? You might choose to install a clean copy of Windows XP on a system containing DOS, Windows 3.1, or Windows for Workgroups 3.11, and Winnt.exe gives you the means of starting Setup. It also lets you specify several options to control how Setup runs.

SEE ALSO   For the complete syntax of both versions, Winnt.exe and Winnt32.exe, including descriptions of all their optional command switches, see Tables 3.1 and 3.2 in Chapter 3.

Some of the options are the same in both Winnt.exe and Winnt32.exe, but Winnt32.exe offers additional switches not supported by Winnt.exe. In both cases, most of the switches are geared toward distributed or unattended setup. For that reason, all of the switches are explained in detail in Chapter 3.

Migrating Applications Manually

When you perform an upgrade, Setup migrates all of your applications to Windows XP so you can begin using them as soon as the upgrade is complete. In fact, that's one of the main reasons to perform an upgrade rather than a clean install. It's a real hassle to have to reinstall applications, particularly if you work with as many as I do.

TIP   Before you jump through the hoops to manually migrate an application, make sure it's really necessary. Copy the folder containing the program's executable file to your computer and double-click the executable. If the program runs without problems, consider yourself lucky. You probably don't need to tweak the Registry or do anything else to continue using the program. Also, see Chapter 12 to learn about tools in Windows XP that you can use to transfer settings, applications, and documents between computers.

If you have to perform a clean install and you can't simply copy the application's folder to your new system, you might be able to migrate some of your applications manually and avoid having to reinstall them. The ability to migrate an application manually can be a real time-saver, but it can be a lifesaver, too. What if you've lost the original distribution CD or diskettes for the program, or they've been damaged? With a little luck, you might be able to copy the files from another system, tweak a few settings, and continue using them.

TIP   Migrating an application manually can be time-consuming and is useful generally only when you can't reinstall the application because of lost or damaged distribution media. Reinstall, if possible.

Whether or not you'll be able to migrate an application without reinstalling depends in large part on three main points, summarized in the following list:

Custom DLLs   If the program includes custom DLLs located somewhere other than in the application's folder, you'll need to locate the DLLs and place them in a location where Windows XP can access them.

Installs as a service   If the program installs as a service, you'll have to manually register the service in Windows XP.

Requires Registry settings   Many programs store settings in the Registry. You'll have to copy the Registry key for the application from the original computer or OS to the new one.

TIP   If you're going to reformat the drive when you install Windows XP, make sure to back up the folder containing the application and any subfolders. Also back up your current Windows or Winnt folder, as some of the application's files might be located in the system root folder.

First, determine if the application uses settings in the Registry. Generally these settings are stored in the \HKEY_LOCAL_MACHINE\Software and/or \HKEY_CURRENT_USER\Software Registry keys. Before upgrading to Windows XP, click Start ➢ Run, enter **regedit** in the Run dialog box to open the Registry Editor (Figure 2.5), and then look for a key for the application. If you find one, select the key and choose File ➢ Export Registry File to open the Export Registry File dialog box (Figure 2.6).

FIGURE 2.5:

Use the Registry Editor to export the application's Registry key.

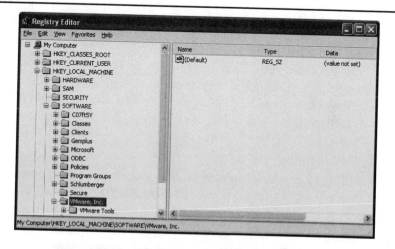

FIGURE 2.6:

Save the application's Registry key to a file.

WARNING   Make sure you select the application's key rather than a higher-level key. For example, don't select the \HKEY_LOCAL_MACHINE\Software key, but instead select, for example, \HKEY_LOCAL_MACHINE\Software\Adobe\Photoshop. Also, make sure you export *only* the selected branch rather than the entire Registry. Exporting then importing into Windows XP the wrong key or the entire Registry could prevent you from booting Windows XP.

Once you've selected the appropriate key in the Export Registry File dialog box, enter a file name for the REG file, select the Selected Branch option, and click Save. Make sure you save the file to a location where you'll be able to read it after installing Windows XP.

Next, locate the folder containing the application and copy it to your new installation. This might require some planning before you install Windows XP, as you might need to back up the application's folder to a CD, network drive, or other media if you plan on reformatting the disk during installation. Place the folder in the same location as on the original installation. For example, if the folder was located in the \Programs Files\Adobe\Photoshop folder, place it there again, creating folders as needed.

If you located and exported a Registry key for the application, import that key now. Simply locate the REG file you previously created and double-click it to add it to the current Registry.

The next step is to try running the application by double-clicking its executable. If the program runs without any problems, you can stop here. If you receive error messages that the program can't find a DLL, note the name of the DLL and copy it from the original system or your backup copy. Repeat the process for any other missing DLLs.

Cloning an Existing Installation

You might be a little worried about installing a new version of Windows if your old version is working just fine. What tempers my concern is the fact that by the time I'm ready to install a new OS on anything other than a test computer, I've been using the operating system in beta for the better part of a year. So, I know what to expect.

In some cases, you might want to clone your existing operating system. This lets you keep the old OS with all settings and applications intact, while still upgrading it to avoid having to reinstall applications. In effect, you're making a copy of your existing OS and upgrading the copy. There's one catch to this concept, however. Windows stores certain applications in the Program Files folder. When you upgrade to Windows XP, Setup upgrades these applications. The new version might not be compatible with your old versions. That's why it's always best to install operating systems in their own partitions and keep the Program Files folders for each separate from one another.

Cloning an operating system implies that you will boot more than one OS on your computer (at a minimum, the existing OS plus your new installation of Windows XP). For that reason, I cover OS cloning in Chapter 4.

Updating the System

Microsoft is constantly fixing bugs and adding features to Windows and makes these updates available for download from its website. In previous versions of Windows, you just pointed your web browser to `http://windowsupdate.microsoft.com` and a web-based interface helped you select operating system updates to install. Windows XP uses the same mechanism, but Microsoft has fine-tuned the notification process that Windows XP uses to let you know when updates are available. You can also use an alternative to the Windows Update site if you need to update multiple computers or simply prefer to download and save the updates so you can apply them when needed (such as after reinstalling your system).

Configuring Windows Update

After you install Windows XP and log in, Windows displays a balloon on one of the tray icons, prompting you to configure Windows Update. You can click the balloon to start the Windows Update Wizard, which lets you configure how Windows Update functions. You can also configure Windows Update through the System object in Control Panel. The only difference is that after configuring settings, the wizard launches your web browser and points it to the Windows Update website. This section explains the Control Panel method.

Open Control Panel and double-click the System icon. Or, right-click My Computer and choose Properties. Then, click the Automatic Updates tab on the System Properties dialog box, as shown in Figure 2.7.

TIP   If your Control Panel is configured to show categories, you'll find the System icon under the Performance And Maintenance category.

Use the following four settings on the Automatic Updates tab to configure Windows Update for Windows XP:

Download the updates automatically and notify me when they are ready to be installed.   Windows XP scans for and downloads updates automatically and then prompts you to allow the updates to be installed.

Notify me before downloading any updates and notify me again before installing them on my computer.   Windows XP asks if you want to download updates rather than performing the scan and download automatically. It then prompts you to allow the updates to be installed.

Turn off automatic updating. I want to upgrade my computer manually.   Windows XP will not scan for or download updates.

Restore declined updates   Click to add to the available update list those updates you have previously declined; allows you to download declined updates.

You can also check for and apply updates at any time. To do so, just click Start ➢ All Programs ➢ Windows Update to open the Windows Update website to review and download updates.

TIP   Access the Windows Update site by pointing your web browser to `http://v4.windowsupdate.microsoft.com`.

FIGURE 2.7:

Use the Automatic Updates tab to configure Windows Update.

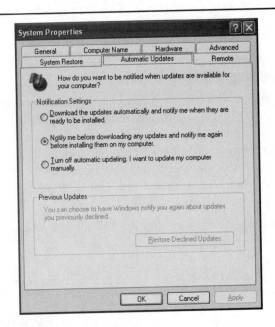

Using the Corporate Update Site

When you use the Windows Update site, Windows XP downloads and installs the updates without giving you the ability to save the download for installation later or on another system. If your job is to manage multiple PCs, or you just like to maintain a library of updates you can apply at any time, you need an alternative to the Windows Update site. That alternative is the Corporate Windows Update site, located at `http://corporate.windowsupdate.microsoft.com`.

The corporate site lets you select updates and download them without installing the updates. This lets you save the updates for installation on other computers, distribute them by CD or other means, or simply save them for installation on your computer at a later time.

To use the corporate update site, point your web browser to the URL and follow the prompts provided to search for and download updates. Double-click a downloaded update to install it.

Windows Product Activation

Microsoft introduced a new feature in Windows XP called Windows Product Activation (WPA) as an effort to control piracy and prevent users from installing a single copy of Windows XP on multiple computers. WPA works much like product activation for other products such as Office 2000 and Office XP. After logon, Windows XP determines whether the product has been activated yet. If not, it directs you to either connect to Microsoft over the Internet or call Microsoft to activate Windows XP.

WPA binds each installation of Windows XP to a specific PC. WPA takes an inventory of a system's hardware and generates a 50-digit string. This string is used to register the product through Microsoft, which provides a 42-digit value for activation. Attempts to activate Windows XP with the same 42-digit value will fail unless the machines are essentially identical.

When you upgrade the system by adding new hardware, Windows XP doesn't perform activation again to change your activation code. In fact, you can make all the changes you want to the system after you activate Windows without affecting your system in any way. However, if you have to reinstall Windows XP, there is a good chance that WPA will not recognize the system as being the same if there are too many hardware changes, such as a different video adapter, different network adapter, new SCSI host adapter, and so on. The end result is that activation will probably fail. That's not really a problem, however, because you can call Microsoft to activate the software. Just tell the technician you have upgraded the system and are reinstalling Windows XP. You'll receive a new activation code for your new configuration.

WPA is targeted primarily at the retail market, however. Copies of Windows XP that you purchase through volume licenses such as the Microsoft Open License, Microsoft Select, or Microsoft Enterprise Agreement programs are not subject to WPA and don't require the same activation steps. If you will be purchasing any retail versions of Windows XP, keep the activation requirements in mind. Otherwise, simply ensure that you purchase Windows XP through a volume license mechanism and avoid a mix of open-license and retail copies to eliminate the licensing confusion it would cause.

Chapter 3

Reaping the Rewards of Network, Automated, and Unattended Installations

Installing Windows XP on one or just a handful of computers isn't much of a task. You pop in the CD, answer a few questions, and let Setup do its thing. You can be up and running after a donut and a cup of coffee. But if, like me, you frequently need to install Windows XP on 50, 100, or even more computers, installation becomes a headache if your only option is to install on one computer at a time. That many donuts would kill me!

Fortunately, Windows XP gives you several options for installing the operating system in a wide variety of situations. For example, you can install Windows XP from a network share across the network, which eliminates the need for a local CD. You can even integrate service packs and other updates to create a *slipstream installation* share that lets you install Windows XP along with updates and service packs in a single operation—a great timesaver.

You can also create custom Setup files to install Windows XP with custom options in automated or unattended installations. This means you can build an answer file to provide responses to all of the questions Setup asks during the installation process. Automated and unattended installation is a handy means for deploying Windows XP across a large number of computers, particularly in situations where the users are not technically adept.

A third and extremely powerful option is Remote Installation Services (RIS), included with Windows 2000 Server and .NET Server. RIS lets you automatically install Windows 2000 and XP to client computers across a network, even if the client computer's hard disk is blank. RIS is very useful for deploying an operating system to new hires and for performing disaster recovery. When you combine RIS with the ability to install applications automatically through Microsoft's IntelliMirror technologies, you can essentially automate the entire process of installing the operating system and all applications for a user.

Finally, a handful of options let you create an image of an operating system and deploy Windows XP simply by copying that image to each computer. Each computer receives an exact duplicate of the operating system and applications. This is a great solution for labs and other organizations where you need to install the same set of applications for a large number of users.

I explore all of these installation methods in this chapter, starting with the many switches you can use with the Windows XP Setup programs. You'll use these switches for many of the Setup options discussed in the chapter, so consider them a foundation for the rest of the chapter.

Taming Setup with Switches

As I explained in Chapter 2, there are two versions of Setup, `Winnt.exe` and `Winnt32.exe`. The first is for use on 16-bit operating systems, including DOS, Windows 3.1, and Windows for Workgroups 3.11. `Winnt32.exe` is for all 32-bit operating systems including Windows 9*x*, Me, NT, 2000, and XP.

The syntax for `Winnt.exe` is

```
winnt [/s[:sourcepath]] [/t[:tempdrive]] [/u[:answer_file]] [/udf:id[,UDF_file]]
[/r:folder] [/r[x]:folder] [/e:command] [/a]
```

The syntax for `Winnt32.exe` is

```
winnt32 [/s:sourcepath] [/tempdrive:drive_letter] [/unattend[num]:[answer_file]]
[ic:ccc][/copydir:folder_name] [/copysource:folder_name] [/cmd:command_line]
[ic:ccc][/debug[level]:[filename]] [/udf:id[,UDF_file]]
[/syspart:drive_letter][ic:ccc] [/checkupgradeonly] [/cmdcons] [/m:folder_name]
[/makelocalsource] [ic:ccc][/noreboot]
```

Table 3.1 summarizes the optional command switches for `Winnt.exe`, and Table 3.2 summarizes the optional switches for `Winnt32.exe`.

TABLE 3.1: Winnt.exe Command Switches

Option	Function
/s[:sourcepath]	Location of Windows XP source files; must be full local or UNC pathname.
/t[:tempdrive]	Location for temporary Setup files and installation partition.
/u:[answer_file]	Performs unattended Setup using specified answer file; requires /s option.
/udf:id[,UDF_file]	Specifies unique ID and uses Unique Database File (UDF) to modify answer file for unattended Setup. ID determines which answers in UDF file are used.

Continued on next page

TABLE 3.1 CONTINUED: Winnt.exe Command Switches

Option	Function
/r[:*folder*]	Creates optional folder that remains after installation; specify folder name as *folder*.
/rx[:*folder*]	Copies folder during Setup but deletes after installation.
/e	Specifies command to be executed after GUI-mode Setup completes.
/a	Enables accessibility options.

TABLE 3.2: Winnt32.exe Command Switches

Option	Function
/s:*sourcepath*	Location of Windows XP source files; specify multiple sources with multiple /s switches.
/tempdrive:*drive_letter*	Location for temporary Setup files and Windows XP installation partition. You must use the /sypart switch with this switch.
/unattend	Upgrade previous version of Windows XP in unattended Setup mode; implies acceptance of EULA.
/unattend[*num*]:[*answer_file*]	Performs a clean install in unattended mode; *num* is seconds between end of file copy and system restart, and *answer_file* is the file specifying Setup options.
/copydir:*folder_name*	Copies optional folder specified by *folder_name* to the system root folder during Setup; use multiple switches to copy multiple folders. Such a folder is not removed after completion of Setup.
/copysource:*folder_name*	Copies optional folder specified by *folder_name* to the system root folder during Setup; use multiple switches to copy multiple folders. Such a folder is deleted after completion of Setup.
/cmd:*command_line*	Executes the command specified by *command_line* after Setup but before final system restart.
/debug[*level*]:[*filename*]	Logs information to specified file; 1 = errors, 2 = warnings, 3 = information, 4 = detailed.
/udf:*id*[,*UDF_file*]	Specifies unique ID and uses Unique Database File (UDF) to modify answer file for unattended Setup. *ID* determines which answers in UDF file are used.
/syspart:*drive_letter*	Copies Setup startup files to drive and marks the drive active for install in another computer. Setup continues on boot on the other computer. Requires /tempdrive switch. Not available for Windows 9x or Me.
/checkupgradeonly	Analyzes the system for upgrade compatibility but doesn't install Windows XP; creates Upgrade.txt (Windows 9x) or Winnt32.log (Windows NT) log file in current OS system root folder.

Continued on next page

TABLE 3.2 CONTINUED: Winnt32.exe Command Switches

Option	Function
/cmdcons	Installs Recovery Console during Setup.
/m:*folder_name*	Copy files from *folder_name* if it exists rather than from the default source location.
/makelocalsource	Copies all installation source files to local hard disk.
/noreboot	Doesn't restart system after final Setup phase.
/dudisable	Prevents Dynamic Update from running during Setup and instead installs only using existing source files. This option prevents Dynamic Update from running even if you specify Dynamic Update options in an answer file.
/duprepare:*pathname*	Prepare a distributed installation folder so it can be used with update files you've downloaded from the Windows Update website.
/dushare:*pathname*	Specifies a network share in which you have downloaded Dynamic Update files from the Windows Update website, and which you've prepared with the /duprepare switch. Use this switch during installation to direct Setup to use the updated files in the specified directory.

As you can see from these two tables, both Winnt.exe and Winnt32.exe support several switches you can use to control the way Setup works and installs Windows XP. I explore all of these switches in the following sections, organized by the function each switch performs.

NOTE   The following sections focus on Winnt32.exe rather than Winnt.exe because you are more likely to be running Setup on a 32-bit operating system.

Specifying the Location of Source Files and Destination

Setup, by default, looks in the same i386 folder where the Setup file (Winnt.exe or Winnt32.exe) is located, for the Windows XP source files. In some cases, you might want to specify a different location, such as a network share or a folder on a local hard disk. You might also want to copy all of the source files to the local hard disk if the original location (network drive or CD) won't be available after the system restarts to complete Setup.

Use the /s switch to specify the folder where the Windows XP source files are located. The /s switch not only lets you specify a different location for the Windows XP source files, but also lets you speed up the file copy process and distribute the load to more than one installation share on different servers. How? You can specify up to eight /s switches with a single command. Setup will copy files from each simultaneously, which speeds up copying and provides load balancing on the installation servers. The following is an example that uses the /s switch to install from three different servers:

```
winnt32.exe /s:\\server1\xpshare /s:\\server2\xp /s:\\server3\xpfiles
```

You can use the /t switch with Winnt.exe to have Setup place temporary installation files and install Windows XP to the specified drive. This is the same as the /tempdrive switch for Winnt32.exe. When you use /tempdrive, you also need the /syspart switch. The following example would install Windows XP from a network share and place the OS on drive D:

```
winnt32.exe /s:\\server1\xpshare /tempdrive:d /syspart:d
```

> **TIP**   Both /tempdrive and /syspart must point to the same primary partition on the target drive.

You can use the /m switch to make Setup copy files from an alternate location rather than the specified or default source folder. For example, assume you've created a folder containing updated driver files and want Setup to use those rather than the ones included with Windows XP. If you specify the /m switch, Setup looks in the specified folder for a file and copies it from that location rather than the default. Otherwise, Setup copies the file from the default location. Here's an example:

```
winnt32.exe /s:\\server1\xpshare /m:\\xpupdates
```

Copying Folders During Setup

Another task you might want to perform during installation is to create optional folders and copy existing custom folders to the target system. For example, maybe you have a set of common documents you want everyone to have, or you need to copy a folder for a custom application as part of the installation process. Maybe you need to install custom drivers during Setup.

You can use the /r and /rx switches with Winnt.exe to create folders during installation. With /r, Setup creates the folder and leaves it in place after installation is complete. With /rx, Setup creates the folder during installation but deletes it upon completion. The corresponding switches for Winnt32.exe are /copydir, which copies the folder and leaves it after installation, and /copysource, which copies the folder during installation but deletes it on completion.

There is a key point to understand when copying folders with these switches. The folders are always created under the *%systemroot%* folder on the target system—the folder containing Windows (such as \Winnt or \Windows.) So, if you want to move the contents of the folder to another location, you need to use the /cmd switch to execute a command to move the files when Setup completes.

Executing Commands After Setup

Let's say you've copied a folder to the *%systemroot%* folder during installation with the /copydir switch, but you want the contents of the folder stored in a different final location. Or maybe you want to run a batch file that sets up a certain folder structure on the user's computer or copies certain files from a network server to the user's computer. Both Setup programs give you a switch you can use to execute a command after Setup completes.

The Winnt.exe switch is /e:*command*, and the Winnt32.exe switch is /cmd:*command*. Enclose the command in quotes if it includes embedded spaces, as in the following example:

```
winnt32.exe /cmd:"move c:\windows\CommonDocs c:\CommonDocs"
```

TIP   If a path in the command includes spaces, such as c:\Program Files\CustomApp, you can use the short 8.3 folder name in the command rather than the long name. For example, the \Program Files folder on almost any system will have the short name \PROGRA~1 because Windows uses a common naming convention when creating short names.

In addition to or instead of using the /e or /cmd switches, you can use a Cmdlines.txt file to execute commands or include a command in the [SetupParams] section of an answer file.

SEE ALSO   See "Customizing Setup," later in this chapter, to learn how to use alternatives such as Cmdlines.txt and answer files to execute commands and perform other automated Setup tasks.

Prepping a Drive for Another System with /syspart

You can use the /syspart switch with Winnt32.exe to perform the initial installation steps on a secondary hard disk in preparation for moving that drive to another computer. After you install the drive on the other system and boot that system, Setup continues and completes the installation process. So, /syspart gives you a means of prepping drives for other systems without creating a duplicate image of an existing system. This option is handy if you need to install Windows XP on several new systems that have varying hardware (which makes drive imaging impractical) and can't use RIS or other automated/network-based methods to complete the installation.

The following example would perform an initial installation to drive D: from a network distribution share:

```
winnt32.exe /s:\\server1\xpshare /tempdrive:d /syspart:d /noreboot
```

NOTE   You must use the /tempdrive switch and point it to the target drive when using /syspart. You can use an unattended Setup file as well to provide answers to questions that the end user would otherwise see during the final stages of Setup.

Use the /noreboot switch to prevent the computer from rebooting after Setup completes. Also, you should shut down and remove the second drive before rebooting the computer, because Setup marks the drive as active in preparation for booting on the target system.

Managing Dynamic Update

Three switches for Winnt32.exe let you control Dynamic Update during installation. Normally, Setup runs Dynamic Update near the end of the installation process to download and install updates from the Windows Update site. However, you can download updates separately and incorporate them into the installation source files to provide an up-to-date installation in the first pass.

The /duprepare switch modifies an existing Windows XP installation share, adding a dudrvs folder to the share and populating it with update files. You would use the /duprepare switch when setting up a distribution share that will later be used by clients to install Windows XP. The syntax for using this switch is:

    winnt32.exe /duprepare:FolderPath

Replace the *FolderPath* variable with the local or network path to the folder that contains the Windows XP installation files.

Use the /dushare switch when you run Setup to specify the location of the folder you've prepared with /duprepare. The syntax for using this switch is:

    winnt32.exe /dushare:FolderPath

Again, *FolderPath* is the local or, more likely, remote network path to the folder containing the Windows Update files.

One additional switch, /dudisable, lets you prevent Windows Update from running during Setup. This speeds up the installation process and allows you to control when and if Windows Update executes.

Miscellaneous Switches

There are a handful of additional switches you can use with Winnt32.exe:

/debug This switch lets you log information to a file during Setup. You can specify one of four logging levels using the numeric variable that goes with the switch:

Level	Logging Performed
1	Log errors that occur during installation.
2	Log warnings that occur during installation.
3	Log informational messages generated during installation.
4	Log detailed information generated by Setup during installation.

/cmdcons   Use this switch to install the Windows XP Recovery Console during installation. You can install the RC along with Windows XP or use this switch to install it at any time after installing XP.

SEE ALSO   For detailed information on installing and using the Recovery Console, see Chapter 47.

/checkupgradeonly   Use this switch to analyze your current OS for compatibility with Windows XP. When you use this switch, Setup doesn't install Windows XP but instead analyzes the system, generates a report, and stores the report as `Upgrade.txt` in the existing operating system's root folder (such as `C:\Windows` or `C:\Winnt`.)

SEE ALSO   The following section provides information on how to use the `/unattend` and `/udf` switches to perform unattended installations.

Customizing Setup

The switches explained so far let you control how Setup works. In some cases, you'll use these switches as the only method for customizing Setup. In most cases, however, you'll use custom Setup files to control the way Setup runs and the actions it performs. I explain in this section how to create and use custom Setup files.

Overview of Automated and Unattended Setup

Normally, Setup asks several questions during installation to determine how you want it to install Windows XP. If you're installing Windows XP on one or two systems, you'll probably just sit through the installation process and provide the answers yourself. If you need to install on several systems or need to perform additional tasks during Setup, a custom Setup file is the way to go.

SEE ALSO   Creating and using unattended Setup files is a complex task. You'll find a good overview of the process in this section. For a more detailed look at using unattended Setup files, see *Windows 2000 Automated Deployment and Remote Administration* by Christa Anderson (Sybex, 2001).

Setup Answer Files

An *answer file* is a text file that contains the answers to questions that Setup normally asks during installation. An answer file contains several sections, each identified by a section name in square brackets. Each section can contain one or more settings. The following listing is a fragment from a typical unattended Setup file:

```
;SetupMgrTag
[Data]
    AutoPartition=1
    MsDosInitiated="0"
    UnattendedInstall="Yes"

[Unattended]
    UnattendMode=FullUnattended
    OemSkipEula=Yes
    OemPreinstall=No
    TargetPath=\WINDOWS

[GuiUnattended]
    AdminPassword="BLINKY"
    EncryptedAdminPassword=NO
    OEMSkipRegional=1
    TimeZone=20
    OemSkipWelcome=1

[UserData]
    ProductID=12345-ABCDE-67890-FGHIJ-12345
    FullName="Jim Boyce"
    OrgName="Jim Boyce, Inc."
    ComputerName=*
```

You can use an unattended Setup file by itself to perform automated or semi-automated installations. All parameters defined by the file will be the same on all systems on which you install Windows XP using the file.

The following example would install Windows XP using the unattended Setup file named custom.txt on a network server:

winnt32.exe /unattend:\\srv1\install\custom.txt

In some situations, you might need to modify the contents of the Setup file during installation to further customize the OS installation. You can use a UDF file for that purpose.

UDF Files

UDF stands for *Unique Database File*. A UDF file modifies the answers in the custom Setup file. Think of it this way: the Setup file can specify all of the answers, but the UDF file replaces some of those answers during installation, overriding selected answers on a per-computer basis. For example, you might use a UDF file to specify computer name, time zone, and a few other properties during installation for each computer.

The UDF file uses the same general format as an answer file. The [UniqueIds] section of the file lists each of the unique sections in the file and typically lists the section where the settings for a particular computer are located. This means you can use a single UDF file to modify any number of individual installations.

Take a look at the following UDF sample:

```
[UniqueIds]
    COMPUTER1=UserData,GuiUnattended
    COMPUTER2=UserData,GuiUnattended
    COMPUTER3=UserData,GuiUnattended
[COMPUTER1:UserData]
    ComputerName=Joe
[COMPUTER1:GuiUnattended]
    AdminPassword="dif984z9"
    TimeZone=" (GMT-05:00) Eastern Time (US & Canada)"
[COMPUTER2:UserData]
    ComputerName=Jane
[COMPUTER2:GuiUnattended]
    AdminPassword="fkuer837x"
    TimeZone=" (GMT-06:00) Central Time (US & Canada)"
[COMPUTER3:UserData]
    ComputerName=Bart
[COMPUTER3:GuiUnattended]
    AdminPassword="8djf7rlcf"
    TimeZone=" (GMT-07:00) Mountain Time (US & Canada)"
```

This example accommodates three different computers, specifying the computer name and an appropriate time zone for the computer during installation, along with the password for the local administrator account. This is a simplistic example, but you can see that it's possible to provide answers for more than one computer in a single UDF file.

To use the UDF file during installation, you need to specify the name of the unattended file, the UDF file, and the unique ID that labels the section you want Setup to use for the current installation. The following code (ignore the fact that this line wraps in print) would install Windows XP on Jane's computer based on the previous UDF example (assuming the file is named custom.udf):

```
winnt32.exe /unattend:\\srv1\install\custom.txt
    /udf:COMPUTER1,\\srv1\udfs\custom.udf
```

Tools for Creating Custom Setup Files

You could create unattended Setup files manually with a text editor. You could also try to stack all the grains of sand on the beach one at a time, but why on Earth would you want to when you could use a bulldozer? That Setup bulldozer is the Setup Manager tool, which

Microsoft includes on the Windows XP CD. You'll find Setup Manager in the file `\support\tools\deploy.cab`. To extract Setup Manager, open a command console and execute the command in the following example. Change the path to the CD drive on your system as needed, and specify the location where you want the file copied for the variable *destination:*

```
expand e:\support\tools\deploy.cab -F:setupmgr.exe destination
```

Next, double-click the extracted `Setupmgr.exe` file to start Setup Manager, which functions as a wizard. As you move through the wizard, you can specify several settings to define the contents of the Setup file.

You can create a new answer file with Setup Manager or modify an existing answer file, and that's the first choice you need to make in the wizard. The second decision you need to make is the type of installation for which the answer file will be used. I'm assuming at this point you're using Setup Manager to create a file for use in an unattended installation, but you can also create a file for a Sysprep or Remote Installation Services installation. These types of installation are covered later in this chapter.

Within the wizard, you can create a distribution share or direct that the answer file will be used to install Windows XP from a CD. After you answer a handful of other questions in the wizard, Setup Manager displays the dialog box shown in Figure 3.1.

You can click Next to move through the settings pages or use the tree pane at the left to select the settings you want to modify. At the end of the process Setup Manager prompts you for the name of a setup file and creates the text file based on the answers you provided.

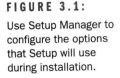

FIGURE 3.1:

Use Setup Manager to configure the options that Setup will use during installation.

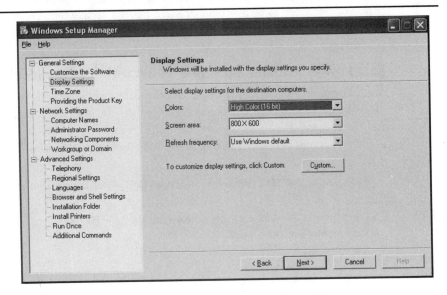

Setup Manager doesn't create UDF files, but you can use Notepad or any text editor to create the file. Use Setup Manager to create the unattended Setup file you'll use with the UDF file, then extract to a separate file those sections you need to modify.

Run Commands with Cmdlines.txt

A common task you'll probably want to perform during an unattended installation is to execute commands. For example, you might want to copy folders, install drivers, set file or folder permissions, or perform other tasks from a command line. I previously explained the /e and /cmd switches you can use with Winnt.exe and Winnt32.exe to execute commands. You can also use the Cmdlines.txt file to execute commands during the GUI portion of Windows XP Setup.

Cmdlines.txt is a text file that contains a single section labeled [Commands], followed by each command on its own line, in quotes. Commands you include in Cmdlines.txt need to run in quiet mode without requiring user interaction, or use scripting to accomplish the same results.

Create the folder OEM in the Windows XP distribution folder and place Cmdlines.txt in that folder. Then add the line OEMPreinstall=Yes to the [Unattended] section of your unattended Setup file.

TIP   The commands in Cmdlines.txt execute after Setup finished but before the system reboots. This means that network shares are unavailable, so the commands and any supporting files need to be available locally. If necessary, use the /copydir or /copysource switches or other method to copy the files to the local system.

Running Applications Once after Setup with [GuiRunOnce]

Another option you have for running applications during Setup is the [GuiRunOnce] section of the answer file. Commands you specify in this section execute after Setup completes and the system reboots, but before the user logs on. The [GuiRunOnce] section corresponds to the commands you specify using Setup Manager's Run Once option. They are added to the Registry key

\HKEY_LOCAL_MACHINE\Software\Microsoft\Windows\CurrentVersion\RunOnce

TIP   Programs and commands that you execute through [GuiRunOnce] need to run in quiet mode without any user input.

Using Sysprep

Sysprep is another tool included with Windows XP that you can use to deploy the operating system. You create an image of an existing Windows XP installation using Sysprep, then replicate the image to other systems using third-party disk cloning software. The target systems must have identical hardware configurations as the source system, making Sysprep useful for deploying Windows XP to multiple computers in a lab situation where you purchase similarly configured PCs in large quantities.

Each Windows XP system needs a unique security identifier (SID). Two computers on the network with the same SID will cause conflicts and lead to problems for both systems. So Sysprep configures the target image to create a new, unique SID at boot.

Here's the process for duplicating Windows XP using Sysprep:

1. Install Windows XP on the source system. The computer should be a workgroup member (not a domain member), and the administrator password should be blank.

2. Install applications on the source system.

3. Test the source system and remove any remaining temporary files.

4. Defragment the disk (optional).

5. Use System Manager to create a `Sysprep.inf` answer file to automate the installation (if desired).

6. Run Sysprep, using switches as needed (described shortly).

7. Duplicate the disk using a third-party utility such as Symantec Ghost.

8. Install the target drive in the target system and boot it.

When you boot the target system, Setup creates a SID and runs a Setup wizard that prompts for any remaining information.

TIP   You can use the `Sysprep.inf` file to provide those answers, if you prefer, bypassing the Setup wizard. If you choose to use `Sysprep.inf`, create the file with Setup Manager. Then place the file in the *%systemroot%*\Sysprep folder prior to creating the image.

The syntax for `Sysprep.exe` is:

```
Sysprep [-quiet] [nosidgen] [-reboot] [-noreboot] [-pnp]
```

Table 3.3 describes the purpose of each switch.

TABLE 3.3: Optional Switches for sysprep

Option	Function
-quiet	Run in silent mode without displaying any information dialog boxes.
-nosidgen	Do not generate a unique SID the next time the system starts.
-reboot	Reboot the system when Sysprep is finished.
-noreboot	Do not reboot the system when Sysprep is finished.
-pnp	Force Plug and Play enumeration on the next reboot.

You'll find `Sysprep.exe` on the Windows XP CD in `\Support\Tools\Deploy.cab`. Use the Extract command to extract the file from the archive.

Integrating Service Packs in a Slipstream Installation

At this point, there is no service pack for Windows XP, but there no doubt will be in the relatively near future. Integrating service pack files is an important consideration when you're dealing with Windows XP installations on multiple computers.

Normally when you install Windows, you first install the operating system and then apply the latest service pack (SP) and any post-SP updates. This is fine for a handful of systems but can be time-consuming if you're installing Windows XP on multiple systems. While you could use a combination of Remote Installation Services and IntelliMirror to deploy the operating system and updates automatically, this method still requires a separate Setup pass to install the SP. To save time, you can create a *slipstream* copy of Windows XP.

A slipstream copy is one in which you've applied a given set of service packs or other modifications to the source files. In other words, it's a copy of the Windows XP source files where the files included in the SP have replaced their original versions. After you create the slipstream copy, you can place it on a network share or burn it to CD for distribution (assuming you've satisfied the necessary licensing requirements).

To create a slipstream Windows XP installation source, first create the folder that will contain the copy (assume `c:\slipstream` for this example). Use the following command to copy the Windows XP source files from the CD in drive D: to the slipstream folder:

```
xcopy d:\i386 c:\slipstream\i386 /e
```

If you have the downloaded version of the service pack, create the folder `C:\SP` and then execute the following command from the directory containing the service pack download to expand the SP files. When prompted, specify `C:\SP` as the location for the extraction.

```
wxpsp1.exe /x
```

NOTE Because there are no service packs for XP as I write this, I'm guessing about the file-name for the SP archive file. Replace `wxpsp1.exe` with the filename of the SP download.

Next, switch to `C:\SP` and execute the following command to copy the service pack files to the slipstream folder:

```
c:\sp\i386\update\update.exe -s:c:\slipstream
```

TIP Replace the path to `Update.exe` if you are using the Service Pack CD rather than the downloaded version.

Finally, copy the contents of the `c:\slipstream` folder to the network share from which users will install Windows XP, or burn the folder to a CD.

Deploying Windows XP with RIS

Setting up systems can take a huge amount of your time, particularly if you need to install Windows XP on many systems. Installing the OS is also a key task in disaster recovery, not just something you perform for new users or when existing users receive new computers. Although new systems will typically come preconfigured with the OS of your choice, you might prefer to provide a custom installation for feature or security reasons.

SEE ALSO *Windows XP Power Tools* focuses primarily on Windows XP rather than Windows 2000 Server or .NET Server. For that reason, this section provides a good overview of Remote Installation Services (RIS) so you'll understand what it is and what it can do, but doesn't explain the specific steps to go through to install a RIS server. For detailed information on setting up and using RIS, see *Mastering Windows 2000 Server* by Mark Minasi (Sybex, 2001).

When a system goes down because of a drive failure and needs a replacement, you can take a couple of different directions to bring that system back online. One approach is to have spare drives on hand with OS images already ghosted onto them. This requires essentially identical systems throughout the organization and is often impractical. If you're using remote OS installation, however, you can simply put in a blank drive and let the installation happen almost automatically. The advantage is that the operating system is installed clean on the system and accommodates disparate hardware while requiring little or no interaction with the user or support staff.

TIP The primary benefit of using remote OS installation is reduced IT support time. Whether you're installing systems for new users or existing users, you reduce to almost zero the amount of time required to deploy a new system.

Remote OS installation requires of a handful of key Windows 2000 Server technologies and features. Remote Installation Services (RIS) is an optional component in Windows 2000 Server that works with other Windows components to allow Windows XP to be installed across the enterprise in an automated fashion. This means that you can deploy Windows XP easily to a large number of systems in the enterprise with little administrative interaction, but it also is a means by which you can deploy Windows XP to diskless workstations—those without diskette or CD-ROM drives.

NOTE   Windows .NET Server also includes RIS, and you can deploy Windows 2000 and XP from Windows .NET Server RIS platforms. For the purpose of explanation, I'm assuming that you're using Windows 2000 Server as your RIS platform. However, the .NET implementation should be very similar, if not identical.

RIS requires support for the Preboot Execution Environment (PXE), a standard that allows a user to boot directly from a PXE-compliant network card to initiate an operating-system installation or repair. When a PXE-compliant system boots, it uses DHCP to request an IP address lease from a DHCP server, as well as the address of available RIS servers. It passes its globally unique ID (GUID), which is defined in the system's BIOS. RIS servers listen for that query and respond by providing their IP addresses and the name of the boot image file that the client system can request.

The RIS server then looks up the GUID in Active Directory to determine if there is a pre-staged account for that GUID/computer. The RIS server downloads the Client Installation Wizard to the computer, which prompts the user to log on. Using the logon information provided, the RIS server looks up the account in AD to determine which installation options it should offer to the user, and then offers those through the wizard. If no options are configured in AD for the user, RIS starts the installation process without prompting for options, although it does warn the user that the system's hard disk will be reformatted and offers the option of canceling the installation. If no GUID was found in AD that matches the one provided by the client computer, the RIS server creates a computer account in AD with a unique computer name and starts an unattended installation using that name.

What if your systems—or at least some of them—are not PXE-compliant? You can still take advantage of remote OS installation, because RIS can generate boot diskettes that provide PXE emulation. Rather than boot from a PXE-compliant network adapter, noncompliant systems can boot from the emulator diskette to access the RIS server and its services.

Because you as an administrator can control the options that are offered to the user on his logon account, you can control which operating system options are installed. Although this requires a little planning and configuration beforehand, you still gain the advantage of simplified installation.

RIS relies on Active Directory and group policies to implement the remote OS installation. You don't apply policies at the user level, which means you don't have to pre-stage installations for every user. Instead, you typically apply the necessary group policy object (GPO) at the organization unit (OU) level, adding or moving users to the OU as needed. If you prefer, you can apply the GPO at the domain or site level depending on the needs of your users and whether those needs are consistent across those levels.

More Information on RIS

If you decide that RIS sounds like the method you want to use to deploy Windows XP, start by becoming familiar with RIS and how to deploy it. On your Windows 2000 Server, use the Add Or Remove Programs object in Control Panel to add the RIS service and its online help. Browse the help to become familiar with the process of installing and configuring the server. Once you've accomplished all the initial planning, the actual process of setting up RIS and creating deployment images isn't difficult. You'll also find more information on RIS at

www.microsoft.com/WINDOWS2000/en/server/help/sag_RIS_Architecture_Overview.htm

Other Installation Methods

You can consider a handful of other options to automate and customize the Windows XP installation process, including some useful tools from third-party vendors.

Systems Management Server (SMS)

Systems Management Server is an alternative to RIS. You can use SMS, a Microsoft product, to deploy operating systems, updates, and applications. Unlike RIS, which is limited to installing Windows 2000 and Windows XP, SMS can install other operating systems such as Windows 9x and Windows Me.

This ability to install other operating systems is SMS's prime advantage. If you only need to deploy Windows 2000 and XP, my choice would be RIS because it is (in my opinion) much easier to manage. You can incorporate automatic application deployment through IntelliMirror (group policies) in conjunction with RIS to provide complete system setup for new installations and disaster recovery.

TIP   Because of the management overhead involved, you shouldn't try to use both SMS and IntelliMirror to deploy applications. Select the one that best suits your needs and standardize on it.

You'll find more information about SMS at www.microsoft.com/smsmgmt/default.asp

Symantec Ghost

One very popular third-party application for disk imaging is Symantec Ghost. While earlier versions of Ghost functioned primarily to mirror drive images, the latest version is a full-featured tool that lets you deploy Windows XP and other operating systems and applications across the network automatically. Unlike RIS, Ghost doesn't require Windows 2000 Server or .NET Server, so you might find it to be an attractive and less expensive alternative to RIS if you're working in a smaller network or don't currently have a RIS-capable server platform.

Ghost functions essentially in two parts: console and client. The console computer serves as the point of control from which you manage client computers. This computer stores the disk images, configuration settings, and other data that you use to create or deploy OS images to client computers.

Using the Ghost console (Figure 3.2) you can remotely clone existing Windows XP workstations, deploy OS images to client computers, apply Registry changes, migrate user data and settings, and deploy applications and updates. You can easily clone multiple workstations and then make changes as necessary to TCP/IP settings, workgroup, domain membership, and other properties.

For more information on the Symantec Ghost Corporate Edition, visit

```
http://enterprisesecurity.symantec.com/products/products.cfm?productID=3
```

FIGURE 3.2:

Ghost gives you a single point of control for remotely deploying Windows XP, applications, and settings.

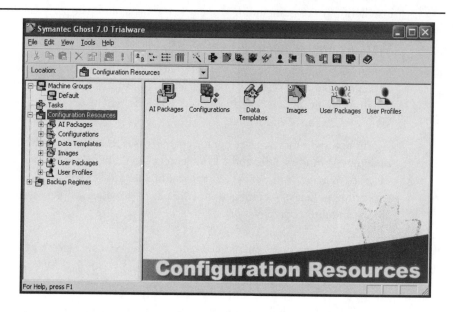

PowerQuest DeployCenter

 PowerQuest's DeployCenter is another alternative to RIS for deploying Windows XP and applications across the enterprise. Like Ghost, DeployCenter doesn't require Windows 2000 Server or .NET Server. With DeployCenter, you can create operating system images and deploy them to client computers remotely. One very nice feature that DeployCenter offers is a web-based interface that lets you create and deploy operating systems from a remote location via the Internet. So, you could even manage OS installations when you're on the road.

Another benefit you'll find in DeployCenter is support for PXE-compliant systems. DeployCenter can install Windows XP across the network to systems with no operating systems if those systems include PXE-compliant network adapters. Support for PXE significantly simplifies deploying Windows XP to new systems and performing disaster recover. For more information on DeployCenter from PowerQuest, visit www.driveimage.com/ deploycenter/.

SEE ALSO   For more information on PXE, see "Deploying Windows XP with RIS," earlier in this chapter.

CHAPTER 4

Running Multiple Operating Systems on a Single PC

I write about lots of different operating systems, so I need to be able to run most versions of Windows, both desktop and server platforms. Occasionally, I also need to run Linux. But I can't afford a different computer for each operating system. You're probably in the same boat—you need to run Windows XP alongside a different operating system but can't or don't want to install XP on a separate computer. Maybe you need to keep your existing operating system for compatibility reasons. Maybe you're installing Windows XP to get up to speed with it but need to continue to use a different OS for your day-to-day work.

There are a handful of solutions for running multiple operating systems on the same computer. Some don't require any third-party software, while others do. Some solutions involve boot managers that hide one operating system from another, while others let your different operating systems coexist.

The latest—and in my opinion the best—solution is an application that lets you run another operating system in a virtual machine. For example, you might use Windows XP as your base operating system but run Windows 9x, Windows NT, or even Linux on the computer at the same time. Third-party applications such as VMware and Virtual PC let you do just that. You gain the ability to run multiple operating systems on one computer, but best of all, you can run them concurrently and switch back and forth with a simple keystroke at any time. This is great when you need to test software, get up to speed with a particular operating system, or provide support for users who have differing operating systems.

In this chapter, I explain all of these options to help you decide which method(s) will work best for you. First, let's take a look at some of the advantages and disadvantages of running multiple operating systems.

Understanding Advantages and Limitations

Wouldn't it be great if everyone used the same operating system? You wouldn't have to worry about compatibility, and providing support to other users would be a snap—you could always count on them having the same functionality and seeing the same dialog boxes. Unfortunately, that just doesn't happen much in the real world. Running more than one operating system is often a real necessity.

One of the main advantages to running more than one operating system on the same computer is reduced cost. You don't have to buy another computer for each operating system. Even if the cost for additional hardware isn't a consideration for you, running all your operating systems on one computer can really simplify your life. You need only one keyboard, one mouse, and one monitor—you can really unclutter your office.

As handy as it is to run multiple platforms on one PC, there are still some disadvantages. If you're not using a virtual machine (VM) manager like VMware or Virtual PC, you can run only one OS at a time. That's fine if you don't need to switch very often—you just reboot whenever you need to switch. If you switch often, however, this limitation can be a real drag (and the key advantage to using a VM manager).

If you decide on a VM manager to run multiple operating systems, you'll probably need to add some additional hardware to your system. Typically, the base operating system needs at least 128 MB of RAM to run well, and each additional OS you run concurrently will probably need at least 64 MB if not more. If you're only running two operating systems at one time, that means a total of 256 MB is fine. As you add more operating systems, however, you'll quickly find that you need 512 MB or more.

You also need to consider disk performance if you choose a VM manager. SCSI drives generally provide the best performance, and it's a good idea to put each virtual machine on its own SCSI drive. SCSI drives are more expensive than IDE drives, so this pushes up the cost a bit. Adding more memory and disks to a system is still cheaper than buying an entire system, however.

SEE ALSO I cover performance issues in more detail later in this chapter in "Running Virtual Machines."

Application compatibility and migration is another big issue. If you need to use the same application on more than one operating system, you'll often need to install the application in each one. In most cases you can install the application to the same folder, unless the program implements OS-specific features. If not, you'll have the added hassle of installing and managing multiple copies of the application.

SEE ALSO Check out Chapter 2 for some additional tips on how to run applications on another operating system without reinstalling them.

If you need to run multiple operating systems on one PC and don't want to use a VM manager for performance or compatibility reasons, I recommend you use a third-party boot manager and keep each operating system in its own partition. This limits potential compatibility problems and is the cleanest solution. However, I still cover, in this chapter, a few methods for managing multiple OSes on one computer without a boot manager.

File System Considerations

An important consideration when setting up multiboot systems is the file system(s) you need to use for each operating system and whether or not they are compatible (or need to be) with one another.

Windows XP supports all FAT file systems, including FAT32. It also supports NTFS, just like Windows NT and 2000. If you choose FAT32 as your file system for Windows XP, then any Windows 9x or Me installation will be able to see the volume, as well. For example, assume you have Windows 98 installed on drive C: and add another drive as drive E: for Windows XP. You format E: using FAT32 and install Windows XP to it. Now the OSes can see more than just their own drives: When you run Windows 98, you'll be able to see drive E:, and Windows XP will be able to see drive C:.

FAT32 Issues

Unlike Windows NT, Windows XP and Windows 2000 both support FAT32. This means that you can install XP into an existing FAT32 partition created with Windows 9x/Me. It also means you can create a FAT32 partition for Windows XP during Setup, if needed. However, Windows XP can sometimes fail during reboot with a disk configuration error if you have created the FAT32 partition during the text-mode portion of Setup. This problem occurs most with partitions larger than 2 GB. The solution is to create the partition with FDISK in Windows 9x/Me and then install Windows XP to it.

TIP Another reason to create the FAT32 partition outside of Windows XP is capacity. Windows XP limits your ability to create FAT32 partitions to 32 GB. Windows 95 OSR2.X, Windows 98, and Windows Me can create FAT32 partitions up to the maximum theoretical size of 2 TB (terabytes). Windows XP has no problem accessing FAT32 partitions larger than 32 GB that were created with other operating systems.

If your current Windows 9*x* system uses a FAT file system other than FAT32, consider upgrading the partition. You can use the Drive Converter tool in Start ➢ Programs ➢ Accessories ➢ System Tools under Windows 98 to convert the volume prior to installing Windows XP.

Converting and Resizing Partitions

PartitionMagic by PowerQuest is a great tool for creating and managing partitions for almost all operating systems. Not only can you create partitions with it, but you can merge and resize partitions dynamically—including NTFS partitions—without losing any data. PartitionMagic also includes BootMagic, which lets you select the boot partition, making it much easier to work with multiple operating systems on one computer. For more information, visit www.powerquest.com/partitionmagic/.

NTFS Issues

When you add NTFS to the mix, the situation becomes a little trickier. Windows 9*x* and Windows Me do not support NTFS. So, using the same sample configuration, Windows 98 would see its own volume (C:) but not drive E:. Windows XP would see its own volume as well as C:.

NTFS versions are another consideration. If you have Windows NT installed on the system and choose to install Windows XP, understand that XP uses NTFS version 5, which incorporates several new features. You need to install Service Pack 4 or later on your NT installation to upgrade the NTFS volume and avoid potential problems in accessing one NTFS volume from another.

TIP   If you haven't installed SP4 for NT yet, I recommend that you don't, but instead install SP6a. You'll find the service pack at www.microsoft.com/ntserver.

Think about how you want your operating systems to be able to see each other's file systems. Then decide which file system you'll use for each based on that consideration. You might find that you don't need to see your Windows XP NTFS partition from your Windows 9*x* or Windows Me installation. If that's the case, you can simply add a new drive, format it as NTFS, and install Windows XP on it.

Reading NTFS Volumes from Windows 9*x* and Me

Winternals has developed a handy tool that lets your Windows 9*x* and Me installations see NTFS volumes on the local computer. NTFS for Win98 installs as a driver on the Windows 9*x*/Me system and uses some of the existing Windows XP NTFS driver files to allow the operating system to see the NTFS volume(s). NTFS for Win98 is a great solution when you want to be able to see your NTFS volumes from a Windows 9x/Me installation on the same computer. For more information, visit

```
www.winternals.com/products/fct/ntfswin98.asp
```

Choosing the Installation Order

Unless you use a boot manager or manually activate a partition and reboot, the system uses the same partition as the boot partition for all operating systems. In most cases, this means you need to install operating systems in a specific order, generally from earliest to latest. For example, you would install Windows 3.1, then Windows 98, then Windows NT, then Windows 2000, and then Windows XP (assuming you needed all five on one system). You use this order because each OS potentially overwrites the previous OS's boot sector, and later versions can detect the existence of a previous operating system and accommodate it.

In some cases, you might need to install another operating system *after* Windows XP rather than before. For example, maybe your system came preconfigured with Windows XP, and you need to install Windows 9x. You can generally install the other operating system second, but there is a possibility you will need to repair the Windows XP installation to restore the boot sector. If so, run Windows XP Setup and choose the option it offers to repair the installation. Setup might need the Windows XP Automated System Recovery disk, so make sure you update the repair disk before you install the other operating system.

TIP   Run Backup and choose Tools ➢ ASR Wizard to create the disk. Also, take the precaution of backing up your critical documents and other files before installing the other operating system.

Where Should You Install?

Another question you need to answer is where you will install each operating system. You would generally have no problems installing multiple operating systems in one partition except for one thing: the Program Files folder.

Every Microsoft operating system since Windows 95 has used \Program Files to store applications, including essentially all of the applications that come bundled with the OS. Microsoft tweaked the location a bit starting with Windows NT, placing the bundled accessories in \Program Files\Winnt\Accessories rather than \Program Files\Accessories as in Windows 9x/Me. What does that mean to you? It means you can typically run Windows 9x/Me from the same partition as Windows NT, Windows 2000, or Windows XP, because the accessories for each are in different folders.

Because NT, 2000, and XP all use the same location for these files, there is some potential for compatibility problems among these platforms. In my experience, though, you only run into problems if you install an earlier operating system after a later one. For example, you'll certainly run into problems if you install Windows XP and then install Windows NT. It's difficult to even accomplish that, however, because Windows XP detects when you're about to install an earlier version and prevents it. So, about the only way to get in this situation is to manually replace files in the `\Program Files\Windows NT` folder with older versions—something I trust you won't do!

Where this becomes a possible issue is cases where a Windows XP application won't work properly with Windows NT or Windows 2000. I doubt you'll run into such problems, but keep in mind that it's a possibility as you decide where to install your operating systems.

An alternative to installing multiple operating systems in one partition is to separate them into different partitions. For example, install Windows 98 and Windows 2000 on one partition, and install Windows XP onto a separate partition. Assuming drives C: and E: for the partitions, C: would function as the boot partition, and E: would serve as the system partition for Windows XP. You can choose the installation partition in the Setup wizard.

Another alternative is to change the active partition each time you want to change operating systems. Whichever partition is active is the one whose operating system boots. You can manage partitions manually, but I recommend a boot manager such as BootMagic (discussed earlier in this chapter) if you choose this route.

TIP   Unless you need to run a particular operating system directly on the system rather than in a virtual machine, I recommend a third-party VM manager like VMware or Virtual PC. These utilities offer a lot of flexibility and simplify any multiboot scenario by letting you standardize on one primary OS.

Cloning Existing OS Installations

You've certainly heard the saying, "You can't eat your cake and have it too." You can't keep your existing operating system and upgrade it at the same time, can you? Of course you can! But why would you want to?

Let's say you've installed Windows 98 and have lots of applications installed. You need to keep Windows 98 for compatibility reasons with a particular application or just aren't ready to give it up. But you also need to get up to speed with Windows XP. Wouldn't it be great if you could upgrade the Windows 98 installation to Windows XP to easily migrate all of your applications but still keep it intact so you could use it? The answer is to clone the existing OS.

For example, assume you install a second hard disk in your computer and you're going to install Windows XP on that new drive. But you want to include all of your existing applications in the Windows XP installation. The answer is to clone your existing Windows 98 installation to the new drive, then upgrade the original copy. You could also clone the existing OS even if you have only one drive. You just need to clone the OS to a different folder.

To use the cloning technique I describe in the next two sections, you need to be able to perform a global search and replace in the Registry, changing references to the old OS location to point to the new one. There are a handful of Registry tools that let you do this, but the one with which I'm familiar is the Registry Toolkit from Funduc Software.

Global Registry Search and Replace

 Registry Toolkit lets you perform global search and replace in the Registry for Windows 9x/Me/NT/2000/XP. The program also lets you preview changes and undo them. Registry Toolkit functions on the local Registry as well as remote registries, assuming you have the appropriate permissions in the remote Registry. For more information about this utility, visit

www.funduc.com/registry_toolkit.htm

TIP   If during the following procedures you find yourself unsure of which copy of an OS you're running, open a command console. Execute the command **ECHO %WINDIR%**. Windows will display the location of the current Windows system folder.

Cloning Windows 9x or Me

You can use the xcopy32 command from a DOS console inside Windows 9x/Me to clone the operating system files to a new folder. There are several additional steps you need to take, all outlined in the following procedure:

NOTE   The following assumes you're cloning Windows 9x, but the procedure is the same for Windows Me. You can replace C:\Win9x with C:\WinMe in all the following steps, if desired.

1. Create a bootable Windows 9x diskette that you can use, if needed, to boot the system. This is a precaution, but it's one step you shouldn't bypass. Also back up your documents and critical files for safekeeping.

2. Install the Registry tool you'll be using to perform the global search and replace in the Registry.

3. Create a new directory named Win9x to contain the cloned copy of Windows, substituting a different name if you want.

4. In Windows, open an MS-DOS command console and execute the following command (change the paths if your folders have different names):

```
xcopy32 C:\windows C:\win9x /h /i /c /k /e /r /y
```

5. When the files are all copied, open My Computer and open the root of drive C:. You need to configure folder options to show hidden files if you haven't already done so.

6. Create the folder `C:\Win9x\boot`.

7. Copy the files `io.sys`, `msdos.sys`, `autoexec.bat`, and `config.sys` to `C:\Win9x\boot`.

8. Right-click `msdos.sys` in the root folder (the original file) and choose Properties. Clear the Read-Only attribute.

9. Open `msdos.sys` in Notepad. Change the values of WinDir and WinBootDir to point to `C:\Win9x`. Save the file, but don't reapply the read-only attribute to the file yet.

10. Restart the system, which will boot the cloned copy in `C:\Win9x`.

11. Replace all instances in the Registry of `C:\Windows`, replacing them with `C:\Win9x`. Use the Registry Toolkit or other third-party Registry editor to accomplish this. Open `System.ini` in Notepad and change any instances of `C:\Windows` to `C:\Win9x`. Do the same for `Win.ini`.

12. Open `msdos.sys` in Notepad again. Change the values of WinDir and WinBootDir back to `C:\Windows`.

13. Reboot the computer to boot the copy of Windows in `C:\Windows`.

14. Insert the Windows XP CD and upgrade the copy of Windows in `C:\Windows` to Windows XP.

WARNING Don't convert the file system to NTFS, as that would prevent you from booting Windows 9x.

15. After Windows XP is installed, configure folder options to display hidden and system files, and then create the folder `C:\Windows\boot` and copy `autoexec.bat` and `config.sys` to that new folder. Then, copy the files `C:\Win9x\boot\autoexec.bat` and `C:\Win9x\boot\config.sys` to `C:\`.

TIP To view hidden and system files, open My Computer and choose Tools ➢ Folder Options. Click the View tab, then select the Show Hidden Files And Folders option and clear the Hide Protected Operating System Files options.

16. Open `autoexec.bat` and `config.sys` in Notepad and change any occurrences of `C:\Windows` to `C:\Win9x`. Also add the command `win` as the last line of `autoexec.bat`,

which will cause Windows 9*x* to start when you select the option to boot the original operating system.

17. Clear the Read-Only attribute from boot.ini in the root folder of the boot drive, then open boot.ini in Notepad. Add the following line in the [operating systems] section of the file, then save the file and restore the Read-Only attribute:

    ```
    C:\"Windows 9x"
    ```

18. Reconfigure folder options to hide protected operating system files, and if desired, not show hidden files. Then, restart the computer and attempt to boot Windows 9*x*. When Windows boots, check all of the shortcuts in the Programs menu to point them to C:\Win9x instead of C:\Windows.

TIP The MS-DOS Prompt shortcut is a good example of a shortcut in the Programs menu that points explicitly to the C:\Windows folder. Most of the accessory applications, however, point to the C:\Program Files\Accessories folder.

19. Reboot the computer to Windows XP and verify that that OS works properly.

Cloning Windows NT or 2000

You can clone Windows NT or Windows 2000 using a similar but slightly different technique from the one for cloning Windows 9*x*/Me. Just as you do when cloning Windows 9*x*/Me, you'll need a third-party application capable of performing a global search and replace in the Registry.

1. Update your system Emergency Repair Disk (ERD) using the command **rdisk /s** in Windows NT or using the Backup utility in Windows 2000. Also make a backup of all documents and other critical data files as a precaution.

2. Create the directory C:\WinXP to contain Windows XP.

3. In your current operating system, open a command console and execute the following command to duplicate all of the files from the existing installation to the C:\WinXP folder (change the path to point to your existing OS if it isn't installed in the Winnt folder):

    ```
    xcopy C:\Winnt C:\WinXP /h /i /c /k /e /r
    ```

4. Open My Computer and configure folder options to display hidden and system files. Then, clear the Read-Only attribute on boot.ini in the root folder of C:.

5. Open Boot.ini in Notepad. In the [operating systems] section, copy to the Clipboard the line that references your current OS installation. The following is a typical example:

    ```
    multi(0)disk(0)rdisk(0)partition(1)\WINNT="Microsoft Windows 2000
    Professional" /fastdetect
    ```

6. Add a new line below the existing line and paste the line from the Clipboard. Modify the line you just inserted, pointing it to the `WinXP` folder instead of the `Winnt` folder, as in the following example:

   ```
   multi(0)disk(0)rdisk(0)partition(1)\WINXP="Microsoft Windows XP" /fastdetect
   ```

7. Save `boot.ini` and restore the Read-Only attribute.

8. Hold down the Shift key and insert the Windows XP CD (holding Shift prevents the CD from autoplaying). Open a command console, switch to the `i386` folder on the CD, and execute the following command to install the Recovery Console:

   ```
   D:\i386>winnt32 /cmdcons
   ```

9. Restart the system and boot the Recovery Console.

10. Select the backup copy in `c:\WinXP` when prompted for which copy of Windows 2000 to start. There will be no SAM (xcopy can't copy it), so you won't be prompted for a password.

11. Change to the `\Winnt\System32\config` folder. Use the `copy` command to copy all of the files in this folder to `\WinXP\System32\config`, which copies the Registry from the original installation to the backup copy.

12. Reboot the computer and select Microsoft Windows XP to boot the copy of Windows 2000 in `C:\WinXP`.

13. Log on as administrator, install the Registry Toolkit, and perform a global search and replace in the Registry, changing all instances of `C:\Winnt` to `C:\WinXP`. Adjust accordingly if your original installation of Windows NT or Windows 2000 is installed in a folder other than `C:\Winnt`.

14. Reboot the computer and boot the option Microsoft Windows XP, log on as administrator, and upgrade the installation to Windows XP.

Configuring Boot Options

Like Windows NT and Windows 2000, Windows XP uses a `Boot.ini` file to provide boot options. The entries in `Boot.ini` determine which operating system starts by default, which other operating systems are defined, and optional switches that control how each operating system starts (this last aspect applies to NT, 2000, and XP only.) The `Boot.ini` file also determines the length of time the boot menu appears on the screen before the boot loader boots the default operating system if you don't select one from the menu.

If your computer contains multiple operating systems, one change you might want to make is to specify a different default OS from the current one. The entry `default` in the `[boot loader]` section of the file specifies the default operating system. Clear the Read-Only attribute on Boot.ini, open it in Notepad, and change the value of default to specify the OS you want your computer to boot by default.

SEE ALSO   For detailed information on Boot.ini options and how to configure them, see Chapter 5.

Using Third-Party Boot Managers

Another option to consider when you want to host multiple operating systems on one computer is a third-party boot manager. A boot manager manages the boot files for multiple partitions. Typically, the partition manager displays a menu at boot from which you select the operating system you want to use. When you select one, the boot manager then activates the necessary partition and copies boot files into place (if necessary) to allow the selected OS to boot. I recommend a boot manager in most situations where you need to run multiple operating systems on one computer and don't want to use a virtual machine manager like VMware or Virtual PC.

PowerQuest BootMagic

BootMagic is an integral part of PartitionMagic, from PowerQuest. BootMagic provides a graphical interface—complete with mouse and keyboard support—that allows you to select the operating system you want to boot. BootMagic manages the partitions and keeps the OSes separate from one another, preventing possible compatibility problems. You can even password-protect the boot process to prevent unauthorized access to your system. For more information, visit www.powerquest.com.

V Communications System Commander 7

System Commander 7, from V Communications, is another good third-party boot manager. The program provides a wizard to automatically prepare a system and partition for a particular operating system, and you can override the wizard to customize the installation whenever necessary. The program includes a full copy of Partition Commander; can create, copy, and resize partitions; and supports all FAT file systems as well as NTFS. It includes an NTFS converter to convert from NTFS to FAT32 and can handle NTFS partitions for both Windows NT and Windows 2000/XP. For more information, visit www.systemcommander.com.

Running Multiple Operating Systems

I've been using Windows 2000 Professional as my base operating system on a day-to-day basis since the last release candidate was issued in the Windows 2000 beta (before that it was

Windows NT Workstation). I've also been using Windows XP since the early beta stages, but still haven't switched to it from Windows 2000 on my primary system. How is it possible I "wrote the book on Windows XP" but still use Windows 2000? I'm not a one-platform kind of guy!

Because I write about a broad range of topics, I frequently need to use other operating systems, including Windows XP, Windows NT Server and Workstation, Windows 2000 Server, Windows 2000 Advanced Server, and Windows 98. Very occasionally, I also need to run Linux. I could use a boot manager and switch back and forth between them, but this isn't practical for me because I need to run certain applications all the time (such as Microsoft Word and Outlook) while doing development or testing in a particular OS.

In the good old days, I used to run more than one computer in my office—one as my working system and at least one other for whatever OS I was writing about. I ended up using KVM switches, pcAnywhere, and all sorts of other methods to try to simplify the process. Finally, I came across a solution that let me reduce the number of computers in my office to just one—a VM manager.

You might not know it, but each 32-bit Windows application you run on your Windows operating system, from Windows 9*x* through Windows XP, runs in its own *virtual machine*. A virtual machine in effect simulates a stand-alone computer, but does so in your physical PC's memory. One of the reasons for running applications in a VM is to separate them from one another so if a particular program fails, it doesn't take down any others. It sounds great in theory and usually works well in practice.

A VM manager such as VMware or Virtual PC creates a virtual environment complete with its own BIOS, virtual hardware, and operating system. Rather than running as a stand-alone operating system on your PC, the operating system runs in a virtual machine. This means you can run multiple operating systems on one PC at the same time, each in its own window, switching back and forth as needed, or even switching a particular OS to full-screen mode.

One particularly handy capability is virtual network support. If I need to write an article or chapter about a server-side topic that involves multiple network interfaces, I can create a virtual server in a matter of minutes. For example, if I'm writing about routing and remote access under Windows .NET Server, I can quickly add one or two additional network adapters to a virtual server just by editing a text file and restarting the VM. Voila! I have a server with three network cards without spending a single penny on additional hardware.

A VM manager is a perfect solution when you need to run multiple operating systems at the same time. For example, if part of your job is providing technical support for people using a range of operating systems, you can use a VM manager to run each potential OS. You don't need to put the caller on hold while you reboot your computer to the appropriate operating system.

VMware

VMware Workstation runs on Windows NT, Windows 2000, Windows XP, or Linux as the base operating system. The program lets you run essentially any PC-based operating system in a virtual machine. VMware also markets virtual server software. Figure 4.1 shows VMware running on a Windows 2000 platform with Windows XP running in a window. You can find more information about VMware at www.vmware.com.

Connectix Virtual PC

Virtual PC runs on Windows Me, Windows NT, Windows 2000, or Windows XP as the base operating system. Like VMware, Virtual PC lets you run any PC-based operating system in a virtual machine. Connectix also markets licensed OS packs with specific operating systems preinstalled and configured. You only need to copy a file from a CD to your hard disk to install and start using a specific operating system. Figure 4.2 shows Virtual PC running on a Windows 2000 platform with Windows XP running in a window. Check out www.connectix.com for more information.

FIGURE 4.1:
VMware Workstation lets you run multiple operating systems at one time.

FIGURE 4.2:

Virtual PC lets you run multiple operating systems at one time.

CHAPTER 5

Gaining Control of Windows XP Startup and Shutdown

Windows XP offers several methods for controlling the way the operating system starts and shuts down. For example, the `Boot.ini` file contains a small number of settings that you can edit, either directly or through the Windows XP graphical user interface (GUI), to specify startup options, such as the length of time the boot menu remains on the screen.

In addition, like other versions of Windows, Windows XP provides a `Startup` folder that lets you start applications automatically at logon. Although there are no settings to configure for the `Startup` folder, you can specify a different location for it, if desired. You can also bypass the `Startup` folder at logon to prevent applications contained in it from starting automatically.

Windows XP also lets you execute scripts at system startup, user logon, user logoff, and system shutdown. In addition to creating scripts to perform a wide variety of actions, you can configure several policies that determine how and when these scripts execute.

This chapter examines these startup and shutdown options, explaining why you might want to change them as well as how to accomplish the change. In most cases, these options are available in both Windows XP versions, but some features that rely on group policy are not available in Windows XP Home Edition.

TIP   Features specific only to Windows XP Professional are identified where applicable in the chapter.

Configuring Boot and Recovery Options in the GUI

Although you can set some boot options by directly editing the Boot.ini file (covered later in this chapter), the Windows XP GUI offers the easiest means of controlling a system's startup options. The boot options include the ability to choose the default operating system, the length of time the Windows XP displays boot menu options, and what actions, if any, XP should take if the system fails. I examine each of these issues in detail in this section.

Setting System Startup Options

You can set a small number of settings in Windows XP through the GUI; for instance, you can specify which operating system will be treated as the default system on multiboot installations or set the length of time Windows XP displays the boot menu for normal and recovery boot options.

TIP   You must be logged on as a member of the Administrators group to configure these settings.

You set system startup options in the Windows XP GUI through the Systems Properties dialog box, shown in Figure 5.1. You can open this dialog box in one of two ways. The first is to right-click My Computer, choose Properties, and then click the Advanced tab. Or simply open the System object in Control Panel, which takes you directly to the Advanced tab of the System Properties dialog box. (Microsoft's official term for System Properties is a *property sheet*, but for familiarity's sake, I usually refer to it as a dialog box.) Then, click Settings in the Startup And Recovery control group to display the dialog box shown in Figure 5.2.

FIGURE 5.1:

Use the Advanced tab of the System Properties dialog box to access startup options.

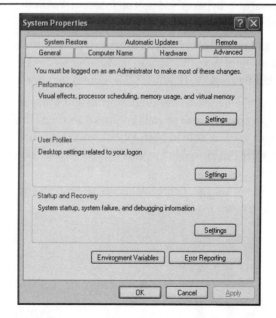

We'll come back to these two dialog boxes several times in this chapter. The following few sections describe specific options available to you here.

Set the Default OS

Use the Default Operating System drop-down list to select the OS you want Windows XP to boot by default if no other option is selected in the boot menu. This selection corresponds to the value of the `default` entry in the `[boot loader]` section of `Boot.ini`.

If Windows XP is the only operating system installed, there is no need to change the default operating system. However, you might be using Windows XP on a system that also contains Windows 98 or another OS. If that's the case, Windows XP displays a boot menu when you start the system that allows you to select which operating system will boot. The default OS is the one that will start if you take no action in the boot menu. You'll probably want to configure the boot options to specify as the default the operating system you use most often.

FIGURE 5.2:

Configure startup options for the system through the Startup And Recovery dialog box.

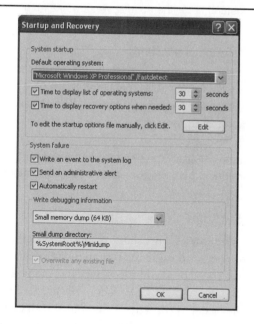

TIP   You can also use the `Msconfig.exe` utility included with Windows XP to modify the `Boot.ini` file.

Control Boot Menu Delay

Select the Time To Display List Of Operating Systems check box, and specify a value in seconds with the associated spin control, to define the length of time the boot menu will remain on the screen before Windows XP boots the default option. Setting the value to zero or deselecting this option disables the boot menu and causes Windows XP to boot the default operating system immediately. This setting corresponds to the timeout value in the [boot loader] section of Boot.ini.

TIP   Selecting an option in the boot menu with the arrow keys stops the timer and keeps the boot menu on the screen until you select an option and press Enter.

If you use the default operating system most of the time, you can speed up the boot process by reducing the menu display interval from its default setting of 30 seconds, to, say, only a few seconds. This makes Windows XP boot almost right away, but still gives you the option of selecting a different boot option if you need to.

TIP   If you have only one operating system installed, Windows XP does not display a boot menu. Instead, it begins booting Windows XP immediately.

Control Recovery Menu Delay

You might also want to change the length of time that Windows XP displays the boot menu for recovery operations. Use the Time To Display Recovery Options When Needed option to specify how long you want Windows XP to display recovery boot options when the system executes automated recovery.

SEE ALSO   See "Setting Startup Options in Boot.ini Manually," later in this chapter, for details on modifying Boot.ini to include additional boot options.

Setting System Failure Options

Although Windows XP is a stable operating system, sooner or later an errant program or another problem will cause the system to fail. While these failures will generally be few and far between, you should consider reviewing and possibly changing the options that determine the actions Windows XP takes in the event of a failure. You configure these settings by opening the System Properties dialog box shown earlier (shown previously in Figure 5.1), then clicking Settings in the Startup And Recovery section to open the Startup And Recovery dialog box (Figure 5.2). The options in this dialog define three possible actions that Windows XP can take in the event of a system failure:

Write An Event To The System Log   Select this option to have Windows XP write an event to the System event log, which you can then view using the Event Viewer console. The event can indicate the source of the failure, although in some cases the system will be unable to write an event depending on the nature of the failure. This value corresponds to the Registry value

`\HKEY_LOCAL_MACHINE\SYSTEM\CurrentControlSet\Control\CrashControl\LogEvent`

Send An Administrative Alert　This option causes the system to generate a network broadcast message to members of the administrative group. This corresponds to the Registry value

`\HKEY_LOCAL_MACHINE\SYSTEM\CurrentControlSet\Control\CrashControl\SendAlert`

Automatically Restart　Select this option if you want Windows XP to automatically reboot the system when the failure occurs. Generally, you enable this option for servers and other systems that need to be online as much as possible or that are not readily accessible to administrative staff who can initiate a reboot. However, you should deselect this option if you're attempting to capture the stop message that is generated when the failure occurs (commonly called the Blue Screen of Death, or BSOD). This setting corresponds to the Registry value

`\HKEY_LOCAL_MACHINE\SYSTEM\CurrentControlSet\Control\CrashControl\AutoReboot`

Winternals BlueSave

One utility that allows you to capture the BSOD to a text file is BlueSave, from Winternals (www.winternals.com). This utility saves the information in the BSOD to a text file, enabling you to review it, send it to Microsoft or a third party for debugging and troubleshooting, and so on. The program requires a system drive with a disk miniport driver that is crash dump–capable.

Setting Startup and Failure Options Remotely

As you might have surmised from the Registry information provided in the previous list, you can set these options through Registry modifications as well as through the GUI. If you're setting the options for a single computer, you should generally use the GUI rather than digging into the Registry, because directly editing the Registry is always a somewhat risky proposition; you might make a mistake when changing values and affect the system's operation—or in the worst case, prevent the system from booting at all.

If you want to configure these settings for multiple computers (and setting them though the GUI isn't practical), you have a couple of options. First, you can use the Registry Editor to connect to another computer's Registry to make the change across the network. To do so, click Start ➤ Run, and enter **regedit** in the Run dialog box. In the Registry Editor, choose File ➤ Connect Network Registry to display the Select Computer dialog box (Figure 5.3). Then, type the name of the computer you want to manage and press Enter or click OK. The Registry Editor adds the remote computer's Registry as a separate key (Figure 5.4). You can then make changes as needed to the remote Registry.

FIGURE 5.3:

Specify the name of the computer whose Registry you want to modify.

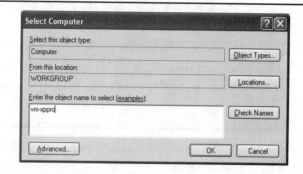

FIGURE 5.4:

Open the key containing the remote Registry and modify settings as needed.

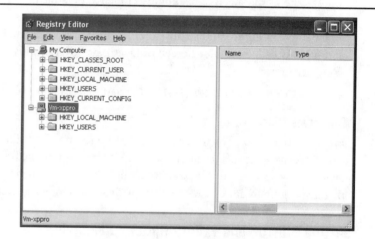

TIP   You can connect to and manage the Registrys of Windows 2000, Windows NT, and Windows XP systems from Windows XP systems, and vice versa.

WARNING   Systems that are configured for Simple File Sharing (SFS) authenticate all network access against the Guest account, so you will be unable to manage a remote system's Registry if that system is configured for SFS. You could allow Guest access to the Registry, but doing so is an invitation to disaster and should be avoided at all costs. Instead, reconfigure the system for regular file sharing.

Another option for modifying the Registry of a remote system is to use Remote Desktop to connect to the remote computer, and then open either the Registry Editor or the System Properties dialog box to accomplish the changes. The remote computer must be running Terminal Services (Windows .NET Server computers) or must be running Windows XP

Professional with access through Remote Desktop enabled. Managing settings in this way is no different from managing the settings on the local computer, with the exception that you must first establish a Remote Desktop session to the remote computer.

NOTE　　Currently there are no group or local policies that define the startup or system failure options. While you could apply the Registry changes through Windows NT–style policies, I don't recommend mixing NT policies with Windows 2000/XP group policies, for administrative reasons.

SEE ALSO　　See Chapter 21 for detailed information on how to configure Windows XP systems for remote Registry access, and Chapter 30 for in-depth discussion of configuring and using the various remote access and management capabilities provided with Windows XP.

Setting Startup Options in Boot.ini Manually

As explained previously in this chapter, some of the settings you configure for startup are stored in the system's Boot.ini file. You should make common startup changes through the GUI rather than modifying Boot.ini manually and, due to the potential for disastrous mistakes, only modify Boot.ini yourself when you need to accomplish a change that isn't offered through the GUI. This section explains how to modify Boot.ini, which changes you can make, and why you would make those changes to control startup. For example, you'll need to modify Boot.ini to include the boot entries for another operating system if you clone the existing OS as I explained in Chapter 2.

Modifying Boot.ini

Boot.ini is located in the root folder of the boot volume. You can edit the file in Notepad, WordPad, or any other text editor capable of reading and writing text files. You can open Boot.ini directly from Notepad, or you can access it for editing through the System Properties dialog box. On the Advanced tab of System Properties, click Settings in the Startup And Recovery group, then click Edit in the next dialog box (Figure 5.2). Windows XP opens Boot.ini in Notepad.

WARNING　　If you're using a program other than Notepad, make sure you don't save Boot.ini in any format other than as a text file. For example, don't use Word to edit the file and then save it as a Word document. Doing so will prevent your system from booting until the Boot.ini file is restored.

SEE ALSO Windows XP includes a command-line utility called Bootcfg that allows you to make changes to Boot.ini.

The Read-Only and Hidden attributes of Boot.ini are set, and you must change the Read-Only attribute if you edit the file outside of the Startup And Recovery dialog box (such as directly in Notepad). Configure the system's folder options to display hidden files, and then right-click Boot.ini and choose Properties. Deselect the Read-Only option and click OK. Open the file in Notepad, make the desired changes, and save the file as you would any other text file.

TIP If you open Boot.ini from the Startup And Recovery dialog box, Windows XP automatically removes the Read-Only attribute from Boot.ini to allow you to make changes. It does not restore the attribute when you close Notepad, so consider resetting the Read-Only attribute on the file after you make changes—to prevent unintended changes to it in the future.

Modifying Boot.ini Settings

There are several settings you can modify or add to Boot.ini to change the way the system boots. For example, you might add a second entry in the file, an entry that points to your existing Windows XP installation but boots it with certain troubleshooting options. Maybe, to troubleshoot a problem, you have to boot the system several times in safe mode. You can add one or more entries to Boot.ini that let you select the safe mode boot options from the main boot menu. This eliminates the need to press F8 during boot to display such options.

The Boot.ini file contains two sections: [boot loader] and [operating systems].

The [boot loader] Section

This section contains settings that control the way the boot process works. Settings in this section specify the operating system that the boot loader boots by default and the length of time the boot menu is displayed. The [boot loader] section can contain two settings:

timeout   This value specifies the length of time the boot loader waits for you to make a selection from the boot menu. A value of 0 causes the boot loader to immediately boot the operating system using the entry in [operating systems] defined by the value of the default setting. A positive value specifies the number of seconds to display the menu. You can specify a value of –1 to cause the boot loader to wait indefinitely for a menu selection, although you must modify Boot.ini manually to do this, as the GUI will not accept a negative value for setting.

default   This value specifies the entry in the [operating systems] section that the boot loader will boot if no other selection is made.

The [operating systems] Section

This section defines the available operating systems and options for each. By default, this section contains only one entry, which boots Windows XP using all default settings. This section contains other entries if other operating systems such as Windows 9*x*, Windows Me, or Recovery Console are present.

The format for an entry in the [operating systems] section depends on the target operating system. Windows NT/2000/XP operating systems use the Advanced RISC Computing (ARC) path format for entries. The default entry for Windows XP specifies the physical drive and partition where the operating system is located along with the /fastdetect switch (explained shortly.) A default entry takes a form similar to the following:

```
multi(0)disk(0)rdisk(0)partition(1)\windows="Microsoft Windows XP Professional"
    /fastdetect
```

The part of the string to the left of the equal sign defines the path to the Windows XP system folder. The data in quotes specifies the description that appears in the boot menu, and the /fastdetect switch disables serial mouse detection on all COM ports (explained in more detail shortly).

Boot.ini Syntaxes

There are three syntaxes that can be used in a Boot.ini file to define the ARC path to the system folder. The following sections explain each one in detail.

Multi Syntax

The multi syntax was originally valid only for IDE and ESDI volumes but was expanded to include SCSI (Small Computer System Interface) devices in Windows NT 3.5. When the boot loader boots an installation of Windows XP using the multi syntax, it relies on the system BIOS to load the files necessary to boot the operating system. The Ntldr program uses standard INT 13 BIOS calls to locate and load the Windows XP kernel file Ntoskrnl.exe and other files (such as drivers) needed to boot the system. The following is an example of the multi syntax:

```
multi(W)disk(X)rdisk(Y)partition(Z)
```

The following list explains the variables:

Variable	Description
W	Specifies the number of the adapter; typically 0.
X	Specifies the physical disk; always 0.
Y	Specifies the logical disk number; a value from 0 to 3.
Z	Specifies the partition number.

For all syntaxes, the first valid value for *W*, *X*, and *Y* is 0, and the first valid value for *Z* is 1. Primary partitions are numbered first, then logical drives.

Typically, the system BIOS identifies only a single adapter for INT 13, which means that the multi syntax can boot Windows XP only from one of two possible disks, on either the primary or secondary IDE chain or on the SCSI bus. The multi syntax supports up to four IDE devices, two each on the primary and secondary chains. The syntax supports the first two drives on the first SCSI adapter, which is the adapter whose BIOS loads first. When the system contains multiple adapters, whether IDE or SCSI, this syntax works only for devices on the first adapter.

SCSI Syntax

This syntax allows the Ntldr program to load a SCSI device driver to access the boot partition rather than rely on INT 13 calls. The following is an example of the SCSI syntax:

```
scsi(W)disk(X)rdisk(Y)partition(Z)
```

The following list explains the variables:

Variable	Description
W	Specifies the controller number.
X	Specifies the physical disk number.
Y	Specifies the Logical Unit Number (LUN) for the disk; usually 0.
Z	Specifies the partition number.

Signature Syntax

The signature syntax allows Windows XP to support Plug and Play systems in which the SCSI adapter number can potentially vary each time the system is booted. Rather than rely on a static SCSI adapter number, this syntax causes Ntldr to search for and boot from the disk containing the specified signature. The following is an example of the signature syntax:

```
signature(W)disk(X)rdisk(Y)partition(Z)
```

The values for *X*, *Y*, and *Z* are the same as for the SCSI syntax. The value *W* specifies the disk signature written to the target disk either during the text mode portion of Setup, or through another installation of Windows XP, or through a previous installation of Windows 2000. The signature—a hexadecimal value—is stored in the Master Boot Record (MBR) of the disk. Windows XP uses the signature syntax only if the system or boot BIOS does not support Extended INT 13, and only if the specified disk is larger than 7.8 GB or the ending cylinder number is higher than 1,024.

Boot.ini Switches

`Boot.ini` supports several switches that you can add in order to control the way Windows XP boots. While you will most likely use the default value created by Setup to boot the operating system, you might add other boot menu selections so you can boot the system differently when needed. For example, you might add an entry that starts a multiprocessor system in single-processor mode, or specify the maximum amount of RAM that Windows XP can use if you suspect a physical memory problem. Table 5.1 lists the available switches and their functions.

TABLE 5.1: Boot.ini Switches and Functions

Switch	Function
/3GB	Moves the 1 GB of kernel and executive components to the 3 GB memory location, allocating 3 GB to user-mode applications (increases user-mode memory from 2 GB to 3 GB).
/BASEVIDEO	Starts Windows XP using the standard VGA driver. Use when a new video driver is preventing Windows XP from starting properly.
/BAUDRATE=*nnnn*	Specifies the baud rate to use for debugging through the system's COM ports. The default rate for a modem is 9,600 and for a null-mode cable is 19,200. This setting causes the /DEBUG switch to activate (see the /DEBUG entry).
/BOOTLOG	Enables boot logging to *%systemroot%*\ntbtlog1.txt.
/BURNMEMORY=*n*	Specifies the amount of RAM (MB) that Windows XP can use. Use this switch to limit physical memory for troubleshooting purposes.
/CRASHDEBUG	Loads the debugger at boot, but the debugger remains inactive unless a kernel error occurs. Use for troubleshooting kernel errors.
/DEBUG	Loads the debugger and allows it to be activated by any host debugger connected to the system. Use this switch when debugging reproducible errors.
/DEBUGPORT=COM*n*	Specifies the serial port to use for debugging, such as COM1. This switch causes the /DEBUG switch to activate.
/FASTDETECT= [COM*n* | COM*x*,*y*,*z*...]	Disables serial mouse detection on the specified port(s). Used by itself, the /FASTDETECT switch disables mouse detection for all ports. Use this switch to speed boot when a device other than a mouse is connected to the specified port(s) at startup.
/MAXMEM:*n*	Specifies the maximum amount of RAM Windows XP can use. This switch is helpful for troubleshooting physical memory problems.
/NOGUIBOOT	Hides the startup progress bitmap during boot.
/NODEBUG	Specifies not to use debugging.
/NUMPROC=*n*	Forces a multiprocessor system to use a specified number of processors. This switch is useful for troubleshooting processor errors and multiprocessor applications.

Continued on next page

TABLE 5.1 CONTINUED: Boot.ini Switches and Functions

Switch	Function
/PCILOCK	Prevents Windows XP from dynamically assigning IRQ and I/O resources to PCI devices, instead allowing the BIOS to assign resources
/SAFEBOOT:*switch*	Forces Windows XP to boot in safe mode using the specified *switch*, which can be `minimal`, `network`, or `minimal(alternateshell)`.
/SOS	Displays device drivers as they are loaded by the boot process. Use this switch to troubleshoot drivers that might be causing a system or boot failure.
/PAE	Allows the system that supports Physical Address Extension (PAE) mode to boot normally. PAE allows software to use more than 4GB of physical memory

SEE ALSO   For more information on PAE and advanced memory issues, consult "Enterprise Memory Architecture" in the *Microsoft Windows Datacenter Server Manual*, included with Datacenter Server and available from TechNet and other Microsoft resources on the Web.

To use any of the switches, simply edit the `Boot.ini` file, adding other entries as needed and including the appropriate switches, or modifying existing entries to include the necessary switches.

TIP   The best way to create a new entry for an existing operating system installation is to copy and paste from an existing entry. When you add or modify an entry, make sure to change the description so you'll be able to easily identify the function of the entry in the boot menu at startup.

Modifying Boot.ini with Bootcfg

Windows XP adds a new utility that you can use to modify the `Boot.ini` file. This tool—`Bootcfg.exe`—is a console utility you can run from a command console within Windows XP, from Recovery Console, or in a batch file. You can use this command to modify the local `Boot.ini` file or the `Boot.ini` file of a remote computer across the network. That means you can change the way a computer on the other side of the world boots without hopping a plane, train, or slow boat.

SEE ALSO   See Chapter 47 for detailed information on Recovery Console.

Granted, it's so easy to modify a local `Boot.ini` on a working system that you will likely not use Bootcfg to do so very often (instead preferring to use Notepad or the options in the System Properties dialog box). But in some cases, Bootcfg offers the best (or only) solution for modifying `Boot.ini` files. For example, if you are managing several systems and need to make modifications across the enterprise, Bootcfg allows you to do so through startup scripts, a Telnet session, or other means. You can also use it to make modifications to a local `Boot.ini` file when you're troubleshooting the system from Recovery Console.

The Bootcfg tool is fully documented in the Windows XP Help documentation. Rather than duplicate that information here, I'll just direct you to the appropriate place. Click Help And Support in the Start menu and perform a search on **bootcfg**. You'll also find Bootcfg listed in the Windows XP Command-Line Reference.

Working with the Startup Folder

Like earlier Windows platforms since Windows 9*x*, Windows XP provides a `Startup` folder that you can use to start programs automatically when a user logs on. The `Startup` folder is actually two folders, one for the current user and one for all users. Therefore, when you log on, Windows XP will start applications located in both folders—one might start from your personal `Startup` folder and another might start from the common `Startup` folder. The combined contents of both `Startup` folders are displayed when you click Start ➢ All Programs ➢ Startup.

There is nothing magical about the `Startup` folders, other than the fact that Windows XP searches them at logon and opens any items it finds inside them. These items can be programs, batch files, documents, scripts, or shortcuts—in short, anything you can execute in Windows.

Defining the Location of the Startup Group

The user-specific `Startup` folder is located by default in

> `\Documents and Settings\`*user*`\Start Menu\Programs\Startup`

where *user* is the user's logon name. The common `Startup` folder is located in

> `\Documents and Settings\All Users\Start Menu\Programs\Startup`

TIP   On systems upgraded from Windows NT, the Startup folders are located in *%systemroot%*\ Profiles*user*\Start Menu\Programs\Startup.

In most cases, you won't need to modify the location of the `Startup` folders, but there is one instance where you might: when you need to redirect several users to the same `Startup` folder(s) across the network. For example, you might want all users to have their own Startup folder on their computers but provide a common Startup folder—located on a network server—that is shared by all. This would provide all users with the same common startup items and offer an easy way to manage and customize startup items for several users.

Relocation by Group Policy

You have a couple of options for redirecting Startup folders. Group policy offers the best solution for computers in a domain, provided you want the whole Start menu redirected to a common location, not just the Startup folder. For example, you can use this option to redirect user folders to a common folder on a network server to give them a common set of applications and shortcuts. Or you might redirect each user's Start menu to the user's home folder on a server.

NOTE   Windows XP Home Edition does not support group policies. To redirect the Startup folder on a Home Edition system, you must edit the Registry, as explained in the following section.

SEE ALSO   This chapter assumes you have some familiarity with group and local policies and how to modify them. For a more detailed discussion of these topics, see Chapter 42.

If you want to redirect the Startup folder through policies, open the Active Directory Users And Computers console on a domain controller in the desired domain, right-click the container where you want to apply the redirection policy (domain or organizational unit), and choose Properties. Then click the Group Policy tab, shown in Figure 5.5.

FIGURE 5.5:

Use the Group Policies tab to specify group policy that redirects folders.

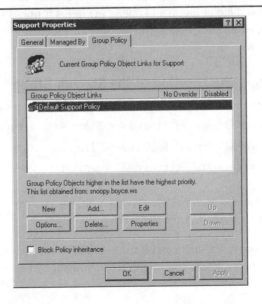

You can apply group policies locally if you prefer not to assign policies at a higher level, or if you are working in a workgroup. Run `Mmc.exe` and add the Group Policy snap-in to the console focused on the local computer. The settings described in the following procedures are available through the Local Computer Policy branch.

Use the Active Directory Sites And Services console if you want to create a group policy object (GPO) that assigns policies at the site level.

Select an existing policy, or if you have no policy already defined, click New to create a new one. Then, click Edit to open the Group Policy editor shown in Figure 5.6.

FIGURE 5.6:

Edit GPOs through the
Group Policy editor.

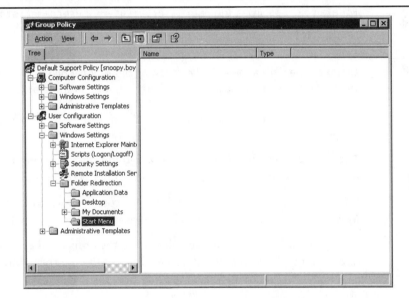

In the Group Policy editor, open the branch \User Configuration\Windows Settings\ Folder Redirection\Start Menu. Right-click in the right pane and choose Properties to open the Start Menu Properties dialog box. Then, select one of the following options from the Setting drop-down list:

"No administrative policy specified"   Folders will not be redirected unless this policy is defined at an overriding level.

"Basic—redirect everyone's folder to the same location"   Redirects folders to a common location for all users who are under the policy's scope of management to a single, common folder. You can specify a Universal Naming Convention (UNC) path or specify a local folder. If you specify a local drive and path, group policy will redirect the Start menu to the matching path on the user's local system, so the specified drive and path must exist locally for each user under the scope of the policy. Specify the path in the Target Folder Location field or click Browse to browse for the folder.

"Advanced—specify locations for various user groups"   Redirects folders to a specified location based on group membership. You add security groups to a list and then specify the redirected folder to be used for each group. Click Add when the Security Group Membership options appear and select a security group and a path to associate with that group. You can specify multiple security groups and paths in a single GPO.

TIP   You can use the %username% variable in the policy to redirect folders based on user name. For example, specifying the path \\server\users\%username%\start would cause the folder to be redirected for a user named jboyce to \\server\users\jboyce\start.

TIP   Group policies are applied in the following order: local policy, site policy, domain policy, OU policy. Therefore, policies applied at the OU level override policies at the site level.

After you specify the path(s) as needed, click the Settings tab of the Start Menu Properties. You can then choose one of the following two options:

"Leave the folder in the new location when policy is removed"   The folder will remain in its redirected location even if the policy is removed.

"Redirect the folder back to the local userprofile location when policy is removed"
Move the user's folder back to their local profile location when the policy is removed.

After you finish configuring the policy, close the property sheet and the Group Policy editor. Keep in mind that you can, if needed, link a GPO to other containers in Active Directory. This allows you to use the same GPO for several OUs or domains.

SEE ALSO   For more information on group policies, see Chapter 42. For more information on redirecting folders and other ways to manage user settings and data, see Chapter 44.

Relocation by Registry Changes

Group policy offers the best way to redirect folders for multiple users. You can also redirect folders by editing the Registry—a handy method when you only need to make the change for a small number of users or when you are not using group policies.

The individual user Startup folder is defined by the Registry value *userprofile*\Start Menu\Programs\Startup, where *userprofile* is replaced by the user's current user profile location, describing the Startup folder in the context of the current user profile. For example, this variable points to Documents and Settings*user* for clean installs or systems upgraded from Windows NT. You can change the portion of the string after the variable to relocate the Startup folder to a different location within the user's profile, or replace the whole string to completely relocate the Startup folder.

The Registry entry for the common Startup folder is defined by the value *allusersprofile*\\ Start Menu\\Programs\\Startup, where *allusersprofile* points to the Documents and Settings\\All Users folder.

WARNING Improperly editing the Registry can cause various system problems, including the inability to boot the system. Make a backup of your system's Registry before making any changes. See Chapter 21 for detailed information on working with, backing up, and restoring the Registry.

The value for the individual Startup folder is located in the Registry value

\\HKEY_CURRENT_USER\\SOFTWARE\\Microsoft\\Windows\\CurrentVersion\\Explorer\\
User Shell Folders\\Startup

The value for the common Startup folders is located in the Registry value

\\HKEY_LOCAL_MACHINE\\SOFTWARE\\Microsoft\\Windows\\CurrentVersion\\Explorer\\User
Shell Folders\\Common Startup

Open the Registry Editor, then locate and open the desired key. Make a backup copy of the key, then apply the change. Log off, then log back on to see the change take effect.

Bypassing the Startup Group

Occasionally you might want to bypass the Startup group and prevent the applications in it from starting automatically when you log on. For example, a startup application might be causing Windows XP to hang. Or perhaps it takes several seconds for the applications to start, and you want to bypass them to speed up logon.

To bypass the Startup folder, hold down the Shift key while logging on. For example, when Windows XP displays the logon dialog box, enter your user name and password. Then, hold down the Shift key and click OK. Continue holding down the Shift key until the Desktop appears and the logon process is complete.

There are a handful of alternatives to the Startup folder that can cause applications to start automatically at logon. These alternatives—and how to bypass them—are covered in the following section.

TIP If you decide you want to permanently prevent a specific application from starting through the Startup folder, open the Startup folder, right-click the item, and choose Delete. This deletes the shortcut from the menu but does not uninstall or delete the application itself.

Alternatives to the Startup Folder

In addition to the two Startup folders (one common, one individual), Windows XP provides other ways to start applications automatically at logon. For example, Windows XP also executes applications listed in the following Registry keys:

```
\HKEY_LOCAL_MACHINE\SOFTWARE\Microsoft\Windows\CurrentVersion\Run
\HKEY_LOCAL_MACHINE\SOFTWARE\Microsoft\Windows\CurrentVersion\RunOnce
\HKEY_CURRENT_USER\Software\Microsoft\Windows\CurrentVersion\Run
\HKEY_CURRENT_USER\Software\Microsoft\Windows\CurrentVersion\Runonce
```

If you're trying to bypass the startup applications, and one or more continues to start even though you've either cleared out or bypassed the Startup folders, open the Registry Editor and check the contents of these keys. Make a backup of the Registry key, and then delete the values in this key for those applications you don't want to start automatically. When you're ready to have the applications start automatically again, simply restore the Registry key, log off, and log back on.

Services can also impact the system at logon. Some applications—including Windows XP components and third-party utilities—are configured to start and run as services. Regardless of the source of the service, you can temporarily configure it to not start automatically, if needed. To do so, open Computer Management Console and then open the Services branch. Locate and double-click the service that you want to temporarily reconfigure. On the General tab, set the startup type to Manual, then click Stop to stop the service. When you're ready to have the service start automatically again, set its startup type to Automatic and restart the service or log off and then log back on.

NOTE   If you've upgraded from Windows 9x, you might also want to check the contents of the WIN.INI file for run= or load= lines that start applications. WIN.INI is located in the system root folder (typically, \WINNT or \WINDOWS).

Startup and Shutdown Scripts

Windows XP supports four types of scripts: startup, shutdown, logon, and logoff. You can use these four types of scripts to automate processes such as mapping drives, starting applications, and so on. You can accomplish a very broad range of tasks with scripts, so this chapter doesn't discuss specific script tasks but instead focuses on the mechanics of creating and assigning startup and shutdown scripts.

SEE ALSO   See Chapter 44 to learn how to create and manage scripts that run at logon and logoff.

You can assign scripts through group policy. Because group policy is not supported for Windows XP Home Edition, you can only use policies to execute startup and shutdown scripts under Windows XP Professional.

TIP   You can emulate the function of logon scripts in Windows XP Home Edition using the Startup folder: create a batch file and include it in that folder. Use the Registry keys referenced in the preceding section to emulate startup scripts under Home Edition.

When you're ready to create and assign a startup or shutdown script, start by creating the CMD or BAT file that contains the script commands. Then, test and troubleshoot any problems with the script.

SEE ALSO   For detailed information on creating batch files, see CD bonus chapter, "Batch Programming." See Chapter 10 for information on specific console commands.

When the scripts are working, decide where you will assign the scripts, whether at the site, domain, OU, or local level. If assigning the policy at the domain or OU level, open the Active Directory Users And Computers console on a domain controller in the domain and open the GPO where you will assign the policy. Open the Active Directory Sites And Services console if you're assigning the policies at the site level. Or, to modify the local policy, run Mmc.exe and load the Group Policy snap-in focused on the local computer (Figure 5.7).

FIGURE 5.7:

Use the Group Policy snap-in to modify the local policy.

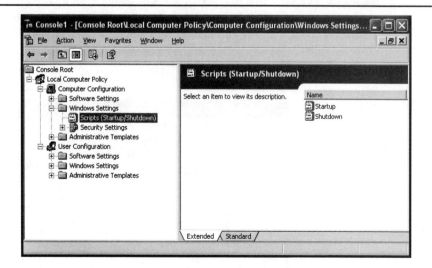

In the policy, open the \Computer Configuration\Windows Settings\Scripts branch. Double-click the Startup policy to open the Startup Properties dialog box. Click Add to open the Add A Script dialog box. In the Script Name field, type the path to the script or click Browse to browse for it. Add any additional parameters for the script in the Script Parameters field and click OK. Repeat the process to add other startup scripts as needed, then close the Startup Properties dialog box.

To specify scripts that run when the system shuts down, double-click the Shutdown policy in the \Computer Configuration\Windows Settings\Scripts branch. Use the same steps as described above to assign shutdown scripts to the computer.

Controlling Script Execution

Policy-defined startup scripts, which execute before other types of scripts, execute synchronously and hidden. The user doesn't see the startup scripts execute, and each script must complete before the next executes. Because the scripts execute synchronously, the logon dialog doesn't appear until all startup scripts have executed.

In most cases, you probably don't need to see the startup scripts execute. However, in cases where you're trying to troubleshoot problems that might be related to the startup scripts, being able to see them execute is critical.

You can control startup script behavior by editing the Registry, but a better solution is to use group policies. Open the MMC, add the Group Policy snap-in focused on the local group policy object (GPO), and drill down to the \Computer Configuration\Administrative Templates\System\Scripts branch (Figure 5.8). Enable the policy Run Startup Scripts Visible to be able to view the scripts as they execute. Enable the policy Run Startup Scripts Asynchronously if you want startup scripts to be able to run concurrently.

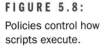

FIGURE 5.8:

Policies control how scripts execute.

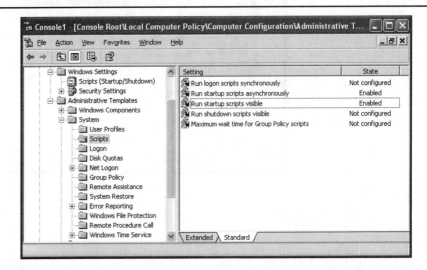

You can use the policy Maximum Wait Time For Group Policy Scripts to specify the maximum amount of time Windows XP will wait for policy-defined scripts to execute. If scripts have not completed execution by the specified time, Windows XP stops script processing and logs an error to the event log.

Restricting Shutdown

In most cases, you'll want everyone to be able to shut down a computer. There are some cases, however, where it's desirable to prevent certain users from being able to shut down a computer. This is certainly true with servers, but can also be true for workstations. For example, a particular workstation might be sharing a set of folders that need to be available at all times. Or a computer might be serving as your fax machine and need to be on all the time to receive faxes. So you might consider restricting the ability to shut down that particular computer only to administrators.

NOTE   You can't control system shutdown for Windows XP Home Edition systems, because they do not support group or local policies.

You restrict the ability to shut down the computer through user rights assignment. Assign these rights through a group policy or local security policy. The right Shut Down The System is located in the \Security Settings\Local Policies\User Rights Assignment branch in the Local Security Policy console or in the \Computer Configuration\Windows Settings\Security Settings\Local Policies\User Rights Assignment branch for group policy.

By default, members of the Administrators, Users, Power Users, and Backup Operators can shut down a system. In most situations, you can simply deny the Users group that right. If users other than those in the Administrators, Power Users, or Backup Operators groups need the ability the shut down the system, create a group specifically for that purpose and grant that group the right to shut down the system.

To configure the right, open the applicable group or local policy branch as described previously. Locate and double-click the Shut Down The System policy. You can use the resulting dialog box to both remove and add users or groups. Click OK when you're satisfied with the changes, then close the policy editor.

PART II

Running and Customizing Windows XP

CHAPTER 6

Shortcuts for Working in Windows

You really can't consider yourself much of an advanced user unless you know a few of these: the Windows XP shortcuts. You know the guilty pleasure you get when you close a program with the Alt+F4 key combination—the program vanishing magically, mouse barely within earshot—and someone over your shoulder says, "Hey, how'd you do that?" "It's simple, really," you say, and you explain, and you instantly become the computing equivalent of Martha Stewart, sharing a recipe that delights and entertains. "Cool," your colleague says, and in a display of subconscious gratitude picks up your latte tab next time the two of you are out.

So while at times they seem little more than diversions, at the end of the day, the shortcuts presented here are to help you spend less time with your computer. Or, more specifically, to spend more time getting actual *work* done rather than the laboring over the tedious administrivia that can sometimes accompany your experience with Windows.

It's worth mentioning that "shortcuts" can mean different things to different people. It can mean an alias file, a custom setting, or series of steps that avoid monotonous work. However, I am using the catch-all definition of the word; for Chapter 6, a shortcut is any speedier way to get things done or to achieve an end result. Don't confuse the term shortcut with *keyboard shortcut*, which is just a smaller subset of available Windows XP shortcuts. Some of the shortcuts presented here are indeed keyboard shortcuts, but for the most part, we are discussing time- and headache-saving procedures.

Working with Shortcut Files

Technically speaking, a shortcut file is just another file on your computer, stored on the Desktop or in a folder somewhere, just like all the other files on your hard drive. This file is saved and identified by the operating system by its .lnk extension. Less technically, the shortcut is simply a placeholder, a tabbed page, in your filing system. The shortcut really has no functionality other than to point to another file or to a directory in your folder tree. The purpose of the shortcut is to allow an object to be, for all intents and purposes, in two places at once.

For example, you usually carefully arrange the folders and files on your computer's hard disk so that you can easy locate resources when you need them. However, this folder hierarchy may not be the best way to access a particular file when it is time to use it. You may want to create a shortcut on the Desktop. This lets you conveniently open the file by simply double-clicking the icon on the Desktop, which is usually easier to get at than a file buried several folder layers deep.

You can recognize a shortcut by the curving arrow in the bottom-left corner of its icon. The shortcut icon otherwise looks just like the icon of the object it points to—whether it be a document, a folder, or an application. And, just as with all other files stored on our system, we can create, delete, move, copy, and rename shortcuts from within Windows Explorer.

Changing the My Computer Icon Label

As you know already, the icon titled "My Computer" is just a representation of your actual computer name. To find out your computer's actual name, you have to look at the Computer Name tab of the System Properties (right-click My Computer and choose Properties to open this dialog box). When you deal with a single computer, you probably have little problem remembering your computer name (unless you accepted the cryptic name Setup offered when you installed Windows XP.)

However, if you are a network administrator, you are probably used to dealing with computers named Sys212, Comp11, TK429, or Admiral Ackbar. There are times when knowing the computer name right away, without having to open System Properties, can be a real time-saver. This is especially true when trying to perform remote support. If you can configure the computers so that the real computer name is used to label the My Computer icon, it can reduce much of the headache when taking support calls.

It takes a Registry tweak to include the computer name under the My Computer icon. Here's how to do it:

1. Open `Regedt32` and expand this Registry branch:

       `\HKEY_CLASSES_ROOT\CLSID\{20D04FE0-3AEA-1069-A2D8-08002B30309D}`

2. Make a backup copy of the Registry key by choosing File ➤ Export, and specifying a name.

3. In the right pane, double-click the LocalizedString value to open the String Editor dialog box.

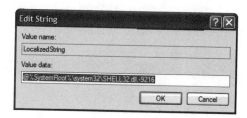

4. Press Ctrl+C, or right-click the value and choose Copy, to copy the value to the Clipboard.

5. Click Cancel and delete the LocalizedString value, then create a new LocalizedString value as a REG_EXPAND_SZ value.

6. Press Ctrl+V, or choose Edit ➢ Paste, to paste the previously saved value.

7. Move the cursor to the end of the string and add a space, followed by `%computername%`.

Now users can just read you what's under their My Computer icon, and remote assistance personnel will know exactly which computer is having problems.

Preventing a Name Change

Now, once you change the computer name, you'd probably like to make sure it stays changed. It would certainly defeat the purpose of your crafty My Computer labeling change if the user went in and changed the computer name to honor his favorite Babylon 9 character.

Preventing a computer name change is relatively easy. Just change the permissions on the Registry key that defines the name, giving users only Read permission on the key. To do this, open `Regedt32` and select this branch:

    \HKEY_LOCAL_MACHINE\SOFTWARE\Classes\CLSID\{20D04FE0-3AEA-1069-A2D8-08002B30309D}

Select Security ➢ Permissions. Remove the Everyone group, add Authenticated Users, and configure permissions such that the Authenticated Users group has Read permission but not Full Control.

Working with Applications

There are several ways to start applications automatically when Windows XP starts. Putting a shortcut to an app into the `Startup` folder is generally the method of choice, because it provides the easiest means of control over the apps. It is also relatively easy to manage the shortcuts kept here, the folder is specific to individual users, and most users are comfortable with the concept of shortcut files. You can manage the Startup folder by looking under this folder path

`\Documents and Settings\%username%\Start Menu\Programs\Startup`

and then editing the shortcuts contained therein, as shown in Figure 6.1.

FIGURE 6.1:

The Startup folder determines what applications load at boot time.

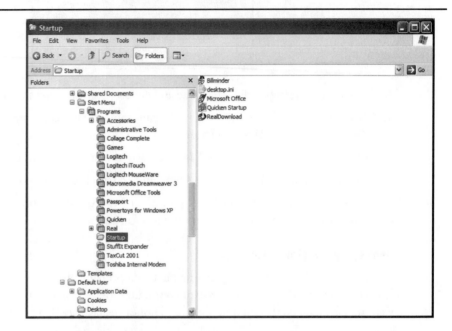

Each item in the Startup folder requires some time to load at boot. If you want a quicker way to start Windows while keeping the contents of Startup intact, simply hold down the Shift key while starting; Windows XP will ignore the folder. If you find that the reduction in startup time is to your liking, you can remove items from the Startup folder to prevent them from starting in subsequent sessions.

Registry Changes to Affect Startup Behavior

Applications don't always use the Startup folder, however. Some applications—particularly system-level utilities—use Registry keys to automatically run. These applications can sometimes seem like monsters that won't die when you're trying to figure out how to prevent them from starting. The key to your control over this startup behavior is to remove their Registry entries from the appropriate key. These entries will be in one of the following places:

```
\HKEY_LOCAL_MACHINE\SOFTWARE\Microsoft\Windows\CurrentVersion\Run
\HKEY_CURRENT_USER\Software\Microsoft\Windows\CurrentVersion\Run
\HKEY_USERS\.DEFAULT\Software\Microsoft\Windows\CurrentVersion\Run
```

Examine these keys and take note of the application entries contained in them. Locate the application you're trying to kill, and delete its entry. Before you do so, however, it would be good computing practice to export a copy of the Registry key (File ➢ Export Registry File) to make it easy to restore the application entry, as well as any others you delete from the Registry.

The System Configuration Utility

There is an easier way to make the kinds of Registry changes just mentioned without having to manually edit the Registry. An excellent benefit of the System Configuration tool is the ability to make the edits without actually having to remove Registry entries. In order to use the System Configuration Utility, you must be logged on to your computer with an owner account.

You will run the System Configuration Utility by opening a Start ➢ Run dialog box and typing **msconfig.exe**. There is no Start-menu shortcut for this tool, and Microsoft does not include documentation about this utility in the first few pages of the user's guide. This is likely because it has incredible power to let less-knowledgeable users make devastating changes to the system with a few ill-advised mouse clicks. This tool's stated purpose is to let users automate the routine troubleshooting steps used when Microsoft Product Support Services technicians diagnose Windows configuration issues. It lets a user easily modify the system configuration through a series of check boxes, reducing the risk of typing errors.

However, you can also use it to change startup behavior of the computer without going into the Registry and without making extensive shortcut edits. From this tool's Startup and Services tabs, as shown in Figure 6.2, you can prevent the loading of certain applications and services with the click of a mouse.

FIGURE 6.2:

Startup items can be enabled and disabled in the System Configuration Utility.

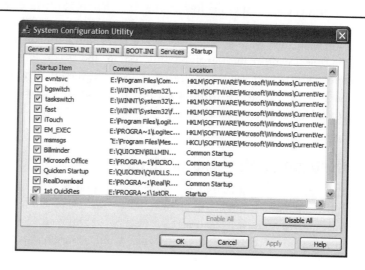

You can also use System Restore right from this interface, by clicking the Launch System Restore button on the General tab.

SEE ALSO   For more information on System Restore, please see Chapter 45.

WARNING   Microsoft cautions you not to use the System Configuration Utility to modify the Boot.ini file. As you learned back in Chapters 4 and 5, an incorrect entry in this startup file can render your computer unusable.

Making Quick Interface Changes

If you're a Microsoft PowerToys fan, you'll no doubt remember the Quickres utility, which let you quickly change screen resolution. For the uninitiated, the Quickres tool loaded in the notification area, allowing users to make resolution changes without having to open the Control Panel Display Properties applet. Furthermore, Quickres let users make these changes without restarting the computer or even verifying the change. For users who made screen resolution changes often, such as those doing graphics work and testing, the default method of changing resolution in Windows quickly became an annoyance.

Unfortunately, though, the Quickres tool included with the Windows 9x PowerToys doesn't work with Windows XP, because of differences in display drivers between 9x and XP. But before you fire off that nastygram to Microsoft, take heart—even though the Quickres PowerToy no longer works—an even better solution exists.

A utility called 1st QuickRes, from Green Parrots Software (www.greenparrots.com), not only lets you quickly change screen resolution just like the Microsoft tool, but also refresh rate, wallpaper, color schemes, screen savers, and other display-related settings. I've installed the free, downloadable version on my system, and as you can see in Figure 6.3, a variety of screen settings are easily configured. This Light version gives you most of the program's features, but to get switch-without-confirmation-benefits, along with a few other nifty features, you'll have to license the Pro version. At $25, it's not a bad deal.

Customizing the Send To Menu

You can use the SendTo folder to quickly send a file to a floppy disk, to your desktop, to another person through e-mail, or to the My Documents folder. What's more, the contents of the Send To menu are customized for every user on your computer; in other words, this menu's contents become part of the user profile (more on profiles in Chapter 41).

FIGURE 6.3:

1st QuickRes allows
for speedy resolution
changes.

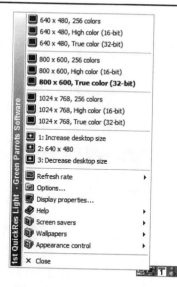

You will find that the addition of alternate locations in the Send To menu is convenient if you frequently perform file-management tasks, especially of you are sending files to locations other than the defaults already mentioned. When you add new locations to the SendTo folder, they appear on the Send To menu when you right-click a file. This can be particularly time- and effort-saving if you back up files on another network computer every day. Imagine if you had to back up several files from different locations of a directory structure that was relatively flat, meaning that you would potentially have a lot of scrolling to do in order to get your files to the desired location. In this case, having the network location on the Send To menu can save you time.

To add a location to the Send To menu:

1. Open My Computer.

2. Double-click the drive where Windows is installed (usually drive C:, unless you have more than one drive on your computer).

TIP   If you can't see the items on your drive when you open it, then under System Tasks, click Show The Contents Of This Drive.

3. Double-click the Documents and Settings folder.

4. Double-click the folder of a specific user.

5. Double-click the SendTo folder.

TIP   The SendTo folder is hidden by default. If it is not visible, choose Tools ➢ Folder Options. On the View tab, click Show Hidden Files And Folders.

6. Choose New ➢ Shortcut from either the File menu or the right-click context menu. Alternatively, you can add a subfolder to the SendTo folder. After this step is completed, any location that you add to the SendTo folder should appear in the Send To menu when you use the shortcut menu from within Windows Explorer.

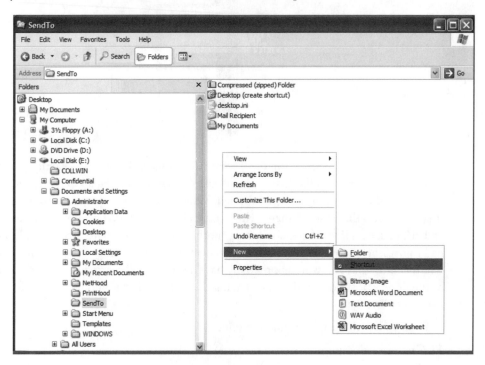

7. Follow the instructions of the Create Shortcut Wizard.

Customizing the Places Bar in the Open Dialog Box

By now, you've opened a document or two in your career as a Windows user, normally by choosing File ➢ Open from most any application. You have also, no doubt, noticed the Places bar on the left edge of this Open dialog box, populated by default by icons for the History, Desktop, My Documents, My Computer, and My Network Places folders. This bar makes it easy to open documents stored in those common folders, but these might not be where you store most of your day-to-day files. You are probably used to getting such files by browsing through the drop-down menu until your desired folder is found.

The content of the Open dialog box is generated by a file called `Comdlg32.dll`, a standard XP system component, and although Windows XP doesn't provide a means in the GUI to customize the Places bar, you can customize its contents by manually modifying the Registry. This might sound like a bit of a pain; after all, how hard is it to click a drop-down menu to find what you are looking for? But, once you've modified the Places bar through the Registry, you'll enjoy those modifications for all Windows XP applications that use `Comdlg32.dll` to generate the Open dialog box (and most do).

To modify the Places bar for XP applications, follow this procedure:

1. First open the Registry, using either `regedit` or `regedt32`.

2. Create this key:

   ```
   \HKEY_CURRENT_USER\Software\Microsoft\Windows\CurrentVersion\Policies\
   ComDlg32\Placesbar
   ```

   You'll need to first create the ComDlg32 subkey, then the Placesbar subkey. This key does not exist by default, and creating it causes the Places bar to be empty initially, but you'll be filling it up shortly.

3. To verify that your key is correct, open Notepad and choose File ➤ Open. The Places bar should now be empty.

The Places bar can contain up to five icons. The Registry values that reference these icons and their associated folders are named Place0 through Place4. Adding your own folders to the Places bar is therefore a relatively simple matter of creating these five entries in the Placesbar key.

You can reference folders either by their absolute path string or by the system ID for the folder. Using the string is best for folders that don't change location based on current logon and for non-system folders. Using the ID is best for system folders such as `My Documents`, because the path can vary based on current logon and for other reasons.

4. Now add an item to your Places bar, using one of these techniques:

   4a. To add a standard storage folder, open the Placesbar key, right-click in the right pane, and choose New ➤ String Value. Name the value Place0, and set its value to the path to the desired folder. For example, you might enter **C:\Urgent** to add the `Urgent` folder to your Places bar.

   4b. To add a *system* folder to the Places bar, right-click in the right pane and choose New ➤ DWORD Value. Set the name to Place1 (or Place2, etc...), and set the value to the ID for the folder. Use the list in Table 6.1 to help you locate the correct ID number of the system folder you are trying to add.

TABLE 6.1: System Folder ID Numbers for Commonly Used Folders

System Folder	ID Number
Favorites	6
Fonts	20
History	34
My Computer	17
My Documents	5
My Network Places	18
My Pictures	39
Network and Dial-Up Connections	49
Printers	4
Recycle Bin	10
Send To	9
System root (Winnt)	36

Now the Places bar will be much more useful for your individual working environment. To test your new creation, open a standard Windows XP application, choose File ➢ Open, and verify that your folders are correct. Adjust and correct values as needed.

TIP   By the way, if you ever want to restore the default Places bar back to the boring one you've just taken the time to modify, simply delete the Registry key \HKEY_CURRENT_USER\Software\ Microsoft\Windows\CurrentVersion\Policies\ComDlg32.

Using Command Keys with Folders

As a general rule, the more adept and familiar you are with the operating system, the more you will keep your hands at the keyboard. Reducing the number of trips your hand makes for the mouse can, over the long haul, reduce fatigue and improve efficiency when working at the computer.

Most power users quickly learn many of the Ctrl and Alt shortcuts that make computer operation easier. For example, the drafting of this chapter is made much easier because I can quickly jump between words and paragraphs by holding the Ctrl key while using the keyboard arrows. Similarly, these users can likely rattle off the uses for Ctrl+Z, +X, +C, and +V more easily than they could give the names of their elected representatives.

Here's how you can take advantage of the Ctrl, Shift, and Windows keys to speed up your file and folder navigation.

Using the Ctrl and Shift Keys

As you are likely aware from earlier versions of Windows, you can configure Explorer such that when you double-click a folder, it opens the folder either using the current window or in a new window. To configure this, you select one of the Browse Folders options from the Folder Options dialog box, as shown in Figure 6.4.

FIGURE 6.4:

This dialog box is opened by choosing Tools ➤ Folder Options from Windows Explorer.

Which option you use is mainly a matter of personal preference. The former keeps your Desktop uncluttered, while the latter lets you keep the current folder open, which is handy for copying or moving documents between folders.

What many users don't realize is that you can modify the opening behaviors of the folders with the Shift and Ctrl keys. For example, let's assume you've configured the system to open new folders in the current window. This is the default behavior of Explorer. You have a folder open and want to go back to the parent folder without closing the current one. You don't want to open a second instance of Explorer, start from the root and work your way down again. Instead, just hold down the Ctrl key and click the Up button on the folder's toolbar.

You can also hold down Ctrl while you double-click a folder, which will again change the configured behavior. Using the same setting as above, this keeps the current window open and opens the selected folder in a new window.

If you have multiple windows open, closing each one by clicking the X (close) button in the top-right corner can be an exercise that leads to a repetitive-motion injury. Using the Shift key, you can close all open parent and child folders with a single click. Just hold down the Shift key and click the X to close a folder. All windows of parent folders should also close at the same time.

Using the Windows Key

Another key that has several shortcuts associated, yet is often forgotten, is the Windows key. The Windows key is included on most keyboards sold today, sitting next to the Alt key on either side. (Laptop computers vary on where they have room to locate this key—on mine, it's crammed in the top-right corner and is about the size of a fingernail clipping—so its access is not quite as easy on mobile systems.)

You have probably been curious by now enough to hit this Windows key and see that it displays the Start menu. This can be a good way to launch a program without having to reach for the mouse (or pointstick).

Another helpful shortcut you can use with the Windows key is to combine it with the M key. This is the command to "minimize all windows," otherwise known as the "Quick, here comes the (boss, spouse, etc.)" command, or more simply the "Oh, (insert explicative)" key.

To restore all windows after hidin—excuse me, minimizing your work, use the Windows+Shift+M key combination.

Other useful Windows-key shortcuts:

Shortcut	Action
Windows+Break	Opens the System Properties dialog box
Windows+D	Shows the Desktop
Windows+E	Opens My Computer
Windows+R	Opens the Run dialog box
Windows+F1	Opens the Windows Help And Support Center

TIP   For a complete listing of all the wonderful things you can so with the Windows key, perform a search in the Help and Support Center on **keyboard shortcuts**.

Adding Context Menu Items

You've probably heard the bromide by now: when in doubt, right-click. A right-click brings up a menu called the context menu, and even if Windows XP is your first operating system, you are probably familiar with these by now.

You have also likely noticed by now that the contents of these menus are pretty much set by the operating system, although some program installations like to add their own shortcuts as well. When you right-click an icon, the resulting context menu gives you a list of actions that apply within the context of the selected object. For example, you can use the context menu for a document to print that document via the Send To menu.

Wouldn't it be great if you could customize this menu just the way that programs do? Well, guess what: you can. This might be especially helpful if you have a folder that you often are saving files to, perhaps a backup location. With a quick change to the Registry, you can do just that:

1. Open either Registry Editor and select this branch:

   `\HKEY_CLASSES_ROOT\AllFilesystemObjects\shellex\ContextMenuHandlers`

2. Add a subkey named Copy To. Select the newly created key and double-click the Default value for the key. Edit the value to the following, including the curly braces:

   `{C2FBB630-2971-11D1-A18C-00C04FD75D13}`

3. Next, add another subkey under ContextMenuHandlers named Move To. Open the key, double-click the Default value, and set it to the following, again remembering to include the curly braces:

   `{C2FBB631-2971-11D1-A18C-00C04FD75D13}`

   (The only difference between this value and the preceding one is the last digit of the first group.)

4. Close the Registry Editor and right-click a document. You should find two new additions to the context menu that let you move and copy the selected object to a folder of your choosing.

Working with the Recycle Bin

File deletion is a part of computer use, just as surely as file installation. (There is probably a "Circle of Life" metaphor that could be inserted here, but I'll let you do the intellectual heavy lifting needed for that.) Suffice to say that the deletion of old files serves a couple of purposes: It clears unwanted and unneeded files away so you don't confuse them with useful files, and it reclaims disk space that these files occupy.

There have probably been times that you have been thankful that Windows makes it so hard for you to delete a file from your hard disk. Four separate actions need to be done, as you probably know, to actually eliminate a file of folder. To review:

- First, you need to either select the item and press the Delete key or right-click it and choose Delete from the pop-up context menu.

- You are then asked to confirm your choice of deletion. After these initial steps are complete, you are only halfway there in the deletion process, as the item now is sent to the Recycle Bin.

- To complete the process, you need to empty out the Recycle Bin by right-clicking its Desktop icon and choosing Delete, or by first opening the Recycle Bin and deleting individual files and folders or emptying the Bin.

- Then you confirm that decision again in a dialog box.

As you may have encountered, this rather lengthy process can occasionally be a lifesaver, giving files a "presidential pardon" from accidental deletion. It can also be time-consuming and tedious. It can be especially irritating for more experienced computer users, who wish to delete files right away.

Furthermore, you should probably understand that deleting a file from the Recycle Bin doesn't actually destroy the physical information on the disk. Rather, Windows marks the file's disk space as available for the storage of other files. It is unlikely that the disk space that is marked as available will be written over soon. This is why organizations and individuals with the right software tools are able to access hard disks where files have been deleted, and still retrieve those files.

Eliminating Confirmation of Delete Operations

Here's a quick and easy keyboard shortcut: If you want certain files and folders gone right away, without any of those tiresome confirmation dialog boxes, simply hold down the Shift key while you drag files and folders onto the Recycle Bin icon. (Beware: you should be *very sure* that you want to delete any such files, as any files that you delete holding down the Shift key will be permanently gone, just as if you had emptied the Recycle Bin. Of course, this is just my version of a "confirmation dialog box.")

> **TIP**   You can also type Shift+Delete, for a deletion that is almost as quick. However, with this method, you have to click a Yes button in a confirmation dialog box; the objects then are truly deleted and not just thrown into the Recycle Bin.

Like most other objects in windows, the Recycle Bin has properties. To display them, right-click the Recycle Bin icon on the Desktop and choose Properties from the pop-up context menu. The Properties dialog box of the Recycle Bin has a Global tab plus a tab for each partition of each hard disk on your system. So even if your system has a single hard disk that has been partitioned into two logical drives, you will see two local disk tabs, with each tab representing the drive letter for an individual partition. We'll be looking at this tab a couple of times in the following procedures, so here it is in all its glory, in Figure 6.5.

FIGURE 6.5:

The Recycle Bin Properties lets you make changes to deletion behavior.

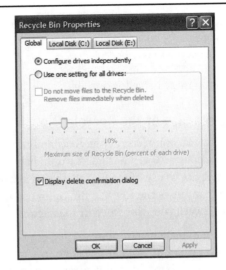

You can also eliminate the confirmation dialog box when sending items to the Recycle Bin. This behavior becomes a part of your user profile, so it won't necessarily affect all users of the computer (unless they use the same username and password). To do so, complete the following steps:

1. Right-click the Recycle Bin icon on the Desktop; choose Properties from the context menu. You will see the dialog box shown in Figure 6.5.

2. From the Global tab of the dialog box, uncheck the box labeled Display Delete Confirmation Dialog. Then click OK to accept the new change.

From now on, you won't be asked if you are "really sure" that you want to delete something when sending it *to* the Recycle Bin. You will still need to confirm when you delete something *permanently*, which is performed by emptying out the Recycle Bin.

However, this behavior is modifiable as well. If you are *really* into slash-and-burn techniques when deleting files—if you are *really* sure that you know what you're doing each and every time you hit the Delete key, that you want to use it like you used the Hyperspace button in Defender—you can skip the Recycle Bin step all together.

To stop sending deleted files to the Recycle Bin at all, right-click the Recycle Bin icon and choose Properties. From Global tab, select the Use One Setting For All Drives radio button, and check the box labeled "Do not move files to the Recycle Bin. Remove files immediately when deleted." Then click OK.

Alright, Nietzsche, now you're ready to go. After you have completed this procedure, any files that you delete from the hard disk are treated like floppy drive deletions—that is, when they are gone, they are gone.

NOTE   Files that are already in the Recycle Bin are unaffected by this procedure; they won't immediately be zapped, and will remain in the Recycle Bin until you empty it, restore the files, or move them to another folder.

You can undo these behavior settings simply by unchecking the boxes listed.

Changing the Size of the Recycle Bin

By default, the maximum size of the Recycle Bin of any hard disk is 10 percent of the disk itself. For example, a 20 GB hard disk would have a maximum Recycle Bin size of 2 GB—quite a bit of space to use of for files that you have decided to delete. If you ever decide to delete a file that causes the Recycle Bin to exceed its allotted 10 percent size (by default), Windows will warn you with an error message.

Configuring a smaller maximum size for the Recycle Bin forces good housekeeping on your drive; you will tend not clutter up your hard disk with useless files that you have marked for deletion. You also might simply want to lower space allocated for the Recycle Bin because disk space is getting low. Conversely, you may decide to raise this limit because you don't want to lose any of the files currently in the Recycle Bin. You can do either of these tasks by first right-clicking the Recycle Bin and choosing Properties, as you have seen in the previous two examples. Then choose one of these:

Set all drives at once   You can change the maximum size of the Recycle Bin for all of your hard disk drives at once. Select the Use One Setting For All Drives radio button on the Global tab. Set the maximum as the percentage of total drive space by moving the slider in the middle of the Global tab. Click OK when you are done.

Set drives individually   If you'd like to change the maximum Recycle Bin size for just a single drive, or want various drives to have different maximums, select the Configure Drives Independently radio button on the Global tab. Click the tab of the drive you want to change, and set the slider on the particular tab. Click OK to apply your changes.

WARNING   If you set the Recycle Bin size to zero, all its contents are lost once the changes are applied. This is yet another way to immediately delete items on the drive without the Recycle Bin providing its stay of execution, as described in the previous section. Setting the size to zero in effect does away with the Recycle Bin, although you will still see the icon sitting uselessly on the Desktop.

Shortcut Grab-Bag

There's always more to learn when it comes to increasing your efficiency. This chapter ends with a grab-bag of some handy shortcuts.

Speeding Up Menu Display

Sometimes, especially on slower computers, XP will take its own sweet time in displaying windows—you know, when you click the Start button and have time to shave before the menu appears. To speed up the way menus display in Windows XP, you can use this tip:

1. Click Start ➤ Control Panel ➤ Performance And Maintenance ➤ System.

2. Click the Advanced tab, and under Performance, click the Settings button. This will bring up the Visual Effects tab, which lets you configure a host of appearance-related settings.

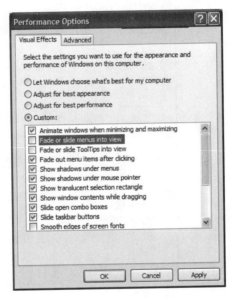

3. To speed up menu display, clear the Fade Or Slide Menus Into View check box, and then click OK.

From now on, any time you bring up a collapsed menu, it will expand without delay. This is especially useful on systems without the latest and greatest display adapters and CPUs, as will be the case with many laptops. XP's enhanced visual eye candy, including the "fading in" menu effect, can put a strain on both.

Putting Familiar Icons Back Where They Belong

If you have a child in your household, you may have experienced this before: The Desktop icons have gone AWOL after some creative time at the computer. (This will be "creative" until they are about 10 or so, after which point I'm told it will become "annoying.") Fortunately for you, there is a quick way to replace all of your favorite Desktop icons from previous versions of

Windows. This also might be especially effective on shared computers, where less experienced users may be comfortable only with launching programs from the Desktop. XP offers an easy way to bring the icons My Computer, My Network Places, and My Documents back to the Desktop, no matter why they have been removed. To do this:

1. Right-click the Desktop, and click Properties.

2. Click the Desktop tab, then click Customize Desktop.

3. Put a check mark in the box next to My Document, My Computer, My Network Places, or Internet Explorer, to add those familiar icons to your Desktop.

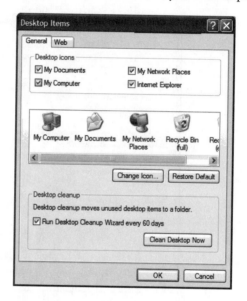

Changing the Contents of Details Shown

You can add other columns to the Details view of the files contained in Windows XP folders, such as Comments, Description, Category, and many others. To add new columns:

1. Right-click the column header of the files list, then either click one of the fields listed or click More.

2. In the Choose Details dialog box, you can reorganize the order of column headers, specify column widths, and add columns to display details for the files in that folder.

3. When you click the new column header, the width of the selected column is displayed in pixels in the Choose Details dialog box.

CHAPTER 7

Customizing the Interface

There are three main components that will, by and large, define how you interact with the XP operating system: the Taskbar, the Start menu (which is actually a part of the toolbar, but because so much activity happens here deserves its own topic), and the Desktop. One of the cool things about the interface components is that they are completely customizable. If there's something that you think you want to change in the look and feel of the Windows experience, you probably can.

The default interface you see when XP is installed actually has a name: Luna. However, its brighter, louder color settings and its newly designed Start menu might not be for everybody—so just like Coca-Cola with its beverage, Microsoft hasn't thrown out the old recipe for the Windows interface. You can quickly switch back to "Classic Windows" if you desire. But this just scratches the surface of all the available user-interface changes. This chapter will describe these main interface components and will discuss how they can be changed to suit your own personal preferences.

The Start Menu

The Start menu is certainly not new to Windows XP—it has been around since you were lining up at your local retailer for a copy of Windows 95—but its appearance and behavior is. In fact, the XP Start menu has been completely redesigned and now bears a likeness to previous Start menus in name and location only.

One of the goals of the redesigned Start menu is to keep the Desktop uncluttered with icons. Toward this end, programs that you use most often have been made easily accessible by moving these program shortcuts to the "opening page" of the Start menu, shown in Figure 7.1. Less often used programs are now hidden under the All Programs section, and accessing these commands takes a bit more effort than the ease offered by the opening page.

The Start menu is actually just a portion of the Taskbar, whose job it is to show you what programs are currently running. As with the Start menu, Windows XP has rearranged the Taskbar slightly, putting multiple windows of the same program under a single Taskbar button. The Taskbar normally resides at the bottom of the screen, but you can move it, expand it, shrink it, or even make it go away. I discuss the Taskbar in detail later in this chapter.

First, let's take a closer look at the items appearing on the Start menu under normal circumstances (and, because you can customize the Start menu, you will get to define what is normal):

All Programs   As mentioned previously, this is where your less frequently used programs will live quiet lives, waiting to be found. These program shortcuts live in the Programs folder, despite the "All Programs" caption here. You can change the contents of the All Programs menu at will.

FIGURE 7.1:

The Windows XP Start menu is a panel, rather than just a list.

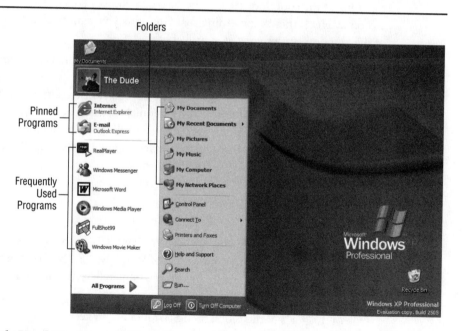

Frequently Used Programs   This is the popular section, for the programs to whom you show the most love. The area on the middle-left of the Start menu, above the All Programs selection, lists the programs you use most frequently. Windows XP runs an algorithm in the background to populate this area based on how often and how recently you have used these programs.

Pinned Programs   At the top-left portion of the Start menu, these programs are the ones you have designated to be "pinned," and yes, it's kinda like that ridiculous act that occurs on college campuses. These are the programs you have made a commitment to and that will always appear in the Start menu, regardless of the number of times you have used them. You can add and remove pinned programs as you please.

Folders   This area lists the special folders that a Windows XP installation creates: My Documents, My Pictures, My Music, My Network Places, My Recent Documents, and My Computer. You can click any of these selections to see the contents of the folder in a Windows Explorer interface.

Control Panel   This item launches Control Panel, which helps make a host of configuration changes to your computer, including installing software and changing Windows settings.

Connect To   This selection provides a submenu that lets you quickly make network connections, such as to a VPN. This submenu should display all connections configured in the Network Properties dialog box (you can right-click My Network Places and choose Properties, or get there from Control Panel), with the exception of the current connection you are using.

Printers And Faxes   This item opens—yes, your intuition serves you well—the Printers And Faxes folder. This folder will look very familiar to users of Windows since the 9x variety, and you can do pretty much the same things here that you have always done.

Help And Support   Clicking here displays the online help. Use of the Windows XP Help options will be discussed later in this chapter.

Search   This word opens a Windows Explorer window in which you can search for files, folders, and other computers.

Run   This link lets you launch a program by typing the name of the file that contains the executable. It is a favorite for opening up a command prompt and for connecting directly to other computers.

Log Off   Enables a user to end a session, so that another user can log on and establish a session of her own.

Turn Off Computer   When you select this item, you get three options: Stand By (or Hibernate or Suspend), Turn Off, and Restart.

As mentioned, the new Start menu will work on your behalf to keep the most frequently used programs close at hand when opening up the Start menu. But one of the first things you can do to make the Start menu more useful is to make sure that frequently accessed programs are available right away, without having to wait for the Windows algorithm to add it to your list of favorites.

You can do this by "pinning" the program to the Start menu, which effectively elevates its priority by putting it at the top of the menu list. This also ensures that the program will not be bumped by other programs, even if you use the others more frequently. To pin a program, right-click the link to your favorite program on the Start menu and select Pin To Start Menu. Your program will be moved permanently to the top part of the list, just below your browser and e-mail programs.

Going Back to the Classic Start Menu

The All Programs menu is a list of potential programs that can be run from your XP system, and is the area of the Start menu that is most like previous versions of Windows. As with previous versions, the XP Start menu is hierarchical and can be customized at any level.

TIP   In Windows XP, Microsoft has jettisoned the "smart menu" feature, which hid many of the menu options that were infrequently used, ostensibly to simplify the Start menu interface in previous versions of Windows. If, however, you still pine for the feature, it will be enabled automatically when you use the Windows Classic interface.

And while we're on the topic of the old Windows interface, here's how to turn the look of the XP Luna Start menu back to the stately Cornflower Blue and Gray of Windows 2000:

1. Right-click the Start button and click Properties.

2. Click Classic Start menu.

3. Click the Customize button to select items to display on the Start menu.

Be aware that when you configure XP to use the Classic Start menu, you will also be making changes to the Desktop: by default, Windows Classic will add the My Documents, My Computer, My Network Places, and Internet Explorer icons to your Desktop.

Rearranging the Start Menu

You are able to customize almost all menus and submenus of the Start menu. There are a few exceptions: The Turn Off Computer, Help And Support, Search, and Control Panel items cannot be removed or reorganized. (Actually, you can govern the display of items such as Control Panel or the Turn Off Computer option through group policies in a Windows 2000 or .NET domain, but that is a topic for another book.) Everything else is fair game.

OK, OK, just so you don't have to go out and get that other book... if your XP clients are part of a Windows 2000 Active Directory domain, you can administer Desktop settings centrally by application of a group policy. The Group Policy editor is an MMC snap-in that lets you configure a host of administrative options, including the ability to distribute software remotely, set up auditing, control how data will be encrypted by your computer when communicating over the network, and yes, adjust the appearance and behavior of the user interface, to name but a small fraction of what can be configured.

Group policies can be set on several objects in an Active Directory domain: on local machines, sites, domains, and organizational units. They are also applied in just that order, so that if any conflicts exist between policy settings, the last policy setting to be applied is the effective setting. (Example: if a policy setting has been applied to the domain object such that the Internet Explorer icon is removed from the Desktop for all users of a domain, but a user account is in an organizational unit where the policy says that the IE icon *will* appear on the Desktop, the icon will appear when the user logs on. This is because the organizational unit policy is applied after the domain policy and trumps any settings configured at the domain level.) Naturally, this behavior is modifiable; domain admins can set the domain policies so that they cannot be overridden, but... well, that really *is* a topic for another book.

If your system does not reside in an Active Directory domain, the only group policy settings that can be applied are from local group policies.

Now, without going into each and every GPO setting, you can change what displays on the Start menu by opening up the Group Policy MMC and making changes to the Start menu settings. To do so, follow these steps:

1. Choose Start ➢ Run and type **MMC**. This will open a blank MMC, waiting for snap-ins to be added to give it functionality.

2. Choose File ➢ Add/Remove Snap-In, then click the Add button in the dialog box.

3. From the Add Standalone Snap-In dialog box, select Group Policy, click the Add button, and then make sure that the policy settings will be configured for the local computer, which will be the default. Click Finish when you are done, and then click Close.

4. You should now see the Group Policy snap-in in the list of snap-ins from the Add/Remove Snap-In dialog box. Click OK to begin working with the group policy.

5. To make changes to the Start menu, expand the Local Computer policy node, then expand the User Configuration node, and then expand Administrative Templates. You should then see a node titled Start Menu And Taskbar.

6. Select the Start Menu And Taskbar node; in the Details pane, you will see a list of the configuration changes possible (and there are many).

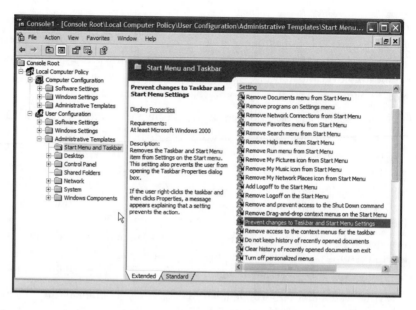

7. By selecting a setting, you will see a description on the left side of the Details pane. Most of the setting titles are self-explanatory. For example, the setting called Prevent Changes To Taskbar And Start Menu Settings will do just that.

8. To make a configuration change, double-click a setting to open its Properties dialog box, and then make the selection to enable or disable the setting.

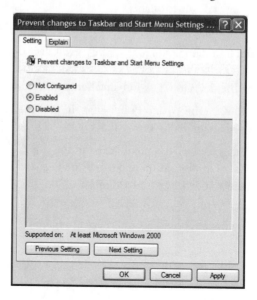

TIP   There is little practical need to disable most Group Policy settings, just as there is little need for the Deny security setting. Use of the Disabled setting usually serves to complicate administration of Windows settings.

There are three ways you can edit the contents of the Start menu areas that you are able to edit, without having to edit a group policy (you may not have privileges to do so anyway): by dragging and dropping, by cutting and pasting, and by making edits in an Explorer window. Which one you use is completely up to you, but from personal experience, the drag-and-drop is awfully easy. Whichever way you select to make Start menu changes, know that you are just making changes to the arrangement of *shortcuts* to programs, not to the programs themselves. You can't do any long-term harm to the system by changing the Start menu. You can make the computer a lot more painful to use, yes, but even if you delete every deletable item on the Start menu, there is nothing that can't be reversed.

Here's a summary of what changes are possible on the Start menu:

Add an item to the top-left area of the Start menu   Right-click a shortcut or an executable (.exe) file. Choose Pin To Start Menu from the context menu.

Add an item to the All Programs menu   Drag a shortcut, or a program's executable, to the Start button and hover there. After about two seconds, the Start menu will expand. You can then hold the dragged shortcut over the All Programs menu until it opens, and so on, until you have found a new home for the shortcut.

Remove an item from the Start menu   Right-click the item and choose Remove From List from the context menu. To remove an item from the All Programs menu, right-click it and select Delete.

Rename a menu item   Right-click the item and choose Rename. Type the name, and press Enter when you are done.

You can create a Start menu entry for almost any item simply by dragging its program file to the Start button. This will work for files, folders, programs, and even other shortcuts. Furthermore, you can drag items from either the Windows Explorer interface or from the Desktop itself.

And here's another effective—no, the most effective—shortcut-dragging method: right-click when you drag instead of left-clicking. That way, you will get a small context menu when you let go of the mouse button, giving you the option to either move or copy your shortcut (or even create a shortcut to your shortcut). This way, you can leave the original shortcut in place while creating a new one in another location. This is my favorite technique when

I move often-used Administrative Tools to the Quick Launch toolbar—the original menu stays intact.

Another way to reorganize the All Programs menu and any of its submenus is to use an Explorer window, as mentioned above. When you are using this method, you are just performing file management in Windows Explorer as you have probably done hundreds of times in previous iterations of windows. The files you are working with here are just the shortcut files.

You can display the Start menu folder in a Windows Explorer window by right-clicking the Start menu and choosing Open or Explore from the context menu; this brings up the Explorer window shown in Figure 7.2.

FIGURE 7.2:

The Start menu content can be edited in Windows Explorer.

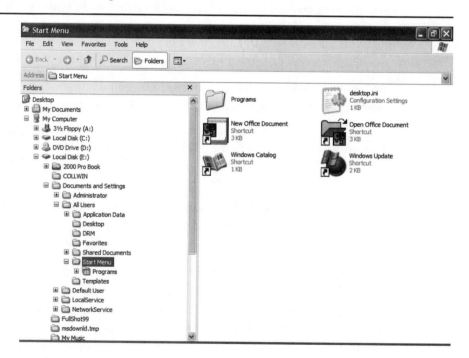

It is important to know the difference between two similar context-menu options. One choice is to Open or Explore, and the other is to Explore All Users. When you select the first option, you are making changes to the Start menu, and these changes will be specific to the account of the user who's currently logged on. When you select Explore All Users, any changes you make to the folder that is opened will affect—that's right—all users of the computer. Be sure you know which you are working with before beginning to move, delete, or rename the shortcuts.

NOTE   The Start menu and its contents are more than just regular folders. For example, you can move the `Programs` folder out of its original location, and you will still see the All Programs menu on the Start menu. Now, I'm not in any way recommending that you change the location of the `Programs` folder, because it can cause problems that are very difficult to fix, unless you're into self-torture. (I mean, you can delete Registry keys too, and can even recover from that as well, but that isn't something I recommend, either.)

As you probably have experienced already, if you have ever installed a piece of software, the installation will often create one or more items to the Start menu, and will almost always create a submenu on the All Programs menu. You may prefer to put these items in other locations on the Start menu or just remove them from the menu altogether. You can do so using any of the methods outlined above.

A pop-up window displays every time a new software installation is performed, notifying you that, yes, indeed, a new software installation has been performed. This is actually meant more for users in Active Directory domains to be made aware that a piece of software has been installed through a group policy, and not for stand-alone users who know exactly when they have installed a piece of software because they have either downloaded it or popped the CD into the machine.

It is possible, however, to get rid of that little window. If you find that it is getting in your way, you can simply turn it off completely by performing the following steps:

1. Click Start, right-click at the top of the Start menu where your name is displayed, and then click Properties.

TIP   Where you click on the Start menu affects what shows in the Properties dialog box. If you click a menu item, you will see the properties of that particular shortcut; if you click the name section or the Start button itself, you get the properties of the Start menu, where you can set the options discussed.

2. In the Taskbar And Start Menu Properties dialog box, on the Start Menu tab, click Customize.

3. Click the Advanced tab, and then clear the Highlight Newly Installed Programs check box.

4. Click OK, and then click OK again.

Adding Other Content to the Start Menu

It is also possible to edit the properties of the Start menu so that additional content appears. One of the most useful procedures for advanced users of XP is the ability to display the

Administrative Tools, which are normally only available through Control Panel. To do so, you will need to do the following:

1. Right-click the Start menu, and then click Properties.

2. On the Start Menu tab, click Customize.

3. Click the Advanced tab, and under Start Menu Items, scroll to System Administrative Tools.

4. Click the "Display on the All Programs menu and the Start menu" option to show the Administrative tools.

Simpler now? Of course! You can now navigate to the Administrative Tools right from the familiar interface of the Start menu, without having to open and close Control Panel each time. You will also probably find it easier to rearrange the Administrative Tools from the Start menu so that the most commonly used tools are easily accessible.

Making Changes to Context Menus

Most computer users today have been familiar with the use of *context* menus for years. It's assumed by the time you have come to XP that the use of context menus is second nature; even if XP is your first *experience* with a Windows operating system, you have by now very likely used context menus in others OSes, such as the Mac OS and Unix (or at least the popular GUI shells that sit atop of the Unix environment). Context menus are the ones that appear when you right-click a Windows object. These menus are subject to modification depending on the object you are right-clicking, yet at the same time will show you some action choices that are always the same. You might hear these menus referred to by other names—action menus, shortcut menus, pop-up menus, context-sensitive menus—but these are all the same thing.

SEE ALSO Find out how to add items to the context menu, with a few edits in the Registry, in Chapter 6.

WARNING You've likely seen this warning before, but it bears repeating: you should treat editing the Registry like brain surgery, because it is like brain surgery to your computer. Damage to the Registry means damage to your system.

The Taskbar

The Taskbar is the row of buttons and icons that usually appears at the bottom of the Windows Desktop; it has served as a nexus of activity for interaction with all versions of Windows since Windows 95. Most user actions in the Windows family begin at the Taskbar. As Microsoft itself has famously put it, it's where you "Start Here." The XP version consists of four parts: the Start button (usually at the left end), the toolbar, the task buttons, and the notification area (at the right).

You can easily customize the Taskbar by moving it, changing its size, and defining exactly what appears on it. It is also common to see chevrons (double-arrow symbols) on the Taskbar, reflecting buttons, shortcuts, or other information available but out of sight. These chevrons work to keep the Windows Desktop uncluttered (in what will become a recurring theme).

There are five toolbars that install with Windows XP:

Quick Launch   A personal favorite for keeping icons off the Desktop and for easily launching commonly used programs. The Quick Launch toolbar will install with three shortcuts: Show Desktop, Launch Internet Explorer, and Windows Media Player. Later we will look at how to edit the contents of this toolbar.

Address   This element works much like the Run command from the Start menu. The Address toolbar contains a text box where you can type a URL for a web page, or a file pathname to open up a local file.

Links   A favorite of Microsoft shareholders. This toolbar displays a button for each of the web pages Microsoft would like you to visit to increase their revenue stream. You can remove these links and add your own list of favorites.

Desktop   Here, Windows displays a button for each icon on the Desktop. If a chevron appears, click it to display items that don't fit on the Taskbar.

Language   This lets you easily switch among the installed languages or among any keyboard or input options that you have added using the Text Services And Input Languages dialog box, which is found in Control Panel. Note that you won't have this toolbar option available unless you have installed support for additional languages and/or keyboard layouts.

Customizing the Taskbar and Toolbars

By default, Windows XP locks the Taskbar so that changes cannot be made. This is done to prevent accidental changes to the Taskbar made by dragging and dropping. When the Taskbar is locked, you cannot move it, resize it, or make any changes to content. You can still control which toolbars display in the Taskbar, though.

When it's time to start making changes to the content of the toolbars, you will need to first unlock them, using the following steps:

1. Begin by right-clicking an unoccupied area of the Taskbar (use the area right next to the clock if you're having problems finding unused space), and click Lock The Toolbars to remove the check mark.

2. Once you have done this, right-click the Taskbar again and from the shortcut menu, under the Toolbars section, choose the toolbar you wish to appear on the Taskbar.

3. You will also have the ability to add a new toolbar to the Taskbar. For example, you can add a toolbar that will let you quickly open commonly used folders such as My Music. To do so, select the New Toolbar option and then Browse for the toolbar you wish to create.

4. It's a good idea then to right-click the Taskbar once more and choose Lock The Toolbars to lock them in place, preventing unintended changes.

Modifying Taskbar Display Options

You can change the size and positioning of the Taskbar just as you have with previous versions of Windows: drag its inside edge to one of the edges of the Desktop. You can expand the size of the Taskbar by dragging its top edge, allowing for the display of more than one row of Taskbar buttons. Of course, you will be able to display more information on each Taskbar button with a larger Taskbar area.

You can change the Taskbar options by right-clicking an empty part of the Taskbar and choosing Properties. This selection will display the Taskbar And Start Menu Properties dialog box, as shown in Figure 7.3.

You can also hide the Taskbar altogether in one of two ways: by decreasing its size, or by using the auto-hide option of the Taskbar And Start Menu Properties dialog box.

FIGURE 7.3:

Set your Taskbar and Start menu properties in this dialog box.

To turn on auto-hide, simply select the Auto-Hide The Taskbar check box. With this option enabled, the Taskbar disappears when it isn't being used. When it is out of sight, there are three ways to make it reappear: drag the pointer to the edge of the screen where it was last visible, or press the Windows key, or type the Ctrl+Esc key combination.

TIP   If you can't find the Windows XP Taskbar, move the mouse pointer to the edge of the screen. If the Taskbar has been resized so that it is no longer visible, the pointer will turn into a double-sided arrow that you can click and drag to increase the Taskbar's size.

You can choose whether you want the Taskbar to be covered by other windows by selecting the check box "Keep the Taskbar on top of other windows," which is selected by default. When the option is selected, the Taskbar will always appear over any application windows you have running. When selected, the Taskbar in effect serves as the bottom of your screen.

If you have unchecked this option and the Taskbar gets covered up, you can display the Start menu by pressing the Ctrl+Esc key combination, or can just display the Taskbar by pressing the Esc key.

A new feature of Windows XP is the ability to group Taskbar buttons. This feature puts multiple windows opened by the same program together in one Taskbar button. It is another option that is turned on by default.

If the Taskbar becomes crowded, the Taskbar buttons from a single program are collapsed into a single button, as shown in Figure 7.4.

FIGURE 7.4:

Multiple program windows are now grouped under a single button.

Notice that the button for a *group* of windows has a down arrow on its right side. Click this button to see the list of individual program windows, and select the one you want. Some people might find this feature annoying, such as users who have to constantly switch back and forth between two items within the same application. To turn off this feature, you can deselect the check box in the Taskbar And Start Menu Properties dialog box.

You can move toolbars to different areas of the Taskbar (changing their order or size), or onto the Desktop itself, by dragging their handles, which are represented by lines of vertical dots. Note that the toolbar handles don't appear when the Taskbar is locked.

To move a toolbar off the Taskbar completely, drag its handle right onto the Desktop. Each toolbar will create its own window of options on the Desktop, like the one shown here, complete with a Close button in the top-right corner.

To reverse this procedure, just drag the title bar of this toolbar window back to the Taskbar—its shape will change when it is placed back in the Taskbar. (It will take up the entire edge of the screen if it is moved to an edge other than the Taskbar.)

If you right-click the Taskbar and look at the shortcut menu that appears, you will notice several options beyond just Properties. Figure 7.5 shows you this Taskbar context-sensitive menu.

The following choices in this menu affect the overall look and feel of the Taskbar:

View   Allows you to display either large or small icons.

Open Folder   Opens the folder where that toolbar's shortcuts are stored, so you can directly edit the contents of the toolbar. You can add and delete shortcuts directly to this folder to change the behavior of the Taskbar.

Show Text   Turns off or on the display of the name of the toolbar.

Close Toolbar   Removes the display of the toolbar from the screen.

Toolbars   Allows you to display a new toolbar that is not currently displayed. There's more on the toolbar configuration options in the next section.

FIGURE 7.5:

The context menu of the Taskbar makes many customization options available.

Mapping a Drive with the Toolbar

You also have the ability to quickly map a drive by adding a menu item to a toolbar, rather than performing the task from My Network Places. If you find yourself often needing to map drives or supporting end users who do, you can use the following technique to add a Map Drive button to the toolbar.

1. If necessary, first unlock the toolbars (right-click an unoccupied area of the Taskbar and uncheck Lock The Toolbars).

2. Right-click the toolbar again and click Customize.

3. Under Available Toolbar Buttons, locate Map Drive, and drag it into the position you want on the right under Current Toolbar Buttons.

4. Click Close, click OK, and then click OK again.

You will now have a drive-mapping button on your toolbar, so you can map drives from any folder window. To unmap drives, follow the above procedure, selecting Disconnect under Available Toolbar Buttons.

The Desktop

Most people are much more comfortable, and effective, with their computers if they know how to configure the Desktop to suit their own personal preferences. Let's go over how to customize a Desktop theme, background, screensaver, icons, and other visual references to give your system a familiar look and feel that is uniquely yours.

First of all, know that users of XP Professional won't even *see* the Desktop without first supplying a valid username and password. So one of the initial things you can do as a user of a stand-alone XP installation is to configure XP for auto-logon—that is, remove the requirement for a user to supply a username and password when using the system. This can be effective when you are the only one who will be using the computer, as is the case for most home and laptop computers, and the use of a logon name and password serves no practical security purpose.

To enable auto-logon for your Windows XP Professional installation:

1. Click Start ➤ Run and enter **control userpasswords2** to open the Windows 2000–style User Accounts application.

2. On the Users tab, clear the "Users must enter a user name and password to use this computer" check box and then click OK.

3. In the Automatically Log On dialog box that appears, type the user name and password for the account you want to be logged on each time you start your computer.

SEE ALSO   You can also accomplish the Autologon objective through one of the PowerToys utility options, which are discussed in Chapter 6.

Changing the Look and Feel of the Desktop

You will configure your Desktop and monitor by and large from one place: the Display Properties dialog box. It can be launched the same way it has for years, by right-clicking the Desktop and choosing Properties. (For those who prefer the scenic route, you can get to this properties sheet from Control Panel as well.)

The Display Properties dialog box has five tabs, and sometimes more, depending on the software that has installed with your video adapter. Here's what you should see no matter what video card is running:

Themes   Controls the Desktop themes.

Desktop   Allows you to choose icons and background pictures.

Screen Saver   Offers several preinstalled screensavers (which are unnecessary and waste energy) and automatic settings for turning off your monitor (which will win you points with me and Ralph Nader).

Appearance   Controls the color, size, and font of every type of object in the Windows interface.

Settings   Lets you set the size of the Desktop, choose the number of colors used, and configure monitor performance settings, such as display refresh rate. The refresh rate is one of the most important options for day-to-day usability of the monitor, as a higher setting can greatly reduce eyestrain from sitting in front of a computer all day.

As you probably know, when you change the settings on any one of these tabs, you make changes to how Windows looks and behaves from a user-interface standpoint. Settings from the Display Properties dialog box are discussed throughout the next few sections.

Choosing a Desktop Theme

You can change the appearance of just about anything on your Desktop, although making individual changes to font, color, icons, background, mouse pointers, and so on, generally isn't worth the effort, and could potentially be as time-consuming as dental school. To make several changes that affect the overall look and feel (and even sound) of Windows XP all at once, Microsoft has provided a set of *themes*.

To change a Desktop theme, go to the Themes tab of the Display Properties dialog box. Simply select a theme from the Themes drop-down list. A preview will appear in the Sample box, and you can click OK or Apply to enforce your selection.

There are websites where people with a lot of spare time have created and given away hundreds of themes that can be applied to XP, as well as previous versions of Windows. Two of the most popular of these sites are www.tweakxp.com and www.xp-erience.org. There are many others that you can find on the Internet. A personal favorite of mine is the Aqua theme, which makes XP do a pretty good impersonation of a Macintosh (which Mac zealots would argue Microsoft has been trying to do for years anyway).

Changing Fonts

You also can easily make sweeping changes to the overall size and appearance of the fonts used in menus, title bars, dialog boxes, and other system text. These changes are made from the Appearance tab of the Display Properties dialog box, and you have no doubt experienced this in previous iterations of Windows. You can even take this customization a little further, if you wish, and make changes to text used in specific contexts, and not just to overall appearance.

New to Windows XP is an Advanced button on the Appearance tab of the Display Properties dialog box. (There is an Effects button as well, where you can change the way menus fade or scroll, and opt to use ClearType fonts, which are discussed shortly and which I highly recommend.) The Advanced Appearance dialog box then gives you much more control over the individual Windows fonts. From this dialog box (Figure 7.6), you can change the appearance of certain text—for example, the font used in the title bar of a window—while leaving other text items alone. To change the font, size, or color of text that Windows uses for a particular item, just select that item in the upper part of the Advanced Appearance box or in the Item drop-down list.

FIGURE 7.6:

Change the font of specific aspects of your Desktop with the Advanced Appearance options.

The first line of boxes refers to the item itself. The second line of text boxes and buttons refers to the text, if applicable, that's displayed on the item. You can make changes to any and all of these boxes to change the look of the selected item. As always, click Apply to see what your settings look like in action; when you are done fooling around, click OK to impose your changes.

One of the changes to the appearance that is most useful is the ability that Microsoft has developed to make text more readable on monitors. This technology is a font setting known as ClearType. It is a way of displaying text more brilliantly and visibly, and works to smooth out font edges. ClearType was developed for use in e-books, and is especially good for LCD or flat-panel displays, which have been in use on laptops for years and are becoming more common in desktop monitors. This technology alone may be worth the price of the XP operating system for laptop use.

To get your computer to use ClearType, take the following steps:

1. From the Display Properties dialog box, click the Appearance tab. Then click the Effects button.

2. With the "Use the following method to smooth edges of screen fonts" check box selected, choose the ClearType option from the drop-down box. (Standard can also be used, and does a pretty good job, but I think you'll find the ClearType to be far superior in terms of readability.)

3. Click OK in both the Effects dialog box and the Display Properties dialog box, to apply your change.

Changing the Background

The background of the Desktop is the pattern, picture, or other element that sits there behind all the windows, icons, and menus on the Desktop. One could even be inclined to say that is serves as the... background for Windows activity.

You can easily select any color, image, or pattern to serve as your background, again from the Display properties dialog box, this time from the Desktop tab. The Background button of that tab lists all the "wallpaper" images that Windows has been made aware of. When you select one of these from the drop-down list, the image will be displayed in the upper (preview) portion of the Desktop tab.

You aren't limited, however, to the background images that are provided with Windows. You can use any image that can be stored as a digital file, such as a scanned photo. In face, to make this easier, Windows automatically places any picture stored in the My Pictures folder appear on the list of Background images on the Desktop tab. If the file is located somewhere else on your system, you can click Browse and locate the image in the dialog box that appears.

You can also find background-image software posted on the Internet. One of the most often downloaded programs in existence is Webshots Desktop, which you can get from `www.webshots.com` or the major download sites. Once you install this application, you can manage and apply a wide variety of images that have been captured and optimized for use as Desktop backgrounds. You will also be able to link to the Webshots website and search through thousands of individual screen shots and even entire screen shot collections, all of which can be downloaded for free.

Furthermore, your Desktop background can be a page from the Internet, or can contain items that have content regularly updated from the Internet, such as stock tickers, news reports, or sports scores.

You can add any web page to the background by first selecting the Desktop tab of the Display Properties dialog box, and then by clicking the Customize Desktop button. The Desktop Items dialog box appears; select the Web tab.

The Web tab offers you the My Current Home Page selection, which will display the same page that is displayed when you open Internet Explorer. You can add any other web page you choose to the Web Pages list by doing the following:

1. On the Web tab, click the New button. The New Desktop Item dialog box appears.

2. Type the URL of the web page into the Location dialog box, or choose an item from your `Favorites` folder by choosing Browse and then selecting it.

3. After making your selection, click OK in the New Desktop Item dialog box. A confirmation will appear; click OK again. The item will now appear in the Web Pages list with its check box selected.

4. When you have made your selections, click OK to close the Desktop Items dialog box, and then OK or Apply in the Display Properties dialog box to have your changes "take." You computer will attempt to connect to the Internet and find the page you have chosen.

You will also notice a button on the New Desktop Item dialog box titled Visit Gallery. This button will take you to a Microsoft website where you can find other web-enabled items to add to your Desktop, such as weather maps and stock tickers. (No betting lines, if you're wondering.) You will find the instructions appropriate for installation at the website.

Once you have added Web content from the Desktop Items dialog box, you can remove it from your Desktop easily by unchecking its check box in the Web Pages list.

CHAPTER 8

Controlling Windows Explorer

If you've worked with Windows for any length of time, you know that using Windows Explorer is central to your comfort level with the operating system. You may also be aware that the Explorer interface was ported to the administrative tools used with the Windows 2000 operating system and recent releases of BackOffice Server products.

However, most user interface tools have changed significantly in this new flavor of the Windows operating system, and the changes to Explorer can be some of the most disorienting at first pass. Because so much of day-to-day file and folder management is performed through the Explorer interface, this chapter takes you on a guided tour, showing you some cool tricks that will make the Explorer interface do exactly what you want.

What Is Windows Explorer?

So just what is this beast anyway? More than one advanced Windows user doesn't even know that this tool has a name. Windows Explorer is the graphical file and folder management utility that is seamlessly integrated into the operating system. I'm describing it as seamlessly integrated because you can open it from almost anywhere. Right-click the Start button, for example, and you are using the Windows Explorer utility to view the contents of the Start menu.

You can open the main Windows Explorer window in a couple of ways. For example, you can choose Start ➢ All Programs ➢ Accessories ➢ Windows Explorer. However, most Windows veterans long ago discovered other, less click-intensive ways to get to an Explorer window. My favorite way is to right-click My Computer and then choose Explore from the shortcut menu. We'll look at some modifications available with this method later in the chapter.

One of the first things you will notice about this new Explorer is that the left side looks different from the interface in previous versions of Windows. The Explorer interface is still split into two panes, one on the left and one on the right. The left pane used to be the stomping grounds of something called the Tree pane or the Node pane, and the right side was filled with the contents of your selection in the Tree pane. Now, however, the left side is by default populated with a new pane called a Task pane, as shown in Figure 8.1. You can use the Task pane to perform a series of tasks on the objects listed in the Details pane (which is pretty much unchanged from previous versions of Windows). These tasks include copying and moving files, sending e-mail messages, displaying pictures and slide shows, and playing music, to name only a few.

Just as you must do in other areas of the Windows XP interface that are a departure from the traditional, one of your first decisions is whether you want to use the new feature. In Windows XP, you can quickly and easily switch back to the classic interface of previous versions of Windows.

If you decide that the Task pane, which is turned on by default as shown in Figure 8.1, is not for you, you can turn it off by following these steps:

1. In Windows Explorer, choose Tools ➤ Folder Options to open the Folder Options dialog box.

2. Click the General tab, if necessary.

3. Click the Use Windows Classic Folders option, and then click OK.

Keep in mind that this decision affects all instances of Explorer; it cannot be set on an individual folder.

FIGURE 8.1:

The Task pane on the left side is new in the Windows Explorer interface.

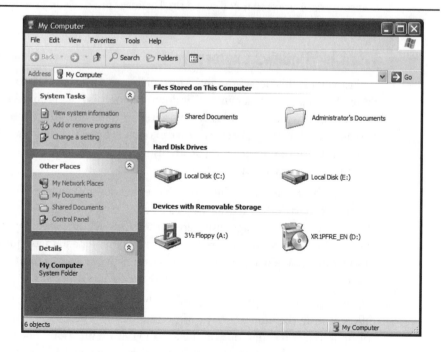

TIP If you find that you are making frequent trips to the Folder Options dialog box, you can place a shortcut to it on the Explorer toolbar.

You will notice rather quickly that the Task pane does not have a Close button. If you want to see the Task pane some of the time, but not all the time, you could flip back and forth by returning to the Folder Options dialog box. But there is a better way. If you click the Folders button on the Windows Explorer toolbar, the Task pane is replaced by the Folders bar, a familiar sight to even casual users of previous versions of Windows. Click the Folder button again to display the Task pane.

TIP You can use both varieties of the left pane (the Task and Folder views) even if XP is set in all other ways to use the Windows classic interface.

If you look at the bottom portion of the Task pane, you'll see the Details section. You can think of this section as a mini-Properties dialog box. Click Details to display useful information about the currently selected item. The lower the screen resolution, the less likely you will be able to see the contents of the Details section without scrolling. (XP will put up a fight when you try to use less than 600×800 resolution.)

Working with Explorer Views

You can display information in the Details pane of Windows Explorer in the following six views:

- Details
- List
- Thumbnails
- Tiles
- Icons
- Filmstrip

NOTE Filmstrip view is available only in the My Pictures folder or any folder that is customized as a pictures folder. I'll show you how to customize a folder as a picture folder later in this chapter.

To select a view, you can click the View menu or click the Views button on the toolbar, as shown in Figure 8.2.

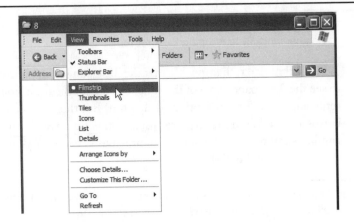

I assume that you are familiar with the List and Details views from earlier versions of Windows. These two views are essentially the same, except that the Details view displays information about the file's attributes, such as the creation date and modification date, and is still
my personal choice for that reason. Remember that when you are working with the Details
view, you can sort any of the items by simply clicking the column heading. You can sort by
date, filename, or file size.

You can also customize the columns that appear in Details view. To do so, choose View ➢
Choose Details to open the Choose Details dialog box. The list of descriptors about a file is
extensive. Further, you can rearrange the order of columns that the Details view displays in
this dialog box. Select a detail from the list, and then click the Move Up or the Move Down
button. It's easier to rearrange columns though by clicking and dragging column headings in
the Explorer window.

The Thumbnails view displays previews of file contents if at all possible. This view can be
especially effective for web developers and others who work with large volumes of graphics
files; a miniaturized version of the file is displayed in the Explorer Details pane.

NOTE   Windows old-timers will notice that the Large Icons and Small Icons views have gone the
way of the dodo.

Understanding the New Views

New to the Windows XP operating system is the Tiles view, which is essentially the replacement view for the Large Icons view and is also the default view. (And which, in my opinion,
has XP doing a pretty fair impersonation of a Mac.) In Tiles view, XP displays as many as

three lines of text to describe each file, showing you more information about the file than was previously available with either of the Icons views. Exactly what information displays depends on the type of file selected. For example, if you select a Windows Media Audio (.wma) file, not only will the filename display, but also the artist name (helping you recognize all the Vanilla Ice tunes you've saved to your hard drive).

Also new is the Filmstrip view. In Filmstrip view, as shown in Figure 8.3, the currently selected figure displays larger than its folder companions and is centered in the window. Below the selected picture, you will see four buttons. You use the first two to flip through the picture display as easily as you would flip through a stack of pictures fresh from the developer. You use the other two buttons to manipulate picture display. You can rotate pictures clockwise or counterclockwise, rather than having to tilt your head when looking at the monitor.

FIGURE 8.3:

Filmstrip view is ideal for working with saved images.

If Filmstrip is not available on the View menu and the selected folder contains images, you can make Filmstrip view available by "telling" the folder that it holds image files. To do so, follow these steps:

1. In Windows Explorer, choose View ➤ Customize This Folder to open the Properties dialog box for the selected folder at the Customize tab.

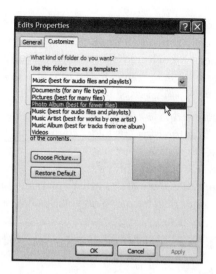

2. In the Use This Folder Type As A Template drop-down list box, select either Pictures or Photo Album.

3. Click OK. You'll now see the Filmstrip option in the View menu.

Using the Same View for All Folders

Windows XP has a great memory when it comes to views: it will remember any view changes you make to a particular folder and then show you that view when you are looking at its contents. You can, therefore, have several views in effect when looking through the contents of a drive.

But what happens if you want to set up all folders to display using the same view, so that you will have a consistent look and feel across the entire drive? Explorer makes this easy to accomplish. Follow these steps:

1. In Explorer, select a folder, and then select the view.

1. Choose Tools ➢ Folder Options to open the Folder Options dialog box.

2. Click the View tab.

3. Click the Apply To All Folders button, and then click OK.

Following these steps effectively resets the default view of Explorer from Tiles to whatever you choose. And you can still apply distinct views to individual folders. Just go to the appropriate folder and change the view again. You can also return all folders to their default views by clicking the Reset All Folders button on the View tab of the Folder Options dialog box.

Sorting Icons

Earlier we looked at ways to customize and sort the properties displayed in the Details view. In other views, you can also sort contents by choosing View ➤ Arrange Icons By and then selecting an arrangement from the submenu. The options depend on the current view for the folder.

For example, you can use the Show In Groups command to arrange icons by a category of your choosing. This is especially useful when working in a folder that has a large number of files or subfolders; it takes the place of the Search feature, which can be much slower to execute.

Opening Explorer for Specific Targets

When you open Explorer, a target folder also opens. Which target folder opens, however, depends on how you open Explorer. For example, when you open Explorer from the Accessories menu, Explorer opens the My Documents folder, but the My Documents folder also opens in Explorer when you right-click My Documents on the Start menu and then choose Explore from the shortcut menu. If you right-click My Computer and choose Explore from the shortcut menu, Explorer opens at the My Computer folder. Right-clicking the Start button and choosing Explore from the shortcut menu opens Explorer at the Start Menu folder under the profile of the currently logged-on user.

Although it is far more common to launch Explorer using one of the methods I've already described in this chapter, you can also open Explorer from a command prompt or by using the Run dialog box. When you use either of these methods, you can use a handful of switches to control how Explorer works and to open Explorer at a specific target. This approach is especially handy for power users who often find themselves working from the command prompt.

The program that launches Windows Explorer is explorer.exe, and by default it opens at the My Documents folder. However, you can use a switch to specify that it open at the My Computer folder instead or at any other folder. You can also direct Windows Explorer to select a folder or file when it opens. The syntax is as follows:

```
explorer.exe [/n][/e][,/root,][[,/select],]
```

Table 8.1 lists and describes the switches.

TABLE 8.1: Command-Line Switches for explorer.exe

Switch	What It Does
/n	Opens Windows Explorer in single-pane view, similar to the view you see when you double-click the My Computer icon from your Desktop.
/Explorer	Opens Windows Explorer in multipane view, which is the default view when you open Explorer using any of the methods described in this chapter, including through the Start menu.
/root	Modifies the target at which Explorer opens. For example, you might specify a UNC path to open Windows Explorer with the shared network folder as root of the view.
/select	Tells Windows Explorer to select the file or folder specified by the path following the switch.

Controlling the Explorer Bar's Contents

Like its Windows predecessors, Windows XP includes a status bar. The status bar displays useful information about a selected file or folder, such as the number of objects selected, the total size of the selected object or objects, and the source of the selection (such as My Computer or Local Intranet). Unlike previous versions, however, this status bar is not visible by default. To display it, choose View ➤ Status Bar.

When you choose View ➤ Explorer Bar, you can select from five additional Explorer bars: Search, Favorites, Media, History, and Folders. (If you see yet other bars on this menu, they have been placed there by applications installed on your computer.)

When you select an Explorer bar, it appears on the left side of the Explorer window, replacing the Task pane if it is selected. Figure 8.4 shows what this will look like, for example, with the Favorites bar selected. You will notice right off the bat that, as in other areas of Windows Explorer, the interface is exactly that of Internet Explorer.

The Search Bar

When you select the Search bar, you will also see the Search Assistant (no relation to Office Assistant, thank you very much), an aid to help you find what you are looking for. Choosing the Search bar has the same effect as choosing the Search option from the Start menu, with the exception that the Search Assistant, when launched from Windows Explorer, is automatically configured to restrict its search to the currently selected folder. The results of the search are shown in the Details pane on the right side of the Explorer window.

To close the Search bar (or any other Explorer bar, for that matter), click its Close button or click the Back button on the Standard toolbar. You can also toggle the Search bar on and off by clicking the Search button or by pressing Ctrl+E.

FIGURE 8.4:

The Favorites bar
appears on the left in
Windows Explorer.

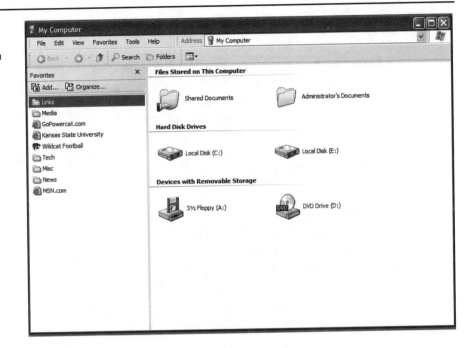

The Favorites Bar

In Windows XP, the contents of your Favorites menu become a part of your user profile. (This is one of the best arguments for using a roaming profile, in my opinion.) By default, this location is in the Favorites folder, which is found under \Documents and Settings\ %Username%\Favorites, unless you are using a roaming profile. And, because the operating system and the web browser are the same thing, the contents of the Favorites folder are used to populate both your Internet Explorer Favorites menu and your Windows Explorer Favorites bar. But, even though you will normally keep Internet shortcuts in the Favorites folder, you can place shortcuts to other information there. For example, if you frequently access a particular folder (especially if the folder is buried deep in the directory structure of the drive), you can create a shortcut to that folder in your Favorites folder and then use the Favorites bar to navigate to it in just a couple of clicks, rather than many. It can be toggled if you remember the keyboard shortcut Ctrl+I.

The Media Bar

The Media bar is more marketing leverage than anything else. It provides links to various places within the WindowsMedia.com website. There is no keyboard shortcut and no toolbar button that will toggle the Media bar.

The History Bar

The History bar is another that you have likely used in working with Internet Explorer. In Windows Explorer, the History bar displays Internet pages you've visited, along with any document files recently opened. It doesn't matter whether you opened the documents locally or over a network connection. This feature can be especially helpful if you are trying to locate a document that has been removed from the My Documents list on the Start menu. You can toggle the History bar by pressing Ctrl+H.

TIP if you click a website from within the History bar, the web page displays in the Windows Explorer window, not in Internet Explorer.

The Folders Bar

The Folders bar is probably the most useful of the Explorer bars; it is really helpful for folder and file management, which is what you open Explorer for in the first place. The Folders bar displays all your storage resources, both local and remote, in a tree structure that has remained, for the most, part consistent since Windows 95.

It seems that Microsoft also considers the Folders bar especially useful; a shortcut button to the Folders bar appears on the standard Explorer toolbar. However, there is no keyboard shortcut.

Navigating the Folder Structure

Windows XP also includes a cleaner way of navigating the Folders bar, called the Simple Folder View. Here's how it works. With the Simple Folder View enabled, clicking a folder in the Folders bar displays the contents of the folder in the right pane of Windows Explorer and expands the folder you've clicked. But when you click another folder, Windows Explorer closes the Folder branch you were just viewing and opens the one you clicked in its place. Thus, only one folder is open when you are looking at the directory tree. (You can modify this behavior somewhat: click the plus sign instead of the folder name to expand a branch without closing the previous one.)

This feature can be a big navigation aid if you are looking through folders that have several subfolders, but at times you might want the Simple Folder View turned off. To set the folder expansion options as they were in previous versions of Windows, follow these steps:

1. In Windows Explorer, choose Tools ➤ Folder Options to open the Folder Options dialog box.

2. Click the View tab.

3. In the Advanced Settings list, clear the Display Simple Folder View In Explorer's Folders List check box.

4. Click OK.

Configuring Toolbars

Windows Explorer includes three toolbars:

- Standard Buttons
- Address Bar
- Links

Using and configuring these toolbars is similar to using Internet Explorer's toolbars of the same names. As in Internet Explorer, you can choose to hide or display these toolbars in any combination. The easy way to control what is displayed is to right-click an empty area of a toolbar and than make a selection from the shortcut menu, but you can also access the same options by choosing View ➤ Toolbars.

Furthermore, you can change the size or location of the toolbars by simply clicking and dragging them. Just look for the handle that appears, as shown in Figure 8.5.

FIGURE 8.5:

Use the handlebars to expand, collapse, and move Explorer toolbars.

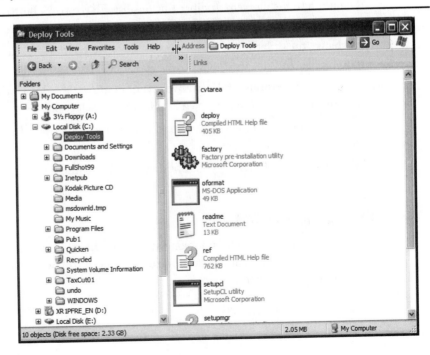

If you don't see the toolbar handles, the toolbar is probably locked. To unlock the toolbars, choose View ➤ Toolbars ➤ Lock The Toolbars.

In addition to repositioning the toolbars, you can customize what is on them. To do so, follow these steps:

1. Right-click an empty area of the toolbar, and choose Customize from the shortcut menu to open the Customize Toolbar dialog box:

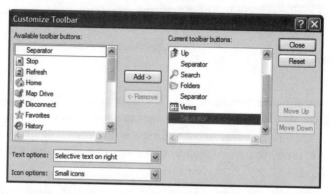

2. In the Available Toolbar Buttons list, select a button, and then click the Add button to add the button to the Current Toolbar Buttons list. To remove a button from the toolbar, select it from the Current Toolbar Buttons list, and click the Remove button.

3. To change the ordering of the buttons on the selected toolbar, select a button in the Current Toolbar Buttons list, and click either Move Up or Move Down.

4. To change the position of descriptive text or eliminate the descriptive text altogether, click the Text Options drop-down list and make a selection.

5. To change the size of the toolbar icons, click the Icon Options drop-down list and make a selection.

6. When you have selected all your options, click the Close button.

Customizing Explorer

So far in this chapter, we've been looking at some of the more common ways to customize the contents of Explorer, but you customize Explorer in still other ways. In this section, we'll take a look at some of them.

Using Tweak UI

Tweak UI (see Figure 8.6) is a program that you can use to customize almost all aspects of the user interface, but it is not formally supported by Microsoft. If you're really into manipulating the user interface and find that the Control Panel options just aren't up to your standards, Tweak UI is the program for you. You can download Tweak UI at

www.microsoft.com/ntworkstation/downloads/PowerToys/Networking/NTTweakUI.asp

As of this writing, version 1.33 was the latest and greatest.

One of the cool things about Tweak UI is that you can use it to customize the Save and Open dialog boxes. If you use the Microsoft Office suite of programs, you know that the Open and Save dialog boxes in those programs offer far more flexibility than the ones used by most Windows programs. Using Tweak UI, you can give Windows' Save and Open dialog boxes more the look and feel of those dialog boxes in Office.

Using Windows Blinds

You can change the entire user interface of Windows in still other ways. Using a program called Windows Blinds, you can apply "skins" to the entire GUI. This program makes XP behave much like programs such as WinAmp, RealPlayer, or Internet Explorer, programs whose look and feel has been modified for years by individuals who are fans of alternative bands or science fiction movies.

FIGURE 8.6:

Using Tweak UI, you can specify many user interface settings.

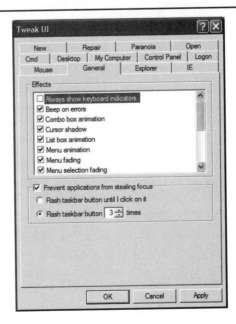

You can download Windows Blinds at `http://download.cnet.com`. When you install the software, you will find that there are a number of sites that store skins for you to download and install with Blinds. In fact, the Windows Blinds installation will direct you to a few.

Using Microsoft Plus! for Windows XP

Many of you are probably familiar with Plus! for previous versions of Windows. Plus! is now available for Windows XP, and you can use it to add desktop themes and multimedia enhancements. The XP edition is fundamentally the same as its predecessors; you just have a few new looks to choose from. You can purchase Plus! at `www.microsoft.com/windows/plus/default.htm`.

CHAPTER 9

Controlling Printing

In this chapter, we'll take a look at how you can optimize printing, all the way from printer setup to configuration to management. You'll learn to manage how and when printer software communicates with printer hardware, how to set up printer pools and priorities, and how to take advantage of printer spooling. Network printing requires a decent amount of configuration, and in this chapter you'll learn how to make a printer available on the network, how to connect clients to it and set permissions, how to configure a printer to print to the IP address of a network interface print device, and how to redirect print jobs. The chapter ends with a section on Internet printing.

Before you roll up your sleeves, best read the first section, which provides all the background you'll need to get started controlling your printers.

Printing Primer

Much of the discussion about printing in Windows XP is initially a language lesson. It's a necessary evil, however; in order to understand printing, we have to be specific with our terminology. We have to be clear, for example, whether we are talking about a piece of software (the printer) or the piece of hardware that applies ink to a page (the print device), because we will perform different administrative tasks on both. Following is a quick review of the terms used in a Windows XP print environment.

Printer   A piece of software that provides the necessary translation so that a Windows can send information to a print device. The printer is there to provide access to the print device on your desk.

Print device   What is normally referred to (before this section, anyway) as the printer. The piece of equipment that turns your electronic files into readable output on a sheet of paper.

> **TIP**   Now, just so you know... it isn't considered proper etiquette to correct people on their use of the terms "printer" and "print device." The terms are really distinguished only for purposes of discussion in computer book chapters that deal with the task of getting ink on a page. So unless you enjoy the role of pariah at social gatherings, keep the distinction between printers and print devices to yourself.

Printer driver   A part of the printer installation that translates document formats into a language that the printer can understand. In other words, because of the work that printer drivers do, all documents look the same to the printer no matter what application they are sent from.

Print server   A computer that has made the printer software resource available on the network by sharing it. Print clients and print servers use the same language to speak to one another, the same one that they use to share and request file resources. Therefore, the client and server components between computers must be compatible in order for print clients to submit jobs to a print server. All Windows 9x and later computers can be print servers.

Port   A printer needs a way to get its translated information to the print device. It accomplishes this through a specifically defined pathway, known as a port. These pathways of information can be of several varieties, as you'll soon learn.

Print spooler   A print spooler is an area of buffer storage (usually an area on a disk) where documents wait to be serviced. The printer pulls the waiting jobs off the buffer at its own rate. This line-up of print jobs is known as the *print queue*, and the two terms are often used interchangeably. Because the documents are in a buffer where they can be accessed by the printer, you can perform other operations on the computer while the printing takes place in the background. Spooling also lets you place a number of print jobs in a queue instead of waiting for each one to finish before specifying the next one.

Now that we have established that a printer is a piece of software and not a piece of hardware (don't walk around correcting your grandmother on this; the social consequences can be harsh), it really shouldn't be too much a leap of faith to imagine that this piece of software, the printer, is just another disk resource that can be shared on a network, as mentioned earlier. We also need to be aware when we configure printing that print devices come in three varieties:

Local   Local printers are devices managed by the software physically installed at your computer. Traditionally, local printers submit their jobs through a parallel port to a device that is sitting right next to your desk, although that isn't always the case (I'll discuss this further in the section on network printing).

Network   These print devices are managed by printers that aren't directly installed on your system. They are accessible over the network, however, as their name implies, and may or may not be located in the same room.

Virtual   These printer types show up as printing options in the Print dialog box of software applications and also are represented as icons in the Printers And Faxes folder. These printers don't send jobs to a device that puts ink on paper, but rather they convert a document to a widely readable format. A primary example of a virtual printer is the PDF Writer, which converts documents into the Adobe Acrobat .pdf format.

The command-and-control center for printing and faxing is the `Printers And Faxes` folder, which you can open from Control Panel by clicking the Printers And Faxes icon. If you are using Control Panel in Category view, you will find the Printers And Faxes icon in the Printers And Other Hardware category.

However, you might also want to add a Start Menu shortcut to the `Printers And Faxes` folder, a shortcut that was present in previous versions of Windows. To do so, follow these steps:

1. Right-click anywhere on the Taskbar or on the Start menu and choose Properties from the shortcut menu to open the Taskbar And Start Menu Properties dialog box.

2. Click the Start Menu tab.

3. Click on the Customize button to open the Customize Start Menu dialog box.

4. Click the Advanced tab, and then, in the Start Menu Items section, scroll down the list and ensure that the Printers And Faxes check box is selected.

5. Click OK to close the Customize Start Menu dialog box, and then click OK again to close the Taskbar And Start Menu Properties dialog box.

Now you have an easier way to open the `Printers And Faxes` folder, which is shown in Figure 9.1.

FIGURE 9.1:

Windows XP lets you track and manage printers and fax devices from a single folder.

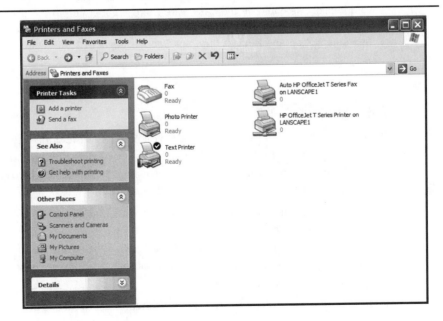

Quick Printing Tips

Usually, the first step in setting up a print environment is to install and configure a local printer, a task that you have likely performed many, many times. To briefly review, you add a printer to the Printers And Faxes folder by using the Add Printer Wizard. To start the wizard, open the Printers And Faxes folder, and click Add A Printer in the Printer Tasks bar. At the Welcome screen, click Next. The wizard then gives you the choice of adding either a local printer or a network printer, depending on where the printer (software) is located.

The remainder of the screens in the Add Printer Wizard depend on whether you choose to install a local printer or a network printer. If you are setting up a local printer, next you'll select a port that the print device is connected to (usually LPT1) and then find the printer drivers to install. Many of these drivers are included with the XP operating system and will also be included on the disk that ships with the print device.

Of course, most printers (whoops, *print devices*) today come with their own setup routine that will take you through this process, even configuring several printing options and settings, without ever having to visit the Printers And Faxes folder to launch the Add Printer Wizard. So if you've been able to print successfully for years but have never seen the Add Printer Wizard at work, you are not alone, and there's no need to worry. The idea is to get the thing to work.

TIP   By the way, if the thing won't work, that is, if your document won't print, it's possible that it has become "stuck" in the print queue (quotes because it's not *physically* stuck as the word implies, as could be the case were there a paper jam in the physical print device). Try opening the Services MMC snap-in from Control Panel (or Administrative Tools), and then select Stop And Restart the Print Spooler Service. That seems to fix a lot of these types of printing problems.

Managing Printers

Because the printer is a piece of software, you manage it the same way you manage other pieces of software stored on your XP machine—by configuring options in the software's Properties dialog box. You can set several attributes in this dialog box, and in this section I've compiled some of the more interesting and/or useful.

Many advanced print configurations rely on your understanding that a printer is a piece of software. Therefore, you can install two or more printers on a system and configure the printers so that both print to the same print device. The configuration options for each printer can be completely different, yet send output to the same machine.

Using two printers to print to the same device can be a great advantage when you quickly want to make several changes to the way a job is printed. Most of today's printers support a wide array of options for paper tray, page size, page orientation, half-toning, print optimization, and so on. For example, one change that I regularly make is to configure a printer to either use or not use photo-quality output. Although the Properties dialog box interface makes it relatively easy to change such printer settings when needed, it can be a little time-consuming when frequently switching printer settings, particularly if you are trying to change multiple settings at once.

So, to easily switch between separate sets of printer settings, configure multiple printer instances for the same physical print device, printing to the same print port, each with its own settings. Give each printer instance a name indicating its function, such as Photo Printer and Text Printer, to make it easy to determine which one you want to use. Then, simply select the printer instance by name in the application's Print dialog box.

To add and configure a printer instance, follow these steps:

1. Open the `Printers And Faxes` folder, run the Add Printer Wizard, and install the printer a second time.

2. When asked if you want to keep the existing driver files or install new ones, keep the existing files.

3. Right-click the newly installed instance and choose Properties from the shortcut menu to open the printer's Properties dialog box. Configure the printer's settings as desired, including assigning a descriptive name, and then close the Properties dialog box.

Follow these steps again to add other instances as needed, configuring their settings as required. You will end up with a Properties dialog box that lists multiple printers for a single port, as shown in Figure 9.2.

FIGURE 9.2:

You can configure two or more printers to use the same port and therefore the same print device.

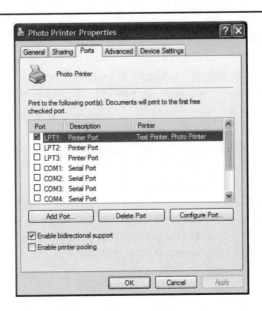

Hours of Availability

You can further manage the use of two or more printers that print to the same device by setting hours of availability for each. Continuing the example from the previous section, I would expect the Photo Printer to print much slower than the Text Printer because of its higher resolution. In this example, let's further assume that there is no urgency to the jobs sent to the Photo Printer and that the Text Printer needs to be more readily available. You don't want to wait several minutes for photos to print when you need to print a letter or an invoice and go on to the next task.

In a scenario such as this, it will be useful to configure a schedule for the Photo Printer so that the print device is not tied up while the Text Printer is trying to have a job serviced. To set printer availability, follow these steps:

1. Right-click the desired printer you want to configure, and choose Properties from the shortcut menu to open the Properties dialog box for the printer.

2. Click the Advanced tab.

3. The default option for the printer is Always Available. To change this setting, select the Available From radio button, and then set the time when the printer will be available to service jobs.

4. Click OK.

TIP   The printer will still be available to receive jobs even when the printer is not available. These jobs will simply wait in the print queue until the printer becomes available.

Pooling and Priority

Printer pools and print priorities are typically used in high-volume printing environments, where many printers or many print devices service the printing needs of network users. The two technologies are really two sides of the same coin, as you will see.

Print pooling associates a single printer with multiple print devices. You typically use a printer pool when many print devices of the same type are located on the network, so that they all understand the instructions of one type of printer driver. The first available print device services the print jobs submitted to a pool. When you configure printer pools, however, you cannot specify which print device will receive the job.

TIP   For the reason I just mentioned, it is wise to place pooled print devices in close physical proximity to one another, unless you are trying to incorporate your printing scheme with some kind of corporate exercise program.

To configure a printer pool, follow these steps:

1. In the printer's Properties dialog box, click the Ports tab, as shown in Figure 9.3.

FIGURE 9.3:

Configuring a print
pool involves just a
few clicks.

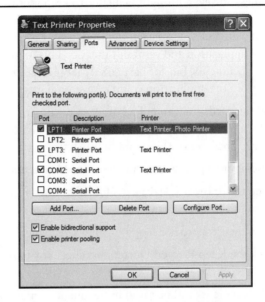

2. At the bottom of this tab, click the Enable Printer Pooling check box, and then select the check boxes of all the ports you want the logical printer to send its ones and zeros from. If you do not select the Enable Printer Pooling check box, you will only be able to configure one port per printer.

3. Click OK.

The flip side of printer pooling is printer priority. Much like configuring a schedule for a printer, you can configure multiple printers to use a single print device. When you set printer priority, you specify how print jobs are sent to the device.

Again, you configure the priority of a printer on the Advanced tab of the printer's Properties dialog box. Using the Priority spin box, you rank the priority of the printer from 1 to 99. The default priority for a printer is 1, the lowest ranking. Any printer that has a higher ranking gets first dibs on the port for which that printer is configured. When the Print Manager on the system polls for print jobs, the printer with the higher priority will always print jobs in the queue before jobs in the lower priority printer.

The Print Queue

The print queue is where print jobs go to stand in line before being serviced by the print device. By default, the jobs are deleted from this queue after they have been sent to a print device. This behavior is useful; it keeps the queue from filling up with old documents and consuming unnecessary disk space.

At times, however, it might be better to keep jobs in the print spool even after they have been sent to the print device. For example, if you have a problem with a print job that allows it to complete but not satisfactorily (the printer runs out of toner, for example), you have to open the application and resubmit the job. This might not be a problem for most applications or documents, but for particularly large documents and some applications, reprinting the job from the application could take several extra minutes.

As a safeguard, you can tell XP to keep documents in the queue. Doing so lets you resubmit a document right from the queue rather than having to open the application. If you often print large documents, this could be a real timesaver.

To configure a printer's queue to retain documents, follow these steps:

1. Open the `Printers And Faxes` folder from your location of choice. (I like to keep a shortcut to this on the Start menu.)

2. Open the Properties dialog box for a selected printer, and then click the Advanced tab.

3. Click the Keep Printed Documents checkbox found near the bottom of the dialog box, and then click OK.

Now documents will be saved in the queue even after printing. Keep in mind that this does require additional disk space and that you will need to manually remove documents from the queue after they are successfully printed.

Spooling

Like other operating systems, Windows XP supports print spooling. Rather than print directly to the printer, applications send translated, ready-to-print jobs to an area of disk space. The print spool is managed by Windows XP, which in turn then takes care of sending the print job to the physical print device. The advantage is that the application doesn't have to wait for the document to finish printing before you can continue using the application. As far as the application is concerned, once the document is in the spool, it's printed. The application can then go about its main function again.

For most people the default settings for print spooling work just fine. In some cases, though, you might need to tweak the settings or turn off spooling. You configure spool settings on a per-printer basis. Follow these steps:

1. Open the `Printers And Faxes` folder, right-click the desired printer, and choose Properties from the shortcut menu to open the Properties dialog box for the printer.

2. Click the Advanced tab.

3. Click the Print Directly To The Printer option.

4. Click OK.

If you choose to use spooling, you can specify that Windows XP start printing as soon as the data starts flowing to the queue, or you can specify that the entire document moves to the spool before printing starts. Specifying the latter option can overcome printing problems, particularly with long documents.

TIP   There is little reason to change the default spooling options. The time savings gained by sending a job right to the printer is barely measurable, and remember, the spool lets the application get back to business as quickly as possible.

Network Printing

If you are familiar with the concept of sharing folders over a network, you already have the fundamentals of network printing. Just as file sharing is the act of making a file resource available on the network, print sharing makes a print resource available to users who have connectivity.

Making a Printer Available on the Network

You can share a printer right when you set up the printer, or you can do it later from the printer's Properties dialog box. To make a printer available for network printing after setup, click the Sharing tab in the printer's Properties dialog box (see Figure 9.4), click the Share This Printer radio button, enter a name for the printer in the Share Name box, and then click OK.

FIGURE 9.4:

You specify a share name after you share the printer.

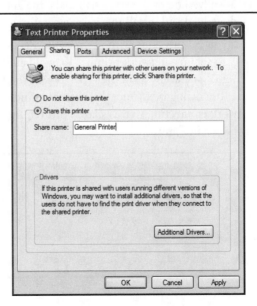

Remember, users will use the share name to make a network connection to the printer. It doesn't have to match the actual printer name, but use intuitive names when possible. Also keep in mind that any MS-DOS clients of your shared printer will not be able to see names longer than eight characters.

Connecting to a Network Printer

Once you share a printer on the network, print clients can connect to it and send documents to it. If you're setting up a network printer, you are telling the print drivers on your system to send the print job over the network to be managed by a printer that lives elsewhere on a print server. (This is why the language lesson was first.) To add a network printer to a client's `Printers And Faxes` folder, follow these steps:

1. In the `Printers And Faxes` folder, click Add A Printer to start the Add Printer Wizard.

2. At the Welcome screen, click Next to open the Local Or Network Printer screen.

3. Select the A Network Printer, Or A Printer Attached To Another Computer option, and then click Next to open the Specify A Printer screen.

3. You can enter a UNC name for the printer, browse the network for a printer, or connect to a printer on the Internet by entering a URL. You can also to search through the Active Directory (if you're a part of an Active Directory domain) to find a printer after you select Browse For A Printer.

When you confirm you choice, the appropriate print drivers for the network printer will need to be installed on your local machine. In a Windows-only environment, this will happen automatically: The print server will make the appropriate print drivers available, and the client will download and install these drivers automatically.

Now that you've learned how to use the Add Printer Wizard, I want to show you an even quicker way to set up a network printer. To avoid all that clicking, just enter the UNC path of the printer (if you know it) in the Open box in the Run dialog box. (Choose Start ➢ Run to open the Run dialog box.) Yep, that's it; the printer will be set up automatically. Upon successful network connection to this shared printer, the contents of the print queue will be displayed, as shown in Figure 9.5.

FIGURE 9.5:

You can simply enter the UNC path to quickly and easily set up a network printer.

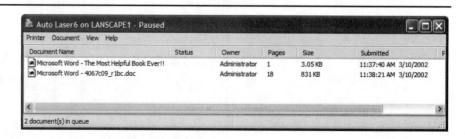

You can also connect and install a network printer by browsing for it in Windows Explorer. In the My Network Places folder, double-click the printer you want to set up. After connection is established, you'll see the window shown in Figure 9.5.

Setting Permissions on Network Printers

When a printer is made available from a print server, default printer permissions are assigned that allow the Everyone group (that is, all users) to print and that allow select groups to manage the printer, manage documents sent to it, or all the above.

Because the printer is available to all users on the network, you might want to limit access for some users by assigning specific printer permissions. For example, you might give all normal users in a department the Print permission and give all managers the Print and Manage Documents permissions. In this way, all users and managers can print documents, but managers can also change the print status of any document sent to the printer. Furthermore, by default the Creator Owner special group has the Manage Documents permission. This means that users can manage all documents that they own. For example, the owner of a document can send a job to the print queue and then cancel its printing if they change their mind.

This behavior is a departure from the behavior of NTFS and Share permissions, in which the Everyone group has the Full Control permission until an administrator tightens security settings. For this reason, you typically won't have to do much configuring of the security permissions of printers.

You control which users have access to a shared printer that you make available from your print server through the Security tab of the printer's Properties dialog box, as shown in Figure 9.6.

To change the permission settings for a printer, you must have the Manage Printers permission, and then follow these steps:

1. Open the `Printers And Faxes` folder, right-click the printer, and choose Properties from the shortcut menu to open the Properties dialog box for the selected printer.

2. Click the Security tab, and then click Add to open the Select Users Or Groups dialog box.

3. In the Enter The Object Names To Select box, enter the names, separating them with a semicolon. Click OK.

4. In the Permissions section of the Properties dialog box, click the Allow or Deny check box for each permission as appropriate.

6. Click OK.

FIGURE 9.6:

You configure the security settings for a printer using the options on the Security tab.

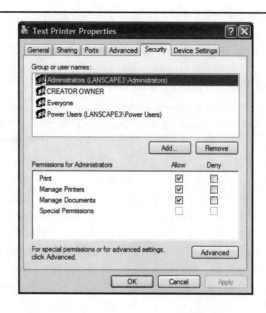

> **TIP**   If your Windows XP system is part of a domain, the Security tab is automatically displayed in the printer's Properties dialog box. But Windows XP does not display a Security tab in the printer's Properties dialog box if you are using Simple File Sharing *and* are operating in a Workgroup environment. To see whether you are using Simple File Sharing, look at the list of Advanced settings on the View tab of the Folder Options dialog box. You will need to make sure that the Simple File Sharing (Recommended) option is cleared in order to display the Security tab.

Network Interface Printing

The printer that is being used doesn't physically have to be connected to your computer or to any other computer in the network. Many companies use the services of a *network interface* print device, which is simply a print device with a NIC (network interface card).

The network interface print device is assigned an IP address, just like any other computer in the network with a NIC, and you configure your printer (the software) to print to this address, rather than to a local port such as a parallel or USB port.

Now here's where it gets a bit tricky—the IP address is also considered a *local* port! Huh? Even though you are sending a print job over the network, technically you are not printing over the network. The printer is still managed locally, not on a remote print server. (However, a remote print server can certainly print to a TCP/IP port the same as you.) I've beaten it into your head by now (I hope), but it bears repeating: the local and network printing are distinguished by the location of the *software*, not the hardware.

To configure a printer to print to the IP address of a network interface print device, you must set up and configure a standard TCP/IP port. Follow these steps:

1. Start the Add Printer Wizard, and at the Welcome screen, click Next to open the Local Or Network Printer screen.

2. Select the Local Printer Attached To This Computer option, clear the Automatically Detect And Install My Plug And Play Printer option, and then click Next to open the Select A Printer Port screen.

3. Select the Create A New Port option, and then in the Type Of Port drop-down list, select Standard TCP/IP Port. Click Next to start the Add Standard TCP/IP Printer Port Wizard.

4. At the Welcome screen, click Next, and then on the Add Port screen, enter the IP address of the print device and give the device a name, as shown in Figure 9.7.

FIGURE 9.7:
You add and name a TCP/IP port on the Add Port screen of the wizard.

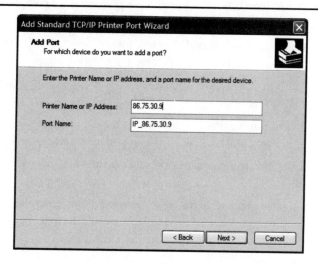

4. Click Next, and the wizard's final screen shows you settings information that confirms successful communication with the print device. Click Finish to complete the process.

TIP   Most network interface print devices can self-generate a configuration report, so you can know the IP address of the device. The print device's manual should tell you how to get this report.

Redirecting Print Jobs

The technique of sending print jobs to printer ports that will then send the jobs to network print devices (see why all the terminology was important?) can be a useful troubleshooting workaround. For example, it can ensure uninterrupted printing when used to redirect the contents of the print queue because a print device is malfunctioning (it's out of toner, there is a paper jam, or various other problems are occurring). You can also use this technique to change the port a printer is configured to use even after the printer is installed. Many network interface print devices also can be connected directly to a computer and may have started life on the network in this way.

To change the port a printer is using, you use the options on the Ports tab in the Properties dialog box for that printer. You are configuring software. Let's say, for example, that your coworker has just kicked the print device connected to your computer in a fit of rage over the latest BCS standings. (Were this coworker in Cleveland, he would probably pelt you with beer bottles.) Now the device is not working, and you have a big report that needs to be printed. However, your coworker has set up a printer on his computer and shared it when he wasn't listening to sports talk radio. Here's what you can do to solve the problem:

1. Open the Properties dialog box for the printer, click the Ports tab, and then click the Add Port button to open the Printer Ports dialog box.

2. With the Local Port option selected, click the New Port button to open the Port Name dialog box.

3. In the Enter A Port Name box, enter the name of the port. Use the UNC syntax of *servername**printer*, just as if you were setting up a network printer.

4. Click OK to close the Port Name dialog box, close the Printer Ports dialog box, and then click OK to close the printer's Properties dialog box.

You have now set up the new local port. And remember, even though print jobs will now be sent over the network, the port is considered local because the printer software installed locally at your machine manages these print jobs.

Internet Printing

Windows XP supports the Internet Printing Protocol (IPP), which lets documents be sent over the Internet to printers that are available through a TCP/IP connection. So how are printers available on the Internet? Glad you asked. The ability to print over the Internet is an integral part of the setup of Internet Information Services (IIS). By default, the installation of IIS is supposed to make shared printers accessible through the Internet, and any subsequent printers that are added and shared will be Internet-available as well. However, whether this happens depends on which version of Windows you're installing, as I'll explain in the next subsection. For now, let's just assume that things are working as advertised.

Once IIS is set up, users who have the appropriate permission levels can view and manage printers from a web browser window. All they have to do to connect to a printer over the Internet is to open a browser window and enter **http://*hostname*/printers** in the Address bar. The *hostname* portion of this URL is the name of the print server on which IIS is installed and can be either a name or an IP address, just like when connecting to a website. In this syntax, the printers portion of the URL is literal; you type the word **printers**. After you enter this URL and press Enter, your browser displays the page shown in Figure 9.8. From here, the printing options are fairly intuitive; if you can click around on Yahoo to get information, you should have little trouble with the options on this page.

TIP   The process I describe in this section also works on an intranet if you have HTTP connectivity.

FIGURE 9.8:

To install and manage printer, follow the links on the home page of Internet printing on a print server that has IIS installed.

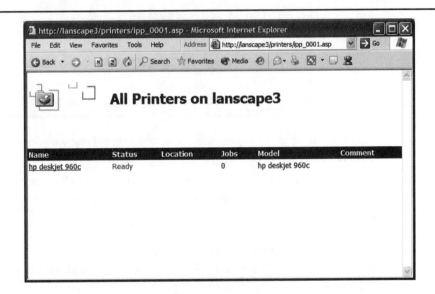

This web page also presents an easy way to set up a network printer on your system. The Printers home page will present you with a hyperlinked list of all shared printers. Simply follow the link of the printer you want to install, and then choose Connect on the next page (it will be at the bottom of the Printer Actions list, as shown in Figure 9.9) to install and set up the printer for your use. You might be prompted to select drivers for the printer you are setting up as part of the installation.

You can install the
printer if it is not
already set up.

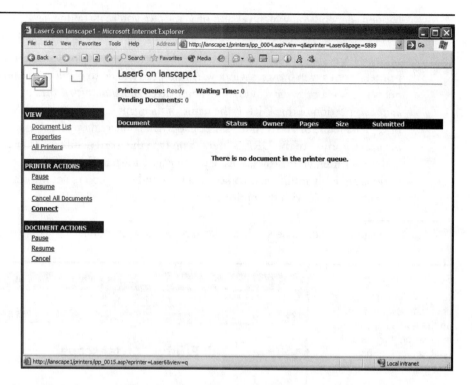

You can also modify the syntax in the Address bar slightly if you want to connect directly to
an available printer, bypassing the home page: **http://***servername***/printers/***printername*.

After the Internet printer is installed, you can use the IPP printer exactly the same as you
would any other printer installed on your system, either attached locally or available on the
network.

Setting Up the Printers Virtual Directory

Here's a bug (feature?) that you will likely encounter when you install IIS under Windows
XP Professional. If you notice the setup options for the World Wide Web Publishing Service, as you configure IIS from the Windows Components Wizard, you will see the check
box selected that tells you that the Printers virtual directory will be created.

This directory is created and configured correctly when you install IIS on a 2000 Server
machine, and Internet printing works exactly as described without further exertion. However,
when you try to connect to this print server using a web browser as outlined earlier, you may
see a "Page Not Found" error message. In this case, a quick glance at IIS will confirm that the
directory has not been set up. In Windows XP, as well as in Windows 2000 Professional, you

must configure the Printers virtual directory manually, despite what setup tells you, to enable printing from across the Internet.

Fortunately, setting up Internet printing under XP Professional is fairly easy. Follow these steps:

TIP   You can follow these same steps to enable Internet printing in Windows 2000 Professional.

1. After you install IIS on the XP system, open the IIS console, right-click the website where you want to add printing capability (normally it will be the Default site), and choose New ➢ Virtual Directory to start the Virtual Directory Wizard.

2. Under the site, add a virtual directory with an alias of Printers that points to the %system-root%\Web\printers directory.

NOTE   This directory is in a completely different location from the directory set up by the IIS installation, inetpub. Not very intuitive, I know, but I didn't write the software.

3. Set the permissions to include Read and Run Scripts.

4. Open the Properties dialog box for the Printers virtual folder and click the Documents tab.

5. Click Add to open the Add Default Document dialog box.

6. Enter the name **page1.asp**, and click OK.

7. Click the up arrow button to move page1.asp to the top of the default documents list. Click OK to apply the change.

8. From a client machine on the LAN or on the Internet, connect to http://hostname/printers, as discussed earlier, and the printers page should be displayed.

TIP   If you can't see the printers from the client browser, stop and restart the website in the IIS console. The client must support IPP to take full advantage of printing across the Internet. Windows XP and 2000 clients natively support IPP. You can find a Windows 9x client for IPP on the Windows 2000 Server CD in \Clients\Win9xipp.cli. There is currently no IPP client for Windows NT, and at last word Microsoft was not planning to release one.

CHAPTER 10

Command Console Survivor's Guide

Some people still swear by it: typing commands to the operating system so that they can be carried out. This ensures, so the argument goes, error-free navigation and execution in the computing environment, because you have to know exactly what you're doing in order to tell the computer what to do. Things can't be messed up by a few inopportune mouse clicks.

Another reason that the command prompt is sometimes preferred is, believe it or not, speed. Not so much the speed of the user typing the commands, but the speed at which the commands are carried out. It takes far less computer horsepower to process a string of text than to paint a picture on a screen and present a graphical user interface.

Whatever your reason, it is likely that even if you just started using computers today, you will still be required at some time or another to use the command prompt, which is Windows XP's way of handing off text instructions to the operating system for execution. Entire books (older ones) have been written about navigating in one command environment or another, and what follows is a brief discussion of some of the things that should make your life easier when working with the XP command prompt. We'll be looking at some commands that will help you navigate your computers drives and directory structure, at some of the ways to modify and customize the command interface, and at some methods to reduce the time spent hunting and pecking for keys when telling the operating system exactly what to do. (And in case you're wondering, read my mind is *not* one of those commands.)

Getting Started with the Command Prompt

If you've become accustomed to using the command prompt when performing administrative tasks, you won't need to change your ways when performing these same tasks with

Windows XP. With Windows XP, you can open up multiple command prompt sessions, and each session is launched in its own memory space, protected from any failures that might occur in other sessions. To get started working with the command prompt, you first need to open a command session. You can do so in several ways:

- Choose Start ➤ All Programs ➤ Accessories ➤ Command Prompt.

- Choose Start ➤ Run to open the Run dialog box, type **cmd** in the Open box, and press Enter.

- Double-click the cmd icon in your \System32 folder.

- Double-click any shortcut you create for the cmd.exe utility.

As I mentioned earlier, you can open as many Command Prompt windows as you want. Each additional window starts an additional command prompt session. But what good is this? Why might this be a good idea? You might want multiple Command Prompt windows in several instances.

For example, you might want to open two Command Prompt windows to see the contents of directories in side-by-side windows. You also might want to be doing two things at once. Just as you have likely used two graphical applications at the same time, say browsing the Internet and working on a spreadsheet, you also might want two command-based utilities to run simultaneously.

You can easily open a second, third, or fourth instance of the command prompt using one of the methods listed earlier or by using one of the following techniques from within your current command session:

- At the command prompt, type **start** and press Enter.

- At the command prompt, type **start cmd**.

These two commands produce the same result. XP assumes that if you don't provide a program name after typing **start** at the command prompt, you want to start a new instance of cmd.exe.

Now that you've opened your command sessions, how do you close out of the command prompt? When the Command Prompt window is active, you can end a command session in any of the following ways:

- Type **exit** at the command prompt.

- Click the Close button.

- Click the Control Menu icon, and choose Close from the Control menu.

- Double-click the Control Menu icon.

TIP   If you are running a character-based program (an older MS-DOS program) from the Command Prompt window, use that program's normal `exit` commands before you actually close the Command Prompt window. In other words, quit the program before you quit the command prompt. If you don't take this important step, you can lose unsaved data in that character-based program.

A bit of a failsafe is built in to the procedure mentioned in the preceding note, and it is this: if a character-based program is running and you try to quit the Command Prompt window without first closing the program, a dialog box should appear asking if you really want to terminate the program.

Using the Command Prompt's Online Help

When using the command environment, you can type /? at the end of any command for help. For example, say you want to convert the file system on one of your partitions from FAT to NTFS, but you can't quite remember the syntax of the `convert.exe` utility. To get the exact syntax, at the command prompt type **convert /?**. (Yes, there's a space between the *t* and the /.)

A list of help items then appears and included are all the switches available and the proper syntax for each. You can also interpret the correct syntax for the `convert` utility in general. If you are a command prompt junkie, you've used this help feature dozens of times.

TIP   You can also type **help** with no arguments to display a list of all the internal commands and utilities provided with the XP operating system. But be careful—the list is long. You might consider using some of the switches (which I'll discuss later in this chapter) that control how the output is printed to the screen when issuing this command. These switches, however, are less important than they used to be because of the scrolling capabilities of the Windows XP command prompt.

In most respects, using `cmd.exe` or `command.com` is similar to using the text-based interface or command interface of any popular operating system, be it MS-DOS, OS2, or Unix. The concept is straightforward: instead of clicking buttons and icons to get the computer to perform activities, you are literal in your instructions to the computer. In other words, you simply tell the computer what to do. And if your experience with the command prompt is with other operating systems and if you are used to one command prompt, you shouldn't have much trouble with the XP version. Furthermore, every operating system, no matter how advanced or colorful the graphical user interface, includes a command-line interface that you can use to create directories, delete files, copy files, rename files, and so on. The exact commands and the names of the utilities might differ from platform to platform, but the general content remains the same.

TIP Sometimes the list of contents displayed by a command utility can be long. For example, the dir command from the \winnt directory produces a huge list of files and directories, too many to be viewed on one screen. To display the output one screen at a time, type the command followed by **| more**. For example, type **dir /? | more** for help on the dir command, displayed one screen at a time.

Because Windows XP shares it lineage with MS-DOS, the commands and features available in Windows XP closely resemble those used since MS-DOS 5. So if you are one of the lucky ones whose use of Microsoft operating systems began before there was such thing as a window, you probably won't have much trouble picking up the commands of the XP command prompt.

The Difference between Using cmd.exe and command.com

So what's the difference between cmd.exe and command.com? A good way to think about the difference is to ask, What's the difference between XP and MS-DOS? A holdover from MS-DOS, command.com is a 16-bit command processor that has been in use since Microsoft was shipping operating systems on floppy disks.

On the other hand, cmd.exe is the 32-bit Windows XP command processor. Both processors take text commands and submit them to either the operating system or a text-based program for execution. Because of its 32-bit capabilities, cmd.exe is the command processor of choice in the XP environment. XP still supports command.com, but it should be used only if you have legacy applications that require it. Unless you are trying to run a 16-bit text-based program from your computer, use cmd.exe whenever possible.

Although you can use most of the commands available to command.com with cmd.exe, the latter also includes a few internal commands that are not available in command.com.

Another of the more easily recognizable differences between the two command processors is that only cmd.exe understands long file names (this is due to its 32-bit nature; 16-bit command.com can only deal with DOS 8.3 naming conventions) and most any command syntax that can be currently run in an XP environment.

Tips for Using Console Commands

If you've had any experience with a Microsoft command environment, the dir (pronounced "dirrr," like Steven Zahn does in *Saving Silverman*) command is one you probably think very little about. That's because it was likely one of the first two or three commands you used.

Think back to the first time you toyed with a command environment: you opened the prompt, typed **dir**, pressed Enter, and whammo! There's your file and folder list. However, advanced users should realize that dir offers several additional switches that control the resulting output of directory contents.

One of the switches you should know right away, before we look at any of the command-line utilities, is the /? switch, which helps users help themselves. You can use the /? switch at the end of almost any command to display a listing of all the switches associated with a particular utility, their purpose, and their proper syntax. I mentioned this earlier, but is worth repeating. You will find yourself coming back to the /? switch often when working in the command console. What follows in this chapter, then, is not an exhaustive examination of each and every command-line utility along with lengthy explanations and the syntax of all associated switches; you can access the help files as easily as I can. Instead, this chapter explains a few of the switches that I think you will find most useful and suggests when you might be most likely to use these switches.

The dir /x Command

Typing **dir** all by itself displays the date, time, size, and long file name for each file or directory. In many cases, however, you might also want to see the short 8.3 filenames generated automatically by Windows XP for each file. To see these backwardly compatible filenames (which are used when working with command.com), use the command dir /x to display the short name as well. If a file or a directory has no short name, dir pads the line with spaces.

The dir /q Command

The dir /q command is another handy variation. The /q switch causes dir to also display the file's or directory's owner. This can be a timesaver when you're working in a command console and don't want to switch back to the GUI to look up the properties of a file.

The dir /t Command

One additional switch I believe you'll find useful is the /t switch. You can use this switch to specify the time field that is displayed or used for sorting the directory list. Use the command dir /t timefield, in which timefield is one of the following:

c   Creation date

a   Last access

w   Last written

When using the dir command, as you likely did when getting comfortable with the command environment, you noticed that, by default, dir sorts its output alphanumerically in ascending order. You also probably took note that directory (folder) names are mixed in with filenames—dir makes no distinction between directories/folders and files in its output listing. That default behavior is fine when the directories/folders contain relatively few files. But, if the directory/folder contains several folders or files, or if you're looking for a specific folder or file, you will find it helpful to be able to sort the output of dir.

The dir /o Command

Used with dir, the /o switch sorts output according to additional parameters you specify. For example, if you issue the plain vanilla command of dir /o, folders are first in the list, followed by files, and the list is in alphanumeric order.

You can, however, use additional parameters to control the sort operation. The n parameter, for example, sorts the output according to name. The g parameter places directories at the top of the list, rather than interspersing them. The s parameter sorts by size, listing the smallest files first.

You can also combine sort parameters so that multiple sorts occur simultaneously. For example, the command dir /oge places folders first in the list, and then groups the listing according to extension, with extensions grouped in alphanumeric order. For a list of all sort parameters, remember to issue the command dir /?.

Using AutoComplete

Many advanced computer users are most comfortable with, and swear by, a command-based interface. It ensures security, and it is a lot harder to mess things up if you don't know what you're doing. But even if this describes you, and even if you're a Mavis Beacon disciple on top of that, you probably like to save keystrokes whenever possible. Using AutoComplete is a way to avoid repetitive typing.

Even if you're not a command prompt devotee, you are probably familiar with the Auto-Complete feature, as it rears its head in applications such as Microsoft Word, Excel, and Internet Explorer. For example, the AutoComplete feature of Internet Explorer, which is turned on by default, saves a lot of time when typing frequently used text, such as text used in filling out forms, stock quotes, and even entire website addresses. (You might, like me, find that AutoComplete works as a sort of History and Favorites hybrid and that it's many times faster than reaching for the mouse and clicking on either menu.)

The command console also supports a form of AutoComplete that automatically completes folder and file names. The command console feature actually goes by a nom de plume that is, intuitively, called File And Directory Name Completion. And unlike its cousin that works behind the scenes, the command console's AutoComplete feature is turned off by default. You shouldn't find this much of a hurdle, however, because it's easy to activate using the /f: mode switch. To turn on AutoComplete, use the cmd /f:on command.

To turn the feature off, use the same command, this time with the switch set to off. Once in the console, you can tell AutoComplete to work its magic by pressing Ctrl+D to complete folder names and pressing Ctrl+F to cycle through file and folder names. You can cycle through names by repeatedly pressing either Ctrl+D or Ctrl+F, as appropriate. You will also notice that after you turn on this feature, the status of the command is listed in the console window's title bar, as shown in Figure 10.1.

FIGURE 10.1:

The console window's title bar reminds you that AutoComplete is on.

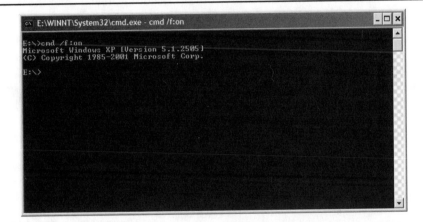

Although executing the cmd /f: mode switch is easy enough, you'll probably want to modify the shortcut you use to start the console so that AutoComplete is enabled each and every time you launch a console window. For instructions on how to modify the properties of a Command Prompt shortcut, see the "Setting Console Properties and Startup" section later in this chapter.

TIP   The command prompt also recognizes wildcards in file and path specifications. For example, typing **cd pro*** might take you to the Program Files folder.

You may find using the Ctrl+D and Ctrl+F keys is a bit of a pain. Fortunately, there's a way to change these default completion keystrokes. If you want to use a different character, specify the hex value of the character in the following two Registry values:

- For the file completion key, use

    \HKEY_LOCAL_MACHINE\Software\Microsoft\CommandProcessor\CompletionChar
- For the directory completion key, use

    \HKEY_LOCAL_MACHINE\Software\Microsoft\CommandProcessor\PathCompletionChar

Now you know the hard way to change the completion key. Want to know the easy way? Use the Tweak UI utility. You can control the command prompt completion key through a simple drop-down dialog box, as shown in Figure 10.2. You will need to navigate down the list on the left to the Command Prompt section; the Completion section contains entries for file and folder name completion keys.

And here's yet another trick that makes all of the above unnecessary and saves you from having to find out anything about hexadecimal notation: use the Tab key. When you use the Tab key (and this works only with cmd.exe, *not* with command.com), you can scroll through all the files and folders in a directory alphabetically. If you enter the first letter or two, Tab fills in the rest of the file or folder according to what you have typed. Folder names may appear in quotation marks; files will not. To scroll backward through a file and folder list, use the Shift+Tab combination.

FIGURE 10.2:

Use Tweak UI to easily change the XP command prompt completion character.

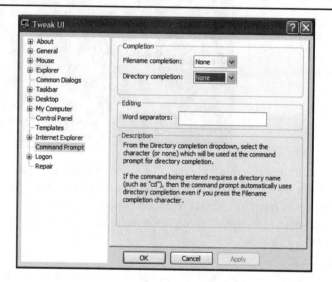

Controlling Command Execution

Although Windows XP makes it easy to customize certain aspects of the command console such as font, color, window size, and so on, other properties are not easily changed. For example, perhaps you want to execute a certain command each time a command console starts, such as configuring a custom command prompt with the prompt command. Or maybe you want to use the cd command to start the command console in a specific folder, launch a driver or other application without intervention, or perform some other task automatically.

To adjust these more complex command prompt properties, you will need to edit the Registry. The following Registry key defines command console parameters and behavior:

`\HKEY_CURRENT_USER\Software\Microsoft\Command Processor`

Within that key, the Registry value for AutoRun lets you define a command string to execute each time the command console starts up. To configure settings in this key, follow these steps:

1. Open the Registry, and drill down to the following:

   `\HKEY_CURRENT_USER\Software\MicroSoft\Command Processor\AutoRun`

2. Enter the internal command or external application executable (`.exe`) file you want to run automatically when the console starts.

3. If needed, include any command line parameters or switches for the command in the AutoRun value.

Setting Console Properties and Startup

You can customize the appearance of the Command Prompt window using several methods. You can change its size; you can change its fonts and use different colors. You can save these settings independently for each shortcut that launches a command prompt session. Thus, you can have multiple command prompts each looking and feeling a different way. To customize a Command Prompt window, you make the setting changes in a Properties dialog box, as shown in Figure 10.3.

FIGURE 10.3:

Customize the Command Prompt window using the settings in this Properties dialog box.

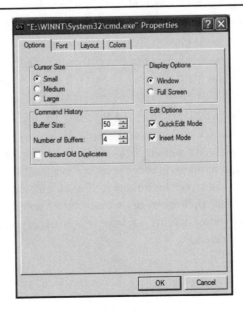

You can open the Properties dialog box shown in Figure 10.3 using any of the following methods:

- Right-click in a shortcut that opens a Command Prompt window and choose Properties from the shortcut menu. Any changes you make to this Properties dialog box affect all future command prompt sessions launched from this shortcut.

- Left-click the Control Menu icon (that little C:\ button in the upper-left corner) in a Command Prompt window and choose Properties from the menu. There is a difference between this method and the one mentioned previously: changes you make here, by default, affect the current session only. However, when you close the Properties dialog box, you will be given the option of propagating your changes to the shortcut from which the session was launched. This will make the changes effective for all future sessions as well.

- Click the Control Menu icon in a Command Prompt window, and choose Defaults from the menu. Changes here do not affect the current session, but instead affect all future command prompt sessions. However, any command sessions launched from a *shortcut* whose individual properties have been modified will be unaffected by the change. In other words, changes made at the individual level will still be trump.

One of the settings of the Options tab is that the prompt runs in Full Screen mode, rather than from a window within the XP interface. This makes the XP operating system resemble an MS-DOS computer, and some MS-DOS programs work best when launched in this mode. If Command Prompt is running in full screen mode, press Alt+Enter to switch to a window display. In this way, you can get to the Properties Control menu. To change the screen position of a newly launched command window, open the command window Properties dialog box and click the Layout tab, as shown in Figure 10.4.

On the Layout tab, you can specify two different sizes: the screen buffer size and the window size. The width for both box sizes is specified in numbers of columns, and the height is specified in numbers of rows. The screen buffer settings control the size of the virtual screen, which is the maximum extent of the screen. The standard screen sizes include 80×5, 80×43, or 80×50, but you can set your Command Prompt screen to any size you please.

In most cases, you will want the same size screen buffer, but if your screen becomes crowded, you can reduce the window size. When you reduce the window size, scroll bars are added so that you can scroll to different parts of the virtual screen. The window size settings cannot be larger than the screen buffer size settings. Unlike most of the applications you are used to working with, applications in a Command Prompt environment display only one font at a time. Your choice of fonts is relatively limited, as you will see when you click the Font tab in the Properties dialog box.

You can also set the color of the text and the background for the Command Prompt window using the options on the Colors tab, as shown in Figure 10.5.

FIGURE 10.4:

The settings on the Layout tab define how the Command Prompt window will appear.

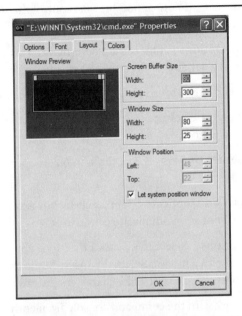

FIGURE 10.5:

Use the options on the Colors tab to change the look and feel of the Command Prompt window.

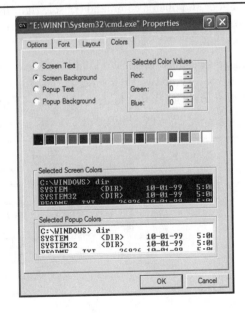

The Options tab in the Properties dialog box offers you a variety of other options that affect your overall experience with the command prompt:

Cursor Size   These option buttons control the size of the blinking cursor in a Command Prompt window.

Display Options   This setting determines whether your command prompt session appears in a window or occupies the entire screen.

Command History   These options control the buffer used by Doskey.

Buffer Size   Click the spin box to specify the number of commands to memorize in each command history.

Number Of Buffers   Click the spin box to specify the number of command history buffers to use.

Discard Old Duplicates   If this check box is selected, it uses the history buffers efficiently by not saving duplicate commands.

Edit Options   Select the Quick Edit Mode check box if you want a fast and easy way to copy text with a mouse. Select the Insert Mode check box if you want to insert text at the cursor position. To overstrike characters instead, clear the Insert Mode check box.

If you work with the command console frequently, at times you'd probably love to be able to click a folder and open a command console right there, without having to open the Command Prompt window and then issue cd (change directory) after cd command to get to the desired location.

Although in previous versions of Windows you could modify the Registry to add this capability, doing so in Windows XP is much easier. To open a Command Prompt window from a specific folder, right-click that folder in Windows Explorer, and choose Open Command Window Here, as shown in Figure 10.6.

FIGURE 10.6:

Selecting the Open Command Window Here item is a convenient way to open the Command Prompt window.

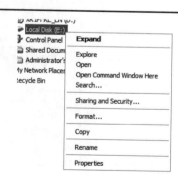

The Command Console and the Clipboard

It is possible to take text from the Command Prompt window and copy it to the clipboard, for use in other Windows applications. Doing so can be useful if you want output generated by a command to be manipulated further in another program. When you paste text into Microsoft Word, for example, you can then apply special formatting to it and print it in several ways, options that are not available from within the command environment.

You can also use the Clipboard when using a lengthy command many times in multiple command windows (or even the same window). Instead of retyping each time you use the command, you can simply paste the contents of the Clipboard at the prompt.

To copy text to the Clipboard from your command sessions, follow these steps:

1. Right-click the title bar of the Command Prompt window, point to Edit, and then click Mark.

2. Click the beginning of the text you want to copy.

3. Press and hold down the Shift key, and then click the end of the text you want to copy (or you can click and drag the cursor to select the text).

4. Right-click the title bar, point to Edit, and then click Copy. (Alternatively, you can press Enter after highlighting the text.)

The text is now on the Clipboard, and you can insert it in another application using that application's Paste command. In Word, for example, position your cursor where you want the text, and choose Edit ➢ Past or press Ctrl+V.

If you are copying text from one Command Prompt window to another or inserting the material in an MS-DOS program, right-click the title bar, point to Edit, and then click Paste.

You can also do the reverse: take text from a Windows program and paste it into the Command Prompt window. Follow these steps:

1. From the Windows program, select the text you want to use in the Command Prompt window and copy it to the Clipboard using the copy method of choice.

2. Position the mouse somewhere in the active Command Prompt window and right-click.

That's it! The text is inserted at the insertion point, wherever the blinking cursor is.

This is a painless technique if someone has sent you instructions in an e-mail message or a Word document or has otherwise typed a command in another program, and you want to use it in the Command Prompt window without retyping.

Tips for Specific Console Commands

You have probably used the Find feature of many popular programs to locate specific words, strings, or other search criteria within the program's documents. Word, for example, can search multiple file types including all Office types, text files, web pages, and more. However, if you don't have Word on your system or simply prefer to search from a command console instead, in Windows XP you can use a couple of command-line tools.

The find command searches for a text string in one or more files. You can configure find to display all lines containing the specified string, display all lines *not* containing the string, or show the count of lines that contain the string. The find command can also search the text typed at a command prompt or piped in from another command, as well as search a file. Open a command console and type **help find** for syntax and options.

The findstr command, short for "find string," provides several options not included in the find command. For example, findstr can list only filenames for files that contain the specified string and can take the list of search strings and search paths from text files. Using this command is particularly handy when you need to perform a complex search or perform a search on a regular basis and don't want to type the information each time. As with find, you can view syntax and options for findstr by entering **help findstr** at a command prompt.

Command-Line Recovery Tools

Before discussing recovery tools, remember the administrator's first rule of thumb: there's no substitute for a good backup set when something goes wrong. But, in certain situations even a backup set can't help, such as when you've modified an important document since the last backup. In such a case, you will need to make every attempt to recover your environment, and the command prompt is the likely interface you will use. Here are some tools that can aid in disk recovery:

- If the problem is disk-wide, recovery tools such as chkdsk and chkntfs could be the solution. These tools create and display a status report for a disk based on the file system. The chkdsk tool also lists and corrects errors on the disk. If used without parameters, chkdsk displays the status of the disk in the current drive.

- If on the other hand, the problem is localized to one file or to a small selection of files, or if you need to recover only a few files and can restore the rest from your backup set, the recover command can be a good solution. It reads a specified file sector by sector, recovering the data from the available good sectors. Data in bad sectors is lost, but between your backup set and the recovered data, you just might be able to piece the document back together.

- Using the `recover` command is simple. Simply execute `recover` *pathname*; *pathname* is the path to the file you want to recover. You can't use wildcards with `recover`, but instead must recover the files one at a time.

Using the tree Command

One of the advantages of working in the Windows Explorer when you're looking for files or folders is that you can see directory structure fairly easily. This is handy when you need to move files, delete them, or just locate a particular file.

If you work from a command console frequently, being able to view the same directory structure can be useful for those same reasons. But how? With the `dir` command, you can see only one directory at a time. The `tree` command, which has been around since long before Windows Explorer, is your solution. Whatever your purpose in using it, the `tree` command does a nice job of displaying a directory structure, complete with file list if you need it. The syntax for `tree` is:

```
TREE [drive:][path] [/F] [/A]
```

Used by itself with no switches, `tree` displays a directory list starting at the current directory. You can first change to the directory you want as the root of the list or specify the drive and path to that root. The /f switch causes `tree` to display the names of files in each folder as well as the directory structure. The /a switch directs `tree` to use ASCII characters instead of extended characters for the structure lines, which can be useful if you're importing the list into an application that doesn't handle the extended characters. Use redirection (>) to redirect the list to a text file if you need to import it into an application.

Changing the Prompt

Like all other versions of the Windows operating systems, the command console displays a command prompt that defaults to the current drive letter, current directory, and a right chevron, such as C:\ WINNT>. This is evident if you use the Open Command Window Here menu item, as described earlier in the chapter.

In some situations, though, you might want more information displayed in the command prompt than the default of drive letter and directory. For example, if you're working in a full-screen console for an extended period of time, you might want to add the current time to the command prompt. Or, perhaps you want the input line to appear on a blank line under the prompt (great when you're working with a long directory string). You might also want less information in the prompt rather than more, such as a single character as the prompt.

Whatever change you'd like to make to the console prompt, you can likely achieve the result you want through the prompt command. For the syntax and options for prompt, open a command console and enter the command **help prompt**. To restore the prompt to its default, execute prompt with no switches. The prompt command can change your command interface to look like that shown in Figure 10.7.

FIGURE 10.7:

Use the prompt command to change the input prompt.

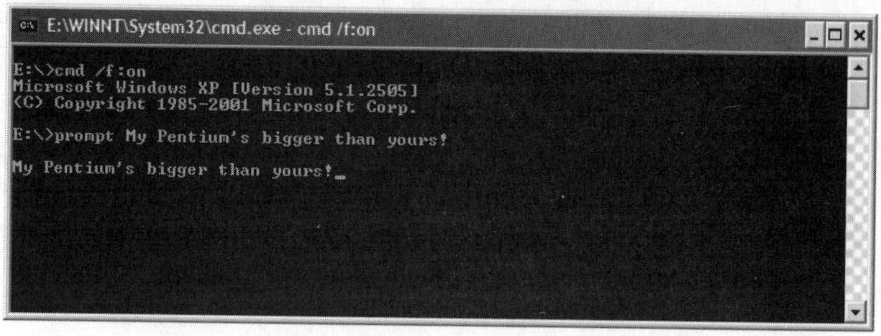

```
E:\WINNT\System32\cmd.exe - cmd /f:on

E:\>cmd /f:on
Microsoft Windows XP [Version 5.1.2505]
(C) Copyright 1985-2001 Microsoft Corp.

E:\>prompt My Pentium's bigger than yours!

My Pentium's bigger than yours!_
```

CHAPTER 11

Using and Customizing Help

Even if you're the type who would never pull over to ask for directions, you have probably had to consult Help from time to time. All versions of Windows have always shipped with Help. The kind of help shipped with previous versions of Windows was *local*, meaning the contents were stored on the local computer and could be accessed without retrieving data from an outside source. Microsoft has always referred to the local help content as *online help*.

With the new version of help in Windows XP, called Help And Support Center, the scope of what is considered online has blurred considerably. Because Windows XP assumes that Internet connections are now ubiquitous, the help tools allow you to connect to additional resources, integrating content from the Microsoft website with the local help content.

Also new to XP is a utility called Remote Assistance, which lets a family member or a colleague provide remote help for connected computers. Remote Assistance allows others to take control of your computer (or vice versa) in order to fix software problems, install programs, or step through a tutorial. If you've ever used a program such as pcAnywhere or Carbon Copy, you are familiar with this technology.

SEE ALSO See Chapter 31 for a complete discussion of Remote Assistance and how to use it.

Working with the Help And Support Center and Adding and Customizing Content

The Help And Support Center contains a collection of web pages that will help guide you to answers to most of your questions. The web pages that first appear are considered online, because they already exist on your local drive. These pages display in a web browser, although it doesn't look much like Internet Explorer or other browsers with which you have worked. It won't take you long to learn your way around the new interface, so I'll just give you some pointers rather than cover the interface in detail.

You access the Help And Support Center by choosing Start ➤ Help and Support. The home page displays first, and its contents are shown in Figure 11.1.

The Help And Support Center home page shows a list of topics on the left side of the window and a list of tasks on the right side. Click a topic to display a sub-list of more specific topics; click a task to begin that particular task

TIP	The general rule of thumb is that you can click an underlined word or words to display more information about that topic, just as when you're browsing the Internet.

FIGURE 11.1:

You access contents from the home page of the Help And Support Center

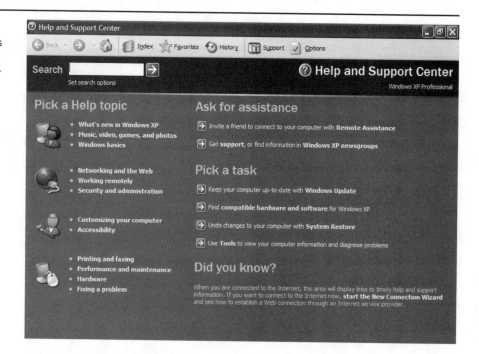

The Home Page

The new version of help behaves differently from what you're probably used to in other Windows versions. Because so much is new in the XP version of help, let's spend a little time here getting familiar with the new sections. Four sections of the Help And Support Center can get you on your way to answering your questions:

Pick A Help Topic   This section presents a list of common help issues. From this list, you can get immediate help when setting up XP to network with other computers, including remote computers, and when setting up the system to print and fax; you'll also find tips to help you customize your computer. This list replaces the Help Content screen you know and love from previous versions of Windows.

Ask For Assistance   This section guides you through a couple of options for getting outside help using your computer. The first option steps you through the process of getting someone to remotely control your system as if they were using the computer themselves. This feature can require knowledge of several networking technologies. I'll present an overview of it later in this chapter, but, as mentioned, Chapter 31 is the place to go for a thorough discussion. Clicking the second option in this section takes you to the Support page, which you can directly access by clicking the Support toolbar button (more on the toolbar, as well as the Support options, later in this chapter).

Pick A Task   The tasks listed in this section will help you keep XP running smoothly and help direct you to hardware and software products that should not create problems upon installation. This is also a place where you can roll back changes to the operating system if hardware or software installations do cause problems.

Did You Know?   This list, located in the lower right corner, contains headlines provided by Microsoft support. Third parties can also customize this content, so if you're using a PC with Windows XP already installed, it's possible that the DYK content has been modified with links to a system manufacturer's web content.

NOTE   If you are running an OEM version of Windows XP, you may see more, fewer, or other sections on the home page.

TIP   If your computer is connected to the Internet, Windows will automatically update the content of the Did You Know? section with news and updates each time you open the home page.

The Windows XP Help And Support Center relies on two modules: the Help And Support Center executable (`helpctr.exe`) and the Help And Support Center Service (`helpsvc.exe`). If two or more instances of `helpctr.exe` are running at the same time, the Help And Support Center may not run at all. To remedy this condition, follow these steps:

1. Press Ctrl+Shift+Esc to open Windows Task Manager.

2. Click the Processes tab, and then click the Image Name heading. Clicking any heading on this tab sorts the list in alphabetic order based on the heading you choose.

3. Find and highlight each instance of `helpctr.exe`, and then click the End Process button. Repeat this step until all instances of the executable have been removed.

4. Choose Start ➢ Control Panel to open Control Panel.

5. Click the Performance And Maintenance link, click the Administrative Tools link, and then double-click Services to open the Services window.

6. In the list of services, right-click Help And Support, and choose Restart from the shortcut menu. The Help And Support Center should now be able to run.

The Toolbar

The home page contains a toolbar that includes several icons you are used to seeing in an Internet Explorer window, including the Home, Favorites, Back, and Forward buttons, and you use these navigation items in the same way you use them when surfing the Internet.

TIP   You can save time when working with Help And Support Center by adding content to the Favorites list. The Help And Support Center contains content for more than 10,000 topics that have been put together from more than 200 compiled help (.chm) files. When you place items in your Favorites list, be sure to give them meaningful titles. Items saved in the Favorites list are placed there in the order in which they are saved, and there is no way to rearrange them.

Using the Search box, located in the upper left corner of the Help And Support Center, is straightforward; if you've used a search engine before, it will be second nature. Using Search is much faster than fishing through each and every topic, looking for the item that will be most helpful.

Once you enter a phrase or topic to search against, the search results are displayed in three groups, as explained next. Figure 11.2 shows the results of one such search, with the search text highlighted.

Suggested Topics   This group is populated by comparing the search terms you entered with an index of keywords defined in the compiled help files. Because this index is searched and not the entire contents of the Help And Support Center, the Suggested Topics list is generated rather quickly.

Full-Text Search Matches   This group displays topics for which the content of the help file matches exactly with the phrase entered in the Search box. The search body is much larger in this case, and you should find that it takes longer to generate than the Suggested Topics list.

Microsoft Knowledge Base   This last group looks out at Microsoft's collection of technical articles that isn't available in the local help files, but rather is found by searching through the Knowledge Base at the Microsoft website. The Knowledge Base isn't really a help file, but rather a collection of articles that have been written over the years by tech support people and experts at Microsoft. Some of these articles can be just the cure for what ails your computer, giving you clear, step-by-step instruction on how to remedy an "issue." Getting through other articles is like trying to crack the enigma code. The real challenge is locating the article for the problem you have, and now the Help And Support Center will try its best to find the right one. If you've tried to find answers in the Knowledge Base before, you know exactly what I'm talking about. If not, just take my word for it, and I wish you the best of British luck. The list of displayed articles matches the search terms used and uses the settings configured on the Options page. (I'll discuss the Options page in a later section in this chapter.)

You can search the entire contents of the Help And Support Center or only a portion thereof. To search everything, enter the search terms on the home page of the Help And Support Center. For more specific searches, first select a specific Topic, and then enter your search term(s) and perform the search. To turn off this default behavior, clear the Search Within Previous Results check box located just beneath the Search box.

TIP   Search terms are not case sensitive. Also, if you enter two or more words, the search algorithm is smart enough to look first for topics containing the exact combination of the two words before returning results for each word separately.

FIGURE 11.2:

Search results are displayed in three groups.

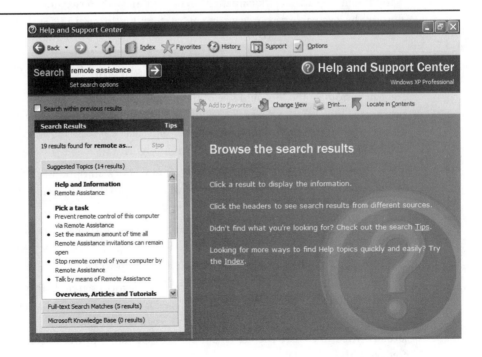

The Scenic Route

The Help And Support Center is also a place where you can let the operating system take you on a guided tour or provide tutorials on certain tasks. When you install Windows XP, you have the opportunity to be given a tour of available features. However, if you need to take this tour at any time *after* installation, follow these steps:

1. From the home page of the Help And Support Center (you can click the Go To The Help And Support Home Page button from the toolbar if you're not there already), click What's New In Windows XP.

2. Click the Taking A Tour Or Tutorial link to display a list of topics.

3. Simply click an item from the list to start the tour or tutorial.

You can also get a quick overview of every wizard used in Windows XP. To do so, follow these steps:

1. In the Help And Support Center, click the Index button.

2. In the Type In The Keyword To Find box, enter **wizards**, which will then display a series of subtopics under the Wizard category.

You'll find step-by-step documentation here of more than two dozen Windows XP wizards. This can be a valuable resource when you're stepping through a wizard for the first time.

Customizing the Appearance of the Help and Support Center

You can customize the look and feel of the Help And Support Center interface just as you can customize other Windows interface components, as was discussed extensively in Chapter 7. To customize the Help And Support Center interface, click the Options button on the toolbar to display the Options page, which is shown in Figure 11.3.

You can configure three areas of options. Simply click an option from the Options list on the left to display a further list of options on the right. Click an option to select it or to clear it if it is already selected.

Clicking Change Help And Support Center Options displays a list of settings that primarily affect cosmetic changes to the interface. For example, if you select the Small or Medium font size, you can squeeze more information into each window.

Also notice that you can hide the display of the Favorites and History buttons, although you cannot hide the toolbar itself. (You can reduce the amount of space taken up by the toolbar, though.) I think you'll find that if you can comfortably change the Windows display settings, you can change the Help And Support Center appearance settings to suit your preferences without incident.

FIGURE 11.3:

Use the Options page to customize the Help And Support Center interface.

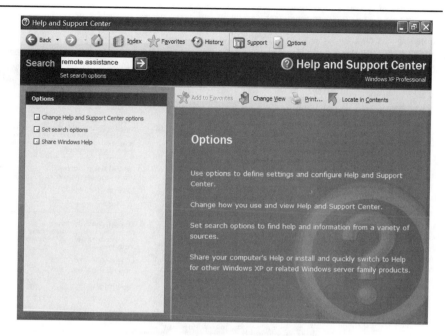

You will likely find that many of the options that directly affect the functionality of the Help And Support Center are set from the Set Search Options page, which is shown in Figure 11.4. The options on this page have a big impact on overall operation because you will usually begin to use the Help And Support Center by searching its contents.

You can set the following options on the Set Search Options page:

Return Up to *xx* Results Per Provider   This is one of the first changes I make. The default value of 15 is too small, I've found, for any comprehensive search. You can set this number up to 999, but I think you'll find a setting of about 50 more functional.

Suggested Topics   This option is selected by default and will cause Windows XP to use the index of keywords with every search. Clearing this check box removes the ability to restrict a search to a specific topic.

Full-Text Search Matches   Also selected by default, this option and its two sub-options let you refine the way searches are performed. The Search In Title Only option does just that. The Match Similar Words option matches words such as *computing* when you enter a word such as *computer*.

Microsoft Knowledge Base   The options here will look familiar if you have ever searched the Knowledge Base from the Microsoft website. You can specify a product to search on, and you can choose, for example, to search for any of the words in a phrase or for the exact phrase. To maximize your chances of finding what you need, search on all products.

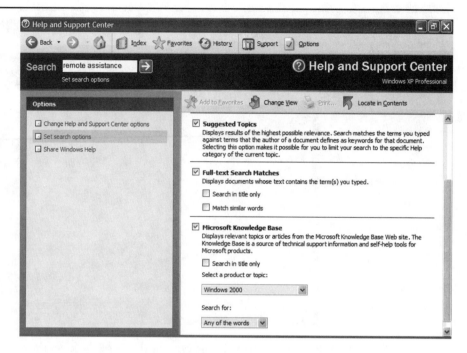

Getting Help on the Web

Clicking the Support button on the toolbar displays the Welcome To Support page, which has three options, all directing you to resources outside your system to resolve an issue.

The first is Ask A Friend For Assistance, which starts the Remote Assistance process. I'll discuss this a bit later in this chapter and then in more detail in Chapter 31.

To use the selections under the second option, Get Help From Microsoft, you must have an active Internet connection. If your PC is online, you can retrieve help information from the Microsoft website. There is one caveat: you must first sign up for a Microsoft .NET Passport. Orwellian connotations notwithstanding, signing up for a passport can be a good thing. It stores information about your account (such as what issues you have needed help with) and allows Microsoft to provide more streamlined service.

After you obtain your passport, you can contact a Microsoft support technician, check on the status of problems you've submitted, and even download and install software that allows Microsoft to upload files from your computer in order to resolve an issue. (You follow that? It means that you can give a Microsoft technician the ability to grab a log or dump file necessary to troubleshoot especially nasty software problems.)

Clicking the third option, Go To A Windows Web Site Forum, displays a single hyperlink, Go To Windows Newsgroups. You can post questions to the newsgroups, and usually someone out there has run across the same issue.

Adding New Content

In Windows XP Professional only (not Home Edition), you'll see a third option, Share Windows Help. One of the main purposes of this feature is that it allows access to Windows XP Professional help files from a Windows XP Home Edition computer. However, you can use this feature to add help files from Windows XP programs, custom help files that you develop, or other Windows XP-compatible help content.

To add the Windows XP Home Edition help content to a Windows XP Professional system, first make sure that you have the Windows XP Home Edition CD nearby, and then follow these steps:

1. From the system running Windows XP Professional, in the Help And Support Center, click the Options button to open the Options page.

2. Click Install And Share Windows Help from the Options list, and then click Install Help Content From A CD Or Disk Image. The view of the pane switches to a list of installed help versions on the XP Professional system, as shown in Figure 11.5. The first time it is run, this list will be empty.

3. Click the Browse button to open the Browse For Folder dialog box. Locate the \I386 folder on the Windows XP Home Edition CD, click OK, and then click the Find button to open the Install Help From Disk window.

4. Select Windows XP Home Edition from the list of available help versions, and then click Install. When the process is complete, the Status column will read Already Installed.

You will now be able to return to the Help And Support Center at any time and switch between help versions. This functionality is of benefit to Help Desk staff who can look up help information for XP Home Edition machines without leaving their XP Professional installation. It can also come in handy if your small home network has multiple installations of both XP Professional and Home.

To switch back and forth between the different versions of help content, follow these steps:

1. Go back to the Install And Share Windows Help dialog box again, click the Options tab, and then select the Switch From One Operating System's Help Content To Another option. The Switch Help Version dialog box will display a list of available help files.

2. Repeat this process to switch back to the XP Professional help files.

FIGURE 11.5:

Any installed versions of help are displayed in this menu.

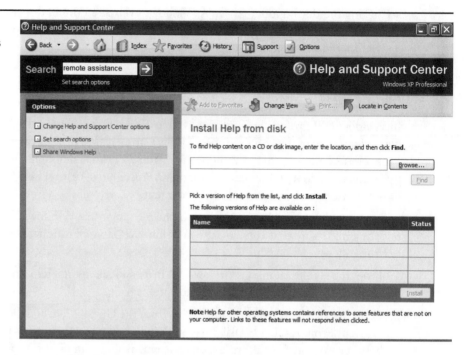

Be aware, however, that the sharing of help files is limited. Only systems that are running XP and .NET can share help files. You can't install previous versions of Windows help files onto the XP machine. Likewise, previous versions of Windows, such as 2000 or 9*x*, cannot load the help files from Windows XP. This is due to the radically different nature of the help files and help centers of previous Windows versions when compared with XP.

Creating Custom Content

If you are developing applications, you will no doubt want to create help content. Development environments such as Microsoft Visual Studio generally provide the necessary tools.

If you are looking to create help content outside the context of application development—such as creating a help system that explains to your users how to use network resources, apply office or company policies, and so on—you'll need an HTML help-development tool.

In Windows' early days, creating online help was a real challenge because of the lack of help-development tools. Today, you can choose from a range of help-development platforms. Before you jump into the fray, however, understand that the Windows help system has changed over the years, and you need a help-development tool that supports the new help engine.

Microsoft introduced HTML-based help content with Windows 98, and Windows XP expands on that help engine. Help content development tools let you use word processors, HTML development tools, and other resources to create the content for the help file. The content is then compiled into a help file with a `.chm` file extension. The Windows XP help engine can display these types of help files.

Many third-party help-development tools don't stop at creating HTML-based content for Windows. Many can also compile the content into the older Win Help format used by Windows 3.*x* and Windows 95. Some also support output to PDF files and other formats, as well as HTML for display on the Web.

When you're looking for a help-development tool to create custom help content for Windows XP users, make sure the tool can output the compiled HTML help files used by Windows XP. Also look for features such as an integrated editor, support for additional output formats, and other key features you consider useful for your needs.

Here's a brief overview of some of the help-development options that can provide usable output for XP. Which one you choose depends on your individual help customization requirements.

Microsoft HTML Help Workshop   You can download this free tool from the Microsoft website and create HTML-based help content. The HTML Help Workshop includes the compiler that creates the final help file. Some third-party applications also use the HTML Help Workshop as their compiler rather than include their own.

Go to `www.microsoft.com` and search on **html help workshop** to locate the HTML Help Workshop downloads and other data. You can also try this URL (although the Microsoft URLs have a tendency to change):

```
msdn.microsoft.com/library/default.asp?url=/library/en-us/htmlhelp/html/
hwMicrosoftHTMLHelpDownloads.asp
```

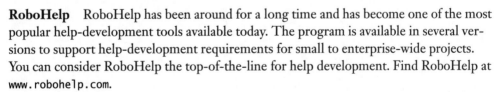

RoboHelp   RoboHelp has been around for a long time and has become one of the most popular help-development tools available today. The program is available in several versions to support help-development requirements for small to enterprise-wide projects. You can consider RoboHelp the top-of-the-line for help development. Find RoboHelp at `www.robohelp.com`.

Help and Manual   This help-development tool not only lets you create HTML-based help content, but also provides features for developing content for the Web, the older Win Help engine, Microsoft Word (RTF output), native PDF, and even an e-book format. You'll find more information about the product at `www.ec-software.com/hmpage.htm`.

Help Development Studio   This tool supports both the Win Help and HTML help formats. It provides an integrated development environment, keyword editor, macro editor, and other handy components. It lets you manage content as a project for ease of development. The program also supports a plug-in system. Find more information about Help Development Studio at www.divcomsoft.com/helpstd.htm.

HelpKit   This tool from DevComponents.com includes an integrated HTML development environment, HTML source editor, cascading style sheet editor, ActiveX control wizards, spell checker, and much more. The program makes it easy to create What's This? content as well as context-sensitive help. You can find more information at www.devcomponents.com/helpkit.

Windows Help Designer/HTML Edition   This help-development tool provides full support for HTML help development and includes an image map editor, a screen capture utility, a style sheet editor, a report generator, and other handy resources. You can use it to create new HTML content, but the tool also lets you import and convert Format-format content to HTML format. Find more information at www.visagesoft.com/whdhtml/index.htm.

Part III

Managing the System and Applications

CHAPTER 12

Minimizing the Aches and Pains of Application Installation and Configuration

Although Windows XP includes a lot of accessory applications, it's a sure bet it doesn't include everything you need. So you'll no doubt have to install at least one application, and more likely install several.

Over time, the number of applications you'll install will probably become overwhelming. Managing applications can become a real nightmare, particularly if an application doesn't provide uninstall support or doesn't do a good job of removing itself from your computer when you uninstall it. Windows XP includes a feature called System Restore, which takes a snapshot of your system's state and lets you restore to that state. This can be handy for uninstalling applications that don't offer their own reliable means for removal.

In some situations, you might also need to move your applications and settings from one computer to another. For example, maybe you're getting ready to buy a new computer and want an easy way to move all of your e-mail accounts, documents, dial-up connections, and other information to the new computer without having to set all of it up manually. To that end, Windows XP provides the Files And Settings Transfer Wizard.

In this chapter, I'll give you some tips on installing and uninstalling applications as well as on what to do when you uninstall an application but it doesn't all go away. I also touch on a very powerful tool for deploying applications across the network to multiple computers: Microsoft's IntelliMirror. This core technology in Windows 2000 Server and Windows .NET Server lets you automatically deploy applications for new installations and disaster recovery.

Tips for Installing and Uninstalling Applications

Usually, there isn't much to installing or uninstalling an application. You pop in the CD and let the Setup program auto-play, or you double-click the program's Setup executable file. You typically only have to worry about where to install the program and what options you want installed along with it. However, there are some things you can do to ensure a trouble-free installation and to make it easier to remove applications if something goes wrong with the program's built-in removal procedure.

Keep a log   First, keep a record of changes you make to your system. This can be the single most important tool for helping you troubleshoot problems that occur after you install software. Make note in your log of each application you install, changes you make to your existing Windows XP installation, Windows XP components that you add or remove, and any other changes to the system's configuration.

TIP   You can use Notepad or WordPad to keep an electronic log of system changes. Create a blank text file with .LOG (case sensitive) as the first line of the file, followed by a carriage return, and then save and close the file. Double-click the file to open it and notice that Notepad appends the current date and time to the end of the file and places the cursor on the line after.

Standardize location   Most applications use Program Files as the default location to install their folders. Unless you have some compelling reason to place a program else-where, I recommend you install all applications into Program Files. This keeps all of your applications in one place, which simplifies backup. You need to back up your applications only when you add one or make global applications changes that need to be archived, and placing all programs in Program Files gives you an easy way to exclude them in your regular backups.

TIP   If you run out of space on the drive where Program Files is located (probably drive C:), you can copy the contents of Program Files to a new drive and then mount that drive to an empty Program Files folder on the original location. See Chapter 25 for detailed information on how to accomplish this bit of magic.

Always use System Restore   Perhaps the best bit of advice I can offer is to make reli-gious use of the System Restore tool included with Windows XP (Figure 12.1), every time you install an application. System Restore lets you create a system *restore point*, which is like a snapshot of your system's current state. Take a snapshot before installing any application. Then, if you need to restore the system to the point where it was before you installed the program, you can simply reset the system back to the appropriate restore point.

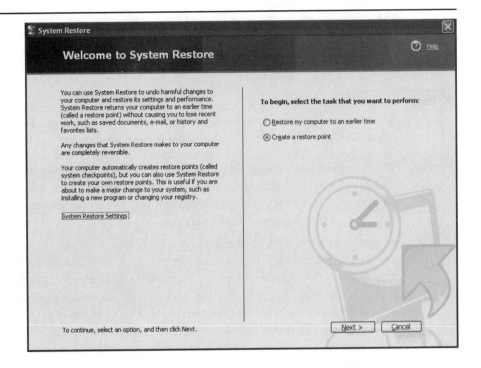

SEE ALSO See Chapter 46 for details on using the System Restore tool.

Cleaning Up Improperly Uninstalled Applications

Times have changed. Only a few years ago, many programs included their own installation mechanism and offered no means for uninstalling the program. This meant that uninstalling applications was sometimes a dicey proposition. You could never be quite sure if the program removed all of itself from the file system or the Registry. Today, most applications use the Windows Installer or a third-party installer to help automate the installation process and provide a means for thorough removal.

TIP Whenever possible, use the Add Or Remove Programs object in Control Panel to remove an application.

Occasionally, a program might still have problems during removal and leave fragments of itself in the file system or in the Registry. Both can have consequences. Leftover files are generally not a problem unless they are dynamic link libraries (DLLs) that are registered as services and therefore get loaded when Windows XP starts. In most cases, you can un-register these files using the `Regsvr32.exe` tool. However, you need to know not only the name of the DLL but also sometimes the name of an uninstall procedure within the DLL. For that reason, you'll probably have to check the program's documentation or support staff for additional help. Many vendors provide instructions on how to manually remove an application should the need arise.

> **WARNING**   Before manually removing an application, check the program's documentation or website to determine if there is a recommended procedure. Improperly removing some applications can leave your system unstable or break certain features.

If you do need to manually remove an application and can't obtain a recommended procedure from the vendor, there are a couple of common steps you can take. First, use the System Restore tool to take a system snapshot to allow you to restore the system in the event your removal procedure doesn't work as intended.

Second, take a trip through the Registry to delete the program's keys and values, if any. Most programs write their Registry settings to `\HKEY_LOCAL_MACHINE\Software\`*vendor*, where *vendor* is the software company's name. You should make a backup copy of the Registry key before you delete it, just in case you need to later restore it. To do so, open the Registry Editor and select the key you're going to delete. Then, choose File ➢ Export to open the Export Registry File dialog box shown in Figure 12.2. Choose the Selected Branch option, specify a file path and name, and click Save. After you export a copy of the key, select the key in the Registry Editor and press Delete to remove it.

> **TIP**   If you later need to restore the Registry key, just locate the REG file you exported and double-click the file to restore it.

You should also check out the following Registry keys for any remnants of the program that are being started automatically when you log on, and delete their entries from the key:

```
\HKEY_LOCAL_MACHINE\SOFTWARE\Microsoft\Windows\CurrentVersion\Run
\HKEY_CURRENT_USER\Software\Microsoft\Windows\CurrentVersion\Run
```

> **TIP**   Check the `Startup` folder for shortcuts associated with the program and delete those, as well.

When you're satisfied that the program is gone, you should also take the time to remove it from the Add Or Remove Programs list in Control Panel. You can't do this through Control Panel, but instead must edit the Registry to remove the entry. Open the Registry Editor and then open the following key:

```
\HKEY_LOCAL_MACHINE\SOFTWARE\Microsoft\Windows\CurrentVersion\Uninstall
```

Look through the key to find the entry for the application you just removed. Delete the value from the key to remove the entry from the Add Or Remove Programs list.

FIGURE 12.2:

Use the Registry Editor to save a Registry key before deleting it.

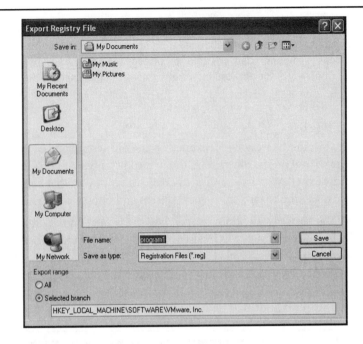

| TIP | Some software products install keys with names such as {03E27B32-28C0-11D3-8F72-00C04F8DD7E3} instead of something readable like Microsoft NetShow Player 2.0. You may need to manually inspect the contents of each bizarrely named key to find the proper key to delete. |

Using the Files and Settings Transfer Wizard

When you get a new computer, the pleasure of having a new system is always tempered by trying to migrate your existing documents, e-mail accounts, and other settings from your old computer to your new one. Accomplishing the move manually is a real pain.

Windows XP includes a wizard you can use to easily transfer files and settings between two computers. It's called the Files And Settings Transfer Wizard—no surprise there. You can use it to transfer files, program settings (such as e-mail accounts), accessibility settings and other Windows system settings, and specific folders (such as the Desktop and My Documents), from any Windows 95 or later platform to a Windows XP system. The amount you can transfer depends on the location you use for the files. Although you can use a floppy disk, you won't get much on it. A network connection works best; if you don't have a network, you can use large removable media such as a Zip disk.

TIP   Before you rush out and buy a removable-media drive to transfer your documents and settings, however, think about setting up a direct cable network. You can use two network cards and a crossover cable to connect the computers, or use a null-modem cable. See Chapter 33 for detailed information on setting up such a network.

I won't cover the wizard in detail because you should have little trouble following it to get your data moved. Let's just cover a few high points.

You run the wizard twice: once on the old system and once on the new one. When you run the wizard on the old system, the wizard prompts you to select the items you want to migrate (more on that shortly) and then creates a set of files that contains your data and setting. You then run the wizard on the new system and import the data.

You have three options for running the wizard on the old system. The first option is available only on Windows XP: just select Files And Settings Transfer Wizard from the Start menu. For other systems, you can run the wizard on the new computer and use it to create a wizard diskette that you use to run the wizard on the old computer. Or, you can run the wizard from the Windows XP CD (Figure 12.3). Insert the CD in the old system, let it autoplay, select Perform Additional Tasks, and then select Transfer Files And Settings.

FIGURE 12.3:

You can choose to run the Files And Settings Transfer Wizard from the Windows XP CD.

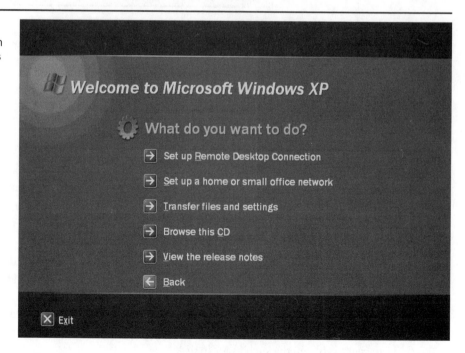

When you run the wizard on the old computer, you need to specify what data and settings you want the wizard to export. You can export files, settings, or both (Figure 12.4). Select the custom list option; the wizard displays a Select Custom Files And Settings dialog box you can use to pick individual folders, files, and file types, as seen in Figure 12.5.

FIGURE 12.4:

Select the items you want to export.

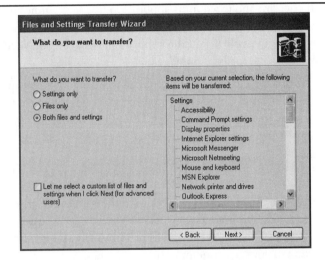

FIGURE 12.5:

You can select a custom set of folders and files to export.

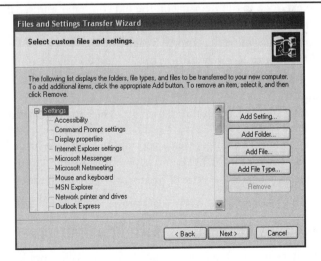

When you click Next, the wizard collects the files and settings and exports them to the target location you've selected. You then run the wizard on the new computer and import the files and settings.

Moving Applications Between Computers Manually

In some situations, you might need to move applications manually between two computers. For example, you can't use the Files And Settings Transfer Wizard to move the Registry key for an application, which means you can't transfer an application not specifically supported by the wizard and listed in its application list. Many times it's just as easy to install the application on the new system as to move it from the old one. In some cases, however, you might not be able to easily install the application—maybe you've lost the CD or installation diskette, or the media is damaged.

The first step in moving an application manually is to copy the files from the old system to the new one. You can use a network connection, direct cable connection, or high-capacity removable media such as Zip or CD to copy the files. Copy the files to the same location on the new computer as on the old one.

SEE ALSO   See Chapter 33 for detailed information on setting up a network.

After you move the files, try running the application by double-clicking its executable file. As long as the program doesn't use Registry keys or custom DLLs that are stored outside of the program's folder, the program will probably run just fine. All that's left is to create a shortcut in your Start menu to the program.

Next, look in the Registry on the old computer and see if the program uses Registry keys. Generally, an application stores its settings in \HKEY_LOCAL_MACHINE\Software*vendor*, where *vendor* is the software company's name. If you find a key for the program, export the key to a REG file with Registry Editor; on the new computer, double-click that file to add it to that computer's Registry.

WARNING   Make sure you export only the selected branch, rather than the entire Registry.

If you receive an error that a certain DLL can't be loaded when you run a program, search the old system for the DLL and copy it to the same location on the new computer. Try the application again, and repeat for any other DLLs the program complains it can't find.

Deploying Applications with IntelliMirror

Another option for deploying applications to Windows XP clients in a network is IntelliMirror, a group of Microsoft technologies that work together to simplify system administration and deployment. Through IntelliMirror, you can set up application packages on a server, and then have those applications installed automatically when a user logs on. IntelliMirror's use of group policies means you can control which applications each user receives. Because this book focuses on Windows XP rather than Windows 2000 Server or Windows .NET Server, I won't cover IntelliMirror in detail. Instead, here's an overview of what's involved to help you determine whether IntelliMirror is right for you.

TIP Deploying applications with IntelliMirror not only simplifies setting up a new computer, but also makes for easy disaster recovery. Whether you're installing applications because you have a new system or because the old one cratered, IntelliMirror can install those applications automatically.

IntelliMirror relies on either Windows 2000 Server or .NET Server to function as the application server. In addition, IntelliMirror relies on group policies to control which applications are available to specific users. You can apply the policies at the site, domain, or organizational unit (OU) level, which gives you good control over who gets what. For example, you might create an Accounting OU to assign applications to the accounting staff and create a Sales OU to assign applications to the Sales department.

Here's the process in a nutshell for implementing IntelliMirror:

Configure Active Directory The first step is to structure AD to accommodate the way in which you need to install applications. This means creating OUs or restructuring domains so you can apply application installation policies at the appropriate levels. For example, if you need to install different sets of applications to four different departments, you would create four OUs, one for each department.

TIP You use the Active Directory Users And Computers console on the server to manage AD in preparation for deploying applications with IntelliMirror.

Publish or assign applications You can either *assign* or *publish* applications. Applications that you publish are available for installation by users who fall under the scope of the policy. The application is listed in the user's Add Or Remove Programs list in Control Panel, allowing the user to install it when needed.

Applications that you assign appear as if they are already installed on the user's system. When the user attempts to open an assigned application that isn't already installed, Windows Installer performs a just-in-time installation of the application.

TIP You assign or publish applications through the group policy editor on the server when you create the group policy object for a given site, domain, or OU. To package the applications, you use a tool such as Windows Installer or a third-party application such as Wise for Windows Installer (www.wisesolutions.com) or InstallShield (www.installshield.com).

Log on to install applications   To actually install applications through IntelliMirror, all you need to do is have the user log on to the domain. As part of the logon process, Windows XP processes group policies that apply to the user's account through its location in AD. The application installation policies take care of setting up the applications on the user's computer.

What Do You Need?

Deploying applications through IntelliMirror isn't really difficult. It's very easy if the application already includes a Windows Installer package you can use for it. If not, or if you need to customize the package, you'll need an external application to build one. To customize Microsoft Office, you can use the customization wizard included in the Microsoft Office Resource Kit to make a variety of changes to the package. For other applications, you can use one of the third-party packaging applications I mentioned earlier in this chapter or a package such as Microsoft's Visual Studio.

The process is much easier for instances where you don't need customized packages. Here's a rundown of what you'll need to deploy applications through IntelliMirror:

Packaging application   Use an app such as Wise for Windows Installer, Visual Studio, etc., to customize Windows Installer packages if the default package will not suit your needs or the application does not include an Installer package.

Windows 2000 Server or Windows .NET Server   Both of these server platforms include the features that make possible application deployment through IntelliMirror. Support for application deployment installs by default when you set up a domain controller; support for Remote Installation Services (RIS)—which makes remote operating system deployment possible—is an optional component.

Domain-based network structure   Group policies are an integral part of a domain-based network, so you must use domains rather than workgroups for your network clients.

Windows 2000 or Windows XP clients   Windows 2000 was the first OS to support group policies, and Windows XP also includes group policy support. Although you can browse and access Active Directory from other platforms (assuming you install the AD client on those systems), only Windows 2000 and XP clients can receive group policies.

SEE ALSO   For more information on Windows 2000 Server, group policies, and IntelliMirror, refer to *Mastering Windows 2000 Server* by Mark Minasi (Sybex, 2002).

CHAPTER 13

Yes, You Can Run Legacy and Non-Windows Applications in Windows XP

You would think that a program written for Windows would work on any Windows operating system, right? Well, that isn't necessarily the case. A program written for Windows 95 might work on Windows XP, but there is at least some chance that you'll have problems running the application. Forcing all Windows users to upgrade all of their applications each time a new operating system version came out would be a horrible marketing strategy for Microsoft, so they've addressed application compatibility with most Windows releases, and Windows XP is no exception. In fact, Windows XP makes it even easier than previous versions to make applications compatible with the operating system, and this chapter brings you up to speed on how to do that.

You'll also find tips in this chapter about running Linux on your Windows PC. An alternative to running Linux or Unix on your PC is to run an X Window terminal emulator program under Windows that provides access to a Unix- or Linux-based server where the application runs. I'll touch on X Window briefly in this chapter and point you to some X Window solutions for Windows XP.

Using the Program Compatibility Wizard

Windows 2000 introduced a tool called Application Compatibility (Apcompat.exe) that allowed you to specify certain compatibility options for a program to allow it to run properly under Windows 2000. Windows XP also includes an application compatibility tool, making it available both as a wizard and directly through the properties for a program's shortcut.

First, let's take a look at the basic options you have for setting compatibility options under Windows XP. Then, I'll discuss compatibility issues in more detail.

Basic Compatibility Options

The Program Compatibility Wizard lets you specify the operating system that Windows XP should emulate for the application as well as a handful of other properties such as screen resolution and color depth. The OS options provided by the wizard include the following:

- Microsoft Windows 95

- Microsoft Windows NT 4.0 with Service Pack 5

- Microsoft Windows 98 / Me

- Microsoft Windows 2000

   To run the Program Compatibility Wizard, click Start ➢ All Programs ➢ Accessories ➢ Program Compatibility Wizard. The wizard prompts you to select the application for which you want to set compatibility options. You can select an installed program, select a program on a CD, or locate the program manually. The wizard then prompts you for the desired compatibility settings (Figure 13.1). After you specify the settings, the wizard gives you the opportunity to test the application to make sure it works before finalizing the settings.

FIGURE 13.1:

Use the Program Compatibility Wizard to make a program compatible with Windows XP.

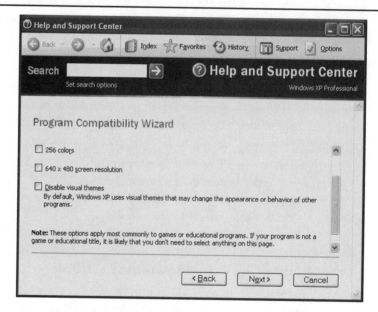

   If you prefer, you can set program compatibility options manually through the properties for a program's executable or a shortcut to the program. Right-click the program's icon and choose Properties, then click the Compatibility tab. You can specify the OS as well as the same additional compatibility options provided by the wizard. The only difference is that you don't have the option of testing the settings. However, you can simply open the properties again and change them.

TIP   You can set properties for an application on a CD, but compatibility settings are saved only for programs installed on a hard disk.

Compatibility Options in Windows 2000

The Windows 2000 Resource Kit includes a tool that you can use to configure certain compatibility options for applications in the same way as Windows XP. This Resource Kit tool adds a Compatibility tab to the properties sheet for a shortcut to an application, allowing you to set the compatibility mode for the application. To install the tool, first install the Windows 2000 Resource Kit. Then open a command console and execute the following command:

```
regsvr32 c:\winnt\apppatch\slayerui.dll
```

After the DLL is registered, create a shortcut to the application's executable file. Right-click the shortcut and choose Properties. Click the Compatibility tab and use the options it provides to select the compatibility mode for the application.

Advanced Compatibility Options

In order to understand advanced compatibility options for Windows XP, you need to understand the reasons why program compatibility is a potential problem. Some applications expect a specific OS version to be running and balk if the OS returns a different version number. A program might call a Windows API that returns data in a particular format that has changed in a later OS version, or which gives unexpected results because of differences in hardware. For example, early versions of a program might not gracefully handle high-capacity disk drives.

Another potential problem is a change in the location of user data and the desktop. Windows 2000 and Windows XP both store user data by default in the \Documents and Settings*user* folder, where *user* is the current logon account. Windows 98 used the \Profiles*user* folder or \Windows\Personal folder for user data.

Windows XP addresses compatibility issues during Setup. It uses two database files, MigDB.inf and NTCompat.inf, to check for hardware and software compatibility problems and reports those problems to the user. MigDB.inf supports upgrades from Windows 9*x*/Me, and NTCompat.inf supports upgrades from Windows NT.

The file *%systemroot%*\AppPatch\SysMain.sdb contains compatibility information and fixes for specific applications. The fixes in SysMain are program-specific and can apply any of several compatibility fixes when the program is loaded, from something as simple as reporting a specific version of the OS the program all the way up to changing the way memory and other system resources are reported to or used by the program.

Windows XP uses Dynamic Update and Windows Update to get the program compatibility information necessary to determine whether a program can run successfully under XP. Dynamic Update works during Setup, downloading updates from the Microsoft Windows Update website. Setup downloads updated drivers, core Windows XP files, and software patches, integrating these updates into the Windows XP installation process. Dynamic Update naturally requires that an Internet connection be available when Setup runs.

Windows XP can also check for compatibility updates when you install an application well after Setup is complete. Windows XP checks the Windows Update site for the same types of updates as Dynamic Update. The only difference is that it checks for the updates during program installation rather than Windows XP installation. So, Windows XP uses both the SysMain database and Windows Update to apply compatibility fixes.

Application Blocking

When Windows XP detects a program with a compatibility problem, the OS can take one of two actions: apply a fix to the program and run it, or block the program from running. Windows XP displays a dialog box telling you the application is incompatible with Windows XP. Depending on the program and its compatibility problems, Windows XP will either let you run the program anyway or will block the program from running. If the program is blocked, you'll have to obtain an update for the program.

Compatibility Modes

A *compatibility mode* is a group of fixes that emulate a specific operating system. Compatibility modes are also called *layers*. Each of the OS choices you see in the Program Compatibility Wizard is a compatibility mode. The Windows 95 compatibility mode, for example, applies roughly 50 different fixes to allow programs written for Windows 95 to run on Windows XP. The fixes that each mode applies varies, but common fixes include reporting the selected version of Windows to the application, changing the way Windows manages memory, and specifying the location of data folders. Each mode is naturally tailored to the target operating system to allow the application to run under Windows XP in the context of that target OS.

Windows XP provides three types of compatibility modes:

End-user   These are the default modes you'll find on the Compatibility tab and in the Program Compatibility Wizard.

System   These include the end-user modes as well as the Limited User Account Security mode, which allows a program to run under a limited security context for a user, and the Profiles mode, which controls the way the program works with Windows XP user profiles.

Custom   Windows XP provides a CompatAdmin tool you can use to create a custom compatibility mode to apply to a specific program.

It's possible for more than one set of fixes to apply to a program. For example, when Setup installs Windows XP and detects an incompatible problem, it can apply a fix through the SysMain database. You might also apply compatibility options through the Program Compatibility Wizard. Windows XP combines the compatibility settings and applies them all to the program.

Customizing and Extending Compatibility Features

The Program Compatibility Wizard and the Compatibility tab of a program's properties give you the means to set basic compatibility properties. Microsoft offers additional tools you can use to customize and extend compatibility features. You can download these tools as part of the Windows XP Application Compatibility Toolkit from

```
http://msdn.microsoft.com/downloads/default.asp?URL=/downloads/sample.asp?url=/
msdn-files/027/001/685/msdncompositedoc.xml
```

The Application Compatibility Toolkit includes several documents that explain program compatibility issues, offer an overview of the compatibility features in Windows XP, and define test procedures you can implement to determine a program's compatibility with XP. The toolkit also includes a list of other online resources that will help you test and manage program compatibility under Windows XP.

The following sections explain the tools included in the Application Compatibility Toolkit. You can install the tools by downloading the file and simply double-clicking it.

TIP   You can launch the tools from the C:\Program Files\Application Compatibility Toolkit\default.htm page after installation, or click Start ➢ All Programs ➢ Application Compatibility Toolkit.

Compatibility Administration Tool

The Compatibility Administration tool (also called the Application Fix Management Console), shown in Figure 13.2, lets you view and enable or disable existing compatibility database entries. You can also use this tool to create custom fixes for specific applications not already included in the SysMain database. Because you can disable an existing entry, you can create a custom entry for a program already included in the SysMain database.

FIGURE 13.2:

Use the Compatibility Administration tool to view, enable/disable, and create program compatibility entries.

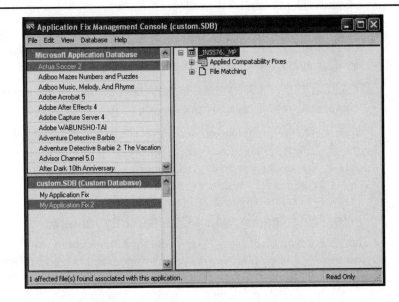

To create a new program fix entry, open the Compatibility Administration Tool and choose Database ➤ Create Application Fix to start the wizard. Select Apply Specific Compatibility Fix from the Create An Application Fix dialog box and click Next. Enter the name of the application and click Next. Browse for or enter the path to the program's executable file, then click Next to display the dialog box shown in Figure 13.3.

You can select any number of fixes to apply to the application; scroll through the list and place a check beside the fixes you want. Then click Next.

The wizard next prompts you to add files to the entry for identification. Windows XP uses these files to automatically detect when the application is installed on a system. Adding other files refines the detection process and is particularly useful when you have more than one application that uses the same executable file name. You can add files to the list manually or click Auto-Generate to have the wizard automatically include support files, such as DLLs, from the program's folder. When you're satisfied with the settings, click Next, then click Finish to create the entry.

When you've finished creating custom program entries in your new database file, choose File ➤ Save to save the database to an SDB file. You can then distribute the database file to other computers to apply the fixes to those systems. You can use the Sdbinst.exe program included with this tool to install the database on the target systems. The syntax is sdbinst .exe *database_file*.

FIGURE 13.3:

Select the specific
fixes to apply to the
application.

Sdbinst.exe installs by default in the *%systemroot%*\System32 folder. This method of installing the database is handy when you need to incorporate a database on a target system through a script. If you prefer, you can simply double-click the database file to add its entries to the Registry. To use this method, place the database file on a network share available to all target users. Send all users an e-mail message containing a link to the database file on the network share (make sure to create the link as a UNC path rather than an absolute path) with instructions to click the link to install the patch.

The Compatibility Administration Tool provides a second view that you can use to search the local computer and connected network drives for programs that use compatibility fixes. This is handy when you need to know which applications have already been fixed and the fixes that have been applied to them. To search for fixed programs, choose View ➢ Search For Fixes. The tool displays a dialog box you use to specify the volumes to search. Place a check beside the volumes to search and click Search. Figure 13.4 shows the results of a search on a typical Windows XP system.

Application Verifier Tool

The Application Verifier Tool gives you the means to test programs for compatibility with Windows XP. After you start the tool, click Add (Figure 13.5) to select the program's executable file. Then select the test settings in the right pane that you want to apply to the program. Click Run to run the program and allow the Application Verifier Tool to capture any incompatibility problems. Click View Logs to view the log and potential fixes for specific problems the tool encountered with the selected program.

FIGURE 13.4:

You can use the Compatibility Administration Tool to search local and network drives for fixed applications.

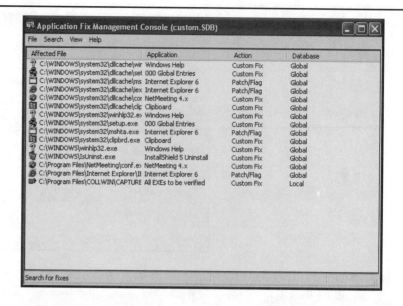

FIGURE 13.5:

Use the Application Verifier Tool to test program compatibility with Windows XP.

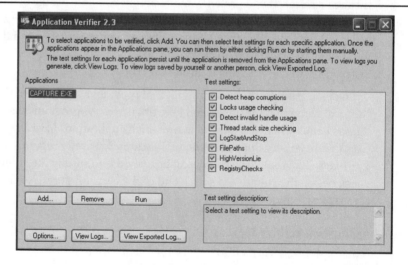

TIP   See the Help file for the Application Verifier Tool for additional information on testing for program compatibility.

QFixApp

QFixApp performs a function similar to the Compatibility Administration Tool. You can use QFixApp to apply fixes for specific programs, test a program, and view results of the test through the QFixApp logs. QFixApp provides two modes: simple and advanced; Figure 13.6 shows the tool in simple mode. The Layers tab lists the available application fix layers. The Fixes tab (Figure 13.7) shows the fixes applied for the selected layer.

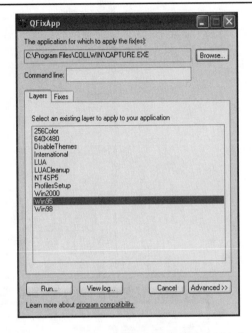

In advanced mode (Figure 13.8), QFixApp lets you specify additional information about the program being patched. This is often necessary if the program uses a common executable name, such as Setup.exe—any name that might be confused with another program that has already been patched or runs correctly under Windows XP. With QFixApp in advanced mode, you can select other attributes such as file size and checksum to further identify the executable to be patched. Click Advanced in the QFixApp window to switch to advanced mode, or click Simple to switch back to simple mode.

While you can use QFixApp to simply view fixes, it's likely you'll want to create fixes for specific programs. QFixApp can generate an SDB file that you can use to install the fix on the local computer or export to other systems. To create the database file, configure the settings and fixes as needed, switch to advanced mode, and click Create Fix Support. QFixApp automatically creates an SDB file in the target program's folder and then asks you if you want to install the fix on the local computer. You can export the SDB file to a network share where it is accessible by other users. Or, if you need to incorporate this fix with others, import the database in the Compatibility Administration Tool and export the fix from there along with any other fixes you need to distribute.

FIGURE 13.7:

Use the Fixes tab to view and select fixes applied for the selected layer.

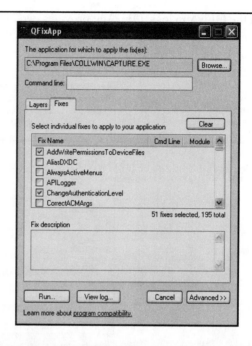

FIGURE 13.8:

Use QfixApp's advanced mode when you need to specify additional information about the program to be patched.

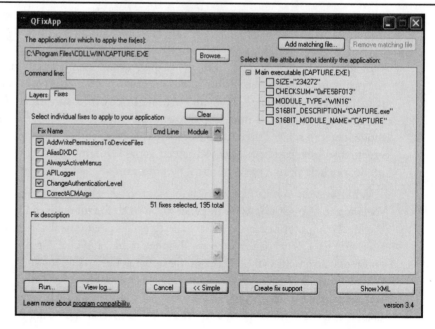

PageHeap

PageHeap is a command-line tool that lets you test a program for heap-related bugs and memory leaks. PageHeap doesn't actually perform any debugging, but instead adds a layer between the application and the operating system to allow the system to verify all memory operations. You must use PageHeap in conjunction with a debugger, so it's a tool primarily for application developers. See the Windows Application Compatibility Toolkit Help file for more information on using PageHeap.

Using Virtual Machines to Run Applications

Chapter 4 discussed two very useful third-party programs, VMWare Workstation and Virtual PC, that let you run other operating systems concurrently under your primary host operating system. These applications create a *virtual machine*, complete with its own BIOS and virtual hardware. The virtual machine (VM) runs in a window under the host operating system just like any other application. The main difference is that the virtual machine contains its own operating system. So, for example, you might run Linux in a virtual machine on your Windows XP host.

These third-party VM managers give you an alternative to the compatibility tools discussed in this chapter for running programs that would otherwise not run properly (or at all) under Windows XP. For example, these tools are perfect for running Linux applications. However, you might also use a VM manager to run *Windows* applications under Windows XP. I use a utility provided by Nortel Networks to manage a handful of routers, and the program only runs under Windows 95. I could hassle with the compatibility tools and try to get it to work under Windows XP, but I prefer to simply open a Windows 95 VM when needed and run the application from there.

> **NOTE**   For more information on VMWare Workstation or Virtual PC, check out www.vmware.com and www.connectix.com, respectively, or consult Chapter 4.

Accessing Unix and Linux Hosts

In some networks, Windows isn't the only platform. Many companies use Unix and/or Linux along with other platforms to provide the applications and server-side features they need. You could dual-boot between Linux/Unix and Windows XP when you needed to run Linux or Unix applications. Or, you might use VMWare Workstation or Virtual PC to run Linux in a virtual machine in order to access programs and other features on your company's

Unix/Linux-based servers. Usually the best option, however, is to use a Windows-based application that ties you into the applications and services on the servers.

A good solution in many cases is an X Window emulator that allows you to access X applications running on a Unix or Linux server from your PC. The X Window emulator runs under Windows XP as a Windows application, giving you a terminal session into your server. You can even copy and paste data between your X applications and your local Windows applications.

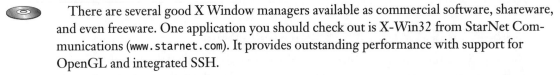

There are several good X Window managers available as commercial software, shareware, and even freeware. One application you should check out is X-Win32 from StarNet Communications (`www.starnet.com`). It provides outstanding performance with support for OpenGL and integrated SSH.

You should also check out the Exceed family of products developed by Hummingbird (`www.hummingbird.com`). Hummingbird offers remote access solutions for a variety of applications and systems.

In addition, a search on the Internet for the keywords **x window**, **manager**, and **software** should turn up several discussion links and other information. Or, check out your favorite download site, such as `www.shareware.com` or `www.tucows.com`.

For character-mode applications, another alternative is Telnet, assuming your Unix/Linux servers provide Telnet services. Windows XP includes a Telnet client you can use to establish a console session on the server to run character-mode applications.

CHAPTER 14

Adding and Removing OS Components

U nlike most earlier versions of Windows, XP provides no custom setup option to let you specify which optional components to install and which to omit. Instead, XP's setup routine installs a one-size-fits-all set of options.

As with almost all clothes, of course, one size never fits all—at least, not comfortably. To get XP working the way you need it to, you're likely to need to add or remove OS components as discussed in this chapter. For example, you might want to add Universal Plug and Play (UPnP) or Print Services for Unix to your installation of XP, or you might want to remove MSN Explorer and all the time-wasting games that the default installation includes.

Even if you're one of the fortunate few for whom the standard installation fully satisfies, you'll need to keep your installation of XP up to date to keep it running smoothly and to minimize security and compatibility problems. For this, XP provides the Windows Update feature. You can make Windows Update run automatically, or run it manually, or prevent users from running it at all.

Adding and Removing Components

XP includes the Windows Component Wizard, shown in Figure 14.1, for adding and removing components. To run the wizard, log on as an Administrator and display the Add Or Remove Programs window by clicking the Add Or Remove Programs link in Control Panel, then click the Add/Remove Windows Components button.

TIP   Instead of going through Control Panel and the Add Or Remove Programs window, you can run the Windows Component Wizard by running the program sysocmgr.exe with the /i switch and the location of the *%systemroot%*\inf\sysoc.inf file—for example, **sysocmgr /i:c:\windows\inf\sysoc.inf**.

FIGURE 14.1:

The Windows Component Wizard is the easiest way to add and remove XP components.

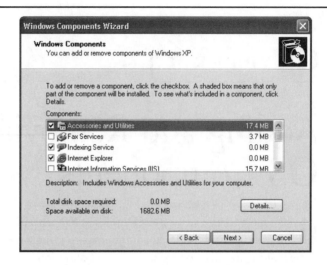

Adding Components

The Windows Component Wizard is easy to use. Each selected check box indicates a component that's already installed. Each grayed check box indicates a component that's partially installed. Each cleared check box indicates a component that's not installed.

To add a component, select its check box. If the wizard makes the Details button available, you can click it to display a dialog box in which you can choose subcomponents of the component. For example, Figure 14.2 shows the details dialog for Internet Information Services (IIS), which lets you select the IIS items you want to install. If a subcomponent itself has subcomponents, the wizard makes the Details button available when you select the subcomponent, and you can drill down to the next level to see your choices. (Some components have subcomponents that aren't selected by default, so you'll need to drill down to the Details level to select all the subcomponents if you want to install the full component.)

Once you've chosen the components to add, make sure your XP CD is in the appropriate drive or that your network installation source is available, and click the Next button. The Windows Component Wizard installs the components, notifies you when it has done so, and returns you to the Add Or Remove Programs window.

Removing Components

The basic way of removing an XP component is, of course, to run the Windows Component Wizard again and clear the check box for the component or subcomponent you want to remove. If another component or service depends on this component or subcomponent, the wizard warns you of the problem and asks if you want to remove the dependent item as well.

FIGURE 14.2:

If the component has subcomponents, choose those you want to install.

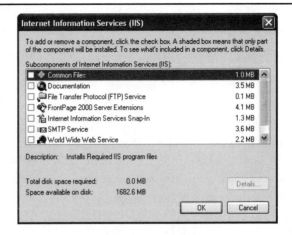

The Windows Component Wizard removes most of the components completely when you ask it to. The exception is Internet Explorer, which is too deeply hooked into Windows to be removed. So when you choose to remove IE, the wizard deletes its Desktop icon and its entry on the Start menu, but all the program files stay in place. This means that "removing" Internet Explorer only gets it out of your interface—it doesn't save you any disk space worth mentioning. (By contrast, removing MSN Explorer nets you a double-handful of megabytes.)

Extending the List of Components in the Windows Component Wizard

As you saw in the previous section, the Windows Component Wizard makes it easy to add and remove components. But it doesn't provide a full list of the components that you can remove. You can actually remove several other components, including Automatic Updates, Windows Messenger, and Pinball. (That's right—you can't remove Pinball by removing the other games. Maybe it was a licensing issue.)

Before using this technique to remove components that the Windows Component Wizard hides, run System Restore and create a restore point so that you can easily recover from any side effects XP suffers from the removal of the component.

These are the components you can remove:

Component	Name in sysoc.inf
Windows Management Instrumentation	WBEM
Windows Automatic Updates	AutoUpdate

Component	Name in `sysoc.inf`
Windows Messenger	`msmsgs`
Accessibility Wizard	`AccessOpt`
multimedia	`MultiM`
Pinball	`Pinball`
WordPad	`MSWordPad`

If you want to remove one of these components, edit the %*systemroot*%\inf\sysoc.inf file in a text editor such as Notepad, and remove the word hide from the line that refers to the component you want to remove. For example, the entry for Pinball appears in a line like this:

```
Pinball=ocgen.dll,OcEntry,pinball.inf,HIDE,7
```

Save sysoc.inf and display the Windows Component Wizard again, and the previously hidden component or components will appear in the list box.

However, XP has other components that you can't remove in this way, such as COM+ (com and CommApps in the sysoc.inf file), Terminal Server (TerminalServer), and Distributed Transaction Coordinator (DTC). Deleting the instance of hide in the line that refers to them makes these components appear in the Windows Component Wizard, but you can't deselect their check boxes.

Installing Service Packs and Updates

To keep Windows XP up to date, you'll need to install such service packs and updates as Microsoft releases to plug security holes, add application compatibility, or add features. XP includes features to check for service packs and updates automatically, but you can check manually if you prefer.

NOTE   Only Administrators can install service packs and run Windows Update.

Using Windows Update

Windows Update is Windows XP's feature for checking automatically for updates and service packs. You can run Windows Update manually or allow the Automatic Updates feature to check for updates periodically. (You can also prevent the user from running Windows Update. I'll discuss how to do this at the end of the chapter.)

Configuring and Using the Automatic Updates Feature

Windows XP's Automatic Updates feature is designed to prod you to keep your installation of XP up to date. Depending on the settings you choose, Automatic Updates can automatically check the Windows Update site for critical updates, download them, and present them to you ready for installation.

Automatic Updates initially appears as a nagging icon in the notification area soon after first logon. When you click the icon, Windows XP displays the Automatic Updates Setup Wizard, whose Notification Settings page contains three largely self-explanatory option buttons:

- "Download the updates automatically and notify me when they are ready to be installed"
- "Notify me before downloading any updates and notify me again before installing them on my computer"
- "Turn off automatic updating. I want to update my computer manually"

Once you've dealt with the Automatic Updates Setup Wizard, you can adjust your Automatic Updates settings on the Automatic Updates tab of the System Properties dialog box (Windows key+R). The Notification Settings group box contains the three option buttons that the Automatic Updates Setup Wizard offers. The Previous Updates group box lets you restore updates you've previously declined.

Accepting or Declining Updates

Unless you turned off automatic updating, Automatic Updates checks the Windows Update Internet site periodically when your Internet connection is open but inactive, to see if new updates are available. When it discovers new updates, Automatic Updates takes the appropriate action depending on the setting you've chosen.

If you chose to download updates automatically, Automatic Update monitors your Internet connection and starts the download when the connection is inactive. If other activity starts on your Internet connection (for example, you start to browse the Web, or your e-mail program checks messages), Automatic Update throttles back its download rate so that it's not hogging all your bandwidth.

When it has downloaded the updates, Automatic Updates displays an Install Reminder icon in the notification area. Double-click the icon to display the Automatic Updates: Ready To Install dialog box.

The three command buttons in the Automatic Updates: Ready to Install dialog box are straightforward:

- Clicking the Install button installs all the updates you've downloaded without showing you details of what they are.
- Clicking the Details button displays details of the updates and lets you choose which to install. (Again, the default setting is to install all the updates.)
- Clicking the Remind Me Later button displays a dialog box that lets you specify a "snooze" time from 30 minutes to 3 days.

If you chose to be notified of available updates without downloading them automatically, you'll see a New Updates Are Ready To Download pop-up from the Windows Update notification area icon. Click the icon to display the Automatic Updates: Updates For Your Computer dialog box (see Figure 14.3), in which you can read brief details of the updates on offer and choose which to download. You can also click the Remind Me Later button to put off downloading the update to a more convenient time.

FIGURE 14.3:

In the Automatic Updates: Updates For Your Computer dialog box, choose which updates to download.

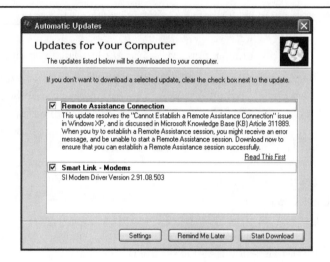

When you choose to download the updates, Windows Update again uses bandwidth throttling to allow you to use your Internet connection through the download. When the download is finished, Windows Update displays the New Updates Are Ready To Install pop-up in the notification area. Double-click this pop-up or its icon to display the Ready To Install dialog box, and proceed as described earlier in this section.

Restoring Declined Updates

If you turn down an update, Windows XP makes available the Restore Declined Updates button on the Automatic Updates tab of the System Properties dialog box. Click this button to make the updates available again.

Pausing the Downloading of Updates

You can tell when Automatic Updates is downloading updates because the Automatic Updates icon appears in the notification area. If you find your bandwidth has suddenly disappeared, check the notification area for this icon. If necessary, you can pause the downloading of updates by right-clicking the icon and choosing Pause from the shortcut menu. To restart the downloading, right-click the icon and choose Restart.

Turning Off the Automatic Updating Service

Even if you choose the Turn Off Automatic Updating option button, Windows XP continues to run the Automatic Updates service, which is called WUAUSERV. This service supposedly consumes minimal resources, but even so, it's not going to speed up your computer. Run the Services console, stop the Automatic Updates service, and configure it for Manual startup so that it doesn't run itself the next time you restart XP.

Running Windows Update Manually

To run Windows Update manually, choose Start ➤ All Programs ➤ Windows Update or open Internet Explorer and choose Tools ➤ Windows Update. Internet Explorer displays the Windows Update website (www.windowsupdate.com), from which you scan for updates or perform any of the actions described in the following subsections.

> **TIP**   If you're connecting to the Windows Update website through an authenticating proxy that uses NTLM proxy authentication, you may need to select the Use HTTP 1.1 Through Proxy Connection check box on the Advanced page of the Internet Options dialog box in Internet Explorer. (Otherwise, if Internet Explorer uses HTTP 1.0, the Windows Update ActiveX controls don't use the right keep-alive headers, and NTLM can't authenticate the client.) After selecting this check box, close Internet Explorer and restart it for the change to take effect.

Reviewing Your Windows Update History

To review your Windows Update history, click the View Installation History link on the Windows Update website.

Downloading Updates So That You Can Use Them on Other Computers

By default, Windows Update doesn't show you the update files it downloads; instead, it gives you details of their contents and lets you choose whether to install them or pass on them. If you have just one Windows XP computer, this is fine, but if you have two or more, it means that you'll need to download the same updates for each computer. Even if you have enough bandwidth to make minor telecoms' entrails churn with lust, multiple downloads of the same files are a waste of time.

To download the update files in a form in which you can apply them to multiple computers, you need to use the Windows Update Catalog, and you need to use it from a computer running XP (rather than an earlier version of Windows).

To do so, click the Personalize Windows Update button on the Windows Update website. Select the "Display the link to the Windows Update Catalog under See Also" check box on the Personalize Your Windows Update Experience page, then click the Save Settings button.

You can then click a link in the See Also area of the left column of the Windows Update page to access the Windows Update Catalog page.

Click the Find Updates For Microsoft Windows Operating Systems link and use the resulting page to search by operating system. Once you've located the updates, use the Add buttons to add to your Download Basket the packages you want to download.

Click the Go To Download Basket link to display your basket. Specify a download location on your computer, and click Download Now to download the update files.

To install a file you've downloaded, double-click it.

> **TIP**   To install a new device driver on multiple computers with the same configuration, use `unattend.txt` to change the Registry setting of the device driver on the computers.

Choosing Which Categories and Updates to Display

You can choose which categories and updates Windows Update should display by using the options on the Personalize Your Windows Update Experience page of the Windows Update website (`www.windowsupdate.com`)

Preventing Users from Using Windows Update

To prevent users from using Windows Update to update their XP installations, take the following actions under \Local Computer Policy\User Configuration\Administrative Templates in the Group Policy snap-in (Start ➢ Run, enter **gpedit.msc**, click OK; see the next chapter for details on the MMC):

1. Under \Start Menu And Taskbar, double-click the Remove Links And Access To Window Update item. In the resulting Properties dialog box, select the Enabled option button and click OK.

2. Under \Windows Components\Windows Update, double-click the Remove Access To Use All Windows Update Features item. In the resulting Properties dialog box, select the Enabled option button and click OK.

3. Under \Control Panel\Add/Remove Programs, double-click the Hide "Add Programs From Microsoft" Option item. In the resulting Properties dialog box, select the Enabled option button and click OK.

XP then removes the Windows Update entries from the Start menu and from Internet Explorer's Tools menu, and blocks users from accessing the Windows Update website manually. (The user can go to the Windows Update website, but they receive an Access Denied message that prevents them from accessing any updates.)

CHAPTER 15

Using and Customizing MMC Consoles

The Microsoft Management Console (MMC) is the framework around which all the tools used to manage Windows XP are built. You use it to create, save, and open collections of administrative tools, called *consoles*. Consoles contain items such as snap-ins, extension snap-ins, monitor controls, tasks, wizards, and documentation required to manage many of the hardware, software, and networking components of your Windows system. You can add items to an existing MMC console, or you can create new consoles and configure them to administer a specific system component.

One thing to understand right off the bat: MMC consoles, by themselves, do not perform any administrative functions. Instead, they provide a backdrop that hosts tools that do, and the primary type of tool you can add to a console is called a *snap-in*. Other items that you can add include ActiveX controls, links to web pages, folders, Taskpad views, and tasks.

The MMC provides a standardized look and feel to all the Windows XP, .NET, and 2000 management tools, which is similar to the look and feel that many are familiar with from working with the file management utility, Windows Explorer. Of course, Windows Explorer, in its current iteration, has been around since Windows 95, so it is assumed that all Windows users are comfortable with this interface. The MMC interface is also not new to the latest versions of the Windows operating systems. MMC consoles began making their first appearances with some of the BackOffice products installed on the NT 4 platform, such as SQL Server 7, SMS 2, and IIS 4. Thus, the MMC tools should be nothing new to most NT 4 administrators.

One advantage of the MMC interface is that it can run on all Windows 9*x* and Windows NT operating systems, allowing you to manage services running on more advanced Windows operating systems from down-level clients.

Many additional benefits are associated with the MMC management interface, including the following:

- It's highly customizable.

- You can save and share MMC consoles with other administrators, and you can send snap-ins as e-mail attachments.

- You can use most snap-ins for remote computer management.

- You can configure permissions so that MMC runs in author mode, which an administrator can manage, or in user mode, which limits what users can access.

In this chapter, we will look at how you can more effectively use this vital management interface. I'll describe the various MMC components, show you how to create your own MMC tools to better manage *your* individual networks, and discuss the modes in which you can work with an MMC and the implications of each.

Working with the MMC

Windows XP comes with several *preconfigured* MMC consoles, from which you can do the bulk of administration on any system. One of the first MMC consoles that users new to XP are likely to work with is the Computer Management snap in. You can open Computer Management, which is shown in Figure 15.1, in a couple of ways:

- Choose Start ➤ Control Panel ➤ Performance And Maintenance ➤ Administrative Tools ➤ Computer Management.

- Right-click My Computer, and choose Manage from the shortcut menu.

Several snap-ins have been added to this preconfigured console. But before I discuss these snap-ins, let's look at a little terminology regarding the MMC. You are likely to hear the parts of the MMC referred to by various names, so there's nothing definitive about the following.

Console tree   Shows the organization of the console and allows for easy navigation between the snap-ins.

Details pane   Displays information related to the currently selected item in the console tree. You can take care of many administrative tasks using the Details pane.

Action menu   Provides commands specific to the current snap-in or the currently selected item in the console tree. In other words, the Action menu contains a list of *actions* that can be performed on the selection.

View menu   Allows you to choose between several ways of displaying information, like its counterpart in Windows Explorer. The View menu might also include a Customize command, which lets you hide or display the console tree, among other things.

Shortcut menus   Contains only items that are relevant to the current context. When in doubt, right-click. You'll likely find that the easiest way to carry out an administrative function is to right-click an item and choose a command from the shortcut menu.

If you're familiar with the NT administrative tools, you are also aware of how different (and much easier to use) the MMC tools are than previous utilities, such as Server Manager and User Manager for Domains. Using the NT administrative tools required that you memorize all the available menus these utilities provided. Conversely, you can use the MMC consoles intuitively by examining the contents of the console tree of a snap-in.

FIGURE 15.1:

The Computer Management snap-in is preconfigured in Windows XP.

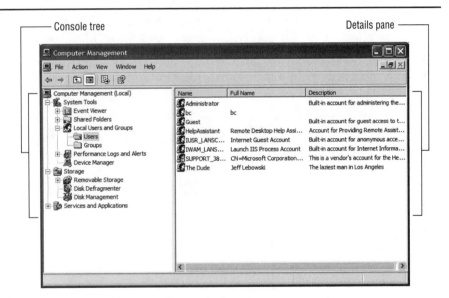

Creating a Custom MMC Console

Although creating a specialized snap-in for the MMC requires knowledge of ActiveX programming, creating a custom MMC console requires no programming background whatsoever. All you have to know is how to point and click. To start to create your own consoles that contain only the administrative tools you commonly need, simply open a blank MMC and add one or more of the snap-ins available on your system. Remember that by itself, the MMC has no functionality; it is just scaffolding around which the management tools are designed. The management usefulness of the MMC depends on which snap-in is loaded.

On Windows XP computers, you can open a blank MMC console (see Figure 15.2) by choosing Start ➤ Run to open the Run dialog box, typing **mmc** in the Open box, and pressing

Enter. When you run this command, you will experience first hand the concept I presented earlier: a blank MMC console is useless until a snap-in provides it with functionality.

Now it's time to give the console something to work on. To add a snap-in to an MMC, follow these steps:

1. From the MMC console window, choose File ➢ Add/Remove Snap-in to open the Add/Remove Snap-in dialog box.

2. Click the Add button to open the Add Standalone Snap-in dialog box.

3. Select the snap-in you want to add, and click the Add button.

4. At this point, you may be asked which computer you want to manage. In most instances, select the local computer. If necessary, click Finish when you have made your choice.

5. Now, the fun part is that you can keep repeating Steps 2, 3, and 4 to add additional snap-ins. In this way, you can create a single MMC that gathers all the tools you commonly use into a single location.

FIGURE 15.2:

A blank MMC console awaits further instructions.

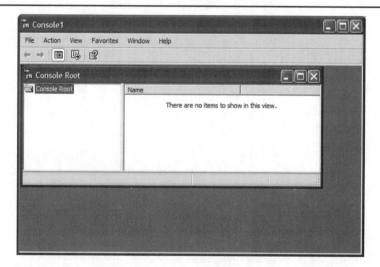

6. After you add the snap-ins you want, you can save the console. Choose File ➢ Save As to open the Save As dialog box. Enter a name for your console, which will be saved with an .msc extension by default.

You can save this newly created, customized console anywhere, but one especially useful place to save it is right on the Desktop, where it becomes a part of the user profile for the current user. An administrator can then access the custom MMC tool anywhere in a domain environment by implementing a roaming profile. From then on, the administrator need only double-click a single icon on the Desktop to perform all day-to-day administrative tasks.

Earlier, in Chapter 7, we looked at how to create a Start menu shortcut to Administrative Tools. These tools are a collection of preconfigured MMC consoles that let users who have the proper rights take care of most administrative tasks.

User Mode versus Author Mode

We've just looked at how to create an MMC console that you can call your own. But you can assign several options to the custom console as you are creating it, and these options define the functionality of the MMC when it is used. Of these options, there are two general access options: author mode and user mode. There is one level of author mode, and there are three levels of user mode:

- Author mode
- User mode, full access
- User mode, limited access, multiple window
- User mode, limited access, single window

You configure these options in the Options dialog box. When you first open a blank MMC, the default option is set to author mode (if it weren't, you would not be able to add snap-ins). To set the MMC console options for a previously saved MMC, open a blank MMC console and then follow these steps:

1. Choose File ➤ Open, right-click the .msc file, and then choose Author from the shortcut menu. You could also choose Start ➤ Run to open the Run dialog box, and in the Open box enter **mmc *path\filename*.msc /a**, if you like to type. Either way, the selected console will open in author mode.

2. Choose File ➤ Options to open the Options dialog box, as shown in Figure 15.3.

3. To change the default mode for which the console is saved, in the Console Mode drop-down list box, select the appropriate mode.

The choices in the Console Mode drop-down list box have the following implications:

Author Mode You can assign author mode to grant full access to all MMC functionality. Doing so grants users who use this MMC the ability to add other snap-ins, add items to the Favorites menu, and so on.

User Mode - Full Access All window management commands and full access to the console tree are provided, but a user is prevented from adding or removing snap-ins or changing the console properties.

FIGURE 15.3:

You can switch between user mode and author mode using the Options dialog box.

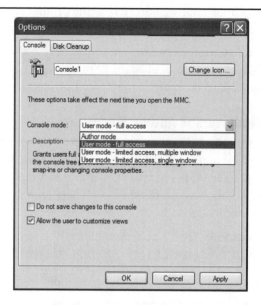

User Mode - Limited Access, Single Window   This mode prevents users from opening additional console windows, as the name implies. Users see only the window that was visible when the console was saved.

User Mode - Limited Access, Multiple Window   Users can create new windows but cannot close windows that were visible when the console was saved.

How console changes are saved depends on the mode in which you are working. When working with a console in author mode, you are prompted to save your changes when exiting the console. However, when working with a console in user mode, changes may be automatically saved. Saving changes is automatic when you close the console if you have cleared the Do Not Save Changes To This Console check box in the Options dialog box.

If the default console mode for the console is one of the user modes, do the following:

- To prevent users from editing the console, select the Do Not Save Changes To This Console check box.

- To enable users to access the Customize View dialog box, select the Allow The User To Customize Views check box.

However, the MMC console always opens in author mode, ignoring the default opening settings when any of the following apply:

- The MMC is already open.

- A console has been opened from a shortcut menu.
- A console has been opened using the /a switch in the Run dialog box.

TIP If it becomes annoying to see the message "Save console settings to..." every time you close a console that was opened in author mode, you can specify that changes to the console are saved every time you close the MMC. To do so, set the default mode for the console to one of the user modes and clear the Do Not Save Changes To This Console check box in the Options dialog box.

Keep in mind that the preconfigured MMC tools are meant to give you easy access to the most commonly performed management tasks without the hassle of adding snap-ins to an MMC each time you want to do something. The best way to use an MMC, probably, is to make your own MMC with the snap-ins you commonly use and then always use that tool. Doing so prevents your having to open multiple preconfigured MMC consoles when you have more than one task to manage. Some preconfigured consoles give you access to one snap-in; others, such as Computer Management, give you access to several.

Creating and Using Taskpads

A Taskpad is a customized page that appears within the Details pane of an MMC snap-in. The big advantage of the Taskpad view is that you can create icons that represent several menus, shortcuts, command strings, and/or scripts. Think of Taskpads as MMC shortcuts. Just as a Desktop shortcut hides several commands that would be necessary to open a file or run an executable, the icons on the Taskpad can hide several steps to achieve a desired administrative goal.

You can create Taskpad views as you are setting up your custom MMC consoles, or you can use previously saved consoles. You can't, however, create Taskpad views in any of the preconfigured MMC consoles. To create a Taskpad view on an existing MMC, open the saved console in author mode using one of the methods discussed earlier, and then follow these steps:

1. In the console tree, select a snap-in item.

2. Choose Action ➢ New Taskpad View (or right-click the snap-in item and choose New Taskpad View from the shortcut menu) to start the New Taskpad View Wizard, which is shown in Figure 15.4.

3. Follow the onscreen instructions.

Now, this procedure will only set up the Taskpad view, not actually create any tasks. If you want to create tasks immediately after you create the Taskpad view, make sure that the Start New Task Wizard check box is checked (it will be by default) in the final screen of the wizard.

FIGURE 15.4:

The New Taskpad View Wizard will help you create a Taskpad view.

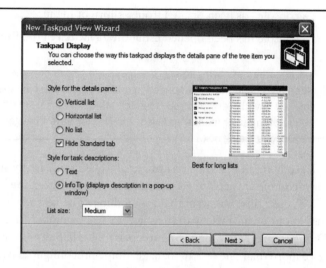

Furthermore, you can add or change tasks to the Taskpad view at any time. To add a task, follow these steps:

1. In the console tree, right-click the Taskpad view, and choose Edit Taskpad View from the shortcut menu to open the Taskpad Properties dialog box.

2. Click the Task tab to display a list of tasks from the selected Taskpad view.

3. Click New to start the New Task Wizard, which will step you through the process. Figure 15.5 shows a screen from the New Task Wizard.

FIGURE 15.5:

Use the New Task Wizard to add or change tasks.

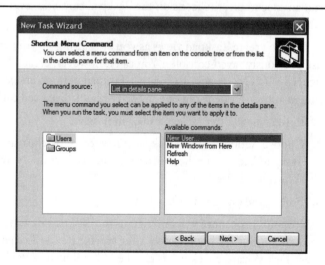

NOTE   To change an existing task, click the Edit button in the Task tab.

Now, a real-world note about Taskpad views: I haven't seen them used often. Because the interface of the MMC is so common for users of the Windows platform, it is easy for most administrators, and even most end users, to learn to use. The prevailing design objective behind the Taskpad view is that a Taskpad might make it easier for novice users to perform their jobs. For instance, you can add applicable tasks to a Taskpad view and then hide the console tree. A user can then begin using tools before they are familiar with the location of particular items in the console tree or operating system.

With that in mind, ask yourself, How often do you delegate administrative tasks to novice users? Probably not often. So even though Taskpad views are relatively easy to set up, and adding tasks is simply a matter of stepping through a wizard, you might not find it worth the extra effort to create a Taskpad and a task when the MMC by itself is so easy to use.

CHAPTER 16

It's All About Control: Tools and Techniques for Managing Services

Although the average user doesn't have to deal with services in Windows XP much, if at all, power users often do need to manage services. For example, you might need to install an application and configure it as a service so it will start automatically when Windows XP starts. Or perhaps you need to configure the account that a service uses to interact with the system. You might even need to start or stop services running on a computer across the network—or even on the other side of the planet.

Like Windows 2000, Windows XP provides a Services MMC console you can use to manage services for both local and remote computers. In this chapter, I explain how to work with the Services console to start, stop, configure, and perform other management tasks for services. You'll also learn about command-line utilities and techniques you can use to manage services both locally and remotely.

Overview of Services

Many core features in Windows XP are implemented as *services*. A service is a process or set of processes that provides support to other applications. In general terms, a service is an application that performs a specific function in the operating system. Some functions implemented by services include logon, networking, the file system, memory management, scheduling, and print spooling, to name only a few. Most devices in Windows XP are implemented as services through their device drivers.

One of the reasons for implementing operating-system functions and applications as services is to allow the OS to manage them automatically. You can configure services for three different startup modes: automatic, manual, or disabled. The automatic and manual modes allow Windows XP or other services to start a given service.

A second reason for structuring the operating system around services is to provide to the OS a high degree of modularity. Services allow the operating system to be built of relatively small and easily manageable core components that can be replaced, upgraded, or supplemented easily without affecting other operating system components. The NTFS file system, for example, is implemented as a service. Other services interact with NTFS to provide other functions. For example, Encrypting File System is a separate service that works in conjunction with NTFS to handle file and folder encryption and decryption.

Another reason for implementing applications as services is to allow them to interact with the operating system within a given security context. Most services interact with the OS using the System account, but there are situations in which you might use a different account for a particular service. For example, the components of a server application such as Exchange Server sometimes require security settings different from the System account or other account under which it might run. So you can create an account with the necessary rights and privileges and let the application use that account to log on and interact with the system.

Why is it important to understand services and how to manage them? If you're a casual user, it probably isn't important. If you need to more closely manage your system or other systems across the network, however, managing services is a core administrative task. You might need to disable a service that is preventing a system from booting properly. You might need to stop a service temporarily while you make system changes. Or maybe you need to install or remove a service. Whatever the case, Windows XP provides a handful of different resources to help you accomplish these tasks. The one you'll use most often is the Services console.

Tips for Working in the Services Console

The Services console is the tool you'll use most often to manage services locally. Services is a snap-in under the Computer Management console. To open the Computer Management console, right-click My Computer on the Start menu and choose Manage. Then, expand the Services And Applications branch to access the Services branch. You can also click Start ➢ All Programs ➢ Administrative Tools ➢ Services to open this console as a standalone console, as shown in Figure 16.1.

NOTE   This chapter covers most, but not all, of the options and functions in the Services console. For information on creating a custom view in the Services console, see the discussion of taskpads in Chapter 15.

FIGURE 16.1:

FIGURE 16.1:

Use the Services
console to manage
services.

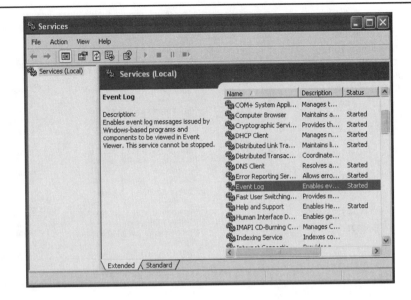

Managing the View

One change in the Services console from Windows 2000 is the addition of the Extended tab
in the right pane. In this view (called a *taskpad*), Windows XP gives you additional information about the selected service, as well as quick links to start and stop the service. The Standard view only lists the five standard columns for each service, which include Name,
Description, Status, Startup Type, and Log On As.

> **TIP** Choose View and then select a different view option to switch among Details (the default
> view), Large Icons, Small Icons, and List.

By default, the Services console sorts the services by the Name column, which is useful
when you want to work with a specific service. However, you can sort the console using the
other columns, as well. For example, whenever I reboot a server, I like to check the Services
console to verify that all of the services that are configured for Automatic startup are running. The easiest way to do that is to click the Startup Type column to re-sort the service list,
as shown in Figure 16.2. I can scan through the list, looking at all of the Automatic services
to make sure they are all started.

> **SEE ALSO** For details on customizing the MMC console, see Chapter 15.

FIGURE 16.2:

Sort the Services console by Startup Type to quickly determine if all automatic services are started.

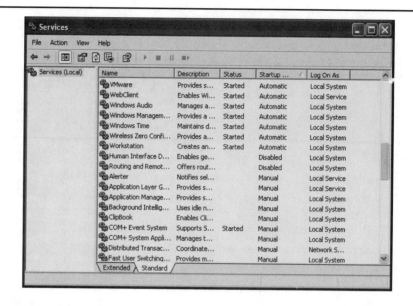

Exporting the List of Services

Occasionally you might find it useful to be able to export a list of the services on a system. For example, maybe you want to create a support database that provides additional information about each service for your support staff and advanced users. Or maybe you need to create a report and need to include a service list in that report.

You can use the Services console to export a list of a system's services to a text file. To do so, open the console and choose Action ➤ Export List to open the Export List dialog box. Select a path and file name for the text file, then select the desired file format from the Save As Type drop-down list. You can choose either comma-delimited or tab-delimited, in either ASCII or Unicode, depending on the requirements of the application in which you'll be using or importing the list. Then click Save to save the file.

TIP   Choose the format for the exported text file according to the application in which you'll use the data. Most database and spreadsheet programs can import both tab- and comma-delimited files.

Configuring Service Startup

Each service has several properties, one of which is its startup type. The startup type determines how (or if) the service can be started. You can configure a service for one of these types:

Automatic   This startup type causes the service to start when the system starts.

Manual   Services with this startup type can be started manually by a user or automatically by a dependent service. They do not start automatically when the system starts.

Disabled   This startup type prevents the service from being started by a user, the system, or a dependent service.

NOTE   The Start button on the General tab of the service's property sheet is dimmed if the startup type is set to Disabled. If you need to start a disabled service, first set its startup type to Manual.

If you want a service to start automatically when the system starts, set its startup type to Automatic. For example, you might want to be able to receive faxes through the Fax service, so you would configure it for Automatic startup. Using this same example, you might set the Fax service to Manual or Disabled if you don't want the computer to receive faxes.

To configure service startup, open the Services console and double-click the service you want to manage. On the General tab (Figure 16.3), select the desired type from the Startup Type drop-down list. If you have no other changes to make, click OK to close the dialog box.

TIP   You can set service properties through Recovery Console as well as the Services console, which is handy when you need to disable a service that is preventing a normal boot. See the section "Managing Services from a Console" later in this chapter for more details. See Chapter 47 for details on RC.

FIGURE 16.3:

Configure service startup on the General page.

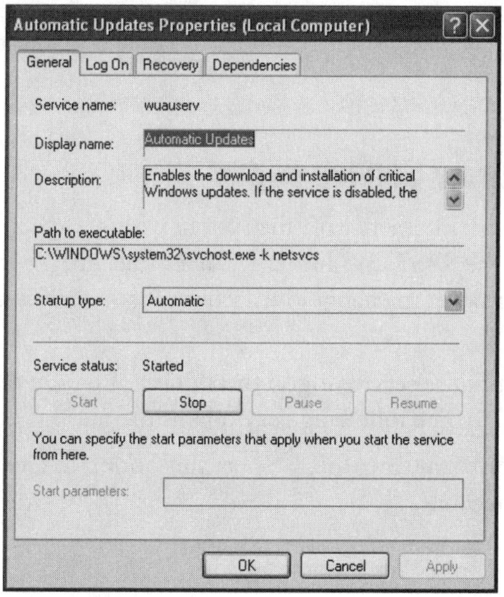

In addition to configuring startup for a service, you can enable or disable a service for a specific hardware profile. For example, you might want your notebook to receive faxes when it's connected to a docking station at the office but not when you're on the road. So you could disable the Fax service for the computer's Undocked profile.

To configure service behavior for a hardware profile, open the Services console and then open the properties for the service. Click the Log On tab (Figure 16.4), select the hardware profile, and click Enable or Disable, as needed.

FIGURE 16.4:

You can enable or disable a service for a particular hardware profile.

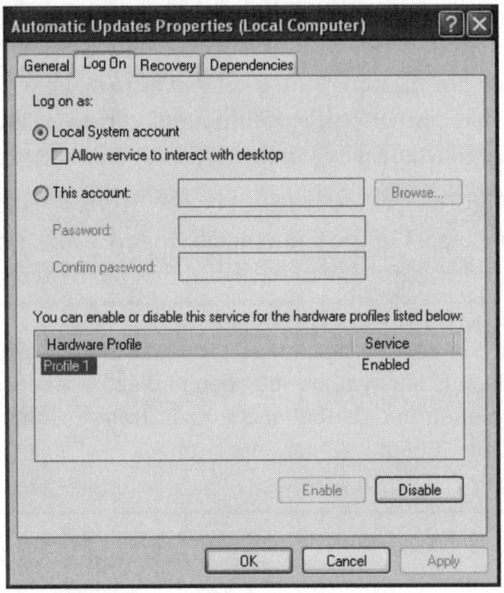

Configuring Service Logon

Each service interacts with the system within a specific security context. Most services log on using the SYSTEM account. That's fine with most services. In some situations, however, you might want to change the account that a service uses to authenticate with the operating system.

You configure service logon through the Log On tab of the service's properties, shown in Figure 16.4. The following list explains the options on this page that apply to service logon:

Local System Account   Select this option to have the service log on using the local SYSTEM account.

Allow Service To Interact With Desktop   Select this option if you want to be able to interact with the service when it is running.

This Account   Use this option to specify an account other than the SYSTEM account for service logon.

Browse   Click to display the Select User dialog box (Figure 16.5), which you use to select a local user or built-in security principal for the service.

Password / Confirm Password   Enter and confirm the password associated with the account you specified with the This Account option.

FIGURE 16.5:

Use the Select User dialog box to browse for and choose the account you want to use for the service.

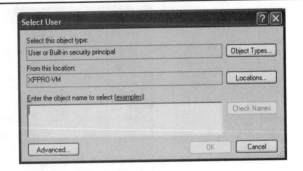

TIP   You don't have to browse for an account if you already know the account name. Just click in the text box beside the This Account option and enter the account name.

Configuring Recovery Options

You'll find that most services keeping running just fine once they are started. Occasionally, however, a service might fail because of problems with the service itself or with an application that relies on the service. In most cases, you don't want the service to just stop and not attempt to recover from the failure, but rather you want it to attempt a restart, generate a notification, or take other appropriate action. You can configure *service recovery* to help Windows XP handle service failures gracefully.

You configure service recovery through the Recovery tab of the service's properties sheet. As Figure 16.6 shows, you can specify the action that Windows XP takes for the first failure instance, for the second failure, and for subsequent failures. Your choices here are described in the following sections.

Service Failure Options

You can choose an option for each failure situation. These options are:

Take No Action   Windows XP does not attempt to recover or restart the service.

Restart The Service   Windows XP will attempt to restart the service after a failure.

Run A File   Windows XP executes the program you specify in the Run Program section of the tab.

Reboot The Computer   Windows XP will reboot the computer if the service fails.

FIGURE 16.6:

Use the Recovery tab to specify how a service should react to a service failure.

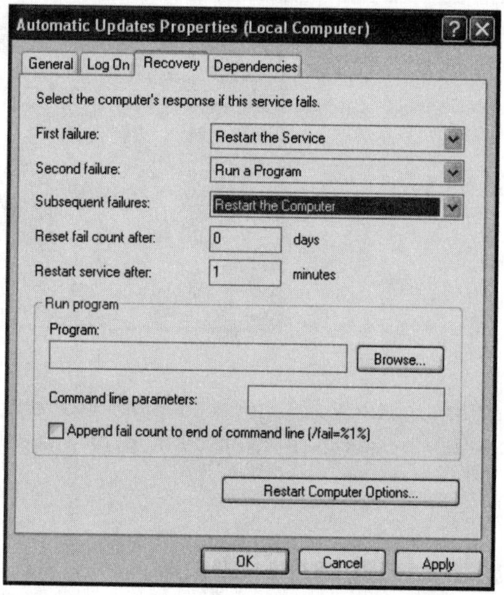

Use the Reset Fail Count After option to specify, in days, when Windows XP should reset the fail counter for the service back to zero. If you select Restart The Service for one of the three failure events, use the Restart Service After option to specify the number of minutes that you want Windows XP to wait before restarting the service. Increase this value if the system needs time to stabilize after the service fails or if the service has dependent services that stop when it fails, giving the other services time to stop before you restart this one.

The Run A Program Option

The ability to run a program on a service failure can be a very valuable tool for handling the service shutdown gracefully. For example, you might use a program to generate an e-mail or pager notification when the service fails, so you'll know about it right away. This is generally more important with servers than with workstations, but the ability is there in Windows XP Professional and Windows XP Home Edition, nonetheless.

To run a program upon service failure, first select the Run A Program option for the desired failure (first, second, or subsequent). Then click in the Program text box and enter the path to the program's executable file, or click Browse to browse for it. If the program requires any additional command-line parameters (such as an e-mail address or pager number), enter that information in the Command Line Parameters text box. Finally, if the program accepts the fail count as a command-line parameter, select the option Append Fail Count To End Of Command Line. Windows XP will append /fail=fc to the command, where *fc* is replaced by the fail count. This allows the specified program to carry out a particular action based on the fail count value.

NOTE   A program must be written specifically to handle the /fail switch.

The Restart The Computer Option

If you choose the option Restart The Computer for a service, Windows XP will reboot the computer if the service fails. You can configure options that specify how soon the computer reboots and whether or not it generates a message before it restarts. For example, assume you're using a Windows XP Professional computer as a file server for a small network. You want everyone on the network to receive a notice five minutes before the server reboots, giving them time to save their documents.

To configure these options, select Restart The Computer from the drop-down list, then click Restart Computer Options to display the Restart Computer Options dialog box. Specify the number of minutes for the restart delay, and select the Before Restart option. Then, type in the text box the message you want others to receive when the service fails. Windows XP automatically provides a default message that you can edit as needed. Click OK and close the service's dialog box.

TIP   Other computers must be running the Alerter service to receive notifications. For that reason, you might want to configure the Alerter service on all computers for Automatic startup type.

Managing Services Remotely

You aren't limited to managing only services on the local computer. In many situations, you might need to manage services for other computers across the network. For example, maybe you need to turn on the Alerter service for all of the computers in the office, but you don't want to have to go to each one physically to do so. Instead, you can start or configure the service remotely from your own workstation.

Configuring Remote Service with the Services Console

You can use the Services console on the local computer to manage services on a remote computer. You have most of the same options and capabilities managing a remote computer as you do when managing the local computer.

To manage a remote computer's services through the Services console, first open the Computer Management console on your local computer. You can right-click My Computer and choose Manage to open the console.

In the console, right-click the Computer Management (Local) branch in the left pane and choose Connect To Another Computer to display the Select Computer dialog box (Figure 16.7). You can enter the computer name in the dialog box or click Browse to browse the network for the computer. After you connect to the remote computer the branch name changes to Computer Management (*computer*), where *computer* is the name of the computer you're managing. At this point, you can manage services just as you would for the local computer. Double-click the service in question and set its properties as needed through its dialog box.

FIGURE 16.7:

The Computer Management console allows you to manage a remote computer as well as the local computer.

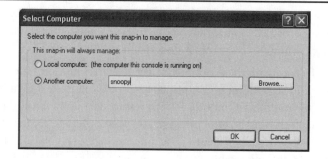

Managing Remote Services from a Console

A second method for managing remote services is to use a console session. However, this requires one of two approaches: either the remote computer must be running as a Telnet server, or you need to use a utility included in the Windows XP Resource Kit.

To use the Telnet approach, you first need to configure the remote computer to function as a Telnet server. Once the remote computer is running the telnet service, you can open a Telnet session on your local computer to the remote computer. The Telnet session is essentially a remote console session. You can then use the net command to start, stop, and otherwise manage services. The net command is explained in a later section, "Managing Services from a Console."

SEE ALSO Chapter 40 explains the ins and outs of setting up a Telnet server.

A second approach is to use the NETSVC.EXE utility included in the Windows XP Resource Kit. You can use netsvc to list installed services, query service status, and start, stop, pause, and continue a service on a remote computer. The syntax for the netsvc command is:

```
netsvc servicename \\computername /command
```

TIP The Microsoft Windows XP Resource Kit is available directly from Microsoft and from book and software retailers. You can view the Resource Kit documentation online and download Resource Kit tools from the Microsoft site at www.microsoft.com/technet/treeview/default.asp?url=/technet/prodtechnol/winxppro/Default.asp.

For example, you would use the following command to start the Alerter service on a computer named SNOOPY:

```
netsvc alerter \\snoopy /start
```

TIP If you're not sure of a particular service's name, use the /list parameter to view the list of installed services.

When you use netsvc, keep in mind that many services have a display name that is different from their service name. For example, the Internet Connection Sharing service (the display name) has the service name SharedAccess. You can use either the display name or the service name with netsvc. Just enclose the display name in quotes if it contains spaces.

TIP For a complete list of netsvc commands and its syntax, execute the command **netsvc /?** in a console.

Managing Services with Remote Desktop Connection

A third option for managing services remotely is Remote Desktop Connection, which allows a client running any version of Windows XP to connect to a computer running Windows XP Professional or a server platform, such as Windows 2000 Server, with Terminal Services installed. In the case of Windows XP Professional, the remote computer must have Remote Desktop Connection enabled for incoming connections.

SEE ALSO You enable incoming remote connections through the Remote tab of the properties for My Computer. See Chapter 31 for detailed information on configuring and using Remote Desktop Connection.

When you connect to a Windows 2000 Professional computer with Remote Desktop Connection, the remote computer's current local logon session is terminated. So using this method works best if there is no one using the computer at the time or the user won't be inconvenienced by being kicked off while you manage the services. Use one of the methods described in the preceding two sections if you don't want to force the remote user to log off.

> **TIP** You manage services through Remote Desktop Connection in the same way you manage local services. Just open the Services console after you establish the remote connection, or open a console and use console commands to manage the services.

Using Remote Assistance to Manage Services

You can use the Remote Assistance feature in Windows XP to manage services remotely. However, this method requires that both the local and remote computers be set up with Microsoft .NET Passports (www.passport.com), and the remote user must request assistance from you. This method is useful when you need to configure services across the Internet and do not have a VPN or Telnet connection to the remote computer.

Managing Services from a Console

You can manage services from a command console as well as from the Services GUI console. Using a command console is a good option if you simply prefer to work in the console rather than the GUI or if you need to manage services through a Telnet session. You can manage services from a console in a regular Windows XP session or from the Recovery Console. Your options are somewhat different for each scenario.

Managing Services in a Windows XP Session

You use the net command to manage services from a command console, whether that console is running on the local computer or you are connected to a remote computer through a telnet session. The net start command lets you view a list of running services and start a service that is currently stopped. Use net start by itself to view the list of running services or use the following syntax to start a service:

    net start *ServiceName*

Replace *ServiceName* with the service or display name of the service. If you specify the display name, enclose it in quotes if it contains spaces.

To stop a service, use the net stop command:

    net stop *ServiceName*

Replace *ServiceName* with the service or display name of the service you want to stop.

Managing Services from Recovery Console

Recovery Console (RC) provides a somewhat different set of tools for managing services. The `disable` command, for example, lets you disable a service. This has the same effect as setting its startup type to Disabled in the GUI. Use the following syntax to disable a service or device driver: `disable` *name*. Replace *name* with the name of the service or device driver you want to disable.

You can use the `enable` command to enable a service that is currently disabled. Unlike the `disable` command, `enable` offers a few options. The syntax for `enable` is:

```
enable {ServiceName | DeviceDriverName} [StartupType]
```

Replace *ServiceName* or *DeviceDriverName* with the name of the service or device driver you want to enable. Then, specify one of the following for *StartupType*:

SERVICE_BOOT_START   Use this option to start a device driver when the system boots.

SERVICE_SYSTEM_START   Use this option to start a device driver when Windows XP starts.

SERVICE_AUTO_START   This option corresponds to the Automatic startup type in the GUI.

SERVICE_DEMAND_START   This option corresponds to the Manual startup type in the GUI.

The third RC command you can use to manage services is `listsvc`, which lists the services available on the computer. The `listsvc` command has no options or parameters, but you can pipe it to the `more` command to display one page at a time:

```
listsvc | more
```

SEE ALSO   See Chapter 47 for details on installing and using Recovery Console.

CHAPTER 17

Monitoring Events

The Windows XP operating system could be considered a busy place, with events of all kinds happening all the time. Some of those events are routine, and some are not. One key to good system management is to keep a historical record of the routine events and know when non-routine events occur so you can respond to them. Windows XP provides two main tools for monitoring events: the Event Viewer and Dr. Watson.

The Event Viewer lets you view events related to the system, applications, and security. Some server applications add their own event logs to the system, and you can view these with the Event Viewer, as well. Applications running under Windows XP Professional or Home Edition, however, are unlikely to have their own event logs but instead will log their events to the global Application event log. This chapter will help you become more familiar with the Windows XP logs, the information they contain, and how to manage those logs.

Dr. Watson, on the other hand, is a debugging tool. Unless you are a programmer, it's unlikely that you will do much with Dr. Watson other than collect some debugging information to send to a technical support engineer. This chapter explains how to do just that with Dr. Watson and will help you understand some of the information that it gathers.

Tips for Working in the Event Viewer

You can open the Event Viewer as a stand-alone console (Figure 17.1) or as a snap-in in the Computer Management console. Double-click the Event Viewer in the Administrative Tools folder to open the Event Viewer, or right-click My Computer, choose Manage, and click the Event Viewer branch.

TIP The Administrative Tools folder doesn't appear on the Start menu or in the All Programs menu by default. You can turn on the Administrative Tools menu through the properties for the Taskbar (right-click the Taskbar and choose Properties).

As Figure 17.1 shows, there are three standard logs: Application, Security, and System. The Application log is where applications—including many of the accessories and tools that are included with Windows XP—write status, error, and other information. This is the log you will use most often when you're trying to troubleshoot a problem with an application.

The Security log maintains security-related events such as logon, logoff, policy change, and a variety of other security/authentication events. You'll use this log to track when other users connect to your computer and monitor other aspects of system security.

SEE ALSO Chapter 19 explains how to configure auditing, which allows you to monitor specific actions such as disk access, logon/logoff, and other important system events and changes.

FIGURE 17.1:

Use the Event Viewer to view information about events that occur in Windows XP.

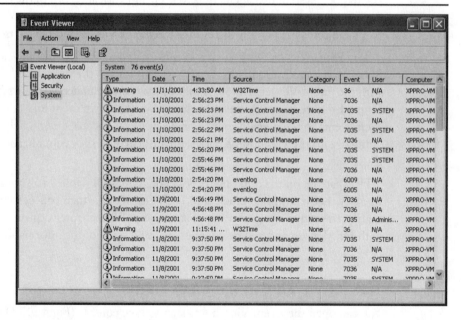

The System log maintains system-wide events that are not related specifically to security or an application. For example, the System log keeps track of when services start and stop, when the system is rebooted, when Remote Assistance sessions start and stop, and many other system-related events. You'll use the System log when troubleshooting system-wide problems, such as a service failing.

To view an event's properties, just double-click the event, or select the event and choose Action ➤ Properties, to display the properties dialog box for the service. Figure 17.2 shows a typical event dialog box.

The event's dialog box contains several items of information about the event:

Date / Time   These two fields show the date and time the event occurred. The Event Viewer by default sorts the event list by date and time, with the most recent events at the top.

Type   This field shows the type of event being logged. The Event Log uses five different event types:

> **Error**   An error indicates a problem that could cause lost data or lost functionality, such as a service failing to start or a service shutting down.

> **Warning**   A warning indicates an item that could cause problems but is not as significant as an error. Examples of events that generate a warning are a disk nearing capacity or the time service being unable to synchronize with a time server.

FIGURE 17.2:

An event's dialog box shows date, time, event ID, and other information about the event.

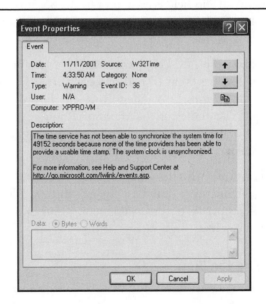

> **Information**   These offer information about successful events for an application, service, or driver. For example, when a service starts successfully, Windows XP logs an Information event to the System log.

> **Success Audit**   These mark successful security events such as logon, logoff, and audited disk access.

> **Failure Audit**   These mark unsuccessful security events. Failure audit events give you an easy way to monitor for attempted security breaches and troubleshoot authentication and other security-related problems.

User / Computer   The User field indicates the security context in which the event occurred. Most system services run in the context of the System account, and events related to these services will list the System account as the user. Application events typically list the application name. The Computer field indicates the computer on which the event occurred. This will almost always be the name of the local computer unless you are managing a remote computer's event logs.

Source   This field lists the application or system component that generated the event. For example, when you install a new application from a Windows Installer package, you'll probably see at least a corresponding event with MsInstaller as the source. Service Control Manager is another common source. Almost all service-related events will have Service Control Manager as the source.

Category   This field is used most by the Security log, but can appear in the other logs, as well. This field categorizes the event with labels such as Policy Change, System Event, and Account Logon.

Event ID   This field uniquely identifies a specific event. For example, a successful account logon is event ID 680, and event ID 7036 indicates a successful service startup. The event ID is useful for identifying specific problems and troubleshooting events. For example, you can search the Microsoft Knowledge Base for specific event IDs associated with a particular component, application, or service to help determine the specific cause of the problem.

Description   This field usually offers the most information. For example, the Description field for a successful audit logon/logoff event lists the user, domain, and other authentication properties for the logon event. Think of the Description field as providing details about the event.

Managing the View

The Event Viewer, like most Microsoft Management Console consoles, lets you sort the view using the various columns displayed in the log. For example, you can click the Date or Time fields to sort the view by those fields. When you're looking for events with a specific ID, you can click the Event column to sort the event list.

TIP   You can choose View ➢ Newest First or Oldest First to specify the chronological order of events in the list.

In addition to sorting the view by column, you can also specify which columns the Event Viewer displays. To do so, select a log and choose View ➢ Add/Remove Columns; use the resulting dialog box to add or remove columns from the view. Select a column and use the Move Up and Move Down buttons to change the column order. For example, you might prefer to have the Date column displayed first rather than the Type column.

Filtering the List

When you're trying to troubleshoot a problem or locate specific events, you can simplify the task by *filtering* the event log. For example, you might want to view only errors and warnings. Or maybe you want to find all events with a specific ID, or all events generated by a specific source. To set a filter, open the log you want to use and choose View ➢ Filter to open a properties sheet similar to the one shown in Figure 17.3.

FIGURE 17.3:

Use the Filter tab to specify filter criteria for the view.

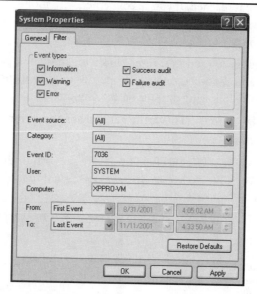

The options on the Filter tab are mostly self-explanatory. Select the event type(s) you want to include in the view, and then select source, category, or other criteria to define the filter. Click OK to apply the filter and modify the view. To clear the filter, choose View ➢ All Records.

Using Multiple Views of a Log

In some situations, it's helpful to be able to view the contents of the log in more than one way at a time. For example, maybe you want to view errors in one view and warnings in another. Whatever the case, you can easily open a new view and configure its view settings as needed. To open a new view, select a log and choose Actions ➢ New Log View. Or, just right-click a log and choose New Log View. Select a view and click the Delete button on the toolbar to close the extra view.

NOTE   You can't delete the standard views.

Managing Log Settings

Each log has several settings that determine how large the log can be, what happens when the maximum size is reached, its display name and location on disk, and other properties. The default size for each log is 512 KB, and Event Viewer overwrites events when the maximum size is reached. If you're concerned with monitoring system security or keeping a longer historical record of the events that occur on a particular computer, you should modify the log settings.

To change log settings, right-click a log in the left pane and choose Properties, or select the log and choose Actions ➢ Properties to open its properties sheet (Figure 17.4). You can change the following options on the General tab:

Display Name   This is the name that appears for the log in the left pane of the Event Viewer.

Log Name   Use this field to specify the path to the log file and the file name. The default location is the *%systemroot%*\system32\config folder.

FIGURE 17.4:

Use the log's properties sheet to change maximum log size and other properties that determine how the log functions.

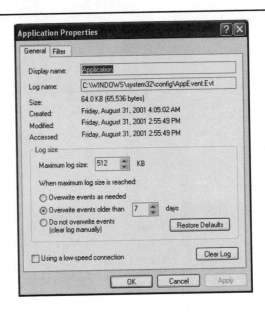

Maximum Log Size   Use this control to specify the maximum size for the log. There is no direct correlation between maximum log size and any time period. A misbehaving service or application could fill a large log file within minutes (although this isn't common). Set the size according to the amount of space you want to allocate to the log. I typically use a log size of 4 MB on a server and the default 512 KB size for workstations.

Overwrite Events as Needed   Choose this option to allow the Event Viewer to overwrite old events with new ones when the log reaches the maximum capacity.

Overwrite Events Older Than *n* Days   Choose this option to allow the Event Viewer to overwrite events older than the specified number of days when the log reaches the maximum capacity. This option lets you specify a "time window" for the log.

Do Not Overwrite Events   Choose this option if you don't want the Event Viewer to overwrite any events. You'll have to clear the log manually when it reaches maximum capacity.

Use A Low-Speed Connection   Use this option if you're viewing the log across a slow connection such as a dial-up. The Event Viewer won't automatically download event information when this option is in effect, but instead waits until you actually open an event.

Restore Defaults   Click to restore the log to its default settings.

Clear Log   Click to clear all events from the log.

TIP	You should save the contents of the log to a file before clearing it, as explained in the next section.

Managing Log Files

As I explained in the previous section, the Windows XP event logs have a specific size limit. When the log reaches that limit, the system takes one of three actions: It overwrites the oldest events with new events, overwrites events older than a specified number of days, or does not overwrite events at all. In the last case, Windows XP displays a message that the log is full. It's then up to you to clear the log so Windows can log additional events.

Clearing and Saving Logs

You can clear the event logs at any time—you don't have to wait until they fill up. For example, it's sometimes helpful when you're troubleshooting a problem to clear the logs so you have a clean slate and can easily and quickly identify new events. When you clear a log, however, you will most likely want to save the existing events in case you need to refer back to them later. Saving your logs is particularly important if you later need to track down a security breach.

You can save a log when you clear it, or save the log without clearing it. Right-click a log in the left pane of the Event Viewer and choose Save Log File As. Select the path and file name for the log (the default extension is .evt) and then click Save.

To save the log when you clear it, right-click the log and choose Clear All Events. Event Viewer asks if you want to save the log. Click Yes and enter a path and file name for the log.

In addition to saving and clearing logs, you can also open an existing log file. For example, maybe you're trying to track down that security breach I mentioned earlier. To open an existing log, just right-click Event Viewer (or any existing log) in the left pane and choose Open Log File to display the Open dialog box. Locate and select the file, then select the log type from the Log Type drop-down list. Change the Display Name if you want Event Viewer to use a different name for the log, then click Open.

Exporting Logs to Other Programs

The Windows XP Event Viewer gives you a reasonable amount of flexibility and capability for viewing and filtering the event logs. In some cases, though, you might want to perform more complex filters or queries on the event logs. You can achieve that by exporting the logs to a database such as Microsoft SQL Server or Microsoft Access. You can also export the events to other programs, as long as those programs can import comma- or tab-delimited text files.

Getting Additional Information About Specific Events

When you're troubleshooting a problem that is dropping event messages in the event logs, and you're looking for more information, the most useful clue is the event ID. The second most useful piece of information is the description. With those items in hand, you can begin searching for answers.

One of the first places to search is the Microsoft website. Open the site and search on **event id nnn**, where nnn is the ID number of the event. In most cases you'll turn up at least a handful of documents, and in many cases, several dozen documents.

If you have a copy of the Windows XP Resource Kit (or Windows 2000 Resource Kit), open the *Error and Event Messages* document. You'll find standard messages and event IDs for the System, Application, and Security logs. You can also search Microsoft TechNet or MSDN for the specific ID and/or a string from the event's description.

When researching events for specific applications, you can check the application's documentation for information about the events. Use the event ID and/or description text to search the application's support website.

To export an event log, right-click the log in the left pane of the Event Viewer and choose Export List to open the Export List dialog box. Specify a path and file name and then select the type of file to create from the Save As Type drop-down list. Click Save to save the file. Then, open the target application and import the data from the file.

Troubleshooting STOP Messages

Windows XP generates a STOP message and halts when the kernel detects an unrecoverable error or the CPU detects an unrecoverable hardware error. STOP messages are referred to fondly by administrators as the Blue Screen of Death, or BSOD, because the system prints the message to the screen in white text on a blue background. The server is dead at this point; thus the name. Figure 17.5 shows a typical STOP message.

FIGURE 17.5:

STOP messages offer information about the error that caused the system to halt.

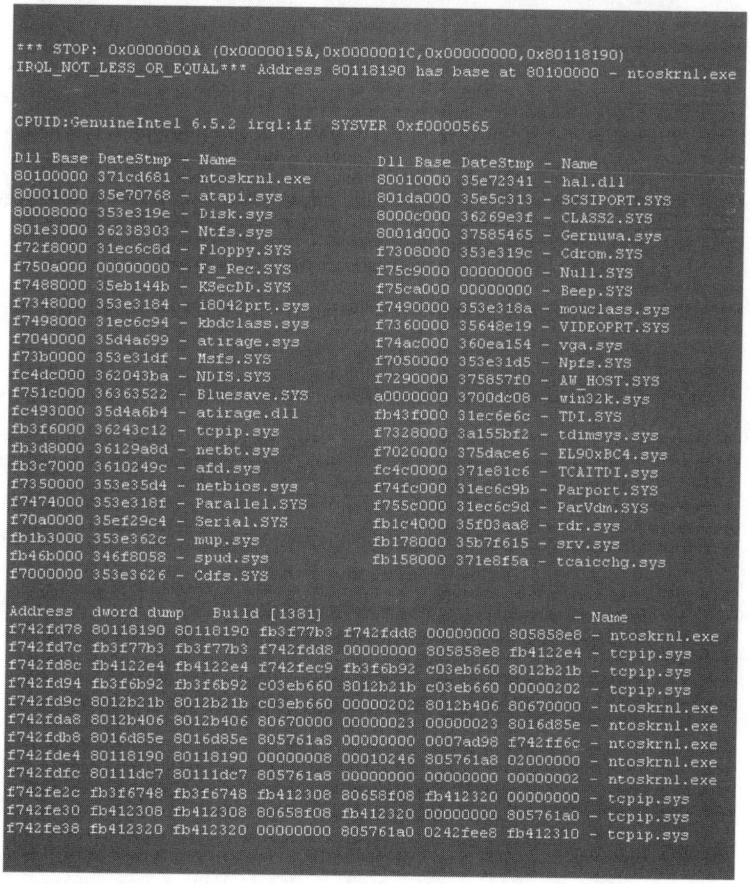

```
*** STOP: 0x0000000A (0x0000015A,0x0000001C,0x00000000,0x80118190)
IRQL_NOT_LESS_OR_EQUAL*** Address 80118190 has base at 80100000 - ntoskrnl.exe


CPUID:GenuineIntel 6.5.2 irql:1f  SYSVER 0xf0000565

Dll Base DateStmp - Name                    Dll Base DateStmp - Name
80100000 371cd681 - ntoskrnl.exe            80010000 35e72341 - hal.dll
80001000 35e70768 - atapi.sys               801da000 35e5c313 - SCSIPORT.SYS
80008000 353e319e - Disk.sys                8000c000 36269e3f - CLASS2.SYS
801e3000 36238303 - Ntfs.sys                8001d000 37585465 - Gernuwa.sys
f72f8000 31ec6c8d - Floppy.SYS              f7308000 353e319c - Cdrom.SYS
f750a000 00000000 - Fs_Rec.SYS              f75c9000 00000000 - Null.SYS
f7488000 35eb144b - KSecDD.SYS              f75ca000 00000000 - Beep.SYS
f7348000 353e3184 - i8042prt.sys            f7490000 353e318a - mouclass.sys
f7498000 31ec6c94 - kbdclass.sys            f7360000 35648e19 - VIDEOPRT.SYS
f7040000 35d4a699 - atirage.sys             f74ac000 360ea154 - vga.sys
f73b0000 353e31df - Msfs.SYS                f7050000 353e31d5 - Npfs.SYS
fc4dc000 362043ba - NDIS.SYS                f7290000 375857f0 - AW_HOST.SYS
f751c000 36363522 - Bluesave.SYS            a0000000 3700dc08 - win32k.sys
fc493000 35d4a6b4 - atirage.dll             fb43f000 31ec6e6c - TDI.SYS
fb3f6000 36243c12 - tcpip.sys               f7328000 3a155bf2 - tdimsys.sys
fb3d8000 36129a8d - netbt.sys               f7020000 375dace6 - EL90xBC4.sys
fb3c7000 3610249c - afd.sys                 fc4c0000 371e81c6 - TCAITDI.sys
f7350000 353e35d4 - netbios.sys             f74fc000 31ec6c9b - Parport.SYS
f7474000 353e318f - Parallel.SYS            f755c000 31ec6c9d - ParVdm.SYS
f70a0000 35ef29c4 - Serial.SYS              fb1c4000 35f03aa8 - rdr.sys
fb1b3000 353e362c - mup.sys                 fb178000 35b7f615 - srv.sys
fb46b000 346f8058 - spud.sys                fb158000 371e8f5a - tcaicchg.sys
f7000000 353e3626 - Cdfs.SYS


Address  dword dump   Build [1381]                           - Name
f742fd78 80118190 80118190 fb3f77b3 f742fdd8 00000000 805858e8 - ntoskrnl.exe
f742fd7c fb3f77b3 fb3f77b3 f742fdd8 00000000 805858e8 fb4122e4 - tcpip.sys
f742fd8c fb4122e4 fb4122e4 f742fec9 fb3f6b92 c03eb660 8012b21b - tcpip.sys
f742fd94 fb3f6b92 fb3f6b92 c03eb660 8012b21b c03eb660 00000202 - tcpip.sys
f742fd9c 8012b21b 8012b21b c03eb660 00000202 8012b406 80670000 - ntoskrnl.exe
f742fda8 8012b406 8012b406 80670000 00000023 00000023 8016d85e - ntoskrnl.exe
f742fdb8 8016d85e 8016d85e 805761a8 00000000 0007ad98 f742ff6c - ntoskrnl.exe
f742fde4 80118190 80118190 00000000 001246 805761a8 02000000 - ntoskrnl.exe
f742fdfc 80111dc7 80111dc7 805761a8 00000000 00000000 00000002 - ntoskrnl.exe
f742fe2c fb3f6748 fb3f6748 fb412308 80658f08 fb412320 00000000 - tcpip.sys
f742fe30 fb412308 fb412308 80658f08 fb412320 00000000 805761a0 - tcpip.sys
f742fe38 fb412320 fb412320 00000000 805761a0 0242fee8 fb412310 - tcpip.sys
```

The STOP message contains three parts: bugcheck information, recommended user action, and debug port information. The bugcheck information, located at the top of the message, provides a value called the bugcheck ID. This information can contain up to four developer-defined parameters enclosed in quotes and includes a symbolic name for the error. A common symbolic name for driver-related errors, for example, is IRQ_NOT_LESS_OR_EQUAL.

The first hexadecimal value in the bugcheck string is often the most useful for identifying the cause of the problem, or at least in finding more information about the potential cause. You can perform a search in Microsoft TechNet, the Knowledge Base on the Microsoft website, or other sources for information about the error. Perform a search on the string **STOP:** *error*, where *error* is the hexadecimal value.

The bugcheck section can also contain the hexadecimal memory address associated with the problem and the device or driver experiencing the problem. This information is useful in helping you narrow the list of possible causes.

The recommended user action section describes steps you can take to try to overcome the problem. Some STOP messages display problem-specific resolution steps, but unfortunately, many display the generic information. In most cases, your first step is to restart the computer to determine if the problem reoccurs. If not, consider yourself lucky. If you see the error again after restarting, you'll need to start troubleshooting the problem. Use the symbolic error name and the hexadecimal value to search the appropriate support site for the STOP message and its potential causes.

TIP   The Windows XP Resource Kit document *Error and Event Messages Help* contains STOP error descriptions, including an explanation of the error and the actions you can take to rectify the problem.

In many situations, the STOP error is caused by installing new hardware or device drivers that are either incompatible with Windows XP or buggy. In these situations, and in situations where the problem is caused by a corrupted Registry, you can boot the system using the Last Known Good Configuration. This replaces the current \HKEY_LOCAL_MACHINE\System\Current-ControlSet Registry branch with a backup copy from the last successful boot, thereby replacing any changes that were made when you installed the new device or device driver.

TIP   To boot from the Last Known Good Configuration, press F8 during boot, select Last Known Good Configuration from the boot menu, and press Enter.

Third-Party Event Management Applications

The Event Viewer is a good tool for browsing and monitoring events on the local computer, but isn't really geared toward in-depth analysis or for gathering information from other computers across the enterprise. There are several third-party tools that extend your ability to monitor and analyze the event logs for both local and remote systems. Most achieve this capability through added services that actively monitor and harvest events from the event logs on multiple systems and then add those events to a database. This gives you the ability not only to view events from a pool of computers, but also to perform much more extensive analysis of events through advanced database queries.

EventAdmin   (Aelita Software, `www.aelita.com`) Works in conjunction with Aelita's Enterprise Directory Reporter product to collect data from Windows, Novell NDS, and Unix platforms. You can use EventAdmin to collect, consolidate, archive, and analyze information from event logs and performance counters. The Reporting Console, included with the product, provides 800 customizable reports.

Argent Guardian   (Argent Software, `www.argent.com`) Provides a very scalable collection and monitoring solution for networks of any size, from small to enterprise. It supports remote and agent-based monitoring of a wide variety of services and applications, not limited to Exchange Server, SQL Server, all Windows event logs, services, SNMP devices, routers and hubs, and NetWare.

LogCaster   (Ripple Technologies, `www.rippletech.com`) A suite of network services that perform real-time monitoring and reporting of Windows event logs, TCP/IP devices and servers, Windows system and application services, SysLog devices (Unix/Linux systems, routers, etc.), and other devices and services. LogCaster stores collected data in ODBC-compliant databases that you can access through any database or web connection or through Crystal Reports, which is included with LogCaster. The product includes over 100 predefined templates, and you can create or modify templates to create custom reports.

Using Dr. Watson

Dr. Watson is a debugging tool that is included with Windows XP. Although you probably won't use Dr. Watson very often, it's a good idea to understand what it is and how it works. You might need to collect debugging information from Dr. Watson to send to support engineers when you're troubleshooting a problem with Windows XP itself or with a specific application. If you know ahead of time how to install debugging symbols, configure Dr. Watson, and collect the resulting data, the support engineer can focus on the problem instead of on helping you set up the system for debugging.

How It Works

Well-designed applications include their own error handlers to detect and perform recovery from specific errors. Here's a simplistic example: If you attempt to open a document file of the wrong type for an application, the error handler prevents the application from opening the file and displays a message to you that the document type can't be used with the application. The difficulty in writing bulletproof programs is anticipating every possible error and incorporating code in the application's error handler(s) to catch and deal with the error so it doesn't crash the program or, worse yet, your system.

An *unhandled error* is one that isn't detected or handled by the application's error handler. When unhandled error occurs, Windows XP looks in the Registry \HKEY_LOCAL_MACHINE\ Software\Microsoft\Windows NT\CurrentVersion\AeDebug for a program error debugger. The value Debugger in this key defines the error handler (and points by default to Dr. Watson). The Auto value determines how the debugger functions:

Value	Description
0	The system displays a dialog box indicating that an error has occurred and includes two buttons, OK and Cancel. Click OK to terminate the program or Cancel to start the debugger.
1	The system automatically starts the debugger without displaying the informational message. This is the default setting.

Although you can manually modify the Registry to configure these default settings, there's an easier way. Open a command console and type the following command:

```
drwtsn32 -i
```

This means that Dr. Watson starts automatically if an application crash occurs. It creates a text-based log file named Drwtsn32.log in the \Documents and Settings\All Users\ Application Data\Microsoft\Dr Watson folder, and you can view the file with Notepad or any other text editor. Dr. Watson also can optionally create a binary crash dump file that a support engineer can load into a debugger to analyze the cause of the crash. Dr. Watson also writes an event to the Application log, which you can view with the Event Viewer.

TIP   You can change the log and crash dump name and path, as explained a little later in this section.

Installing Debugging Symbols

Without any other configuration, Dr. Watson collects and logs useful but somewhat limited information. In order to capture additional and more targeted information, you need to install debug symbols on the system. You can download these symbol files from www.microsoft.com/ddk/debugging/symbols.asp.

Installing the debugging symbols is a two-step process. First, you need to copy the symbols to a folder on the system. Then, you need to set an environment variable to point Windows XP to them. So, first create the folder *%systemroot%*\symbols, then copy the entire symbol folder/ file structure to this folder.

Next, right-click My Computer and choose Properties to display the System Properties sheet, then click the Advanced tab and click Environment Variables to display the Environment Variables dialog box shown in Figure 17.6.

FIGURE 17.6:

Add the environment variable through the Environment Variables dialog box.

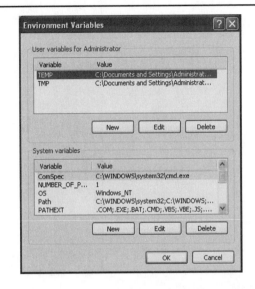

Under the System Variables list, click New to open the New System Variable dialog box. Type **_NT_SYMBOL_PATH** in the Variable Name text box, and then enter the path **%systemroot%\symbols** in the Variable Value text box.

In addition to the Windows XP symbols, you can also install debug symbols for specific applications. This is generally most common on a server but is also possible for Windows XP Professional. You install these application debug symbols in much the same way as the system symbols. Copy the symbol files to their own directory, and then add the path to the _NT_SYMBOL_PATH environment variable, separating each path from the next by a semicolon.

Configuring Dr. Watson

You can configure several options that control the way Dr. Watson functions. To do so, click Start ➢ Run and enter **drwtsn32.exe** to display the dialog box shown in Figure 17.7. The options you can configure are:

Log File Path   This is the path to Dr. Watson's log file. The default path is

```
\Documents and Settings\All Users\Application Data\Microsoft\Dr Watson
```

There is generally no reason to change the path unless you want to store the log in a secure folder. However, you need to make sure the system has the necessary permissions to write to the folder. The log file name is `Drwtsn32.log`.

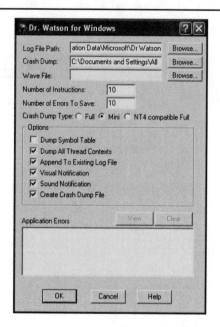

Crash Dump   If the Create Crash Dump File is enabled, you can specify the path for the binary crash dump file. The default location is the same as for the log file. The crash dump file can be quite large (many megabytes), so make sure you choose a location on a volume with adequate space.

Wave File   If you enable the Sound Notification option, use the Wave File text box to specify the path to the WAV file that you want Windows XP to play when the error occurs.

Number Of Instructions   This value specifies the number of instructions before and after the current program counter that Dr. Watson will disassemble for each thread state dump.

Number Of Errors To Save   This value specifies the maximum number of errors that Dr. Watson records in the log file. This number naturally affects the overall log size.

Crash Dump Type   Use this option to specify the type of crash dump file to capture. Pick the type requested by the support engineer.

Dump Symbol Table   You can enable this option to have Dr. Watson include the symbol dump table, which includes the address and name for each symbol, in the dump file. Including the symbols considerably increases the size of the file.

Dump All Thread Contexts   Select this option to have Dr. Watson log the state for each thread in the program that generated the error. If you deselect this option, Dr. Watson logs the state of only the thread that caused the error.

Append To Existing Log File   Enable this option to have Dr. Watson append each new crash log to the existing log file. Deselect the option if you want Dr. Watson to overwrite the existing log. Appending to the file can make it very large, so a good practice is to immediately move the log file to a different folder for analysis as soon as the dump occurs. The next crash will then create a new log file.

Visual Notification   Select this option to have Dr. Watson display a dialog box when the error occurs. The dialog box closes by itself after five minutes if you don't close it yourself.

Sound Notification   Select this option to have Dr. Watson play the WAV file specified in the Wave File text box when the error occurs.

Create Crash Dump File   Select this option to have Dr. Watson create the crash dump file when the error occurs. If this option is not selected, Dr. Watson only creates the log file.

Application Errors   This text box displays all of the errors for the Event Viewer and Dr. Watson from the system's event logs.

Collecting and Submitting the Data

Unless you are a developer, you will likely not work with the log and crash dump files yourself but will instead send them to a support engineer, who will use a debugger to troubleshoot the error and hopefully provide a fix for the problem. I've dealt with Microsoft on several support issues that required me to send debug files to a support engineer. Generally, the engineer provides an FTP site you can use to upload the files, or will sometimes have you e-mail the files, depending on the size. Because the files can be so large, you'll need to compress the files using a tool such as WinZip or PKZip. Send the files on their way and try to wait patiently while the engineer resolves the problem.

CHAPTER 18

Monitoring Performance

Regardless of the operating system or PC we use, many of us treat optimal system performance like the digital equivalent of the Holy Grail: always pursued yet difficult to obtain. We worry that certain processes slow us down, wonder whether we can eke out just a bit more speed, and debate whether a change in memory or CPU is having the effect we want. This means we need ways to monitor the behavior of various aspects of our system as it performs its work. Tools within Windows XP aid you in doing just that.

For those of you primarily familiar with the consumer side of Windows (95/98/Me), you realize that measures of operating performance in the form of utilities usually fell to external applications that you found and installed to allow you to monitor CPU utilization, disk usage, network efficiency, and the like. However, Windows NT 4.0 and later have offered a feature called a system monitor and at least a core set of measurement checkers, called counters, that allow you to keep an eye on key functions that give you an idea of your system's activity. Those already familiar with NT and 2000's Performance monitoring should be able to transition quickly to the changes here, but may want to review this chapter to refresh their memory.

The Windows XP Performance tool has two primary components: System Monitor, which reports levels of real-time activity for critical features such as CPU, disk, available memory, and network; and Performance Logs And Alerts, used to track user-configured data about system performance and to notify you when potentially important situations arise. Both are available from the Performance option in Administrative Tools in Control Panel.

Windows XP, like add-on utilities that can monitor this, works by *sampling* data, or taking a discrete time-slice representation of the actual activity of the feature or function being monitored. For some tests, you might want samples taken every 5 seconds, while for others, you may want to sample far more rarely. With many options, you can adjust the sampling rate to fit the situation.

In this chapter, you'll learn about using System Monitor and the Performance Logs And Alerts features to help you understand how your system is performing as you work. As you read, don't lose sight of the fact that this data can be terribly useful not just in overall efficiency, but in monitoring components and services as you troubleshoot problems on that system.

Before You Monitor Performance

Before you begin a systematic analysis of your overall performance and establish a baseline efficiency level from which you can compare earlier and later results, Microsoft recommends you take certain steps spelled out in Help under the Performance section. These include:

- Adjusting the paging file to 1.5 times the amount of physical memory installed on the system
- Turning off any unnecessary services
- Turning off screensavers
- Using Registry Editor to check and note the non-zero values for the following subkeys:

    ```
    \HKEY_LOCAL_MACHINE\SYSTEM\CurrentControlSet\Control\SessionManager\
    Memory Management
    \HKEY_LOCAL_MACHINE\SYSTEM\CurrentControlSet\Services\LanmanServer\
    Parameters
    ```

> **NOTE**   As you begin to work, realize, too, that it will be important for you to identify which information to monitor or which log is required to produce the data you most need to analyze. If you're trying to track specific memory utilization, for example, there are many options that simply won't be necessary to employ, and you may not want to clutter your resources (system and mental) in watching them. You'll learn more about the best counters to use in the next section.

Using System Monitor to Check Real-Time Performance

System Monitor is the part of XP performance monitoring that allows you to get a real-time view of specific aspects of a system or network's activity. Simply put, System Monitor differs from Performance Logs And Alerts in that you use it to determine what's happening *now*, rather than the more historical view offered by Performance Logs (described in detail in the next section). In this way, they complement each other in helping you perform your analysis.

However, in using either or both tools, there are some basic concepts you must understand. The work of both is based on items called *performance objects* and *performance counters*.

Performance objects refer to categories of data Windows XP checks through the Windows Registry and collects from monitoring the behavior of select components installed to your system, such as the CPU (processor), memory, disks, and so on. For each performance object, there exists a set of performance counters that can be applied to the object to measure its activity or efficiency.

Here's an example: You want to check the bandwidth and the number of packets received per second on your network interface. The Network Interface would be the performance object you select, and from that, you would choose to monitor the Current Bandwidth counter and the Packets Received/sec counter (from a drop-down list of 17 counters).

NOTE　Performance objects aren't exclusively hardware: processes and services (such as Indexing, Terminal, and RSVP) qualify as well, and both allow you to choose counters under such objects to measure.

Configuring System Monitor

Open System Monitor by choosing Administrative Tools in Control Panel, and clicking Performance. Then select System Monitor from the Console Root.

TIP　To open System Monitor from the command line, type **perfmon.msc**.

System Monitor installs with certain basic information already being monitored, as shown in Figure 18.1. These include CPU usage (% Processor), the average disk queue length for the physical disk in use, and the number of pages per second moving in and out of memory.

Familiarize yourself with the System Monitor screen, from the selections available on the Toolbar in the Monitor window itself (major functions are described under Views), to the information display window (in which your view is presented in one of the three formats listed next), to the statistics windows, and the object information panel at the bottom (not available in Report view). Then choose a view that works best for you.

FIGURE 18.1:

System Monitor defaults to monitoring several counters.

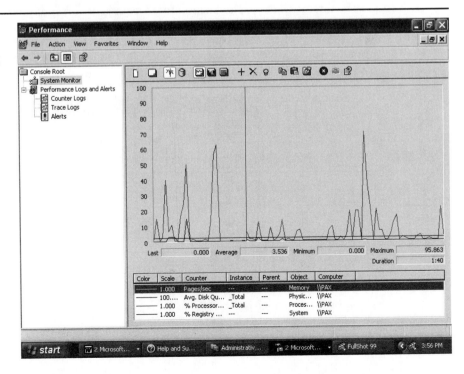

Different Views

You can observe your System Monitor information in one of three different views:

Graph   (Ctrl+G, or the Graph icon on the Toolbar) Records the typical peaks and valleys graphical representations of the data being tracked.

Histogram   (Ctrl+B, or the Bar Chart icon on the Toolbar) Reports the data in classic bar format.

Report   (Ctrl+R, or the Report icon on the Toolbar) Shows the data in text format.

Also important, you can perform the following key functions using these keys or icons:

Action	Keyboard Shortcut	Button
Clear Display	Ctrl+D	Clear Screen icon
View Current Activity	Ctrl+T	Graph Background icon
View Current Log	Ctrl+L	Round Bar icon
Add Counter	Ctrl+I	Plus sign
Delete Counter	Delete	*X* sign

Adding and Removing Counters

To add a counter for an object to be monitored from your current System Monitor screen:

1. Click the Plus sign to add a new counter.

2. From the Add Counters window, choose whether to use the local computer's counter or to choose from a list of recognized systems on the network.

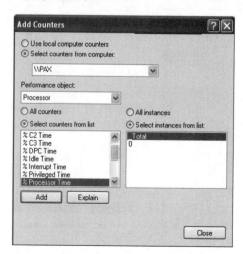

3. Click to open the drop-down list under Performance Object, and select the object you want to track.

4. Click All Counters available for that object, or select a specific counter from the drop-down list.

5. Click Add, and then Close or repeat, as needed, until you have all the objects—and their associated counters—you want.

TIP With so many different objects and counters, it can be hard to choose what is most relevant to monitor. Check the "Monitoring for Specific Performance Issues" section, later in this chapter, for recommendations, and then feel free to experiment to find what gives you the best data for your particular situation.

Uncertain what a specific counter will measure? Click the Explain button under the Counters list and you'll get a pop-up like this one.

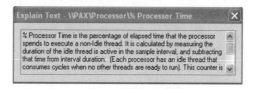

To remove a counter, try one of the following:

- From Graph or Histogram view, select the counter to remove in the bottom object information panel, and click the X on the Monitor toolbar.

- Also from Graph or Histogram view, select a counter in the bottom object panel, right-click, choose Properties, locate the counter to remove, and click Remove. Click Close.

To change the appearance or properties of a counter in System Monitor:

1. Right-click the counter in the bottom object information panel and choose Properties.

2. Select among the following tabs and make changes, as needed:

Tab	Functions
General	Basic display options
Source	View, add, or remove data sources (monitor, logging, or database)
Data	Counters being used for that object

Tab	Functions
Graph	Graph customization options
Appearance	Change background appearance and font

3. Click OK.

Using Performance Logs And Alerts

As with System Monitor, Performance Logs And Alerts uses both performance objects and performance counters as part of its feature-set to specify which information must be tracked, logged, and if necessary, to notify you of special problems.

Logs are stored by default in the *[drive letter]*:\PerfLogs folder and store data in a comma- or tab-separated format suitable for importing into applications such as spreadsheets or SQL-capable databases, for long-term tracking and reporting purposes. Also, logs may be started automatically or manually, and they can be viewed both during the collection process and after collection has finished. Through System Monitor, these can be viewed by clicking the View Log Data icon (Ctrl+L) and choosing the log to review, or by choosing the appropriate log under the Performance Logs And Alerts section of the MMC console.

Counter logs   Stores information collected by the counters you establish.

Trace logs   Collects and stores information from system application events tied to one of the following: errors or problems such as page faults, or more normal operations such as disk I/O activity tied to such an event.

Alerts   Sends a message via the Messenger service to alert you when conditions being monitored and logged meet conditions, or threshold limits, that you establish.

Setting Up Counter Logs

To establish a counter log (multiple counters can be tracked through each), follow these steps:

1. In the Performance MMC, highlight Performance Logs And Alerts, then choose and right-click Counter Logs.

2. Select New Log Settings.

3. Provide a name for the log (must be unique).

4. From the General tab of the next window, note the full log name, then Add Objects and Add Counters, as desired. At least one counter must be selected before you can proceed. Make changes to sample data intervals and units as needed.

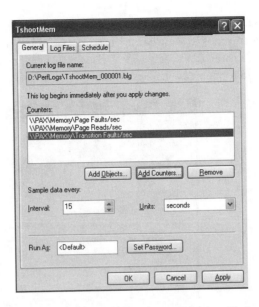

5. From the Log Files tab, make any changes as required for log file format (binary, binary circular, tab- or comma-delimited text, or SQL database) and for naming of automatic logs.

6. From the Schedule tab, set the schedule for this logging procedure. Click OK.

NOTE   By default, the following counters are included in basic logging: Memory\Pages/sec, PhysicalDisk(_Total)\Avg. Disk Queue Length, and Processor(_Total)\% Processor Time.

WARNING   Although both Windows 2000 and Windows XP name their binary performance log files with the .BLG extension, the two formats differ. You cannot directly read XP-created BLG files with Windows 2000. You must either view these files exclusively on XP machines or use the Relog.exe command to convert the XP-created BLG to a Windows 2000–compatible format (*.csv or *.tsv). Here's an example: **relog *oldname.blg* -f CSV -o *newname.csv*.**

Setting Up Trace Logs

To configure for a new trace log, perform these steps:

1. Choose and right-click Trace Logs from Performance Logs And Alerts in the Performance MMC.

2. Select New Log Settings.

3. Provide a name for the log (must be unique).

4. A tabbed window appears with the full current log name displayed. From the General tab, click Provider Status to see what services are available. Then either choose Events Logged By System Provider (and enable TCP/IP, etc., as needed), or choose Nonsystem providers and click Add to include those you want.

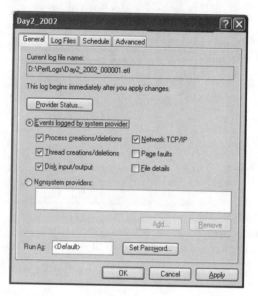

5. From the Log Files tab, make any needed changes to log file type (sequential trace or circular) and naming convention.

6. Under the Schedule tab, establish the time(s) you want this to run.

7. On the Advanced tab, you may adjust file buffer sizes. Click Apply, then click OK.

WARNING   Depending on how you have configured your performance tracking, logs may not be immediately available for viewing after you start the tracking process. Most require at least two data samples to be collected to establish the validity of the logging information.

TIP   To quickly change parameters for a log, locate it in the list, right-click it, and choose Properties.

Setting Up Alerts

To configure Windows XP to issue an alert to you when conditions match watch criteria you set, do this:

1. Choose and right-click Alerts from Performance Logs And Alerts in the Performance MMC.

2. Select New Alert Settings.

3. Provide a name for the alert (must be unique).

4. From the General tab, configure the criteria for the alert, based on the counter.

5. From the Action tab, indicate what XP should do when it determines an alert is necessary (just log, send a network message, start a specific log, or run a program, for example).

6. From the Schedule tab, make changes as needed to the schedule for alert scanning. Click Apply, and then OK.

WARNING   Messenger must be installed and you must be signed into the service in order to receive Performance alerts. For those who try to disable or remove Messenger because they want to use another Internet/network message service, be aware that this will disable your alerts, too.

Monitoring for Specific Performance Issues

As I mentioned, some counters (and their associated performance objects) are likely to be of more express use to you than others; some you may rarely, if ever, try. Table 18.1 offers the top 12 counters you should consider when looking at performance in the typical key areas, such as disk access and memory.

TABLE 18.1: Top 12 Performance Counters

Issue/Object	Counter	Significant Result
Disk	Physical Disk\% Disk and % Idle	Any major changes
Disk	Physical Disk\Disk Reads/sec and Disk Writes/sec	Below disk manufacturer's specifications
Disk	Physical Disk\Avg. Disk Queue Length	No. of spindles + 2
Memory	Memory\Available Bytes	< 4 MB
Memory	Memory\Pages/sec	20 is average; monitor and review paging activity
Network	Network Interface\Bytes Total/sec, Bytes Sent/sec, and Bytes Rec'd/sec	Look for slowdowns
Overall System/Paging	Paging File\% Usage	Above 70%
Printing	Print Queue\Bytes Printed/sec	Any sustained reduction in print capacity
Printing	Print Queue\Job Errors	Sustained or recurring errors may indicate misconfiguration of printer
Processor	Processor\% Processor Time	80 and above—find what is grabbing the CPU's time

TIP If you want to establish a baseline operating performance review, monitor the system while it is engaged in routine operations. You can monitor again during more extreme periods of activity or for troubleshooting, and compare the results against the baseline. From such a comparison, you may be able to see if your system or some component or service therein simply isn't functioning well under serious workloads (and thus, may need replacement or tweaking).

WARNING Be aware that monitoring many aspects of performance at once can by itself affect overall system efficiency. Reduce your monitoring overhead by using Report view rather than graphical mode, and prioritize the counters you load.

Third-Party Monitoring and Performance Tuning Applications

One of the advantages to the performance monitoring capabilities built into Windows XP is that you have a reasonably broad set of tools already available to you, without buying or installing a separate package. In talking with several IT professionals and super users in preparing this, for example, most admitted that they either used what was already in XP or used an additional one or two monitoring tools (for instance, a network diagnostics utility such as the type you find on a 3Com or other network manufacturer's install CD) besides those within XP itself.

However, regarding optimization and tuning, XP mostly just makes recommendations, either by default settings Microsoft feels is the most advantageous for the largest number of users, or through threshold and acceptable limit settings specified when you look under Help And Support.

Get the Right Tool for the Tuning Job

You have the option to use a third-party package or single-use application to do all of what System Monitor and Performance Logs achieve, and beyond to performance tweaking.

The following paragraphs describe some of the more commonly available Windows XP performance monitoring and tweaking/tuning tools that I worked with in preparing this chapter. Many of these are shareware and can be downloaded online from sites such as IT Pro Downloads at `www.itprodownloads.com`, or CNET's Download.com at `www.download.com`.

Also, you'll find that various websites provide some optimization and performance tweaking or at least provide suggestions after performing an online analysis of your system. The most popular of these—and one that hasn't disappeared over time as so many others have—tends to be PCPitstop at `www.pcpitstop.com`.

Event Reporter

(Adiscon, shareware) Event Reporter is an alternate event logging and monitoring system for those who want to use a central syslog daemon to report alerts to e-mail or server; the data seems easier to digest and analyze with this interface than straight Windows.

TechFacts

(winutils.com, shareware) TechFacts offers both alternative monitors (network, software changes, etc.) and system benchmarks.

Tweak-XP

(Totalidea Software, commercial) Tweak-XP is a system optimization wizard (memory, cache, and more) and monitoring tool.

VBSys Windows System Monitor

(Michael Krane, shareware) VBSys Windows System Monitor checks for CPU and disk usage, swap file, and free memory.

X-Setup

(Xteq Systems, freeware) X-Setup recommends optimum performance settings for hundreds of Windows processes and events; this is excellent for at least providing some ideas for where you may lose some overall performance.

Optimization Tool Profile

Beyond the programs listed in the preceding section, one package is probably the best known as well as the most frequently recommended. However, until recently, it was not updated to work well with recent versions of Windows, much to the consternation of its many fans among the power users who liked it and used it since its debut in 1995.

This package is Windows PowerToys, a suite of utilities for optimizing and fine-tuning a whole range of Windows interface, usability, and performance issues. These were developed by Microsoft Windows programmers as sort of "side" utilities for Windows 95 that have always stayed separated out of the standard Windows installation. But Microsoft is promising to make an XP package available for download at

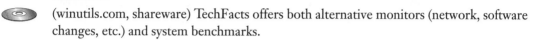

    http://microsoft.com/windowsxp/pro/downloads/powertoys.asp

While many of the tools within this suite are meant more for making you happier with your desktop experience, the crown jewel of this package was and is TweakUI, a stand-alone program that allows you to tweak a huge number of settings that mostly affect your personal performance and preferences for how Windows works and looks.

For example, rather than learning all the intricacies of best CD burning performance and what modifications you can make to the Windows Registry and interface, you can use TweakUI to swiftly adjust your CD writing cache to see if you can improve overall efficiency when writing to your CD burner.

One caveat: if you have a previous version of TweakUI or any of Windows PowerToys installed, fully uninstall it before you install the XP-specific version (which will *not* be backward compatible with previous versions of Windows).

TIP   It may be your experience—as it is for many of us—that there are few performance tuning or tweaking applications that do as good a job as what a knowledgeable user or administrator can accomplish by knowing what to change. Still, many of us don't have the time to investigate every possible setting and Registry tweak. What some of us do is use these extra tools to identify the types of things we can modify, and then use that information to do it ourselves. Always read the utilities' documentation to see if you can pick up some smart tips.

Before you obtain and install a third-party package for system monitoring and tuning, consider these points:

- Perform a full backup prior to installing any third-party applications of this type, particularly with performance tuners that may alter key settings.

- For comparison of monitoring and performance utilities, be sure to run each under the same types of operating conditions, or the results may be too dissimilar to be useful.

- Those written specifically for Windows XP (or 2000) are apt to run the best and report more accurately.

- Where possible, avoid using more than one monitor at a time. As noted, intensive performance monitoring can actually draw further upon strained resources.

- Review the documentation carefully before installing—or removing—any of these.

CHAPTER 19

Auditing the System

Chapter 17 explained the importance of monitoring and responding to events generated by the system, applications, and security processes such as logon and resource
access. Chapter 18 explained the importance of monitoring system performance.

When you are concerned with system security, you need to go one step further and
audit the system. Auditing in Windows XP provides the means by which you can track
resource usage, attempted security breaches, and a wide variety of other events that occur
on a system that would not otherwise be logged in the system's event logs. For example,
perhaps you have a set of folders shared on a computer and want to keep track of unsuccessful attempts to access that folder. Or maybe you want to keep track of unsuccessful
logon attempts or other possible security breaches. Auditing lets you do just that.

This chapter first gives you an overview of why auditing is important and how it works.
Then you'll learn how to enable auditing for general events as well as audit specific folder
resources. If you haven't already done so, you should read Chapters 17 and 18 to get a better
understanding of events, performance issues, and the tools provided in Windows XP to
monitor both.

> **NOTE** Windows XP implements auditing through group or local security policy. For that rea-
> son, it is available only on Windows XP Professional. Windows XP Home Edition does
> not support auditing because it does not implement policies.

Understanding Auditing

In Chapter 17, I defined an *event* as any significant occurrence in the operating system or
an application that requires users (usually administrators) to be notified. When a service
stops, for example, that's certainly something that needs to be logged to the System event
log, at least. You can keep track of a computer's health by monitoring the event logs and
performance counters.

Auditing, however, lets you track the success or failure of specific types of events. For example, maybe you need to monitor logon attempts to determine not only who is logging on successfully, but also when unsuccessful logon attempts occur. Unsuccessful logons might point to attempts to breach a computer's security, or perhaps to something far less sinister, such as a user who has forgotten his or her password and is too embarrassed to admit it.

Logon and logoff are by no means the only events you can audit in Windows XP. You might also need to audit access to a shared folder to keep track of who uses the folder and the actions they take in it. There are many different types of events you can audit in Windows XP, in several categories:

Account Logon Events   Monitor user logon and logoff through a user account.

Account Management   Monitor when user accounts or groups are created, modified, or deleted. Monitor when user accounts are renamed, enabled, or disabled. Monitor when a password is set or changed.

Directory Service Access   Monitor access to Active Directory.

Logon Events   Monitor authentication of non-local entities, such as network user of a network share or other resource, or a remote service that logs on using a local account (such as the SYSTEM account).

Object Access   Monitor access of specific objects such as folders, files, and printers. Auditing in this category also requires configuring auditing properties on the object itself.

Policy Change   Monitor when user rights or audit policies are modified.

Privilege Use   Monitor occurrences of a user exercising a right that is not associated with logon or logoff.

Process Tracking   Monitor process execution, such as an application being started.

System Events   Monitor global system events, such as startup, shutdown, restart, or events that are related to the system security log or to overall security.

Each of these categories includes several types of events, some of which are general in nature and others that are specific to certain objects. In all cases except object access, auditing is a global action—when you enable auditing for system events, for example, that results in a range of events being audited. You can't audit one type of system event and not another. The exception is object access, which you enable globally for the system, but must also turn on auditing for specific objects (more on this a bit later).

Rather than cover every type of event audited for each category, I'll instead explain how to enable and configure global auditing policies in this chapter. You'll also learn how to configure auditing for individual folders, files, and printers.

Enabling Auditing

As I explained previously, you enable auditing by configuring a local or group security policy. For all auditing except object access, setting the policy is all you need to do. The system then begins placing events in the event logs as audited events occur. (Object auditing requires one extra step, as I'll explain in the next section.) First, you need to understand how to configure auditing policies.

If you want to perform auditing on all computers in a given organizational unit, domain, or entire site, you should enable auditing through group policy at the appropriate level. For example, assume you want to audit account logon throughout your entire organization. You would enable that auditing policy setting at the site level, or at the domain level if all of your computers/users are members of the same domain. To audit account logon only for a specific group of users, you would instead place those users in an organizational unit in the Active Directory and then enable the audit policy for logon in that OU.

Because this book focuses primarily on Windows XP and not Windows 2000 Server or Windows .NET Server, I'll assume that you will be configuring auditing at the local level rather than through group policies.

TIP   If you need to configure auditing through group policy, open the Active Directory Users And Computers console, open the properties for the container (OU or domain), and create or modify a group policy object (GPO). In that GPO, locate and enable the policy settings for the type(s) of auditing you want to perform.

To configure auditing at the local level, open the Local Security console from the `Administrative Tools` folder. Then, expand the \Security Settings\Local Policies\Audit Policy branch as shown in Figure 19.1.

As Figure 19.1 illustrates, there is one policy setting for each of the auditing categories discussed previously. Each of these policies has three possible settings: No Auditing, Success, and Failure. The default value for each policy is No Auditing, so you don't need to take any action if you're not interested in auditing a particular category. Otherwise, double-click the policy for the category in question to open its property dialog box as shown in Figure 19.2.

A key point to understand when you enable auditing is that you can audit two different types of events, success and failure. You don't have to audit both for a given category. For example, you might only audit failure for account logon events to help detect attempts to hack into the system or to identify users who are having difficulty remembering their passwords (or accounts that are being used to attempt a break-in), but not audit successful logons. On the other hand, perhaps you simply want a record of when each user logs on and from which computer but are not interested in unsuccessful logon attempts. If that's the case, you would audit success for this category and not audit failure.

FIGURE 19.1:

Use the Local Security console to enable auditing.

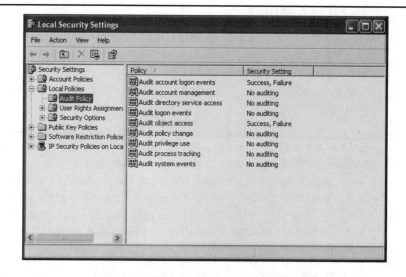

FIGURE 19.2:

Enable success and/ or failure auditing through the policy's properties.

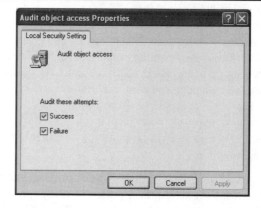

As you're rummaging through the audit policies trying to decide which event categories to audit and the type of auditing you want to perform in each one, keep in mind that auditing can generate a huge amount of log activity. For that reason, you should only audit those types of events that have a true relevance to your system, network, or security needs. Otherwise, you might spend quite a bit of your time clearing out the logs.

NOTE   Consider whether or not you're willing to take the time to actively review the logs for the audited events. If all you're doing is filling the logs with events that are never reviewed, reconsider your auditing plans. Decide what's relevant, and then actively monitor and analyze that information.

When you've configured the auditing policies as needed, close the policy console. Windows XP will begin logging events to the event logs according to the policies you have specified.

TIP   One final step you should take is to make sure you have configured the logs' maximum size and overflow behavior so you won't end up with full logs or begin to lose older events as they are overwritten by newer ones (unless that's the behavior you want). Open Event Viewer, right-click the Security log, and choose Properties to set log behavior.

Auditing Object Access

When you enable success or failure in the audit policy for object access, you are only making auditing possible. That action alone doesn't cause any object access events to be logged to the event logs. This is in contrast to the other auditing categories, which begin generating audit events as soon as you configure the policy. So, auditing object access is a two-step process. First, you enable auditing for object access (success, failure, or both), and then configure auditing for specific objects. For example, if you want to audit access to a shared folder, you must configure auditing properties for that folder before the system will log access to it.

TIP   If you're concerned that users or administrators are making changes in the Registry, you can turn on auditing in the Registry on a key-by-key basis. The section "Auditing Registry Access," later in this chapter, explains how.

Auditing Folder and File Access

You enable auditing for a file or folder through that object's properties. Open My Computer and browse to the folder or file. Right-click it and choose Properties to open its properties sheet. Then click the Security tab (Figure 19.3).

NOTE   You won't see or be able to access the Security tab unless you configure the computer to use regular file sharing instead of simple file sharing. Configure this option through the folder options. In any folder choose Tools ➢ Folder Options, click the View tab, scroll to the bottom of the list to locate the setting Use Simple File Sharing, and turn it off. Also, you can configure object access only for NTFS volumes. Auditing is not available for FAT volumes.

The Security tab lets you configure access permissions for specific users or groups. Click Advanced to open the Advanced Security Settings dialog box, and then click the Auditing tab (Figure 19.4) to configure auditing for the selected folder or file.

FIGURE 19.3:

Configure security settings for a folder through the Security tab.

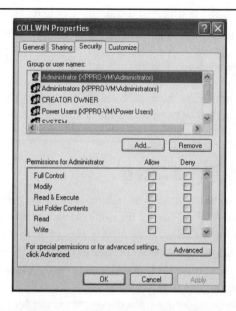

FIGURE 19.4:

Enable or disable auditing of a folder or file through the Advanced Security Settings dialog box.

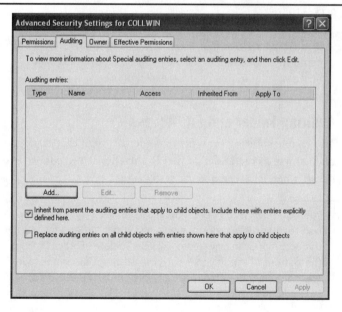

Click Add in the Advanced Security Settings dialog box and enter the name of the user or group whose access you want to audit. Or, click Advanced in the Select User Or Group dialog box to browse for a user or group. When you click OK, Windows XP opens the Auditing Entry dialog box, shown in Figure 19.5.

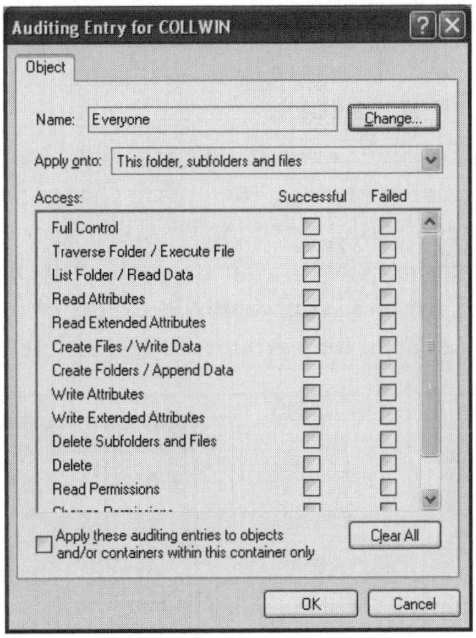

FIGURE 19.5:

You can audit a broad range of actions for the selected folder or file.

TIP   To audit all users, audit the Everyone built-in group.

In the Auditing Entry dialog box, select Successful for each event for which you want to monitor successful access to the object. Select Failed for each event for which you want to monitor unsuccessful access. The Apply Onto drop-down list lets you specify how the audit settings are applied to the folder, its contents, and subfolders. For example, if you want to audit only the files in the folder and not subfolders, you can select the Files Only option. Select the option This Folder, Subfolders, And Files if you want to audit the current folder, its contents, and the contents of all subfolders. The option "Apply these auditing entries to objects and/or containers within this container only," if selected, restricts auditing to only the selected folder. The contents of subfolders are audited if this option is not selected.

Back on the Advanced Security Settings dialog box (Figure 19.4) are a couple of options that control how auditing entries are applied throughout the folder structure. You'll probably puzzle over these settings:

"Inherit from parent the auditing entries that apply to child objects"   When this option is turned on, the selected folder inherits the auditing settings from its parent folder. Clear this check box if you don't want the folder to inherit the auditing settings from its parent.

"Replace auditing entries on all child objects with entries shown here that apply to child objects"   Turn on this option to clear audit settings in child objects (such as subfolders) and apply the audit settings for the current folder to those child objects.

After you click Apply or OK, Windows XP begins auditing the folder and its contents according to the settings you have specified.

Auditing Printer Access

You can audit printer access in much the same way you audit file or folder access. For example, you might want to monitor attempts to change permissions or take ownership of a printer. To set printer auditing, open the `Printers and Faxes` folder, right-click the printer, and choose Properties. Click the Security tab, then click Advanced. Click the Auditing tab, and add a user or group as you would for a folder or file. As Figure 19.6 indicates, the types of events you can audit for a printer are very different from a folder.

FIGURE 19.6:

You can audit a hand-ful of events for a printer.

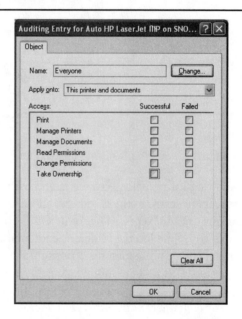

As with folders and files, you should be judicious in how you apply printer auditing, particularly in a busy network with lots of printing going on. Monitor only those types of events that will help you track printing problems and potential security issues that are applicable to your network.

Auditing Registry Access

You can use the same basic steps to enable auditing for a Registry key that you use to set up auditing for folders, files, and printers. Open the Registry Editor, right-click a Registry key, and choose Permissions. You can use the resulting dialog box (Figure 19.7) to restrict access to the selected key.

Use the Permissions dia-
log box to limit access to
a Registry key.

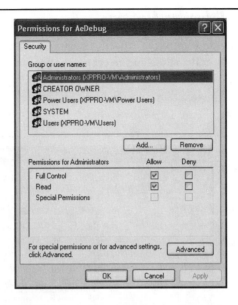

Click Advanced in the Permissions dialog box, then click the Auditing tab and add a user or group using the same method described previously for a folder or printer. The options that Windows XP offers for a Registry key are naturally different from other types of objects, as you can tell from Figure 19.8. As with other types of objects, you can apply the auditing settings to just the selected object or also include child objects, which in this case include subkeys and values.

You can audit a wide
range of events for a
Registry key.

Tips for Effective Auditing

Just turning on auditing for specific events or objects is pointless unless you follow up with active review and analysis of the events that occur. Windows XP records audited events to the Security log, so you can use the Event Viewer to view these events. Audited events show up with a Type of either Success Audit or Failure Audit, depending on the success or failure of the event. Figure 19.9 shows a handful of audit events in the Security log.

FIGURE 19.9:

Audited events appear in the Security log.

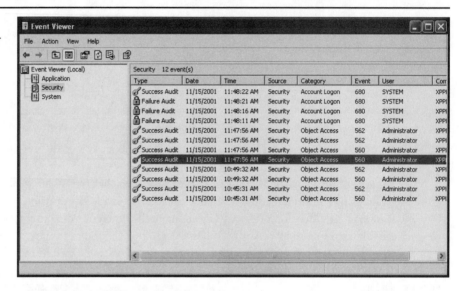

The Event Viewer works fine when you need to review audited events on a small scale or only on a single computer. When you need to expand auditing and analysis to a range of computers or even the entire organization, you'll have to turn to other tools. The third-party tools that let you collect data and analyze the event logs give you the same capabilities for analyzing audited events. Check out Chapter 17 for some suggested third-party applications that will let you do just that.

If you choose to enable auditing, there are a handful of approaches you can take:

Audit nothing You can take the approach that you won't audit any events or objects. This is a valid approach if you're working in a very small network that doesn't have frequent or continuous Internet connections and where none of the users ever have problems or could be considered even a potential security risk. If you have such a network, congratulations! You don't really need auditing. If your network and users are in the real world, however, it's likely you'll need at least some level of auditing.

Audit everything In networks that must be completely secure, you can consider auditing all events. Keep in mind that this will generate a huge amount of log traffic, so you'll need to adjust your log size accordingly and aggressively archive and analyze your logs. I strongly recommend a third-party solution like those discussed in Chapter 17. You might also consider auditing only failure events and not success events, unless you need a historical record of successful logons or other actions.

Audit specific users   Another approach is to audit only specific users or groups of users. For example, you might audit users who you feel pose an extra security risk or who frequently cause problems by purposely or accidentally attempting to access restricted resources or perform tasks for which they are not authorized. Keeping records like this will help you guide these users more effectively and, if the need arises, provide a historical record to support termination or other actions.

Audit administrative actions   Except in small networks with only one or two administrators, you should generally monitor actions taken by administrators as well as the attempted unauthorized use of administrative privileges. The latter is important in any size network. In particular, monitor logon for the administrative account or group(s), plus actions taken such as policy changes, account creation or modification, and other administrative tasks that you feel might pose a risk to your network.

Audit folders and files   If you provide access to sensitive documents across the network, you should monitor access and use of those documents. In addition to tracking access, keep a close eye on attempts to change ownership or permissions on a folder or file, both of which can have unwanted security consequences.

What to Audit for Optimum Security

You may be tempted to audit every resource in sight, but this is almost never a good idea for a couple of reasons. First, auditing a large number of events may slow the computer down, because it has to perform more actions. Second, for auditing to do you any good, someone will have to go through the resulting logs and identify problem events. If that person is you or someone you supervise, you'll want to minimize the amount of time involved in the review.

This section discusses which events to audit for maximum security on your Windows XP Professional systems, and suggests remedies to try for various types of hazards. The section is broken down by the types of threats the auditing is intended to counteract or minimize.

Dictionary, Hybrid, or Brute-Force Password Attack

To detect attacks aimed at finding a password by trying a list of words until one works, audit account logon events for failure. (A *dictionary* attack uses known words from one or more languages. A *hybrid* attack mixes numbers, letters, or symbols into known words to search for disguised passwords. A *brute-force* attack tries every possible key combination.)

If you detect failed attacks (or even if you don't), review your password policies carefully to make sure that you're requiring all users to use passwords of at least six characters that include numerals and symbols, to change passwords frequently, and to prevent users from reusing passwords they've used before. If you need truly strong security, consider replacing your passwords with biometric authentication devices.

Entry Using a Stolen Password

To learn when someone has entered the system using a stolen password, audit account logon events for success. Because auditing account logon events for success will show you all successful logons by authorized users as well, you'll need to do some sleuth work to sort the authorized logons from the unauthorized.

If you detect an unauthorized entry, assess the damage and determine effective countermeasures. At the very least, you'll need to force a password change for the user account involved. If in doubt about unauthorized entries, force all users to change password immediately.

User Using a Computer They're Not Authorized to Use

To check for users using computers they're not authorized to use (for example, workstations in the wrong section of the network), audit account logon events for success. If you discover users using computers they're not authorized to, close the loophole by changing the appropriate policy.

Misuse of User Privileges

To check for users misusing their privileges, audit the appropriate privilege uses for success. Curtail or remove the appropriate privileges from offending users.

WARNING   Don't audit privilege use continuously, because doing so will produce massive amounts of data, and you'll need to trawl through large numbers of legitimate events to uncover any instances of abuse.

Misuse of Administrator Privileges

To check for administrators misusing their privileges or unintentionally making changes they shouldn't, audit account-management events and policy changes, both for success. Boost your communication channels or rein in your administrators as necessary.

File Security Breaches

To check for breaches to your file security, audit the appropriate files and folders for success and failure of access and change. For example, to find out who has been viewing the files in a particular folder, audit the folder and its files for List Folder/Read Data access for success; to find out who's been trying to view the files, audit List Folder/Read Data access for failure.

To prevent access to the files and folders in question, remove permissions for their folders from everyone but those users and groups allowed to access them. For greater security, locate the files or folders on another drive or server to which the offending users do not have access.

Printer Efficiency and Security

To find out whether users are having problems with certain printers, audit printer failure events. If you detect problems, fix the printers or the users' access to them.

In most cases, you won't want to audit printer success events, because if your printers are used moderately or heavily, the auditing will log a large number of events. However, you may want to audit printer success events for a short period—especially for printers that use expensive media—to determine whether users are using printers they're not supposed to print to. If they are, remove their permissions to do so.

User Running Unauthorized Programs/User Monitoring

To detect users running unauthorized programs, or to monitor a user for unauthorized actions, audit process tracking for success. If the program is installed on the user's computer, remove it and use policies to prevent them from reinstalling it or installing other programs. If the program is installed elsewhere, remove the user's access to it.

Virus Threat

To detect unauthorized processes being run by a virus, script, or other malware, audit write access for program files (EXE and DLL files) for success and failure and process tracking for success and failure. Monitor the System log actively while doing so.

CHAPTER 20

Using Disk Quotas

In a small network with one user per computer, controlling disk space is not generally a big issue. If someone fills up a disk, you or that user can clear out old documents or unused applications as needed. As the network begins to grow and as multiple users begin to use the same computer, controlling disk space becomes increasingly important.

Limiting disk usage is also important on a server. You don't want one user filling up the server with MP3 or AVI files. Disk usage is just one reason; that kind of activity also indicates a (to be diplomatic) lack of sufficient focus to the job. By limiting disk activity, you can not only prevent users from carelessly filling up a disk, but also limit their ability to purposely load up the server with junk.

You can impose *disk quotas* to control the amount of space a user can use on a local computer as well as a server. You can control disk quotas in a few different ways depending on where the volumes are located and which users should be affected. In this chapter, I explain three different quota methods: setting them directly, using mounted volumes, and applying them through group policy.

Understanding how to set disk quotas is an important issue even if you have a relatively small network with no dedicated server. You might have in place now, or put in place down the road, a Windows XP Professional computer to act as a file server. If that's the case, you should consider applying disk quotas to the computer to avoid potential problems later. A disk filling up isn't just an inconvenience to the user, but can cause services to fail and in some situations render the computer effectively useless. That makes disk quotas doubly important.

Applying Quotas to a Disk

A *disk quota* is just what its name implies: It's a limit—or quota—on the amount of disk space a given user can fill on a volume. You apply disk quotas on a per-volume, per-user basis. This means that the quota defines the total amount of space that the user can have on the volume. It is not limited to a specific folder, but rather to the volume. You can set two different quota levels. The first acts as a warning level; when it is reached, Windows XP issues a warning message to the user that the quota level is being reached. This gives the user the opportunity to do their own housecleaning and weed out old documents or other files.

> **TIP**   The term *volume* refers to a physical or logical drive, such as C:, D:, and so on.

The second limit acts as a stop on the user's ability to store files on the computer. Windows XP issues a message to the user that the maximum amount of space has been used and prevents any further additions to the volume by that user. This forces the user to clean up their act. While quotas won't eliminate an administrator's need to monitor disk usage, they do put the impetus on the users to manage their own folders more effectively.

> **TIP**   Quotas work equally well on Windows XP Professional and Home Edition. If you have children who share a computer, it's a good idea to set quotas to prevent one or two from using up the entire volume with games, downloads, or other files. It also helps teach them good work habits and computer management skills.

Quotas function through junction points in the file system, which allow specific file-system features to be implemented by drivers other than the primary file-system drivers. Quotas are one example of the use of junction points; encryption is another. Because quotas rely on junction points, which rely on the NTFS file system, you can apply quotas only to NTFS volumes. You can't apply quotas on a FAT volume.

Setting Global Quota Settings

Perhaps the easiest way to set disk quotas is directly through the properties for the volume. Open My Computer, right-click the volume, and choose Properties. Then click the Quota tab (Figure 20.1).

Setting up disk quotas for a volume is really a two-step process. You first configure the general settings that apply for all users. Then, you add users to the quota entry list and specify the amount of space they can use. If a user doesn't have an explicit quota entry for a volume, you can configure the volume's global quota properties to include default values for quota and warning limits, and have those settings apply to new users. Windows XP checks the quota entries and, if it doesn't find one for the user, creates one based on the default settings. This gives you the means of automatically applying the same quotas for all users without having to create individual quota entries.

> **TIP**   As you'll learn in the next section, you can modify the quota entry for any user. So a good plan of attack is to set reasonable quota defaults and then modify individual user quota entries as needed to increase or decrease the quota settings for users who need more or less than the default amount of disk space.

Use a volume's Quota
tab to set quotas.

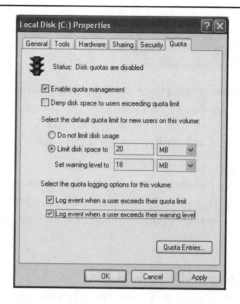

To enable quotas, select the Enable Quota Management option on the Quota tab. This
makes available the remaining options on the tab. These options are explained in the following sections.

"Enable quota management"   Use this option to enable or disable quotas for the volume. When this option is enabled, Windows XP applies the quota settings for the volume.
Clear this option if you don't want any disk usage limits applied to the volume.

"Deny disk space to users exceeding quota limit"   Enable this option if you want
Windows XP to prevent users from using any more space on the volume if they exceed
their quota limit. Clear this option if you only want to warn users but not impose a physical
limit. In a way, not denying space defeats the purpose of disk quotas, so I generally recommend that you enable this option unless you have a compelling reason to warn rather than
enforce.

"Do not limit disk usage"   Select this option if you don't want to apply a disk quota to
new users who have no disk quota yet on the volume. In general, I don't recommend using
this option, but instead suggest you apply a default setting using the following setting.

"Limit disk space to"   Select this option to set a default quota for any user who doesn't
have an existing quota entry for the volume. This value specifies the maximum amount of
space the user can fill. If you select the Deny Disk Space… option described previously, the
user is denied the ability to use more space when this limit is reached.

"Set warning level to"   Use this option to set the amount of space used that will generate a warning message. As with the preceding setting, this sets the default value for new users who have no existing quota entry on the volume. Windows XP creates a new quota entry for the user with this setting and the Limit Disk Space To setting on first access.

"Log event when a user exceeds their quota limit"   This option adds an event to the System log when a user exceeds the quota limit specified in their quota entry for the volume. This option gives you a means of notification and analysis to help plan and manage disk usage, particularly if you use a third-party event-log analyzer like those discussed in Chapter 17.

"Log event when a user exceeds their warning level"   This setting adds an event to the System log when a user exceeds the warning limit specified in the quota entry for the volume. Use this option in conjunction with the preceding one to plan and analyze disk usage.

Setting Quota Limits for a User

As I explained in the previous section, you can set default quota values for a volume and let Windows XP apply those quotas to everyone. You don't have to ever set individual users' quota settings unless they need custom values. A second approach is to manually create quota entries for specific users and not apply default settings to other users. This, in effect, applies quotas to a selected group of users but lets all others use as much space as they want on the volume. Think about how you want to restrict disk usage and choose a method accordingly. Just remember that even if you decide to use default settings and apply quotas to all users, you can modify the settings for any user as needed.

To modify quotas for a user or to create an explicit quota entry, open My Computer, right-click the volume in question, and choose Properties. Click the Quota tab, then click Quota Entries to display the dialog box shown in Figure 20.2.

The Quota Entries dialog box shows all existing quota entries for the volume and useful information such as the settings for the user, amount currently used, percent used, and the status, which indicates whether the user is within quotas or has exceeded the warning or limit levels.

Double-click any quota entry to open the Quota Settings dialog box (Figure 20.3) for the user, to enable/disable quotas or to set the warning and limit levels for the selected user.

To create a new quota entry for a user, choose Quota ➤ New Quota Entry. Windows XP opens the Select Users dialog box, which you use to enter or browse for the user account. After you select the user, Windows XP displays a dialog box similar to the one in Figure 20.3. Set the warning and limit values and click OK.

FIGURE 20.2:

You can view, add, and modify quota entries for users as needed.

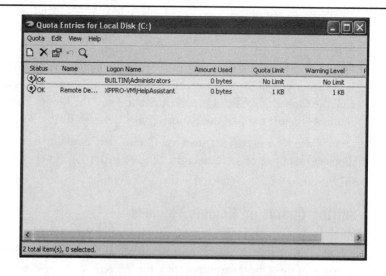

FIGURE 20.3:

Change a user's settings through the Quota Settings dialog box.

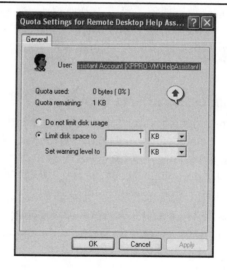

TIP   You can't apply quotas to groups. So the Select Users dialog box limits the search to user accounts and excludes groups.

Copying Quotas from Volume to Volume

Let's say that over time you have fine-tuned the quota settings on a particular volume, but even with quotas in place, you still need to add more disk space. So, you decide to add a new volume to the computer. You don't want to have to set up all of the quotas again, but instead want to impose the same quotas for the new volume as for the old one. Windows XP makes it easy to do just that.

You can export the quota entries from a volume to a file, and then import those settings in the other volume. To export the settings, open the properties for the source volume and click the Quota tab. Click Quota Entries to open the Quota Entries dialog box, and choose Quota ➤ Export to open the Export Quota Settings dialog box.

Once you have exported, open the Quota Entries dialog box on the target volume and choose Quota ➤ Import. Select the file you exported and click Open to add the quota entries.

Setting Quotas on Remote Volumes

You can apply quotas to a remote volume in much the same way you apply quotas to a local volume. The remote volume must be shared at the root of the volume, and you must be a member of the Administrators group for the remote computer.

To set quotas on volumes that fit those criteria, first open My Computer and map a local drive letter to the remote share. Then right-click the mapped volume in My Computer and choose Properties. Use the Quota tab of the remote volume's properties to set quotas just as you would for a local volume.

How Compression Affects Quotas

Disk compression is a feature of NTFS volumes that allows a file to use less space on the disk than it would if uncompressed. When Windows XP tracks disk usage for quotas, it considers the uncompressed size of the file, not the compressed size. A 100 MB file that compresses down to 60 MB would still count as 100 MB against the user's quota, so you (or the user) can't use compression to get around the quota limit for files.

However, Windows XP does consider the compressed size of *folders* rather than the uncompressed size. A compressed folder that takes up 400 MB compressed but would have an uncompressed total usage of 700 MB only counts as 400 MB against the quota.

SEE ALSO   See Chapter 25 for a more detailed discussion of compression.

How Conversion Affects Quotas

You can convert FAT volumes to NTFS without a loss of data. FAT volumes don't track file ownership, but NTFS volumes do. So when Windows XP converts a FAT volume to NTFS, it needs to assign ownership to each file on the volume. It automatically makes the

Administrator the owner for all files. If you enable quotas on the converted volume, this means that all of the existing files will count against the Administrator account's quota limit. This typically isn't a problem, because in most cases you won't apply a quota limit for administrators. If you need to apply a limit, however, check the total disk usage right after converting the volume. Then add that amount to whatever quota limit you plan to give administrators.

How Ownership Affects Quotas

As the previous section hints, quotas are directly tied to ownership. So ownership is an issue you consider when setting quotas. Conversely, you need to consider quotas when changing ownership of a folder or file. If you change ownership, that folder or file will be counted against the new owner's quota limit. If that's not a problem, you don't have to worry about it. Otherwise, you might need to either increase the new user's quota or not make the ownership change.

Applying Folder-Specific Quotas with Mounted Volumes

As I explained previously, quotas are volume-specific. You can't set one quota on a folder and set a different quota on a different folder. For example, you can't have a 20 MB limit in C:\Program Files and a 200 MB limit in C:\users\you. At least, that's the case if both folders reside on the same physical disk. But how can you have two folders in the same directory structure (both appearing under C:, for example) that actually reside on different physical disks? You use one or more mounted volumes, another feature made possible by NTFS 5 junction points.

A *mounted volume* is a volume that you mount into an empty NTFS folder. For example, assume a computer's physical drive C: is running low on disk space. You need to add several additional applications. You can install a new disk, move the contents of the existing C:\Program Files folder to the new disk, and then mount the new disk in the now empty C:\Program Files folder. To the user, it appears that drive C: suddenly has lots more free space. In reality, it's a different disk.

One side benefit of mounted volumes is that the mounted volume can have different quota settings from the host volume. So, you might mount a volume as C:\Users with a completely different set of quotas from the settings applied to the physical C: volume. For example, users might have a 5 MB limit on the host volume but a 200 MB limit on the mounted volume, which appears as C:\Users.

There isn't anything magical about setting up different quota settings for mounted volumes. However, you might need to change the way you get to the quota settings. You can mount a volume to an empty NTFS folder, and that mounted volume does not have to have a drive letter. So you can't just right-click the volume in My Computer to access the Quota tab in its properties. Instead, you need to use the Disk Management console. Right-click My Computer, select Manage, and click the Disk Management branch in the Computer Management console. Right-click the mounted volume and choose Properties. You'll then have access to the volume's Quota tab, where you can set quotas as you would for a nonmounted volume.

SEE ALSO   For a detailed discussion of how to configure and use mounted volumes, see Chapter 25.

Applying Quotas with Policies

Although you can apply quotas manually, as explained earlier in this chapter, there are many situations where you might prefer to apply quotas through group or local policy. For example, let's say that you have 50 workstations shared by several hundred users (a computer lab in a school would fit that scenario). You want to impose a disk quota so that each user can have only 5 MB of data. You could go to each computer and manually configure the quota default settings, but there is a much easier way, provided those computers are domain members. You can apply the quota settings through group policy, which allows you to configure the settings once from a central location and have them applied to all of the computers.

You can apply quotas through group policy or local policy. The former requires the Active Directory Users And Computers console, and the latter requires the Group Policy console focused on the local computer. Setting quotas through local policy rather than group policy is your only policy-based method of imposing quotas if the computers belong to a workgroup rather than a domain. It takes just as long—if not longer—to set local quotas through local policy as it does to set them through the volume's properties. The benefit is that any new volumes that you add to the computer will have the same quotas automatically, without the need to set them. This isn't a major advantage, but it is helpful, nonetheless.

Set Quotas with Group Policy

You can set group policy at the site, domain, or organizational unit (OU) level. This section assumes you're setting the policy at the OU or domain level. If you're setting quotas at the site level, use the Active Directory Sites And Services console rather than the Active Directory Users And Computers console.

To set policies, open the Active Directory Users And Computers console on a domain controller, then right-click the domain or OU and choose Properties. Click the Group Policy tab (Figure 20.4) and open an existing group policy object (GPO) or create a new one.

TIP   You can't apply a GPO to the built-in Users container. If you need to apply quotas or other policies to a group of users, create an OU and move their accounts to that OU.

FIGURE 20.4:

Use the Group Policy
tab to access and edit
group policy objects.

In the Group Policy editor (Figure 20.5), expand the \Computer Configuration\Administrative Templates\System\Disk Quotas node. You'll find five policies that correspond to settings on a disk's quota tab. These group policy settings are self-explanatory. Just double-click a policy and set its value as needed. The last policy, Apply Policy To Removable Media, if enabled, causes the quotas to be applied to removable media in addition to fixed media.

FIGURE 20.5:

Use the Group Policy
editor to modify policies.

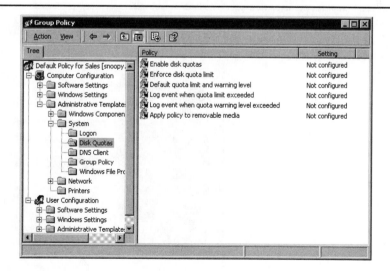

Set Quotas with Local Policy

To set quotas with local policy, click Start ➢ Run and enter **MMC** in the Run dialog box. When the MMC opens, choose File ➢ Add/Remove Snap-In. Click Add and choose Group Policy from the Add Standalone Snap-In dialog box (Figure 20.6), then click Add.

FIGURE 20.6:

Select Group Policy from the Add Standalone Snap-In dialog box.

The console automatically focuses the snap-in on the local computer, as shown in Figure 20.7. Click Finish to add the console, then click Close, followed by OK to return to the console.

FIGURE 20.7:

Group policy is automatically focused on the local computer.

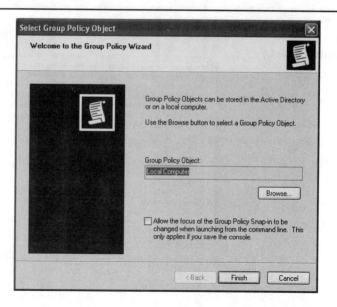

Next, expand the \Local Computer Policy\Computer Configuration\Administrative Templates\System\Disk Quotas node, and set the policies in that node as needed. See the previous section if you need an explanation of the individual policies. Then close the Local Computer Policy console.

Applying Quotas from a Command Console

In some situations, you might find it helpful to be able to manage quotas from a command line. For example, perhaps you need to incorporate quota tasks in a batch file, or want to manage quotas on a remote computer from a Telnet session. The `fsutil` command lets you do just that.

> **TIP** You can use `fsutil` as part of an administrative script to create quota reports or set disk quotas as part of the setup process when you add a new user.

`fsutil` has several uses. The following list the syntaxes for it:

```
fsutil quota disable VolumeName
```

Use this syntax to disable quota tracking and enforcement on the volume specified by *VolumeName*.

```
fsutil quota enforce VolumeName
```

Use this syntax to enforce quota tracking and limits on the volume specified by *VolumeName*.

```
fsutil quota modify VolumeName Threshold Limit [UserName]
```

Use this syntax to modify an existing quota entry or create a new one on the volume specified by *VolumeName*. The *Threshold* value specifies the value at which Windows XP issues a quota warning. The *Limit* value specifies the hard quota limit for the entry. *UserName* specifies the domain or user name for which to apply the settings.

> **TIP** Specify the values for *Threshold* and *Limit* in bytes.

```
fsutil quota query VolumeName
```

Use this syntax to list quota entries on the volume specified by *VolumeName*.

```
fsutil quota track VolumeName
```

Use this syntax to track quotas on the volume specified by *VolumeName*.

```
fsutil quota violations
```

Use this syntax to search the application and event system logs for quota violations or threshold limits being reached.

PART IV

Hardware

CHAPTER 21

Understanding and Managing the Registry

In the good old days of Windows 3.x, Windows stored the majority of its settings in text-based INI files. Some Windows applications still use INI files to store application settings. However, the majority have moved their settings to the Windows Registry. As this chapter explains, the Registry serves as the main data repository for the Windows XP operating system and for application settings.

Most tasks that you'll need to perform don't require that you really know much at all about the Registry. Although it's where most settings are stored, various elements in the GUI give you the means of modifying these settings. When you make changes in a Control Panel applet, for example, you're actually indirectly modifying settings in the Registry.

In some situations, however, modifying the Registry is the only way—or the quickest way—to make system or application changes. You need an understanding of how to work in the Registry for that reason alone. In addition, you need to know how to back up and restore the Registry. This chapter explains the Registry and how to work with local and remote registries. For detailed information on backing up and restoring the Registry, see Chapter 45.

Understanding the Windows XP Registry

The Windows XP Registry stores information about the operating system configuration, system hardware, security settings, rights, working environment settings (Desktop properties, for example), and many other types of information. Setup creates the Registry when you install Windows XP, and the operating system modifies the Registry when you add or remove hardware or modify hardware or operating system settings. Most applications also modify the Registry to store their settings.

The Windows XP Registry is a single logical entity, comprising five subtrees. Each subtree contains keys, which can contain subkeys and values. A subkey is just a branch of a subtree. Values are the actual items in the Registry that store data.

The Registry includes two physical subtrees, HKEY_LOCAL_MACHINE and HKEY_USERS. These are often abbreviated as HKLM and HKU. The HKLM subtree stores hardware- and system-related data; HKU stores user-related data.

These two physical subtrees are divided into five logical subtrees, called *hives*. Microsoft defines a hive as a body of keys, subkeys, and values rooted at the top of the Registry hierarchy. The five logical hives are:

HKEY_LOCAL_MACHINE   This hive stores information about the local hardware and operating system configuration. These settings are not user-specific but are instead the same regardless of the current user.

HKEY_CLASSES_ROOT   This hive, abbreviated HKCR, contains the settings that define file association data. This hive is created from \HKLM\Software\Classes and \HKCU\Software\Classes. The values in the HKCU key take precedence over the HKLM key, making the values user-specific. So Windows XP can store different file association data for each user.

HKEY_CURRENT_USER   This hive stores the current user's profile, which includes the desktop settings, Start menu, application settings, and so on. This hive is an alias of the \HKU*SID* key, where *SID* is the current user's security ID.

HKEY_USERS   This hive stores the user profiles for users who log onto the computer locally. This includes the default user profile. There are individual keys for each user SID.

HKEY_CURRENT_CONFIG   This hive stores hardware information such as installed devices, device drivers, device settings, and so on. This hive is an alias of the key

```
\HKLM\System\CurrentControlSet\Hardware Profiles\Current
```

Each hive comprises two files. These are the Registry file and the log file, both of which are stored in the *%systemroot%*\System32\Config folder. The Registry file contains the Registry structure and values for the hive, and the log file functions as a transaction log for hive modifications.

TABLE 21.1 REGISTRY HIVE FILES

Hive	Files
\HKEY_LOCAL_MACHINE\SAM	Sam and Sam.log
\HKEY_LOCAL_MACHINE\SECURITY	Security and Security.log
\HKEY_LOCAL_MACHINE\SOFTWARE	Software and Software.log
\HKEY_LOCAL_MACHINE\SYSTEM	System and System.log
\HKEY_CURRENT_CONFIG	System and System.log
\HKEY_CURRENT_USER	Ntuser.dat and Ntuser.dat.log
\HKEY_USERS\DEFAULT	Default and Default.log

TIP You'll also find `.sav` files in the `Config` folder. These are backup files created after the text portion of Setup and are used only if the GUI portion of Setup fails.

The majority of these files reside in the *%systemroot%*\System32\Config folder. The exceptions are the `Ntuser.dat` and `Ntuser.dat.log` files, which reside in the user's profile folder. On a system with a clean install of Windows XP, the profile folder is \Documents and Settings*user*, where *user* is the user's logon name. On a system upgraded from Windows NT to Windows XP (or from NT to 2000 and then to XP) the user profiles are stored in %systemroot%\Profiles*user*.

Figure 21.1 shows the Registry Editor (covered later in this chapter) to illustrate the Registry's logical structure.

FIGURE 21.1:

The Registry comprises five logical hives.

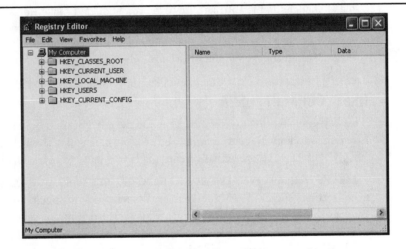

HKEY_LOCAL_MACHINE

The HKLM hive stores hardware and operating system settings that are system-wide. The HKLM hive contains a handful of subkeys:

HARDWARE Stores hardware configuration information. Windows XP creates the contents of this key when the system boots.

SAM Contains security data for local user accounts and groups.

SECURITY Defines the local security policy.

SOFTWARE Contains data about installed applications.

SYSTEM Contains values for device drivers, startup, services, and other system-wide values.

The settings in HKLM are used if there are no corresponding settings in the HKCU key. Otherwise, the settings in HKCU take precedence. However, some items—such as device drivers—always come from the HKLM key and not the HKCU key.

HKEY_USERS

This hive stores information about users who log on to the computer locally. The first key in this hive is the .DEFAULT key, which stores the default user profile that Windows XP uses to create the profile for a user the first time that user logs on. The rest of the keys in this hive define the profile for specific users. Each user's settings are stored in a separate key, which has the user's unique SID as its key name.

TIP   In most cases, you won't be able to identify a user from a SID, which makes it difficult to make changes in the HKU key. However, you shouldn't make Registry changes directly in most cases, anyway. If you need to change values for a user, log on as that user and make the changes through the Control Panel or other GUI methods. Or, log on as the user and make the changes in the HKCU hive, which points to the current user's key in HKU.

HKEY_CURRENT_USER

This key is an alias for the \HKU*sid* key for the current user. So when you log on, the HKCU hive points to your Registry key in the HKU hive. If you make a change to keys or values in HKCU, the changes are actually being made to \HKU*sid*, where *sid* is your security ID.

HKCU contains several subkeys. The AppEvents subkey, for example, contains application event settings such as WAV files that are associated with specific operating system events (such as that annoying startup sound). This key also contains several other subkeys that define the command console, Control Panel, working environment, identities (such as for Outlook Express), network settings, remote access settings, and much more. In essence, all user-specific settings are visible through HKCU.

HKEY_CLASSES_ROOT

This hive stores file associations. Windows XP builds this hive from \HKLM\Software\Classes and \HKCU\Software\Classes. Values in HKCU take precedence over HKLM, giving each user custom file associations. This means that one user can have a particular file type associated with one program, while another on the same computer can have a different application associated with that same file type.

HKEY_CURRENT_CONFIG

This hive stores hardware configuration data such as device drivers, device settings, and so on. HKCC is an alias of \HKLM\System\CurrentControlSet\Hardware Profiles\Current.

HKCC contains two main keys, Software and System. The Software key contains settings for system fonts and a few applications. The System key stores a partial copy of \HKLM\System\ CurrentControlSet.

Working with Keys and Values

A Registry key is really just a container for other keys and for values. Keys provide the structure for the Registry, and values store the data. You can create several types of values in the Registry:

REG_BINARY   Stores a single item of data in binary format. The Registry Editor displays these values as hexadecimal numbers.

REG_DWORD   Stores a single data item as a four-byte number. The Registry Editor can display these values using binary, hexadecimal, or decimal formats.

REG_EXPAND_SZ   A variable-length string that stores information with expandable variables (thus the name). The variables are enclosed in percent signs and expanded at the time of use by the system or an application. For example, the *%systemroot%* variable expands to the actual path to the Windows XP system folder.

REG_MULTI_SZ   Stores multiple string values as a single Registry value. The strings are separated by commas, spaces, or other character delimiters.

REG_SZ   Stores fixed-length strings, one string per value. It is the most common type of Registry value.

REG_FULL_RESOURCE_DESCRIPTION   Stores nested arrays. This value type is commonly used to store the resource list for a device driver or hardware component.

SEE ALSO   You'll learn in the next section how to create and modify keys and values in the Registry.

Using the Registry Editor

Previous versions of Windows, including Windows 2000 and Windows NT, provided two different programs for editing the Registry. Windows XP combines (finally!) the features in both of these Registry editors into a single one. You can use the Registry Editor (Figure 21.2) to browse the Registry to check settings, create, modify, or delete keys and values, and set permission on keys. You can also use the Registry Editor to manage a remote Registry.

SEE ALSO   See the section "Managing a Remote Computer's Registry," later in this chapter, for information on how to access and manage a remote Registry.

As Figure 21.2 illustrates, the Registry Editor shows the five Registry hives as expandable branches in the left pane. You can navigate the Registry structure in the left pane and view subkeys and values in the right pane.

The Registry Editor is easy to use, so I won't cover it in detail in this chapter. Instead, I'll give you a few tips on using it more effectively.

FIGURE 21.2:

Use the Registry Editor to view and make changes to the Registry.

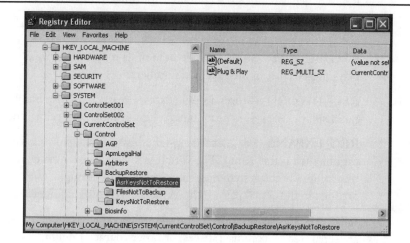

Copying Key Names

When you're working with the Registry, it's sometimes useful to be able to extract the key name. For example, maybe you need to document a particular change and want to reference the Registry key in the document. You could open the Registry Editor and the document and manually type the key in the document, character by character. Or, you can simply use the Clipboard.

Just select the desired Registry key and choose Edit ➤ Copy Key Name to copy the key name to the Clipboard. Then switch to the document where you want to use the key name and paste the text into the document.

Favorite Registry Keys

The Registry Editor in Windows XP lets you maintain a list of "favorite" Registry keys. I realize that Registry keys are probably your least favorite thing, but the ability to save a key to a Favorites list helps you navigate quickly to frequently used keys. Some of the keys you'll use more often than others are buried pretty deep in the Registry structure and you can click your fingers raw getting to them.

To add a key name to the Favorites list, browse to the key and choose Favorites ➤ Add To Favorites. Specify the name you want to appear in the list and click OK. Choose Favorites ➤ Remove Favorite to open a dialog box you can use to remove an entry from the Favorites menu. Adding a Registry key to the Favorites menu adds it to the Favorites menu in the Registry Editor, not to your Favorites folder where URLs are stored.

TIP If you want to copy your Registry favorites from one computer to another, export the Registry key \HKEY_CURRENT_USER\Software\Microsoft\Windows\CurrentVersion\ Applets\Regedit\Favorites and import it on the other system.

Last Used Key

Another feature that the Registry Editor implements by default is to automatically open the key that you had open when you last closed the Registry Editor. This can be handy, particularly if you are experimenting with a setting and need to make frequent changes to it. However, it can also be a security risk. You might not want someone else to open the Registry Editor and see where you were last working.

You can prevent the Registry Editor from keeping track of the previous key from session to session. First, open the Registry Editor and locate the key

\HKEY_CURRENT_USER\Software\Microsoft\Windows\CurrentVersion\Applets\Regedit

Double-click the value LastKey, clear the value, and click OK.

Next, you need to set permissions on the Regedit key to prevent it from displaying the last used key. In other words, if a particular user doesn't have Full Control in this key, the Registry Editor can't read the LastKey value and therefore can't display it. Right-click the key

HKEY_CURRENT_USER\Software\Microsoft\Windows\CurrentVersion\Applets\Regedit

and choose Permissions. Remove the Full Control permission for any user you don't want to be able to see the previous session's last used key.

TIP As an alternative, you can simply collapse all branches and select My Computer in the left pane prior to closing the Registry Editor.

Exporting and Importing Registry Keys

There are lots of situations in which you will want to export or import a portion of the Registry. For example, you can move application settings from one computer to another by exporting the appropriate portion of the Registry. It's even possible to avoid reinstalling certain applications by simply copying their files and Registry key to the other computer.

When you export a portion of the Registry, the result is a text file with a .REG extension. Here's a sample of a portion of a typical REG file:

```
Windows Registry Editor Version 5.00

[HKEY_CURRENT_USER\Software\Microsoft\Windows\CurrentVersion\Internet Settings]
"User Agent"="Mozilla/4.0 (compatible; MSIE 6.0; Win32)"
"IE5_UA_Backup_Flag"="5.0"
"NoNetAutodial"=dword:00000000
"MigrateProxy"=dword:00000001
"EnableNegotiate"=dword:00000001
"ProxyEnable"=dword:00000000
"EmailName"="IEUser@"
"AutoConfigProxy"="wininet.dll"
"MimeExclusionListForCache"="multipart/mixed multipart/x-mixed-replace
multipart/x-byteranges "
"WarnOnPost"=hex:01,00,00,00
"UseSchannelDirectly"=hex:01,00,00,00
"EnableHttp1_1"=dword:00000001
"PrivacyAdvanced"=dword:00000000

[HKEY_CURRENT_USER\Software\Microsoft\Windows\CurrentVersion\Internet
Settings\5.0]

[HKEY_CURRENT_USER\Software\Microsoft\Windows\CurrentVersion\Internet
Settings\5.0\Cache]
"Signature"="Client UrlCache MMF Ver 5.2"
...
```

The lines contained in square brackets [] define a Registry subkey. The lines that follow the key name are the settings that are included in the specified branch.

When you export from the Registry, you can export the entire Registry or just the selected branch. I can't think of a situation in which you would want to export the entire Registry. You'd end up with a huge REG file. You could export the Registry as a backup, but you're better off using the Backup applet to back up the system state data.

To export a portion of the Registry, open the Registry Editor and select the key you want to export. Choose File ➢ Export to open the Export Registry File dialog box. Enter a name for the REG file, verify that the Selected Branch option is selected, and click Save.

When it comes time to import a REG file, you have two options. You can open the Registry Editor and choose File ➢ Import, then select the file. The easier method, however, is to simply double-click a REG file. Windows XP then imports the contents of the file (after prompting you to verify the import).

In some situations, you might want to distribute a REG file to multiple users. For example, let's say you're creating a custom category list in Microsoft Outlook, and you want everyone in the company to use the same categories. There are a couple of ways to distribute the categories. You can either create an e-mail with the categories assigned, or simply export the part of the Registry where the categories are stored.

To distribute a REG file, you can attach it to an e-mail and send it to everyone who needs it. If your mail server blocks REG attachments (which I strongly recommend), you can instead place the REG file on a network share and then e-mail a link to the UNC path of the REG file. Recipients can then click the link to download and import the Registry file.

Setting Permissions on Registry Keys

Just as you can with many other objects in Windows XP, you can apply permissions to Registry keys to specify the actions that specific users or groups can take in the selected Registry key. For example, you can prevent others from accessing your Registry remotely by changing the permissions on the winreg key (explained later in this chapter).

Setting permissions can also have implications for you as well as for other users. For example, in the section "Last Used Key," earlier in this chapter, I explained that you can prevent the Registry Editor from automatically opening the last used key in the next session by simply setting permissions on the key where that information is stored. So, if the Registry Editor can't read that key, it can't open the last used key and instead opens at the root of the Registry.

WARNING   Be judicious in your application of permissions in the Registry. Incorrectly applying permissions could prevent you from accessing important keys in the Registry or even stop your system from functioning.

You can use the same method in either Professional or Home Edition to set permissions on a Registry key. Open the Registry Editor, select the key on which you want to set permissions, and choose Edit ➤ Permissions to display the dialog box shown in Figure 21.3.

You can use this dialog box to add or remove users and groups and to modify the permissions that each of those users or groups has in the selected key. The Permissions dialog box gives you access to only a few permissions. To set advanced permissions, click Advanced to open the Advanced Security Settings dialog box. The Advanced Security Settings dialog box includes two options that determine how permissions are applied:

"Inherit from parent the permission entries that apply to child objects"   When this option is enabled, the selected key inherits permissions from the parent key.

"Replace permission entries on all child objects with entries shown here that apply to child objects"   Select this option to apply the selected Registry permissions to all subkeys of the currently selected key.

You can also apply special permissions when you need to fine-tune access to a particular key. In the Advanced Security Settings dialog box, select a user or group and click Edit to display the Permission Entry dialog box shown in Figure 21.4. Table 21.2 lists the advanced permissions and their effect.

FIGURE 21.3:

Use the Permissions dialog box to restrict access to a Registry key.

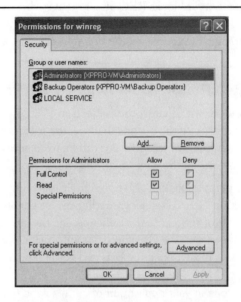

FIGURE 21.4:

You can set several advanced permissions on a Registry key.

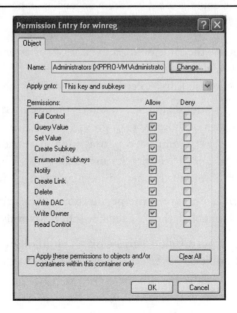

TABLE 21.2: Registry Permissions

Permission	Effect
Query Value	View the key.
Set Value	Set Registry values.
Create Subkey	Create keys.
Enumerate Subkeys	List/view subkeys.
Notify	Open the key with Notify access.
Create Link	Create links to a key.
Delete	Delete a key.
Write DAC	Determine who has access to a key.
Writer Owner	Determine key ownership.
Read Control	Remotely access Registry objects.

Working with Hive Files

Another capability the Registry Editor gives you is the ability to open, modify, and save a hive separate from your computer's own current Registry hives. While you might puzzle over why you would want to do this, there are actually a handful of very good reasons. For example, let's assume that you have a system that won't let anyone log on because of an improper Registry change. The problem computer boots and can be seen on the network, however. The solution is to load the appropriate Registry hive file, make the modifications, and close the file.

TIP   If one of your computers won't boot because of a Registry problem, you can use the Recovery Console to copy the hive file from the problem computer to a working computer, make the necessary changes, and then replace the damaged copy. Because the hive file is probably larger than the capacity of the computer's floppy drive, you'll have to copy it to a removable media such as a Zip disk. Or, if the system uses FAT instead of NTFS, you can boot the system to a Windows 9x boot disk and install a minimal network client on the computer so you can access the files across the network.

You can also use the Registry Editor to open a user's portion of the Registry to make changes for a particular user. The user portion of the Registry is contained in Ntuser.dat, which Windows XP stores in the user's profile folder, such as \Documents and Settings*user*.

To load a hive and modify it, open the Registry Editor on a working system. Click either HKEY_LOCAL_MACHINE if you're opening a system hive or HKEY_USERS if you're opening a user hive. Then, choose File ➢ Load Hive to display the Load Hive dialog box. Browse for and select the hive file and click Open. The Registry Editor prompts you for the hive name. Enter the name under which you want the hive to appear in the editor. For example, if you're opening Joe's user hive, you might use the name Joe's Hive.

> **TIP**   You can open a hive only if it is not in use. If you are opening a user hive from a remote computer, that user cannot be logged on at the time.

The added hive appears under the selected key, as shown in Figure 21.5. You can expand the hive to access keys and values just as you would for a local hive. As with a local hive, Windows XP immediately applies changes to the added hive's file when you make those changes in the Registry Editor. When you are finished working with the hive, select it in the left pane and choose File ➢ Unload Hive.

FIGURE 21.5:

You can load and modify an external hive in the Registry Editor.

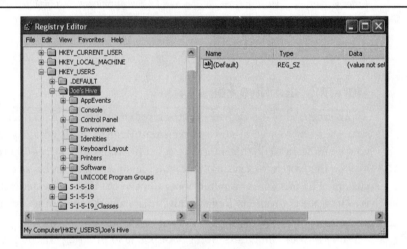

Managing a Remote Computer's Registry

You can use the Registry Editor to view and modify a remote computer's Registry in much the same way you modify a local Registry. For example, you might want to apply a Registry change to several computers across the network and find that the easiest method is to simply make the change through the Registry Editor. Or, using the example in the previous section of a computer that won't allow local logon but can still boot, you could connect to the remote computer's Registry to change the setting that is preventing logon.

Accessing a Remote Registry

Modifying a remote Registry through the Registry Editor is easy. Just open Registry Editor on your local computer and choose File ➢ Connect Network Registry to display the Select

Computer dialog box. Enter the remote computer's name, or browse for the computer and then click OK. Registry Editor adds a new branch to the left pane that includes two subkeys: HKEY_LOCAL_MACHINE and HKEY_USERS. You can then use the same methods in these subkeys to modify keys and values in the remote Registry as you would for the local Registry. Figure 21.6 shows Registry Editor with two remote registries opened.

FIGURE 21.6:

Each remote Registry appears under its own branch in the Registry Editor.

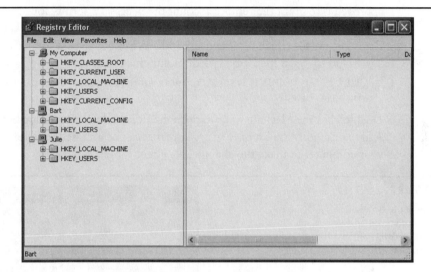

When you've finished viewing or making changes to the remote Registry, choose File ➢ Disconnect Network Registry. Select the Registry you want to disconnect and click OK.

Restricting Remote Registry Access

Your ability to access a Registry remotely depends on the permissions you have in the remote Registry. The permissions on the key

```
\HKEY_LOCAL_MACHINE\System\CurrentControlSet\Control\SecurePipeServers\winreg
```

control which users can access a Registry remotely. By default, the Administrators group has Full Control and can therefore access the Registry remotely. The Backup Operators group has Read permission, as does the LOCAL SERVICE group.

To restrict access or to grant a specific user or group the ability to access the Registry remotely, you must modify the permissions on the key. Open the Registry Editor, select the key

```
\HKEY_LOCAL_MACHINE\System\CurrentControlSet\Control\SecurePipeServers\winreg
```

then choose Edit ➢ Permissions. Use the Permissions dialog box to add users or groups and assign the desired permissions.

In many situations, you will probably want to allow limited remote Registry access. For example, the Directory Replicator service needs remote access to perform replication, and the Spooler service on a remote computer needs remote access to your Registry to be able to print to your shared printer(s).

You can take two approaches to allowing selected remote Registry access. The first approach is to grant the remote account the necessary permissions to your Registry. This is generally not very practical. Instead, you can use the AllowedPaths key to specify specific Registry keys for which remote users and services can bypass the security set on the winreg key. To do so, open the Registry Editor and open the key

```
\HKEY_LOCAL_MACHINE\System\CurrentControlSet\Control\SecurePipeServers\
winreg\AllowedPaths
```

Double-click the Machine value to open the Edit Multi-String dialog box shown in Figure 21.7. Add to or modify the list of Registry keys that can be accessed remotely, then click OK. Restart your computer to make the change take effect.

FIGURE 21.7:

The list of accessible keys is stored as a REG_MULTI_SZ data type.

The Remote Registry Service

Windows XP uses the Remote Registry service to enable remote computers to access the local Registry. The Remote Registry service starts automatically. If you stop this service, remote users and services will not be able to access your local Registry. This can add an additional layer of security for your system as long as your local computer provides no services to other computers on the network (such as printing, replication, etc.). If that's the case, you can configure the Remote Registry for Manual startup to prevent it from starting when the system boots.

NOTE   Windows XP Home Edition does not include the Remote Registry service, so you can't remotely manage the Registry of a Home Edition computer.

CHAPTER 22

Working with Device Manager

Managing hardware in Windows hasn't always been an easy task. Prior to Windows 9*x* and the introduction of Device Manager, managing devices was primarily a matter of kicking real-mode drivers in `Autoexec.bat` or `System.ini` when the devices needed configuration changes. Device Manager made that task much easier by putting a graphical interface on the process.

Windows XP has its roots in Windows NT, and while device management in NT isn't all it's cracked up to be, Windows 2000 made a big leap with its own Device Manager console. You'll find the same console in Windows XP, making device management in Windows XP relatively easy.

As a power user, you won't have any problem working in Device Manager to manage hardware settings, so I don't cover the nuts-and-bolts of it in this chapter. Instead, I focus on ways to make it easier to use Device Manager, such as changing the way it displays information to help you identify and manage resources. This chapter also explains how and why to create device logs with Device Manager to provide a historical record of changes you make to systems.

In larger organizations, the ability to remotely manage systems can be a real boon to power users and system administrators. So this chapter also covers some of the remote-management options.

Tips for Running Device Manager

Windows XP includes Device Manager as a snap-in for the Computer Management console, as shown in Figure 22.1. To open Device Manager, right-click My Computer, choose Manage, and then click the Device Manager node in the left pane.

The Computer Management console is a catch-all, containing management tools you might not use very often. For example, I never use the Indexing Service, WMI Control, or Removable Storage consoles on a Windows XP system. While they certainly apply to XP systems—and you might have need of them—there are probably just as many people who don't use them. So, when you're working with devices, you might want to either work solely with Device Manager or incorporate it into your own custom console.

You'll find the Device Manager in the Computer Management console.

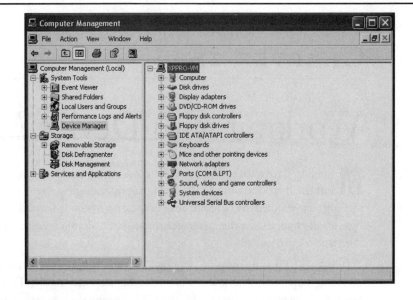

Using Device Manager by Itself

Device Manager is a standard MMC console contained in the file Devmgmt.msc, located in the %systemroot%\Sytem32 folder. You can open this console file to work with Device Manager by itself. One way to do that is to create a shortcut to Devmgmt.msc on your Desktop or in the Start menu. Or, you can simply double-click the MSC file to open the console. Figure 22.2 shows Device Manager running by itself.

You can use Device Manager by itself.

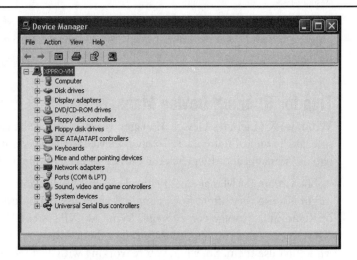

TIP You can also add the Device Manager snap-in to a new console. In most cases, you'll also be adding other snap-ins to the console, which is covered in the next section.

Creating a Custom Management Console

Device Manager lets you view and set properties for a device, such as IRQ usage, DMA, and other resources, as well as install or update drivers. When you're managing devices, however, it's sometimes helpful to have other consoles at hand. For example, you might need to stop and start services when you modify hardware settings, so having the Services console and Device Manager together can come in handy. I prefer Device Manager, Services, and Event Viewer in one console when managing devices. This mix gives me access to all of the information I need to troubleshoot a device, locate an available resource, and otherwise manage the system's devices (Figure 22.3).

FIGURE 22.3:

Create a custom console to include the snap-ins you use most frequently.

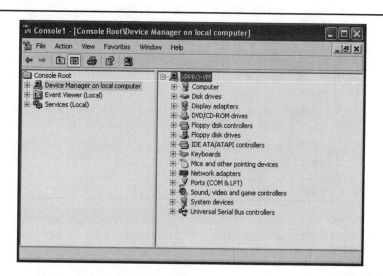

You can easily create your own custom console with these snap-ins, or with any combination you choose. Click Start ➢ Run and enter **MMC** in the Run dialog box. Choose File ➢ Add/Remove Snap-In, then click Add and add the desired snap-ins. For each, Windows XP asks for the focus for the snap-in. Select the Local Computer option when prompted to choose the focus.

TIP If you need to compare the settings on a remote computer with those on the local computer, add two instances of Device Manager—one focused on the remote computer and one focused on the local computer.

Running Device Manager in Administrator Context

When you log on using an account that is a member of the Administrators group, you increase the security risk to your system because applications that run when you are logged on can run in an administrator context. This means the applications have the potential to make changes you might not like. For example, you might connect to a malicious website that downloads and executes an application on your computer that deletes files or compromises your system security in other ways. You also give Trojan horse applications and worms greater access to the system and therefore greater potential to do damage when you run in the Administrator context. For that reason, you should use an account that is a member of the Users or Power Users group for regular work and use an Administrator account only when you need to make system changes.

When you do need to make a change, however, it can be a real hassle to have to close all your programs, log off, and then log on again. Fortunately, you can take a different approach—just run Device Manager or other administrative application in the Administrator context. You use the runas command to do that.

> **TIP**   You can use runas to run any application in a different user context. This chapter focuses on Device Manager.

You can use one of two methods to launch Device Manager in an Administrator context. If you have the Administrative Tools folder on the Start menu, click Start ➢ All Programs ➢ Administrative Tools. Then hold down the Ctrl key and right-click Computer Management and choose Runas from the context menu. In the Run As dialog box (Figure 22.4), select The Following User and then select the Administrator account from the drop-down list.

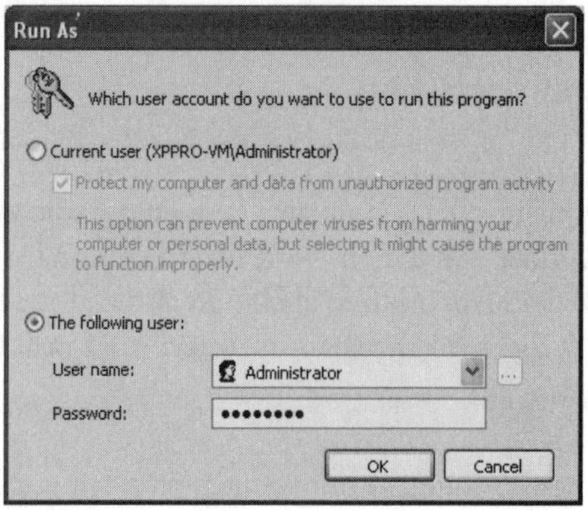

FIGURE 22.4:

Use the Run As dialog box to select an account with administrative privileges.

You can also use the `runas` command in a command console to launch the Device Manager console. Open a command console, change to the *%systemroot%*\System32 folder, and issue the following command:

```
runas /user:administrator "mmc.exe devmgmt.msc"
```

Windows XP will prompt you for the password for the administrator account. After you enter the password, Device Manager will open and you can then manage the system as if you were logged on as an administrator.

NOTE   On a Windows XP Home Edition system, the Owner account serves as the administrator account. Replace administrator in the command line with owner on a Home Edition system.

Controlling Device View

Device Manager, by default, lists the system devices sorted by device type, such as computer, disk drives, display adapters, and so on. This view is useful when you need to locate a specific device. But this isn't the only view Device Manager offers. Its other views can come in handy when you need to manage devices in other ways.

For example, maybe you're trying to resolve an IRQ or a DMA conflict between devices. Rather than search through each device to find its resource settings, you can change the view to show resources by type and view a list of IRQ assignments and the devices that use them. This is a much better view for identifying resource conflicts.

Device Manager provides four views:

Devices By Type   This default view, shown in Figure 22.2, lists devices by their type, such as monitor, display adapter, disk drive, CD-ROM drive, keyboard, and so on.

Device By Connection   This view shows devices according to their connection to the computer. All devices connected to a SCSI adapter, for example, appear together under that adapter. All devices connected to the IDE controller on the motherboard would show up under the IDE controller. Other devices would appear under their respective connections. Figure 22.5 shows Device Manager in Device By Connection view.

Resources By Type   This view shows resource usage sorted by device. The resource categories include Direct Memory Access (DMA), Input/Output (I/O), Interrupt Request (IRQ), and Memory. Each category shows the resources used and the device that is using each one. Figure 22.6 shows the Resources By Type view. You might use this view when trying to identify an available resource.

FIGURE 22.5:

Use the Device By Connection view to show devices according to the way they are connected to the computer.

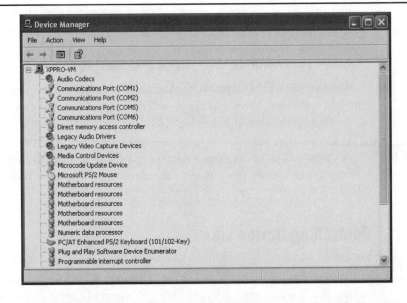

FIGURE 22.6:

Use the Resources By Type view to determine which resources are assigned to which devices.

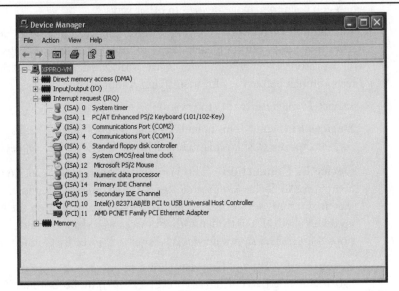

NOTE   This view doesn't show unallocated resources. Unused IRQs, for example, do not show up in the IRQ list.

Resources By Connection This view (Figure 22.7) shows resource use sorted by device connection. It's similar to the Resources By Type view, except that the resource list is organized by device connection rather than device type. You might use this view when you're trying to determine the resources being used by all devices on a given connection (such as all devices on a SCSI or IDE host adapter).

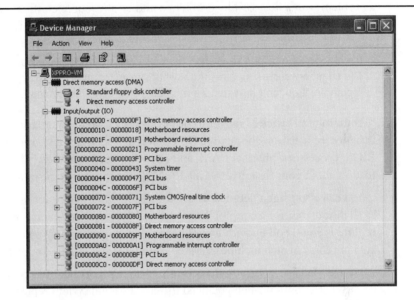

Showing Hidden Devices

Device Manager, by default, hides certain types of devices, such as all non–Plug and Play drivers. This includes the IPSec driver, NDIS system driver, TCP/IP protocol driver, and several others. Device Manager also hides a handful of other devices.

In most situations, you won't need to view or work with the hidden devices. If you do, however, you can easily configure Device Manager to show them. To do so, choose View ➤ Show Hidden Devices. The hidden devices will then show up in your view.

SEE ALSO For more information on working with hidden devices, see Chapter 23.

Creating Device and Configuration Logs

Windows XP can create system restore points that enable you to easily restore the system to a specific condition. For example, assume you're about to install some software or new device. To be safe, you create a system restore point prior to making the change. Then, you install the software or device. If the system is unstable after the change, you can restore the system to the previous state, which is defined by the restore point. Chapter 49 covers System Restore in detail.

In addition to using System Restore, you should also create device configuration logs that will help you troubleshoot problems that might occur with your system's hardware. For example, assume you change a device's DMA or memory settings and a few days later notice a problem with a device. The problem could be a resource conflict. Having a record of the change that you made can help you locate and troubleshoot the problem.

TIP   It's a good idea to print a system summary before taking your computer to be serviced. The summary serves as a record of what's in your computer. While most repair shops are reputable, it doesn't hurt to have a hardcopy on hand just in case.

You can use Device Manager to print or save a system summary. The system summary includes information about your OS version and service packs, registration information, BIOS, processors, physical RAM, and other system properties. The summary also lists information about your disk drives, CD-ROM drive, and device resource usage.

You can also print a detailed listing for a specific device or for an entire device class (such as all disk drives, for example). In most cases, I don't recommend printing a device or class report, as you'll end up with lots of pages. This is particularly true if you print a complete system report, which includes a system summary and details for every device.

Device Manager gives you the means to print a report but not save it to disk, the latter being a much better option when you need to generate a full system report because of the quantity of data. However, you can get around that limitation by printing the report to a generic text printer. If you haven't already done so, run the Add Printer wizard and create an instance of the Generic / Text Only printer pointed to FILE as the port. Then, print the report to a file.

To print a report, open the Device Manager and choose Action ➤ Print to open the Print dialog box (Figure 22.8). Choose a report in the Report Type group, choose the printer, and click Print.

Managing Devices on a Remote Computer

Device Manager lets you connect to a remote computer and view devices and their settings on that remote computer. However, Device Manager operates in read-only mode when connected to a remote computer. In effect, you can look but not touch—you can only make changes through Device Manager on the local computer, not a remote computer. That isn't very convenient when you need to troubleshoot a computer located in another part of the building, and it's really a drag if that computer is on another continent (unless you're shooting for a company-paid vacation).

FIGURE 22.8:

You can print three types of reports in Device Manager.

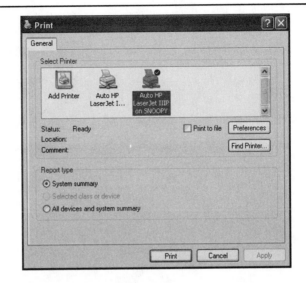

You have a few options for managing devices remotely, most of which require some means of remote access other than a plane ticket. The first (and easiest) option is to use Remote Desktop Connection to connect to the remote computer. You can then open Device Manager on the remote computer and make whatever changes are needed, just as if you were sitting at the remote computer. You can use other remote-access tools instead of Remote Desktop Connection to connect to and manage a remote computer; third-party tools such as pcAnywhere and VNC are good examples.

SEE ALSO   See Chapter 31 for detailed information on setting up and using Remote Desktop Connection.

You have a couple of options for managing remote systems from a console, although this is limited primarily to stopping and starting services. You can connect to the remote computer using a Telnet session (if the remote computer is acting as a Telnet server), or use the netsvc command to manage the remote services.

SEE ALSO   See in Chapter 16 for details on remote service management tools, including netsvc.

CHAPTER 23

Configuring Hardware

Some people love to tinker with computer hardware; others hate it. The rest of us think about our computer's hardware only when one of two things happens: we need to add a new gadget, or one that is already installed fails and needs to be replaced. Windows 2000's incorporation of Device Manager and Plug and Play (PnP) support went a long way toward simplifying device installation and management. Windows XP builds on those capabilities to make device management just as easy.

In order to effectively manage computer hardware under Windows XP, you need to understand some basic concepts. In the first few sections in this chapter, I take you through device drivers and PnP to give you the background you'll need to add, remove, and configure devices under Windows XP. You'll also learn how to update and replace device drivers.

Installing devices is an easy task in Windows XP, so you shouldn't have any trouble with the mechanics of adding or removing devices. So, rather than focus on device installation, this chapter explains how to disable and enable them. The ability to disable devices lets you prevent XP from using a device without actually having to remove it. This is handy when a device would otherwise conflict with another in the system. You can disable one of the devices to avoid the conflict, enabling it and disabling the other when you need to use it. It's also handy when you're experiencing problems with the system, and you want to temporarily shut down a device for troubleshooting.

Resource usage is another important hardware topic you need to understand to effectively manage hardware. In this chapter, I explain how devices often use DMA, I/O, IRQ, and memory resources and how to configure them. For example, you might need to change the DMA channel a device uses to prevent a conflict with another device. This chapter explains how.

Working with Drivers

You don't need to know the ins and outs of Windows XP device drivers and how they work to manage devices. It is important, however, to have a basic understanding of the function that device drivers play and how to work with them.

Understanding Drivers

A *device driver* is a program, usually small, that serves as a means of communication between a device and the operating system. Typically vendors implement device drivers as .sys files, sometimes supplementing them with Dynamic Link Libraries, or DLL files. With a few exceptions, the device driver loads at system startup, enabling Windows XP to communicate with the associated device.

Windows XP includes a large library of drivers for generic equipment types as well as specific third-party devices. These drivers are stored in the %systemroot%\Driver Cache\i386\ driver.cab file. When Windows XP detects a new device, the operating system looks in the driver.cab file for an appropriate driver and, if it finds one, installs that driver and any associated files for the device. If Windows XP can't find a driver, it prompts you to specify the location of the driver files. Some devices provide a Setup program that takes care of installing the driver and any other support software. You've no doubt been through these processes before, so it won't be anything new to you.

In Windows XP, as in Windows 2000, drivers are either *signed* or *unsigned*. Microsoft implemented driver signing to provide additional security for the operating system, but mainly to improve system stability.

Signed drivers have a digital signature attached to them. The signature signifies that the driver has passed certain compatibility and performance requirements from Microsoft's Windows Hardware Quality Labs. The signature also ensures that the driver hasn't been modified by a virus or Trojan horse application or subjected to other unwanted changes. Digital signing doesn't guarantee that a driver is completely free of bugs, but it certainly reduces the likelihood. Later, in the section "Signed vs. Unsigned Drivers," I explain the mechanism that Windows XP provides to prevent unsigned drivers from being installed and the issues to consider when installing drivers.

Viewing Device Driver Properties

Before you go through the trouble of searching for an updated device driver, take the time to determine what version you have now. You don't want to go through the hassle of updating a driver only to find that you already have the latest version.

To view the driver's properties, open Device Manager and locate the device. Double-click the device to open its properties sheet, and then click the Driver tab (Figure 23.1).

As Figure 23.1 shows, the Driver tab lists general information about the provider, driver date, version, and whether or not the driver is signed. You can click Driver Details to display a dialog box that shows the path to each of the files. Click a file to view its version, provider, and other information.

NOTE   Some drivers consist of a single file. Others use two, three, or more depending on the device.

With the version information in hand, you can check the vendor's website or other sources to determine whether a newer version of the driver exists.

FIGURE 23.1:

You can manage a device's driver through the Driver tab.

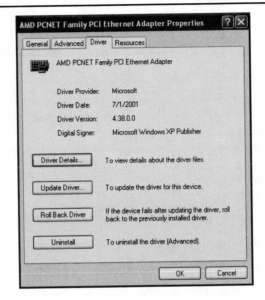

Getting Device Information with driverquery

Windows XP Professional includes a command-line tool you can use to get information about the drivers on a system. You'll find the program Driverquery.com in the %systemroot%\System32 folder. The syntax for the command is:

```
driverquery [/S system [/U username [/P [password]]]] [/FO format]
[/NH] [/SI] [/V]
```

Table 23.1 lists the parameters and variables.

TABLE 23.1: driverquery Parameters

Parameter	Description
/S system	Specify the system from which to display driver information. Omit to use the local system. Specify system in the form *computer* or *domain\computer*.
/U username	Specify the user context in which the program will run.
/P password	Specify the password for the user name specified with the /U switch. Omit to be prompted for the password.
/FO format	Specify the format for the driver information output. Replace *format* with TABLE, LIST, or CSV.

Continued on next page

TABLE 23.1 CONTINUED: driverquery Parameters

Parameter	Description
/NH	Suppress column header for TABLE or CSV formats.
/SI	Display information about signed drivers.
/V	"Verbose;" display detailed information.

When used without any parameters, Driverquery lists information about drivers on the local system as shown in the following sample output using the default TABLE output mode:

```
Module Name   Display Name             Driver Type   Link Date
===========   ======================   ===========   ======================
AFD           AFD Networking Support   Kernel        8/17/2001 8:30:36 PM
AsyncMac      RAS Asynchronous Media   Kernel        8/17/2001 3:55:29 PM
atapi         Standard IDE/ESDI Hard   Kernel        8/17/2001 3:51:49 PM
Atmarpc       ATM ARP Client Protoco   Kernel        8/17/2001 3:46:40 PM
audstub       Audio Stub Driver        Kernel        8/17/2001 3:59:40 PM
Beep          Beep                     Kernel        8/17/2001 3:47:33 PM
cbidf2k       cbidf2k                  Kernel        8/17/2001 3:52:06 PM
Cdaudio       Cdaudio                  Kernel        8/17/2001 3:52:26 PM
Cdfs          Cdfs                     File System   8/17/2001 10:33:34 PM
Cdrom         CD-ROM Driver            Kernel        8/17/2001 3:52:25 PM
Disk          Disk Driver              Kernel        8/17/2001 3:52:31 PM
dmboot        dmboot                   Kernel        8/17/2001 3:58:34 PM
dmio          Logical Disk Manager D   Kernel        8/17/2001 3:58:27 PM
dmload        dmload                   Kernel        8/17/2001 3:58:15 PM
Fastfat       Fastfat                  File System   8/17/2001 10:39:54 PM
```

Verbose mode displays considerably more information, such as start mode, state, status, the amount of memory used by the driver, and more. Verbose mode generates a wide listing that you will have difficulty viewing in a console, but you can redirect the output to a file and view it in Notepad. The following example redirects to a file:

```
driverquery /V > DriverInfo.txt
```

Use the LIST output mode when you want to display the driver information in a vertical list, with each driver separated from the next by a blank line:

```
Module Name:    Update
Display Name:   Microcode Update Driver
Driver Type:    Kernel
Link Date:      8/17/2001 10:53:56 PM

Module Name:    usbhub
Display Name:   USB2 Enabled Hub
Driver Type:    Kernel
Link Date:      8/17/2001 4:03:11 PM
```

```
Module Name:      usbuhci
Display Name:     Microsoft USB Universal Host Controller Miniport Driver
Driver Type:      Kernel
Link Date:        8/17/2001 4:03:04 PM

Module Name:      VgaSave
Display Name:     VgaSave
Driver Type:      Kernel
Link Date:        8/17/2001 3:57:51 PM

Module Name:      vmx_svga
Display Name:     vmx_svga
Driver Type:      Kernel
Link Date:        11/1/2001 12:11:15 AM
```

Use the CSV format when you want to output the information in comma-delimited format for import into a spreadsheet or database. Generally, you will redirect the output to a file rather than the display when using the CSV mode. The following is a sample output using CSV mode:

```
"Module Name","Display Name","Driver Type","Link Date"
"AFD","AFD Networking Support Environment","Kernel ","8/17/2001 8:30:36 PM"
"AsyncMac","RAS Asynchronous Media Driver","Kernel ","8/17/2001 3:55:29 PM"
"atapi","Standard IDE/ESDI Hard Disk Controller","Kernel ","8/17/2001 3:51:49 PM
"
"Atmarpc","ATM ARP Client Protocol","Kernel ","8/17/2001 3:46:40 PM"
"audstub","Audio Stub Driver","Kernel ","8/17/2001 3:59:40 PM"
"Beep","Beep","Kernel ","8/17/2001 3:47:33 PM"
"cbidf2k","cbidf2k","Kernel ","8/17/2001 3:52:06 PM"
"Cdaudio","Cdaudio","Kernel ","8/17/2001 3:52:26 PM"
"Cdfs","Cdfs","File System ","8/17/2001 10:33:34 PM"
"Cdrom","CD-ROM Driver","Kernel ","8/17/2001 3:52:25 PM"
"Disk","Disk Driver","Kernel ","8/17/2001 3:52:31 PM"
"dmboot","dmboot","Kernel ","8/17/2001 3:58:34 PM"
"dmio","Logical Disk Manager Driver","Kernel ","8/17/2001 3:58:27 PM"
"dmload","dmload","Kernel ","8/17/2001 3:58:15 PM"
"Fastfat","Fastfat","File System ","8/17/2001 10:39:54 PM"
"Fdc","Floppy Disk Controller Driver","Kernel ","8/17/2001 3:51:22 PM"
```

TIP Use the /NH parameter if the program in which you will be importing the information does not need the first line of the file to include the column or field names. For example, exclude the column headings if you are importing the data into an existing database that already has the fields defined.

The Driverquery tool can be a truly useful tool for displaying information about drivers on a local or remote computer, but is most useful for gathering information for analysis in a database, spreadsheet, or other data analysis tool.

TIP   You can use the Driverquery command from a local console to retrieve information about drivers on a remote system that is located on your network. For systems not on the local network, connect with a Telnet session and use the Driverquery in the Telnet session to retrieve information from those remote systems. Keep in mind that you need to make a connection only to a Telnet server on the remote LAN, and can use the Driverquery tool to retrieve driver information from any computer on that remote LAN—you don't need a Telnet session to each remote computer.

Driver Compatibility

In general, Windows XP is particular about the drivers you install, and whenever possible you should use a driver written specifically for Windows XP. In a pinch when no XP driver is available, however, you should be able to use a Windows 2000 version of a driver without any problems. Although there is the possibility of an exception, most drivers written for Windows 9x and NT will not work well, if at all, under Windows XP. If you have a device you need to use under Windows XP and the vendor doesn't offer a 2000 or XP driver, you can certainly try installing the driver. However, back up your critical files and/or create a system restore point before installing the driver. Then, test the system fully after installation to make sure everything is working properly.

SEE ALSO   See Chapter 46 for detailed information on creating system restore points and restoring a system using this method.

Updating/Replacing Device Drivers

Most hardware vendors continue to improve on their drivers after the initial release, incorporating bug fixes and in some cases adding support for new features. So it's a good idea to check periodically for updated drivers and replace them if you're looking for additional features. This is particularly true if you're experiencing a problem with a device. Check the vendor's website for driver updates, and also check your computer manufacturer's site for updated drivers. You'll need the device name and model, which you can generally find in Device Manager. Just expand the device branch to view the device name and model of devices under the selected branch.

WARNING   I subscribe to the old adage, "If it ain't broke, don't fix it." Not the most grammatically correct bit of wisdom, but still good advice. If you're satisfied with the way a device is working, don't go looking for updates. You might find that a new driver introduces problems you didn't have before.

When you're ready to upgrade the driver, you can take one of two methods depending on the way the vendor has packaged the driver. In some cases, the vendor includes a Setup program that you can run to update the driver. If so, just run the Setup program and follow its prompts to install the update. Otherwise, you can update the driver through Device Manager.

> **TIP**   Installing or removing devices requires administrator privileges. You must either log on as a member of the Administrators group or supply the administrator password when prompted by Windows XP.

First, open Device Manager and locate the device whose driver you want to update. Double-click the device to open its properties sheet, and click the Driver tab. Then, click Update Driver to start the Hardware Update Wizard.

Follow the prompts provided by the wizard, pointing it to the location where your new driver files are located. If you have a CD or floppy, browse the disk for a Windows XP folder, and lacking that, a Windows 2000 folder (or a folder obviously intended for those platforms, such as W2K or WXP). If you downloaded the files to your hard disk, select the download location, instead.

Rolling Back after an Upgrade

Windows XP keeps track of changes that you make when you update a driver or add a new device. So, if you update a driver and find that it doesn't give you the performance or features you were looking for, or it introduces new bugs or problems you didn't have before, you can easily roll back the system to use the previously installed driver. This is similar in a way to restoring the system from a restore point, but rolling back a driver affects only the selected driver. It has no other impact on the system state.

To roll back a driver, open Device Manager and then open the properties for the device. Click the Driver tab, then click Roll Back Driver. Windows XP prompts you to confirm that you want to perform the rollback, then accomplishes the task for you.

> **TIP**   If you have not updated the driver for a device, and therefore no backup driver exists, Windows XP displays a dialog box that gives you the option of launching the Troubleshooter to troubleshoot the device. Click No to cancel or Yes to start the Troubleshooter.

Uninstalling a Driver

There are a handful of circumstances in which you might want to uninstall a driver. You might want to remove it to reinstall the driver from scratch. You might not be using the device and want to prevent the device driver from loading or consuming any system resources. Or perhaps you've determined that the current driver is buggy and want to remove it until you can obtain an updated driver. Uninstalling the driver prevents the driver from loading but does not remove the device. When it's time to get the device going again, you only need to reinstall the driver, not the device. This can save you a bit of time.

To uninstall a driver, open Device Manager and open the properties sheet for the device. Click the Driver tab and then click Uninstall. Windows XP prompts you to confirm the deletion and then removes the device driver's files and corresponding Registry entries.

If you're removing the driver for a PnP device, the device must be plugged in. So for removable devices such as PC Card network adapters, modems, and so on, make sure the device is plugged in and then remove the driver. You can unplug the device after removing the driver.

TIP	You can reinstall drivers for a PnP removable device without removing and then reinserting it. Just open Device Manager and choose Action ➤ Scan For Hardware Changes. Windows XP will redetect the device and install its driver.

Signed vs. Unsigned Drivers

As I explained previously in this chapter, driver signing helps ensure that drivers are fully compatible with Windows XP and have been through testing for performance and reliability. It's therefore always preferable to use signed drivers rather than unsigned ones.

In some situations, however, you find that you cannot get a signed driver for a device. Maybe the device manufacturer chose not to go through the added effort and expense to have the driver certified and signed (not a good indication of quality, unfortunately). Or maybe the device is relatively old and the manufacturer chose not to write a driver for Windows XP, or the company is out of business. Whatever the situation, you can use unsigned drivers. You can also control the way Windows XP handles unsigned drivers.

Controlling Driver Signing Locally

If you attempt to install an unsigned driver, Windows XP displays a warning dialog box that gives you the option of either continuing with the installation or canceling it. You can configure other behavior for unsigned drivers, as well. To do so, open the System properties sheet from Control Panel and click the Hardware tab. Click Driver Signing to open the dialog box presented in Figure 23.2.

You can choose one of three options: have Windows XP ignore driver signing and always install drivers, have it prompt you (the default), or always prevent unsigned drivers from being installed. If you are logged on as an administrator, you can choose the option Make This Action The System Default to apply the setting to all users of the local computer.

FIGURE 23.2:

Configure how Windows
XP handles unsigned
drivers through the
Driver Signing Options
dialog box.

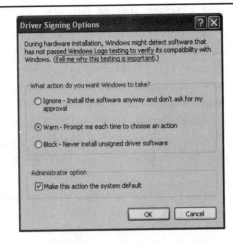

Controlling Driver Signing with Group Policy

In a large network, it isn't usually practical to configure Windows XP's driver signing behavior through the method I described previously. In these situations, it's much easier and more effective to apply the behavior through a group policy.

NOTE   You can apply the behavior locally by modifying the local policy. Open the MMC and add the Group Policy snap-in focused on the local computer. Then modify the policy as explained in this section for group policies.

To configure group policies for driver signing, open the Active Directory Users And Computers console on a Windows 2000 or Windows .NET domain controller for the applicable domain. Right-click the domain or organizational unit and choose Properties. Click the Group Policy tab, then edit an existing group policy object or create a new one. Expand the \Computer Configuration\Windows Settings\Security Settings\Local Policies\Security Options branch. Open the Unsigned Driver Installation Behavior policy and select Define This Policy Setting. Then, choose one of the following from the drop-down list:

Silently Succeed   Allow unsigned drivers to be installed without prompting or warning.

Warn But Allow Installation   Prompt the user to allow or prevent the driver to be installed.

Do Not Allow Installation   Block unsigned driver installation.

TIP   You can define the policy at the site level to apply to all domains, if desired. Use the Active Directory Sites And Services console to set the policy rather than the Active Directory Users And Computers console.

Stopping and Starting Device Drivers

Although you will most often disable a device to prevent Windows XP from using it, you might occasionally want to stop or restart a device driver. You can determine which device drivers can accept a stop or start command by listing the services with Driverquery (explained in detail in a previous section). Use the /V switch to create a verbose listing, then check the value for the service in the Accept Stop column. If this value is TRUE, you can stop and start the service.

You can stop and start certain services through Device Manager. Choose View ➤ Show Hidden Devices to display the non-PnP devices. Open the properties for the device whose driver you want to stop, then click the Driver tab. Click Stop or Start as appropriate.

TIP   If you want to test your ability to stop and start a service, try stopping and starting the Beep driver. It's a relatively low-priority service that won't be missed.

You can also stop and start drivers using the NET command. Open a console, then type **net stop *driver***, where *driver* is the device driver's name. Use **net start *driver*** to start the driver again.

SEE ALSO   For more information on working with services and the `net` command (as well as its remote cousin, `netsvc`), see Chapter 16.

Managing Plug and Play

In its earliest incarnation, Plug and Play (PnP) worked sporadically at best. Over time, however, manufacturers and Microsoft have worked together to improve PnP's performance from the system, device, and operating system perspectives.

PnP has several requirements in order to work properly and allow automatic installation and configuration of hardware. First, the system's BIOS must support PnP. All new systems support PnP, as do many older systems. A quick scan through an older system's BIOS setup program for PnP-related settings will tell you whether the system supports PnP.

The second requirement to support PnP device management is a PnP-compliant operating system. Windows 95 was the first of Microsoft's OSes to support PnP, and support has only improved in later versions, including Windows XP.

Third, the device itself must support PnP. This means that the device must be able to provide an identification string to the operating system so the OS can identify the device manufacturer, type, model, etc. The OS needs this information to automatically install support for the device (more on this shortly). Also, the device must be able to provide the OS with a list of its required resources, including such system resources as DMA channel and IRQ, but also the drivers it requires. Finally, the device must be designed to detect and respond to PnP events such as directives to power down the device (where applicable) or other hardware control events. With a true PnP-compatible device, Windows XP can dynamically load and unload drivers as needed. Unplug a PC Card network adapter, for example, and Windows XP can shut down the driver until the device is reinserted, at which time it restarts the driver.

ISA-bus devices (8-bit or 16-bit ISA adapters) generally do not support PnP. Most PCI-bus devices do support PnP. PC Card (formerly PCMCIA) and USB devices are by definition PnP devices. So with rare exceptions, all of the devices sold today that connect to the system through PCI, PC Card, USB, or FireWire (IEEE 1394) interfaces support PnP. Devices that connect through a standard serial or parallel port can support PnP, but the likelihood is less than for the other interface types.

PnP Device Installation

The beauty of PnP is that it automates the device installation process. So, there isn't really a lot for me to tell you about installing PnP devices, except briefly how it works.

When you install a PnP device and boot Windows XP (or simply connect the device to a PnP-compatible bus such as USB), the operating system reads the ID string stored in the device's firmware or BIOS. XP then looks in its driver index—which it builds from the files in the *%systemroot%*\Inf folder—for a match. If it finds one, it installs the appropriate driver file(s) and makes any other needed system modifications to support the device. When the process is complete, Windows XP displays a message informing you that the installation is complete.

TIP   Many PnP devices require that you install the software that comes with the device before installing the device itself. This adds the driver files to Windows XP's driver index and allows the OS to install the drivers automatically.

If Windows XP can't find a driver for the PnP device, it starts the Found New Hardware Wizard, which prompts you for the location of the drivers for the device. This is the same method XP uses for non-PnP devices that it is able to detect.

NOTE   Windows XP detects non-PnP devices in much the same way it detects PnP devices, querying the devices for ID strings. The main difference is that the PnP devices allow Windows XP to automatically configure the device. Non-PnP devices don't support configuration by the OS. However, Windows XP is at least able to identify and install the appropriate driver for most non-PnP devices and enable you to specify any required settings such as IRQ or other resources.

Managing Devices

As I explained in the chapter introduction, I don't cover adding and removing hardware per se in this chapter, because you shouldn't have any problems accomplishing it. Instead, this section focuses on how to manage devices that are already installed in the system.

Enabling and Disabling Devices

Occasionally you might have two devices that need the same resources, or have a device that seems to be preventing an application or another device from working properly. Although you could remove the device, you might prefer to simply disable it. This shuts down the device but makes it an easy matter to get it going again when you need it—just enable it again.

TIP If two devices conflict with one another and you don't need to use them at the same time, you can create two hardware profiles and disable one device in each profile. Then, boot with the appropriate profile when you need to use a specific device. I cover hardware profiles in Chapter 24.

To temporarily disable a device, open Device Manager and open the properties for the device to be disabled. On the General tab, select Do Not Use This Device (Disable) from the Device Usage drop-down list and click OK. To reenable the device, open the General tab again and select Use This Device (Enable) from the drop-down list, then click OK.

Device Resource Use

Most devices use some type of system resource. These resources include Interrupt Request Line (IRQ), Direct Memory Access (DMA) channel, I/O base address, and memory address. The system has a limited amount of each resource type, and as you add more devices, the potential for resource conflicts increases. You might occasionally need to modify the resources used by a device to overcome a resource conflict.

Fortunately, resource conflicts in Windows XP are rare unless your system contains multiple legacy devices (non-PnP adapters). Most devices don't require DMA, so the system can usually accommodate all DMA-needy devices with the available DMA channels. The same is generally true for devices that require an I/O base address or a memory range.

The exception to this plethora of resources is the IRQ resources available on the system. With earlier systems, IRQ allocation was a real problem, and finding an available IRQ for a device in an already heavily populated system was difficult. Thankfully, Windows XP takes advantage of the fact that most of today's devices that require an IRQ are PCI devices, and that most of today's motherboards provide Advanced Configuration and Power Interface

(ACPI) compliance, which enables them to share IRQs among multiple devices. So it's not at all uncommon to see two or three devices in a Windows XP system using the same IRQ.

> **TIP** Although some devices support sharing IRQs, they also refuse to work correctly if sharing an IRQ. Everything might look good with the device's drivers and resources, but it still might not work. Sharing IRQs can be a hit-or-miss proposition.

Configuring Resource Settings

The combination of PnP and ACPI means that you seldom have to make any resource configuration changes for devices in Windows XP. In fact, you often can't change resource settings directly in Device Manager but instead must force changes by removing a specific IRQ from PnP availability in the system's BIOS. But changing resource settings is necessary when you have one or more non-PnP devices in the system. The following section explains how to view and change resource settings.

> **TIP** If you open the Resources tab of a device's properties sheet and the Use Automatic Settings check box is selected and dimmed, you can't modify the resource settings for the device.

To change resources for those devices that support it, open Device Manager and open the properties sheet for the device. Then click the Resources tab (Figure 23.3).

FIGURE 23.3:

The Resources tab shows resource usage.

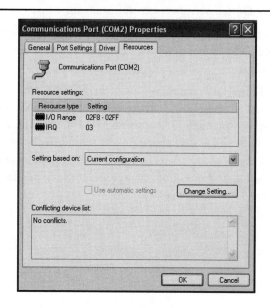

TIP If the device isn't using any resources, the Resources tab contains a single button, Set Configuration Manually. Click this to make the tab change to appear like the one in Figure 23.3.

If the option Use Automatic Settings is selected, clear it. Then, select the resource (I/O range, IRQ, etc.) from the Resource Settings list and click Change Setting. If you receive the error, "You cannot modify the resources in this configuration," you must select a different configuration from the Settings Based On drop-down list. In the resulting dialog box—which differs slightly according to the resource type—choose the resource setting you want to use and click OK.

NOTE If the resource value you select is already in use by another device, Device Manager shows the conflicting device in the Conflict Information list. You can then either select a different value or change the resource usage on the other device.

Managing Hidden Devices

I've already discussed, to some degree, the existence of hidden devices in Windows XP and the fact that you can view and manage them in Device Manager. Hidden devices are primarily non-PnP drivers, but there are a handful of others.

To view the hidden devices, open Device Manager and choose View ➤ Show Hidden Devices. Device Manager then refreshes the display to show additional branches and devices.

You can manage hidden devices in much the same way you manage other devices in Device Manager. The General tab for a hidden device's properties sheet, for example, lets you enable or disable it.

The Driver tab, though, is somewhat different from the Driver tab for other types of devices. For most hidden devices, you can use the Driver tab to stop and start the driver as well as configure its startup method. In general, you will probably not have to stop or start these devices except in the situations I suggested earlier in this chapter. Unless you're directed to do so by a support engineer, I don't recommend changing the startup type for a service unless you understand the implications of the change and how it will affect not only the device, but also other devices and system services.

Chapter 24

Using Hardware Profiles

If you use a desktop computer with no removable devices, it's unlikely that you ever need to disable devices unless two devices in the system conflict with one another. Notebook users, on the other hand, often switch devices through the notebook's PC Card slots. For example, maybe you connect to two different networks with your notebook and get tired of switching network settings. Whatever the situation, you can use hardware profiles to provide a specific hardware configuration when you need it.

Unfortunately, you can't switch between hardware profiles dynamically. Instead, Windows XP will automatically choose a profile based on the hardware it detects at startup. You can also select a profile yourself at startup.

Working with Hardware Profiles

When Setup installs Windows XP, it creates a default hardware profile named Profile 1. Because there is only one hardware profile, Windows XP always boots with that profile. By default, all hardware in the system is enabled for the default profile. You can view the profile through the System properties sheet. Right-click My Computer and choose Properties, or double-click the System icon in Control Panel, to open the System Properties dialog box. Then, click the Hardware tab and click Hardware Profiles to display the dialog box shown in Figure 24.1.

This dialog box lists all hardware profiles that exist on the computer and allows you to view their properties, create new profiles by copying existing ones, remove profiles, and rename them.

FIGURE 24.1:

Use the Hardware Profiles dialog box to create and manage hardware profiles.

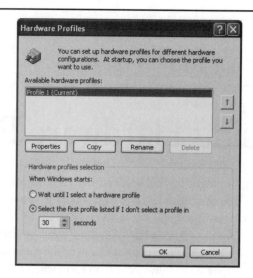

The following two options on the Hardware Profiles dialog box control the way Windows XP handles hardware profiles at startup if it can't automatically determine the appropriate profile based on the hardware's configuration:

"Wait until I select a hardware profile" Select this option if you want Windows XP to wait indefinitely until you select a profile from the proffered list.

"Select the first profile listed if I don't select a profile in" Select this option if you want Windows XP to automatically select the first profile in the list if you don't make a selection in the time specified.

Changing Profile Properties

The first step you might want to take is to view and possibly change the properties of the default profile. Select the profile and click Properties to display its properties sheet (Figure 24.2).

If you're viewing the profile on a portable computer, select the option This Is A Portable Computer. Then choose one of the following options:

The Docking State Is Unknown Windows XP selects this option automatically if it can't determine whether the computer is connected to a docking station.

The Computer Is Docked Select this option if the computer is connected to a docking station.

The Computer Is Undocked Select this option if the computer is not connected to a docking station.

FIGURE 24.2:

Use the Profile 1
Properties dialog box
to configure the way
Windows XP uses the
profile.

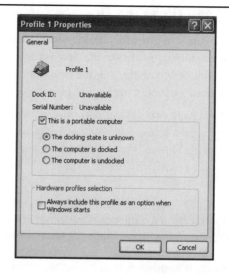

The latter two settings let you explicitly set the docked state for the hardware profile. If you don't have a docking station and Windows XP isn't able to detect the docked/undocked status, choose The Computer Is Undocked. If you want Windows XP to consider the computer to be docked whenever the selected profile is used, select The Computer Is Docked.

The last option on the profile's property sheet—"Always include this profile as an option when Windows starts"—forces Windows XP to display this hardware profile during boot, even if Windows XP detects that a more appropriate profile exists (one that more closely matches the current hardware). Even if you don't select this option, Windows XP still might display this profile if it can't determine whether or not the profile is appropriate to the current hardware configuration.

Creating Profiles

If you experiment in the Hardware Profiles dialog box, you'll find that you can't delete the current hardware profile, which means that initially you can't delete the original profile because it's the only one. This makes sense, as Windows XP needs at least one hardware profile from which to boot.

Another protection that Windows XP offers to keep you from trashing your system is the fact that you can't create a hardware profile from scratch. Instead, you have to copy an existing profile. To do so, open the Hardware Profiles dialog box, select a profile, and click Copy. Windows XP prompts you for a new profile name and then creates the new profile with that name, using the selected profile as the basis for the new one.

Enabling and Disabling Devices for a Specific Profile

When you create a new profile, it's identical to the source profile. So all devices that are enabled in the source profile are enabled in the new one. Likewise, all devices that are disabled in the source are disabled in the new one. This prompts the question, "Why would you disable a device in a profile in the first place?"

Let's say you have two devices that otherwise conflict with one another. You only use one infrequently. The solution is to create two hardware profiles, one with Device A enabled and another with Device B enabled (and the conflicting device disabled in each). Then, when you need to use a particular device, you simply boot the system with the applicable hardware profile.

SEE ALSO Network adapters in a notebook are another scenario in which you might disable a device in a particular profile. See Chapter 29 for an explanation.

Performance is another reason to disable certain devices. A poorly written device driver might impose an unacceptable load on the computer, but it's the only driver available. If you don't use the device often, you can disable it in the main profile and enable it in a secondary profile. When you need to use the device, you simply boot using the secondary profile.

You can enable and disable devices only in the current profile. So to disable a device in a specific profile, you must boot the computer with that profile. Create the profile if you haven't already done so. Then, boot the computer using the profile in which you want to disable a device (or enable a currently disabled device).

TIP When you boot the computer, Windows XP should display both profiles, since they are initially identical. If one profile doesn't appear for some reason, open the profile's properties and select the option "Always include this profile as an option when Windows starts."

You don't enable or disable devices through the Hardware Profiles dialog box. Instead, you accomplish this task through Device Manager. Open Device Manager and open the properties for the device you want to modify. On the General tab (Figure 24.3), select the desired option from the Device Usage drop-down list.

SEE ALSO See Chapter 22 for tips on working with Device Manager.

FIGURE 24.3:

Enable or disable a
device through the
General tab in its
Device Manager
properties sheet.

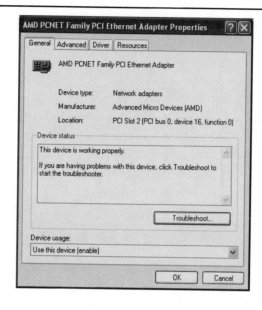

CHAPTER 25

Managing the File System

There are several advanced features in Windows XP that can baffle even the most experienced users. IPSec, encryption, and some other features can seem like a foreign language.

There are also a couple of *basic* features that can confuse users, and the file system is one such feature. In order to choose between FAT and NTFS file systems, for example, you need to know the advantages and disadvantages of each. In order to set up a fault-tolerant volume, you need to understand not only what RAID is all about, but also understand the difference between basic and dynamic disks.

This chapter explains several key features associated with the file system options in Windows XP, beginning with a discussion of the pros and cons of FAT and NTFS to help you decide which file system is right for a particular computer. I also cover, in this chapter, how to configure disks and volumes, including how to use compression and how to optimize volumes in other ways.

Another feature you'll find handy for NTFS volumes is the ability to mount a volume to an empty NTFS folder. You could, for example, increase the apparent size of drive C: when it nears capacity by installing a new drive and mounting it into a folder in drive C:. This would let you go from, say, a nearly full 4 GB disk to a 40 GB disk without replacing the existing drive or moving any files.

Windows XP also supports Redundant Array of Independent Disks (RAID), which lets you extend and protect volumes. Windows XP Professional supports RAID level 0, which offers improved performance but no fault tolerance. I discuss RAID levels in detail later in the chapter.

Windows XP adds some new wrinkles for sharing folders and files, and I try to iron out those wrinkles for you in this chapter, as well. The new Simple File Sharing can be difficult to understand (paradoxically), particularly if you are experienced with the file sharing mechanisms in Windows 2000 and other platforms. I'll even show you a trick to get around Simple File Sharing in Windows XP Home Edition when you need better sharing security.

Choosing the Best File System

You have two choices for file systems in Windows XP: FAT or NTFS. Each has certain advantages and disadvantages in terms of performance and security. The following sections offer a look at each.

File Allocation Table (FAT)

FAT stands for File Allocation Table, which is the mechanism this type of file system uses to store information about files and folders. I won't cover FAT in detail, but you need to understand the high points to make an informed choice between FAT and NTFS.

First, there are various flavors of FAT, including FAT, FAT16, FAT32, and a few others not worth mentioning. FAT32 is the most efficient in terms of storage capacity and performance. FAT32 was introduced in one of the maintenance releases of Windows 95. Windows NT doesn't support it, but Windows 2000 and Windows XP do.

NOTE   Windows NT does support FAT, as do all other Microsoft operating systems going back to the first incarnations of DOS.

The main advantage that FAT file systems offer is compatibility. For example, in a system with a dual-boot configuration with Windows XP on an NTFS volume and Windows 98 on a FAT volume, the Windows 98 installation can't "see" the Windows XP's NTFS file system. Because Windows XP supports FAT, however, it's perfectly happy working with the Windows 98 volume as well as its own. As long as you don't need to use the NTFS volume from Windows 98, you're in good shape.

 Winternals offers a tool called NTFS for Win98 that enables Windows 98 to read and write to NTFS volumes. Rather than include its own NTFS drivers, it hooks into the existing Windows XP NTFS drivers. Check out www.winternals.com if you have older systems that would benefit from NTFS access. Winternals also offers a tool called FAT32 for Windows NT 4.0 that lets NT systems use FAT32 volumes. Finally, keep in mind that the local file system type is irrelevant in terms of access from other computers on the network (except where security is an issue, but more on that later).

File system compatibility can also be a concern during system recovery. If your system won't boot but has a FAT file system, you can boot the computer using a DOS or Windows 9x boot disk and get access to your files. You can even load a small DOS-based network client to enable you to copy files to or from other computers on the network. If the computer uses NTFS instead, recovery can be a little more difficult.

In the past, FAT sometimes offered the advantage of better performance than NTFS, although with the speed of today's computers and hard disk subsystems, it's unlikely that you would notice any performance differences. One area where FAT does lag a bit behind NTFS is in efficiency. Because of differences in the way the two systems allocate space on the disk, NTFS volumes do not become as fragmented as FAT volumes. So, you need to defragment NTFS volumes less frequently if you want to optimize capacity and performance.

SEE ALSO   Many users have the misconception that NTFS volumes don't become fragmented. They do, just not to the degree that FAT volumes do. See "Optimizing Disk Performance" later in this chapter for details on defragmenting disks.

Another disadvantage of the FAT file system is a complete lack of security. FAT offers no means for assigning ownership or access permissions to folders or files, making it almost impossible to prevent a local user from accessing any folder or file on the system. This means that anyone with the ability to log on to the computer can access all of your documents, delete system or other critical files, and generally wreak havoc on the system and compromise your data's security. It also means that if you leave your system logged on while you're away and don't protect it with a screensaver, anyone can slip a disk in a removable drive and copy files to their heart's content.

TIP   The network services built into Windows XP do provide a limited amount of security for folders and files that others access from across the network. See "Understanding and Implementing Sharing" later in this chapter for details.

New Technology File System (NTFS)

NTFS stands for New Technology File System, and this "new technology" has actually been around quite a while, having been introduced in Windows NT. The version included with Windows XP is NTFS 5.

NTFS uses a different on-disk structure from FAT, which offers several benefits. First, NTFS provides excellent security mechanisms to protect folders and files from local access. You can apply permissions to folders and files (or even the entire volume) on a per-user or per-group basis. This means that unless another user has the necessary permissions in your folders, they can't access your data even if they can log on to your computer. It also means that non-administrators can't do any damage by deleting critical system files.

Compression is another benefit offered by NTFS. Although Windows 9x supports compression on FAT-based volumes, Windows XP does not. However, NTFS supports on-the-fly compression and decompression, increasing storage capacity transparently to the user. You can apply compression on a per-volume, per-folder, or per-file basis.

Encryption is another benefit provided by NTFS. As with compression, encryption is completely transparent to users. Just set the encryption attribute on a folder and all files created in that folder are automatically encrypted so that only you—or someone with whom you share your encryption key—can read them. Decryption happens automatically, as well. You don't need to do anything special to open an encrypted document, for example, nor does the program need to know anything about encryption. The operating system handles the entire process at the file system level.

Another benefit of NTFS is its support for mounted volumes. You can mount any volume into an empty NTFS folder, making the volume appear as if it were part of the directory structure in which it is mounted. For example, let's say your computer's drive C: is nearly full. The Program Files folder is using several gigabytes that you need for more documents, and you also need to add more programs (more is always better, right?). No problem! Just add a new volume and, instead of using it as drive D:, move your existing Program Files folder to it and mount it under the now-empty folder on drive C:. Your drive C: now has lots of free space and you can add new programs to the Program Files folder, which is actually now on a completely different disk.

> **TIP** Spanned volumes are another solution to dwindling disk space. You can install a new drive and span it with your existing drive C: to make a logical drive C: that has the total capacity of both disks. See "Managing Spanned Volumes" later in this chapter for details.

Mounted volumes can also simplify the file structure for inexperienced users. For example, you might mount a reference CD or other volume under drive C: so users don't have to work with more than one volume. See "Using Mounted Volumes" later in this chapter for details.

So, what's the bottom line? Since you're reading this book, you're probably a power user and won't have any problems working with permissions or the other advanced features offered by NTFS. In fact, you'll probably find at least some NTFS features indispensable. I recommend NTFS even if you're setting up a system to use at home, particularly if others (such as your children) will be using the computer. NTFS will enable you to secure documents and prevent unwanted changes to the system. If you do have systems that dual-boot between Windows 9x and Windows XP, and these systems contain NTFS volumes that you need to access from Windows 9x, you can always use Winternals' NTFS for Win98.

> **TIP** If you decide to use FAT initially, you can still convert to NTFS later if the need arises. Windows XP can convert FAT volumes to NTFS without much effort and without losing any data.

Configuring Disks and Volumes

The Disk Management console is the main tool you'll use to manage disks and volumes. It's included in the Computer Management console, or you can add it to your own custom console. Figure 25.1 shows the Disk Management console with the Disk List view in the top pane and Graphical View in the bottom pane.

Disk Management offers three views:

Disk List   Organizes the view as a list by physical disk.

Volume List   Organizes the view as a list by logical volumes.

Graphical View   Shows physical disks and logical volumes using a graphical view rather than a list.

Hidden   This option hides the bottom pane.

FIGURE 25.1:
Use the Disk Management console to partition, format, and perform other disk operations.

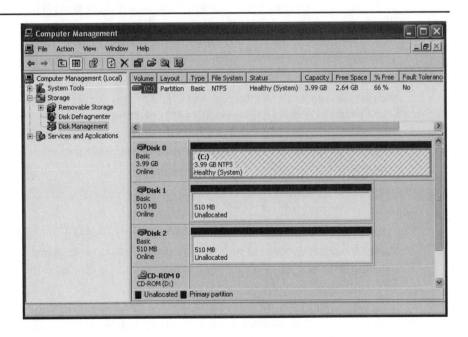

TIP   You must be logged on with an account that has administrator privileges in order to run Disk Management. You can use the runas command to launch the console in an administrative context if your current logon account doesn't have it. See the section "Running Disk Defragmenter in Administrator Context" later in this chapter to learn more about runas.

Some disk operations, such as setting the volume label, aren't covered in this chapter because they are relatively basic and easy to accomplish. You should have no problems with those tasks. Instead, the remainder of the chapter focuses on more advanced disk topics and those that are not self-evident from the Disk Management console.

> **WARNING** If you're coming to Windows XP from Windows NT, understand that Windows XP commits all disk changes as soon as you make the changes in the Disk Management console. This is different from Windows NT, which requires that you manually commit disk changes (such as deleting a partition) to make them take effect.

Understanding Basic and Dynamic Disks

The disks supported by DOS and all versions of Windows prior to Windows 2000 are now called *basic disks*. Non-Itanium, 32-bit systems (your average PC) support a maximum of four partitions per basic disk. These partitions can be either *primary partitions* or *extended partitions*. A primary partition functions as a single logical drive. Extended partitions can contain multiple logical volumes. A disk can include up to four primary partitions, or up to three primary partitions and one extended partition.

Systems with a 64-bit Itanium processor also support both basic and dynamic disks. These systems also support a new type of disk partitioning schemed called GUID Partition Table (GPT), which supports a theoretically unlimited number of unique partitions per disk. GPT also supports volumes up to 8,192 EB (exabytes) in size, and primary and backup partition tables for redundancy. Windows XP 64-Bit Edition runs on Itanium processor-based systems. It can read/write but can't boot from a basic disk.

> **TIP** GUID stands for globally unique ID.

Windows 2000 introduced a new type of disk called *dynamic disks*, and Windows XP Professional carries forward support for dynamic disks. Professional supports features on dynamic disks that it doesn't support on basic disks. This includes the ability to create the following types of volumes:

Simple This volume type comprises space from a single dynamic disk. It can use a single region on a disk or multiple regions on the disk that are linked together. You can extend a simple disk to include additional space, and extending a simple volume onto other physical disks makes it a spanned volume.

Spanned These volumes comprise space on more than one physical disk, enabling you to create a larger volume than what's available on a single disk. You can extend an existing spanned volume to further increase its capacity.

Striped   This type of volume provides better performance by striping the data for a single logical volume across two or more disks. The performance increase comes from distributing read/write load across multiple disks. Striped volumes don't offer any fault tolerance. If one disk in a striped set fails, the entire volume is lost.

RAID   There are several levels of RAID, but Windows XP Professional only supports RAID level 0, or striped volumes (see the previous item). RAID 0 doesn't provide any fault tolerance. To gain that, you need to move up to RAID 1, disk mirroring, or RAID 5, stripe sets with parity. These RAID levels are supported by Microsoft's Server platforms, such as Windows 2000 Server.

NOTE   Windows XP Home Edition does not support dynamic disks, and therefore does not support the features made possible by dynamic disks such as spanned and striped volumes. Throughout the remainder of this chapter, any discussion of spanned and striped volumes or of dynamic disks applies only to Windows XP Professional.

SEE ALSO   See "Creating and Managing Advanced Volumes" later in this chapter for more details on RAID levels and their benefits.

Compatibility is the main advantage offered by basic disks. Systems with operating systems prior to Windows 2000 don't support dynamic disks. This is an issue only on systems that dual-boot between Windows XP (or Windows 2000) and Windows NT, Me, or 9x. If you are only running Windows XP on the computer, you don't have to worry about compatibility, except in one situation: disaster recovery. If you're using basic disks with a FAT file system and something happens to a system that prevents it from booting, you can boot with a Windows 9x or DOS boot disk and still gain access to the files. On systems with NTFS, you can use Recovery Console to attempt to recover the system.

NOTE   Windows NT supports simple, spanned, striped, and RAID volumes, but not through dynamic disks. Windows 2000 and Windows XP support existing volumes of these types on basic disks but require a dynamic disk to create new ones.

When you're deciding which disk type to use, consider whether or not you want to create spanned or striped volumes. If so, you'll need to convert your disks to dynamic disks.

Converting Between Basic and Dynamic Disks

You can convert a basic disk to a dynamic disk without losing any data on the disk. Open the Disk Management console and change the view to show either Disk List or Graphical View. Both of these views show the disk type for each physical disk (Figure 25.2). Right-click the disk and choose Convert To Dynamic Disk. Disk Management displays a dialog box with all drives listed. Place a check beside each disk to convert and click OK.

TIP	When Disk Management converts the disk from basic to dynamic, it must dismount the disk, making it unavailable. If you're sharing folders on the disk, first disconnect all users. You can use the Shared Folders branch of the Computer Management console to close files and disconnect users.

You can revert a dynamic disk to a basic disk, although the volumes on the disk must be empty. To revert a disk, first back up all of the volumes on the disk and remove the volumes and partitions. Then, right-click the disk and choose Convert To Basic Disk. Disk Management reverts the disk without any additional prompts or input.

FIGURE 25.2:
The Disk Management console identifies a disk's type.

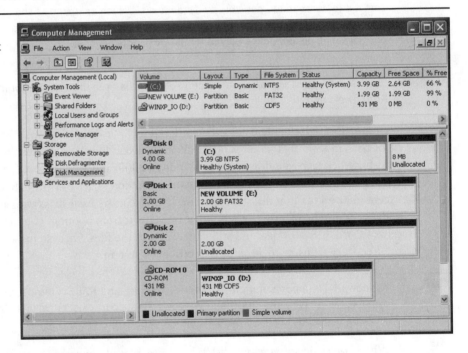

Creating and Activating Partitions

It's a simple matter to create a partition. Just right-click the disk and choose New Partition to start the New Partition Wizard. The wizard prompts you for the partition type, size, driver letter or path (explained in the next section), format, and compression attribute. You should have no trouble creating partitions with the wizard.

You do need to keep one thing in mind, however. If you're going to boot from a partition, that partition must be active. I can't tell you how many times I've cloned a disk to replace an existing smaller drive and forgotten to activate the boot partition on the new disk!

It's easy to activate a partition. Open Disk Management, right-click the partition, and choose Mark Partition As Active. When you reboot, the system will boot from the active partition.

TIP You can also use the FDISK console utility to activate a partition.

Changing Drive Letter or Path

Each volume can have a drive letter associated with it, be mounted in an empty NTFS folder, or both (or neither). You can also create a volume that has no drive letter or path association, although there isn't any way to use it, so that's an unlikely scenario.

To assign a different drive letter to a volume, regardless of the drive's type (hard disk, CD, etc.), open Disk Management and right-click the disk, then choose Change Drive Letter And Paths to open a dialog box.

Click Change if you want to modify the existing drive or path assignment, or click Add to add one. The resulting dialog box is essentially the same except for its title (Figure 25.3). Both of the options are available only if you currently have no letter or path assigned to the volume. Otherwise, the one you currently *don't* have will be available. Choose a drive letter from the drop-down list or enter the path to an empty NTFS folder, then click OK.

FIGURE 25.3:

Use the Add Drive Letter Or Path dialog box to add or change drive letter assignments.

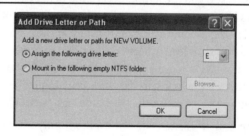

TIP To remove a drive letter or path assignment, open the Drive Letter And Paths dialog box, select the item to remove, and click Remove.

Formatting Volumes

Earlier in this chapter I discussed the pros and cons of FAT and NTFS. You can format a volume as FAT, FAT32, or NTFS, and have three methods for formatting volumes. The first is to use the Disk Management console. Just right-click a volume and choose Format. Click Yes when asked if you're sure you want to format the partition. You'll see the Format dialog box shown in Figure 25.4.

FIGURE 25.4:

Use the Format dialog box to specify file system and other properties for the volume.

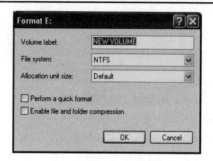

The dialog box contains two options worth singling out here:

Perform A Quick Format   Select this option if you simply want to clear out the file allocation data and not check the disk for errors. This speeds up formatting on a drive that has previously been formatted.

Enable File And Folder Compression   Select this option to enable the compression attribute for the volume. All folders and files created on the volume will be compressed by default.

In most cases, you can simply accept the default allocation unit (cluster) size suggested by Windows XP, but you can manually select a value if you want a specific cluster size. The smaller the cluster size, the more efficiently (in most cases and up to a point) the disk can store data. Larger cluster sizes lead to wasted space due to *cluster slack*. Here's why: when you create a new file, Windows XP allocates space on the disk in clusters. Let's say the disk's cluster size is 32K. You create a file that is 2K in size. The remaining 30K is wasted—Windows XP can't allocate the remaining space to another file, although it can use the space if the file grows in size.

Having a small cluster size can lead to highly fragmented files, reducing performance. That's why I recommend that you let Windows XP choose the cluster size for you. Storage efficiency usually isn't a big deal unless you're really cramped for disk space. With today's inexpensive cost of high-capacity disks, cluster size won't have enough impact to make it worth worrying about. You'd be better off using the time you spend worrying about cluster size cleaning off all the unused files and other junk littering your hard disk.

The second option you have for formatting a disk is to simply right-click the disk in My Computer and choose Format to open the Format New Volume dialog box shown in Figure 25.5.

Use this option when you want to ensure high security for the volume. You can apply whatever permissions are necessary after convert finishes its job.

By default, convert will prompt you whether or not it should dismount a volume before converting it. Dismounting the volume makes it unavailable and is a good idea to help ensure a problem-free conversion. You can use the /X parameter to direct convert to dismount the volume without prompting you.

> **NOTE**   The time required to convert a volume depends almost entirely on the amount of data on the disk. If you're converting a volume that others need to access, and it contains lots of data, consider converting the data after hours when it won't be missed.

 Unfortunately, convert will not convert a volume from NTFS to FAT. In Windows XP itself, there is no way to convert an NTFS partition to FAT or FAT32. Without a third-party utility, you must back up the volume, reformat it, and restore the files. You can, however, use a utility such as PowerQuest's PartitionMagic (www.powerquest.com) to convert the file system, with a few caveats. The NTFS partition can't contain compressed files, sparse files, reparse points, or encrypted files. The NTFS partition also must be error-free, so you might need to perform a check and repair on the volume with chkntfs before performing the conversion.

> **TIP**   NTFS reparse points are the mechanism by which Windows XP implements several file system features. These include mounted volumes, compression, encryption, sparse files, and offline storage. In effect, reparse points are like flags in the file system that direct Windows XP to pass processing of the data that follows to a different file system driver. When the NTFS driver comes to a reparse point indicating an encrypted file, for example, it passes the operation to the EFS subsystem for processing.

Another advantage that partitioning tools like PartitionMagic provide is the ability to merge NTFS partitions. You could merge two 4 GB partitions on the same disk into a single 8 GB partition.

> **WARNING**   When you convert an NTFS partition to FAT or FAT32, extended NTFS data such as permissions, alternate data streams, and quotas are lost.

Optimizing Disk Performance

Even with the relatively low cost of high-capacity disks, it's still important to optimize disk capacity and performance. In this section, I examine two methods for improving disk capacity and performance: defragmentation and compression.

Disk Capacity and Fragmentation

In order to understand why fragmentation occurs and what impact it has on the system, as well as how allocation size affects capacity, you first need to understand a little about disk structure.

A *sector* is the smallest unit of storage space on a disk. The sectors are arranged in circular *tracks* around the disk. The tracks from one platter to another form a *cylinder*. When Windows XP allocates space on disk, it does so using *clusters*. A cluster is a group of sectors. The number of sectors in a cluster is defined when you format the disk. Remember the allocation unit size I described earlier in the section on formatting? That's the cluster size.

The cluster size has a lot to do with disk capacity. Let's say you format a disk with a large cluster size—64K in this example. So, the smallest amount of space that Windows XP can allocate is 64K.

You create a new file that is 20K in size. When Windows XP stores the file, it allocates one cluster, or 64K, for the file, and the 20K of data goes into the 64K cluster. The end result is that the OS has wasted 44K of space, since Windows XP won't store any other data in the unused space in the cluster. It's like putting a small present in a large box—you're wasting the additional space inside the box.

TIP This disk capacity waste is often called *sector slack*.

Many people have the misconception that NTFS is more efficient than FAT because of its difference in file system structure. In fact, NTFS is just as susceptible to sector slack as FAT. The reason NTFS is more efficient is that it uses a smaller default cluster size that ranges from 512 bytes to 4 KB. Using a smaller cluster size means less sector slack and more efficient storage.

NOTE FAT can't address as many clusters as NTFS, and is therefore forced to use larger cluster size as the disk size increases. The result is increased sector slack and less efficient storage.

On the other side of the efficiency coin is *fragmentation*. Windows XP tries to allocate contiguous clusters for a file, or clusters that reside side-by-side in a track on the disk. This makes for faster reading and writing, because the disk heads don't have to move as much to write or read the file. As files change or more files are added to an already fragmented drive, a file can become fragmented—that is, stored in noncontiguous clusters. This reduces performance because the OS has to skip around the disk to pull back together all the pieces of the file. The more file changes that occur, the more fragmentation becomes a potential problem.

Cluster size is the common thread between disk capacity and fragmentation. A small cluster size leads to less sector slack and higher capacity, while a larger cluster size leads to less fragmentation. This might seem like a Catch-22 if it weren't for the availability of a defragmentation tool for Windows XP. You can use a small cluster size to improve disk capacity and efficiency and still avoid excess fragmentation, as long as you periodically defragment the disk.

TIP   When you format an NTFS volume, let Windows XP use the default cluster size or manually specify a cluster size of 4K or less for best performance.

Another disadvantage to using a cluster size larger than 4K on an NTFS partition is that you can't use compression on the volume. So I recommend you stick with the default cluster size for NTFS partitions.

Tips for Defragmenting Disks

Windows XP includes a tool to analyze fragmentation on FAT and NTFS disks and to defragment them, if necessary. The Disk Defragmenter is a console snap-in that resides in the Computer Management console by default. However, you can create your own MMC console and add the Disk Management snap-in to it, if you wish. Figure 25.6 shows the Disk Defragmenter console.

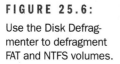

FIGURE 25.6:

Use the Disk Defragmenter to defragment FAT and NTFS volumes.

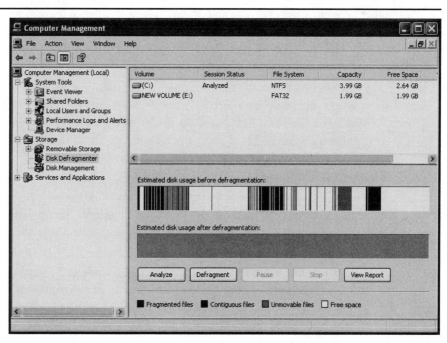

It isn't difficult to figure out the Disk Defragmenter—just right-click a volume and choose Analyze to create a fragmentation report, or choose Defragment to start the defragmentation process. Disk Defragmenter handles the task without any further intervention from you. For that reason, I'll just offer some tips on defragmenting drives rather than explain in detail how to use this tool.

Running Disk Defragmenter in Administrator Context

First, you must be logged in as administrator (or Owner for Home Edition systems) in order to defragment a disk. This doesn't necessarily mean that you must log off and log on again with an account with administrator privileges. Instead, you can use runas to launch the Disk Defragmenter console in an administrator context.

Open My Computer and browse to %systemroot%\System32. Hold down the Ctrl key, right-click Dfrg.msc, and choose Run As to open the Run As dialog box. Select the option The Following User, select Administrator from the drop-down list, and type the appropriate password. Then click OK to launch Disk Defragmenter.

Automatic Defragmentation

Unfortunately, there isn't any mechanism in Windows XP to schedule the Disk Defragmenter to run automatically. Although the Disk Defragmenter console actually uses two other programs, Dfrgfat.exe and Dfrgntfs.exe, neither of these support command-line operation, which would make it possible to schedule the defragmentation with the AT command, Scheduled Tasks folder, or other mechanisms. So, defragmenting a disk is purely a manual process with the Disk Defragmenter console.

In order to gain the ability to defragment automatically, such as at a scheduled time, you need to move to a third-party tool such as Executive Software's Diskeeper. Diskeeper was the first defragmentation tool for NTFS and continues to be a leader in defragmentation technology for Windows platforms. You'll find more information about Diskeeper at www.diskeeper.com.

Using Disk Compression on NTFS Volumes

Windows XP supports on-the-fly compression that lets you increase a disk's apparent capacity. Unlike compression methods for Windows 9x and Me, compression in Windows XP doesn't require that you compress an entire volume. Instead, you can compress specific folders or even individual files.

There is one limitation for disk compression in Windows XP—you can't compress FAT volumes. You can only compress folders and files on NTFS volumes. This isn't much of a drawback, because NTFS is a better choice than FAT in almost all cases, anyway.

Compressing a volume, folder, or file is easy. To compress an entire volume, open My Computer, right-click the volume, and choose Properties. On the General tab (Figure 25.7), select the option Compress Drive To Save Space and click OK.

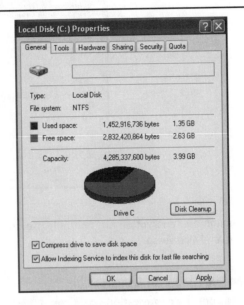

Windows XP next displays the Confirm Attribute Change dialog box. You can apply compression to only the root of the volume or to the entire volume. If you select the latter, all existing folders and files on the volume are compressed, and any new folders or files you create will also be compressed.

TIP   You can set a volume's compression attribute when you format the volume. Look for the Enable File And Folder Compression or Enable Compression check box in the Format dialog box (depends on whether you're formatting from My Computer or Disk Management).

You use a similar method to compress a folder or file. Just right-click the item and choose Properties. On the item's General tab, click Advanced to display the Advanced Attributes dialog box (Figure 25.8). Select the option Compress Contents to Save Disk Space and click OK. As when compressing a volume, Windows XP prompts you to choose whether to compress subfolders and their contents or not.

The reason I've used the term *set the compression attribute* rather than *compress the folder* is that unless you direct Windows XP to compress the subfolders and their contents, the only thing that happens is that Windows XP sets the value of the folder's compression attribute. It doesn't actually compress anything. When you create new files in the folder, however, they are compressed because Windows XP checks the compression attribute and acts accordingly.

FIGURE 25.8:

Use the Advanced Attributes dialog box to set the compres- sion attribute for a folder or file.

TIP   Compression and encryption are mutually exclusive. You can compress a file but not encrypt it, and vice versa.

Moving and Copying with Compression

You need to consider compression when you move or copy files between folders and volumes. When you move or copy a file, those files take on the compression attribute of the target folder, with a few exceptions (explained shortly). For example, copy a file from an uncom- pressed volume to a compressed volume, and the new copy of the file will be compressed. Likewise, copy a compressed file to an uncompressed volume, and the file is uncompressed.

There are two exceptions to this behavior:

- The object retains its original compression attribute if the target folder is on the same volume as the source folder.

- The object is uncompressed if it is copied or moved to a FAT volume, because FAT does not support compression under Windows XP.

Identifying Compressed Folders and Files

By default, compressed folders and files look just like their non-compressed counterparts. You can configure Windows Explorer to display the title under compressed folders and files in blue to identify them as compressed. With any folder open, choose Tools ➢ Folder Options, then select the option Show Encrypted Or Compressed NTFS Files In Color from the View tab.

Working with Zipped Folders and Files

Windows XP supports a second kind of compression that you can use on both FAT and NTFS volumes that doesn't function at the operating system like NTFS compression.

You're probably familiar with ZIP files, which are compressed archives that can contain files and folders. The ZIP format is a standard compression format supported by several software vendors and has become the most popular choice for compressing files for distribution. One of the most popular tools for zipping and unzipping files is WinZip (www.winzip.com).

Windows XP adds support for zipped archives, treating them like compressed folders. You can view a ZIP file's contents as if it were a folder. Just double-click the folder and Windows XP opens a window to display its contents, just as it does for a regular folder. Zipped files appear as an icon with a zipper, as shown in Figure 25.9.

In most cases, you can work with a ZIP file and its contents just like a regular folder. To extract a single file, for example, just open the ZIP file and drag the file to the Desktop. You can also right-click a ZIP file and choose Extract All to extract the entire ZIP file contents to a folder. The Extraction Wizard prompts you for the destination and lets you specify a password for password-protected ZIP files.

The main advantage to using Windows XP's ZIP capabilities is that you don't need to install an application such as PKZIP or WinZip to handle archives. However, Windows XP's ZIP capabilities are rather limited. If you want the full complement of features—such as ability to span disks, perform encoding, or apply a password—you need a third-party tool.

FIGURE 25.9:

Windows XP lets you work with ZIP files without any add-on software.

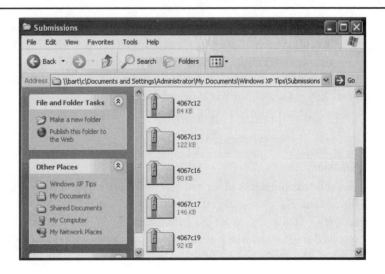

To add a new ZIP file, right-click in a folder and choose New ➤ Compressed (Zipped) Folder. Specify a name for the file, and after it's created, just drag files to it to add them to the archive.

TIP   If you decide to install a third-party ZIP application like WinZip, keep in mind that the direct access you have in Windows XP will no longer be available. Instead, the ZIP application takes over all ZIP file actions. However, some of the third-party applications offer the same capability to treat ZIP files as folders.

Managing Volumes from a Console

Windows XP includes a couple of tools you can use to manage volumes from a command console. You will probably do most of your disk management from the GUI, but you might occasionally need to perform tasks from a console or to incorporate functions into a batch file. The two tools are `fsutil` and `diskpart`. Both offer gut-level access into the file system.

The fsutil Command

`fsutil` lets you manage both FAT and NTFS file systems. This utility gives you quite a bit of power over the file system, so you should use it with care.

TIP   You must be logged on as an administrator to use `fsutil`.

`fsutil` is actually a set of commands rather than a single command. The following sections briefly explain each of the subcommands you can use with `fsutil`. The `fsutil` command is fully documented in the Windows XP Help system, so I won't cover these options in detail here. For information on specific options or usage, open Help And Support Center in Windows XP and search for the keyword **fsutil**.

The syntax for using `fsutil` is:

```
fsutil subcommand options
```

behavior

Use this subcommand when you want to query or set certain properties or behavior of the file system. For example, you can control how Windows XP uses short 8.3-format file names, enable or disable update of the Last Access Time (LAT) attribute for a folder or file, set the reserved size for the MFT zone, and specify how often quota violations are logged to the system log (the default is one hour).

You can view short filenames with the `dir` command. Open a command console and execute the command **dir /X**. The fifth column in the resulting output shows the 8.3 short filename.

dirty

The `dirty` subcommand lets you query or set the value of a volume's *dirty bit*. When the dirty bit is set, it indicates that the file system could be in an inconsistent state. For example, there might be corrupt directory entries, or data might be waiting in the write buffer that hasn't been committed to disk. When the system boots, the Windows XP kernel calls `Autochk.exe` to check volume status. If the dirty bit is set, `Autochk` initiates a check of the disk with `chkdsk /f`.

You can query the status of a volume's dirty bit with the `dirty` subcommand. You can also use it to set the bit to force a check of the volume when the system reboots. The following two examples would check the bit and set it, respectively:

```
fsutil dirty query c:
fsutil dirty set c:
```

You can specify the drive letter followed by a colon, as in these examples, or specify a mount point or volume name.

file

Use the `file` subcommand to perform a range of file operations. The following list explains the options you can use with the `file` subcommand.

createnew   Use this option to create a file of a specified length that contains all zeros for its data. For example, you might use `createnew` to create a large file to test file system performance.

findbysid   Use this option to find files by the security ID (SID) of the user who owns the files. This is useful for listing all files on a volume that are owned by a given user.

queryallocranges   Use this option to query the allocated ranges for a file, which is useful if you're trying to determine whether a file contains sparse regions (regions with all zeros for data).

setshortname   Use this option to set the short 8.3-format filename for a file.

setvaliddata   Use this option to specify the valid data length (VDL) of a file on an NTFS volume.

setzerodata   Use this option to replace a range of data in a file with zeros. If the file is a sparse file, setting a range to zeros has the effect of releasing the clusters used by the range back to the OS, making them available for other files.

fsinfo

The fsinfo subcommand of the fsutil command lets you query information about drives, volumes, and file system statistics. The fsinfo subcommand offers several options.

drives   This option simply lists all of the drives on the system.

drivetype   This option displays the drive type of a specified drive, for example showing Fixed Drive for a hard disk, Removable Drive for a floppy drive, or CD-ROM Drive for a CD drive.

ntfsinfo   Use this option to list detailed information about an NTFS volume, such as number of sectors, total number of clusters, free clusters, and location of the MFT zone.

statistics   This option lists file system statistics, such as log file, metadata, and MFT reads and writes.

volumeinfo   This option displays information about the volume, such as the name, serial number, and file system type.

hardlink

Use the hardlink subcommand to create *hard links* to a file. A hard link is a directory entry for a file. On NTFS volumes, each file has at least one hard link, but can have multiple hard links, enabling it to appear as if it resides in multiple directories. However, there is only one copy of the file. Users can use a file through any of its hard links—they are handled at the file system level and are transparent to the user, who simply sees a file in the directory where the hard link exists. Windows XP deletes a file only after all hard links to it are deleted.

objectid

Object identifiers (OIDs) are used by the Distributed Link Tracking Client service and File Replication Service to track objects such as files, directories, and links. You can use the objectid subcommand to create, delete, query, and set OIDs, but it's unlikely that you will ever need to do so. In fact, you can wreak havoc on the file system by incorrectly modifying OIDs, so stay away from it!

quota

The quota subcommand offers several options to help you manage quotas on NTFS volumes. You can use quota to disable, enforce, modify, query, or track quotas on a specified volume. You can also use it to search a volume for quota violations.

reparsepoint

Reparse points are objects in the NTFS file system that act as flags to the operating system; such a flag indicates that the file or directory associated with the reparse point needs to be handled by a different driver or subsystem. For example, encryption is implemented using reparse points. The NTFS driver begins to read an encrypted file and comes to the reparse point that contains data indicating the file is encrypted. NTFS then passes the operation on to the EFS subsystem, which takes care of decrypting the file on the fly. Other features such as mounted volumes and the Distributed File System (Dfs) rely on reparse points. You can use the reparsepoint option to query or delete reparse points on an NTFS volume.

sparse

A *sparse* file is one that contains one or more regions of unallocated space. The unallocated space would otherwise be filled with zeros or no data. Sparse files enable Windows XP to more efficiently manage disk space, because the space that would otherwise be used by the file for the empty data isn't allocated to the file. Instead, only the space required for the non-zero data is allocated, along with a relatively small amount for the reparse points that enable the operating system to recognize the sparse data areas.

You can use the sparse subcommand to query for and set sparse ranges in a file.

usn

This subcommand lets you manage the update sequence number (USN) change journal, which maintains a complete log of all changes to files on a given volume. Several services use the USN change journal, including the Indexing Service, File Replication Service, Remote Installation Service, and Remote Storage. Although you can use the usn subcommand to create, delete, and query in the USN change journal, you will probably never have to do so.

volume

Use the volume subcommand to dismount a volume or query the amount of free space on the volume. Dismounting a volume makes it unavailable but is necessary for certain actions such as converting a volume from FAT to NTFS.

The diskpart Command

The diskpart command isn't new to Windows XP—it was previously included in the Windows 2000 Recovery Console. What's new is its presence in Windows XP outside of Recovery Console.

diskpart lets you perform a wide range of disk management tasks, which you can accomplish dynamically from a command console or through a script or batch file. You can create diskpart scripts as text files and run them through diskpart to automate disk management tasks. diskpart returns an error code when it encounters an error, enabling you to troubleshoot problems with the script.

TIP In addition to the syntax diskpart *subcommand*, It's also possible to use this by simply typing **diskpart** at the command line and hitting Enter. The prompt will change to DISKPART>. You can then type subcommands directly or type **?** for a list of available commands.

The following list summarizes the subcommands supported by diskpart and the functions they perform. For a detailed discussion of each subcommand, open the Help and Support Center in Windows XP and search for the keyword **diskpart**.

active   Use this subcommand to mark a partition as active. A partition must be active to enable the computer to boot from the partition.

add disk   Use this subcommand to add a disk to a mirror set. You can only mirror simple volumes on dynamic disks. Neither Windows XP Professional nor Home Edition support mirrored volumes; this subcommand applies only to Windows 2000 Server and .NET Server platforms. You can, however, manage mirrored volumes on a server from a Windows XP workstation.

assign   You can assign a drive letter or volume mount point to a volume with this subcommand. You can't assign a different drive letter to the system or boot volumes, to the volume that contains the paging file, or to any OEM partition or GPT partition other than a basic MSDATA partition.

break disk   Use this subcommand to break a mirrored volume. This subcommand applies only to Windows 2000 Server and .NET Server platforms (see the add disk subcommand).

clean   You can remove all partitions and formatting from a volume with the clean subcommand. On MBR-based disks, the MBR and hidden sector data are overwritten. On GPT disks, the GPT partition data (including the Protective MBR) is overwritten. You can use the all parameter with the clean subcommand to replace all data on the disk with zeros, effectively wiping the disk's contents.

convert basic   Use this subcommand to convert a dynamic disk to a basic disk. The dynamic disk must be empty.

convert dynamic   Use this subcommand to convert a basic disk to a dynamic disk. diskpart retains any existing data on the basic disk during the conversion.

convert gpt   This subcommand lets you convert an empty, basic MBR-based disk on an Itanium-based computer to a basic disk with GPT partition style.

convert mbr   Use this subcommand to convert an empty, basic disk containing a GPT partition to a basic disk with an MBR partition.

create partition efi   This subcommand creates an Extensible Firmware Interface (EFI) system partition on a GPT disk. This subcommand only applies to Itanium-based systems.

create partition extended   Use this subcommand to create an extended partition. A disk can contain only one extended partition, although the extended partition can contain multiple logical drives.

create partition logical   Use this subcommand to create logical drives in an extended partition.

create partition msr   This subcommand creates a Microsoft Reserved (MSR) partition on a GPT disk. The subcommand applies only to Itanium-based systems.

create partition primary   Use this subcommand to create a primary partition on a basic disk. A disk can contain up to four primary partitions.

create volume raid   This subcommand creates a RAID 5, or striped set with parity, volume on a Windows 2000 Server or .NET Server platform. Windows XP does not support RAID 5 volumes.

create volume simple   Use this subcommand to create a simple volume on a dynamic disk. Simple volumes can comprise a single region on a disk or multiple regions on the same disk.

create volume stripe   This subcommand lets you create a striped volume using two or more dynamic disks. Striped volumes represent RAID 0, which offers performance improvements but no fault tolerance.

delete disk   Use this subcommand to delete a missing dynamic disk from the disk list. You can use the override parameter to delete all simple volumes from the disk.

delete partition   You can delete a partition on a basic or dynamic disk using this subcommand. You cannot delete the system partition, boot partition, or partition containing the paging file.

delete volume   Use this subcommand to delete a volume. You can't delete a system or boot partition, or the partition containing the paging file.

detail disk   This subcommand displays detailed information about the selected disk and its volumes.

detail volume   Use this subcommand to list the disk on which the current volume resides. For example, you would use this command to view the disks used by a spanned volume.

exit   This subcommand exits the diskpart command.

extend   Use this subcommand to extend the current volume. You can extend a volume on a basic disk only to unallocated space on the same disk, but volumes on dynamic disk can be extended to any dynamic disk.

help   Use this subcommand (or /?) to display a list of diskpart commands.

import   Use this subcommand to import a foreign disk group into the local computer's disk group.

list disk   This subcommand displays a list of the disk on the system and information about them, such as size, free space, and partition style.

list partition   Use this subcommand to list the partitions in the current disk.

list volume   This subcommand lists the volumes on all basic and dynamic disks.

online   Use this subcommand to bring an offline disk or volume online.

rem   Use this subcommand to add comments to a Diskpart script, just as you would add comments to a batch file.

remove   You can use this subcommand to remove a drive letter or mount point from the current volume. Use the all parameter to remove all drive letters and mount points.

rescan   Use this subcommand to scan the computer for new disks that have been added.

retain   This subcommand prepares a simple volume on a dynamic disk to be used as a boot or system volume. For *x*86-based computers, retain creates a partition entry in the MBR. On Itanium-based computers, this subcommand creates a partition entry in the GPT.

select disk   Use this subcommand to select a specific disk and shift the focus of diskpart to it. Most of diskpart's subcommands operate on the disk with the current focus.

select partition   This subcommand lets you select a partition and shift focus to it.

select volume   Use this subcommand to select a volume and shift focus to it.

Using Mounted Volumes

Mounted volumes are a handy feature introduced in Windows 2000 and carried over into Windows XP. Essentially, mounted volumes enable you to mount any volume into an empty NTFS folder. The volume then appears as a part of the directory structure of the hosting volume. For example, let's assume the one hard disk in your computer is running low on space. You have all the programs you need, but you're running low on space for documents. So, you add a new hard drive to the computer, move the contents of the Documents and Settings folder to it, and mount the new drive into the now-empty Documents and Settings folder. The result is that you now have lots of space for documents and other data.

Mounted volumes offer one other useful capability. Quotas apply at the volume level, so there is no way to apply quotas to a folder that are different from the volume hosting the folder. You can get around that limitation by applying the different set of quotas to another volume, then mounting the volume into an empty NTFS folder on the host volume. The result is that the mounted volume has different quota settings from the host volume, even though the mounted volume appears as a folder on the host volume.

Setting up mounted volumes is easy. You can mount any type of volume; it doesn't have to be NTFS. However, the host volume must be formatted with NTFS, because mounted volumes rely on reparse points, a feature supported only by NTFS. Also, the directory in which you mount the volume must be empty.

First, create the target folder on the NTFS host volume, or empty an existing folder. Then, open the Disk Management console, right-click the volume to be mounted, and choose Change Drive Letter And Paths. Click Add to open the Add Drive Letter Or Path dialog box (shown earlier in Figure 25.3).

Type the path to the empty NTFS target folder or click Browse to browse for it. Then, click OK and close the Change Drive Letter Or Path dialog box. The mounted volume is represented by a drive icon rather than a folder icon (Figure 25.10) in the host directory structure when you view the folder locally as well as across the network.

FIGURE 25.10:

The mounted volume is represented by a drive icon rather than a folder icon.

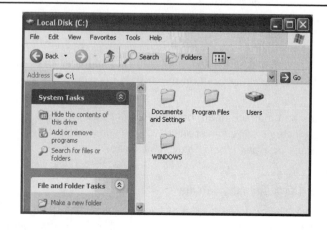

Creating and Managing Advanced Volumes

As I mentioned previously, in the section "Understanding Basic and Dynamic Disks," Windows XP Professional supports two advanced volume types: spanned volumes and striped volumes. This section explains how to manage these types of volumes.

NOTE Unlike Windows 2000 Server and .NET Server platforms, Windows XP does not support mirrored volumes (RAID 1) or stripe sets with parity (RAID 5). The highest level of RAID supported by Windows XP is RAID 0—striped sets. Windows XP Home Edition does not support dynamic disks, spanned volumes, or striped volumes. Also, Windows XP Professional lets you create advanced volumes on dynamic disks but not on basic disks.

Managing Spanned Volumes

A spanned volume is one that uses space from two or more disks to create a single logical volume. Why would you do such a thing? Let's say you're running out of space on drive E: (your main data drive) and you need more space. You could install a new hard drive and mount it into an empty NTFS folder on drive E: to increase the apparent size of the volume. This has the potential disadvantage that most of your free space is now available only in the mounted volume. A better solution would be to add a new drive and create a spanned volume, giving you a logical drive E: that encompasses the space on both drives. You can add up to 32 disks to a spanned volume to create a potentially huge volume (although a couple is probably all you'll ever use).

WARNING If you dual-boot the computer with an operating system such as Windows 98 that doesn't support dynamic volumes, don't convert the drive to a dynamic disk. If you do, the other operating system will no longer work.

If you decide to create a spanned volume, keep in mind that it doesn't offer any fault tolerance. If one disk in the spanned set dies, you'll lose all of the data in the spanned volume, including the data stored on the disk that is still functioning.

TIP You can manage spanned volumes created on basic disks with Windows NT, but you can't create or expand spanned volumes on basic disks with Windows XP. Instead, you must create or expand them on dynamic disks.

Creating a Spanned Volume

You use the Disk Management console to create a spanned volume. In the console, right-click the unallocated area on the disk that will serve as the first part of the spanned volume and click New Volume to start the New Volume Wizard. Click Next, choose Spanned, then click Next.

In the Select Disks screen (Figure 25.11), select the other disk to add to the volume set and click Add. If you don't want to add the entire disk to the set, change the space allocation using the control labeled Select The Amount of Space In MB. Then, click Next. Specify the drive letter or mount point, then follow the remaining prompts to complete the process.

FIGURE 25.11:

You can use only a portion of a disk for a spanned volume by changing the amount allocated.

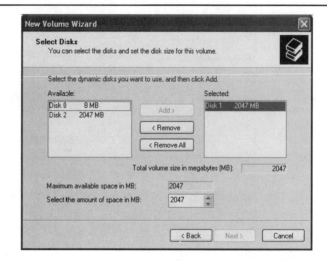

TIP   If you have only one drive with available disk space, you need to extend an existing volume rather than create a new one.

The new volume appears in My Computer as a single volume. In Disk Management's graphical view, the volume is labeled as a single volume, but you can view and work with the individual disks (Figure 25.12).

Extending a Simple or Spanned Volume

You can increase the size of a simple or spanned volume, adding additional unallocated space to it, by *extending* the volume. For example, assume you added a new disk to a computer. Now, you want to add the new disk to your existing simple volume to create a spanned volume. You do that by extending the existing volume to include the additional space.

NOTE   If you extend a simple volume, it becomes a spanned volume. You use the same process to extend both simple and spanned volumes.

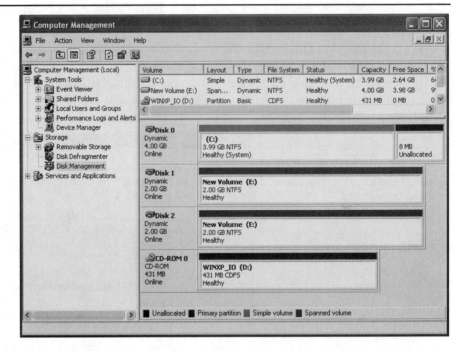

The process for extending a volume is a lot like that for creating the spanned volume. Open Disk Management, right-click the existing volume, and choose Extend Volume to start the Extend Volume Wizard. Click Next, select the disk containing the unallocated space that you want to add to the volume, and click Add. Adjust the amount of space to be allocated, if desired, then click Next. Click Finish to complete the task.

Following are a few notes that apply to extending volumes:

- A volume must contain no file system (unformatted) or must be formatted as NTFS to be extended. You must convert FAT/FAT32 volumes to NTFS before you can extend them.

- You can't extend a simple volume on a disk that was upgraded from a basic disk to a dynamic disk. You can extend only volumes created on a dynamic disk.

- You can't extend system or boot volumes.

- You can't extend striped volumes.

- If you extend a simple volume onto multiple disks, it becomes a spanned volume and can't be striped.

- You can't delete any portion of a spanned volume. Instead, you must delete the entire volume.

Managing Striped Volumes

A *striped volume* in one in which the data is written across multiple disks that appear as a single logical volume. Unlike a spanned volume, in which a file would probably reside on only one disk, files in a striped volume are typically spread across all drives in the set because Windows XP distributes the write operations to multiple disks.

Striped volumes, which represent RAID 0, provide increased performance, particularly on systems with SCSI drives. These disks can read and write independently of the other disks in the system. With the file system distributed across multiple disks, read/write times decrease and performance increases because the workload is divided among the disks in the set. However, striping offers diminishing returns as more drives are added to the set, so a set of two or three drives is optimal.

Striped volumes offer no fault tolerance, however. If a single disk in the set fails, the volume is broken and all data is lost. Before you rush off and stripe your disks, understand that you'll gain performance but will still need to rely on backups or other methods to ensure survivability of your files in the event of a disk failure.

TIP   To gain fault tolerance, you need to move up to RAID 1 (mirroring) or RAID 5 (stripe sets with parity). Neither of these is supported by Windows XP, although you can install RAID hardware in a computer to implement them. There are other levels of RAID, as well, but they pertain mainly to server environments and therefore fall outside the scope of this book.

You use much the same method to create a striped volume as you do to create a spanned volume. The only difference is that you select Striped in the New Volume Wizard. See the earlier section "Creating a Spanned Volume" if you need more information.

Understanding and Implementing Sharing

It isn't difficult to share a folder with other users on the network, but there are some security issues to consider, particularly if you are not familiar with NTFS permissions. Windows XP also adds a new twist on sharing by introducing Simple File Sharing. This section of the chapter focuses mainly on Simple File Sharing and security, but still explains briefly the process for sharing folders in Windows XP.

Understanding File Sharing Options

Before you begin sharing files, you need to choose between the two sharing methods: classic or Simple File Sharing.

Share Permissions vs. NTFS Permissions

The classic sharing mechanism in Windows XP is the same as that in Windows 2000 and Windows NT, and functions as a combination of *share permissions* and *NTFS permissions*. When you share a folder, you can set limited permissions for the share itself. These permissions include Full Control, Read, and Change. The share permissions control access to the share from the network. For example, if a user is assigned Read permission in the share, he can only read the data but not modify it.

NTFS volumes offer an additional layer of security that provides much more granular—that is, detailed—control over folder and file access. In addition to setting share permissions on a folder, you can also set NTFS permissions on the folder and/or its contents. For example, assume you are sharing the folder C:\Docs on your computer. The folder contains several other folders. Some users need access to some of the folders, while other users need access to different folders. You also want to restrict users to only the folders they specifically need. The answer is to use NTFS permissions.

To enable all of the users to access the shared folder across the network, you grant Full Control to the built-in Everyone group when you share the folder. Then, you remove the Everyone group from the NTFS permissions for each folder and add the users who need access to each item, giving them whatever level of access is appropriate. The end result is that the share permissions allow everyone to get into the share, but NTFS permissions control what they can do once they're in.

TIP   NTFS permissions apply to local as well as network access of a folder or file and are the mechanism by which you can secure folders or files against local access from others who log on to your computer. NTFS permissions are available only on NTFS volumes. FAT volumes support only share permissions and therefore provide no local security.

It's important to understand the interaction between share permissions and NTFS permissions. The most restrictive permission applies, so you might grant Everyone Full Control through share permissions but grant only Read permission through NTFS permissions. The result is that unless a user is a member of another group that explicitly has less restrictive permissions, he will only have Read ability in the folder.

NOTE   Also take into account group membership when setting up sharing. Group membership is cumulative, and a user receives the permission granted to his account as well as the permissions granted to each group of which he is a member.

Simple File Sharing

Now, enter Simple File Sharing, or SFS. I believe that Microsoft introduced SFS mainly to insulate Windows XP Home Edition users from the intricacies of NTFS permissions. Sharing a folder with SFS enabled is easy and requires only a few clicks of the mouse. The disadvantage is that you have much less control over access. SFS controls access to folders using the system's Guest account, so all users have the same level of access in the folder, either Full Control or Read, depending on how you share the folder.

You can easily share your own documents with other users on the network with SFS. You can also make your My Documents folder private, which prevents other users from accessing it locally. I cover each of these tasks later, in the section "Sharing and Securing Folders and Files."

Choosing a File Sharing Method

Windows XP Professional includes in the GUI the ability to switch between classic sharing and SFS. To switch, open the Folder Options dialog box (choose View ≻ Folder Options from any folder or use the Folder Options icon in Control Panel) and click the View tab (Figure 25.13). Scroll to the bottom of the Advanced Settings list and use the Use Simple File Sharing check box to enable or disable SFS.

Windows XP Home Edition users don't normally have the ability to disable SFS, which would make it seem that SFS is the only way share files. Although SFS is the default mechanism in Home Edition, you can still use classic sharing. The secret is safe mode.

FIGURE 25.13:

Use the View tab to configure SFS.

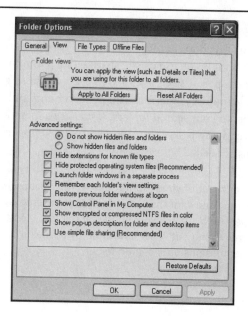

When you boot a Home Edition computer in safe mode, the sharing mechanism reverts from SFS to classic. If you right-click a folder and choose Sharing And Security, you'll see the same Sharing tab that Windows XP Professional users see when SFS is turned off. You can assign share permissions, selectively apply access, and configure NTFS permissions for the folder. When you reboot the computer in normal mode, SFS once again becomes the default sharing mechanism.

So what happens to folders you share in safe mode and reboot in normal mode? The changes you made still apply. If you open the sharing properties for the folder, you'll see the usual SFS interface with the folder shared. Whatever NTFS permissions you applied will still be valid.

As an advanced user, I prefer classic sharing because I'm used to it, but also because I prefer greater control over what I share. Nevertheless, SFS is a good option for inexperienced users who only need to share a folder occasionally on their systems and don't need the added security offered by NTFS permissions.

TIP   Certain features are difficult or impossible to implement if SFS is enabled. For example, you can't configure NTFS permissions if SFS is enabled. All access to the computer from the network is authenticated with the Guest account when SFS is enabled, and this affects the ability to access a Registry remotely and other network features. If you enable SFS and then down the line can't get a feature to work as you might expect, try turning off SFS to see if the problem goes away.

Sharing and Securing Folders and Files

There isn't much to sharing folders. The process varies slightly depending on whether you are using SFS. If you use classic sharing, keep in mind that Windows XP controls access based on the permissions assigned to accounts or to groups. If your computer belongs to a domain, Windows XP uses the domain accounts and groups to authenticate access by network users to your shared folders. If you are a member of a workgroup, you need to use local accounts and groups to control access to shared folders. If the latter is the case, create accounts or groups as needed before diving into sharing.

WARNING   Take the threat of viruses and worms into account when you configure sharing and permissions. A new method of attack that viruses such as Nimda take is to search for improperly secured network shares and infect files they find there. You can avoid a lot of aggravation and potential downtime by removing the Everyone group from sharing and NTFS permissions on a shared folder.

Classic Sharing

You can use classic sharing whether or not you are sharing from an NTFS volume. However, if you're sharing from a FAT volume, you won't have any additional options using classic sharing than you would using SFS. Keep that in mind when you decide which sharing method to use.

To share a folder, first set the necessary NTFS permissions on the folder and its contents to control access (assuming you're sharing a folder on an NTFS volume). Locate and right-click the folder and choose Properties. Click the Security tab (Figure 25.14), add or remove users or groups as necessary, then assign them the desired permissions. Click Apply when you're happy with the permissions.

WARNING The reason I always set NTFS permissions first is you're securing the folder and files before making them available on the network. It's like closing each horse's stall before opening the barn door—they won't get out unless you let them out. If you share the folder first, you might forget to apply NTFS permissions and expose your data to unwanted access.

Next, click the Sharing tab (Figure 25.15) and select Share This Folder. Windows XP uses the folder name as the default share name, but you can change it if you wish. This is the name by which users on the network see the folder when they browse the network.

If you wish, you can limit the number of concurrent connections to the folder. Windows XP supports up to 10 concurrent connections, so choosing Maximum Allowed will allow up to 10 connections. In most cases, this won't put much of a burden on your computer or the network, but you can select Allow This Number of Users and specify a lower number, if desired.

FIGURE 25.14:

Use the Security tab to configure NTFS permissions.

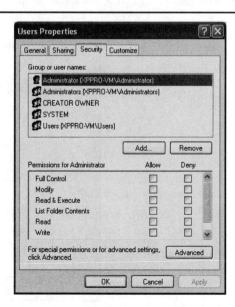

FIGURE 25.15:

Use the Sharing tab to share a folder.

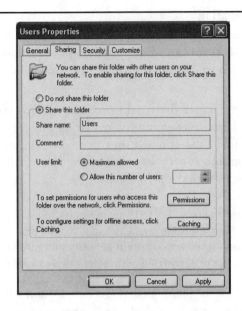

You'll need to move up to Windows 2000 Server or .NET Server if you need more than 10 concurrent connections.

Click Permissions if you want to change share permissions. In the Permissions For Users dialog box (Figure 25.16), add and remove users or groups and assign permissions as desired. Click OK, then click OK to close the folder properties and begin sharing the folder.

FIGURE 25.16:

Use the Permissions For Users dialog box to set share permissions.

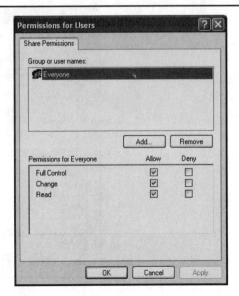

Sharing with SFS

The process is a bit simpler with SFS. Right-click the folder and choose Sharing And Security to open the Sharing tab shown in Figure 25.17. Select Share This Folder On The Network, then change the share name, if desired. Choose the option Allow Network Users To Change My Files if you want to grant Change permission in the folder. Click OK to start sharing the folder.

What's the effect in terms of classic sharing? When you share a folder with SFS enabled, Windows XP shares the folder and grants the built-in Everyone group Full Control if you selected Allow Network Users To Change My Files. If you don't select this option, XP grants the Everyone group Read permission.

If the folder resides on an NTFS volume, Windows XP sets the access control lists (ACLs) on the folder to give Everyone Modify permission if you selected Allow Network Users To Change My Files. If not, Windows XP sets the ACLs to grant Read & Execute permission.

FIGURE 25.17:

Use the Sharing tab to
share a folder with
SFS enabled.

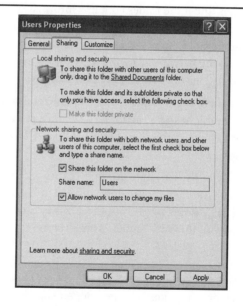

Sharing or Making Private Your Documents

Regardless of which sharing method you use, you'll find your documents available directly through My Computer. You can share your documents folder or make it private. To share it, right-click the folder and choose Sharing And Security. Use the same method to share the folder as you would for any other.

TIP   To quickly share your documents, just drag it to the Shared Documents folder. This creates a shortcut in Shared Documents to your documents folder.

To make your documents folder private, choose the option Make This Folder Private. Then, click OK.

NOTE   This option is available only if the folder you're attempting to change is located in the \Documents and Settings*username* folder for the username you are currently logged in as. This option also requires NTFS. Also, keep in mind that even Administrators can't gain access to the contents when made private. It's the equivalent of granting NTFS Full Control permissions to *System* and *Username* and granting no one else has any rights at all.

Hiding Shares

When you share a folder, it is visible to other users who browse your computer on the network. This is fine if the folder contains information you want to share with everyone, or if you don't mind that those people who don't have access can still see the folder on the network. In some cases, however, you might want to hide the folder so that don't appear when users browse the network. Anyone who knows that the folder is there, however, can still connect to it if they have the necessary permissions.

Hiding a share is easy—just add a $ character as the last character of the share name. For example, you might share the folder Docs on a computer named Bart as Docs$. When someone needs connect to the share, they can map a drive or browse to \\bart\docs$ and work with the folder.

The ability of the $ to hide the share exists because, although remote Windows computers *do* see your share, they simply don't display it. Unix/Linux computers running a Samba client can see all Microsoft shares, even those with a $ on the end. Be sure not to relax your security just because you think it's hidden from everyone.

TIP   Windows XP creates administrative shares for each disk in the system. Drive C:, for example, is shared as C$. XP shares the *%systemroot%* folder as ADMIN$. Windows XP also creates a handful of other hidden shares depending on the services that are running. You can connect to these shares on a remote computer as long as you are a member of the Administrators group on the remote computer.

Command-Line Tools for Sharing

You might occasionally find it useful to share folders or map a drive letter to a remote share from a command console. You can use the `net` command to do just that. To share a folder, use the following `net` syntax:

```
net share sharename=drive:path
```

Replace *drive:path* with the path to the folder you want to share. You can use some additional parameters to control the number of connections, add a description for the share, set offline cacheing options, and so on. Execute the command **net help share** at the command console to view the syntax for these parameters.

To map a local drive letter to a remote network share, use the following syntax:

```
net use drive: \\server\share\subshare\...
```

Replace *drive:* with the local drive letter to map to the remote share. Replace *server* with the name of the computer sharing the folder. Replace *share* with the name of the share on the remote folder, and replace *subshare* with the name of a folder inside the remote share. You can specify multiple *subshare*s to drill deeper into the remote share's directory structure.

TIP	For a list of available `net` subcommands, just type **net** with no other parameters. Then, type **net help *subcommand*** to get more information about the syntax and use for specific subcommands.

PART V

Communications and Networking

CHAPTER 26

Modem and Dial-Up Networking Configuration

There usually isn't much to setting up a modem and making dial-up connections work. In most cases, Windows XP will automatically recognize the modem and install the appropriate driver for it. Setting up a dial-up connection is then just a matter of specifying the phone number, server type, and other general properties.

For those reasons, I won't cover modem or dial-up connection configuration in detail in this chapter, but instead focus mainly on related topics. For example, I explain why dial-up connections don't work sometimes even if your modem is dialing and attempting to connect to the remote server. The chapter also covers scripting, dialing rules, and other more advanced topics.

If you have more than one modem, or are willing to invest a little money in another modem to improve your dial-up connection's performance, you'll be interested in the section on multilink. This feature in Windows XP lets you aggregate together two or more dial-up connections to increase overall throughput. For example, you might aggregate two 56K dial-up connections to achieve a theoretical connection speed of 112K. That's still not as good as a broadband connection such as DSL, but any improvement is usually worthwhile.

Modem Configuration Tips

Modem installation and configuration in Windows XP is generally easy, but there are a few issues to consider and a few potential problems. This section offers tips for these situations.

TIP   The Phone And Modem Options object in Control Panel gives you access to the majority of modem configuration tools and properties.

The Standard Modem

As I mentioned in the introduction, there isn't much to setting up a modem in Windows XP. In most cases, Windows XP automatically recognizes the modem and installs support for it. Sometimes, however, Windows XP won't properly recognize a modem and installs it as a Standard modem using a generic driver. I used to own and operate an ISP with about 1,000 customers (I'm glad that's over!), and it's my experience that the Standard modem often causes connection problems. Whenever a customer called Support with a connection problem, the first thing we checked was the modem type. Installing the right driver invariably fixed the problem and allowed the customer to connect without further problems.

Check your system to make sure it is using the right modem driver. If Windows XP didn't correctly detect your modem and instead installed one of the Standard modem drivers, update the driver. If you can't get a new driver from the modem manufacturer, consider replacing the modem for a new one.

> **NOTE**   To update the driver, open the properties for the driver in Device Manager or in the Phone And Modem Options object in Control Panel. Click the Driver tab, click Update Driver, and follow the wizard's prompts to install the new driver.

Performing Diagnostics and Logging

On those rare occasions when you need to troubleshoot a modem connection, you can use a couple of Windows XP features that simplify the process.

Query the Modem

First, you can query the modem to make sure Windows XP is communicating with it. To do so, open the Phone And Modem Options object in Control Panel and click the Modems tab. Select the modem in the list and click Properties, then click the Diagnostics tab (Figure 26.1). Next, click Query Modem. Windows XP queries several registers in the modem and displays information about the modem and its configuration in the dialog box.

If Windows XP is unable to query the modem, either your modem isn't working or is not properly connected to the computer (external). If you're setting up the modem and it hasn't worked successfully, there is also the chance that you have it configured incorrectly. Check the COM port assignment to make sure you're using the right port. Also check in Device Manager for a COM port conflict.

> **TIP**   If you install an internal modem on a particular COM port that your computer also has enabled on the motherboard or an add-on card, you should disable that system COM port to avoid potential port conflicts.

Use the Diagnostics
page to query the
modem.

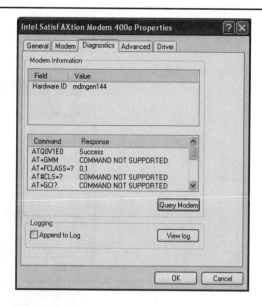

Send Commands to the Modem

Another troubleshooting technique is to communicate directly with the modem, sending it configuration and test commands to determine whether the computer can communicate with the modem and the modem can dial out.

You can use HyperTerminal, which is included with Windows XP, to communicate with the modem. Click Start ➢ All Programs ➢ Accessories ➢ Communications ➢ HyperTerminal. The first time you run HyperTerminal, Windows XP asks if you want it to be the default Telnet program. I prefer the command-line version, but HyperTerminal works well as a Telnet client—the choice is up to you.

After you respond to the prompt, HyperTerminal displays the Connection Description dialog box. Enter a name for the connection, such as Modem Direct, choose an icon for the connection, and click OK. In the Connect To dialog box (Figure 26.2), choose from the Connect Using drop-down list the COM port assigned to the modem. Then click OK.

In the Port Settings dialog box, select a port speed from the Bits Per Second drop-down list. I recommend 9600 for testing purposes. Use the default settings (8, none, 1, hardware) for the other settings and click OK.

When you click OK, HyperTerminal starts a connection to the modem. Type **AT** and press Enter. You should receive the response OK. If you don't see the AT as you type it, you need to turn on local echo. Choose File ➢ Properties, and then click the Settings tab. Click

ASCII Setup to display the ASCII Setup dialog box (Figure 26.3). Select Echo Typed Characters Locally and click OK. Click OK to close the properties sheet and try the AT command again.

FIGURE 26.2:

Select the modem's COM port from the Connect Using drop-down list.

FIGURE 26.3:

Use the ASCII Setup dialog box to enable local echo of typed characters.

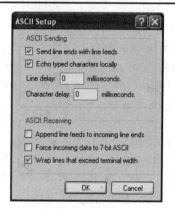

If you receive OK in response to the AT command, try dialing. Issue the command **ATD-number**. Replace *number* with the phone number you want to dial. If the modem starts dialing, you can type **ATH** to hang up the connection. If the modem successfully dialed, the problem likely lies in your communications program. There's an outside chance that the modem driver is wrong, but I'd look at the connection settings before looking for problems with the driver.

TIP   You can use lots of other commands to initialize or configure a modem. Check your modem manual for a complete list of commands.

If you receive an error message in response to AT, you likely have a problem with the modem itself, with the driver, or with the connection between the computer and modem. Check these and try again. If the modem responds to AT but gives you an error, such as no dial tone, check the connection between the modem and phone line.

> **TIP** You can shut down the computer and then start it again to reset an internal modem. For an external modem, cycle power on the modem and then use Device Manager to scan for device changes to redetect the modem. Check the connection again after the reset.

Check the Modem Logs

Another modem-troubleshooting technique you can use in Windows XP is to check the modem logs. Windows XP creates a log when it detects a modem, and you can use this log to identify potential problems with detection. Check the file %systemroot%\ModemDet.txt for the port on which a modem was detected and other status messages.

Windows XP also creates a modem log for each modem as you use it. The modem logs are located in the %systemroot% folder and are named ModemLog_*ModemName*, where *ModemName* is the name of the modem. For example, the log file for the ancient but functional Intel 400e I use for incoming faxes is named ModemLog_SatisFAXtion Modem 400e.txt.

> **NOTE** I'm hanging onto the Intel 2400 baud external modem I have just in case Intel wants it for their corporate museum some day. I would entertain bids, however. The worst thing is that I fondly remember the days when 2400 baud was fast enough for anything you cared to do online.

Each log file contains the initialization commands that Windows XP sends to the modem, as well as modem responses and other information. The log can be particularly useful in tracking down initialization or communication problems.

Using Additional Configuration Strings

In some cases you might need to use additional configuration strings for a modem. To put it simply, these are additional modem commands that you direct Windows XP to send to the modem when it initializes the modem to start the dial-up session. For example, you might need to enable error-correction methods or change other settings that aren't available through the GUI.

Check the modem documentation to determine the commands you need to send to the modem. Then, open the properties for the modem and click the Advanced tab. In the Extra Initialization Commands text box, type the initialization string you need to send to the modem. You can also click Change Default Preferences to change properties such as initial port speed, data protocol, flow control method, and other properties.

Configuring Dial-Up Connections

Setting up a standard Internet connection is relatively easy to accomplish, and in most cases you can simply run the New Connection Wizard and let Windows XP create the connection based on the information you provide, such as phone number, account name, and password. This section of the chapter focuses on the additional issues you might face for certain connections or when using a connection from a different location.

> **TIP**   To run the New Connection Wizard, click Start, then right-click My Network Places and choose Properties to open the Network Connections folder. Click Create A New Connection in the left pane to start the wizard.

Setting Dialing Rules

Dialing rules allow you to specify the way Windows XP dials a connection—for example, using a credit card to dial, dialing the area code, dialing a prefix to access an outside line, disabling call waiting when it initiates the call, and other dialing tasks. Dialing rules are based on calling location, so if you are calling from a particular area code, a hotel, or location that requires other special dialing steps, you can specify a set of rules accordingly.

Basic Rules

To configure dialing rules, open the Network Connections folder, right-click the connection, and choose Properties. Or, in the Connect dialog box prior to dialing, click Properties. On the General tab of the connection's properties, click Use Dialing Rules. Then, click Dialing Rules to open the Phone And Modem Options dialog box. Select an existing location and click Edit, or click New to create a new dialing location. Figure 26.4 shows the resulting Edit Location dialog box.

> **TIP**   You can also access the Phone And Modem Options dialog box from Control Panel.

Use the General tab to specify the dialing location name, area code, prefixes to dial for local and long-distance calls, and a handful of other settings. The settings on the General tab are self explanatory.

Area Code Rules

Use the Area Code Rules tab to create rules to govern the way Windows XP treats specific area codes for the selected dialing location. For example, if you are dialing from area code 218 and need to dial other numbers in the 218 area code, you might need to specify which ones should be dialed as long distance and which ones should be dialed as local calls without the area code. Click New to open the New Area Code Rule dialog box (Figure 26.5) to enter the area code and specify which prefixes should be dialed as long-distance numbers. To dial only certain prefixes as long-distance numbers, choose Include Only The Prefixes In The List Below, click Add, and add the prefixes.

FIGURE 26.4:

Use the Edit Location dialog box to specify dialing rules.

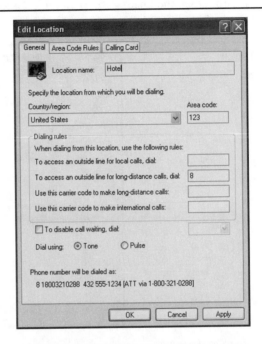

FIGURE 26.5:

Use the New Area Code Rule dialog box to specify prefix rules.

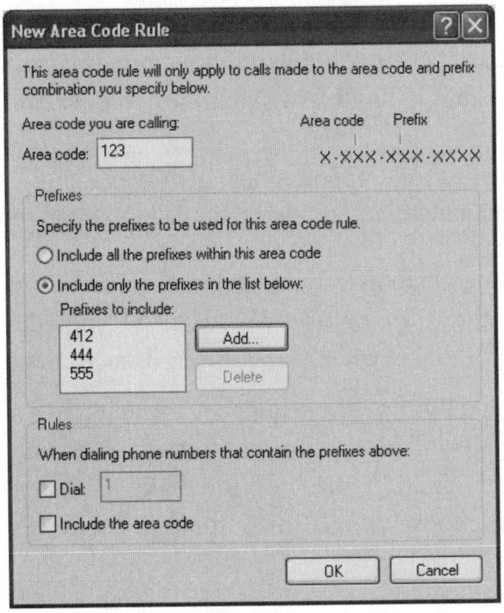

Calling Cards

Setting up Windows XP to use a calling card to dial a number is perhaps the most difficult rules task. Windows XP includes several predefined card types to make it easier to set up your own card. Open the Dialing Rules tab, select a location, and click Edit. Then click the Calling Card tab (Figure 26.6).

FIGURE 26.6:

Windows XP includes several calling card types.

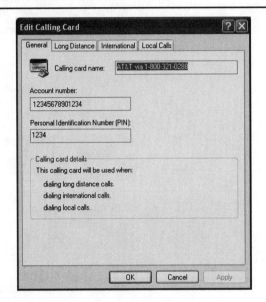

Look through the list of predefined cards to see if yours is included. If so, select the card from the list and then enter the account number and PIN (if any) in the text boxes on the Calling Card tab. If you need to fine-tune the card's settings, select the card and click Edit to open the Edit Calling Card dialog box (Figure 26.7).

TIP   The process for creating a new card is much the same as editing an existing card. Just click Add instead of Edit and then fill in the desired settings.

The General tab lists the card name, account number, and PIN. Click the Long Distance tab to change the access number Windows XP should dial to use the card and/or the other information to be dialed when using the card, such as the sequence in which it dials specific items.

The dialog box lists the sequence in which items are dialed when using the card. You can use the Move Up and Move Down buttons to change the sequence as needed. Click an item's button if you need to add that item to the dialing sequence; in some instances, this brings up a dialog box to choose details for that item. For example, click Wait For Prompt if you need

Windows XP to wait for a response or for a message to end before sending the next dialing string. When you click Wait For Prompt, Windows XP displays the dialog box shown in Figure 26.8.

FIGURE 26.7:

You can edit an existing card to suit your specific needs.

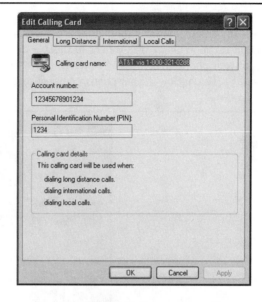

FIGURE 26.8:

Use the Wait For dialog box to include a pause in the dialing string.

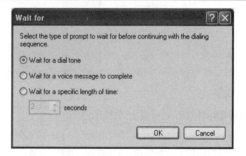

If you simply need to dial a string of numbers or the * or # characters, click Specify Digits to enter the digits to be dialed. Windows XP dials those digits at the specified point in the dialing sequence.

The settings on the International and Local Calls tabs are the same as on the Long Distance tab. However, these settings apply when Windows XP detects that you are dialing an international or a local call, respectively.

The best way to check the number sequence without actually dialing it is to open the connection after you set the dialing rules, then check the numbers shown in the Dial drop-down list (Figure 26.9). You can also click Dialing Rules to view the dialing string.

TIP	Calls that come in when you are online can disrupt the connection if call waiting is enabled. You can disable call waiting for the duration of the call through the General tab of the Edit Location dialog box. Select To Disable Call Waiting Dial, then enter the dialing string for your phone system that disables call waiting. Common strings include *70, 70#, and 1170. Check with your phone company to determine the appropriate string.

FIGURE 26.9:

The Dial drop-down list shows the number to be dialed.

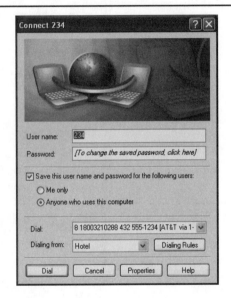

Manual or Operator-Assisted Dialing

In some cases, you might find it easier to simply dial the connection yourself or have an operator do it rather than let Windows XP do it. This is particularly true if you only need to use the calling card a couple of times—in a lot of cases, you can dial the connection yourself and be finished with the dial-up session in the amount of time it would take to finish setting up the card.

Setting up manual/operated-assisted dialing isn't exactly intuitive, because Windows XP doesn't offer those settings through the dial-up connection's properties. Open the Network Connections folder and choose Advanced ➤ Operator-Assisted Dialing. Double-click the connection you want to dial. Pick up the handset and dial the number, calling card, and any other dialing strings, and then click Dial. You can hang up the handset after the modem takes over the line (immediately in almost every case). To disable operator-assisted or manual dialing, open the `Network Connections` folder and choose Advanced ➢ Operator-Assisted Dialing to remove the check from the menu.

Choosing Authentication Settings

Windows XP supports several authentication methods for dial-up connections, and you can assign multiple authentication methods for a dial-up connection. Windows XP attempts the connection using the authentication methods in decreasing order of security provided. You configure the method(s) for a connection through the Security tab for the connection (Figure 26.10).

FIGURE 26.10:

Use the Security tab to configure authentication methods for the connection.

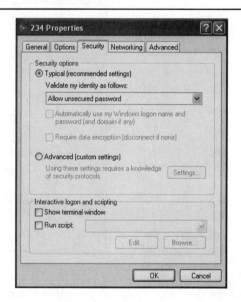

The Security Options group gives you access to three authentication options:

Allow Unsecured Password   This option allows the use of Password Authentication Protocol (PAP), which transmits passwords in plain text. This option provides the least security because passwords can be easily sniffed from the PPP packets. Windows XP will also attempt a connection using CHAP, SPAP, MS-CHAP, and MS-CHAP v2 with this option selected.

Require Secured Password   With this option, Windows XP attempts a connection using CHAP, MS-CHAP, and MS-CHAP v2 (all explained later in this section). The password is encrypted, providing much better security and considerably reducing the possibility that the password will be compromised. PAP and SPAP are not attempted.

Use Smart Card   This option offers excellent security for systems that contain a smart card reader. Windows XP uses the credentials stored in the smart card to authenticate the connection to the remote server. Windows XP uses EAP for authentication (more on this later).

You can also set advanced authentication methods—for example, restricting the connection to a specific authentication method, or using a method such as EAP that provides better security. Click Advanced on the Security tab, then click Settings to display the dialog box shown in Figure 26.11.

FIGURE 26.11:

Set authentication options through the Advanced Security Settings dialog box.

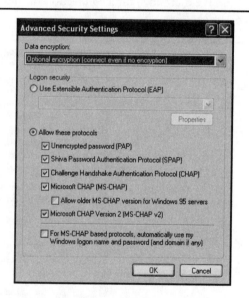

The Data Encryption drop-down list lets you specify whether or not Windows XP uses encryption for the connection. You can choose between the following:

No Encryption Allowed   Windows XP drops the connection if the server requires encryption.

Optional Encryption   Windows XP attempts encryption but allows the connection even if the server declines encryption.

Required Encryption   Windows XP disconnects the connection if the server doesn't offer encryption.

Maximum Strength Encryption   This option requires 128-bit encryption.

Whether or not you choose to use encryption depends on whether the server supports it and you require maximum security for data.

Another choice you need to make if setting authentication from the Advanced Security Settings dialog box is the protocol(s) to use for the connection.

PAP   (Password Authentication Protocol) This protocol uses plain text to transmit the password to the dial-up server. This makes the password susceptible to compromise, so you should use PAP only in situations where it is unlikely that someone can intercept your password or where the remote server only supports PAP.

SPAP   (Shiva Password Authentication Protocol) This was developed by Shiva Corporation, a remote-access technology company that has since been acquired by Intel. SPAP allows connections to Shiva products such as the Shiva LAN Rover. Like PAP, SPAP provides lower security than the other authentication methods offered by Windows XP, so you should use it only when connecting to a Shiva access device that doesn't offer a stronger security.

CHAP   (Challenge Handshake Authentication Protocol, also known as MD-5 CHAP or simply CHAP) It uses a standard mechanism for encrypting the authentication process. CHAP is supported by various remote access servers, including non-Microsoft servers. It offers better security than PAP or SPAP because of its encryption, but doesn't provide the same level of encryption—and thereby increased security—as that offered by either MS-CHAP version or by EAP.

TIP   If you are configuring a Windows 2000 Server or Microsoft .NET Server computer to support CHAP, keep in mind that password must be stored on the server using reversible encryption. You can enable reversible encryption for each account through the Store Password Using Reversible Encryption option on the Account tab of the user's properties (Active Directory Users And Computers console). You can also configure reversible encryption on a global basis through group policy in the \Security Settings\Account Policies\Password Policy.

MS-CHAP   (Microsoft Challenge Handshake Authentication Protocol) This is a version of CHAP developed by Microsoft and supported by their remote-access platforms (such as Windows 2000 Server RRAS). With this protocol, the authentication server sends the client a challenge containing the session ID and an arbitrary challenge string. The client responds with the user name assigned to the dial-up connection and an encryption of the session ID, challenge string, and password. The server validates the credentials and authenticates the session if they match the credentials stored on the server. This protocol provides better security than CHAP.

MS-CHAP v2   Version 2 of the Microsoft Challenge Handshake Authentication Protocol improves on MS-CHAP's security. With this protocol, the remote server sends the client a challenge containing the session ID and an arbitrary challenge string. The client responds with the user name, an arbitrary peer challenge string, and a one-way encryption of the server's challenge string, peer challenge string, session ID, and password. The server validates the response and returns a success/failure and an authenticated response based on both challenge strings, the encrypted client response, and the password. The client validates that authentication data and accepts the connection if it is valid. The client terminates the connection if it can't validate the authentication data provided by the server. So, MS-CHAP v2 offers two-way authentication and therefore excellent security.

EAP   (Extensible Authentication Protocol) EAP allows the client and server to negotiate an authentication method from the methods supported by the server. The client and server must both support the same EAP types in order for authentication to succeed.

Windows XP supports two EAP types: EAP-MD5 CHAP and EAP-TLS. EAP-MD5 CHAP works much like CHAP but sends challenges and responses as EAP messages. EAP-MD5 CHAP authenticates clients using user names and passwords.

EAP-TLS uses certificates to authenticate remote clients, using a secured private key exchange between the client and the server. EAP-TLS is the most secure method of authentication offered by Windows XP because it uses certificates for authentication. Windows 2000 Server and Microsoft .NET Server platforms support EAP-TLS only in domain environments—the Routing and Remote Access Service (RRAS) does not support EAP-TLS on a standalone RRAS server.

Configuring Authentication

Choosing and setting up authentication methods for a dial-up connection is usually easy. If your dial-up server doesn't have advanced authentication requirements (you're dialing an ISP, for example), you can generally leave the settings at their default values. In those cases where stronger security is needed and is supported by the dial-up server, you can use the Advanced Security Settings dialog box previously shown in Figure 26.11.

Select the desired encryption option from the Data Encryption drop-down list. If you are not using EAP, select the protocol(s) you want the connection to be able to use in the Allow These Protocols list. If the user credentials on the dial-up server are the same as your local user credentials, select the option "For MS-CHAP based protocols, automatically use my Windows logon name and password." This causes Windows XP to use your local user name and password for authentication.

For dial-up scenarios requiring EAP, select the Use Extensible Authentication Protocol option and then choose the EAP method from the drop-down list. If you choose the Smart Card Or Other Certificate option, click Properties to display the dialog box (Figure 26.12).

The following list summarizes the options on this dialog box:

Use My Smart Card   Select this option if you have a smart-card reader on the local computer and want to authenticate on the remote server using the credentials stored in your smart card.

User A Certificate On This Computer   Select this option to use a certificate installed on the local computer to provide authentication.

Validate Server Certificate   Select this option to check that the certificate on the server has not expired.

FIGURE 26.12:

Configure the EAP
certificate and other
options in the Smart
Card Or Other Certifi-
cate Properties
dialog box.

Connect Only If Server Name Ends With   Use this option to specify a domain name for the remote dial-up server and prevent a connection if the server does not reside in the specified domain. If you were connecting to a server in the sybex.com domain, for example, you would enter sybex.com in this check box.

Trusted Root Certificate Authority   Select the root certification authority (CA) in the certification hierarchy for the server's certificate. This requires that the server's certificate be verified for authenticity against the specified root CA.

Use A Different User Name For The Connection   Select this option if the user name stored in the smart card or associated with the certificate is not the same as the user name on the remote server.

SEE ALSO   See Chapter 48 for detailed information on obtaining and installing certificates on your computer.

Scripting

Most dial-up servers don't require connection scripts, but there are a few holdouts and older servers that still require scripts. For example, you need a script to connect to CompuServe's network.

Windows XP includes four predefined scripts that you can use for connecting to specific types of servers. These scripts are stored in *%systemroot%*\System32\ras:

Cis.scp   Use this script to connect to CompuServe.

Pppmenu.scp   Use this script to establish a PPP connection to a remote-access server that uses a menu to offer connection options.

Slip.scp   Use this script to connect to a server that uses Serial Line Interface Protocol (SLIP) to establish the connection.

Slipmenu.scp   Use this script to establish a SLIP connection to a remote-access server that uses a menu to offer connection options.

In most cases, you can use the scripts as-is or make only minor modifications to the scripts to apply them to your situation. To select a script, open the Security tab of the connection's properties and click Run Script. Click the drop-down list to select the desired script, or click Browse to browse the computer for it. After you select the script, you can click Edit to open the script in Notepad for editing.

TIP   You can view the script in action to troubleshoot the script or simply watch its operation. Select the Show Terminal Window option on the Security tab to monitor the script's progress.

It's unlikely that you will need to do anything other than make minor changes to existing scripts, and you will likely not need to create your own from scratch. For that reason, I'll just point you in the right direction for more information rather than offer pages and pages of content on scripting here. In Windows XP, open the Help And Support Center and search on the key phrase **connection script**. The document "Basic Structure of a Script" under the Suggested Topics category offers a good introduction to scripting. You'll also uncover several additional documents that explain scripting commands and syntax.

TIP   Although I haven't run across this problem yet with Windows XP, it's my experience that Windows 2000 sometimes has problems in getting the password to authenticate for a CompuServe connection. You could try re-creating the connection, but my preferred solution has always been to simply modify the Cis.scp file to explicitly send the password rather than use the $PASSWORD variable to pull it from Windows XP. If you choose this route, edit Cis.scp and replace $PASSWORD with your actual password in quotes. Note that this exposes your password to anyone who has access to the script file. To avoid that, store the password in an NTFS folder with permissions set to prevent access by unauthorized users.

Using Callback for Security and Cost

Like Windows 2000, Windows XP provides callback features to enable a remote-access server to call back your computer to initiate a connection. There are two reasons to use callback: cost and security.

Having the server call you back reverses any long-distance charges that might otherwise apply. Naturally, for this to work the remote server must be configured for callback and must be able to dial a long-distance call. Commercial remote-access services are very unlikely to support callback at all, much less callback to a long-distance number. Instead, reversing long-distance charges through callback is applicable only to remote-access services provided by your company. Unfortunately, Windows XP doesn't support callback as a dial-up server, so you'll need to use Windows 2000 Server or Microsoft .NET Server platforms (or third-party RAS servers) as your remote-access servers to enable callback.

Security is another reason to use callback. You can configure remote-access policies on a Windows 2000 or Microsoft .NET RRAS server to call a user back at a specific number. This ensures that the user can connect only from a specific location, and considerably lessens the possibility that someone else could obtain the user's credentials and use them to gain unauthorized access.

NOTE   You configure callback for a specific user through the Dial-In tab of the user's account in Active Directory on the server.

To configure a dial-up client to use callback from Windows XP, right-click My Network Connections and choose Properties to open the Network Connections dialog box. Choose Advanced ➤ Dial-Up Preferences and click the Callback tab. You can choose from three options:

No Callback   You connection will not use callback, even if offered by the server.

Ask Me During Dialing When The Server Offers   Windows XP displays a prompt asking if you want the server to call you back. The prompt appears only if the server offers callback.

Always Call Me Back At The Number(s) Below   Use this option if you want the server to call your computer back at a specific number. If your computer has more than one modem and the server supports multilink, you can specify the number for each modem and have the server call back each one to create a multilink connection.

A Windows 2000 or Microsoft .NET RRAS server supports three callback options: No Callback, Set By Caller, and Always Callback To. The first option prevents the user from being called back by the server. The second option, Set By Caller, allows the server to call the user back at the number from which the user called (requires caller ID) or at the number requested by the caller (which could be different from the dialing number). The third option, Always Callback To, lets the RRAS server administrator specify a number for the user that the server always uses to call back the remote user, even if his computer requests a different number.

Improving Performance with Multilink

In the previous section, I touched briefly on multilink, which lets you aggregate together two or more connections to create a single logical connection with a bandwidth equal to the added bandwidth of all connections. For example, you might aggregate two 56K connections for a theoretical connection speed of 112K.

There are two requirements for using multilink on a dial-up connection:

- Your computer must have two or more modems, each connected to a different phone line.
- The remote server must support multilink connections.

The actual throughput you get depends on a variety of factors. As you experiment with multilink, you might find that it doesn't offer a noticeable improvement in through-put, particularly if you are aggregating two 33.6 Kbps or 56 Kbps modems. Still, it's worth a try if you're trying to get the most possible bandwidth out of your existing dial-up connection.

Also, keep in mind the requirements of the dial-up server and the way the service bills you for the multilink connection. You can't use two or more different accounts to establish a mul-tilink connection. Instead, each call uses the same user credentials to authenticate. This means you can't use your and your neighbor's dial-up accounts to make multilink work. It also means that the dial-up provider needs to deal with the fact that you are using one account to dial into more than one modem at a time. ISP that offer unlimited access are very unlikely to support multilink because it reduces their customer-to-modem ratio without increasing revenue. Some support multilink but charge you for two accounts. Those ISPs that offer metered (time-limited) access are much more likely to support multilink. In this situation, your account is debited time according to the number of connections you are using. Use two connections for an hour, and you are docked two hours on your account.

Setting Up a Multilink Connection

First, install all of the dial-up devices you want to use for the connection. Then open the properties for the connection. On the General tab (Figure 26.13), place a check beside each of the devices you want to include in the connection. Select the option All Devices Call The Same Numbers if you use a single dial-up number to connect to the RRAS server. Otherwise, clear this option, click a modem in the list, and enter the phone number it should dial in the Phone Number field. Click the next modem and enter its dial-up number. Then click OK.

TIP   You don't have to use multilink every time you use a connection that is configured for multilink. Just deselect one of the modems and then dial the connection.

FIGURE 26.13:

Use the General tab to configure multilink.

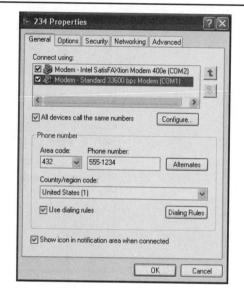

Dynamic Multilink Connections with BAP/BACP

Windows XP, like Windows 2000, supports Bandwidth Allocation Protocol (BAP) and Bandwidth Allocation Control Protocol (BACP). BAP enables multilink to be adaptive to bandwidth requirements. If bandwidth utilization drops below a certain point, BAP enables multilink connections to be dropped to reduce cost. BAP also allows multilink connections to be added as bandwidth utilization grows.

BACP performs a single function. If both peers of a multilink / BAP connection send a request for adding or dropping a link at the same time, BACP elects one as a favored peer and responds to its request, rejecting the request for others. This prevents both connections from being dropped or more than one additional link being created at a time.

A computer running Windows XP can use multilink and BAP to aggregate outgoing connections, subject to whether or not the called remote access server supports multilink and BAP. In addition, a Windows 2000 or .NET Server running RRAS and serving as a remote-access server for incoming connections can support multilink and BAP to calling clients.

To configure BAP on a Windows XP client, click the Options tab of the connection's properties. In the Multiple Devices group, select from the drop-down list the method you want to use to initiate the multilink connection. To use BAP, choose Dial Devices Only As Needed. Then click Configure to display the Automatic Dialing And Hanging Up dialog box (Figure 26.14), where you set the parameters the client will use to determine when to request new links or drop existing links. The options on this dialog box are self-explanatory.

FIGURE 26.14:

Configure BAP through the Automatic Dialing And Hanging Up dialog box.

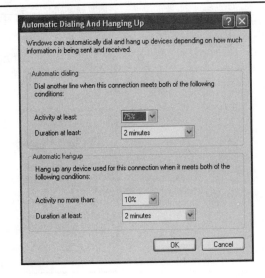

CHAPTER 27

Choosing a Network Topology

Not too many years ago, a network was the exception rather than the rule for small companies, and even some mid-sized companies had limited networks. Today, even many homes have small networks, so networking is becoming much more commonplace and the rule rather than the exception.

In this chapter, I offer tips on choosing and implementing a network. Although wired options provide the best performance, wireless solutions make more sense in some situations, particularly for network installation in existing structures and between buildings. So, this chapter covers both wired and wireless options.

You have other considerations for building your network, including how to tie together all of the computers. Hubs are less expensive than switches, but switches offer better overall performance. I take a look at the pros and cons of each and offer some suggestions on choosing other hardware such as routers and hardware firewalls.

NOTE There are lots of ways to go when developing a network. I focus on the most common and most widely used in this chapter. For example, I don't cover Token Ring networks, because they are increasingly uncommon. Also keep in mind that is a network primer to help you begin to plan your network, not an in-depth treatment of networking.

Wired Options and General Network Considerations

Wiring a network will give you the best network performance and is almost always the best choice for new construction (where you are building a new office, for example). It's also the best choice for installation in existing structures in most cases, although you can run into difficulties with wired connections in some situations. I cover those in the next section.

Network performance boils down primarily to speed, although there are a handful of other considerations. Network speed is traditionally measured in bits per second. Not too many years ago, 10 Mbps networks were the norm. Today, many companies have moved up to 100 Mbps networks for the increased throughput it offers. Most of today's network cards support both 10 Mbps and 100 Mbps speeds, and are commonly referred to as 10/100 cards. You can configure the cards to automatically sense the network speed or set them for a specific speed (forcing a 100 Mbps speed, for example).

The latest development in network hardware boosts speeds up to 1 Gbps (gigabits per second), a huge boost in performance. 1 Gbps networks offer excellent performance for scenarios with very high network utilization, such as those with frequent use of streaming video and audio, video conferencing, and extensive database transactions.

Category 5 (Cat5) cable supports up to 1 Gbps, so you can install a Cat5 network today for a 10/100 network and still upgrade to 1 Gbps in the future without recabling the network. But you may think, why not move up to 1 Gbps today? If you have the need and can afford the additional expense of 1 Gbps switches and network adapters, there is no time like the present. However, many companies—particularly smaller ones—will find that 1 Gbps technology just isn't cost effective today. My recommendation is that you implement a 100 Mbps network today and wait for the 1 Gbps technology to come down in price as more manufacturers start offering 1 Gbps devices.

TIP   It's estimated that up to 90 percent of existing Cat5 installations will adequately handle 1 Gbps speeds, but look at Cat5E if you're installing new cabling.

As you begin planning a wired solution for your network, you need to keep a few important considerations in place. First, look at where and how you will run the cable. A star configuration is the most common configuration for a typical Ethernet network (Figure 27.1). In this configuration, a hub or switch serves as the nexus for the workstation and server runs. This means that the most efficient placement for the switch in terms of reducing cable lengths is to locate the hub or switch centrally within the network.

SEE ALSO   See the section "Hardware Considerations," later in this chapter, for an explanation of the differences between hubs and switches, when each is appropriate, and coverage of other hardware issues.

As the number of computers grows, the structure of the network becomes more complex. For example, you might use a single switch to accommodate computers on two or three floors of a building, assuming the switch had enough ports to accommodate them all (Figure 27.2).

FIGURE 27.1:

A typical Ethernet star network has one hub or switch as its central point.

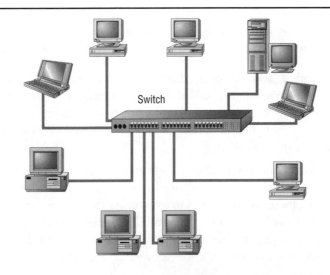

FIGURE 27.2:

Multiple switches can be used in a multifloor installation.

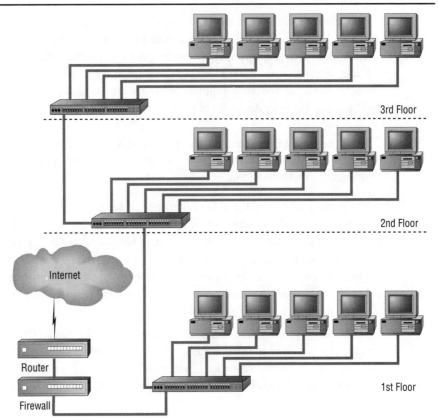

TIP   Cat5 cable runs are limited to 300 meters in an Ethernet network. This would be, for example, the length of cable between the switch and a computer.

In other cases, you might decide that it is easier or more cost effective to put in a hub or switch for each floor. You'll also need to increase the number of hubs or switches for a single floor as the number of computers grows beyond the capacity of a single device. You can use a network configuration similar to the one in Figure 27.2 to service a large number of computers on a single floor.

A key concept you should gain from the previous few figures is that you can chain together hubs or switches—you don't need a single device to service all the computers on the network. In fact, there are advantages to structuring the network using multiple segments. If properly implemented, you reduce the possibility of downtime for all users in the event of a device failure. If everyone goes through the same switch and it dies, for example, all of the users will be effectively off the network. Segmenting the network limits the number of users affected by an outage.

If you choose switches rather than hubs, you can also provide restrictions to network access. For example, you might want to allow all users to access the Internet, but want to prevent one group from seeing other groups' computers on the network. You can create virtual networks with the switches to accomplish that separation. Group A can see the computers in their workgroup, Group B can see the computers in their workgroup, but A can't see B and vice versa. However, users in both A and B can browse the Internet. Figure 27.3 illustrates the concept.

NOTE   Setting up virtual LANs goes beyond the scope of this book, but you should understand the possibilities when planning your network. Virtual LANs offer an excellent means of adding security for networks.

Where you actually run the cable is another important consideration. You need to consult local and state building codes to ensure compliance when you cable. In particular, you need to determine where you need plenum-rated cable and where non-plenum cable is acceptable. Generally, you need to run plenum-rated cable where the space in which the cable runs is considered a plenum area, or an area that serves as an air-distribution space. Plenum-rated cable gives off lower toxic emissions in the event of a fire and is required to ensure greater safety if a fire does occur.

Several other physical cabling considerations come into play. Obviously, you can't run cables under carpet or in other areas where they are subject to traffic and wear, although you can certainly run them along a wall baseboard where there is no traffic. You should also use raceway to conceal and channel exposed cable for aesthetics and to prevent damage to the cables.

FIGURE 27.3:

Virtual networks provide separation of computers on the same physical network.

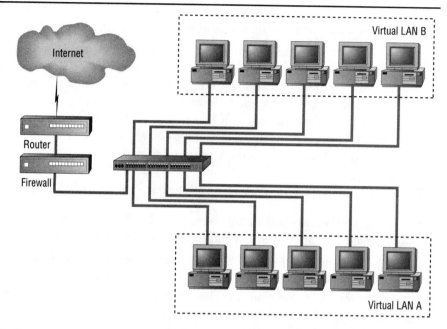

Finally, take into account equipment and light fixtures when running cables. Avoid running cables near fluorescent fixtures if possible, and cross electrical cables at right angles. Also avoid running cabling near heavy equipment that puts out a lot of EMF emissions unless you provide additional shielding for the cables.

Wireless Options

Although a wired solution is the best in terms of performance, it isn't always the most feasible or desirable solution. Installing cabling in some structures can be difficult. For example, it's tough and sometimes more expensive to run cables in buildings with concrete block walls. You can use raceway to run the cables along the outside of walls, but getting connections between rooms and floors can sometimes be difficult.

Wireless networking provides a good solution where the physical constraints of the building make cabled networks difficult or inefficient, or where you need to provide connections between buildings and installing underground cabling isn't feasible.

The main considerations for wireless networking are speed, distance, and cost. The wireless technology in common use as I write this is limited to 11 Mbps, considerably less than the 100 Mbps or even 1 Gbps you can get from wired solutions. Other wireless solutions based on the 802.11a standard are now becoming available that offer up to 54 Mbps throughput, with some vendors claiming as much as 72 Mbps possible. This increase in speed makes wireless solutions all the more attractive, particularly in situations where cabling isn't feasible.

There are other standards such as HomeRF, 802.11b, and Infrared that offer much lower throughput, and I don't recommend them in most cases. You'll also find solutions that use the electrical wiring in the building as the transmission media. The solutions coming available now support up to 20 Mbps theoretical throughput, with an actual throughput somewhere around 14 Mbps. This certainly isn't as good as 100 Mbps wired solutions or the 802.11a wireless solutions, but it's generally inexpensive and a good choice if you can't afford the expense of faster media or the hassle of cabling.

TIP   Before you settle on a wireless solution, make sure the vendor offers Windows XP drivers.

As you evaluate wireless solutions, also take a look at the distance you can achieve and how distances are affected by building structures (going from one floor to another, for example).

You might find that a combination approach works well for you. You can use cabled connections where possible and use wireless solutions to connect buildings or hard-to-reach locations within your building. This gives you the advantage of speed for those users connected by cabling to their servers or to other users while providing connectivity to those who can't be reached with cabling.

TIP   If you use wireless to link buildings and cabling within buildings, consider that intra-building traffic will be faster than inter-building traffic.

Networking for Internet Performance

Network performance for Internet access will likely be an issue that comes to mind when you are planning your network. In almost all cases, the bandwidth a company has to the Internet is considerably less than local network bandwidth. For example, assume your company has a T1 connection to the Internet, which provides about 1.5 Mbps of bandwidth. Compare that to a 100 Mbps LAN or even a 10 Mbps LAN, and you can see that you will get much better performance from LAN traffic than for Internet traffic. So, if you're upgrading to a 100 Mbps network to get better Internet performance, don't bother. You won't see any increase at all. The main point here is that you will improve network performance locally by upgrading your LAN but will likely see no improvement in Internet performance.

When you are hosting your own web servers, however, you should consider networking performance in the context of the Internet. If you anticipate a lot of traffic from the outside world to your servers, isolate them from the LAN with switches so the Internet traffic doesn't saturate your LAN. Figure 27.4 illustrates one possible solution.

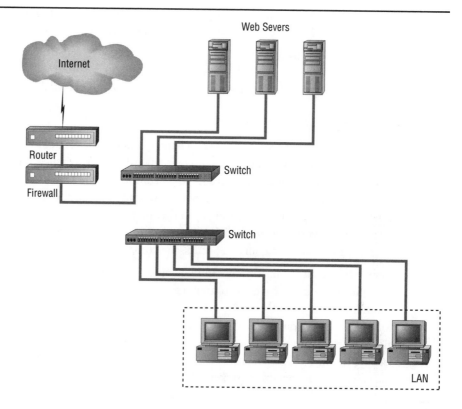

A possible network topology to reduce the impact of Internet traffic on your LAN.

Hardware Considerations

This is the section where I examine some of the hardware you will need for your network and the issues to consider when choosing a particular piece of equipment.

Network Interface Cards (NICs)

The network interface card (NIC) connects a computer to the network. NICs take the form of cards that install in a computer, interfaces built onto the computer's motherboard, PC Cards for a notebook, or external USB devices. I offer two pieces of advice: choose a major vendor, and make sure the device includes Windows XP support.

There are lots of networking hardware vendors, but you should choose one that has been around for a while and will likely be around for the long haul. Some of the ones I can recommend include 3Com, D-Link, Linksys, and Intel, but there are others that would also be good choices. Do your homework and pick a vendor you feel will be around for the long term and has the resources to continue development—you don't want to upgrade to the next version of Windows and find that you have to replace all of your network cards because the vendor doesn't have the resources to develop the necessary drivers.

That also holds true for Windows XP. When you choose network hardware, make sure it includes drivers to support Windows XP. Although you might be able to use Windows 2000 or Windows NT drivers for the device, it's better to have Windows XP drivers to ensure compatibility.

Hubs and Switches

As I explained in the beginning of this chapter, you need hubs or switches to connect the computers on your network. Hubs are less expensive than switches, but they have the disadvantage of forwarding the same traffic to all computers on the LAN. So, if a data stream comes in from the Internet bound for your computer, that same traffic affects all of the other computers on the network, as well, even though they reject the packets. This leads to an increase in *network collisions*, which occur when two or more computers try to transmit data at the same time. When a collision occurs, the computers have to retransmit the data.

Switches reduce collisions by sending traffic only where the traffic is supposed to go. For example, assume you have 24 computers connected to a switch. One computer sends data to another computer on the LAN. The switch receives the data, determines the destination, and forwards the data out the port where the target computer is located. It doesn't forward it to all of the ports. If you used a hub instead of a switch, the traffic would be forward to all ports, leading to more collisions and reduced network performance because each NIC would have to analyze all the incoming packets of data and discard the ones not meant for it.

TIP   Collisions only affect half-duplex connections. The primary advantage to using a switch is that it allows NICs to communicate at full-duplex (something not possible with hubs) which eliminates collisions and more importantly doubles the possible bandwidth (200 Mbps for FastEthernet, 100 Mbps in each direction).

There was a time when switches were considerably more expensive than hubs. The cost of switches has generally dropped, making them much more feasible for even small networks. In fact, small four- to eight-port switches are not much more expensive than similarly-sized hubs, making them a no-brainer for small networks. Whatever your situation, you'll find that switches are a solution for improving network performance.

If you decide to use switches rather than hubs, you'll need to choose between *managed* and *unmanaged* switches. A managed switch provides an interface—often web-based—that you use to configure the switch. For example, you can configure the speed of each port, set up virtual LANs to restrict traffic, and tune other parameters to further increase network performance. An unmanaged switch requires no configuration—you just plug it in and forget it. It doesn't offer the additional features of a managed switch but will likely be much less expensive than a managed switch. Figure 27.5 shows the interface to a typical managed switch to give you an idea of the types of configuration tasks you can accomplish for such a device.

FIGURE 27.5:

The management interface for a managed switch manufactured by Hewlett-Packard.

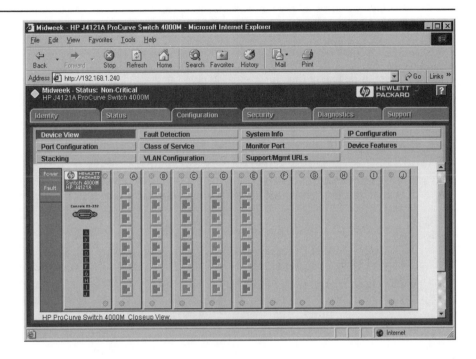

Tips and Tools for Cabling

I've put together a lot of small networks, and my last bit of advice has to do with all the hardware related to cabling and how you terminate the cables. I've already suggested that the hub or switch be centrally located to reduce the length of cable runs. When all that cable comes together at the switch, how should you connect it?

You could simply crimp a connector on the end of the cable and plug it into the switch. Having crimped hundreds of connections, I can tell you I'd rather poke a sharp stick in my eye. It takes time to strip the cable, line up the conductors in the right order, get them into the connector, and crimp the connection. Then, you have to do cut off the connector and do it all over again if you didn't get the wires in the right order or didn't get it crimped properly.

A much better solution is to use a patch panel with impact connections on the back. To make these connections, you strip a few inches of sheathing off the cable, match the color code on a wire to the connector, and then attach it with an impact tool (also called a punch-down tool). I can punch down 10 cables to the back of a patch panel in the time it takes me to make just one crimped connection. Plus, the success rate for completion is always much higher, because the patch panel is almost fool-proof compared to a crimping tool (although nothing is truly fool-proof to a sufficiently talented fool).

Once you have all the connections punched down on the patch panel, use pre-manufactured patch cables (with connectors already on both ends) to connect the ports on the patch panel to the ports on the switch.

> **TIP** Use a mounting rack for the patch panel and attach the cables to the rack with plastic cable ties to eliminate strain on the connections and provide a much neater installation.

At the other end of the connection, you have the same choice—simply crimp a connector on the cable or punch it down and use a patch cable. You'll find several types of modular connectors for wall mount or installation into standard receptacle boxes (like those used by electrical receptacles). Connect the cable coming from the switch to a modular punch-down connector, then use a patch cable to connect the computer to the receptacle.

CHAPTER 28

Configuring LAN Connections

As it does with most other hardware configuration tasks, Windows XP makes it relatively easy to install and configure network hardware. Even so, getting your network up and running the way you want requires that you understand the settings you can configure for your network card and clients, and which protocol(s) to choose. There are also a handful of advanced network settings that you can modify to fine-tune a system's performance.

In this chapter, I explain how to work in and customize the Network Connections folder. For example, you might not realize that you can rename your network connections, or why you'd want to do such a thing.

This chapter also covers network configuration, starting with network adapters. The settings vary from one to another, but there are common settings you can change. You also need to decide which protocols and services to use on your network, and how services should be bound to protocols for each connection. For example, you shouldn't bind the File and Printer Sharing service to TCP/IP for external connections, to avoid someone being able to access your system from the Internet. There are some mitigating factors, however, which I discuss later in the chapter.

This chapter also explains how to configure network clients and change logon options. I round out the chapter with a look at the advanced settings you can configure for your network connections through the Network Connections folder.

Managing the Network Connections Folder

Like its predecessor, Windows 2000, Windows XP integrates your network and dial-up connections into one location. Windows 2000 users will probably be familiar with the Network and Dial-Up Connections folder. Microsoft has opted to rename the folder simply Network Connections, eliminating the distinction between LAN and dial-up connections. Figure 28.1 shows the Network Connections folder on a typical system.

FIGURE 28.1:

Use the Network Connections folder to manage network settings.

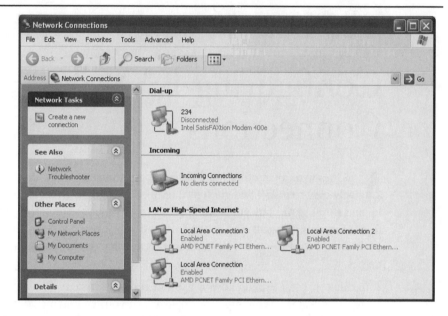

To open the Network Connections folder, click Start, right-click My Network Places, and choose Properties. You can also open it through the Network Connections icon in Control Panel.

Changing the View

Windows XP uses the Tile view as the default for the Network Connections folder. This view shows the connection name, status, and device associated with the connection. If you have several connections or want more information, you might prefer a different view. For example, the Details view includes the same information plus the device type, owner name, and phone number or network address of the connection. Figure 28.2 shows the Details view.

To switch views, just choose View and select the type of view you want. If you choose the Details view and want to customize it, choose View ➢ Choose Details to open the dialog box shown in Figure 28.3. You can select which columns to display and change the order of the columns using the Move Up and Move Down buttons. You can also change the column order and columns displayed directly in the view. Just click and drag a column to change its location. Right-click any column to display a menu you can use to turn on or off the various columns.

FIGURE 28.2:

The Details view offers additional information about connections.

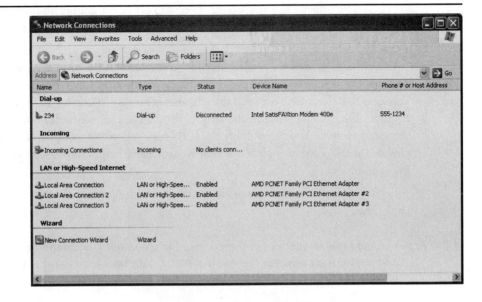

FIGURE 28.3:

Use the Choose Details dialog box to change the columns displayed and their location.

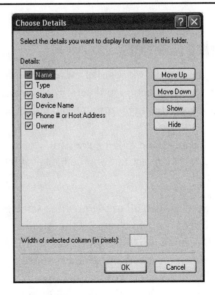

Simplifying the Folder for Multiple Adapters

Although most Windows XP computers will typically have only one network adapter (and possibly several dial-up connections), you might run across a computer now and then that contains two adapters. A good example is a computer that functions as an Internet gateway, sharing its broadband Internet connection with other computers on the network. One NIC connects to the DSL modem or cable modem (or router), and the other connects the computer to the LAN.

Windows XP names the first connection Local Area Connection and names subsequent connections Local Area Connection 2, Local Area Connection 3, and so on. This doesn't make it very easy to differentiate between the adapters. The easy solution is to simply rename the connections. For example, rename the adapter for the Internet connection to WAN, Internet, or something similar. You can simplify the LAN connection's name as LAN, Local, etc. This lets you identify the cards at a glance, which is particularly helpful if you have two identical adapters in the computer.

Just right-click the connection's icon and choose Rename. Type the name you want and click OK.

TIP   I include the IP address in the connection's name if the computer has a assigned address. If the computer has two NICs that both take their addresses dynamically, I include the first three octets of the address. This helps me recall at a glance the NIC addresses.

Configuring Adapters

Most network adapters offer at least a few settings you can configure to change the way the card handles the connection and certain protocols. These settings vary from one card to another, with some being common to all and others implemented only on some cards.

WARNING   If you don't understand a particular setting and don't have a specific reason to change it, leave it alone. You might find yourself juggling the settings to try to get the connection to work again.

It's difficult to explain all of the possible settings because they are device-dependent. One setting you might want to change is the speed and duplex mode of the card. Cards that support both 10 Mbps and 100 Mbps speeds set the speed automatically by default. The cards sense the connection speed and mode at startup and configure the speed accordingly. If you are connecting to a switch with defined speeds and modes for each port (or at least for your port), you can explicitly set the speed and mode for your adapter.

TIP   Check your network card's documentation for information on the other settings offered by your card.

Open the properties for the connection and, on the General tab, click Configure to open the properties sheet for the card. Then click the Advanced tab. Find the setting that offers the following options and select according to your desired configuration:

10 Mbps Full Duplex   The card operates at 10 Mbps and can send and receive at the same time.

10 Mbps Half Duplex   The card operates at 10 Mbps and does not send and receive at the same time.

100 Mbps Full Duplex   The card operates at 100 Mbps and can send and receive at the same time.

100 Mbps Half Duplex   The card operates at 100 Mbps and does not send and receive at the same time.

100 Mbps full duplex offers the best performance, but it requires that the other devices with which you communicate support the same speed and mode.

TIP   In a few cases, I've seen network problems crop up when setting a card to explicitly use 100 Mbps Full Duplex, and resolved the problem by moving either to AutoDetect or 100 Mbps Half Duplex. I've also seen cases where the card autodetected the correct settings but had to have the setting explicitly set to function properly.

The only other settings you are likely to need to change for a network adapter are the resource settings it uses. However, even this is not very likely, as most of today's network adapters fully support Plug and Play, which means that Windows XP can dynamically assign the I/O range, memory range, and IRQ used by the card. If you are working with a legacy card or need to change the properties for another reason, you can do so through the Resources tab of the network card's properties.

SEE ALSO   See Chapter 23 for a discussion of Plug and Play and how to configure resource assignments through Device Manager.

Choosing Protocols

Network protocols are the language by which networked devices communicate. In the earlier versions of Windows, the most common protocol was NetBEUI for Microsoft networks and IPX/SPX for Novell NetWare networks. Over the years and in the past few iterations of the Windows platform, TCP/IP has become the protocol of choice for performance and compatibility reasons.

SEE ALSO   See Chapter 29 for a complete discussion of TCP/IP and its configuration.

Which protocol is right for your situation? Let's take a look at the three most common protocols.

NetBEUI

Although it isn't considered the protocol of choice these days, NetBEUI is still a good choice for small networks because it requires no configuration. However, Windows XP doesn't install NetBEUI by default, so you have to add it manually, which dilutes that ease-of-use a bit. Also, NetBEUI isn't routable, which is both a good thing and a bad thing, depending on what you're trying to accomplish.

Not being able to route NetBEUI is a problem if your network sits on multiple segments and traffic needs to pass through one or more routers. TCP/IP is generally the best bet in these situations.

Where NetBEUI can be handy is in networks that are directly connected to the Internet and in which you want to provide an added measure of security against attacks from the Internet or unauthorized access to files on the LAN. In this scenario, you need two protocols, NetBEUI and TCP/IP. You bind NetBEUI to the File and Printer Sharing service, which means it gets used for file and printer sharing on the LAN. You unbind TCP/IP from the File and Printer Sharing service, which prevents remote users on the Internet from browsing files on your LAN. You could also substitute IPX for NetBEUI and achieve the same results.

NOTE   You might think that this is an unlikely scenario, but I have seen it happen myself over more than one type of broadband connection (such as a home DSL connection). It's also possible over a dial-up connection.

However, I don't recommend this type of poor man's firewall. Windows XP now sports its own firewall, which you can use to protect a small network from various types of attacks. An even better solution is a hardware-based firewall that can provide not only protection from attacks but also offer content filtering to prevent browsing to various "undesirable" sites.

So is NetBEUI still a good choice? If you are setting up a small network that isn't connected to the Internet and don't want to hassle with any configuration at all, it's a good solution. In almost all others, TCP/IP is the way to go.

TCP/IP

TCP/IP is actually a suite of protocols, of which the two primary ones are Transmission Control Protocol (TCP) and Internet Protocol (IP). TCP/IP is the protocol suite used by the Internet and has become almost universal, even for small networks. Windows 2000 used TCP/IP as its default protocol, and Windows XP follows suit.

With TCP/IP, each network device must have a unique IP address, which can be statically assigned or dynamically assigned. There are two means for dynamic assignment: DHCP and APIPA. In the case of the former, a DHCP server manages a pool of IP addresses and assigns an address to a computer (or other device) when it starts up. A device can also release and renew its address. You'll find that most hardware firewalls can act as DHCP servers. A computer that shares its Internet connection through Internet Connection Sharing (ICS) functions as a DHCP server. You might also have one or more computers running one of Microsoft server platforms (such as Windows 2000 Server) on the network and functioning as a DHCP server.

Automatic Private IP Addressing (APIPA) used by Windows XP provides a means for allocating IP addresses automatically without a DHCP server. When the computer boots, it looks for a DHCP server and, finding none, assigns itself an IP address from a common non-routable (private) address range. The end result is that all of the computers on a network can assign their own addresses through APIPA, which means no configuration is required.

Windows XP uses TCP/IP as its default protocol, installing TCP/IP automatically during XP installation. If you do nothing to modify the network installation during installation, Setup will install TCP/IP and configure it for dynamic addressing.

Although TCP/IP requires some configuration and more thought than NetBEUI, I still recommend it in almost all situations. Configuring TCP/IP isn't rocket science, and even novice users can have success with TCP/IP if they understand what's needed.

IPX/SPX

This protocol is primarily in Novell NetWare networks. If your LAN includes one or more NetWare servers, IPX/SPX is a possible protocol. However, NetWare also supports TCP/IP, and TCP/IP is a better choice if only to improve network administration and eliminate the need for multiple protocols for computers that need access to both NetWare servers and the Internet.

What's the bottom line? I recommend TCP/IP in all situations unless you have a compelling reason to use a different protocol. That's why this book focuses primarily on TCP/IP.

Working with Network Clients

In addition to a network protocol, you'll also need a network *client*. The client provides the mechanism for access to shared network resources. So, if you're going to do file or printer sharing on the network, you'll need a client.

Windows XP provides two network clients: Client for Microsoft Networks and Client Service for NetWare. The former lets you access shared resources on a Microsoft-based network, such as one with Windows NT, Windows 2000, or Windows .NET servers. You also use this client to access shared resources on a peer-to-peer network of Windows computers (all versions) with no dedicated servers.

The Client Service for NetWare is the client you'll use in a NetWare environment—one with one or more NetWare servers. The next two sections cover both clients. To add a client, open the properties for the network connection and click Install. Select Client, click Add, and follow the prompts to select and install the client.

Client for Microsoft Networks

You set the properties for the Client for Microsoft Networks through the properties for the connection where it is installed. Open the connection's properties and double-click Client For Microsoft Networks in the General tab. Figure 28.4 shows the resulting dialog box.

FIGURE 28.4:

Client for Microsoft Networks configuration

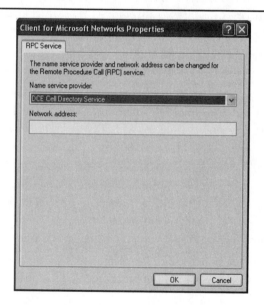

The dialog box contains two settings:

Name Service Provider   This option specifies the method Windows XP uses to locate other computers on the network. Choose between Windows Locator and DCE Cell Directory Service. Windows Locator is the default selection and is applicable to most situations. The other option, DCE Cell Directory Service, enables the computer to communicate with a DCE computer running the Name Service Interface Daemon (NSID), which provides name services for the network.

Network Address   If you selected the DCE Cell Directory Service option from the Name Service Provider drop-down list, you must specify the address of the DCE name server.

TIP   Client for Microsoft Networks corresponds to the Workstation service in Windows NT.

Client Service for NetWare

Unlike the Microsoft client, the NetWare client doesn't offer the ability for configuration through the `Network Connections` folder. Instead, you need to use the CSNW icon in Control Panel to configure the NetWare client. Figure 28.5 shows the resulting dialog box.

FIGURE 28.5:

Use Client Service for NetWare dialog box to configure the NetWare client.

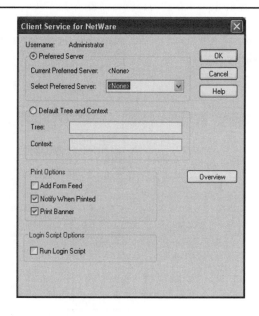

NOTE   The NetWare client does appear in the properties for the connection in the `Network Connections` folder, but you can't configure the client from there.

The Client Service for NetWare dialog box contains the following settings:

Preferred Server   This is the server that your computer connects to by default when you log on and which displays information about the resources available on the NetWare network. Use this option if your NetWare network is not running Novell Directory Services (NDS).

Default Tree And Context   If your network uses NDS, use this option to specify the NDS directory tree and context for your user account.

Print Options   Set various print parameters through these options.

Login Script Options   Select this option if you want your logon script to run each time you log onto a NetWare server or NDS tree.

Setting Advanced Network Properties

There are a handful of advanced settings you can configure for network connections. With the Network Connections folder open, choose Advanced ➢ Advanced Settings to open the Advance Settings dialog box (Figure 28.6).

FIGURE 28.6:

Use the Advanced Settings dialog box to change provider order and other advanced settings.

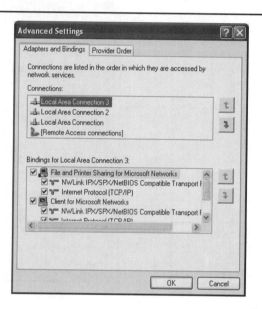

Controlling Bindings

The Connections group on the Adapters and Bindings tab lists the network connections in the order in which they are accessed by network services. In most cases, you will want to keep LAN connections at the top followed by dial-up connections. In a few rare cases—such as when you work primarily through a dial-up connection rather than your LAN connection—you might want to change the order. If that's the case, click a connection and click the up or down arrow to change its order in the list.

When you click a connection, Windows XP displays the *bindings* for the connection in the Bindings group. If a particular client or service is bound to a connection, Windows XP allows that item to function through the connection. For example, if the File and Printer Sharing service is bound to a particular connection, remote users can access your shared files and printers through that connection. However, you generally don't want File and Printer Sharing bound to a public connection such as a dial-up connection or WAN link (the network adapter connected to your cable or DSL modem, for example). The answer is to unbind the service from the connection. That's as simple as clearing the check box beside the File and Printer Sharing service in the Advanced Settings dialog box.

TIP   You can unbind a client or service from a network connection through the connection's properties—you don't necessarily need to use the Advanced Settings dialog box to do it. Just open the properties for the connection from the Network Connections folder, then clear the check box beside the item on the General tab.

Each service or client in the Bindings group of the Advanced Settings dialog box lists the protocols that are bound to it. This is different from the properties for the connection, which only shows whether or not a protocol is enabled for the connection. It doesn't show whether or not a given protocol is bound to a specific client or service the way the Advanced Settings dialog box does.

You can bind or unbind one or more protocols for a specific client or service through the Adapters and Bindings tab of the Advanced Settings dialog box. Just select the connection, locate the client or service in the Bindings list, and clear the check box to unbind it, or place a check beside it to bind it. For example, assume you are using NetBEUI as your local protocol and TCP/IP for Internet connectivity. You would bind NetBEUI to the File and Printer Service but not TCP/IP. Removing the binding for TCP/IP would remove the possibility that remote Internet users could browse your shared resources.

TIP   Using NetBEUI as a local protocol is one way to reduce unauthorized access to a computer's shared resources, but it is no substitute for a firewall.

Setting Provider Order

The Provider Order tab of the Advanced Settings dialog box (Figure 28.7) lets you specify the order in which Windows XP uses network providers when multiple providers are present. For example, if you have both a NetWare and a Windows client, but use the Windows client most often, you can move it to the top of the list, giving it higher priority and therefore making Windows XP access it first by default. This can improve network performance and streamline browsing for resources.

You can also change the order of print providers through the Provider Order tab. Changing the order determines which print method Windows XP will use when multiple providers are available. For example, if you use IPP (Internet Printing Protocol) to print to printers on the network with HTTP rather than use the LanMan print service, you can change the order of the services so HTTP Print Services comes first in the list.

To change provider order, open the `Network Connections` folder and choose Advanced ➤ Advanced Settings. Click the Provider Order tab, select the item whose order you want to change, and then click the up or down arrows to move it to the desired location in the list.

FIGURE 28.7:

Use the Provider Order tab to control the order in which Windows XP uses network providers.

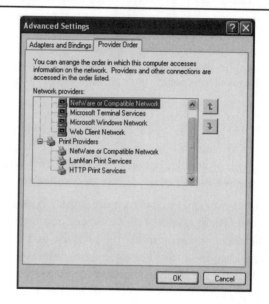

Bridging Connections

In a typical small network, all computers reside on the same media. For example, all of the computers in your office might be connected by twisted-pair cable through a small hub or switch, and all of the computers reside on the same network. Having all computers on the same network in this way is usually the best because it simplifies network setup and management.

The same holds true in a small home network. If all of your computers use the same media and are on the same network, it's much easier to share resources and connect them to the Internet. In some cases, however, it isn't possible or practical to have all computers on the same network. For example, let's assume you have a handful of computers connected in your office through twisted-pair cable on one or two switches. All of the computers have a single network adapter, reside on the same logical network, and can share resources. They can all also access the Internet through a DSL router connected to the network.

However, now you need to add several computers in the manufacturing area, but it's located a hundred feet away in a different building and you don't want to run cable to it. Instead, you decide to use wireless access points to connect the two networks. So, one computer in your office network (computer X) will have two network adapters: one for the wired LAN and one for the wireless LAN. One of the computers in the manufacturing area (computer Y) will also have two adapters: one for its local LAN and one to connect to the office network. The result is three networks: the office network, the network between computers X and Y (the wireless network), and the manufacturing network.

Without bridging connections, X can see Y and vice versa because they are on the same wireless network, but the computers on either LAN are unable to see across the wireless network to the other LAN. Plus, computers on the manufacturing network won't be able to get out on the Internet through the office LAN.

The solution is to *bridge* the connections. In this scenario, you'll actually create two bridges. You would bridge the connections on X to allow the office LAN to see the wireless network, and create a second bridge on Y's two connections to allow the manufacturing LAN to see the wireless network. The end result is that each LAN can now see across the wireless network to the other LAN. Then, all of the computers will be able to communicate and access the Internet.

To bridge connections, you must log on to the target computer using the Administrator account. You can bridge any Ethernet, IEEE 1394, or Ethernet-compatible wireless network adapters, but cannot bridge dial-up, VPN, or direct cable connections. You can't bridge a connection that has Internet Connection Sharing or Internet Connection Firewall enabled.

TIP Although you can bridge an adapter that has a public IP address to an adapter that has a private address—in effect creating an Internet gateway—you should not do so. Instead, use Internet Connection Sharing to create the gateway. Better still, install a hardware-based firewall/router on the network and use that as the Internet gateway.

When you're ready to create a bridge, open the Network Connections folder and select one of the two adapters to include in the bridge. Hold down the Ctrl key and click the other. Then right-click one and choose Bridge Connections. Windows XP creates the bridge and then creates a new section in the folder named Network Bridge. It moves the two bridged connections to this section and creates a new icon to represent the bridge.

You can't make changes to a network adapter's settings directly when it is part of a bridged connection. Instead, you must make changes through the Network Bridge icon. Right-click the icon and choose Properties to display the dialog box shown in Figure 28.8.

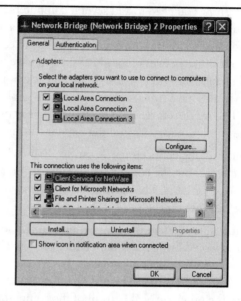

FIGURE 28.8:

Use the Network Bridge
dialog box to modify the
bridge or settings for
adapters in the bridged
connection.

As the figure illustrates, the General tab shows the adapters included in the bridge and the services, clients, and protocols used by it. As with an unbridged connection, you can enable or disable specific items simply by checking or clearing the check box beside the item. To add another adapter to the connection, just place a check beside it.

The Authentication tab configures Windows XP's use of 802.1x authentication. This draft standard was developed by several wireless vendors, Microsoft, and PC vendors in conjunction with the IEEE and addresses the potential security issues that arise from otherwise unprotected wireless LANs. For example, if you have a wireless LAN in your apartment that connects to your DSL connection, it's possible for your neighbors to tie into your wireless LAN and gain access to the Internet through your connection (not to mention possibly access your files).

The Authentication tab lets you specify the types of authentication that the computer will use when connecting to the network. Although the 802.1x security standard is designed for wired LANs, it applies primarily to wireless LANs. For that reason, I cover the options on the Authentication tab in the following section.

Securing a Wireless Network

As I briefly mentioned in the previous section, security for wireless networks is a potential problem and should be a major concern for you if you implement wireless solutions at the office or at home. Without proper security mechanisms in place, it's possible for someone to gain unauthorized access to your network and potentially to your Internet connection, essentially stealing services from you and from your Internet service provider.

A wireless access point—the device through which you connect to the network—broadcasts its service set identifier, or SSID, to potential wireless clients. This makes the wireless network visible to clients looking for a network. There are a few steps you can take to reduce the possibility that an unauthorized user can even identify your wireless network, much less connect to it.

The first change to make is to modify the SSID of your access point(s) to a non-default value that is not easy to guess. For example, set it to an arbitrary string of letters and numbers. Don't use your phone number, address, or other information that an unauthorized user might easily guess. If possible, turn off SSID broadcast. The downside to turning it off is that the wireless network won't appear when you browse for a network in Windows XP when adding a new computer, but the upside is that it decreases the likelihood that an unauthorized user will find your network.

> **WARNING** Windows XP provides the ability to browse for wireless networks and discover SSIDs. There are third-party and freeware applications that can discover wireless networks for other operating systems, so you should do everything you can to inhibit the ability of these platforms to identify your network.

Next, check out the access point to determine whether it allows you to configure the network as either open or closed. In an open network, wireless clients that specify Any as the station name or that specify no station name at all can still connect. In a closed network, the station name must be specified. Select the closed option, if available.

You should also change the default password or community string for the access point. Many default to using the common SNMP community string `public`, making it easy for a savvy user to get into the access point if they succeed in determining the SSID.

Another security step you can take is to switch from dynamic addressing to static addressing. If your network includes a firewall or router that assigns addresses dynamically through DHCP, turn off DHCP and assign addresses in an arbitrary private subnet. Don't use the common 192.168.0.n subnet, for example, but go with something like 192.168.52.n. At the very least, this increases the number of addresses a potential unauthorized user has to go through to find your subnet.

Windows XP supports Wired Equivalent Privacy (WEP), a set of services that provide additional security for wired networks. WEP allows a certificate to be used to authenticate network clients and also supports encryption to secure data from sniffing. To configure the wireless connection, open the `Network Connections` folder and open the properties for the wireless adapter, then click the Wireless Networks tab (Figure 28.9).

Figure 28.9 shows a typical configuration, with an Orinoco PC Card connection to an Orinoco RG1000 Residential Wireless Gateway with an SSID of 089c41. To configure security, select a wireless network from the Available Networks list (multiple networks might be listed) and click Configure to display the Wireless Network Properties dialog box shown in Figure 28.10.

FIGURE 28.9:

Use the Wireless Network tab to configure security for wireless LANs.

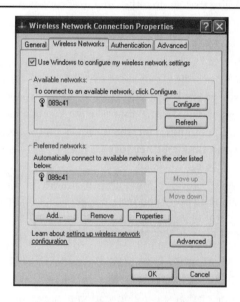

FIGURE 28.10:

Enable WEP and configure security through the Wireless Network Properties dialog box.

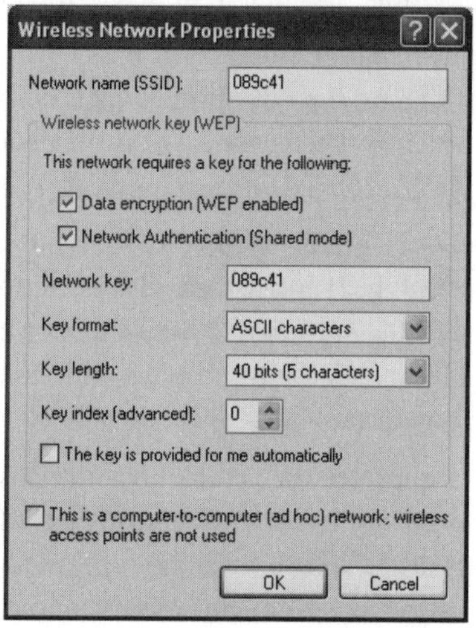

Select Data Encryption (WEP Enabled) to enable WEP. The option Network Authentication (Shared Mode) determines whether a network key is used to authenticate to the wireless network. If your access point requires a network key, select this option. The key itself might be provided on the wireless adapter, and if so, you can use the default option The Key Is Provided To Me Automatically to let Windows XP use that key automatically. Otherwise, clear this option and then specify the network key string, format, length, and index using the options provided.

NOTE   The key is defined by the access point and is often by default the same as the network name. To increase security, consider changing the key from the default value to something difficult to guess, such as an arbitrary string of digits.

The last option on the dialog box specifies whether the connection is to another wireless computer or to an access point. Select this option if you are connecting directly to another computer and not through an access point.

If your access point is configured to not broadcast is SSID, you will need to connect to the wireless network manually. To do so, click Add on the Wireless Networks tab. In the Wireless Network Properties dialog box, enter the SSID of the access point and the authentication information as I described previously. Then click OK.

CHAPTER 29

Configuring and Optimizing TCP/IP

Transmission Control Protocol/Internet Protocol (TCP/IP) is an array of network protocols (sometimes called a protocol suite) essential to Internet and other network communications through the operating system.

Whether you realize it or not, you use it everyday in going online. Yet what is more important for you to understand is that TCP/IP's proper configuration and optimization can be key to achieving the best results (read: the fewest hassles) in your communication.

In this chapter, you'll get a fuller understanding of what TCP/IP is and the job it does, how to configure it, and ways to optimize it for best results. Then, in the following chapter, I'll take you through both the monitoring and troubleshooting of TCP/IP connections.

TCP/IP Overview

If you're looking for a de facto standard for network communication, TCP/IP is it.

As I mentioned, TCP/IP isn't a single network communication protocol. Instead, it is actually an aggregate of different protocols, which work together in providing a host of both simple and advanced communication services and are supported by virtually all current-issue network operating systems and packages. You'll find TCP/IP built into Unix, for example. These different protocols come together under the umbrella of TCP/IP to serve as the protocol "bridge" linking different and divergent systems and networks for communication. The need to interconnect different networks—what eventually became the global Internet—is in fact the reason why TCP/IP was developed. Because of this versatility, TCP/IP has grown to become the dominant technique used in a variety of networking environments, for home users connecting to the Internet as well as small and large organizations.

TCP/IP supports functions and processes such as virtual private networking (VPNs), internal IP routing, network-based printing, and permits multiple addresses to be tied to either one or more network interface cards (adapters) commonly known as "multihoming." Also, various tools built into TCP/IP provide a host of diagnostic and service functions for monitoring and troubleshooting connections and configuration (covered in detail in Chapter 30).

Here are just a few of the protocols bound together under the name TCP/IP:

- Address Resolution Protocol (ARP)
- Internet Control Message Protocol (ICMP)
- Internet Group Management Protocol (IGMP)
- Internet Protocol (IP)
- Transmission Control Protocol (TCP)

Configuring TCP/IP

Since TCP/IP is installed by default with Windows XP, your job becomes configuring it for proper communications.

In this section, you'll learn more about the terminology—and the technology behind the terms—of TCP/IP communications, including IP addresses and their assignment, and the IPConfig tool used to verify the communications. I'll also tell you how to obtain and supply the necessary parameters such as an Internet Protocol (IP) address or whether to obtain one automatically if you're logging onto the Internet from a dial-up Internet provider.

Before we launch into the terms and details, follow these steps to access your current TCP/IP properties:

1. Open My Network Places and right-click the Local Area Connection option. (If you have more than one connection/connection type, you may have more than one TCP/IP configuration in place for each particular circumstance.)

2. Choose Properties.

3. Check the General tab and note the configuration information.

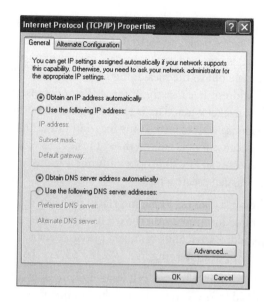

4. Next, click the Advanced button to open the Advanced TCP/IP Settings. You will then see these four tabs:

IP Settings	Used for establishing communications parameters; discussed in the next section.
DNS	Domain Name System; discussed later under "Using DNS."
WINS	Windows Internet Naming Service; discussed later under "Using WINS."
Options	Discussed later under "Configuring Other TCP Properties."

We'll talk about checking and properly configuring these various settings as we go.

Internet Protocol Addressing

Internet Protocol (IP) addresses act as a unique identifier for every computer system connected either to a network or to that bigger network known as the Internet. They have to be unique, of course, because communication would get confusing otherwise. (Just ask George Foreman, the ex-heavyweight champ, who named all his many sons George and one of his daughters Georgetta. Can you imagine answering the telephone in that house?)

Here's a simple example of how IP addressing works. I use a popular network messaging program to send notes back and forth in real time to colleagues and friends. When I send the message, TCP/IP is involved in the process of communicating with my provider and helping to send my message out to the messaging service's server. That message gets stamped with my system's IP address, because the Internet Protocol inserts both the source and destination IP address into a packet when data is sent. So when the other party sees my message and replies, that response arrives back at my location rather than being sent to some user logged in from Tibet, because it gets routed through the Internet to my unique IP address. This is why the uniqueness is so key to proper communications, and why mistakenly duplicating an existing IP address can create a mess.

The IP address gets bound to the interface, such as the installed network interface card (or the NIC integrated into the motherboard itself) or other network adapter. An IP address is always a 32-bit address, usually organized into four *octets* (four sequences of eight bits each) and taking the form of something like 192.168.63.1 or 169.254.0.2.

Configuration within Windows XP (and elsewhere) of TCP/IP and the assignment of these unique IP addresses can be done either automatically through options in XP or manually (see "Manual IP Addressing" later in this chapter).

Every IP address is comprised of two components: a network portion and a host portion. How you determine which sets of numbers are network portions and which are host portions depends on the type, since there are different classes of IP addresses. A Class A IP address uses only the first set of numbers as the network portion, with the rest identifying the host portion; a Class B network portion is defined by the first two octets, while a Class C IP address uses the first three sets of numbers to identify the network.

IP Address Types

There are two major types of IP addresses:

Public IP addresses   These are used for devices connecting to the Internet.

Private IP addresses   These take the same format as public IP addresses, but are specifically used for systems on a network that don't connect directly to the Internet and cannot be accessed from the outside world. For example, if you're on a workstation on a 10-node network, that network really only requires one public IP address to connect to the Internet, while each individual workstation, including yours, just needs its own authorized private IP address.

You should know a bit more about these IP address types, since you may ultimately have reason to use more just than a public IP address, particularly if you're involved in a networked environment. After all, even a small home network can employ more than a few IP addresses, since each node on the network needs (at least) one, and one gets assigned by your Internet provider for connecting online.

TIP   Ever wonder exactly who establishes and keeps track of the untold number of unique IP addresses? This is the job of the Internet Assigned Numbers Authority (IANA), which (along with other organizations it delegates to) provides access companies and others with lists of available public IP numbers for assignment. Permitted address ranges for private IP addresses were established some years ago, and their usage is governed by RFC 1918; these are used and reused over and over, without any need to go through a formal assignment (again) by the IANA.

Public IP Addresses

This is the type of IP address required for access to the Internet, typically assigned by an Internet service provider (ISP) or access company through a list of available IP addresses supplied to them by the IANA.

Public IP addresses can be either *static* (the same IP address is always used, usually because of a fixed connection to the Internet, as occurs through many types of broadband Internet access) or *dynamic* (randomly assigned during each Internet connection, more typical with dial-up Internet access).

Private IP Addresses

Private IP addresses are just that—drawn from a list of available, valid IP addresses identified by IANA. These are typically employed on a network where individual nodes don't have direct Internet connectivity (because they would then need a public ID address).

Does this mean you can't connect to the Internet at all if you use the private IP address route? Absolutely not, because you can configure these nodes to share an Internet connection that has been established on a system (or server) that *does* have a public IP address, using either Windows XP's Internet Connection Sharing or a third-party communications proxy program, such as WinProxy.

IP Address Assignment Methods

Windows XP directly supports four different methods for performing IP address assignment within TCP/IP. These include:

Dynamic Host Configuration Protocol (DHCP)   The default method for IP address assignment under Windows XP, used to automatically configure both IP addresses and other necessary options for all clients in a network based on a DHCP server.

Static IP addressing   This method involves the manual assignment of a fixed IP address, usually used in special circumstances and/or where DHCP and APIPA are unavailable or undesired.

Automatic Private IP Addressing (APIPA)   This is another automatic configuration method, used when a DHCP server is unavailable or unwarranted.

Alternate IP configuration   This new method within Windows XP is used to configure one primary and one secondary IP assignment. Alternate configuration can be helpful when you have multiple connection options, such as when you use your laptop both at work to establish one type of connection and then at home or on the road to connect via another method; the primary configuration is tried first, and if it's not available, the secondary configuration is tried.

Each of these methods is covered in later sections of this chapter.

Manual IP Addressing

As a rule, wherever possible, you should choose automatic IP address assignment over manual configuration.

When you learn more about DHCP-style IP address assignment in the next section, you'll see that Windows XP is automatically configured to make services available for the automatic assignment of IP addresses. Also, be aware that by choosing to manually assign these IP addresses, you become responsible for their validity (i.e., uniqueness, following a valid number range, and so on) and their administration and that you're effectively bypassing the normal safeguarding measures built into TCP/IP.

Thus, if you develop a problem when manually assigning the addresses, you may want to work through or around this by removing these self-enforced assignments and going the automatic route instead to facilitate the establishment of basic network communications. Once you have your setup functioning correctly, you can always go back and tinker.

Also, be aware that you can use a mix of both manual and automatic IP address assignment—this is pretty common practice, in fact, in almost every major network environment.

Disabling Automatic TCP/IP Configuration

In some circumstances, such as certain situations in which you may have to later use static addressing for IP address configuration, you may find it necessary to disable automatic TCP/IP configuration. Now, why would you need to do that, since (as you'll read later under the APIPA section) automatic configuration is ignored when static addressing is used? From what I'm told, this is because you may have an IP assignment situation in which you've set up the static IP address correctly yet the configuration behaves as if it's still using (you suspect) its automatic assignment. The Registry tweak outlined here forces the disabling of automatic configuration in such a case, ruling this issue out in troubleshooting a connectivity issue.

The best way to do this is by editing the Registry, and you should follow the usual precautions in protecting the integrity of your Registry (see Chapter 5 before you start).

Once you've done that, follow these steps to permanently disable automatic configuration:

1. Load the Registry Editor.

2. Locate this Registry key:

    `HKEY_LOCAL_MACHINE\SYSTEM\CurrentControlSet\Services\Tcpip\Parameters`

3. Add the following entry to the key:

    `IPAutoconfigurationEnabled: REG_DWORD`

4. Assign this entry a value of 0.

5. Save your changes and exit the Registry Editor.

Manually Configure Your TCP/IP Properties

If you choose to manually configure your system for special reasons, or because you do not have a situation in which you can use DHCP or APIPA, follow these steps:

1. From Network Connections, right-click the Local Area Connection entry (or the desired one, if more than one exists for your setup) and choose Properties.

2. From the General tab, click to select Internet Protocol (TCP/IP) and click the Properties button.

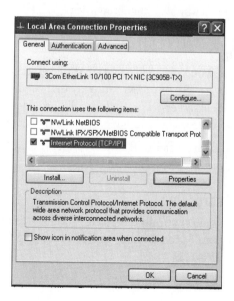

3. From the new General tab, click to select Use The Following IP Address, and then type in the appropriate information, including a value for IP address, subnet mask, and default gateway. Click OK twice to save your changes and exit.

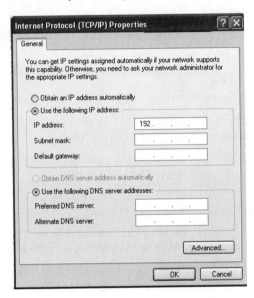

SEE ALSO See "Configuring Other TCP/IP Properties," later in this chapter, for information on configuring the default gateway and other properties.

Static Addressing

One example where you may need to set up static addressing occurs when you have a computer connecting to an ISP or access company that requires you to use a specific, static address to access their servers. They will usually provide this address to you in the documentation or e-mail accompanying the opening of your account with them.

To manually configure a static IP address under TCP/IP, follow the steps in the preceding section and enter the address you need.

Automatic IP Addressing

The chief means of automatically assigning IP addresses are Dynamic Host Configuration Protocol (DHCP) and Automatic Private IP Addressing (APIPA).

Dynamic Host Configuration Protocol (DHCP)

One of the protocols wrapped under the umbrella of TCP/IP, DHCP was first conceived as a common, easily implemented way to allow for automatic configuration of IP addresses and other parameters. DHCP is enabled by default within Windows XP.

This method works under a distributed process called *leasing*, where a DHCP server keeps and manages a list of valid IP addresses available for a network. When a client system logs into the server, the server configures and leases a dynamic IP address to the client, meaning that IP address assignment occurs on the fly and the IP for a particular node on the network can change frequently but automatically without user configuration.

Also, the DHCP leases these IP addresses for a specific chunk of time, referred to as the lease duration. When a client obtains a lease and begins using it, the meter begins running. Halfway through the lease duration, the client automatically sends a request to extend the lease to the DHCP server, to make sure a session doesn't time out or otherwise fail because of an expired lease. The DHCP, on its end, grants that request again and again until the client stops requesting an extension (for example, because the client has been shut down or otherwise removed from the need for an IP address assignment). This helps ensure that leased IP addresses will return to the DHCP queue for reassignment.

By design, DHCP effectively avoids pesky address conflicts and other issues that typically crop up with manual IP address assignment and configuration.

You also don't need an intricate network to make use of the services of DHCP, since Windows XP's Internet Connection Sharing employs it, for example, in distributing Internet access to other systems, even on a small home network. Internet service providers also may use DHCP and require you to adjust your configuration for this process (i.e., Obtain An IP Address Automatically) under your TCP/IP properties.

DHCP does more than assign IP addresses. It manages addresses for features such as print and news servers, as well as configuring other TCP/IP parameters including the default gateway and the subnet mask.

Since DHCP is already installed and enabled for you when you setup Windows XP, it's already there waiting for use. See the next section for instructions for setting up TCP/IP to use this automatic configuration, and for the rules of how Windows XP handles the issue of whether to use DHCP, APIPA, or alternate configuration to assign IP addresses.

Automatic Private IP Addressing (APIPA)

Using APIPA, you can automatically allow Windows XP to configure the system to assign private IP addresses to each node on the network—no DHCP server or manual IP address assignment required.

However, there are some special conditions placed on APIPA's use. Unlike some of the other methods mentioned here, APIPA configures the IP address and subnet mask *only*. Any other settings (such as default gateway and IP addresses for either DNS or WINS servers) are left unconfigured. Thus, it should only be used on a network with just one subnet and where no routers are connected.

Also, because we're talking about the assignment of private IP addresses and without the added configuration setup, it's not wise to use this for either a home area network (HAN) or a small office's LAN where a direct connection to either an intranet or the Internet is used.

I said earlier that Windows XP uses that protocol by default to configure for IP addresses automatically. However, what happens when a DHCP server is unavailable? Windows XP then looks at the Alternate Configuration tab and makes a judgment call whether to use APIPA or these alternate parameters to configure the IP address.

If APIPA is chosen (and under normal conditions, it would be), then an IP address is assigned using a very specific range (169.254.0.1 to 169.254.255.254). These addresses are reserved for APIPA use only and won't be found anywhere on the Internet. APIPA also sets the subnet mask to a default setting of 255.255.0.0.

Because Windows XP looks to DHCP first and falls back then to either APIPA or alternate configuration, how you enable these to work is roughly the same for all three (at least, so long as you have an alternate configuration established). If you choose to force a manual configuration through the use of static addressing, however, all automatic configuration is ignored.

Follow these steps to assign your IP addresses automatically:

1. From Network Connections, right-click the Local Area Connection you want to adjust, and choose Properties.

2. From the Internet Protocol (TCP/IP) Properties window, select Obtain IP Address Automatically.

Configuring for a Default Gateway

A *gateway*, by definition, is any device used for common access to an external source. With Internet Connection Sharing, for example, the single system directly accessing the Internet serves as a gateway to the other systems on the network sharing the service.

But specifically as it relates to TCP/IP, the gateway is the address of a specific, reachable IP router.

Understand that, to add a default gateway, you have to manually configure your TCP/IP properties, including IP address and the subnet mask, as well as add the default gateway information. To do this:

1. From Network Connections, select the connection you want to configure, and then click Change Settings Of This Connection.

2. From the General tab, click to select Internet Protocol (TCP/IP Properties), then click Properties.

3. Click to choose User Configured, click Use The Following IP Address, then supply the IP address, subnet mask, and default gateway. If needed, fill in the primary and alternate information for either or both DNS and WINS servers. Click OK.

What Is a Subnet Mask?

A *subnet* is a subdivision of an IP network—often used for better performance control and security—where all devices share one or more IP address prefixes. For example, nodes on a subnet may all have IP addresses of the form 192.168.0.*xxx*; here, *xxx* will be the unique identifier for each device.

A *subnet mask* is the method of identifying the various devices within a subnet, providing a 32-bit number (usually taking the form of 255.*xxx.xxx.xxx*) needed to allow a device sending an IP packet to identify both the network ID and host ID sections of a particularly IP address for accurate handling and routing. When a device prepares to send an IP packet, it compares the destination IP to its own, trying to first determine whether both are on the same subnet or not. If they are on the same subnet, the device ARPs (see the preceding chapter) for the destination's MAC address and sends it directly. If they are not on the same subnet, the IP packet is sent instead to the default gateway's IP address.

TCP/IP-Based Name Resolution

Ever try to recall—accurately—more than a few IP addresses? Since everything covered here needs an IP address *and* each IP address needs to be unique, you end up with a lot to remember. But for most, they're much tougher to use on a regular basis than a normal name identity.

Thus, it becomes the job of a process called TCP/IP *name resolution* to convert those unique IP addresses into a unique name identity. This gives you the option of looking for a computer called Pax rather than trying to remember 192.168.0.5 (the Pax system's IP address on the network). Although virtually all of the methods discussed here can resolve both from name to IP and from IP to name, these methods are chiefly used for resolving names to IP addresses, and that's why the process is called name resolution.

Windows XP directly supports several types of TCP/IP name resolution, including:

- Domain Name System (DNS)
- Windows Internet Naming Service (WINS)
- HOSTS
- LMHOSTS
- Broadcast

I'll discuss the first two in some detail, and then tell you how the next two are used, while you'll find the last, broadcast, briefly described under LMHOSTS.

Using DNS

Domain Name System (DNS) is a directory service that translates domain names into IP addresses. When DNS is used on a network for name resolution (meaning, whenever you use a domain name), the network looks to a hierarchical, distributed database (called the *domain namespace*) stored either within the network or on the Internet. That database stores specific mappings of DNS domain names to related data, which includes IP addresses and user-friendly names, for easy lookup. When the network queries the DNS server, it's searching on the data stored within that database to try to come up with an IP address linked to that particular domain so that it can convert that domain into an IP address. As soon as an appropriate match is made, the process is finished. If it can't make a match based on the listings contained with the local database, it jumps to other available DNS servers trying to find it. If it can't find a match anywhere, a DNS error is reported back.

DNS is the default name resolution system used with Windows XP clients, and a DNS host name is automatically collected from the client's computer name when XP is installed. To see your DNS host name, double-click the System icon in Control Panel and choose the tab labeled Computer Name.

A primary DNS suffix is used to identify the DNS domain to which a specific host belongs. Under normal conditions, when working with a small network, workgroup, a stand-alone system, or even a Windows NT domain, a DNS suffix may not be needed and would not be established *unless* you manually specify one.

You can either establish your first DNS suffix or modify your existing one by following these steps:

1. Open the System applet in Control Panel and choose the Computer Name tab.
2. Click Change.
3. Click More.

4. From the DNS Suffix And NetBIOS Name window, type the new DNS suffix required, and click OK until you exit.

TIP   To change this setting automatically each time a system changes its domain affiliation (membership), be sure to click to check this option in the DNS Suffix window.

NOTE   A secondary DNS suffix is simply the alternate one to use if the first isn't available.

Using WINS

When you read about DNS in the preceding section, you learned that the distributed database stores results of mapping a *domain* name or host name to other information, including (importantly) the IP address. Now let's look at Windows Internet Naming Service (WINS), which maps *computer* (NetBIOS) names to their respective IP addresses.

WINS is a server-based process that uses a distributed database to track and update these NetBIOS/computer name-to-IP address listings, with the updating part critical, because if DHCP servers are configured to assign IP addresses dynamically, these IP addresses (and the names they associate with) can change from session to session. One strong benefit here is that WINS facilitates the way you can locate computers even on remote networks. Another is that WINS is compatible for use with clients and servers running earlier versions of Windows.

Two different elements comprise what we refer to as WINS:

WINS server   The administrative part, handling the distributed database and responsible for both name queries as well as for name registrations.

NetBIOS over TCP/IP (NetBT, as client)   This network component is used for backward compatibility with non-Windows 2000 and XP systems still using the basic network input/output operating system (NetBIOS) included with earlier versions of Windows and to perform computer name-to-IP address mapping and name resolution.

If DHCP is used for auto-configuration of the IP address, WINS information (server parameters) should be automatically set. However, let's go through the steps of configuring Windows XP to use WINS, while also being sure that you have enabled DHCP. To do this:

1. From Network Connections, right-click Local Area Connection (or the appropriate connection if you use more than one), and choose Properties.

2. From the list of protocols, select Internet Protocol (TCP/IP), then click the Properties button.

NOTE   If you don't use auto-configuration through the DHCP assignment method, you *must* configure your WINS connection manually.

What you do next depends on whether you have a DHCP server already established to work with WINS or not. If you do, choose Obtain An IP Address Automatically, and click OK. If you don't, then follow these steps:

1. From the General tab under TCP/IP Properties, click the Advanced button.

2. Select the WINS tab.

3. Click Add, which opens the TCP/IP WINS Server dialog box.

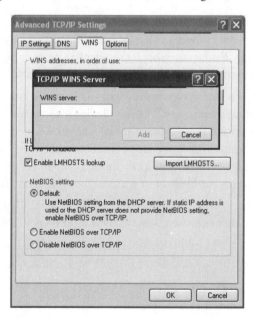

4. Provide the name of the WINS server you want to use, and click Add again.

If you have more than one WINS server you can use, you can add additional ones here. To change the preference order by which Windows XP checks these servers, select the desired server from the list, then click the up arrow to move it higher in the list or the down arrow to move it lower.

Using a HOSTS File

What if you don't have access to a DNS server for domain/host name-to-IP address resolution?

This is the role of the HOSTS file, a table of local host computers that provides host name resolution whenever DNS isn't available (or where it is available but not all hosts may be registered). You can use it to store a list of static entries for the systems to which you regularly connect.

A sample HOSTS file is located in the *%systemroot%*\System32\Drivers\Etc\ folder. A simple text file, this can be edited by you to add the names of remote hosts plus IP addresses to which you connect, or you can use its format to create your own (remember to save it in text-only format). The syntax for an entry for a host named Pax1 at kchase.com might look like this:

```
192.168.68.10          pax1.kchase.com
```

Using an LMHOSTS File

Windows XP sees any system that is neither configured as a WINS server or a WINS client as being something called a *broadcast* or *b-mode* computer, because of the way such a system uses IP broadcasts for NetBIOS name resolution rather than the WINS name resolution type. What's different here is that the system's cache gets called upon to store registered address/name mappings gathered from something called an LMHOSTS file (*LM* stands for local machine, referring to that system's hosts listing).

The LMHOSTS file is simply a straight text file containing the NetBIOS or Microsoft NT domain name as well as the IP address of remote computers or (backup) domain to which you connect. Such computers can be any system inside or outside your local subnet. The contents of this file are read into the cache, and when Windows XP wants to try to identify a remote computer, it looks first in the cache. If it can't identify the remote computer through stored mappings, it then moves to IP broadcasts to try to resolve the name. If that fails, it goes back and parses the entire LMHOSTS file.

A sample LMHOSTS file (lmhosts.sam) is provided for you in the *%systemroot%*\System32\ Drivers\Etc folder. You can edit this version to add necessary computers, but you must save it to lmhosts, rather than lmhosts.sam, to have the file recognized for use.

TIP   For the LMHOSTS file to be most effective, you need to add the NetBIOS name and IP address of every remote system you regularly connect with.

Other TCP/IP Properties and Tools

In the following sections, I discuss a variety of further TCP/IP options:

- Setting up multiple gateways
- Configuring TCP/IP filtering
- Using class IDs
- Taking advantage of IPConfig

Using Multiple Gateways

As was the case in early versions of Windows (including NT 4), you can set up multiple gateways for a single workstation, if necessary. This situation could occur if you have multiple network adapters installed, all pointed at different other systems or devices acting as gateways. This has the added benefit of allowing data to switch to the second gateway, for example, if the first one is unavailable.

Follow these steps to add one or more additional gateways:

1. From Control Panel, click Network Connections.
2. Select and right-click the desired connection, and choose Properties.
3. Select TCP/IP and click Properties.
4. From the General tab, click Advanced.
5. From the IP Settings tab (opened by default), go to Default Gateways, and click Add.
6. From the TCP/IP Gateway window, type in the desired gateway address, and click Add. Click OK.

Using TCP/IP Filtering

Filtering here means a way to try to better control the data traffic reaching the Windows-based machine being configured for TCP/IP.

TCP/IP in Windows XP includes a set of input filters specifically designed to work with local host traffic only; these filters are typically used when you're not configuring for more advanced data traffic management, such as you might have through an external application, Routing and Remote Access, or even IPSec.

By default, TCP/IP filtering is turned off in Windows XP. To turn it on and configure it for use, follow these steps:

1. From Network Connections, select the local area connection you want to modify, right-click, and choose Properties.

2. From the General tab, select Internet Protocol (TCP/IP), and then click Properties.

3. Click Advanced.

4. From the Options tab, select TCP/IP Filtering, and then click Properties.

5. From the TCP/IP Filtering window, click to select Enable TCP/IP Filtering.

6. Under their respective sections, provide the port numbers for all TCP and UDP ports, plus the IP protocols you want to enable filtering to check. You must click Permit Only before you are allowed to add these ports. Click OK until you exit.

NOTE   Concerned about security or have questions about establishing IP security under Windows XP? You'll find this covered in Chapter 50.

Using Class IDs

Starting with Windows 2000, Windows operating systems support the use of class IDs, used by DHCP for distinguishing which class of PCs a particular workstation or client belongs to. Classes can help identify particular groups of devices, such as those residing within a particular department, and customize those locations to which they have access, the priority with which requests are handled, and the length of DHCP lease periods used.

For example, based on class ID, you can give a much longer lease period to people who logon directly through the network than to workers dialing in from home or a remote location.

By design, a DHCP server will handle requests based upon the available class IDs presented to it.

Class IDs are set using the IPConfig tool, discussed in the next section. You must log in on an administrator account in order to set class IDs, and use one of the following syntaxes:

```
ipconfig /setclassid [classIDname]
ipconfig /setclassid [adaptername] [classIDname]
```

WARNING   Failure to specify the new class ID when using the /setclassid option purges any current class ID established.

Using IPConfig

The IPConfig tool is a command-line tool available in Windows XP to help verify the proper setup of TCP/IP and its communication with other systems and networks. Specifically, IPConfig confirms the configuration parameters available on the host, with the host here defined as any device on the network that is not responsible for forwarding data packets between subnets.

NOTE   If you recall the WINIPCFG tool available in earlier versions of Windows, you're probably already aware that it is not included with Windows XP. The IPConfig tool replaces it.

NOTE   Another such tool, the Ping utility, is discussed in the next chapter.

By default, IPConfig displays the following information for each adapter to which TCP/IP has been bound after it has completed its verification (as shown in Figure 29.1):

- Assigned IP address
- Subnet mask
- Default gateway

However, switch options available for use with IPConfig allow you to customize (to some degree) the result output depending on your specific needs. These options are detailed in Table 29.1.

FIGURE 29.1:

IPConfig gives this screen output.

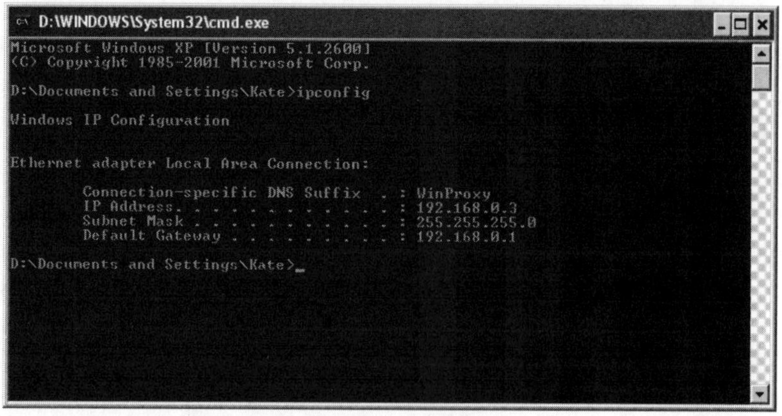

```
D:\WINDOWS\System32\cmd.exe

Microsoft Windows XP [Version 5.1.2600]
(C) Copyright 1985-2001 Microsoft Corp.

D:\Documents and Settings\Kate>ipconfig

Windows IP Configuration

Ethernet adapter Local Area Connection:

        Connection-specific DNS Suffix  . : WinProxy
        IP Address. . . . . . . . . . . . : 192.168.0.3
        Subnet Mask . . . . . . . . . . . : 255.255.255.0
        Default Gateway . . . . . . . . . : 192.168.0.1

D:\Documents and Settings\Kate>_
```

TABLE 29.1: IPConfig Switch Options

Option	Purpose
/all	Displays all available TCP/IP configuration information.
/displaydns	Displays info from the DNS resolver cache.
/flushdns	Clears out the DNS resolver cache.
/registerdns	Reregisters DNS names after it refreshes all DHCP leases.
/release *adapter*	Releases IP address (specified adapter only).
/renew *adapter*	Renews IP address (specified adapter only).
/setclassid	Resets the DHCP class ID to specific setting.
/showclassid	Displays the DHCP class ID(s) available for the specified adapter.
/?	Displays online help; use the |more option to break the text into different screens.

The syntax used in conjunction with IPConfig follows conventions such as these (typed from the command line):

```
ipconfig /all
ipconfig /displaydns
ipconfig /renew adapter_name
ipconfig /setclassid adapter class_ID
```

The results of ipconfig /all are shown in Figure 29.2. When using the /renew switch, replace the variable with the name of a specified adapter, with wildcards supported.

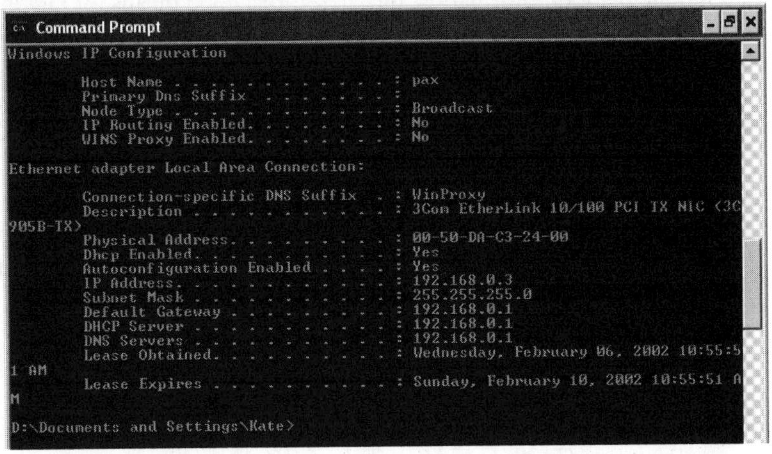

FIGURE 29.2:

ipconfig /all reports all available TCP/IP data.

TIP   If you fail to provide the name of the specified adapter for either /release or /renew, then these will be applied to all adapters bound to TCP/IP.

WARNING   If you force a static IP address assignment, you won't be able to release it with the ipconfig /release command; you must reconfigure the TCP/IP properties instead.

TIP   Need to see if APIPA is currently enabled on the system? Go to the Command Prompt and type **ipconfig /all**. Make sure the entry marked Autoconfiguration Enabled reads Yes and that it provides a valid IP address within the range of 169.254.0.1 to 169.254.255.254.

Switching between Network Settings

In some situations, you might want to use two different sets of network settings on a notebook. For example, assume you connect to your office LAN with a PC Card NIC and use the same NIC for your home connection (or for connection in a different office). But the settings at the office are different from those at home. You have to switch settings each time you move your computer from one network to the other. That can be a real pain.

Windows XP maintains information about the installed PC Cards based on their slot. Using the slot location as an indicator is the best means for managing settings, because you might have two identical adapters in the notebook's PC Card slots. The slot number is a unique piece of information and therefore a good means for tagging the settings.

This bit of behavior means that you can move a PC Card from one slot to another and have Windows XP maintain different settings for it in the new location. As you might have guessed, this makes it easy to switch networks. Just switch the card to the appropriate slot and boot the computer. You don't even need to use hardware profiles to accomplish the change.

Alternate IP configuration is an option under a TCP/IP setup's properties that lets you provide an alternate (secondary) IP address. The PC I'm using right now has one IP address for its primary work and communication, and another (the alternate IP) for sharing broadband Internet services through the main network via WinProxy.

To configure this option, follow these steps:

1. Under Network Connections, right-click the connection to which you want to add an Alternate Configuration, and choose Properties.

2. Click Internet Protocol (TCP/IP), then click Properties.

3. Select the Alternate Configuration tab.

4. Either choose Automatic Private IP Address, or select User-Configured and then provide the desired IP address and other information. Click OK twice.

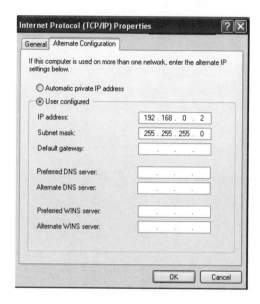

We're done here, but you may be wondering how you can monitor TCP/IP performance and activity, as well as how you can work through difficulties you may encounter both in configuration and use. Jump to Chapter 30, where I'll take you through all that and more.

Troubleshooting and Monitoring TCP/IP Connections

S ometimes, it can be difficult enough resolving what should be a very simple communication between two computers directly connected together. After all, it could be a problem with configuration, with the cable, or many other aspects.

Imagine how much more complicated troubleshooting becomes when a lot more hardware, software, and distance intervenes between two systems trying unsuccessfully to communicate with one another. If you've ever tried to get the IP address for another user on the Internet, you'll often see that your attempts go through any number of "hops"—different locations your data message bounces to en route to its ultimate destination. A problem at any one of those hops could mean data gets rerouted, slowing everything down; or it could be that data just dies out in the ether somewhere, and you have to determine where the problem lies.

Even before we get into a situation where we need to troubleshoot, we tend to want to monitor our data transmissions to make certain they're efficient, that all channels along the route are open and ready to both forward and receive data. This obsession strikes everyone from casual home users who have just installed their first network to seasoned network administrators who always keep their eyes on the data traffic, trying to anticipate a possible bottleneck or connectivity failure before it occurs by watching how swiftly and efficiently data moves.

Such watching—and fixing—is the focus of this chapter. You'll learn about the underlying structure beneath TCP/IP monitoring and troubleshooting, as well as when and how to use the most common relevant commands. At the end, you'll get a quick look at some of the third-party utilities available to cover some of the work done by these commands, but sometimes rolled into one graphical interface.

Internet Control Message Protocol (ICMP)

A major part of how you both monitor and troubleshoot TCP/IP configurations and the overall health of the network (of whatever type) your data moves across is tied to yet another protocol, Internet Control Message Protocol (ICMP). This isn't exclusive to Windows XP, since ICMP is a TCP/IP standard and, as such, crosses platforms, operating systems, and network environments.

ICMP's role is to provide a sort of behind-the-scenes communications system by which both hosts and routers can exchange information related to data control and status, as well as to report errors that are encountered.

Automatically, without your intervention, ICMP issues messages in the event that certain conditions are seen and/or reported. These include:

- An IP datagram can't reach its target address.

- A router or gateway can't forward datagrams at an appropriate transmission speed.

- An IP router, seeing the packets, redirects the host (sender) to use a different (usually more efficient) route to its destination.

NOTE   What's an IP datagram? It's simply a packet of information containing two distinctive parts: an *IP header* containing source and target addresses and other key administrative information, and what is often referred to as the *IP payload*, or the meat and potatoes of the data being transmitted. ICMP messages, by design, are contained within IP datagrams.

Also, different types of ICMP messages are used in this process. The ones discussed most often in this realm are these:

Echo Request messages   Used to determine whether an IP node, host, router, or gateway is available for contact/data transmission.

Echo Reply messages   The reply sent in response to an Echo Request message, reversing the path followed by the Echo Request.

In addition to the situations that cause an automatic ICMP message issuance, the commands discussed in the next section detail ways you can initiate ICMP messages to troubleshoot, because these commands send those messages as part of their run-time process.

But before we move on, I strongly encourage you to try these commands as you go, so you get a feeling for the wealth of information about your connections that can be gleaned from the results—once you train your eye to look through the mass of numbers to see the real data.

TCP/IP Commands

If you've been using the Internet for a while, you may have actually run a few of the various commands that evaluate your connection(s) and data transmission performance, such as `ping` or `tracert`, either to check the status of your Internet service provider's access server or that of a specific website.

There are some commonalities within our work with commands here that is worth noting in one place, rather than under each separate command reference.

First, all of these commands are accessible only from the command line (*not* from Start ➤ Run), and should be executed by following these short steps:

1. Open the Command Prompt.

2. Type the command you want to use, along with switches and the IP address you wish to check. Press Enter.

3. Then check the screen, where the results will be reported.

Also, as with other types of commands, you can stop the actions of many of these commands at the Command Prompt by typing Ctrl+C, or pause them by typing Pause.

You may find it useful to open the Command Prompt console window up to its full capacity, since some of the results from these commands can be rather extensive. However, you may also want to use the pipe symbol (|) with the keyword `more` to break the output into distinct screens, pausing between each. For example, to pause between screens using `tracert`, you could type at the command line **tracert www.kchase.com |more**.

TIP   You can redirect the results of some commands from the screen to a text file (or printer), if desired. For example, to send the results of a `ping` command to a text file called `pinglog.txt` in your Logs folder, you would type **ping>c:\logs\pinglog.txt**.

WARNING   Many of the switch options available for these commands *are* case sensitive. Beware.

NOTE   Typing the command alone (without any parameters at the end) will display information and available options for that command.

To make your job easier when you have some commands that issue routinely every time you run a check, you may want to roll them into a batch file (see CD Bonus Chapter, "Batch Programming").

Finally, be aware that testing network connectivity often involves testing more than one connection once. This means that you're likely to use a mix of these commands as you work, and you may execute them differently (using varying parameters, for example) against each major point along a connection route to try to pinpoint a failure or slowdown. If that last process sounds painstaking, it should, since that is what is sometimes required of you in tracking and resolving a TCP/IP communications issue.

Let's look at the commands you're most apt to use in normal TCP/IP monitoring and troubleshooting, along with when and why you might use them.

ping

The ping command is overwhelmingly the most common of the TCP/IP commands for troubleshooting IP-level connectivity. It works—as many commands do—by sending ICMP Echo Request messages to a destination IP address you want to test, and then reporting some vital facts about what hops the process took and how responsive these were in passing your data (in this case, the ICMP request) along to its intended addressee.

An example of how this is used happens when you can't open a particular website through a browser (even though you can open other sites) or can't connect to a mail server. You would then use the ping command to send a test packet to the problematic server or other destination IP address to see whether you get any response, or whether the operation times out along the way. If it does, other commands you'll find here can help you narrow down whether it's the destination itself that isn't responding, or some point along the way that isn't available for routing your test packet.

The syntax for the ping command is

ping [-*switch switch_value*] *target_IP_address*

For example, using this command

ping −1 30 208.149.106.51

means to ping the IP address 208.149.106.51 (the target) using 30 bytes of data. The results of this can be seen in Figure 30.1.

FIGURE 30.1:

Use ping to test connectivity and response.

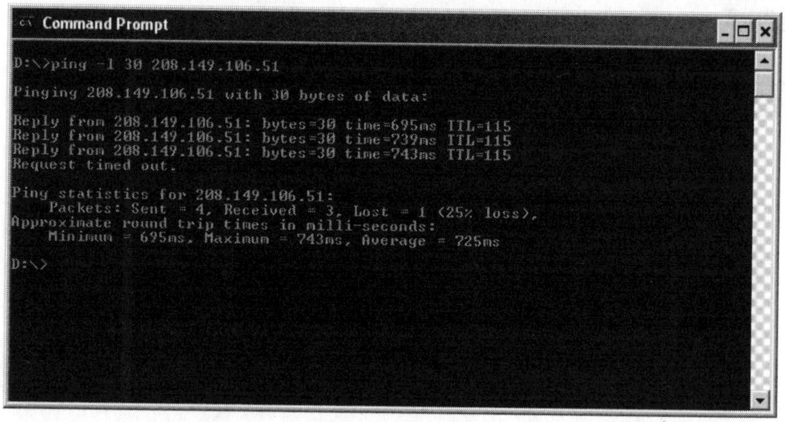

WARNING Use the ping command with care, since repeated, frequent pinging affects overall traffic all on its own, and may interrupt the session of a user logged in at the system being pinged.

TABLE 30.1: ping Switch Options

Switch	Function
-a	Resolves an address to its hostname.
-f	Sets "Don't fragment" flag within the packet to prevent routers along the path from fragmenting it; used for monitoring possible Path Maximum Transmission Unit (PMTU) issues.
-i *value*	Sets value of the Time To Live (TTL) field.
-j *hostlist*	Take a "loose" source route along the *hostlist* (see Chapter 29).
-k *hostlist*	Take a "strict" source route along the *hostlist*.
-l *size_value*	Pings using specified (by *value*) number of bytes for the packet's data field.
-n *count*	Specifies a number (*count*) of Echo Request messages to send; by default, the count value is 4.
-r *count*	Enables the Record Route option within the IP header to chronicle the route taken by the ICMP Echo Request (each hop getting its own entry in the route table); valid *count* is 1–9.
-s *count*	Enables the Internet Timestamp option within the IP header to chronicle the time both the Echo Request and the Echo Reply Request reach each hop along the route; valid *count* is 1–4.
-t	Specifies to keep sending Echo Request messages until interrupted (by Ctrl+Break, Pause, or Ctrl+C).
-v *TOS_value*	Enables and specifies a value for the Type Of Service (TOS) field in the ICMP Echo Request message's IP header; by default, this is set to 0 with a valid range of 0–255.
-w *timeout_value*	Forces a maximum amount of time (in milliseconds) to wait for an Echo Reply message answering an Echo Request message before a timeout is declared; by default, this is set to 4,000 (4 seconds).

pathping

The command pathping is typically used to detect packet loss and monitor network latency (that is, transit time, especially the lag time lost due to bottlenecks or errors). As its name implies, pathping is like the ping command but performs its work by looking at intermediate hops along the route a packet takes. The purpose of pathping is not so much to determine whether there is a data logjam but to identify where things are getting hung up by looking at the path step by step.

When you see the results, note that the information is largely broken into two parts, with the hops path listed first, and then specific statistics per hop, number of packets lost vs. sent, and IP address.

Syntax for this command follows this convention:

```
pathping [-switch switch_options] IP_address_or_name
```

For example, by using this command:

pathping -n -p 500 www.example.com

I am checking (by pinging) all routers along the path, with the -n switch telling it not to try to resolve the IP address of intermediate routers and with -p 500 forcing pathping to wait 500 milliseconds (½ second) between consecutive pings. Table 30.2 lists the switches available to modify the ping command.

TABLE 30.2: pathping Switch Options

Switch	Function
-g *hostlist*	Tells pathping to send ICMP messages using the loose source route option contained in the *hostlist* file.
-h *value*	Specifies the maximum number of hops to use, where *value* equals the number of hops; by default, this is set to 30.
-n	Tells pathping not to resolve the IP addresses of intermediate routers to try to save time.
-p *value*	Sets the amount of time (in milliseconds) to wait before each new ping is issued; by default, this is set to 250 ms (¼ second).
-q *value*	Sets a specific number of ICMP Echo Request messages to transmit to each router along the data path, where *value* equals the number of messages; by default, this is 100.
-r	Forces pathping to check to see if every network device along the data path supports the Resource Reservation Protocol (RSVP), used to reserve a chunk of bandwidth as a dedicated data stream; if you receive a "Destination Unreachable" error, it is usually because RSVP is not supported by one or more hops.
-t	Attaches a tag to the Echo Request message to check each network device along the path to be sure they support layer-2 priority (used to assign a level of priority to a message) functionality; if one or more is found that does not, this could be a point of concern.
-w *value*	Establishes a set amount of time (in milliseconds) to await an Echo Reply message after pinging, where *value* is the number of milliseconds; by default, this is 3,000 ms (3 seconds).

NOTE Only the -p switch option forces pathping to ping each intermediate hop individually.

tracert

The tracert command is used to check the path data takes in trying to reach its destination. It works like the ping command in that it sends multiple ICMP Echo Request as well as Echo Reply packets out and then reports on the results as the data moves through each different router on its journey.

If you're looking for packet-to-router specific information, you'll probably do better using the pathping command (see the preceding section).

The syntax to use with the tracert command follows either of the following two conventions:

```
tracert [IP_address]
tracert -d [hostname]
```

For example,

tracert -d www.example.com

There is only one switch for tracert, and it's described in Table 30.3.

TABLE 30.3: tracert Switch Option

Switch	Function
-d	Restricts the display output from the tracert command for easier readability.

arp

The arp command is used to both reveal as well as to change entries contained within the Address Resolution Protocol (ARP) cache. This cache is used to store tables (one for each installed Ethernet or Token Ring network adapter) containing IP addresses and their respective resolved addresses.

The syntax used for this command follows this convention:

```
arp [-switch option]
arp [-switch option [InetAddr] -switch option [IfaceAddr]]
```

where *InetAddr* stands for an IP internet address and *IfaceAddr* represents a network adapter interface address, which are both shown in decimal notation. You can also use an Ethernet address (*EtherAddr*), presented in hexadecimal notation taking the form of (for example) 00-50-DA-C3-00-24.

NOTE   Under normal conditions, contents of the ARP cache scroll out over time as new entries replace them, with one exception: The -s switch option allows you to make entries to the ARP cache that are static and do not scroll out with time (except when TCP/IP itself is stopped and then started, and you might have with a shutdown/restart). If you have ARP entries that should be added each time TCP/IP restarts, Microsoft recommends that you place them in a batch file (see CD Bonus Chapter, "Batch Programming") and add this batch file to your Scheduled Task entries so that it can be re-executed regularly.

TABLE 30.4: arp Switch Options

Switch	Function
–a *InetAddr*	Used to reveal the most recent ARP cache tables for each installed adapter; often used with the –N switch, as in **arp -a 208.169.62.15 -N 10.0.0.99**.
–d *InetAddr* [*IfaceAddr*]	When used with *InetAddr*, this switch deletes the entry for the Internet address specified; to remove all entries for a specific adapter itself, use –d with *IfaceAddr*.
–g *InetAddr*	Identical to the –a switch.
–N *IfaceAddr*	(Note uppercase.) Typically used secondary to the –a switch to specify the IP address of the network adapter.
–s *InetAddr EtherAddr*	Used to write a static entry to the ARP cache that resolves the IP address of the Internet address to the physical address of the adapter address specified in *EtherAddr*; for example: **arp -s 10.0.0.99 00-50-DA-C3-00-24**.

netstat

The netstat command is used to display information about all active current TCP connections as well as all ports that are engaged in "listening" for transmissions. It also goes well beyond this to show all vital Ethernet statistics (including both total bytes and packets sent/received) and the IP routing table, plus IP protocol version–specific statistics for the connection, including IPv4 and IPv6.

Of specific interest to you in monitoring and troubleshooting may be the information compiled by the command, including these categories:

Proto   Shows the type of protocol in use (TCP or UDP).

Local Address   Lists both the local system's IP address along with the port number in use for the operation; where the port isn't established or available, it will display with an asterisk (*).

Foreign Address Reports both the IP address and the port number for a specific remote system.

State Gives the state of the connection; 10 different states are recognized:

CLOSE_WAIT	FIN_WAIT_1	LISTEN	TIMED_WAIT
CLOSED	FIN_WAIT_2	SYN_RECEIVED	
ESTABLISHED	LAST_ACK	SYN_SEND	

The syntax for this command follows this convention:

```
netstat [-switch switch_option] [interval]
```

For example, the command

```
netstat -e -s 30
```

can be used to display the Ethernet statistics by protocol for all protocols available and then redisplay them every 30 seconds. Running `netstat` without any switches or parameters simply displays statistics for the active connections (as seen in Figure 30.2).

FIGURE 30.2:

Use `netstat` to see Ethernet statistics by protocol.

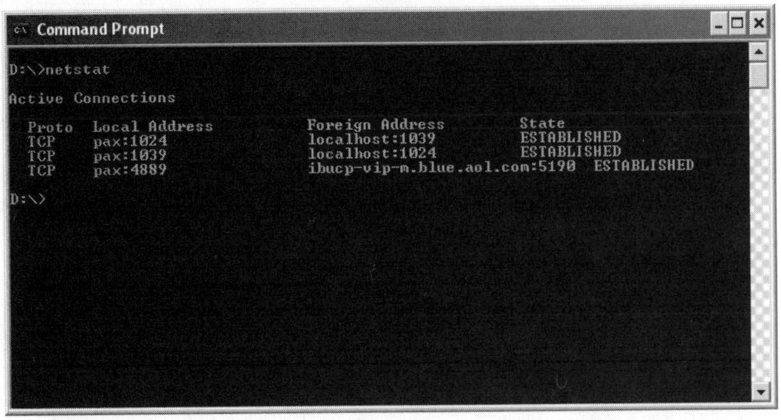

TABLE 30.5: netstat Switch Options

Switch	Function
-a	Results in a list of all current and active TCP connections along with the "listening" TCP and UDP ports.
-e	Displays Ethernet statistics, including how much data (in bytes) has transmitted; often combined with the -s switch option.

Continued on next page

TABLE 30.5 CONTINUED: netstat Switch Options

Switch	Function
-n	Gives a report of all active connections but without resolved names, and with both addresses and port numbers expressed numerically only.
-o	Reports active TCP connections but specifically includes the process ID (PID) for each of these connections. You can then match the PID to corresponding processes contained in the Processes tab in Windows Task Manager.
-p *protocol*	Active connections are shown only for those using the protocol specified by the *protocol* switch (such as TCP, UDP, TCPV6, and UDPV6); when used with; when used with the -s switch option, it can display the connections by various types of protocols (the ones previously stated plus ICMP, IP, ICMPV6, and IPV6).
-r	Works like the `route print` command to display the entire contents of the IP routing table.
-s	Shows statistics by protocol (by default, for TCP, UDP, ICMP, and IP, plus IPv6 if that protocol has been installed under Windows XP).
interval	Use this to tell the command to redisplay chosen data every set number of seconds (with *interval* reporting the exact number).

hostname

The hostname command is used to display the name of a computer (the host); it's useful if you're doing other command-line procedures and need to verify the name of the system for troubleshooting or monitoring.

The syntax of this command is simply hostname. No switches are available for it.

route

The route command, as you might expect, is highly focused on the route a packet of data takes in reaching its destination and then answering back with a reply, as we see with Echo Request and Echo Reply messages.

Specifically, this command can be used to both show and edit entries contained within the IP routing table, where each route identified and taken by your data transmissions gets its own entry in this master routing index of sorts.

You'll find this command a little different than others used in this chapter, because you can actually issue certain commands in conjunction with route, each command performing a specific function (add (entry), change, delete, and print) against entries in the IP routing table. Also, there are other non-switch parameters which can be used with this command, as indicated in Table 30.6.

TABLE 30.6: route Switch and Parameter Options

Switch	Function
-f	Removes entries from the IP routing table except the following: non-host route (defined as a route with a netmask of 255.255.255.255), loopback network route (where the destination is 127.0.0.0 and the netmask is 255.0.0.0), and multicast route (destination 224.0.0.0 and netmask 240.0.0.0). When run with a route-supported command, the entries are cleared before the command is executed.
-p	Used only with two commands: add (where a new route is added and used to initialize the IP routing table anytime TCP/IP is stopped and restarted) and print (where it produces a list of persistent routes—these found in the \HKEY_LOCAL_MACHINE\System\CurrentControlSet\Services\Tcpip \Parameters\PersistentRoutes key within the Windows XP Registry).
Command	As above, with four commands supported: add to add an entry to the IP routing table, change, delete, and print.
Destination	The final destination of the route; can be an IP address for a host route, an IP network address, or a default route destination of 0.0.0.0.
Gateway	Specifies the gateway address (which can be a directly reachable router's IP address, the IP address of a interface attached to the subnet, etc.).
if Interface	Used to specify the interface index for a connection-reachable interface; use the route print command to display a list of interfaces and their corresponding interface indexes to use with this parameter. (Case is not significant for this or the next two options.)
mask Netmask	Used to specify the netmask or subnet mask used for a particular network destination; can be the (sub)netmask of an IP network address, a host route (255.255.255.255), or a default route (0.0.0.0).
metric Metric	A number (integer between 1 and 9,999) used to designate the levels of efficacy in routes to a particular destination appearing within the IP routing table; the lower the metric value, the better (and faster) the route.

The syntax to use for this command is as follows:

```
route [-switch switch_option] [command_and/or_parameter]
```

For example, issuing this command as configured:

route print

allows me to print the entire contents of the IP routing table, while this command:

route delete 10.0

lets me delete all IP routing table entries that start with the IP address of 10.* (wildcards obviously supported).

nbtstat

nbtstat stands for (TCP/IP) *NetBT statistics* and is used to show (in table format) both protocol statistics as well as current connections for any NetBT communications; this is useful for both troubleshooting as well as general information. It can also be used to refresh the NetBIOS name cache as well as registered entries within WINS (see the previous chapter for details)—especially helpful you want to dump current entries in favor of a fresh list. It also works with the NetBIOS name table, which is a listing of the various NetBIOS names representing installed and running NetBIOS applications.

Be aware that with this command, you really need to respect case sensitivity when adding switch parameters, because the case used here can alter the results you get from executing nbtstat. The switches for this command are described in Table 30.7.

TABLE 30.7: nbtstat Switch Options

Switch	Function
-a *RemoteName*	Used to show the NetBIOS name table of the remote computer, where *RemoteName* must be the NetBIOS name of this remote system.
-A *IPAddr*	(Note uppercase.) A variation of the -a switch, where you provide the IP address of the remote system and then get the NetBIOS name table for it.
-c	Shows the entire contents of the NetBIOS name cache (local system), along with both the NetBIOS name table and resolved IP address.
-n	Shows the NetBIOS name table (local system); check the Registered column to see if the NetBIOS name for the system is registered as either broadcast or with a WINS server for name resolution.
-r	Used to view relevant statistics for NetBIOS name resolution; where WINS is used, it provides the total number of names that have been resolved and registered (for either broadcast or WINS).
-R	(Note uppercase.) Dumps the contents of the NetBIOS name cache (local system), then looks in the lmhosts file to reload entries marked with the #PRE tags (see preceding chapter).
-RR	(Note uppercase.) First releases and then reloads NetBIOS names (local system) for a system registered with a WINS server.
-s	Shows information about both NetBIOS client and server sessions, then tries to resolve the destination IP address to a name.
-S	(Note uppercase.) Same as -s, except lists remote systems by the destination IP address (no name resolution).
interval	Provide a value (in seconds) in place of *interval* to force nbtstat to refresh the listing for selected statistics that often.

The syntax to follow for this command is:

nbtstat [-*switch switch_parameter*] [*interval*]

This example, shown in Figure 30.3:

nbtstat -a PAX

would display the remote computer's (whose NetBIOS designation is PAX) NetBIOS name table, while this example:

nbtstat -R

releases all the NetBIOS names currently registered with the designated WINS server and then re-register them all again.

FIGURE 30.3:

Use nbtstat to check IP statistics.

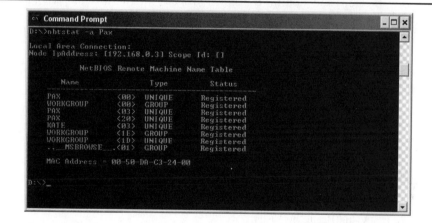

netsh

netsh is a command-line scripting tool that establishes its own console within the command console, so to speak, from which you can see or change the network configuration of the system from which you're working (and you can be working locally—at the keyboard—or remotely). By console within a console, I mean that you execute **netsh** first (or **netsh diag** for diagnostics), and then the command prompt turns into a Netsh (or Netsh diag>) prompt, from which you then run specific netsh commands. Different commands are available depending on the type of network service you're checking, including DHCP, Interface IP, routing, for general diagnostics, and more.

Because of the volume and breadth of commands covered under netsh, you may want to refer to them directly by using Windows XP Help And Support to search on **netsh**. There, you'll find all these commands, their conditions, and switches laid out for you depending on the troubleshooting or modifications you need to perform.

Third-Party TCP/IP Monitoring and Troubleshooting Utilities

Any number of companies—from individual part-time developers to large manufacturers—produce a plethora of network connectivity checkers that work much like what you've learned about in this chapter. Usually, these incorporate several different functions (such as pinging, route tracing, and fast name resolution) under the umbrella of one program. Such utilities include those that can automate the pinging process (called *pingers*), those that map the hops and monitor transmission speed (often called *mappers*), packet monitors (*packet sniffers*), and those that watch the ports on your system (or others) to determine what's open for authorized use—as well as what's open to those who shouldn't have access (*port sniffers* or *network port scanners*).

Many of the downloadable utilities you can find really focus on Internet connectivity, creating visual tracing of routes, and other types of data you might want to see about the efficacy of your connection to your Internet provider and who is connecting back to you, rather than on heavy-duty professional network monitoring. However, many can be used for both.

Some of the best ones I've used are:

NeoTrace Professional by NeoWorx:

`www.neoworx.com/products/neotrace/`

VisualRoute by Visualware:

`www.visualware.com/visualroute/index.html`

NetScanTools by Northwest Performance Software (although I haven't found an XP-specific upgrade for the last version yet):

`www.nwpsw.com`

NScan by Halcyon Data is one I recently discovered that works quite well as a port scanner on networks of varying sizes. I also found that, as advertised, it seems to lay out the transmission route a great deal faster than some of the other tools, especially over some of the command options discussed in this chapter.

Another, Network Information by tulipsystem, (`www.tulipsystem.com`), worked decently, too, employing the same basic set of tools as discussed previously in this chapter to get basic and more advanced communication and configuration information. Less experienced users who tested it with me found it a bit easier to use than the command line.

Also, most of these are available for under $100 (some $20 or less) for registered shareware (for up to 3–5 users on the same license), while many simpler tools are available at no cost (now or later).

Finally, you'll find that many network hardware manufacturers—3Com, LinkSys, and U.S. Robotics among them—provide various network communications tools and monitors as part of the CD packed with the equipment or available for download from the manufacturer's website. Sometimes these are written by someone with the manufacturer, or often enough by a third party who provides a special scaled-down version of the tool for inclusion with the hardware.

WARNING Always verify that such utilities work with Windows XP before trying to use them. In rare cases of OS incompatibility, they can foul up the very process they're installed to check (largely because of evolutionary changes within TCP/IP, and so on).

CHAPTER 31

Remote Access, Monitoring, and Management

Remote access services under Windows aren't completely new, although they've gone through some changes in Windows XP. Formerly, however, they were known strictly as Terminal Services—aptly named as a way to remotely log on via terminal (remote console) to a server or a system acting in that capacity. Seasoned professionals have used something like these remote services for many years to resolve issues remotely for clients and employers, through external applications like pcAnywhere and Carbon Copy.

In Windows XP, the Remote Desktop Connection option noted in this chapter is what was formerly called the Terminal Services client, and Remote Desktop basically uses the same infrastructure.

Terminal Services, however, had a (perhaps undeserved) reputation for being difficult to configure and troubleshoot; it was typically only used in commercial or heavy-duty use environments or by technicians who often had to log on from remote locations to fix problems that others on-site could not.

Remote access services under Windows XP make this a great deal more friendly for the average user looking to increase their control over one or more other systems while sitting at just one PC. For instance, one method allows you to do this from a web browser. Configuring this requires almost no time, and the remotely controlled systems can be non-networked systems within your home or office, or can be located across the state, the country, or the world. The most common use is to provide someone working from home a way to connect with their host system at the office—and not just to exchange files, but to work very much as though you were sitting at the keyboard in the office.

In this chapter, you'll learn about Remote Desktop services, their requirements, how to manage them, how they're configured and used, as well as some troubleshooting techniques to get around common problems related to their use. Then I'll finish by discussing two major third-party applications that largely duplicate the kind of functionality available within Windows XP.

Remote Access Overview

Remote Desktop is actually comprised of two components—Remote Desktop Connection and Remote Desktop Web Connection—and serves as the client front-end for Terminal Services.

There are many situations in which remote access to a Windows XP system might be desirable, including these general categories:

- Working on the office system from home

- Working on the home system from the office

- Evaluating, working on, or repairing someone else's system, much in the way Remote Assistance permits them to get help

- Performing system administration when you're on the road

TIP   Here's a different use. The other night, I had the monitor connected to my XP system flake out. I couldn't get it to stay on consistently, and it's tougher to troubleshoot with no display. I logged on through Remote Desktop over my network and was able to proceed with my work—exactly where I left off.

This is achieved by setting up a Terminal Services server on the XP system, then configuring it to accept incoming connections as well as determining which users should have access in this manner.

Remotely, someone with either Remote Desktop or the older Terminal Services client installed can—with a valid user name and password and access either through the Internet or a network—log on to the remote XP system and work from the same Desktop, with the same applications and files available, as someone sitting at the keyboard of that remote system. In fact, if you come in during the middle of a session being conducted by a user at the console, you receive their working Desktop—populated by its open applications, running processes, and on-screen messages.

But it also raises questions, such as "How will I keep the wrong people out?", "How vulnerable does this leave my system?", and "How do I control the situation remotely?"

Read on to find the answers.

Managing and Securing Remote Access

Clearly, working remotely presents a unique set of problems related to access and security. A way into the system is necessary for those authorized to do so, yet you need to keep everyone else out, including anyone who may try to hijack your transmitted data, your passwords, and even your hardware (some Trojans and computer viruses can act against printers, for example).

Remote Desktop and its associated services for remote access can employ one or more security schemes to try to maintain adequate protection. These include:

- Requiring password authentication at logon (rather than automatic connections)
- Establishing suitable encryption levels for local-to-remote connections and transfers
- Turning off printer and file redirection
- Disabling Clipboard sharing

You can force any of these options—and others—by configuring the Terminal Services Group Policy to enable or disable them. Specific settings for each are included in the next section. You'll learn how to work with this in the next section.

NOTE As you read, you'll see that I discuss two aspects of Remote Desktop: Remote Desktop Connection and Remote Desktop Web Connection. The end-result of both is the same: the ability to log onto your XP machine remotely. The chief difference is that Remote Desktop Connection is accessed as any normally installed program, while Remote Desktop Web Connection can be used from any supporting Web browser, without extra software installed on other systems.

TIP Be sure to read "Adding and Removing Users to Remote Desktop Connections" later in this chapter, because you must add users for access to Remote Desktop Connection and Remote Desktop Web Connection before they can successfully login remotely. If you set all this up and still find you or another user can't connect, look at your user assignments first.

Adding the Terminal Services Snap-In

You can effectively manage and control many aspects of Remote Desktop (including basic configuration) through the Terminal Services group policy (Figure 31.1), available as a snap-in under Microsoft Management Console (MMC). These aspects are *not* configured by default.

The features and functions you can set and manage here include:

- Setting time and requirement limits based on situations and types of users
- Establishing a remote user's range of services (view or full control)
- Permitting or preventing Windows Messenger
- Forcing a program to run each time a remote connection is successfully made
- How the remote Desktop will appear

FIGURE 31.1:

Load the Terminal Services group policy snap-in to configure remote access.

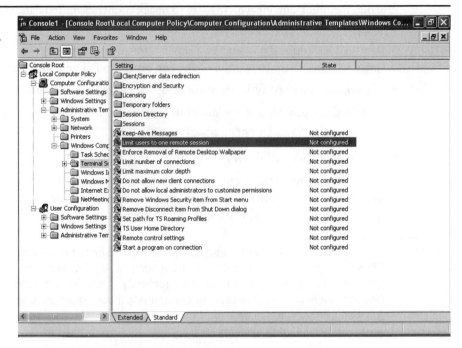

Let's go through the steps for loading this group policy:

1. From a command prompt, type **mmc** to launch the management console.

2. From MMC, choose File ➢ Add/Remove Snap-In, then click Add.

3. From the Add Standalone Snap-In window, click Group Policy, click Add, then click Finish from the Select Group Policy Object window.

4. Back on the Add Standalone Snap-In window, click Close. Click OK to exit the Add/Remove Snap-In window.

5. At the console, click \Local Computer Policy\Computer Configuration\Administrative Templates\Windows Components\Terminal Services.

Later in this chapter, you'll learn about command-line options for managing and controlling your connections as well.

Requiring Password Authentication

A password is required at all times for any user trying to connect remotely. However, Remote Desktop Connection allows users to set up a password that can be automatically used as part of the login process rather than typing it in each time. Doing so, of course, means that anyone with access to the system where that's setup could logon remotely, because the password is provided for them.

To prevent users from bypassing the password screen (and thus, defeating one level of security), use the Terminal Services group policy to require Always Prompt Client For Password, located in the Encryption and Security branch.

Choosing Encryption

Remote Desktop by itself is already equipped to use the highest form of encryption available (the 128-bit standard for financial and other secured transactions). However, you need to enable and enforce it (which you can do using the same process you'll read about in a moment).

However, as you'll soon learn in this chapter, you may need to use the actual (older) Terminal Services client (what Remote Desktop replaces in Windows XP) when connecting remotely to an XP system from a Windows 2000, Windows NT, or even a Windows for Workgroups system. The older client does not by default support 128-bit encryption.

For situations where you're working with the older access client, you can choose to reduce your level of encryption to one called Client Compatible, where Remote Desktop uses the highest level of encryption possible that doesn't interfere with communications between itself and the client (connecting) system. This is accomplished by opening \Terminal Services\Encryption And Security and enabling the option Set Client Connection Encryption Level Properties, as shown in Figure 31.2.

Disabling Redirection

To disable file redirection, select Do Not Allow Drive Redirection in the Client/Server Data Redirection branch from the Terminal Services group policy.

To turn off printer redirection, choose Do Not Allow Printer Redirection.

Use the Do Not Allow Clipboard Redirection option in the Client/Server Data Redirection branch to remove a user's ability to perform this function.

About Firewalls and Remote Access

One of the chief jobs of a firewall, such as the one included with Windows XP or the many others like BlackIce and Zone Alarm that are also available, is to protect your system or network from unwanted access, including port snooping (those who scan your ports trying to find one open so they may enter and/or attack).

Naturally, however, your communication depends on the ability to use necessary ports to exchange data. Thus, a delicate balance must be struck between "open for what you need" and "closed for everyone else." One of the ways we achieve that is through understanding what programs and utilities require exactly which ports to be open. In this way, a firewall can map acceptable use to the necessary ports (so it doesn't block your desired communications) while monitoring anything which goes on with the other ports.

As I walk you through remote access services, including some third-party ones, note that I usually mention the ports typically used by the operation(s). Combine that information with what you will learn about Windows XP's Internet Connection Firewall in Chapter 32, and you can better configure your firewall to keep data flowing unobstructed.

FIGURE 31.2:

Use group policy to determine the encryption level.

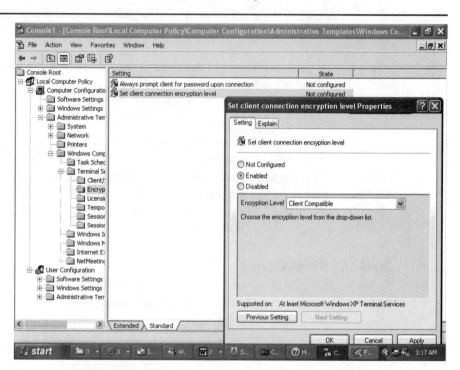

Remote Desktop Connection

Remote Desktop Connection is the client software for remote access. Where you choose to work from something as ubiquitous as a web browser (meaning remote access would be available from devices that are more mobile than a desktop PC), you can also use Remote Desktop Web Connection, discussed later in this chapter.

NOTE   Remote Desktop Connection and its associated Terminal Services initially connect using port 80 and then settle into communications using port 3389. Note these for your firewall configuration.

Remote Desktop Connection Requirements

When I talk about configuring Remote Desktop Connection, I mean a two-step process, because both the primary system you're configuring *and* the remote system have to be set up to work together, and that requires that the remote system have software installed to it that allows this functionality and connection to occur.

The Windows XP system acting as the host for remote connections needs to have Remote Desktop Connection (Terminal Services) installed and set up for use and must have a means—network, dial-up phone line, or broadband continuous connection—for letting remote systems contact it.

The remote system needs one of two client software packages:

Remote Desktop Connection   Already available if not configured under Windows XP, but can be installed using the Windows XP install CD to Windows 95/98 and Windows NT 4 systems following the steps provided under manual installation later in this section.

Terminal Services Client   Available with Windows 2000 server, or which can be installed to Windows NT 3.51; see "Installing and Using Terminal Services Client" later in this section.

But you also need a connection method, as well as a client interface. That can take the form of any of these:

- Virtual private network (VPN)

- Local area network (LAN)

- Dial-up modem connection or broadband access (see "Working with a Dynamic IP Address" later in this chapter)

TIP   Before you install and configure for Remote Desktop Connection functionality, be sure your connection method works properly. By doing so, you'll avoid reaching the point where you're trying to connect remotely, can't, and have to wonder whether it's the connection itself or your configuration of Remote Desktop that's at fault.

Installing Remote Desktop Connection Manually

There are two situations in which you may need to perform a manual installation of Remote Desktop Connection:

- You cannot find Remote Desktop Connection installed to your Start ➤ All Programs ➤ Accessories ➤ Communications menu.

- You need to install it on a non-XP system (95/98 and Windows NT 4) in order to connect with an XP-based Remote Desktop–connected system.

To perform this manual installation:

1. On the non-XP system you want to connect to using Remote Desktop Connection, run Setup from your Windows XP installation CD, and choose Perform Additional Tasks.

2. From the Additional Tasks screen, select Set Up Remote Desktop Connection.

3. When the InstallShield Wizard opens, click I Accept under the License Agreement, then click Next.

4. When prompted, provide your information under Customer Information and then select to install this program either for all users on this system or just for you. Click Next.

5. Click Install.

Configuring Remote Desktop Connection

Follow these steps to configure your client Remote Desktop Connection for connection with the Windows XP–based server:

1. From Windows Start ➤ Programs ➤ Accessories ➤ Communications, select Remote Desktop Connection.

2. From the Remote Desktop Connection window, click Options, which opens up the lower section of the window bearing five tabs.

3. Under the General tab, select the computer you want to connect to, then provide your user name, password, and domain (if applicable). If desired, click Save My Password.

4. From the Display tab, you can adjust your normal viewing settings—useful if the other system being connected to may have a much different quality monitor or display adapter as you and you need to make adjustments for optimal display.

TIP   Those connecting via slower, dial-up connection rates should only use 256 colors; the more colors used, the more bandwidth is required to keep the display fresh in a timely manner.

5. From the Local Resources tab, you can set these options:

   Remote Computer Sound   Determine whether or not to play sound invoked on the remote computer via your local system or at all.

   Keyboard   Modify Windows key combinations.

   Local devices   Check or uncheck access to local devices such as disk drives, printers, and serial ports.

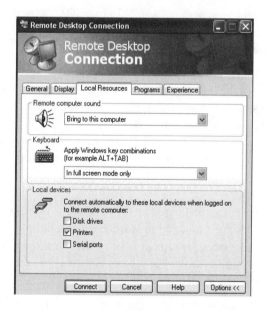

6. From the Programs tab, you can setup a specific program to run every time you connect to a remote system—helpful if you always need to execute the same application or utility each time.

7. From the Experience tab, you can configure how the two systems connect (dial-up modem, broadband, LAN) and whether to allow certain features such as the Desktop background, themes, and bitmap caching during your remote session.

TIP   You can also use the General tab to save your current connection settings, which are then stored to a file ending with .rdp. Use the General tab again, and choose Open to reopen these saved settings.

WARNING   If you hit serious performance problems, turn off "extra" features under the Experience tab such as Desktop background and themes.

NOTE   If you find you can't add an available computer to your connect list, check to be sure that the computer you want to connect to has the Terminal Services client or Remote Desktop Connection installed and/or is configured to allow this access.

Working with a Dynamic IP Address

The best way to use remote access in Windows XP is with existing network or high-speed broadband Internet access, but it's also best if the XP system hosting the remote connection has a static (fixed) IP address or a recognized Internet name.

The problem with a dial-up access situation for the XP host is that you must know the current IP address of the host (which can change with each connection) in order to connect. You can find this by using the ipconfig /all command at the command console, but you need to do this each time a new connection is established if you don't have a static IP address or recognized name for the host system. Otherwise, remote users—including you logging on from another location—won't be able to find the host to connect.

Priority of Access

Since only one user can be logged on (at the console or remotely) to Windows XP at any one time, Remote Desktop Connection and Remote Desktop Web Connection (and Terminal Services) prioritize access by type of user, so that if two people try to log on at the same time, the person with "administrator" access always wins. Its exact behavior, however, depends on whether Fast User Switching is enabled.

When one administrator is already logged on and a second administrator tries to log on, the second administrator has the ability to bump the currently connected user. However, when two users of normal stature conflict, the first person to connect can continue his session while the one who attempts to log on later receives a message that a user (identified) is currently logged on.

One difference between Fast User Switching being enabled or not amounts to how a user's session is terminated in the event of an administrator override. If Fast User Switching is turned on, the user currently on the system will be disconnected but not logged off; they can continue their session later once the administrator has gone. If Fast User Switching is off, the user is logged off and disconnected.

Also, when Fast User Switching is enabled and a second user tries to log on while another user is already logged in, the current user will receive a message like this:

```
<Domain or Computer Name>\<username> is trying to connect to this computer. If
you allow, you will be disconnected, but you can resume later. Do you want to
allow this connection?
```

WARNING Reserve administrator status for a very select few. If others need to log on, they can be given normal user or Remote Desktop user status.

Loading Remote Desktop Connection

First, be certain you have a valid connection in place (dial-up modem, broadband, or network).

To launch Remote Desktop Connection:

1. Choose Start ➤ All Programs ➤ Accessories ➤ Communications ➤ Remote Desktop Connection.

2. From the Remote Desktop Connection window, select the computer's name you want to connect to, and click Connect.

If your connection is good, you're using a valid account (see the following section), and no one else is logged on to the system (see the preceding section), you should be logged on properly and able to begin work as the remote Desktop opens before you.

Adding and Removing Users to Remote Desktop Connections

As I tipped you to earlier, a user cannot connect remotely unless he or she has been added as a user for this service.

When Remote Desktop Connection is installed and configured for use, a new type of user becomes available: Remote Users. Administrators automatically have access to remote connection features, but it's neither good security nor good practice to make everyone who may connect remotely to the hosting XP system an administrator.

By following these steps, you can add new people to your remote access services:

1. From Control Panel, double-click the System icon, and choose the Remote tab.

2. Be sure that the Allow Users To Connect check box is checked, then click Select Remote Users.

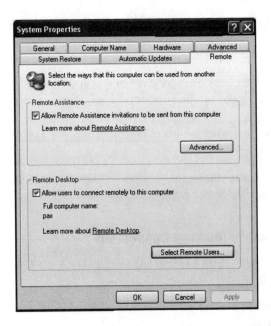

3. From the window labeled Remote Desktop Users, you may already see a list of user accounts currently configured to use Remote Desktop access (by default, this initial listing will only display administrators). To add more, go to Step 4. If you don't need to add any additional users to this list, click Cancel until you fully exit.

4. Click Add.

5. From the Select User window, Users should be listed under Object Type. Click Locations if you need to change the location to look for these users.

6. In the text box named Enter The Object Names To Select, type in the name of a user you want to add and click Check Names.

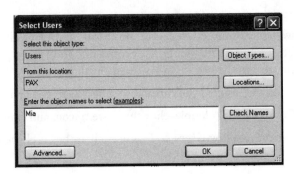

7. If a match is found, click OK in the Select Users dialog box. It is then added to your list. Highlight the name, click Add, then click OK until you exit. If a match is not found, you get the Select User window again with a message telling you to verify the user name.

You can use the same basic process to remove users from your active Remote Users list by clicking Remove rather than Add in Step 7.

Managing Remote Systems Using Terminal Services

With older Windows NT/2000 systems, which didn't include the new Remote Desktop Connection, you'll need to install and configure the Terminal Services client to connect to the XP system.

You'll learn about that in this section, but I'll also tell you about some special commands related to Terminal Services that are available for use from the command console only when you're logged in remotely. These commands can help you exercise control over your remote connections and monitor the connections made to it.

Installing and Using Terminal Services Client

If you want to connect from a system running Windows 2000 Server, you can install and configure Terminal Services for use by performing these steps:

1. Open Windows Explorer and locate the folder named `%systemroot%\System32\Clients\Tsclient`.

2. Right-click this folder, select Properties, then select the Sharing tab.

3. Click to check Share This Folder. Click OK.

If you can't access the option to share this folder, be sure you're logged on with an Administrator, Server Operator, or Power User logon account.

Managing Terminal Services from the Command Line

Certain commands are supported under Terminal Services—and by extension, Remote Desktop—and allow you to monitor, change, and otherwise control the Terminal Services server-client environment and its connections from the command line. You can use them to look up session information by session ID, session name, or even user name. Also, they can be used to copy profiles from one user to another; to kill, shut down, or shutdown and reset connections; and to send messages to other users, among your many options.

How you use these commands is often poorly documented, because some requirements are imposed to be sure that not just anyone logged on can execute them.

Before you can use the Terminal Services commands, you must make sure you're set in three different areas:

1. Enable the use of remote commands under Terminal Services group policy.

2. Be logged onto the remote Windows XP system using the Remote Desktop/Desktop Web/Terminal Services client with an account that allows their use (such as Administrator). This is the only time these commands may be used. If you try to use them outside of this session, you'll receive a message that they aren't recognized.

3. Run them from the command console, either directly or through a batch file (see CD bonus chapter "Batch Programming.")

To enable the use of remote commands (this is disabled by default), follow these steps:

1. Load the Terminal Services MMC snap-in, as described earlier in this chapter.

2. Under \Local Computer Policy\User Configuration\Administrative Templates\ Windows Components\Terminal Services, double-click Remote Control Settings in the right pane.

3. From the Setting tab, click to check Enabled. Under the Options drop-down list, you can choose how these settings are enabled, ranging from View Session Without User's Permission to Full Control With User's Permission. Click OK. You may then close the console.

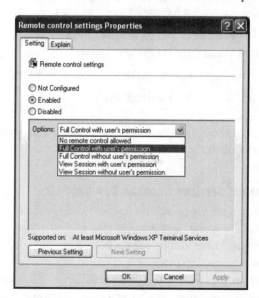

WARNING It may be necessary to shut down and restart Terminal Services—or even to restart the system acting as the server—before this is applied so that remote commands are available to those logging in from the client.

Table 31.1 lists key commands for managing remote sessions from the command console.

TABLE 31.1: Key Commands for Terminal Services

Command	Parameters	Function
change logon	/enable	Allow logons from other users from client sessions (rather than the console).
	/disable	Disallow other users logging on in this same session.
	/query	Determine status (enabled/disabled).
change port	PortA=PortB	Change (map) the serial port specified by *PortA* with the serial port specified by *PortB* (with COM ports 1–4 usually supported).
	/d:porta	Delete the mapping applied to the COM port specified by *PortA*.
	/query	Display mapping information for the port.
change user	/execute	Turn on *.ini file mapping to the home directory (by default).
	/install	Turn off *.ini file mapping to the home directory (this is very necessary when you're installing applications to the terminal server itself).
logoff	SessionID	Log off the session specified.
	SessionName	Log off the session specified.
	/server:ServerName	Specify the terminal server from which the session you want to log off from is running; the current server is used when none is specified.
msg	UserName	Specify the name of the user to whom you want to send a message.
	SessionID	Specify the ID of a session to contact.
	SessionName	Specify the name of a session to contact.
query process	*	Display all processes running for all current sessions.
	/id:nn	Specify the ID of a session whose processes you want to query.
	ProcessID	Identify the ID of the process you want to check.
	ProgramName	Identify a particular program (use full name including .exe file extension) whose processes you need to check.
	/server:ServerName	Specify another server (besides the current one) in the query.
	SessionName	Identify all the processes running in a particular session.
	/system	Include all system processes in the query results.
	UserName	Check all the processes running for a specific user.

Continued on next page

TABLE 31.1 CONTINUED: Key Commands for Terminal Services

Command	Parameters	Function
query session	/connect	Query a terminal server about currently active connection settings.
	/counter	Display information gleaned from current counters, including total count of sessions (created, disconnected, and reconnected).
	/flow	Check current flow control settings.
	/mode	Show line settings currently in effect.
	SessionID	Specify a particular session ID to check in the query.
	SessionName	Specify a particular session name to check.
	UserName	Query about a session by a specific user name.
query termserver	/address	Reveal both network and node addresses for all terminal servers.
	/continue	Turn off a pause between screens when displaying query results.
	/domain:Domain	Specify a particular domain on which to query its terminal servers (useful only if it's not the current domain).
query user	/server:ServerName	Specify a different terminal server in running a user query.
	SessionID	Specify a particular session ID to query for user data.
	SessionName	Specify a particular session name to query for user data.
	UserName	Check by a specific user name.
register	FileName	Register the specific file named by this parameter.
	/system	Not only register the file, but register it as system global resource file.
	/user	Register the specified file as a user global resource.
	/v	Turn on verbose mode for more detailed information.
reset session	SessionID	Reset the session specified.
	SessionName	Reset the session specified.
	/server:ServerName	Specify the server hosting the session you want to reset.
shadow	SessionID	Control the session specified.
	SessionName	Control the session specified.
	/server:ServerName	Identify the terminal server running the session you want to control.

Continued on next page

TABLE 31.1 CONTINUED: Key Commands for Terminal Services

Command	Parameters	Function
tscon	*SessionID*	Connect to session specified.
	SessionName	Connect to session specified.
	/dest:*SessionName*	Specify name of destination connection you want to use.
	/password:*pw*	Connect using password specified by *pw*.
tsdiscon	*SessionID*	Terminate the connection specified.
	SessionName	Terminate the connection specified.
	/server:*ServerName*	Identify the terminal server where the connection is occurring used *if* not the current session (and server) in use.
tskill	/a	Kill the process for all sessions running it.
	/id:*SessionID*	Terminate the process running in the identified session.
	ProcessID	Terminate the process specified.
	ProcessName	Terminate the process specified.
	/server:*ServerName*	Specify a terminal server where the process you want to kill is running, used when this is not the currently used terminal server.
	/v	Turn on verbose mode for more detail.
tsprof	/copy	Copy the user configuration information for the person identified as *SourceUser* to that of the person identified as the *DestinationUser*.
	DestinationUser	Identify the user account you're copying a source user's information to.
	/domain:*Domain*	Specify the domain (when it's not the present one).
	/local	Apply profile operations only to local accounts.
	/profile:*ProfilePath*	Specify Terminal Services profile path.
	/q	Reveal the current profile path of a user.
	SourceUser	Specify the existing user account whose profile you want to perform an operation upon.
	/update	Specify that the profile path information for a specific user name gets updated.
	UserName	Identify a particular user account for updating or query.
tsshutdn	/delay:*LogOffDelay*	While tsshutdn allows an admin to shut down (and reboot, if desired) a terminal server, this switch allows you to specify how much time to wait between logging off users and shutting down.

Continued on next page

TABLE 31.1 CONTINUED: Key Commands for Terminal Services

Command	Parameters	Function
tsshutdn	/powerdown	Shut terminal server completely down (where available, because of hardware/software support).
	/reboot	Specify to reboot the terminal server post-shutdown.
	/server:ServerName	Specify the terminal server to shutdown if not the current one in use.
	/v	Turn on verbose mode for more details.
	WaitTime	Specify a set amount of time between notifying users that a shutdown is about to occur, and forcing their logoff so the shutdown can happen.

TIP   For more information about these and other Terminal Services commands, use Help And Support under Windows XP and search on the phrase in question.

Remote Desktop Web Connection

What makes the Remote Desktop Web Connection (RDWC) not just a cool capability but a useful enhancement to standard remote connections is that you can work remotely through a supporting web browser (such as Internet Explorer 6). If your Windows XP system, for example, has a supporting web server with this installed, you can log on and use your XP system from another computer—say, one at work or at home—using the browser.

The difference, as you might guess, between Remote Desktop and RDWC, because the latter can use a browser as its access medium, is that the web connection requires the service be installed to a supporting web server, such as you find with Internet Information Services (IIS).

Unlike Remote Desktop Connection, this web component is optional and not included in your installation. You must add it through Windows.

Also, the requirements change slightly. For example, the Remote Desktop Web Connection must be installed to a valid web server on one system, where files get copied automatically to the %systemroot%\Web\Tsweb folder to support the process. If you can't install it to a web server, you won't have this functionality.

For clients to work with it, they need the following available:

- TCP/IP connection either to the Internet or a network
- Compatible web browser (Microsoft IE 4.0 or later)

NOTE   You must be logged on as an administrator in order to install and configure this option.

WARNING   You also need to have Windows Internet Naming Service (WINS) or another name-resolution method configured to have RDWC work. See Chapter 29.

Installing Remote Desktop Web Connection

Follow these steps to install the Remote Desktop Web Connection:

1. From Control Panel, click Add Or Remove Programs, then click Add/Remove Windows Components, which launches the Windows Components Wizard.

2. Select Internet Information Services from the list, and click Details.

3. From the resulting Subcomponents window, click to check World Wide Web Service, and then click Details.

4. From the next Subcomponents window, click to check Remote Desktop Web Connection. Click OK, and then click Next.

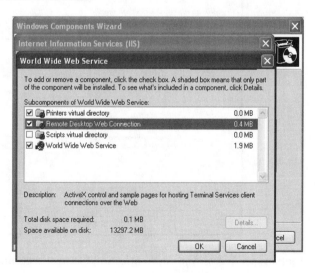

NOTE   When Remote Desktop Web Connection is installed, it brings with it two default web pages (`default.htm`, which can be used as a home page to replace the default RWDC page in the browser, and `connect.asp`, a connection-specific page). These files can be customized for your use.

Configuring Remote Desktop Web Connection

Once installed, you need to adjust settings under Directory Security for your web server/site to allow for anonymous logons. To do this:

1. Launch Internet Information Services (available from the All Programs list under Administrative Tools).

2. Expand the folders until you locate and select *computername*\Web Sites\Default Web Site\tsweb (the Terminal Services web folder), where *computername* is the name of the system on which you're setting up RDWC.

3. Right-click the folder, and choose Properties.

4. Select the Directory Security tab.

5. In the Anonymous Access And Authentication Control section, click Edit.

6. From the Authentication Methods window, click to check the Anonymous Access check box. Click OK twice to apply and exit.

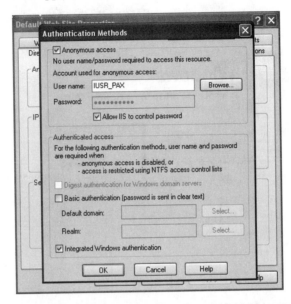

Using Remote Desktop Web Connection

Once you have Remote Desktop Web Connection installed and configured for use on your system, you want to double-check (if possible) that the remote system you want to contact is available online.

When you have done this, make certain you have a valid connection in place (dial-up modem, broadband, or network) and follow these steps to connect to web server where Remote Desktop Web is installed:

1. From the remote or client system, launch Internet Explorer.

2. Type the address for the hosting web server into the browser's Address line, following this format: **http://*name*/*tsweb*/**, where *name* is the name of the web server and *tsweb* is the default web for this purpose.

3. When you connect to the Remote Desktop Web Connection default page, provide the name of the computer to which you want to connect in the Server dialog box.

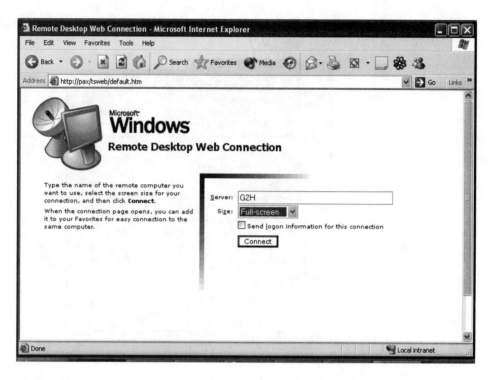

4. Click Connect.

5. Next, you'll be prompted to log on to the other system using a valid user name and password (preferably, one with permissions to allow your work).

NOTE   You can also adjust the screen size by clicking the Screen drop-down box and selecting the size you want to use.

NOTE   You may be prompted during this process to accept the download of a Terminal Services Control (RC2) file. Click Yes to accept it.

Once you've done this, you'll see the Desktop—including open files and applications, if any—available on the other system from your browser, as shown in Figure 31.3. Just start working as you normally would, with this caveat: If someone is on the remote system when you log on, they'll find they are locked out of work (and will be notified of same) until someone with administrator access logs on from the console.

FIGURE 31.3:

Use Remote Desktop
Web Connection to
work from the browser
just as you work from
the Desktop.

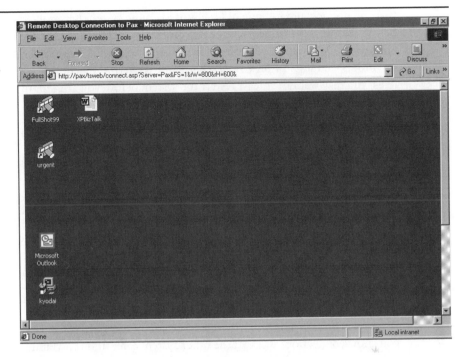

NOTE   Be aware that since Remote Desktop Web Connection is working from a website, port 80
must be available, along with port 3389.

Troubleshooting Remote Desktop

In this section, you'll learn how to troubleshoot some of the more common issues encountered when using Remote Desktop Connection.

Some of the problems that can be encountered are really to be expected. If you're using a slow dial-up connection through an analog modem, for example, you may find your remote connection at times intolerably slow. For very slow dial-ups, you're either going to sit waiting at times or learn to be very moderate in what you run remotely. Where possible, use broadband access for remote work. When my satellite connection is running at its best speed, I notice relatively little difference compared to working at the console directly.

Also, you have to use common sense in working with a remote system. If the remote system tends to run slower anyway, it won't seem any faster through a remote connection. If the remote system is laboring under a borderline amount of installed RAM, you have to respect that and not demand too much. Finally, if a remote system has problems—for example, it's behaving in a flaky manner before you connect—you're going to feel them remotely through your system in the form of errors, slowness, and so on. Likewise, if the system you're connecting with is running low on virtual memory or is overburdened with open applications or problems, you may want to at least restart the system before you attempt the remote connection.

Can't Logon

First, always be sure that you're trying to connect to the right system, and using a valid user name and password for access. Policy settings and permissions may also limit your access to a remote site, so verify them. If necessary, try logging on with an administrator account to see if it's available to someone with advanced privileges and if it is, then the problem may indeed be with policies and permissions limiting the other account you were using.

If you're using Remote Desktop Web Connection, be sure that you're not trying to log on as a remote to the same system on which you are currently working. You can't. Also make certain that you're using the right URL to connect, following the convention of *computername**tsweb*.

Remote Desktop Can't Find XP System

Before you do anything else, try to test the computer name or IP address on a system where you know connections work. If the other system can't find the Windows XP system, then the XP system may be unavailable (it's crashed, for example, or shut down, or something else is preventing Terminal Services from allowing connections). Check the XP system's functionality and remote configuration as soon as possible.

If you can log on in one way or another from a different system, your current system may not be configured for name resolution (see Chapter 29), you may not be using quite the same address, or there may be a problem with your connection. Test it by trying to reach other sites, either through your web browser or other means. If you can't reach anything, restart your system (just to be sure) and then check your communications hardware (modem) for physical connections, as well as review your TCP/IP settings.

Can't Run Programs Remotely

Check the account you're using and its privilege level. Also be sure that you haven't configured anything in group policy that may restrict this.

Try more than one program. If necessary, you can use the `reset session` command in Terminal Services to try to reset the Windows XP–based server. In some of my sessions, I've experienced a short-term lockup, probably due to Internet traffic congestion, and found that one or more programs had a tendency to stall after this. Resetting the server and reconnecting usually gets me back to the point where I can work normally again.

Third-Party Remote Control Applications

In this final section, we'll look at the two most popular third-party remote control PC access applications: pcAnywhere and Virtual Network Computing (VNC), including the versions you need to work with Windows XP.

What is central to both of these applications and different from Windows XP Remote Desktop/Terminal Services is that these apps are designed to work beyond a strict Windows platform, where each remote system needs to be configured for the specific remote services supported under Windows XP. This gives you a bit more flexibility

A third application—lesser known but mentioned a little more these days—is GoToMyPC, from ExpertCity (an online support site), available for demo trial download at www.gotomypc .com. It operates quite a bit differently, however, because the whole remote communication process and most of the work is done by GoToMyPC servers external to you rather than by software installed to your system. It doesn't require any special configuration or changes to your firewall to use. Because it's a hosted solution, I'm going to focus on the other two applications here.

Using pcAnywhere

pcAnywhere has been with us almost as long as the PC; it's a commercial product available from Symantec designed for remote control access and administration of a system from another system. The latest version (10.5) has been updated for compatibility with Windows XP. You can buy and download it directly online from Symantec's site at

```
www.symantec.com/pcanywhere/Consumer/index.html
```

Like XP's Remote Desktop Web Connection, pcAnywhere has a web-based component (pcAnywhere WebCast!) for remote viewing and operation, but with more built-in security features (whereas you're the security configuration master with XP), including authentication and strong encryption capabilities (three levels of encryption supported). The Mandatory Password feature helps avoid some of the convenience workarounds we often try to employ that can really defeat even the best security measures.

One plus about pcAnywhere over Remote Desktop is that you do have more options, including AutoTransfer for files, and more aggressive logging and connection monitoring features that users may find easier to work with that the types of querying you can have with Terminal Services commands. For instance, I can more readily identify unauthorized logon attempts using pcAnywhere than I can using tools within Windows XP; I can find this information through XP, too, but it requires a bit more effort.

NOTE   pcAnywhere requires TCP port 5631 and UDP port 5632. Earlier versions (7.51 and earlier) require TCP 56301 and UDP 22.

Using Virtual Network Computing (VNC)

AT&T's Virtual Network Computing (VNC; Figure 31.4) has been around for some time, in use by technicians and other IT professionals as a remote Desktop solution.

FIGURE 31.4:

VNC can be used for accessing remote systems.

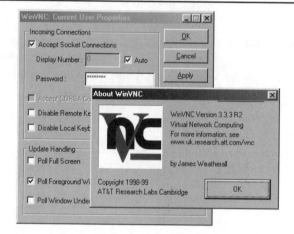

While missing some of the strong encryption of a commercial package like pcAnywhere, the thing many people like about VNC (and WinVNC, its Windows-based counterpart) is that it's free for use. You can download the freely distributed software from AT&T Cambridge Laboratories website at www.uk.research.att.com/vnc—along with the fact that many colleagues often know and recommend the utility for remote purposes. For example, I get some Internet access through a broadband satellite service, and WinVNC is part of my default setup so that the satellite company can check my system remotely if I need to call for assistance.

VNC doesn't have all the extras along with the pleasing interface of pcAnywhere, but it's an excellent, widely used remote access tool that covers all the basics and more.

NOTE   VNC listens on two different ports: 58xx and 59xx, where xx is the display number used. A default display of 0 or 00 is common; often, ports 5800 and 5900 are used.

CHAPTER 32

Configuring and Sharing Internet Connections

Although there aren't as many people with computers connected to the Internet today as you might think, the odds are still good that you either want to connect or improve the connection you already have. For example, maybe you're thinking about installing DSL or cable broadband service and are looking for tips on connecting your home network.

This chapter explains how to configure, optimize, and share an Internet connection. Whether you use a dial-up connection or broadband, you can share that connection with users on your local network. So, everyone on the network can check their e-mail, browse the Internet, and perform other Internet-related tasks even if you have only one modem, one phone line, and one dial-up account.

If you are experienced with networking, you probably won't need any help connecting your network to the Internet. You'll still find lots of useful information in this chapter, such as how to protect your network with a firewall, how to optimize TCP/IP settings for clients on the network, and even how to enable routing on a multihomed computer (one with multiple network adapters).

If you're not up to speed with networking or don't have a network in place now, this chapter will help you connect your network quickly and safely to the Internet. I don't cover general networking topics in this chapter, but you can refer to Chapters 27, 28, and 29 to get the local network operational and ready for the Internet connection.

SEE ALSO See Chapters 26 through 29 for help configuring modem and network connections. Chapter 29 explains how configure TCP/IP connections.

Options for Sharing Internet Connections

How you share an Internet connection with other users depends on the type of connection, how your network is structured, and a few other issues. In this chapter I explain the possibilities and how to configure each one.

SEE ALSO   See the section "Sharing through a Router" if you want an alternative to Internet Connection Sharing.

Internet Connection Sharing

One of the easiest ways to share an Internet connection is through Windows XP's Internet Connection Sharing (ICS) feature. ICS is designed for situations where one computer is connected directly to the Internet and you want to allow the other computers on the network to access the Internet through that computer. The Internet connection can be a dial-up connection or broadband connection. Figure 32.1 shows a typical dial-up scenario, and Figure 32.2 shows one broadband possibility.

FIGURE 32.1:

You can share a dial-up connection with ICS.

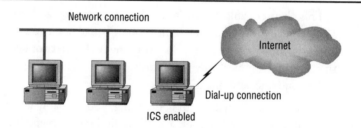

FIGURE 32.2:

You can also share a broadband connection with ICS.

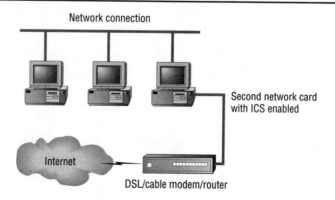

With the broadband scenario, the DSL/cable modem connects directly to the computer through its network card. A crossover cable eliminates the need for a hub or switch between the two devices. In some situations, the DSL or cable modem actually installs directly in the PC and takes the place of a network card. Some broadband modem devices provide the IP address for the connection. Those that don't provide the IP address require a router or network adapter to provide the address.

If your system uses a cable or DSL modem that connects directly to your computer's network interface or installs internally in your computer, you'll need to add another network adapter to that computer and connect it to the rest of the local network. Then, share the Internet connection with ICS. The other computers on the network will connect to the Internet through the second adapter.

Enabling ICS

When you dial into an Internet service provider (ISP), the dial-up connection receives a dynamically assigned IP address that resides on the ISP's subnet. If you have a broadband connection, the DSL or cable modem is assigned an address in the ISP's subnet, either dynamically or statically. In most cases, that's the only IP address you'll get from the ISP. It would be impossible to share one IP address with multiple computers without some means of address translation or routing. ICS uses a combination of routing and NAT.

You enable ICS on the network interface that connects to the Internet. This interface receives an IP address that resides in the ISP's subnet, placing your computer on the ISP's network. When you enable ICS, Windows XP assigns the static IP address 192.168.0.1 to the local network interface. Figure 32.3 illustrates the scenario.

FIGURE 32.3:

ICS assigns a static IP address to the computer.

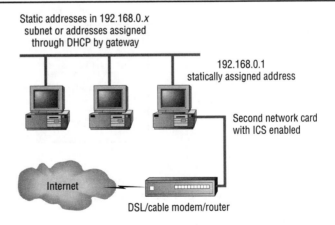

Static addresses in 192.168.0.*x* subnet or addresses assigned through DHCP by gateway

192.168.0.1 statically assigned address

Second network card with ICS enabled

Internet

DSL/cable modem/router

Any other computers on the local network must have an address in the same 192.168.0.*x* subnet (with subnet mask 255.255.255.0), and they must have the ICS computer set as their default gateway. Packets from these other computers go to the ICS computer, which routes them out through the Internet connection. The ICS computer not only acts as a router, but also performs network address translation (NAT), replacing the source computer's IP address with its own. When the packets come back, the ICS computer removes its IP address from the packet, restores the original source address, and forwards the packet on to the client.

To share an Internet connection through ICS, open the `Network Connections` folder on the computer that will share its connection. Right-click the connection to the Internet—whether dial-up or broadband—and choose Properties. Click the Advanced tab. Figure 32.4 shows the Advanced tab for a dial-up connection.

Select the option "Allow other network users to connect through this computer's Internet connection" if you want to share this Internet connection with other computers on the network.

FIGURE 32.4:

Use the Advanced tab to enable ICS.

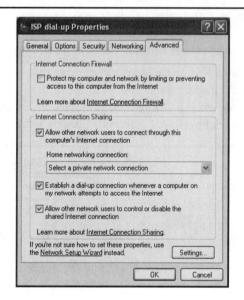

TIP   The Advanced tab is similar for a broadband connection, except the option "Establish a dial-up connection whenever a computer on my network attempts to access the Internet" isn't present.

Controlling Automatic Connection

If you are sharing a dial-up connection, the option "Establish a dial-up connection whenever a computer on my network attempts to access the Internet" determines whether or not your computer will automatically dial the connection. When a client attempts to connect to the Internet through an application such as Internet Explorer, the packets get routed to the ICS computer, which then determines whether or not there is a current connection to the Internet. If not, and this option is enabled, the ICS computer dials the connection. The dial-up remains connected until you manually disconnect it at the ICS computer or it reaches its specified inactivity period and disconnects automatically. If this option is disabled, the client's connection attempt times out and fails.

TIP   See the later section "Configuring Client Timeout" to prevent a client from timing out before the connection is established.

The Establish A Dial-Up… option also applies to a broadband dial-on-demand connection such as a VPN connection to your office LAN. Windows XP will make the connection automatically if this option is enabled and a client attempts to connect to the Internet through the shared connection.

Letting the Client Control the Connection

The option "Allow other users to control or disable the shared Internet connection" determines whether the client can control the connection state of the Internet connection. For example, assume you share a dial-up connection with an inactivity timeout of 20 minutes. Someone else on the network opens Outlook Express to check their e-mail. The session takes less than a minute. They walk away, and the dial-up remains connected for another 19 minutes before finally timing out and disconnecting.

Another potential problem is that the user's session might time out and fail before the dial-up finishes connecting. For example, say it takes 45 seconds for the dialer to connect, authenticate, and establish the Internet connection. But the user's program only waits 30 seconds before it assumes there is no connection and fails.

If you enable the option "Allow other users to control or disable the shared Internet connection," other users on the network can force the connection to dial first before they even open the e-mail program, browser, or other application. They can also disconnect the connection when they are finished, rather than wait for the connection to time out. They connect and disconnect the connection using the Internet Gateway icon in their Network Connections folder.

Sharing through a Router

Broadband Internet connections typically offer other possibilities for sharing. If your system uses a DSL or cable modem that connects directly to your computer's network interface, or which installs internally in place of a network card, then ICS is your means for sharing the connection with others. If a router sits between your computer and the broadband connection, however, you share the connection differently. You also have more options.

Figure 32.5 illustrates a typical broadband connection with a hardware router. You can also install a software-based router such as WinRoute (described later in this chapter) to let one connection work as a router and share its Internet connection. Let's take a look at the hardware solution first.

As Figure 32.5 shows, the router sits on both the ISP's subnet and your own local network subnet. The router might be incorporated into the cable / DSL modem, or it could be a separate piece of equipment.

FIGURE 32.5:

Multiple computers can share a router-based DSL connection.

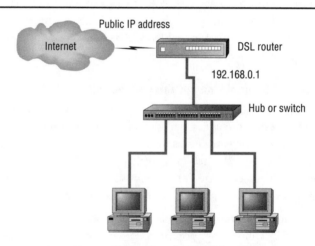

Sharing an Internet connection in this situation is really not much of a chore. Just configure the router's LAN interface with the desired private IP address for your network. Configure its WAN (wide area network) interface with the IP address assigned to you by your ISP. This might be a private or public address, depending on how the ISP has structured its network. It's also possible that the WAN address is assigned dynamically by the ISP rather than statically. In either case, configure the WAN address according to the ISP's requirements.

The next step is to configure your workstations so they reside in the router's LAN IP subnet. For example, assume you assigned the address 192.168.0.1 to the router with a subnet mask of 255.255.255.0. Just assign addresses in that same range and with the same subnet mask to the other computers on the network. Then, specify the router's LAN port address (in this case, 192.168.0.1) as the default gateway for all computers.

The main advantage offered by a router is the flexibility to use different addressing schemes on your local network. ICS forces you to use the range 192.168.0.*x*. With a router, you can use any private address range. For example, perhaps you want to use the 10.10.10.*x* subnet. The router doesn't care—it will translate the traffic regardless of its source address. You just need to make sure the router's LAN interface resides in the same subnet as the local network.

I'm assuming that you'll be connecting a limited number of computers through the shared connection. That makes static IP addressing a workable solution for assigning client addresses. As the number of computers increases, dynamic addressing makes more sense from an administrative standpoint. Without ICS, Windows XP doesn't work as a DHCP server. That means you'll need to install a DHCP server of some kind on the network. Virtually all DLS/cable routers also function as DHCP servers. If you have Windows NT Server, 2000 Server, or .NET Server on the network, you can use its DHCP service to assign client addresses. If not, you can use a third-party DHCP server application to provide dynamic addressing.

SEE ALSO   For a complete description of how DHCP works, see Chapter 29.

A search for DHCP on your favorite download site will no doubt turn up at least a handful of third-party DHCP server applications or integrated server suites that provide DHCP and that run under Windows XP. I cover one of the more popular solutions in the next section.

TIP   Check out www.jhsoft.com for Simple DNS Plus, a server suite that provides DHCP services.

Using a Software-Based Router

 If you want the flexibility of a router without putting in another piece of hardware, consider using a software-based router solution such as Kerio's WinRoute Lite or WinRoute Pro. Both versions provide DHCP, network address translation, routing, and several other features. The Pro version adds an integrated firewall, URL filtering, a proxy server, and several other excellent features.

You'll need two network adapters in the routing computer if you decide to go this route (no pun intended). One interface will connect to the Internet, and the other will connect to the local network.

Configuring Clients to Access the Shared Connection

Getting to the Internet through a shared connection requires that the client computers be configured properly. I've already touched on addressing in the previous sections. The following section explains how to configure the address at the client.

Assigning Addresses

You can assign the other computers on the network the appropriate address range and default gateway manually, or let the ICS computer or your DHCP server assign the addresses. If you prefer to configure the client systems manually and are using ICS, give them a static IP address in the range 192.168.0.*x* with subnet mask 255.255.255.0 and the default gateway 192.168.0.1. You can use a different address range if you have a hardware or software router in place.

The easiest solution, however, is to let the ICS computer assign the IP configuration. ICS lets the connection-sharing computer act as a mini-DHCP server. You configure the client computers to take their IP address dynamically, and the ICS computer assigns the IP address, default gateway, and DNS servers to the clients when they boot or refresh their address lease.

To configure the client settings, open the Network Connections folder and open the properties for the client's network connection. Locate the TCP/IP protocol in the list of installed components, select it, and click Properties.

TIP   For platforms other than Windows XP, right-click the Network Neighborhood folder (or My Network Places) on the Desktop and choose Properties to set the connection properties.

To assign a static IP address, click Use The Following IP Address. Enter the private IP address for the computer in the IP Address field and specify the appropriate subnet mask. Enter the IP address of the router or ICS computer in the Default Gateway field. Then enter the DNS servers your ISP has provided to you in the DNS Server fields.

TIP   Dynamically assigning addresses is much easier. Just select the option Obtain An IP Address Automatically. This also takes care of assigning the DNS servers, assuming the device functioning as the DHCP server has been configured with DNS server settings.

Configuring Client Timeout

After you have used ICS for a while with a dial-up connection, you have probably run across the problem that your client computer often times out waiting for ICS to establish the connection. For example, your web browser might report your home site as unreachable because TCP times out before the server can establish the connection.

TCP sets an initial retransmission timer of three seconds when it attempts the first data transmission for a connection. TCP doubles the retransmission timeout value for each subsequent connection attempt, and by default attempts retransmission two times. So, the first attempt is made at 3 seconds, the second at 3 + 6 seconds, and the third at 3 + 6 + 12 seconds, for a maximum timeout of 21 seconds. Increasing the initial retransmission timer to 5 seconds result in a total maximum timeout of 5 + 10 + 20, or 35 seconds.

To increase the initial TCP retransmission timeout value for a Windows XP computer, use the Registry value

```
\HKEY_LOCAL_MACHINE\System\CurrentControlSet\Services\Tcpip\Parameters\InitialRtt
```

The InitialRtt value is a REG_DWORD with a valid range from 0–65,535 and specifies the timeout in milliseconds.

The number of connection attempts is defined by the Registry setting

```
\HKEY_LOCAL_MACHINE\System\CurrentControlSet\Services\Tcpip\Parameters\
TcpMaxDataRetransmissions
```

The TcpMaxDataRetransmissions value is also a REG_DWORD with a valid range of 0–65,535.

TIP   Neither of these Registry settings exists by default—you'll have to create them.

Firewalls, NAT, and Security Planning

Whether you use a dial-up connection or dedicated Internet connection, you need a firewall to protect your systems from being compromised and your network from denial-of-service and other attacks. Other methods such as network address translation (NAT) can help secure your network from intrusion, but these methods can't offer the same protection as a firewall. Let's take a look at your options.

Windows XP's Built-In Firewall

Windows XP includes its own firewall, called Internet Connection Firewall (ICF), that you can use to protect your systems. In most cases, you need to run it only on the computer that is sharing its Internet connection—you don't need to run it on every computer. In fact, running it on every computer can affect your ability to share files and printers on the network.

Enabling and configuring ICF is relatively easy. To enable ICF, open the Network Connections folder, right-click the Internet connection, and choose Properties. Click the Advanced tab and select the option that begins Protect My Computer And Network.

Allow Access to Internal Services

Next, click Settings to open the Advanced Settings dialog box (Figure 32.6). The Services tab lets you specify port-to-address mapping that allows Internet users the ability to access servers inside your firewall. For example, if you host a web server on your network, you would open port 80 for HTTP traffic to reach the server.

FIGURE 32.6:

Use the Advanced Settings tab to configure services and security.

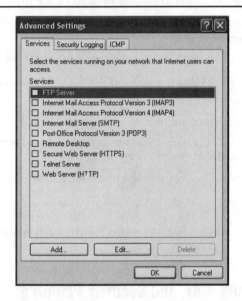

ICF lets you map different services to computers inside the firewall. These services can be running on a single computer or on multiple computers. However, you can only direct traffic for a particular service to a single computer.

Select the service that you want Internet users to be able to access. When you click the check box, Windows XP displays a Service Settings dialog box similar to the one shown in Figure 32.7. As the figure illustrates, you can enter the IP address or host name for the target computer, but you can't change the port assignments.

TIP   If you specify a host name, the ICF computer must be able to resolve that name to a local IP address inside your network.

The Services tab contains nine predefined options that cover the most commonly used services. However, you can add additional services to suit your needs. For example, you might need to add a service option to allow pcAnywhere or VNC connections to an internal server. Or, perhaps you want to redirect all incoming traffic on port 80 to a different port on an internal server. You can accomplish both tasks by creating a custom service.

FIGURE 32.7:

Specify the host name or IP address of the server in the Service Settings dialog box.

> **NOTE**   Why would you have a web server functioning on a port other than 80? Perhaps you've installed a third-party web server on a computer that is also running IIS, which is providing access to the computer's printers. So, you configure the third-party server to use port 8080 (for example) and continue to use port 80 for IIS.

Click Add to open an empty Service Settings dialog box. Enter a name for the service as you want it to appear in the Services tab, and include the IP address or host name of the internal computer providing the service. In the External Port field, enter the port that external computers use to access the service. For HTTP traffic for example, enter 80. In the Internal Port field, enter the port on the internal computer that is listening for the traffic.

Configure Security Logging

Use the Security Logging tab (Figure 32.8) to specify how you want ICF to handle access through the firewall. The settings on the Security Logging tab include the following:

Log Dropped Packets   Record in the log file all packets that the firewall drops (doesn't allow to pass through the firewall). Use this option to maintain a record of potential attempted attacks on your network or to troubleshoot attempts to access services from the LAN that are not allowed by the firewall.

Log Successful Connections   Record all successful connections from both inside and outside of the firewall. This can result in lots of data being logged but is useful for troubleshooting.

Name   Specify the path and name of the log file.

Size Limit   Set the maximum size for the log file. Windows XP drops older log entries when this size is reached.

Configure logging on the
Security Logging tab.

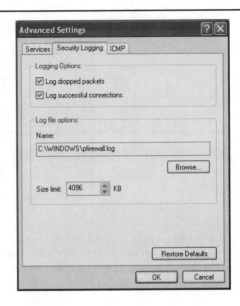

Configuring ICMP

ICMP stands for Internet Control Message Protocol. The ping command is the most common use for ICMP. As Chapter 30 explained, ping lets you troubleshoot connections by sending ICMP echo requests. If the packets come back, you've verified connectivity between the two devices. If you receive a Request Timed Out error instead, there could be a problem with the connection. Another possibility is that a firewall is dropping ICMP packets, because ping is one tool that hackers and other miscreants use to launch a denial-of-service attack on a computer.

The ICMP tab (Figure 32.9) of the Advanced Settings dialog box lets you specify how ICF should handle ICMP packets. Each check box identifies a particular ICMP request, and selecting the option directs ICF to allow the computer to respond to the request. For example, select Allow Incoming Echo Request if you want to be able to use ping from other devices to check connectivity to the local computer.

Third-Party Software-Based Firewalls

ICF is certainly a useful firewall, combining a reasonable level of security with very easy configuration. However, ICF trades features for ease of use. If you need better control over what the firewall does and doesn't allow, or you need to perform more advanced network address translation, you need a different firewall.

One of the most popular third-party software-based firewalls is ZoneAlarm from Zone Labs (www.zonealarm.com). ZoneAlarm is free for personal and non-profit use and provides good protection from intrusion and various attacks. ZoneAlarm Pro adds lots of other features, including expanded e-mail protection, the ability to track the source of an attack, restricted zones, custom security levels, and much more.

Another product worth considering is Tiny Personal Firewall from Tiny Software at www.tinysoftware.com. TPF is free for home use and offers several advanced features including the ability to verify the authenticity of applications. This prevents an application from impersonating an authorized application to infect your system or cause other havoc.

 Also check out Kerio Personal Firewall, on the companion CD and at www.kerio.com. Like TPF, this firewall is easy to configure but offers some advanced features, including application verification.

FIGURE 32.9:

Use the ICMP tab to define how ICF handles ICMP requests.

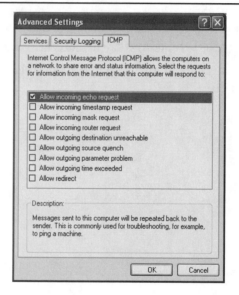

Hardware-Based Firewalls

In many cases, a typical software-based firewall isn't practical or doesn't offer the necessary level of protection. For example, if you're just hooking up a DSL or cable broadband connection, you'll need a DSL/cable router. Why not put in a router that also functions as a firewall and kill two proverbial birds?

One of the features that a hardware-based router offers, that many of the workstation-class, software-based firewalls do not offer, is content filtering. This enables the router to restrict access to specific websites that fall into certain categories, such as those that contain pornography. The firewall maintains a list of prohibited sites and their categories and blocks access to them if you've configured the router to do so. Check out `www.sonicwall.com`, `www.linksys.com`, `www.netgear.com`, `www.dlink.com`, and many other companies for hardware-based firewalls.

Enabling Routing on a Multihomed System

Windows XP does not, by default, providing routing services between two network interfaces. For example, assume you have a computer with one network card at 192.168.0.1 and a second card at 10.10.10.1, connecting together two networks. Windows XP will not route packets between the two networks. You can, however, turn on IP forwarding to enable XP to route the packets.

Open the Registry Editor and then open the branch

`\HKEY_LOCAL_MACHINE\SYSTEM\CurrentControlSet\Services\Tcpip\Parameters`

Look for the setting IPEnableRouter. Set the value to 1 to enable IP routing on all the computer's interfaces.

Supporting Wired or Dial-Up Incoming Connections

All of Microsoft's Windows operating systems have supported incoming connections, either through built-in support or through add-ons. Support for incoming connections lets you set up a Windows XP computer to act as a dial-up server. For example, you might connect a modem to a computer in the office to allow a small number of customers or business associates to access files on that computer. This lets you grant access to the system without putting it on the Internet or going through the hassle of setting up an FTP site or website.

In addition, you can set up Windows XP to support other types of incoming connections. For example, you can use a null-modem cable between two computers to create a small network. So, if you have a notebook without a network adapter, you could connect your notebook to your desktop computer through the serial or parallel port to create a mini-network for sharing files.

An easier solution, if both computers include infrared ports, is to set up infrared connections for sharing. This solution offers the beauty of no cables and very little installation hassle.

This chapter explains how to set up each of these types of incoming connections.

Configuring Incoming Dial-Up Connections

As I mentioned in the introduction, Windows XP can support incoming connections from dial-up lines. For example, you can configure Windows XP to allow remote users to dial into a modem connected to the computer to access its files or even print to its printer. You can use this option when it isn't possible or practical to set up the computer to accept incoming connections through a hardwired connection such as the Internet. For example, you might not have a broadband Internet connection to the computer, or your ISP's firewall might prevent users from connecting to your computer.

TIP   You can use Internet Information Services (IIS) to share files with users on the Internet.

Windows XP can support one incoming dial-up connection. However, it can also support one each of the other types of incoming connections (infrared and direct cable) for a total of three. If you need to support multiple remote users over the same type of connection (such as several concurrent dial-up connections), install Windows 2000 Server or Windows .NET Server, which support an unlimited number of remote-access users.

It's important to understand that in addition to gaining access to shared resources on the computer that is acting as the dial-up server, the remote client can also optionally gain access to the network on which the dial-up server is located. So, a remote client can dial into a Windows XP computer and then use the resources of the LAN as if the remote computer were connected directly to the network. The client could access shared network volumes, shared printers, and other network resources (such as an e-mail server). You control whether or not the remote client has access to the network when you configure the incoming connection (explained shortly).

If you're hoping to provide 56 Kbps dial-up speeds for a remote client, I have to dash your hopes. Providing 56 Kbps dial-up connections requires a digital link from the phone company to the modem pool, which is typically provided by a T1, fractional T1, or other digital broadband connection. You can't simply dial into an analog 56 Kbps modem with another 56 Kbps modem and get 56 Kbps performance. If the two modems are compatible, the fastest connection possible is 33.6 Kbps. In many cases, the best connection you'll get is 28.8 Kbps because of compatibility issues between the two modems.

Even at these slower speeds, a dial-up connection can still offer advantages you can't otherwise enjoy. For example, you might configure your home computer as a dial-up server so you can access your home files, printers, or even shared Internet connection when you're on the road. Or maybe you need to grab a file from the office when you're working at home, and a dial-up connection to your office computer could be the solution.

Understanding the Security Risks

When you configure a Windows XP computer as a dial-up server, by default the computer allows the remote caller to access the local network to which the dial-up server is connected. For example, assume you set up your office computer as a dial-up server. When you connect from home, you can access not only your own computer but also any resources shared on the office network.

The ability to access network resources is an important and powerful tool, but it's also a potential security risk. In order to dial in and connect, the remote caller must have or know an account on the dial-up computer. If one of the accounts is compromised, and that account has been granted dial-in permissions, an unauthorized user can potentially gain access to network resources. Securing all network resources with NTFS and share permissions is one step to securing the network, but you should still consider dial-up servers in a network to be a security risk for shared resources.

Dial-up access also poses other potential risks. Allowing dial-in connections bypasses the firewall if one is in place on your network, providing a potential back door into your network for viruses, Trojan-horse programs, and hackers. For that reason, you should only install a Windows XP dial-up server if you fully understand and accept the security risks involved.

Setting Up the Connection and Using Callback

Your first step in setting up a dial-up server is to install the modem and verify that it is working. You don't necessarily need to dial out with it—just open the modem's properties and use the Diagnostics tab to verify that you can query the device. When the modem is working, you can start setting up the connection.

You configure a Windows XP computer to act as a dial-up server through the Incoming Connections icon in the `Network Connections` folder. By default there is no such icon, so you need to create a new connection to create it.

Log on as administrator, open the `Network Connections` folder, and click the Create A New Connection link in the left pane. Select Set Up An Advanced Connection and click Next. Select Accept Incoming Connections and click Next. The wizard displays the available connection devices, as shown in Figure 33.1. Select the modem and click Next.

FIGURE 33.1:

Select the device(s) that will accept incoming connections.

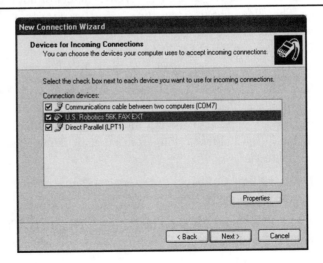

You can specify whether or not the dial-up server will support incoming VPN connections. You don't need to support VPN to allow the remote caller to access the local computer or the LAN, so choose Do Not Allow Virtual Private Connections and click Next. The wizard then prompts you to specify the local users who can dial in (Figure 33.2).

FIGURE 33.2:

Select the users who
can dial in.

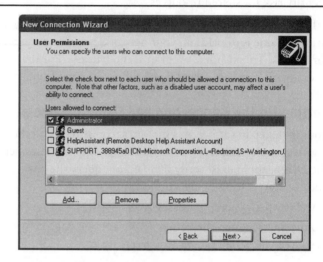

You can select multiple users to grant those users the ability to dial in. You can also change the user's full name or password through the wizard. Just double-click the account to open its properties.

You can use the Callback tab to specify whether or not the server will call back the remote user. This allows you to essentially reverse the connection charges. For example, if you are working from home and need to dial into your office computer to work, and the call is long distance, you can use the Callback properties to configure your office computer to dial you back at home. The company then picks up the tab for the call.

The other reason to use callback is to increase security. You can configure each account to use a specific callback number. This helps prevent unauthorized access to the dial-up computer and LAN, because not only must the remote caller have the necessary logon credentials, but he must also be calling from a specific number. Select one of the following options to use callback:

Do Not Allow Callback   The server will not call back the remote user, even if the remote user requests it.

Allow The Caller To Set The Callback Number   The remote user can specify the number for callback when the initial connection is made.

Always Use The Following Callback Number   The server will call back the remote user at the specified number, even if the user requests a different number.

You don't need to configure any special settings at the client to use callback. Windows dial-up clients automatically attempt to negotiate a callback session. From the remote computer, dial the server. The client and server negotiate a callback protocol, as well as other protocols (such as authentication). After the server authenticates the client, the client, recognizing that the server accepts callback, initiates the callback. A dialog box appears on the client's computer requesting the callback number. Figure 33.3 shows a Windows 98 client in a callback session. If the account requires callback to a specific number, you can't change the number from the client. Otherwise, enter the callback number complete with area code and dialing prefix, if needed. When you click OK, the computers disconnect and the client waits for a call back. The server then dials the specified number to reestablish the connection. You can also click Cancel if you want to continue the existing connection without a callback.

FIGURE 33.3:

Specify the callback number when you first establish the connection.

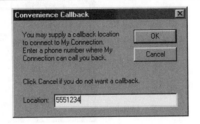

After setting callback options, click OK, then click Next in the wizard. Review the network components that are enabled for the connection in the Networking Software list. Clear the check box beside any item you don't want used for the connection. For example, if you have more than one network protocol installed and only want to use one, clear the other(s). When you're satisfied with the settings, click Next, then Finish.

TIP   If your modem doesn't answer, it could be that the modem initialization string isn't being set to enable auto-answer. On a Windows 98 computer, open the connection's properties and click Configure on the General tab. Click the Connection tab and click Advanced. In the Extra Settings field, type **ATS0=1**, then close the dialog boxes (ATS0=1 sets the modem to auto-answer on the first ring). For Windows XP and 2000 computers, open the modem's properties in Control Panel and set the initialization string through the Advanced tab.

Controlling Access to the Network

As I mentioned earlier in this chapter, you can configure the dial-up server to allow the remote caller to access the network as well as the server. This ability is set on a per-protocol basis. If the client is negotiating two different protocols, one can deny network access and the other can allow it.

Right-click the Incoming Connections icon in the Network Connections folder and choose Properties. On the Networking tab, double-click the network protocol that you want to configure. On the resulting protocol property dialog box, select the option Allow Callers To Access My Local Area Network if you want the remote caller to be able to access network resources. Clear this check box to restrict the remote caller to accessing only those resources available on the dial-up server. Figure 33.4 shows the dialog box for the TCP/IP protocol as an example.

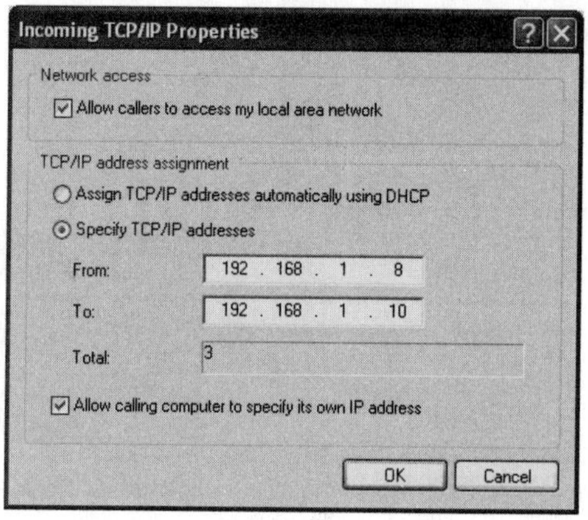

FIGURE 33.4:

Use the properties for the protocol to allow or deny network access.

TIP   If the dial-up server allows multiple protocols, make sure you configure the settings for each protocol to allow or deny access as appropriate for your situation.

Configuring Incoming Hardwired Connections

Although a dial-up connection can be a handy way to connect to a remote computer or network, it doesn't give you stellar data speeds. In some situations you might want to use a hardwired connection between two computers. For example, perhaps you have a desktop computer at home and a notebook that you use at work and at home. You don't have a network in place at home, but you want to connect your notebook and desktop systems at home to share some files or a printer.

You have a couple of different options for connecting the computers. This section explains two options: using network cards and a crossover cable, or using a null-modem cable attached to the computers' serial or parallel ports.

SEE ALSO See the section "Using Infrared Devices and Connections," later in this chapter, if both computers provide infrared support or if you are looking for a solution to allow your notebook or other infrared-capable devices to connect to a computer that currently has no infrared support.

Network Adapters and Crossover Cables

The first option for connecting two computers doesn't require Windows XP's remote access features at all. You only need a network adapter in each computer and a network *crossover cable*. In a crossover cable—unlike a standard network cable—the send and receive lines are crossed. This enables the two computers to communicate without going through a hub or switch. Think of it as holding two phone handsets together, microphone-to-speaker.

The advantage to this method is that you get high data throughput speeds (up to 100 Mbps if the adapters support 100 Mbps speeds). It's also easy to set up. Just install the network adapter, connect the two computers with the crossover cable, and your network is up and running. You avoid the expense of a hub or switch.

TIP You don't need to disconnect the cable from the desktop computer when you are not using the mini-network. Leave the cable connected and accessible so you can easily plug it into the notebook or other computer when needed.

USB-to-USB Connections

Another option to consider if both computers have USB ports is to connect them through USB. Parallel Technologies (www.lpt.com) offers a USB-to-USB cable that lets you connect two computers through their USB ports. The cable, in effect, acts like a pair of USB network adapters. For that reason, this method uses the built-in network features of the two computers' operating systems rather than Windows XP's remote-access features. This USB cable option supports transfer speeds of up to 6 Mbps. The price of the cable is comparable to the price of two network adapters and a crossover cable, making it an attractive alternative to the option I discussed in the previous section.

Serial or Parallel Port Connections

You can also use a serial (COM) or parallel (LPT) port to connect two computers. This option does require Windows XP's remote-access features, as well as an appropriate cable to connect the two computers. Parallel port connections offer faster data throughput than serial connections, so you should choose a parallel connection for best performance.

Your first step in setting up a direct cable connection between the two computers is to make sure you have the right cable. You can purchase a cable or make your own. As with a network crossover cable, I suggest you buy one and avoid the hassles inherent in making the cable. Parallel Technologies (www.1pt.com), which I mentioned in the previous section, sells serial and parallel port cables that work for direct cable connections with Windows XP.

You can also find cables for direct cable connections at most computer retailers. If you're not sure which one to get, either ask the salesperson or check the cable to see that it matches the pin-outs shown in Tables 33.1 and 33.2. You can also point your web browser to

http://support.microsoft.com/default.aspx?scid=kb;EN-US;Q310576

or search the Microsoft Knowledge Base for article Q310576, which shows the pin-outs.

TABLE 33.1: Serial Cable Pin-Outs

9-Pin	25-Pin		25-Pin	9-Pin	Description
Pin 5	Pin 7	connects to	Pin 7	Pin 5	Ground–Ground
Pin 3	Pin 2	connects to	Pin 3	Pin 2	Xmit–Rcv
Pin 7	Pin 4	connects to	Pin 5	Pin 8	RTS–CTS
Pin 1 and 6	Pin 6	connects to	Pin 20	Pin 4	DSR–DTR
Pin 2	Pin 3	connects to	Pin 2	Pin 3	Xmit–Rcv
Pin 8	Pin 5	connects to	Pin 4	Pin 7	CTS–RTS
Pin 4	Pin 20	connects to	Pin 6	Pin 1 and 6	DTR–DSR

TABLE 33.2: Parallel Cable Pin-Outs

25-Pin		25-Pin	Description
Pin 2	connects to	Pin 15	N/A
Pin 3	connects to	Pin 13	N/A
Pin 4	connects to	Pin 12	N/A
Pin 5	connects to	Pin 10	N/A
Pin 6	connects to	Pin 11	N/A
Pin 15	connects to	Pin 2	N/A
Pin 13	connects to	Pin 3	N/A
Pin 12	connects to	Pin 4	N/A
Pin 10	connects to	Pin 5	N/A
Pin 11	connects to	Pin 6	N/A
Pin 25	connects to	Pin 25	Ground–Ground

When you have the right cable in hand, you're ready to hook up the computers. Connect the cable to an available port on each computer.

Set Up the Host

On the computer that will act as the server (host), open the Network Connections folder. If Incoming Connections does not already exist, run the Create A New Connection wizard as explained in the earlier section "Configuring Incoming Dial-Up Connections." When the wizard prompts you to select the connection device or port, select the port to which you've connected the cable. Complete the wizard as you would for a dial-up connection (although you naturally can't configure callback options).

TIP   You actually have two ways to set up the host. When you run the wizard, you can choose the option Connect Directly To Another Computer instead of Accept Incoming Connections. If you choose this route, select Host when prompted to specify whether you're setting up the host or client. When you complete the wizard, you'll have an Incoming Connections icon in the Network Connections folder.

Set Up the Client

The process for setting up the client is very similar. On a Windows XP computer, open the Network Connections folder and run the Create A New Connection wizard. Select the option Connect Directly To Another Computer, then select Guest. When prompted for the name of the computer to which you're connection, you can specify any name—this is the name for the connection, not the host's actual computer name (although they can be the same). Select the appropriate port to finish the wizard.

To set up a client on a Windows 98 or Me computer, first make sure the Direct Cable Connection software is installed. Click Start ➤ Programs ➤ Accessories ➤ Communications ➤ Direct Cable Connection. If this item doesn't exist, open Control Panel and use the Add/Remove Programs applet to add the software. Click the Windows Setup tab and select Direct Cable Connection under the Communications group. After the software is installed, click Direct Cable Connection in the menu to start the connection wizard. Select the Guest option and follow the wizard's prompts to specify the other properties, such as connection port.

Use the Connection

The guest connection works much like a dial-up connection. On a Windows XP client, open the Network Connections folder and double-click the connection's icon. Windows XP displays a connection dialog box (Figure 33.5), in which you enter the user name and password for the account on the host computer. Click Connect to initiate the session.

FIGURE 33.5:

Specify the user name and password for the connection.

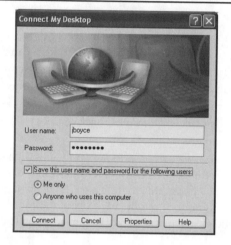

The process is a little different on a Windows 98 or Me computer. Click Start ➤ Programs ➤ Accessories ➤ Communications ➤ Direct Cable Connection. Windows displays a dialog box similar to the one shown in Figure 33.6. Click Connect to initiate the session.

FIGURE 33.6:

Use Direct Cable Connection to connect in Windows 98.

After you connect the two computers, the host appears essentially like a node on the network, just as if it were connected by a standard network connection. You can browse resources on the host through the My Network Places folder and even map local drives to shared resources on the host.

Using Infrared Devices and Connections

If you want to avoid the hassle of cables, you can use infrared to connect two computers to share files and other resources. Most notebook computers include infrared (IR) ports. Typically, the notebook includes a port in front and one in back, and you can specify in the system's BIOS which port to use, switching between them as needed.

Windows XP provides two methods for connecting via infrared. If you only need to send files from one computer to another or to send images from your digital camera to your computer, you can establish an infrared link between the two devices and let Windows XP's built-in infrared file transfer software take care of the transfer automatically.

The second option is to set up an infrared direct connection between the two, using infrared instead of a serial or parallel cable. In this scenario, one computer acts as a host and the other acts as a guest. The guest can access shared resources on the host including its Internet connection.

Using an Infrared Link

Setting up an infrared link really doesn't require much effort. Make sure the infrared ports are enabled on both devices, and then set them up so the infrared transceivers are no more than a meter apart and are pointing at one another. When Windows XP recognizes the other device, it places an infrared link icon in the notification area and displays the Wireless Link icon on the Desktop.

To send files to the other device, double-click the Wireless Link icon. In the Wireless Link dialog box, select the files you want to transfer and click Send. An even easier method for transferring files is to simply drag them to the Wireless Link icon.

TIP   You can also click the Wireless Link icon in the notification area to open the Wireless Link dialog box.

You configure the location for incoming files through the Wireless Link properties. Double-click Wireless Link in Control Panel to display the Infrared tab. Click Browse to select the folder for incoming files. You can also set a handful of other settings, which are generally self-explanatory.

If your digital camera supports the IrTran-P infrared transfer protocol, you can easily transfer images from the camera to your PC. Open the Wireless Link tool and click the Image Transfer tab. Select the option "Use wireless link to transfer images from a digital camera to your computer." Then place the camera's IR transceiver in range of the computer's IR transceiver and initiate the image transfer from the camera.

NOTE   You can't initiate an image transfer from the computer. Instead, you must start the process from the camera.

Using an Infrared Direct Connection

Sometimes you might need to do more with an IR link than just transfer files. For example, you might want to use your home computer's Internet connection from your notebook but don't want to hassle with cables. As long as both computers have functioning IR ports, you can set up a direct connection between the two, just as you would when using a serial or parallel cable.

To create the connection, open the Network Connections folder on the computer that will act as the host. If you have already set up the computer for incoming connections on other ports, right-click the Incoming Connections icon and choose Properties. Place a check beside the IR port and click OK. If you haven't enabled incoming connections yet, run the Create A New Connection wizard as explained in the section "Serial or Parallel Port Connections," earlier in this chapter. Select the option Connect Directly To Another Computer and run through the wizard, specifying the IR port as the connection device.

On the host, run the Create A New Connection wizard and set up the computer as a guest as explained in "Set Up the Client," earlier in this chapter. After you configure the guest and host, double-click the connection in the Network Connections folder on the guest computer to initiate the session.

CHAPTER 34

Optional Networking and Management Components

Windows XP includes several optional networking services. Many of these are general TCP/IP tools. For example, the RIP Listener is a service that lets a Windows XP computer listen for route updates from routers that use the Routing Information Protocol (RIP) version 1. Although you wouldn't need to listen for RIP updates in most scenarios, the service is useful for improving routing and network performance in certain dial-up situations.

The Simple TCP/IP Services included with Windows XP allow an XP computer to respond to requests from other computers for certain optional TCP/IP functions. For example, the Quote of the Day service allows the computer to return quotations taken from a text file. The Simple TCP/IP Services also include Character Generator, Daytime, Discard, and Echo tools, all of which are explained in this chapter. In most cases, these tools are only useful in environments where Unix-based systems are also present.

Simple Network Management Protocol (SNMP) allows remote monitoring and management of devices including routers, switches, computers, and other types of devices. The SNMP service included with Windows XP allows clients to access SNMP data across the network.

Print Services for Unix, another optional networking service included with Windows XP, allows Unix clients on your network to access printers connected to an XP computer. This allows you to share your printer with those Unix systems. The service also enables a Windows XP computer to print to printers hosted by Unix-based hosts.

The Universal Plug and Play service included with Windows XP makes it possible for an XP computer to discover and control Universal Plug and Play devices on the network.

This chapter explains each of these services is found and how to install—and configure where appropriate—those services.

RIP Listener

Routers use one of two methods to route network traffic: static routing or dynamic routing. A *static* route is one that the router administrator manually enters in the router's firmware. *Dynamic* routing allows a router to build its routing table from information it gathers from adjacent routers. This allows routers to respond on the fly to network events such as a new router coming on line or a router going down. Each time a router boots, it rebuilds its routing table. The routing table initially only contains the routing table entries for physically connected networks, but the router can add other routes dynamically as it learns them.

RIP, which stands for Router Information Protocol, is a common routing protocol. A router using RIP periodically broadcasts announcements regarding routes. This enables adjacent routers to modify their routing tables accordingly. Therefore, a router begins using RIP announcements to build its routing table after it boots.

TIP   Each router is sometimes referred to as a *hop*, and a packet's hop count is increased by one each time it passes through another router. RIP is relatively easy to configure but is limited to a maximum of 15 hops, making it suitable mainly for small to mid-sized networks. Any destination more than 15 hops away RIP considers to be unreachable.

RIP also provides for *triggered updates* in addition to broadcast updates. These updates are triggered when a router detects a network change, such as an interface going down. The router then broadcasts the change to adjacent routers, which modify their routing tables accordingly. When the interface comes back up, the router that recognizes the change broadcasts a triggered update to adjacent routers, which again modify their routing tables to accommodate the change.

RIP v2 provides additional features not supported by RIP v1, such as authentication for security, support for Variable Length Subnet Masks (VLSM), and route filtering. RIP v2 also supports multicast broadcast of RIP announcements and several other features. RIP v1 routers are forward compatible with RIP v2 routers, enabling them to coexist.

The RIP Listener service included with Windows XP allows an XP computer to listen for RIP v1 announcements and adjust its routing table accordingly. In the vast majority of situations, RIP Listener isn't needed on a workstation. However, if a multihomed Windows XP computer is serving as a router or connects to a remote network through a dial-up or direct connection, the RIP Listener service can improve network performance by reducing the number of hops required for outgoing packets to reach their destination. Rather than be routed through a less efficient route and require a remote router to reroute the packets, the Windows XP computer can route them according to the new routes defined through the RIP announcements. Using the RIP Listener allows the computer to update its routing table itself, without the need for you to manually add or modify the routing table.

TIP RIP Listener can also listen for RIP v2 announcements that are sent as subnet-level broadcasts, but it does not receive RIP v2 multicast announcements.

One of the most common uses for RIP Listener is to simplify workstation configuration when more than one gateway is available. As Figure 34.1 illustrates, a computer with multiple gateways to other LANs or to the Internet can use RIP Listener to update its routing table based on RIP announcements from its adjacent routers. This helps the computer determine the most efficient route for a given packet.

The main advantage, therefore, to RIP Listener is that traffic gets routed more efficiently, providing faster network response. It also reduces the number of hops for a given packet, which reduces the work load on the routers involved.

FIGURE 34.1:

RIP Listener lets a computer build its routing table dynamically from adjacent routers.

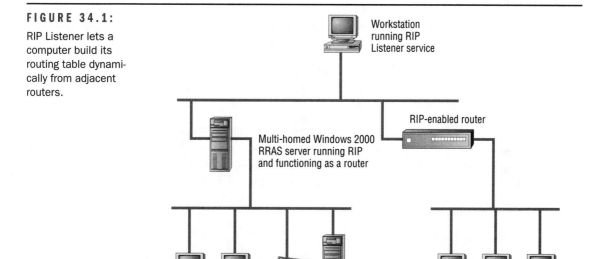

Using RIP Listener on a Windows XP computer is easy because you don't need to configure the service. Just open the Add Or Remove Programs object in Control Panel and click Add/Remove Windows Components. Open the Network Services item and place a check beside RIP Listener, then click OK and click Next. Windows XP will prompt you for the Windows XP CD or location of the Windows XP source files, copy the files, then start the service. You do not need to perform any additional configuration.

TIP The RIP Listener service appears in the Services console. You can stop and start RIP Listener there, if needed.

Simple TCP/IP Services

Windows XP includes a set of services that support features offered by most Unix platforms. These services include the following:

Character Generator   This component sends data from the 95 printable ASCII characters and is useful for troubleshooting printer problems.

Daytime   This component returns messages containing the day of the week, month, day, year, current time, and time zone. It is most often used programmatically to monitor differences in this information with other computers.

Discard   This component discards all messages received on the port without responding to or acknowledging the messages. It can also be used programmatically to discard unneeded messages.

Echo   This component echoes messages that it receives, which is useful for testing and debugging.

Quote of the Day   This component returns one or more lines of text from *%systemroot%* System32\Drivers\Etc\Quotes. Windows XP creates a sample file that you can use as-is or modify to add additional quotes.

If your computer resides in a Unix environment and you want to make use of these components, you can add them through the Add Or Remove Programs object in Control Panel. Click Add/Remove Windows Components, then open the Network Services item. Select Simple TCP/IP Services, click OK, click Next, and insert the Windows XP CD when prompted.

SNMP Service

As I mentioned in the introduction, SNMP stands for Simple Network Management Protocol, an Internet standard for gathering information about network devices and managing those devices. For example, many routers, switches, and other devices use SNMP as the primary mechanism for remote monitoring and management. An administrator doesn't have to be physically present at a router to configure it, but instead can rely on an SNMP-based management tool to interface with and configure the router.

SNMP is also often used to monitor and manage computers. SNMP management applications allow network administrators to gather information about the computers on their networks for inventory and management purposes; often, the application scans the network for SNMP devices automatically. Windows XP doesn't include an SNMP management application, but you can use one of several third-party management tools as well as Microsoft's own

Systems Management Server (SMS). Some network management tools you might want to consider are:

- Tivoli NetView

    www.tivoli.com/products/index/netview

- Hewlett-Packard OpenView

    www.hp.com/products1/softwareproducts/software/openview/index.html

- Computer Associates UniCenter

    www.ca.com

- Microsoft Systems Management Server

    www.microsoft.com/smsmgmt/default.asp

What Windows XP does include for SNMP is the SNMP agent that allows a management application to collect information from the Windows XP computer. This chapter explains how to install and configure the SNMP service on a Windows XP workstation.

Installing the SNMP Services

There are actually two SNMP services for Windows XP. The first is the SNMP agent, which allows SNMP information to be collected and provided to management applications. The second is an SNMP provider, which allows that information to be provided to management applications through the Windows Management Interface (WMI). You need the latter only if you plan to use management applications that use WMI.

You add the SNMP service to a computer in the same way as other optional components. Open the Add Or Remove Programs item in Control Panel, and click Add/Remove Windows Components. Open the Management And Monitoring Tools item and select Simple Network Management Protocol. Also select WMI SNMP Provider if your management applications are WMI-based. Click OK, then click Next, and provide the Windows XP CD or path to the XP installation files when prompted.

Configuring SNMP

After you install the SNMP service, you need to configure each computer for SNMP. This is one of the few Windows XP components that you configure through the Services console. Open the Services console and double-click the SNMP Service to display the properties sheet for the service, and then click the Agent tab (Figure 34.2).

The Agent tab contains the following options:

Contact   Specify the person who is the contact for this computer. You can enter a name, e-mail address, or other identifying information.

Location   Specify the physical location of the computer.

Physical   Select this if you want SNMP to report information about physical devices such as hard disks.

Applications   Specifies that the computer uses applications that send data using TCP/IP.

Datalink And Subnetworks   Specifies that the computer manages a bridged network connection.

Internet   Specifies that the computer functions as an IP gateway for other clients.

End-To-End   Specifies that the computer is an IP host.

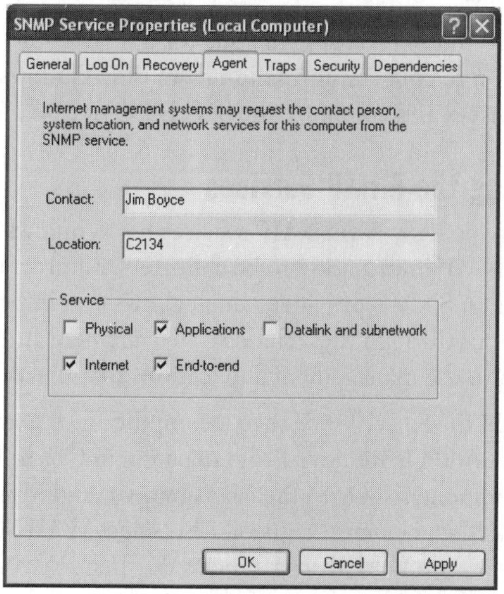

FIGURE 34.2:

Use the Agent tab to configure general SNMP settings and services used by SNMP.

In addition to configuring general information for SNMP, you also need to configure community names and traps. The community name essentially serves as a password. All SNMP devices that need to communicate do so using the community name. Many devices use the community name public by default, although configuring your SNMP devices to use this default community name is a security risk. Instead, you should use an SNMP community name that is not easy to guess.

You configure community names and trap destinations on the Traps tab of the SNMP service properties (Figure 34.3). Type a community name in the Community Name combo box and click Add To List.

TIP You can configure a computer for more than one SNMP community. This enables the computer to communicate in multiple groups of computers and provides a means for administrators to logically group computers for management purposes.

Next, click Add to open the SNMP Service Configuration dialog box. Enter the host name, IP address, or IPX address of the computer that needs to receive SNMP notification messages from the computer. You can add multiple trap destinations to send notifications to multiple computers.

The community names specified on the Traps tab are used to authenticate outgoing SNMP messages only. You configure security for incoming SNMP messages through the Security tab (Figure 34.4).

FIGURE 34.3:

Use the Traps tab to configure SNMP community names and traps.

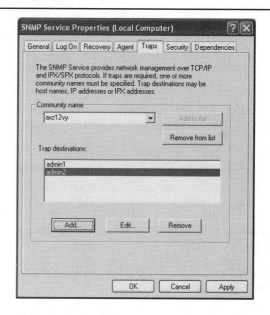

The options on the Security tab include the following:

Send Authentication Trap   Select this option to have the computer send an SNMP authentication trap message to all hosts in the trap list if the computer receives an SNMP request from a host not in the communities listed on the Security tab.

Accepted Community Names   Click Add to add a new community name and specify the community rights, or select an existing community and click Edit to edit the current rights. These rights include the following:

None   This setting prevents the host from processing any SNMP requests.

Use the Security tab to configure properties for incoming SNMP messages.

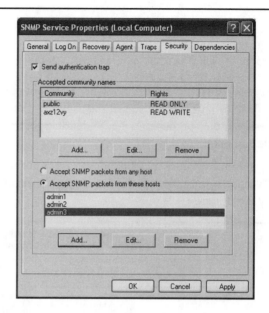

Notify   This setting allows the host to only send trap notifications to the communities configured in its trap list.

Read Only   Select this option if you don't want the host to process SNMP SET requests. In effect, this allows management applications in the specified community to read SNMP information but does not allow them to cause the computer to modify its configuration.

Read Write   Select this option to allow the host to respond to SET requests, enabling management applications to cause the computer to change its configuration through SNMP.

Read Create   Select this option to allow the host to create new entries in the SNMP tables.

NOTE   The communities specified on the Security tab apply to incoming SNMP requests only. Use the Traps tab to configure communities for outgoing SNMP messages.

Accept SNMP Packets From Any Host   Use this option to allow the computer to process SNMP requests from all hosts specified in the Accepted Community Names list.

Accept SNMP Packets From These Hosts   Use this option to apply a higher level of security for SNMP. With this option selected, the computer process SNMP messages only from selected hosts. You specify the host name, IP address, or IPX address of the allowed host(s). Click Add to add a host to the list of allowed hosts.

Setting SNMP Properties with Group Policy

Although you can configure SNMP properties through the properties for the SNMP service, you will find it more efficient to set SNMP properties through group policy if you have a relatively large number of computers in a domain environment. Group policy allows you to apply the SNMP properties across the site, domain, or organization unit (OU) automatically, without requiring that you modify settings at each individual computer.

To configure SNMP policies, edit the group policy object at the desired level (site, domain, OU, or local computer). Open the \Computer Configuration\Administrative Templates\Network\SNMP branch (Figure 34.5). Open the Communities policy and add the communities in which the computer should belong. This setting corresponds to the Accepted Community Names property in the SNMP service.

FIGURE 34.5:

You can configure SNMP properties through group or local policy.

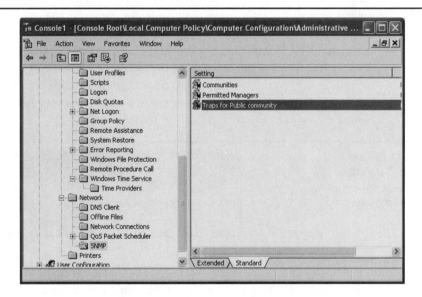

Use the Permitted Managers policy to define the SNMP management hosts to which the client will respond. This policy corresponds to the list associated with the option Accept SNMP Packets From These Hosts in the SNMP service properties.

Use the Traps For Public Community policy to specify the hosts that should receive SNMP traps from the computer. This policy corresponds to the list of hosts in the Traps tab of the SNMP service.

TIP   SNMP properties set through group policy override SNMP settings configured locally on the computer through the SNMP service properties.

Print Services for Unix

Print Services for Unix allows Unix (or Linux) hosts on the network to print to a printer hosted by a Windows XP computer and, vice versa, allows a Windows XP computer to print to a printer hosted by a Unix-based computer that uses line printer daemon (LPD). Print Services for Unix adds support for LPR ports to Windows XP.

To connect to a printer on a Unix host, first install Print Services for Unix. Open the Add Or Remove Programs object in Control Panel, click Add/Remove Windows Components, and add Print Services for Unix, which is located under the Other Network File And Print Services item.

Next, you need to add the printer driver for the remote printer and configure its LPR port. Run the Add Printer Wizard, click Next, and choose Local Printer Attached To This Computer. Clear the option to automatically detect and install the printer, and then click Next. Select Create A New Port, choose LPR Port from the drop-down list, and then click Next. In the Add LPR Compatible Printer dialog box (Figure 34.6), enter the fully qualified host name or IP address of the Unix host that manages the remote printer. Also enter the name of the printer or the print queue on the remote computer, and click OK. Windows XP checks communication with the remote print server and displays a warning if it can't locate the remote server. You have the option to continue anyway.

FIGURE 34.6:
Specify the remote Unix host name and printer or queue name.

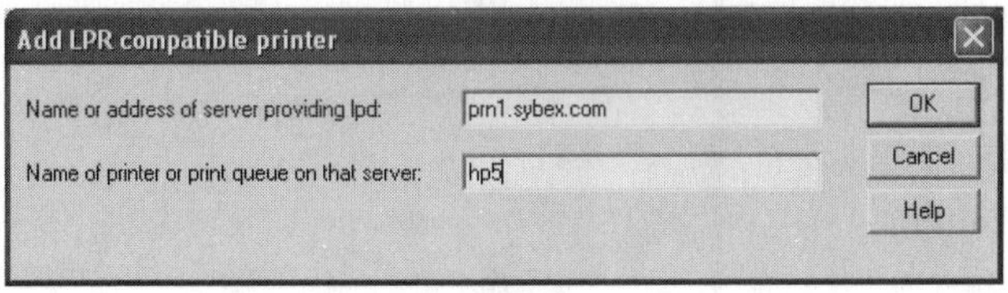

Add LPR compatible printer	
Name or address of server providing lpd:	prn1.sybex.com
Name of printer or print queue on that server:	hp5

> **TIP**   If Windows XP displays a warning that it can't communicate with the remote Unix host, and you discover after installing the printer that the host name or printer / queue name is incorrect, just change those properties. Open the properties for the printer, click the Ports tab, and click Configure Port to change the port settings.

Universal Plug and Play

The Universal Plug and Play service in Windows XP allows a Windows XP computer to detect and control Universal Plug and Play (UPnP) devices on the network. These devices include printers, network storage devices, and other devices that provide resources on the network. When Windows XP detects a new UPnP device, Windows displays notification in the tray. UPnP devices also appear in My Network Places, giving you quick access to these devices and the resources they provide.

UPnP does not install by default when you install Windows XP. This is fortunate, because the UPnP service included with the initial release of Windows XP suffers from an unchecked buffer bug that, if exploited by a hacker, can enable the hacker to gain complete control over the computer. This UPnP service can also be exploited to accomplish a denial-of-service attack against the computer and the network in which it resides.

If you choose to use the UPnP service, you should apply the latest patches to ensure that you prevent the attacks I've described above. To install the UPnP service, open the Add Or Remove Programs item in Control Panel and click Add/Remove Windows Components. You'll find UPnP in the Networking Services item.

After you install UPnP, there are no additional configuration steps you need to take. However, you do need to install the patch. You'll find a detailed description of the problem and the patch in Microsoft Knowledge Base article Q315000:

```
http://support.microsoft.com/default.aspx?scid=kb;en-us;Q315000
```

This article includes links to the patch files. You can also access the updates through the Windows Update site.

PART VI

Internet Applications and Services

CHAPTER 35

Optimizing Internet Explorer

Microsoft Internet Explorer 6.0 is ready to use the minute you finish installing it, which occurs by default. But like so much else in Windows, computing, and even life, Internet Explorer may work a great deal better for you and your specific needs if you explore options for optimization and advanced configuration.

In this chapter, I'll take you through some of the options available to you for advanced configuration, focusing on features such as AutoComplete and Content Advisor as well as security functions. Then we'll finish up with a look at some of the many add-ons programs available for use in conjunction with Internet Explorer (IE).

TIP Throughout this chapter, you'll make most adjustments by opening the Internet Options properties sheet (Tools ➤ Internet Options).

Optimizing IE Advanced Settings

When web browsers first arrived on the scene after the general birth of the World Wide Web in 1993, we were happy to just have them load a web page. Now, especially with the Windows environment, the browser has become the window not just to the rest of the world, but to the Desktop. With this comes a need for more functionality and more options.

Many of the options you can configure within Internet Explorer 6 are self-explanatory. This section will focus on some less-covered but highly useful tools you can enable and configure, such as AutoComplete for assisting with website addresses and web form field entry, and certain advanced options you can set to improve the overall performance, security, or efficiency of the browser.

Working with AutoComplete

The AutoComplete feature has been around for a few Internet Explorer versions now. Its name tells you the function it performs: it tries to automatically complete an entry for you. This entry can be a URL for a website or for a drive and folder on your system, or anything you might type into a field on a form on a website, such as your home or work address, phone number, e-mail address or user name.

AutoComplete works—when enabled—by recording entries you have typed before and storing them in encrypted format as part of your browser history. When you return to a site or folder and begin typing the word, phrase, or address again, AutoComplete performs an ultra-fast search of like entries and expands the field to reveal located possible matches. You can either continue typing or click one of the choices AutoComplete presents to you, as shown in Figure 35.1.

FIGURE 35.1:

AutoComplete presents a list of possible matches.

The vast majority of the time, enabling AutoComplete can be a real time-saver, since it will try to complete not just web addresses but frequently used user names and passwords, too, such as you might use to log on to a secured and/or subscription website.

However, just as with other such convenience options, you run into obvious security problems. If you're logging onto your company's secured website to work from home, enabling AutoComplete means that anyone else who sits down at your system—or connects to your XP system remotely—could access the same site just as easily. For an online vendor site, the user name and password may be tied to a credit card, Social Security number, or other information, which could make it very easy for someone else at your keyboard to access and "borrow" it.

Also, if you're concerned with privacy yet don't happen to clear your AutoComplete entries or IE history before someone else uses your system, they'll be presented with your AutoComplete match list, which might give them a clue where you've visited, along with any phone numbers, addresses, and so on that have been recorded in the course of your work.

NOTE   Website designers who use IIS and who want to suppress a user's ability to use AutoComplete for user names and passwords when visiting their sites should check out Article Q290641 in the Microsoft Knowledge Base at http://search.support.microsoft.com.

Enabling or Disabling AutoComplete

In IE6, AutoComplete is enabled by default, while a sub-component of it called Inline Auto-Complete (used to try to finish a line based on best matches if the user has previously typed a similar line) is not.

To disable AutoComplete for most of what you do (websites), From Internet Explorer, choose Tools ➤ Internet Options. On the Content tab, click AutoComplete, and uncheck all the boxes.

To enable the use of the Inline AutoComplete feature, choose Tools ➤ Internet Options and, from the Browsing group on the Advanced tab, click to check Use Inline AutoComplete. Click OK until you exit.

Modifying AutoComplete Settings

You have some options, although limited, for when and how AutoComplete works. For example, as shown in the previous section, turning it off for Web Addresses turns off its match feature for those items, so it won't try to complete them for you. You can do the same for forms, as well as user names and passwords, by following the instructions for disabling in the preceding section and choosing which options you want to keep.

Deleting AutoComplete Entries

Entries within the Internet Explorer history are kept within a single store, so there is no clean, neat way to remove individual entries expeditiously. What you have is basically two options: clear all of AutoComplete's recorded entries, or remove them one at a time from the match list as it appears.

To empty all of the entries, choose Tools ➤ Internet Options and, from the History group on the General tab, click Clear History. Click OK.

You can remove individual entries from the AutoComplete list, with one caveat. This can only be done while you're in the process of typing in information on a web-based form or user name-password field on a website. As you work and AutoComplete presents you with a match list, locate and select the entry you want to delete, then press the Delete key.

Configuring Advanced Settings

The Advanced Settings tab under Tools ➢ Internet Options (Figure 35.2) lets you specifically configure your browser to use (or to prevent the use) of various supported options, including these major categories:

Accessibility   These are special options for those who don't download images, who use alternative input methods, or who have a physical limitation.

Browsing   Various options are included here, including whether to notify when a download is complete, whether to underline links, and so on.

HTTP 1.1 Settings   Options here are for compatibility with an earlier standard.

FIGURE 35.2:

When a website doesn't act as expected, this tab is the best place to check.

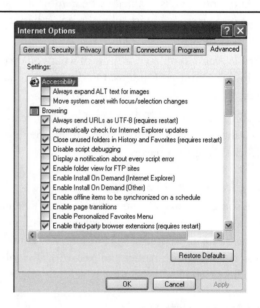

Microsoft VM   This allows the use of the Microsoft-compatible Java Virtual Machine (often used for running Java applets).

TIP   If you can't run Java applets from a website, be sure that JIT Compiler is checked under Microsoft VM.

Multimedia   Check here for entries regarding audio and graphics related to websites and how IE handles them.

Printing   Click to check if you want to print background images from websites.

Search From The Address Bar   Indicate how to handle web searches conducted from here (whether to try to make the closest match to what you typed).

Security   These options are discussed in the next section.

Optimizing Internet Explorer Security

Considering the breadth of the Internet along with the vast number of different types of files that can be run or opened through the browser, it makes sense that security in Internet Explorer would take a categorized approach to how secured options should be handled, based on the type of website or file.

IE does this by dividing its range into distinct zones, each of which can be configured differently depending on the level of restriction desired. You can add specific sites to these zones so that they can be covered by the specific rules configured for that zone.

In this section, we'll tackle zones, talk about cookie management as administered by IE6, and step through the enabling and configuration of Content Advisor, which can prevent the browser from accessing specific sites or types of sites altogether.

Content Zones and Security Settings

Internet Explorer 6 supports five different zones (as did versions 4 and 5), each of which can have its own security settings to configure for individual preferences and needs.

Internet   Settings for generalized Internet use; applies to all sites that you haven't assigned to another zone.

Local Intranet   Specifically websites and pages that are part of an intranet (internal web network).

Trusted Sites   Sites designated as ones that should be safe (containing no offensive or damaging content).

Restricted Sites   Sites that may contain either offensive or damaging content.

My Computer   Effectively displays the entire contents of your PC drives from the web browser.

Except for the last, My Computer, all of these security zones can be user-configured to adjust the security level from virtually none to high. Each zone can be configured differently, if desired (and it frequently is).

NOTE   My Computer can be changed only by using the Internet Explorer Administration Kit (IEAK).

Adjusting IE Security Zone Settings

You can adjust your IE security zones, on the Security tab (Figure 35.3), following these instructions:

1. From Internet Explorer, select Tools ➤ Internet Options.

2. Select the Security tab.

3. Click a zone, then click Custom Level.

4. From the Security Settings window, you can click to check individual options (Disable, Enable, Prompt before doing) under each listing, such as ActiveX downloads, file downloads, and more.

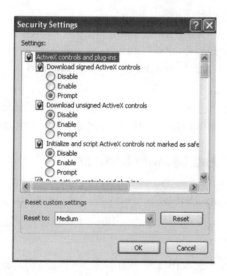

5. Click OK until you exit, or return to Step 3 to repeat this operation for another zone.

NOTE From Step 3, you can also choose Default Level, which restores the zone to its default security status. Likewise, at the bottom of the window described in Step 4, you can Reset Custom Settings, click the drop-down list box to choose your desired security level, then click Reset. This clears your previously configured security back to default levels.

Adding (and Removing) Sites to a Security Zone

Not all zones allow you to add sites under their category—the Internet zone (a catch-all category for all others) and My Computer do not. The rest do, and allow you to remove sites from the same screen you use to add them.

FIGURE 35.3:

Customize your IE
security zones.

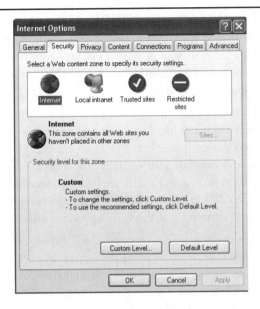

To add a site to a desired zone, or to remove one you've added, open the Security tab of the Internet Options dialog box. Click the desired web content zone, and click Sites. In the resulting dialog box, type the desired web address under Add This Web Site To The Zone and click Add; the URL you typed should then appear in the list of sites for this zone below. Or, select the URL you want to remove from the Web Sites list and click Remove. Click OK.

NOTE   One zone differs from these instructions: Local Intranet Zone has an intervening screen of options specific to sites that may be available on your network or intranet. To add (or remove) sites from this zone, click Sites, and from the Local Intranet screen, click Advanced to reach the add/remove screen.

Working with Advanced Security Settings

When we looked at the Advanced tab under Internet Options earlier in this chapter (Figure 35.2), you saw that it has some security settings available for configuration. Now let's examine some of the terminology provided here, to make sure you understand the implication of some of these settings.

For example, when options refer to certificates, it's important to realize that many (usually commercial) websites like Microsoft and others use security certificates to help identify them as a trusted source. These certificates are issued by an Internet certification authority, such as VeriSign, to attest that a site or a file you download from such a site is from the right source (and not some destructive entity trying to masquerade as a vendor you would trust). This isn't foolproof, since someone a few years ago managed to get a certificate issued to him in the name of a company with which he had no association.

The option identified as Signatures On Downloaded Programs refers to a unique digital signature attached to many types of files that try to verify the author/creator of a file. Visual Basic for Applications, for example, allows you to digitally sign code you develop for Office XP and other applications. Internet Explorer allows a user to establish a trust relationship based on that digital signature, always permitting such a signed file to be downloaded even if others are blocked.

SSL refers to Secure Sockets Layer, a special protocol used with online vendors, financial organizations, and subscription-only sites to try to prevent online snoopers from trying to steal unsecured personal or financial information you may send through the browser. An SSL-enabled website transaction is considered a secure one and is subject to 128-bit encryption.

Managing Cookies

Cookies are text files containing a usually small store of information related to who you are and where you may have visited on a particular website. This information is passed to your browser from the web server hosting a website you visit, and stored on your system for later retrieval.

For example, if you visited the *New York Times* website to read articles, cookies there might store information about which articles you've already read, so that when you revisit, you can tell (by a change in color) whether you've read a particular article. Other cookies are used to pass administrative access to a particular person to work on a secured website.

Cookies are a controversial topic, because many people choose not to have anything on their systems that could track and identify their Internet usage. They feel cookies are an intrusion forced onto their systems and block them at all costs.

Usually, cookies are fairly innocuous in nature (letting a site identify you so they can greet you by name or selected preferences) although the possible information data store on you being kept by vendors who employ cookies on their sites may not be. However, the vendors' accumulation of data on you is more frequently tied to your particular viewing or spending habits and other information they can glean from how you use their site.

Let's go through the cookie management features of Internet Explorer 6.

WARNING   Some sites will block you from accessing parts of the website or the entire website if you choose to block all cookies.

TIP   In the final section of this chapter, you'll find some recommended cookie- and history-cleaning utilities.

Adjusting Cookie Security

By default, Windows XP is configured to handle the acceptance or rejection of a cookie based on the level of security you've set. This runs the range from cookie management turned off (Accept All Cookies), from Low through High, to Block All Cookies.

To adjust your overall cookie security level, open the Privacy tab of the Internet Options (Figure 35.4). Move the slider bar up to increase the security level or down to decrease it (text to the right tells you the significance of each level).

TIP   Click Import to import a set of cookies from another source.

FIGURE 35.4:

Use the Privacy tab to control how IE accepts or reject cookies.

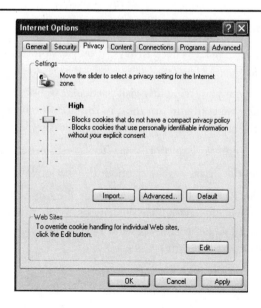

Overriding Windows XP Cookie Management

You have the option of overriding Windows XP's designed (by security level) method of handling cookies To do so, click Advanced on the Privacy tab. In the next screen, click to check Override Automatic Cookie Handling.

You then have the option to choose from the following settings, for both first-party (special to you) and third-party cookies (a third-party cookie is one that is offered to you from a website you're visiting but is actually sent by a third party, such as another vendor or company):

Accept   Automatically receive the cookie.

Block   Automatically refuse the cookie.

Prompt   Ask before accepting.

If desired, click to check Always Allow Session Cookies. Click OK to return to Internet Options.

But what if you frequently visit particular websites that need a separate cookie security level than you configure for most of the sites you browse? Internet Explorer allows you to bypass the regular security level on a site-by-site basis. You can do this by:

1. From Internet Explorer, select Tools ➤ Internet Options.

2. Select the Privacy tab and, under the section labeled Web Sites, click Edit.

3. Under Per Site Privacy Actions, type the name of the website, then click either Allow (if you normally have cookie security set to a high level but want to change it for this site) or Block (if you normally set security very low but you specifically want to reject cookies from a particular site). Click OK.

Note that from this same window, you can Remove one site on your existing list or Remove All sites.

Working with Content Advisor

Content Advisor has also been with us in Internet Explorer for some time, devised as an effort (mostly) to try to keep younger or sensitive eyes from getting access to unwanted content.

Like most content watchdog programs, such as CYBERSitter and Net Nanny, the idea is to develop guidelines for what types of content are deemed acceptable, and then to allow the user to visit only those sites that meet or exceed the configured guidelines (sort of like the movie rating system here in the U.S.). Also like most programs, Content Advisor works only as well as it is configured and managed. This means that if you're a parent using Content Advisor to try to keep your kids out of sexually oriented sites (or an employer trying to do the same for people working in the office), you need to supplement the use of this tool with real monitoring, so that you can catch sites they manage to access around your guidelines, and then change your rules to fit.

When you configure Content Advisor for use, you must provide a supervisor's password, and you must use that password whenever you make changes to the configuration.

Enabling and Configuring Content Advisor

Let's go through the process of enabling Content Advisor, and then configuring it for the job you want it to do. One word of warning before we start: be prepared to go back and adjust your ratings later, as needed. You may have to tweak it a bit before you find the right level of access balanced with restriction.

To set up Content Advisor for use, follow these steps:

1. Open the Tools menu in IE, and choose Internet Options.

2. From the Content tab, under Content Advisor, click Enable. (If you already have Content Advisor enabled, click Settings, then type the supervisor password.)

3. From the Content Advisor window, select the Ratings tab.

4. Click to select a category (Language, Nudity, Sex, or Violence), then move to the slider bar to the right to reduce the exclusion level for that category (as you move the slider, the screen informs you of what each level covers) or to the left to increase the level.

NOTE   Click More Info from the Ratings tab to see additional detailed information about each rating level and how these ratings are determined.

5. Move to the Approved Sites tab, provide the URL of any websites to allow and the conditions for each (Always Allow or Never Allow), or click Remove to remove a website already on the list.

6. Move to the General tab, where you can set user options (such as allowing users to view all non-rated websites), create a supervisor's password, or find more information or configure options under Ratings Systems.

7. Move to the Advanced tab, and select, if desired, a ratings bureau (an organization that creates and manages rating system lists) to use in helping you secure your browser from unwanted sites. You can also import Platform for Internet Content Selection (PICS) rules here.

8. Click OK to close the Content Advisor properties.

TIP If the Settings button under Content Advisor is grayed out, this indicates Content Advisor has not been enabled.

Resetting a Lost Content Advisor Password

What happens when you forget your Content Advisor password? It's probably no overstatement that thousands of people uninstall or reinstall Internet Explorer trying vainly to disable the Content Advisor feature and allow them to work without limitations.

The by-the-book process, from Microsoft, is to call them and they'll walk you through the fix. You can't completely scream at them for this, since Content Advisor was created to help keep children (among others) from visiting sites that might contain inappropriate material. Simply telling everyone how to do this would defeat the whole purpose of having it.

But let's cut to the chase, so to speak, by following these steps to reset your Content Advisor password when needed:

1. Load RegEdit.

2. Locate and double-click the key identified as

    HKEY_LOCAL_MACHINE\Software\Microsoft\Windows\CurrentVersion\Policies\Ratings

3. Delete the key value.

4. Exit RegEdit.

5. Use Windows Explorer or another method to look in your *%systemroot%*\system folder and right-click the file labeled `ratings.pol`. Select Rename, and rename this file.

6. Shut down and restart the system.

7. When the system is back up again, launch Internet Explorer.

8. From the Tools menu, choose Internet Options.

9. Select the Content tab, and click Enable (or Disable) Ratings.

10. When prompted, type in a new password, and click OK.

Internet Explorer Add-Ons

Add-on programs for Internet Explorer abound, and they tend to fall into these basic categories:

Interface changers   Some items change the appearance of the IE browser, from just substituting a different logo or picture in the upper-right corner to effectively changing the whole basic appearance; examples of these are "skins." These are usually the most frequently downloaded types of files, as many people want to change the default look of the browser.

Utilities   Some tools either diagnose or try to resolve problems related either directly to the web browser or to the various functions it performs. These include ad and cookie defeaters, history cleaners, tools for tweaking Registry settings to try to optimize Internet transfer speeds, download and other file handling managers, and more.

Let's look at a few of the utilities I find more useful for taking care of some of the problems (like privacy and cookies) that you've learned about in this chapter.

But permit me a word of caution before you feel inspired to log on and stock up on IE add-ons. Like any other types of software, some of the add-ons available are very good, while some are fairly useless. More importantly, you are apt to find that some you download can behave quite badly (either crashing your browser, acting to slow down rather than speed up your Internet access, or grabbing system resources you could use elsewhere). Also, different add-ons—sometimes even from the same developer or publisher—can conflict with one another. For this reason, I suggest you follow these general guidelines when choosing and installing IE add-ons:

- Read the accompanying (or online) documentation carefully beforehand. If you can't determine not just what it does but how it does it from your reading, you may want to make another choice.

- Look for ones with complete uninstallers; a browser add-on can be very messy to root out manually if you desperately need to get rid of it.

- Never try more than one of these add-ons simultaneously; you run a greater risk of conflicts if you do.

- Familiarize yourself with your IE settings before you install an add-on so that you have more ability to recognize changes an add-on may make to your browser and how it's configured.

Webroot Software's Window Washer 4.1 (shareware, $29.95; www.webroot.com) was one of the better add-on tools for Internet Explorer I've worked with over the years, for tidily cleaning up files and entries associated with web browsing. It's not specific to IE, however, since it works with recent versions of Netscape, MSN Explorer, and the AOL browser. It's like a downloadable search-and-destroy team, appearing to pick up entries that other tools have historically not removed. Something they call a "Bleach" feature can act upon already deleted files to try to make them less recoverable by serious snoops; other extras called Custom Wash plug-ins allow you to clean up the history for other, third-party online tools like RealOne Player.

One that is a big favorite with serious online users is Go!Zilla (freeware; `www.gozilla.com`), whose 4.11 version has been updated for Windows XP/IE6 compatibility. The focus with GoZilla is more efficient downloading (without pretending that it magically speeds up your connection to do so, as so many claim), and it takes care of some functionality that default Windows/IE do not, which is almost anything about download management except the common sense to know when to stop. Foremost is the ability to resume interrupted downloads, available in standard communications since the 1980s but somehow not intrinsic to Windows downloads.

NOTE   There's one exception to this Windows behavior: if you have a file download interrupted in Internet Explorer and you return immediately to the site to try to download it, you will find sometimes or regularly (depending on your system setup) that the transfer will start again where it left off. What it does is start back at byte zero, and then applies the amount of the file already downloaded to the current transfer. However, if you manually delete the partial file or have a cleanup utility that removes incomplete files before you try to resume the download, you'll start from scratch.

PanicWare's Popup Stopper (free and shareware versions, $19.95; `www.popupstopper.net`) is an IE-specific add-on a friend suggested after I complained about the overuse of pop-up, unsolicited ads while browsing. A couple of sites I routinely visit feed them to you en masse, sometimes at a rate of 2–3 per page view. You've seen them: those annoying X10 camera or free metal sunglass ads that often appear when you're visiting a portal site. Other tools I tried usually reduced their occurrence but certainly didn't almost eliminate it. PopUp Stopper Pro did a far better job—just three popped in the time that I often see as many as 24. This can make a true difference in recovering some of the bandwidth lost to ads, particularly if you're using a slower Internet dial-up connection for access.

Looking for an intelligent way to try to organize your ever-growing collection of web links for better retrieval? HydraLinks by iLOR (shareware, $29.95; `www.ilor.com/HL_download.htm`) definitely made the job easier for me in being able to readily locate entries in my 500-plus link collection.

For those who want a free utility for easily clearing out history, cookies, and cache (yet with a small footprint), check out Echo1's Just Clear (check major download sites). Assistance and Resources for Computers' PurgeIE (shareware, $14.95; `www.aandrc.com`) does the same job, plus offers more advanced options for clearing out browsing history.

Outlook Express is actually a built-in add-on for Internet Explorer. In the next chapter, I provide useful tips for using it for more than just reading your e-mail and Usenet newsgroups.

CHAPTER 36

Outlook Express

Outlook Express is the component of Internet Explorer that allows you to send and receive both e-mail and Usenet newsgroup messages.

When you set up your e-mail account here, a wizard guides you through the steps. You supply the necessary information, such as user name and password, as well as mail server names, which you usually determine from previous account settings or obtain from your e-mail provider.

With this kind of ease, we'll turn our attention to slightly more advanced Outlook Express configuration issues, such as creating and managing more than one identity, migrating messages from different mailer software, and setting up special other types of e-mail accounts—such as the free, web-based Hotmail or online service accounts—to send and receive messages through Outlook Express instead.

Account Management in Outlook Express

In this section, I'll take you through the transferring of data (addresses, messages, settings) from a different e-mail program, such as Eudora, into your new base of operations in Outlook Express (OE). Then you'll learn about establishing and using additional identities under Outlook Express to help you manage situations in which more than just you will be using it for your e-mail.

Importing Accounts and Messages

All too often, changing PCs—or even installing a new hard disk in one PC—means you have to either start fresh with your e-mail or go through a moderately complicated process to restore your old settings and messages for use under the newly configured e-mail program.

Outlook Express automates this process in many ways through its Import function, allowing you to bring mail account settings, address book entries, and messages (both e-mail and newsgroup-based) into it using a few simple steps. You can import from all the major mailer programs, including both Microsoft Outlook and Microsoft Exchange, as well as Netscape Communicator and Eudora (and export to these formats, as well).

TIP   What if you have an address book or other entries stored in text format or only available in a non-compatible mailer program? Comma-delimited (.csv) text files can be imported using the same processes described in the next few sections. For incompatible other mailers, try exporting your address book and other data in text or .csv format, then try to import them into Outlook Express.

Importing Account Settings

Account settings specify how Outlook Express communicates with your mail servers (both the outgoing e-mail's Simple Mail Transfer Protocol, or SMTP, and the incoming e-mail's Post Office Protocol, or POP).

Information provided within these settings include:

- User name and password

- E-mail identity (usually, *username@provider*.com)

- Names of the SMTP and POP servers

- Any special accommodations (such as requiring logon authentication)

To import account settings from your currently installed and configured mailer software, do this:

1. In Outlook Express, choose File ➢ Import ➢ Mail Account Settings.

2. When prompted, select the appropriate mailer program to use as the source of the mail account settings you wish to import. Click Next.

3. The mail settings for the other mailer's account are displayed. You can then:

   - Click Change Settings and follow the wizard to make any necessary changes to the existing account settings, or

   - Click Accept Changes to accept them as displayed.

4. Click Next, then click Finish.

The account you imported should now be displayed under Tools ➢ Accounts ➢ Mail.

If your prior mail account is stored elsewhere (for example, on another system) using Outlook Express, follow these steps:

1. On the old system, load Outlook Express.

2. Go to Tools ➢ Accounts and select the Mail tab.

3. Choose the desired mail account (if more than one exists) and click Export. Click OK to finish.

4. Locate the file it exported these to (stored in a file ending in .iaf) and copy it to the system with the new Outlook Express installation.

5. From Outlook Express on this machine, go to Tools ➤ Accounts, select the Mail tab.

6. Click Import, and specify the location of the .iaf file you just exported. Click OK.

Importing Address Book Entries

These steps permit you to import your Address Book from another mailer into Outlook Express.

1. From OE, click the address book icon.

2. From Address Book, choose File ➤ Import ➤ Other Address Book. (If you're importing the contents of another Windows Address Book (.wab) file, choose Address Book (WAB) instead.)

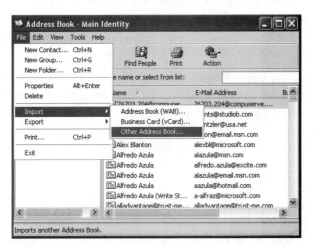

3. Locate and select the other address book you want to bring into Outlook Express, and click Open.

4. You are then prompted to select the type of address book. Once done, click Import.

Importing Mail Messages

If you're anything like me, your mail software becomes something of an historical vault for communications. I frequently back up the message base, and always transfer messages from one mailer to another when I either switch computers or add a new mailer to one of the systems in my office.

But before you get down to the basics of message migration, here are a few recommendations to consider:

- Where possible, perform manual housekeeping on your current message base (and address book) to remove advertising and other material you really don't want to follow you.

- If your current mail software has a Compact or Condense feature, to clean up spaces in the message store index, run it before you import the message store into Outlook Express.

Now, to import messages from your previous mailer into Outlook Express, follow these steps:

1. Use File ➤ Import ➤ Messages.

2. From the Select Program window, choose the program you want to import messages from, and click Next. Verify your selection and click Next again.

3. Next, select whether to Import All Folders (to import every folder available in the other mailer) or Select Folders (to choose from specific folders). Click Next, then click Finish.

Using and Managing Identities in Outlook Express

When you launch Outlook Express for the first time, part of the configuration process involves creating an identity for you. An identity in OE is much like a user profile, storing information specific to the person identified by the label.

With Outlook Express, more than one identity can be established to allow more than one user (or even one user who wants to maintain different accounts and settings under more than one identity) to use the mailer. It can be used by two or more people sharing a single copy of Outlook Express on a PC at home or at work. What this saves is time and foul-ups because without multiple identity support, you would have the pesky issues of manually changing names and mail accounts each time you sent mail on other than your default (primary) e-mail account.

The primary identity in Outlook Express, the one loaded by default when OE launches and used by default when an application doesn't inquire which identity to use for sending mail, is called the Main Identity. Each subsequent identity is labeled by whatever name you provide for it when you add the new identity.

Unlike user profiles, you don't have to log off the Desktop to let another person log in to send e-mail. You can switch identities right from Outlook Express, do your mail, and switch back to the first person with just a few pop-up windows prompting you to choose.

Each identity gets its own:

- Set of folders, such as Inbox
- Sub-folders (if you create them)

- List of contacts
- User settings (under Tools ➢ Options)

The following steps allow you to establish another identity under Outlook Express. If you need more than one, simply repeat the steps.

1. Choose File ➢ Identities ➢ Add New Identity.

2. From the New Identity window, type in the name you want to use for the new identity. If desired, click to check Require A Password.

Once the identity has been created (instantly), you'll be asked if you want to switch to the new identity.

To switch to an identity that has already been created, choose File ➢ Switch Identity. From the Switch Identities window, select the identity to which you would like to switch, and click OK.

NOTE   If you respond Yes to the prompt asking "Do you want to switch identities?" immediately after you create one, you'll be asked for information about this new identity's mail account and Internet connection.

Using Outlook Express for Special Mail Accounts

You can tie special types of e-mail accounts into Outlook Express for centralization. Looking in one location for your mail is always easier than looking in three or four, and that's a major possibility considering many have more than one e-mail account.

By special accounts, I mean one with special considerations, because you're working with either a web-based mailer (popular because you can access mail from wherever you go that has an Internet connection and a web browser) or the proprietary e-mail systems of online service accounts, such as CompuServe and Microsoft's MSN.

I'll start with Microsoft's Hotmail, because it's the most commonly used e-mail address aside from America Online's familiar @aol.com.

WARNING   Mail server information is part of what we discuss here, but be aware that server names can change with relatively little notice. Always consult the frequently asked questions (FAQ) page or customer support area of your online service to double-check specific mail settings if you experience a problem.

Using Outlook Express with Your Hotmail Account

A nice plus of being able to tie your online service or web-based e-mail account to Outlook Express is that you can then read and respond to e-mail while offline (connecting again to send it). Without it, you have to stay online while performing any web-based mail function.

1. Choose Tools ➤ Accounts.

2. From the Internet Accounts window, click Add, then select Mail.

3. In the Internet Connection Wizard, type the name that should be displayed in the From line on messages you send (for example, John Q. Public). Click Next.

4. From the Internet E-mail Address screen, type in your full Hotmail account mailing address (for example, kate_chase@hotmail.com). Click Next.

5. From E-Mail Server Names, click the drop-down box under My Incoming Mail Server Is A, and choose Hotmail. Then under My HTTP Provider Is, select Hotmail. Click Next.

6. From Internet Mail Logon, check that the e-mail address listed under Account Name is correct, and then type your password in the Password field. Click Next, and then click Finish.

The account will then be available for checking under Outlook Express, and listed under your accounts, as shown in Figure 36.1.

FIGURE 36.1:

Hotmail will be listed with other e-mail accounts.

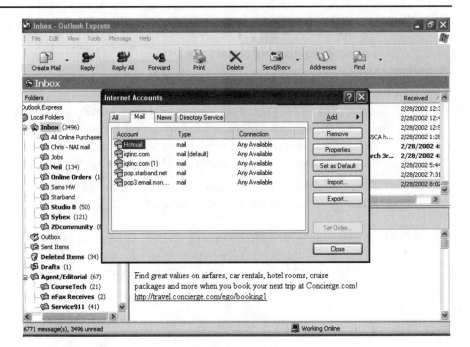

If you want to set up a web-based e-mail account that is not Hotmail but is Outlook Express–compatible, click Other under My HTTP Provider Is in Step 5, and provide the complete URL for that service, following the format *http://www.example.com/mail*.

> **TIP** If you don't have a free Hotmail account but would like to add one as a backup to your regular account, use your Internet connection and browser to visit www.hotmail.com. Click Sign Up. Such accounts can also be useful when you need to provide an e-mail address at a registered website but you don't want to give your main e-mail address for fear of being overrun by unsolicited advertising.

> **NOTE** If for some strange reason, you're choosing to use an older version of Internet Explorer/Outlook Express, be aware that you need at least version 5.5 to configure Hotmail under Outlook Express.

Using Outlook Express with Your Online Service Mail Accounts

Many online service accounts allow you to access your e-mail account with them through Outlook Express. One big benefit here is that Outlook Express makes it a bit easier to filter e-mail into these accounts, by allowing you to block specific senders and create rules to handle mail based on certain conditions (for example, delete all e-mail which lists "Make Money Fast" in the subject line). This is particularly important with online service accounts, where you may be targeted heavily with unsolicited advertising into your electronic mailbox.

Let's take a quick tour through your ability (or inability) to use Outlook Express to connect to accounts through three of the best known online services.

America Online

Although it's been talked about as in development for years, America Online's proprietary e-mail system cannot be configured to work with external mailers, such as Outlook Express. You need to load your AOL software and check it the usual way.

CompuServe

Since CompuServe mail supports the POP3 standard, you can establish your CompuServe mail account under Outlook Express. However, if you're using CompuServe Classic, you must activate this first. To do this:

1. Sign onto CompuServe Classic.
2. From Go, type **GO POPMAIL** and follow on-screen instructions.

Once you've set this up, you'll see additional on-screen instructions for configuring the account for use with Outlook Express.

MSN

For most MSN users, Outlook Express is really the best way to check e-mail (or read news-groups), because MSN's web-based mail can be gruesomely slow, particularly if you're on a dial-up connection.

To configure your MSN e-mail under Outlook Express, do this:

1. In OE, choose Tools ≻ Accounts.

2. From the Internet Accounts window, click Add, then select Mail.

3. In the Internet Connection Wizard, type the name which should be displayed in the From line on messages you send (for example, John Q. Public). Click Next.

4. From the Internet E-mail Address screen, type in your full MSN account mailing address (for example, kate_chase@msn.com). Click Next.

5. From the E-Mail Server Names screen, provide your POP3 server as **pop3.email.msn.com** and the SMTP server as **secure.smtp.email.msn.com**. Click Next.

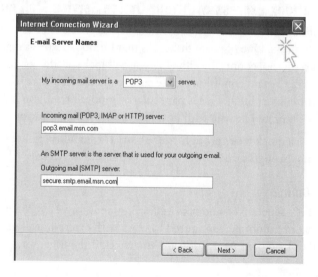

6. From Internet Account Logon, type your user name and password, then click to check Log On Using Secure Password Authentication. Click Next. Click Finish.

CHAPTER 37

Hosting Websites

Windows XP Professional includes Internet Information Services (IIS), a collection of components and services that allow you to host a website on a Professional computer. Although Windows XP Professional is limited to a maximum of 10 concurrent connections, IIS nevertheless provides a means for you to share resources with other users through mechanisms different from those you might otherwise use. For example, you can use IIS to share documents with users across the Internet.

IIS also makes it possible to share printers through TCP/IP, including allowing remote Internet users to connect to and print to your printer. You might use this as an alternative to a fax machine, or simply to provide easy access to printers from the LAN for inexperienced users.

SEE ALSO See Chapter 9 for details on setting up IPP (Internet-based) printing.

This chapter explains installing and configuring IIS, as well as setting up specific web services. You'll find detailed information in this chapter on how to set up a web server, share files with others through FTP, and use FrontPage Server Extensions to support publishing from FrontPage. I'll also explain how you can run CGI and Perl scripts on your computer, which enables you to run counters, submit forms through e-mail, and perform a host of other tasks not possible or practical without a knowledge of programming. If you're looking to secure your website, you'll find information on using certificates and Secure Sockets Layer (SSL).

This chapter also takes a look at a small number of web development tools you might want to consider if you're looking for an easy way to develop your website. You'll find that it's easy to create websites that support Dynamic HTML (DHTML) for special visual effects, serve dynamic content from databases, use feedback forms, and create other high-end content for your website.

Overview of Internet Services in Windows XP

In Windows XP Professional, Internet Information Services (IIS) comprises components and features that allow a computer to function as a web server, FTP server, or SMTP relay agent (relaying e-mail). IIS also includes additional components that support these core services. For example, FrontPage Server Extensions allow a computer running Microsoft FrontPage to publish to the web server. The following sections offer an overview of each component.

NOTE   Windows XP Home Edition does not include IIS or a version of Personal Web Server (PWS). Check out www.tucows.com or other software download sites for freeware and shareware web hosting solutions for Home Edition.

The World Wide Web Service

The World Wide Web Service allows a Windows XP Professional computer to serve a single website. Windows XP Professional is limited to a maximum of 10 concurrent connections, so a maximum of 10 users can access the website at any one time. This is a problem if you are hosting a public Internet site (unless your site is incredibly unpopular) but is a great solution for hosting a site for internal use by other users on your LAN. For example, you might use a Windows XP Professional computer running IIS to provide links to documents, support information, policies, printers, or other information or resources.

TIP   Consider Windows 2000 Server or Windows .NET Server if you need to host more than one website on a single computer, or if you need to provide more than 10 concurrent connections to your web server.

Windows XP Professional can also be useful as a *staging server*. You use a staging server to publish and test a website before publishing it to its final server. Since you are only testing the site, it doesn't matter that you are limited to one site and a maximum of 10 users—unless you are stress-testing the site. If that's the case, you're better off staging to a server that matches closely, in hardware and OS, the final target server.

TIP   You can host more than one website at a time on a Windows XP Professional computer, but only one can be running at a time. See the section "Hosting a Website" later in this chapter for more details.

File Transfer Protocol Service

The FTP Service allows a Windows XP Professional computer to host an FTP site, which lets users share files. If the computer is connected to the Internet, remote Internet users can access the files. FTP provides an excellent means for sharing documents, drivers, or any other type of file that needs to be available to multiple users, but which you don't want to share through conventional means (such as a network share). Users can access the FTP site through a web browser, with a third-party FTP application such as FTP Explorer, or from a command console. As with websites, IIS under Windows XP Professional can serve one FTP site, and the site is limited to a maximum of 10 concurrent connections.

SEE ALSO   See Chapter 39 for details on setting up and managing an FTP site.

SMTP Service

Simple Mail Transfer Protocol (SMTP) is an Internet standard that defines e-mail transfer. SMTP is the most widely-used mechanism for transferring mail across the Internet.

The SMTP Service in Windows XP doesn't give you the means to turn a Windows XP Professional computer into a full-blown e-mail server. It does, however, let you set up the computer for *mail relay*. For example, you might create a form on your website that collects information and forwards it through e-mail. The SMTP Service can receive the message and forward it to its destination or route it to another SMTP server that will process the message.

The SMTP Service also accepts incoming messages. It doesn't provide a mailbox structure like Exchange Server or other e-mail servers, but instead places incoming messages into a drop folder. You can develop applications that monitor the folder and direct e-mail to specific users, or use third-party applications for the same purpose.

Hosting a Website

I've been in the Internet service business for several years, and one of my main experiences in that time has been setting up and managing web servers. So I can offer you some useful insight into hosting websites with IIS. This section not only explains how to set up and configure a single site in IIS, but also explains some ways to work around the one-site-only limitation imposed by IIS under Windows XP Professional.

Installing IIS

IIS installs through Control Panel just like most other Windows XP components. However, you do have some control over which components Setup installs.

To install IIS, open Control Panel and then open the Add Or Remove Programs item. Click Add/Remove Windows Components. If you only select Internet Information Services from the components list, Setup installs the World Wide Web service and support files (such as documentation), but does not install the FTP or SMTP services. If you want to add or remove components, select Internet Information Services and click Details (Figure 37.1). Select the components to install and click OK, then click Next to complete the installation. Windows XP will prompt you for the Windows XP CD or the location of the installation files.

FIGURE 37.1:

You can add or remove components from IIS.

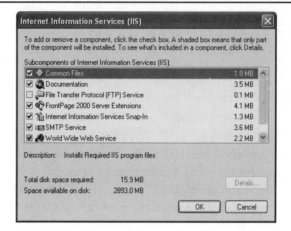

TIP   Make sure you install the IIS snap-in so you will be able to configure and manage your sites.

If you don't plan on publishing to your website using FrontPage, you can omit the Front-Page Server Extensions. If you select FrontPage Server Extensions for installation, Setup automatically sets up the Default Web Site for publishing though FrontPage. You don't have to add the extensions separately.

TIP   Setup does not by default install the Scripts virtual directory for the World Wide Web service. Double-click the service in the components list to open the details for the service, and then select the Scripts item. This causes Setup to create the Scripts virtual folder. However, Setup does not place any scripts in the folder. This simply saves you the trouble of creating the folder if you plan to use it to store scripts for your website.

Setting Up the Site

With IIS installed, you're ready to set up your website. Windows XP automatically creates a site called Default Web Site when you install IIS (Figure 37.2). You can modify this site as needed to define your own site, or delete the site and create a new one. The advantage to keeping the original site and just modifying it as needed is you save yourself the trouble of configuring the basic settings, specifying the site folder, adding FrontPage Server Extensions (if needed) to the site, and other setup tasks. Besides, IIS doesn't give you the means to delete the Default Web Site without having the administration scripts (see the following section), so modifying the existing site is the easiest method by far to customize your website.

To configure the site, open the Internet Information Services console from the Administrative Tools folder. Expand the server and Web Sites nodes, right-click Default Web Site, and choose Properties to display the properties sheet shown for the site.

> **NOTE** The following sections explain how to configure common website properties. See Chapter 38 to learn more about FrontPage Server Extensions. Other configuration issues, such as setting up security for the site, are covered later in this chapter.

FIGURE 37.2:

Use the IIS console to manage the Default Web Site and Default FTP Site.

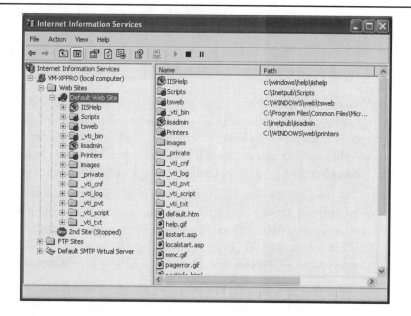

IP Address, Port, and Host Header

Each website has three properties that determine how it responds to client browser requests: the IP address, port number, and host header. You set these on the Web Site tab of the site's properties (Figure 37.3). By default, IIS sets up the site to respond to all unassigned IP addresses. This is really only an issue on a computer with more than one IP address. In this default configuration, IIS will monitor incoming traffic for all IP addresses not assigned to other sites (not really applicable on a Windows XP computer anyway) and respond to requests on those addresses.

FIGURE 37.3:

Use the site's properties sheet to configure the site.

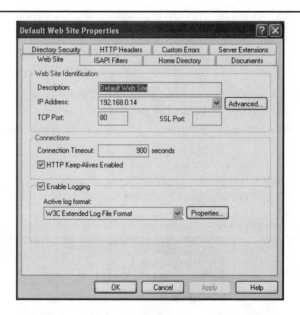

You don't need to worry about changing the IP Address setting under Windows XP, because the default setting will enable IIS to respond to all requests to the site, even if the computer has multiple IP addresses. However, you do need to change the IP address if the computer has multiple IP addresses and you want IIS only to respond to a specific address. Simply select the IP address from the drop-down list if you want to assign a specific address to the site.

The default TCP port for HTTP—the protocol used for web traffic—is port 80. In most cases, you will want to leave your site configured for the default port. This allows a client to connect to your website through a browser without having to specify the port number in the URL. For example, you can get to my website by entering the URL www.boyce.ws. If I changed the port to, say, 8080, you would have to type the URL www.boyce.ws:8080 to get to the site.

You generally only want to change the port number for one of three reasons: to hide the site from casual browsing, to enable the site to run on the same computer as another site with the same IP address and host header, or to enable the site to run on a computer that includes other hosting software—in addition to IIS—that is using port 80. In most cases, you can leave the port at the default of 80.

TIP   If you decide to change the port, you need to tell clients what port to use, or place a link to the URL (with port) on a page served by another server, enabling the client to link to your site.

The host header also serves to identify the website in conjunction with the IP address and port. When a browser connects to a site, it passes the web server the host header, such as `www.boyce.ws`. The web server then checks the host header to determine which site to provide.

The host header isn't really needed if you are only hosting one site. Clients can get to your site either through the IP address or through a URL. The URL can take the form `http://computer`, where *computer* is the network computer name of the Windows XP computer hosting the site. Or, you can create a DNS host record in the DNS zone in which the computer resides and allow the clients to use the host name in a URL. If the host name were www, the URL would be `http://www.boyce.ws`. The host name `jim` would enable the client to use the URL `http://jim.boyce.ws` to reach the site. If you are relying on DNS records to allow clients to reach your site, click Advanced on the Web Site tab of the site's properties, and then click Add. Specify the IP address, port, and host header, and click OK.

TIP   Windows 2000 and Windows XP computers can register their host names with a Windows 2000 Server or Windows .NET Server DNS server automatically. This allows hosts that use DHCP to obtain an address dynamically to still have a valid and current host record in their domain zone records. So, if your IP addresses changes because of an address lease change, remote clients can still connect to your website using your host name or network name, because the record is updated on the DNS server.

Home Directory and Permissions

The Home Directory tab (Figure 37.4) lets you specify the folder in which the website's files are located, as well as general permissions for the folder. You can specify a folder on your local computer as the home directory, use a shared folder on another computer on the LAN, or redirect the site to a different URL.

In addition, you can specify the permissions that clients have on the directory. In most cases, you should grant only Read permission and deny Write, Script Source Access, and Directory Browsing. Restricting the site to Read permission helps protect the site against hacking and other potential security threats.

NOTE   You can configure an application for the site, but in general you don't need to do so for a typical site. It's unlikely that you will run server applications on a Windows XP Professional computer, so application configuration isn't covered in this book.

If you configure a site for Directory Browsing, clients can connect to the site and browse the underlying folder structure. This is generally a bad idea unless you are using the site to provide access to documents, because it exposes all of the files in the site to the client.

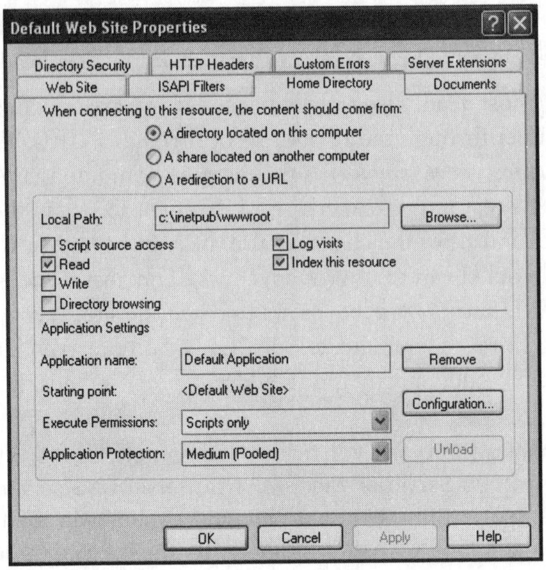

FIGURE 37.4:

Use the Home Directory tab to specify where the site's files are located.

Default Documents

One additional property you need to set initially for the site is the default document, which allows a user to view your default page without having to include it in the URL. For example, assuming your default page for www.boyce.ws is index.htm, a client can point a web browser to www.boyce.ws and IIS displays the index.htm page automatically. This is the same as entering www.boyce.ws/index.htm but eliminates the need for the client to know your main document name.

IIS automatically assigns four default documents to the website: default.htm, default.asp, index.htm, and iisstart.asp. default.htm and index.htm are the most commonly used, but you can use any document for the site. To use a different document, open the Documents tab of the site's properties (Figure 37.5), click Add, and add the document to the list. Use the up and down arrow buttons to change the order of the documents in the list. IIS searches the folder for a matching document in the order listed, and the first one found is served to the client.

Other Site Properties

You can configure many other properties for the site that determine how IIS handles the site and how clients access it. The remaining properties that apply to the types of sites typically hosted on a Windows XP Professional computer are explained later in this chapter as they apply to specific issues, such as providing site security.

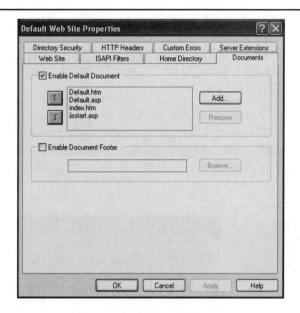

Setting Up Multiple Sites

Windows XP is limited to hosting one site. However, through a little sleight-of-hand you can add the ability to create multiple sites on a Windows XP computer through IIS. The computer will still only support one running site, so to start another site, you must first stop the one currently running. The ability to add multiple sites is useful primarily for staging websites for testing without going through the expense of installing Windows 2000 Server or .NET Server. However, you might find other uses for this ability.

The trick to creating multiple sites under IIS on a Windows XP Professional computer is borrowing the administrative files from a Windows 2000 Server running IIS. When you install IIS on a Windows 2000 Server, Setup creates a virtual directory named IISADMIN, which points to *%systemroot%*\System32\inetsrv\iisadmin. This virtual directory contains files that enable you to manage the web server from a browser. These files ignore the one-site-only restriction IIS imposes on a Windows XP Professional computer, and enable you to create and manage multiple sites on the computer.

To set up a Windows XP Professional computer to manage multiple sites, copy the folder *%systemroot%*\System32\inetsrv\iisadmin from the Windows 2000 Server computer to the Inetpub (by default, C:\Inetpub) folder on your Windows XP computer. Set permissions on the iisadmin folder to grant the local Administrator account full control. Then, open the IIS console on the Windows XP computer and add a new virtual directory that points to the folder (configure it to allow script execution). In the virtual folder properties, configure the folder to deny anonymous access and allow integrated Windows authentication.

SEE ALSO   See the next section to learn how to configure authentication options for a site or virtual directory.

When you want to manage the server to add another site, open the IIS console, open the IISADMIN virtual folder, right-click `default.htm` in the document list, and choose Browse. Your web browser will open the document, and IIS will prompt you to log on. Enter the administrator account credentials. You should then see a web page similar to the one shown in Figure 37.6.

FIGURE 37.6:

Use the administration web page to create new web and FTP sites.

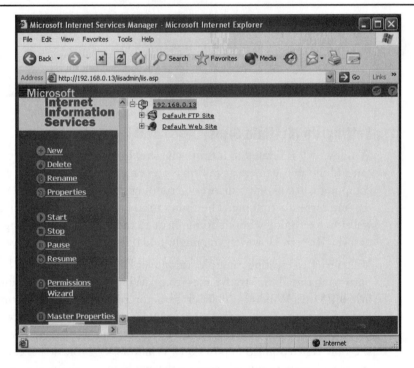

Click New in the left frame to start the New Site Wizard, which enables you to create web and FTP sites on the server. Follow the prompts in the wizard to create the new site. When you're finished, open the IIS console and note that the new site now appears in the console, although it will be stopped (because only one site can be running at a time). You can now set the properties for the site through the console. If you prefer, you can also use the IISAdmin scripts to manage the site's properties.

Providing Site Security

Web server security is an important issue, particularly as the threat of viruses, worms, and hackers continues to grow. It's therefore important that you have an understanding of the security issues involved in hosting a website and how to configure IIS to afford the protection your site requires. This section covers the most common security issues.

General Site Security

First and foremost, I recommend that you host your site files on an NTFS partition to give you control over the files. Without the protection that NTFS provides, it's much easier for someone with access to your computer to modify the files and present site content that could be embarrassing or damaging to you or your company. It's also easier for hackers to exploit potential security holes to access your system and your site's content.

You should also consider how you will make the site available for publishing content. You generally have three options: publish the files locally or through the LAN, use FTP to publish to the computer, or in the case of FrontPage, use FrontPage Server Extensions to publish to the server. Given that the target server is running Windows XP Professional, it's a good bet that you will also be doing your website development on the same computer. So publishing the files locally is the most likely scenario and one that involves the least security risk. As long as you use NTFS for the target partition and make sure you don't grant the Everyone group anything other than Read permissions, you should be in good shape. However, you will also need to grant the IUSR account Read access, as I explain in the next section. You should also review the permissions on the folder to make sure that any other users or groups that should not have Write or Change permission on the folder have the appropriate permissions. This advice also holds true for any situation in which you need to publish to a computer across the LAN. Just make sure you apply the appropriate permissions to the folder and its subfolders, and connect to the share using credentials that have the necessary permissions in the folder.

If you need to use FTP to publish to the server from a different computer, make sure you configure the computer's FTP site to provide the appropriate security, restricting access as needed to the folder containing the website.

SEE ALSO   See Chapter 39 for complete details on hosting and FTP site under Windows XP Professional.

The last option for publishing is to use FrontPage Server Extensions and develop/publish the site from FrontPage. FrontPage Server Extensions provide a means for controlling authoring permissions to prevent unauthorized access.

SEE ALSO   See Chapter 38 to learn how to install and configure FrontPage Server Extensions.

Perhaps one of the most important things you can do is to ensure that you keep your operating system up-to-date with the latest security patches. You can obtain the patches by pointing a web browser to windowsupdate.microsoft.com. You should also consider implementing a firewall in front of the server to help prevent denial-of-service (DoS) and other attacks aimed at your server.

You should also consider implementing auditing for the site in an effort to detect unauthorized access or attempted access. See Chapter 19 for a discussion of how to audit security for Windows XP.

Anonymous Versus Authenticated Access

IIS supports two types of access to a site, anonymous and authenticated, although the former is not a technically accurate description. Anonymous access allows anyone with a web browser to connect to the site without providing any user credentials. IIS doesn't actually allow unauthenticated access, however. When you install IIS, Setup creates a user account named IUSR_*computer*, where *computer* is the computer's name. On a computer named Snoopy, for example, the account would be IUSR_SNOOPY. IIS then uses this account to authenticate all anonymous requests for access to the site.

For authenticated access, the site or page is protected by NTFS permissions and is only accessible to users who specify an appropriate user name and password. This gives you a means of restricting access to a site or page, preventing anonymous users from browsing it. You can protect the site or page with a single set of user credentials or create a separate account for each user.

To configure authentication for a website, open the IIS console, right-click the site, and choose Properties. Then click the Directory Security tab. Click Edit in the Anonymous Access and Authentication Control group to display the dialog box shown in Figure 37.7.

If you don't want to allow anonymous access to the site, clear the Anonymous Access checkbox. You can use the Basic Authentication and Integrated Windows Authentication options if you want to authenticate users against local accounts. With Integrated Windows Authentication (IWA), the client's browser first attempts to authenticate using the current logon credentials. If that fails, the server prompts the client for a user name and password. With Basic Authentication, the server simply prompts for the credentials without attempting to authenticate using the existing logon credentials.

Basic Authentication is less secure because the password is not encrypted. However, Basic Authentication allows for authentication through a proxy server, but IWA does not. If you need to authenticate through a proxy server, use Basic Authentication. Otherwise, use IWA for the additional level of security it provides.

FIGURE 37.7:

Use the Authentication
Methods dialog box to
configure anonymous
and authenticated
access.

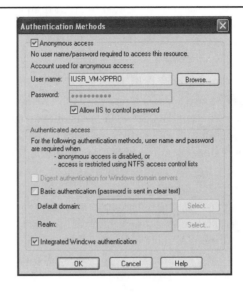

> **WARNING** Although you can change the account that IIS uses for anonymous logon, I don't recommend doing so because it can lead to unforeseen authentication problems.

Restricting Access to Specific Pages or Folders

In some cases, you might want to offer anonymous access to a site but restrict access to certain parts of the site, whether a single page or an entire folder and its contents. If that's the case, configure the site to allow authenticated access and then set the NTFS permissions on the file or folder to remove the IUSR account from the list and add any accounts that need access, granting them the appropriate level of permissions (Read, Change, etc.) depending on the function of the particular item.

You can also apply security at the folder level, whether that folder is a physical folder or virtual folder. Open the IIS console, open the site, right-click the folder, and choose Properties. Use the same procedure to configure security that you use to configure site-level security (see the previous section.)

Restricting Access by Address or Domain

Windows NT Server, Windows 2000 Server, and Windows .NET Server give you the ability to restrict access to a site by the IP address, subnet, or domain of the client. Windows XP Professional, however, does not provide this feature, although the controls for accessing it are located on the Directory Security tab. The controls are disabled. If you need to restrict access based on address, subnet, or domain, you'll need to move the site to a server platform or configure rules in your firewall to control access (which is outside the scope of this book).

Using SSL to Secure a Site

You can use Secure Sockets Layer (SSL) to provide additional security for clients. SSL uses a certificate to encrypt data between the client and server, making that data secure from interception and hijack. For example, you might use SSL to secure the site for authoring, enabling a remote client to publish to the site with greater security.

Obtain the Certificate

In order to use SSL, you must obtain an install a certificate on the Windows XP Professional computer that is acting as the web server. You can obtain the certificate from a public certification authority (CA) such as VeriSign (`www.verisign.com`) or Thawte (`www.thawte.com`). Or, if your network contains a stand-alone or enterprise CA, you can obtain the certificate from the local CA.

> **TIP**   Windows 2000 Server and Windows .NET Server platforms include Certificate Services, which allows the server to function as a stand-alone or enterprise CA. A Windows XP computer can't function as a CA.

The method you use to obtain the certificate varies slightly depending on the CA. The easiest method is to use the IIS console. Open the IIS console and open the properties for the website. Click the Directory Security tab, then click Server Certificate to start the Web Server Certificate Wizard. In the wizard, specify that you want to create a new certificate and that you want to prepare the certificate request now but send it later.

On the next page of the wizard (Figure 37.8), enter a descriptive name such as **Web Server Certificate** in the Name field. It's unlikely that you will need to change any of the other options on this page for a site hosted on a Windows XP Professional computer, so I won't cover those (they would lead to a lengthy discussion of topics outside the scope of this book). The remaining items of information required by the wizard are for the most part self-explanatory or adequately explained by the wizard. When prompted for the Common Name, however, what you enter depends on how the site is accessed. For a site publicly available on the Internet, enter the host header (such as `www.boyce.ws`) as the common name. For an intranet-accessed site, specify the computer's DNS or NetBIOS name. The wizard automatically uses this name unless you enter a different name.

> **TIP**   If users will connect to the secure site through its IP address rather than a host name, use the IP address as the common name.

FIGURE 37.8:

Use the IIS console to create a certificate request.

Next, open a web browser on the computer that will function as a server and connect to http://*server*/certsrv, where *server* is the CA's computer name. The CA presents a web-based wizard that steps you through the process of requesting the certificate (Figure 37.9). Click Next, choose Advanced Request in the wizard, and click Next.

FIGURE 37.9:

The CA uses a web-based wizard to process your certificate request.

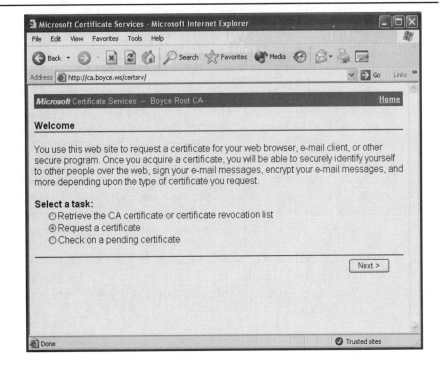

In the following wizard page (Figure 37.10), choose the option to submit a request using a Base64-encoded file. Click Next.

FIGURE 37.10:
Request the certificate using a Base 64-encoded file.

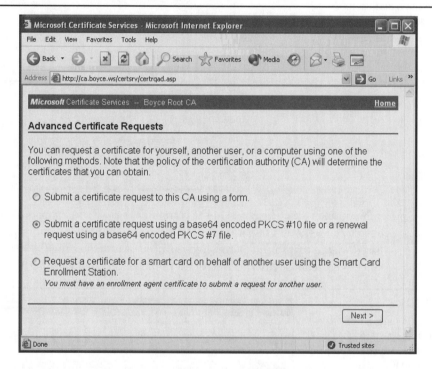

On the next page (Figure 37.11), click Browse to browse for and select the certificate request file you created through the IIS console. Then click Read to enter the data into the form. You can also open the file in Notepad to cut and paste the data. Then, select Web Server from the Certificate Template drop-down list and click Next.

TIP   You won't be able to browse to the file on your local computer unless you add the CA's URL to your list of trusted sites. You do this through the Security tab in Internet Explorer's options. If the CA doesn't use SSL for certificate requests, you need to clear the option "Require server verification for all sites in this zone."

Depending on how the CA is configured, the CA will either provide you with the certificate immediately or will prompt you to return to the CA later to retrieve the certificate after it has been issued by an administrator. If the CA issues the certificate immediately, select the option to download it.

FIGURE 37.11:
Import the request file.

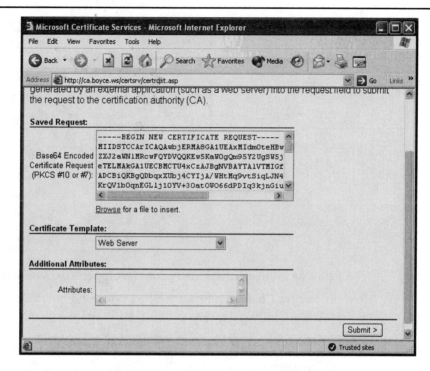

If you use a commercial CA such as VeriSign, you will have to pay for the certificate. These services also use a web-based wizard to prompt you for the information needed to create the certificate. When the certificate is ready, the wizard downloads it to your computer.

After the certificate is downloaded to the server, open the IIS console again and open the properties for the website. On the Directory Security tab, click Server Certificate. Choose "Process the pending request and install the certificate" and click Next. Browse to the location of the certificate file you obtained from the CA. Click Next and follow the remaining prompts to complete the installation.

Configure the Site for SSL

After you install the certificate, you will probably want to modify some of the SSL-related settings for the site. Open the properties for the site in the IIS console and click the Directory Security tab. Click Edit under the Secure Communications tab to open the dialog box shown in Figure 37.12.

FIGURE 37.12:

Use the Secure Communications dialog box to configure SSL settings.

The following list summarizes the options on the Secure Communications dialog box:

Require Secure Channel   Select this option to require the clients to use SSL to connect to the website. Clearing this option allows unsecured and unencrypted access to the site.

Require 128-bit Encryption   Choose this option to require stronger 128-bit encryption.

Client Certificates   Use Accept Client Certificates to enable clients to use client-side certificates to authenticate on the website. Use Require Client Certificates if you want to force the clients to authenticate using a client-side certificate. Use Ignore Client Certificates for a publicly available website.

Enable Client Certificate Mapping   This option maps client-side certificates to local computer accounts on the server, enabling the client to use a certificate to authenticate on the server.

Enable Certificate Trust List   You can enable this option to specify a list of CAs that are trusted by this website. Only certificates issued by a trusted CA will be granted access.

Test It

At this point, you should be ready to test SSL connections to the website. Point your browser to `https://SiteURL`, where *SiteURL* is the URL for your web server. Make sure to use `https` rather than `http` in the URL. If you are unable to successfully connect to the site or receive a warning such as the one shown in Figure 37.13, check the certificate to make sure you specified the appropriate host header in the Common Name field for a public site or the computer's machine name for an intranet site. Note that in Figure 37.13, the only problem with the server's certificate is that it was issued by a CA not explicitly trusted by the client computer. If you obtain a certificate from a public CA instead of issuing your own, public clients will generally not see this warning, as their computers are probably configured to trust the public CA. For internal clients, make sure to add your local CA to the trusted authorities on each client.

FIGURE 37.13:

This warning can indicate an incorrectly configured certificate.

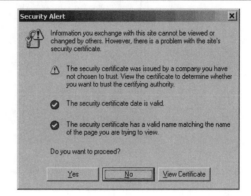

Using Custom Error Pages

IIS provides common error pages for specific errors such as the requested page not existing (the 404 error). Most of these error messages are pretty boring, and you might want to either spice up the error messages a bit or include additional information. For example, you might want to provide a link to your home page or to a corporate page when a 404 error occurs.

The default error pages are stored in *%systemroot%*\help\iisHelp\common as HTML documents. You can either modify these pages or create your own from scratch. If you choose the latter option, create the file and place it in the common folder just mentioned. I recommend you give the file a new name rather than overwrite the default document for the error in question.

Next, open the IIS console and open the properties for the site. Click the Custom Errors tab (Figure 37.14). Select the error for which you want to change documents and click Edit Properties to display the Error Mapping Properties dialog box. Enter the path to the custom file and click OK. Repeat the process for any other custom errors, then close the properties for the site.

FIGURE 37.14:

Use the Custom Errors tab to define custom error documents.

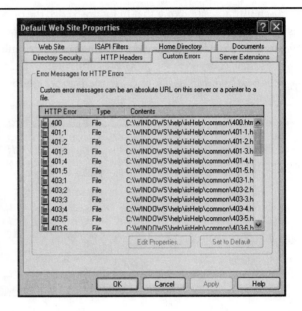

Using Counters

Although your website will be limited to a maximum of 10 concurrent users, you might still want to keep track of how many hits the site gets. You have several options for including a counter on the site. FrontPage, for example, includes a visible counter that you can easily add to a page. To add an invisible counter, you'll either need to code one yourself or subscribe to a service such as thecounter.com that offers site tracking. Many of these, including thecounter.com, offer free visible counters and paid hidden counters. Adding the counter to your site is as easy as copying the script code provided by the counter site to your web page. The counter site will explain the process when you obtain the counter script.

NOTE In most cases, you don't need to add Perl/CGI support to the web server to support a counter. The exception is when the script is written as a Perl script.

Using Perl and Other Server-Side Applications

In some situations you might want to add the ability for your server to process CGI or Perl scripts. For example, maybe you would like to host a bulletin board such as the one offered at www.ikonboard.com. Or perhaps you want to have the clients enter information in a form and have that form e-mailed to you. There are lots of great scripts out there that you can use on your web server, but you need to add script support to your server.

One of the best options is to use ActivePerl, available from `www.activestate.com`. ActivePerl is free for both commercial and noncommercial use.

When you install ActivePerl, Setup creates the necessary application association to handle scripts with a PL extension. If you want to handle scripts with a CGI extension, you need to modify the site's configuration. Open the IIS console and open the properties for the site. Click the Home Directory tab and click Configuration to open the Application Configuration dialog box. Click Add to open the Add/Edit Application Extension Mapping dialog box (Figure 37.15). Enter

```
C:\Perl\bin\Perl.exe "%s" %s
```

in the Executable field and then enter **.cgi** in the Extension field. Enter **GET,HEAD,POST** in the Limit To field, and click OK.

FIGURE 37.15:

Use the Add/Edit Application Extension Mapping dialog box to add a mapping for CGI scripts.

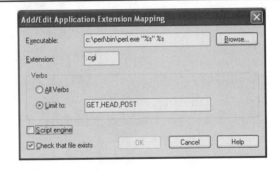

NOTE   Change the path to `Perl.exe` if you installed ActivePerl in a different folder.

After you install Perl and configure the site, create a folder—either physical or virtual—named `cgi-bin`. You can use a different name if you prefer, but this is the most commonly used name. Then place your custom scripts in this folder. Many commercial scripts use their own folder structure, so you can create their folders either under the root of your website or as a subfolder under the `cgi-bin` folder.

Generally, you also need to modify the scripts to specify the path to the script root, as well as specify the path to the Perl interpreter. If you installed ActivePerl in the default location, the path to Perl is `c:/perl/perl.exe`. Change this path in your scripts as needed. The path is specified most often in the first line of the script.

E-Mailing Form Results

One function you might want to perform is to e-mail the contents of a form to someone, whether to yourself or someone else. For example, you might use a form to allow clients to request information about a service, get support, or provide feedback on the site. How you accomplish this bit of magic depends on your development platform.

E-Mail Forms from FrontPage

If you create the site in FrontPage, it's relatively easy to set up a form for e-mail submission. Create the form, the right-click the form and choose Form Properties (Figure 37.16). Choose the Send To option and then enter the target e-mail address in the E-Mail Address field. You can also have the form sent to a file specified by the URL in the File Name field. Clear this field if you only want the form submitted by e-mail.

FIGURE 37.16:

Use the Form Proper-
ties dialog box to con-
figure the target e-mail
address.

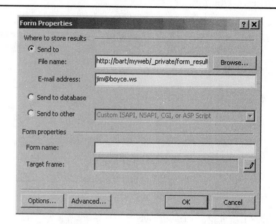

Next, click Options to open the Saving Results dialog box, and then click the E-Mail Results tab (Figure 37.17). Choose the format for the message from the E-Mail Format drop-down list. Select the option Include Field Names if you want FrontPage to include the field name for each field in the message along with the form content. Specify the subject for the message in the Subject Line field and the reply address in the Reply-To-Line field.

Configure form e-mail
properties through the
E-Mail Results tab.

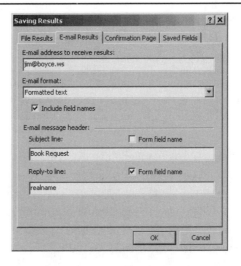

You can perform additional functions through FrontPage with the form. For example, you can redirect the user to a confirmation page after they submit the form. You can also retain values from the form to use elsewhere (such as in the confirmation page). Check the FrontPage documentation, or *Mastering Microsoft FrontPage 2002 Premium Edition* (by Peter Weverka and Molly E. Holzschlag; Sybex, 2001), for more information on using forms in FrontPage.

E-Mail from Non-FrontPage Sites

One of the most popular tools for e-mailing forms on non-FrontPage servers is FormMail, developed by Matt Wright (`www.worldwidemart.com/scripts`). You can use the `formmail.pl` script without charge provided you retain the copyright information and attribution in the script.

On Unix systems, `formmail.pl` relies on the Unix sendmail program to send the message. Windows XP systems don't have sendmail, so you need to take a little different route. There are a handful of different solutions available to you. You can create your own script to send the message through the SMTP service on the server or on a different server. For a sample script and additional information to help you create such a script, see the Microsoft Knowledge Base article Q221495:

```
http://support.microsoft.com/default.aspx?scid=kb;en-us;Q221495
```

The option I prefer is to use a third-party e-mail utility on the computer and use a modified version of `formmail.pl`. There are a few different e-mail utilities but the one I typically use is Blat, which is free. You'll find Blat on the companion CD and at

```
http://www.interlog.com/~tcharron/blat.html
```

To install Blat, copy the `Blat.exe` program executable to the `%systemroot%` folder on the Windows XP Professional computer that is acting as the web server. Then, open a command console on the server and execute the following command to install and configure Blat:

```
Blat -install server sender
```

Replace *server* with the IP address or fully qualified domain name of the SMTP server to be used for sending the e-mail. Replace *sender* with the e-mail address you want Blat to use by default as the sender for the e-mail. To view other options, type **Blat** without any other options or parameters.

Next, you need to obtain and install a copy of `formmail.pl` that has been customized to use Blat. You'll find just such a copy of `formmail.pl` on the *Windows XP Power Tools* CD. Copy the script to your web server's script folder (typically `cgi-bin`). Then, create the form and include the following hidden form fields:

recipient   Specify the e-mail address to which you want the form to be mailed. The following is sample HTML code for the tag:

```
<input type="hidden" name="recipient" value="jim@boyce.ws">
```

required   Specify the names of fields on the form that must be filled in by the user. Typically this includes the user's e-mail address and name, but it can include other fields, as well. Separate the fields by commas, as in the following example:

```
<input type="hidden" name="required" value="realname,email">
```

subject   This field specifies the subject for the e-mail. The following is an example:

```
<input type="hidden" name="subject" value="Book Request">
```

title   This is the title for the confirmation page that the script displays when the message has been sent. The following is an example:

```
<input type="hidden" name="title" value="Thanks for your request!">
```

Add any other fields to the form (as visible fields) that you want included in the message. Then specify POST as the method for the form, and specify the path to `formmail.pl` as the action. For example, you would specify `cgi-bin/formmail.pl` if the `formmail.pl` script is located in the site's `cgi-bin` folder. When the user clicks the Submit button, the form contents are processed by FormMail.

CHAPTER 38

FrontPage Server Extensions

The FrontPage Server Extensions, the 2000 version of which are installed by default as a part of Internet Information Services (IIS) setup, are a set of several server-side programs whose routines perform a variety of useful tasks. These routines let website authors use FrontPage to easily design not only simple, static, web pages, but also more robust web content such as forms, discussion threads, hit counters, and full-text searching. Further, FrontPage Server Extensions allow authors to update the contents of a site directly from the FrontPage interface. Without the server extensions, you must write complex server-side code to incorporate many advanced features.

You can install FrontPage Server Extensions on all popular operating systems—including Windows NT Server, Digital Unix, Sun's Solaris, and, naturally, XP Professional—which allows for cross-platform web server compatibility. The server extensions also support most popular web server software packages, including IIS, Netscape, and WebSite, as well as freeware and shareware web servers such as Stronghold from RedHat. Thus, a great degree of flexibility is built-in when installing these extensions.

One place you should visit right away if you are working with FrontPage (or if you are working with a web developer who is) is Microsoft's FrontPage website at `www.microsoft.com/frontpage`. From there, you can download and install the latest versions of the FrontPage Server Extensions. The most recent version, at the time of this writing, is 2002.

Why FrontPage Extensions?

As mentioned, the FrontPage Server Extensions make it easy for web authors to take web design beyond online brochureware (this is not a word you will find in Webster's; I think we all know one of these sites when we see one, however). In addition, the extensions let website administrators support that increased functionality. The server extensions do the following:

- Let authors collaborate to create and maintain a website

- Let authors edit a website directly on the server computer (saving download time)
- Let authors easily add functions to a website, without doing any programming
- Support hit counters, full-text searches, e-mail form-handling, and other functions that an author can add to a website by using FrontPage
- Work across a number of popular server platforms, such as Windows NT and Unix, as well as on many web server products, as mentioned earlier
- Automatically update hyperlinks after a page in a website is moved, deleted, or renamed (only the page's filename, rather than the entire file, needs to be transmitted to the web server)

TIP   If you have used FrontPage, you probably noticed that publishing a single change to a site can take a long time. So even though the process of publishing directly from FrontPage is easy, you can streamline this procedure somewhat. To do so, create a Web folder on your FrontPage extended web, and use it to publish a single page or only a couple of pages to your server.

You can use several tools to maintain and manipulate the behavior of the FrontPage Server Extensions. If you are installing the extensions on a Windows server (at the time of this writing, the .NET server products were yet to be released in their final versions), you will almost certainly use the FrontPage MMC (Microsoft Management Console) snap-in. With it, you can do the following:

- Extend a virtual server with the FrontPage Server Extensions
- Check and fix the FrontPage Server Extensions on a website
- Upgrade the FrontPage Server Extensions on a web site
- Remove the FrontPage Server Extensions from a website
- Delete a subweb that you have extended with the FrontPage Server Extensions
- Convert a subweb into a folder, and vice versa
- Recalculate all hyperlinks in a web
- Add an administrator
- Enable or disable authoring on a web
- Tune web performance
- Log authoring operations
- Require Secure Sockets Layer (SSL) for authoring

- Specify that a folder can contain executable scripts or programs
- Enable source control
- Set e-mail options

NOTE   We'll look at the FrontPage MMC snap-in in the next section.

You cannot, however, perform the following tasks with the snap-in:

- Administer the FrontPage Server Extensions from a remote computer (use the `fpremadm` utility instead)
- Write command-line scripts (use the `fpsrvadm` utility instead)

We'll look at the `fpremadm` and `fpsrvadm` utilities in detail in the next section.

As you can see, the list of capabilities that the FrontPage Server Extensions provide is extensive. They will almost certainly be part of any site that is designed with FrontPage. Even if you don't use all of them, it is probably worth your while to download and install them on any web server that will be publishing FrontPage material. So, is there any reason you *wouldn't* want to use the FrontPage Server Extensions? Well, yes. In a word, there is no reason to install the extensions if you are not using FrontPage to author your site.

The FrontPage MMC and Other Administrative Tools

The FrontPage MMC snap-in provides a graphical interface that you can use to easily administer the FrontPage Server Extensions. It replaces and significantly improves on the `fpsrvwin.exe` utility, which was an administrative program with a graphical interface that was included with previous versions of FrontPage. However, the FrontPage MMC snap-in runs only on Windows operating systems, and as mentioned, one drawback is that you cannot use it to administer the server extensions from a remote computer. You have to be physically sitting at the server, which is sometimes impractical.

But the FrontPage MMC snap-in is only one of several tools available for administering the FrontPage Server Extensions. Three other tools provide almost the same functionality as the FrontPage MMC snap-in and can operate in environments where the snap-in can't:

- The `fpsrvadm.exe` utility is a command-line program that you can use on XP, Windows NT, and various Unix operating systems. You can use this utility to write command-line scripts. Fpsrvadm is installed automatically when you install the FrontPage Server Extensions, so even if you use the FrontPage MMC snap-in exclusively, it is still there. You cannot use `fpsrvadm.exe` to administer the server extensions from a remote computer.

- The `fpremadm.exe` utility is a command-line program you use to administer the FrontPage Server Extensions from a remote computer. However, `fpremadm` runs only on Windows-based operating systems: Windows XP, 2000 Professional and Server, Windows NT Workstation, Windows NT Server, and Windows 95/98 operating systems, but not on Unix operating systems such as Linux and Sun's Solaris. The `fpremadm` utility is also installed automatically when you install the FrontPage Server Extensions.

- You can also administer the extensions using HTML Administration Forms. This program allow you to remotely administer the FrontPage Server Extensions from a web browser. Future updates to the FrontPage Server Extensions, including the just-released 2002 version, will rely more heavily on HTML forms.

If you work with both IIS and other web servers—such as WebSite or Netscape—you may be aware that the FrontPage Server Extensions 2002 MMC snap-in works differently with IIS 4 or later than it does with the other web servers, including IIS 3.

IIS 4 or later includes a snap-in that snaps in to the MMC. The FrontPage MMC snap-in is constructed so that it snaps into the snap-in of IIS 4 or later. If IIS 4 or later is installed on a computer, the FrontPage snap-in functionality is fully integrated with that of IIS.

If you have worked with the IIS MMC snap-in, you may notice that in the FrontPage Server Extensions MMC snap-in (choose Start ➤ All Programs ➤ Administrative Tools ➤ Server Extensions Administrator) some commands have been added to the Action and shortcut menus and that a Server Extensions tab has been added to the Properties dialog box. The FrontPage Server Extensions MMC snap-in has added this new functionality. If there is overlapping functionality, the IIS command appears, not the FrontPage Server Extensions snap-in command. In the console tree, IIS lists all IIS websites, both FrontPage extended as well as other websites.

If, however, the FrontPage Server Extensions MMC snap-in is installed with a web server other than IIS 4 or later, its functionality is not integrated with that of the web server; in fact, the web server might not even have an MMC snap-in that adds its functionality to the console. In such a case, the console tree lists only FrontPage-extended webs; it does not list all the websites on the computer.

Because web servers are just software applications that make information available using the HTTP protocol, it is quite possible to have more than one web server running on a single machine. In this event, you will see a top-level item for each web server, with its websites listed below it. When you select a site that's on the IIS 4 or later web server and then display the shortcut menu, you see the IIS snap-in commands along with the FrontPage snap-in commands. However, when you select a website that is published with non-IIS web server software and then display the shortcut menu, the commands for administering the FrontPage Server Extensions are contributed by the FrontPage MMC snap-in only.

Installing and Configuring FrontPage Server Extensions

IIS administrators already know this: FrontPage information and capabilities are always rapidly evolving. For exhaustive administrative information about the FrontPage Server Extensions, take a look at the FrontPage Server Extensions Administration Guide, which is at `www.microsoft.com/frontpage/`. Much of the information that was previously included in the Resource Kit is now included in the TechNet area of Microsoft's website.

The FrontPage website is also one of the first places you should visit to get the correct version of the FrontPage Server Extensions for the version of FrontPage you are using. Installing the extensions is simply a matter of locating the correct download from the Front-Page site and then installing the executable file. If you have downloaded and installed anything before, you won't have any problem with this procedure.

And, as you'll see, certain FrontPage Server Extensions are installed automatically depending on which web server version you are running. Installing IIS 5, for example, automatically installs the FrontPage Server Extensions 2000 by default at setup time.

If you installed the FrontPage Server Extensions 2000 on your computer, you can access extensive help information, including overviews and descriptions of administrative techniques. This help file is installed by default at

```
C:\Program Files\Common Files\Microsoft Shared\Web Server Extensions\40\bin\
nnnn\Fpmmc.chm
```

The *nnnn* folder has a numeric name based on the installation language. You don't need to memorize the number, but you should know what you are looking at. For example, in a U.S. English installation, the path is

```
C:\Program Files\Common Files\Microsoft Shared\Web Server Extensions\40\bin\
1033\Fpmmc.chm
```

After you install the FrontPage Server Extensions, you don't administer them directly. Rather, you use one of several tools, whose functionality overlaps. Which tool you use depends on which version of the extensions you are using and/or which settings you are trying to change. If you installed the FrontPage 2000 Server Extensions, one of those tools is the FrontPage Server Extensions MMC snap-in, which is shown in Figure 38.1. This pre-configured MMC snap-in is added to the Administrative tools Menu, as mentioned earlier.

If, on the other hand, you installed FrontPage Server Extensions 2002, you will most likely be performing your administration via a web page. After installation, a shortcut to the Server Administration web page, Microsoft SharePoint Administrator, is placed in the Administrative Tools section of the Start menu. (I'm assuming that as a good power user you configured the Administrative Tools to appear on the Start menu.) Figure 38.2 shows the Server Administration page.

FIGURE 38.1:

You control much of
the behavior of the
extensions using the
FrontPage Server
Extensions MMC
snap-in.

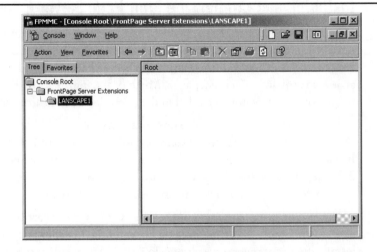

FIGURE 38.2:

Use the Server Adminis-
tration page to adminis-
ter FrontPage Server
Extensions 2002.

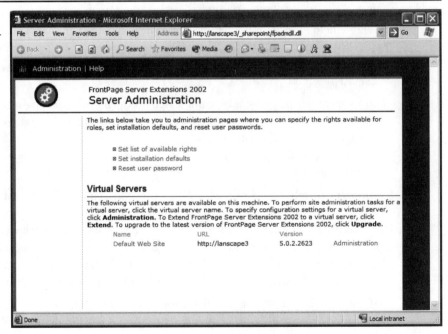

Using the Server Administration page, configuration is simply a matter of following hyperlinks; there is really no administrative tool to learn. For example, if you want to allow (the
default behavior) or disallow anonymous access to the site, click the Change Anonymous
Access Settings to open the page shown in Figure 38.3.

FIGURE 38.3:

Use the options on
this page to toggle
anonymous access.

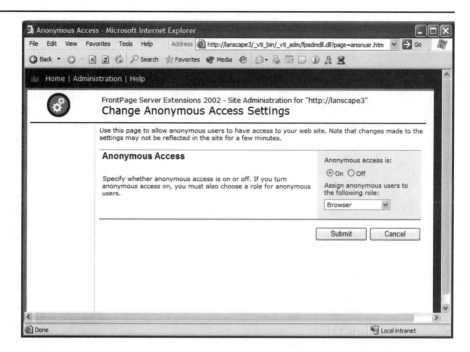

On the Server Administration page, click Help to open the Site Administration Help page, which is shown in Figure 38.4. Clicking the How Do I link on the Site Administration Help page displays a menu of step-by step instructions for performing certain tasks. For example, if you want to create a subweb in FrontPage, simply expand the Manage Webs And Subwebs topic, click the Create A Subweb link, and follow the instructions.

Using Web Folders

Is it possible to develop a web page in FrontPage even if the web server you are publishing to does not have the FrontPage Server Extensions installed? Absolutely, but you should remember a few caveats.

If the FrontPage Server Extensions are not available on the target web server, you can use FrontPage to develop your web pages and publish them to the server using any FTP program or using Web Folders. You'll be able to use Web Folders if the server you're publishing to supports WebDAV (Web Distributed Authoring and Versioning). Web Folders is Microsoft's implementation of WebDAV on the client side. It's a protocol that allows clients to transparently publish content to the Web, just as if they were moving content from one folder to another on their own computer. WebDAV is a cousin of the HTTP 1.1 protocol and offers several features that make it more secure than using the older FTP protocol.

Help on using the
FrontPage Server
Extensions 2002 is
always only a few
clicks away.

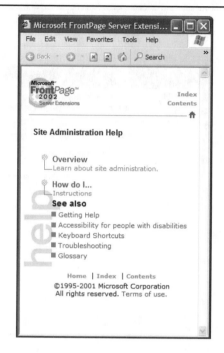

When you use Web Folders, publishing web content becomes as easy as copying files to a location in Windows Explorer, as you will see shortly. The process is similar to mapping a network drive. You copy content to a mapped drive, and then it is copied to a file server somewhere, without the end user necessarily being aware of what's happening under the hood.

For example, you can develop a website using FrontPage and then use Personal Web Server on your XP computer to transfer the web content to the target web server using Web Folders. Keep in mind that you may lose some features or experience some incompatibilities between your working server and the target server.

To create a Web Folder for the purpose of uploading files to be published a web server, follow these steps:

1. Open My Network places, and in the Network Tasks pane, click Add A Network Place to start the Add Network Place Wizard.

2. At the Welcome screen, click Next to open the Where Do You Want To Create This Network Place? screen.

3. Specify the address of a website, a network location, or and FTP site, and click Next.

4. In the next screen, enter the address of a web server that supports Web Folders, and then click Next.

5. Give the shortcut a name, click Next, and then click Finish to complete the wizard.

You'll now see an icon in My Network Places for the shortcut you created.

Now Web Folders is ready to take content from your machine and send it to a web server. Follow these steps:

1. In Windows Explorer, select the document or folder that you want to publish.

2. In the File And Folder Tasks pane, click Copy This File or Copy This Folder to open the Copy Items dialog box.

3. Expand My Network Places, and then click the shortcut folder you just created for web content. Click Copy to compete the operation.

Now you can create content in FrontPage and publish it on a server that doesn't have the FrontPage Server Extensions installed. You can drag and drop files into your Web Folders to publish them to the server that the shortcut folder targets.

TIP You can use almost any FTP application to do the same. Many free graphical FTP applications are available at www.dowload.com.

TIP It is not necessary for all parties to use FrontPage when collaborating on web projects. Each member of the team can use the HTML editor of choice as long as they have Web Folders. By dragging and dropping individual files onto a shortcut Web Folder, each team member can work on pages and publish them without disturbing other work. More on other HTML editors later in this chapter.

Administering the FrontPage Server Extensions

Which FrontPage Server Extensions MMC snap-in menu, command, dialog box, or HTML page do you need to perform your task, and where do you find that particular item? The answer depends on which version of the extensions is installed.

Because the FrontPage 2002 Administrative HTML pages are so intuitive to use, it is better to focus on the FrontPage 2000 Server Extensions MMC snap-in. Here is a brief overview of the three main MMC components that you use to administer the 2000 FrontPage Server Extensions:

- The New menu, from which you can select commands to create a new website, add a new administrator, and so on, depending on the item you select in the console tree.

- The Task menu, from which you can select commands to check and fix, remove, and upgrade the FrontPage Server Extensions, as well as perform other tasks. Again, the item you select in the console tree determines which commands appear on the Task menu.

- The Server Extensions tab, which includes option you can choose to modify the settings of the FrontPage Server Extensions, such as e-mail and security.

With these extensions in place, you'll be able to govern the behavior of the following FrontPage capabilities that *require* FrontPage Server Extensions:

- The Database Results Wizard
- Send To Database Form Handler
- Nested Subwebs
- Lightweight Source Control (Document Check-in/Check-out without VSS)
- Categories Component
- Style Sheet links to multiple files or ASP files

Alternatives to FrontPage

To author a website, all you have to do is be able to write HTML code. You can begin by using an ASCII text editor such as Notepad and design all your sites this way. But you're not quite up to speed in your HTML, you say?

Not to worry. Lots of programs are adept at handling HTML on your behalf. You might be familiar with such graphical code-generating programs if you have ever worked with Microsoft Access, which generates SQL queries in the background as you drag and drop queries against tables. These web-authoring programs are known as WYSIWYG (pronounced "wizzy-wig") editors because What You See (as you are building the web page in the application) Is What You Get (when the HTML code is finally viewed in a web browser).

Most dedicated web designers (good ones, anyway) are fluent in HTML and can edit the HTML code directly. However, many web-authoring applications (including FrontPage) can write HTML code under the hood while you are busy adding graphics, text, or other content, letting you focus on the look and feel rather than the programming of the site.

Moreover, some programs can save content especially for distribution on the web, that is, in HTML format, even if they are not designed exclusively for this purpose. An example is Microsoft Word. When you create a document in Word, you can save the document with an .html extension rather than the default .doc extension. Doing so turns the document into a web page, encapsulating the contents within HTML tags, ready for display in a browser.

Keep in mind, though, that this is a quick-and-dirty way to create web content; the HTML code generated by programs not designed for that purpose tends to be sloppy. The number of unnecessary lines of code makes experienced web designers cringe as though undergoing a root canal.

Following are descriptions of several programs that are better suited (than Word and its relatives) for creating HTML, and they are alternatives to FrontPage. Which is best? All of them, according to the companies that sell them. Evaluation copies of many of these programs are available at the company's website.

HomeSite   A full-featured web page editor from Allaire Software. An evaluation copy is available at `www.macromedia.com/software/homesite`.

HotDog Professional   An HTML authoring tool that features enhancements such as the HTML Property Sheet (which provides access to every attribute for the current tag), tag completion and error highlighting, and wizards for obscure and otherwise exhausting tasks. You can download an evaluation copy at `www.sausagetools.com`.

Cool Page 2.7   A design tool that you can use to create a page simply by dragging and dropping objects into a layout. It also features a Publish button that lets you automatically upload your site to the Internet. Pages designed with Cool Page are compatible with Netscape, Internet Explorer, and the AOL browser. Cool Page has unlimited undo and redo capabilities that allow you to go back to how your page looked at any point in the design process. You can download Cool Page at `www.coolpage.com`.

HoTMetaL Pro   A versatile website authoring tool that lets you learn HTML with study aids and then take advantage of professional features to create sites. If you're creating your first website, the Site Maker can help you build it automatically, or you can try the WYSI-WYG editor. HoTMetaL Pro includes a host of learning tools: context-sensitive tag help, an HTML self-study course, a JavaScript self-study course, HTML and CSS reference guides, and validation and authoring tools. You can find HoTMetaL Pro at `www.softquad.com`.

Netscape Composer   A website editor that is part of the Netscape Communicator suite of programs (including the web browser, Navigator, which in my opinion is one of the most significant inventions of the last 25 years). You can download Composer at `www.netscape.com`.

Dreamweaver   Probably the most popular WYSIWYG web authoring program today, it is available from Macromedia. You can use Dreamweaver to easily include content from other Macromedia programs, such as Flash animations. Macromedia also makes Fireworks, which, unlike other graphics programs, is specifically designed to create and optimize graphics for the web.

GoLive 6   A program from Adobe software, makers of the popular graphics application Photoshop. GoLive 6 lets you quickly design, build, manage, and deploy dynamic content for the Web. GoLive also includes the new Adobe Web Workgroup Server, which offers additional asset management features such as version control. You can try out GoLive at `www.adobe.com`.

CHAPTER 39

Hosting FTP Sites

Internet Information Services (IIS) in Windows XP Professional includes an FTP service that you can use to exchange files with other users. FTP stands for File Transfer Protocol and is an Internet standard. Not too long ago, FTP was the primary means for making files available to other users across the Internet. Today, HTTP is rapidly replacing FTP as the method of choice for publishing files on the Internet. When you link to a file on a web page, far more often than not it's an HTTP link to the file rather than an FTP link.

Even though HTTP is more common for file sharing, FTP is still an important service and an attractive alternative to HTTP, particularly when you need to share a relatively large number of files (particularly binary files). When you set up an FTP site, you only need to create the folder structure under the service and place files in the folders—you don't need to create individual links on a page to each file. With HTTP, you need to either create individual links or enable directory browsing for a folder.

FTP is also a primary means for publishing websites for non-FrontPage servers. All web development platforms—including FrontPage—support FTP as a publishing method. So, if you are using any development tool other than FrontPage, it's a good bet that you will need to set up the FTP service on the server if for no other reason than to publish your website.

This chapter explains how to install and configure the FTP service under Windows XP Professional, set up an FTP site, and provide security for the site. I also offer a few tips for handling a few potential problems you might run across, as well as how to access the FTP site from the client side.

Hosting an FTP Site

Setup does not install the FTP service by default when you install Internet Information Services (IIS), unless you explicitly select the FTP service during installation. To add the FTP service, open the Add Or Remove Programs item in Control Panel and click Add/Remove Windows Components. Expand IIS in the component list and select FTP, and then follow the remaining prompts to install the service. With the service installed, you can begin setting up your FTP site.

Configuring the Default FTP Site

When you install the FTP service, Setup automatically creates a default FTP site. As I explained in Chapter 37, you can use the IISADMIN scripts from a Windows 2000 or Windows .NET Server installation of IIS to create additional FTP sites on a Windows XP Professional computer. However, you can only run one site at a time, so there isn't a lot of utility in creating multiple FTP sites. Although you could create a new site, it's easier to modify the existing site to suit your needs.

TIP   If you need to host multiple FTP sites, switch to Windows 2000 Server, Windows .NET Server, or a third-party FTP hosting application.

To configure the site, open the IIS console (Figure 39.1), right-click the default FTP site, and choose Properties.

FIGURE 39.1:

Use the IIS console to manage your FTP site.

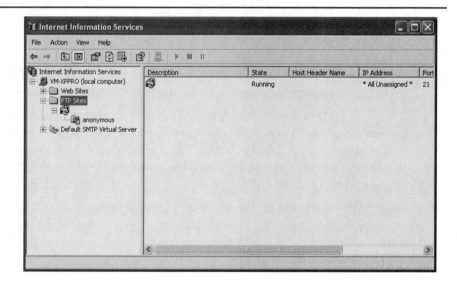

Configuring General Properties

Use the FTP Site tab (Figure 39.2) to configure the site's general properties. The Identification group of controls lets you specify the name for the site as it appears in the IIS console, the IP address it will use, and the TCP port. The default port is 21, and you should use a non-standard port only if clients know the port beforehand or if you create a link on a web page to the FTP site's URL that includes the port. An example of an FTP URL that includes the port number is `ftp://ftp.boyce.ws:10000`.

FIGURE 39.2:

The FTP Site tab controls the general settings for the site.

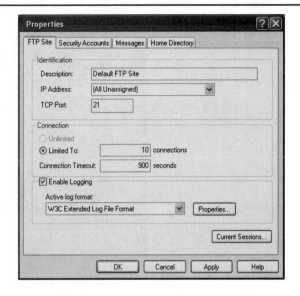

TIP Generally the only reason to use a nonstandard port is if you have another service running on the computer that uses the standard port. This would be the case only if you are running another FTP server on the computer in addition to IIS.

The Connection group lets you specify the maximum number of connections and the connection timeout value. As with a website, Windows XP Professional is limited to 10 concurrent FTP connections, so the only reason to change the number of connections is to limit access to fewer users. The Connection Timeout value controls how long a connection can be inactive before IIS disconnects it, requiring the client to connect again. The default is 900 seconds, but you could consider decreasing the value if you have one or more clients who tend to time out frequently because of network problems. With only 10 available connections, you probably wouldn't want connections tied up because of timeout issues. However, if you set the timeout too low, IIS will drop connections unnecessarily. If you feel you're having problems with connections being unavailable due to timeout, consider decreasing the timeout value to 180 seconds (three minutes).

The Enable Logging option lets you turn on logging of FTP sessions. I recommend you turn on logging unless you do not provide public access to the FTP site, the site is available only to a limited number of people, and you are not concerned about security for the files and/or server. In all other cases, I recommend you turn on logging, if for no other reason than to provide an evidence trail that will allow you to prosecute someone who hacks into or abuses your system. You can choose between the IIS log file format and the extended W3C format, which offers additional formatting options. Select the desired format from the list and then click Properties to display the log properties shown in Figure 39.3.

FIGURE 39.3:

The General Properties tab configures the log frequency and path.

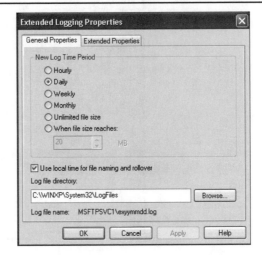

As Figure 39.3 illustrates, you can specify how frequently IIS creates a new log, choosing between log frequency and log file size. If you want to continue with a single log file indefinitely, select the Unlimited File Size option. However, you should periodically check the size of the log to make sure it isn't growing out of control. IIS can log a lot of data in a file without making it overly large, but you should monitor the log file anyway. When the log grows uncomfortably large (takes a long time to load in WordPad, for example), write it to a CD-R or other removable media.

If you choose the W3C log format, IIS displays an additional Extended Properties tab for the log (Figure 39.4). IIS by default logs only certain information about each session. You can choose the Extended Properties option and select additional items to include in the log. I recommend that you at least include the user name in the log if you are providing non-anonymous FTP services, giving you the ability to track who is using the FTP server and when.

Viewing Current Connections

IIS gives you the ability to view the current connections to the FTP server, as well as to disconnect specific users. To view current connections, open the properties for the FTP site in the IIS console and, on the FTP Site tab, click Current Sessions to display a dialog box similar to the one shown in Figure 39.5. If you enable authenticated access to the FTP server, the user's logon name identifies the user. Otherwise, the password that the user enters for the anonymous account identifies the user.

FIGURE 39.4:

Use the Extended
Properties tab to
specify the log's
contents.

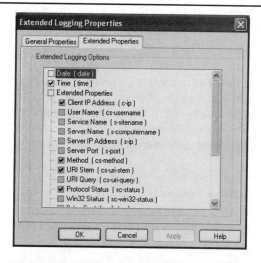

FIGURE 39.5:

Use the FTP User
Sessions dialog box
to view current user
sessions.

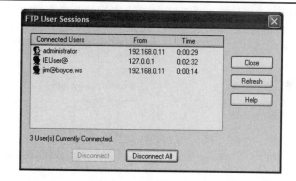

To disconnect a user, click the user in the list and click Disconnect. Or click Disconnect All to close all sessions. Keep in mind that file transfers that are active will be terminated (and incomplete) when you close the connections.

Configuring Authenticated and Anonymous Access

Like the World Wide Web service in IIS, the FTP service supports both anonymous and authenticated access. Also like the World Wide Web service, anonymous FTP access isn't truly anonymous in the sense that IIS uses the IUSR account I discussed in Chapter 37 to authenticate all anonymous users. So, while you might not know who an anonymous FTP user is—since they can provide a bogus e-mail address for the password when they log in— at least IIS is authenticating the access against an existing account.

You should configure the FTP service for anonymous access if you don't care who accesses the site and its files. If you want to maintain control over who has access and who doesn't, you should turn off anonymous access and rely on user accounts to protect your site.

NOTE   One reason to allow *only* anonymous access is to prevent users from logging onto the FTP server with an account that has administrative privileges. Administrative access could present a security risk to the computer and the files hosted on your FTP server, because an account with administrative privileges is likely to have full control over the folders and files, something you might not want.

To configure access methods for FTP, open the IIS console, right-click the Default FTP Site, and choose Properties. Click the Security Accounts tab (Figure 39.6). Select the option Allow Anonymous Connections if you want to allow anonymous users to access the FTP site. This option does not prevent users from logging on with a different, valid user account, however. If you want to prevent users from logging on with anything other than the computer's IUSR account (anonymous access), also select the option Allow Only Anonymous Connections. IIS will then reject any attempts to connect using any user name other than anonymous.

FIGURE 39.6:

Configure access with the Security Accounts tab.

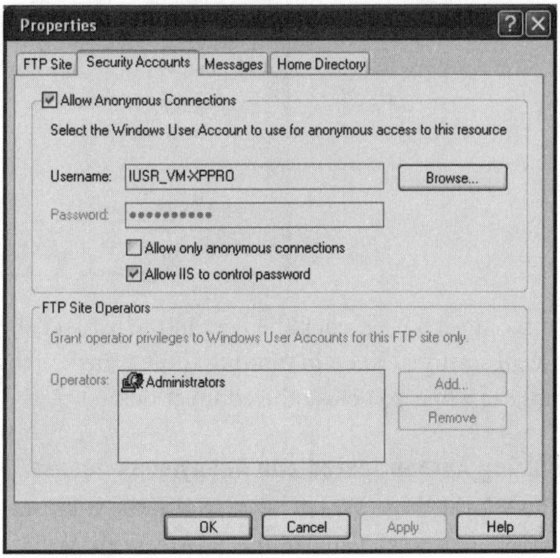

If you want to prevent anonymous access to the site, clear the option Allow Anonymous Connections. Users must then provide a valid local account with the necessary rights to log onto the FTP site (explained shortly).

TIP   Although you could change the account that the FTP service uses for anonymous logon, I don't recommend it. Leave the default IUSR account in place and allow IIS to control the password (through the option of the same name).

For remote users to connect to the FTP service, the account they provide must have the right to log on locally. Setup grants the IUSR account this right when you install IIS. You need to grant this right to any other accounts that are authorized to use the FTP service. You could assign the right on a per-user basis, but I recommend you create a local group named ftp-users (or something similar), grant this group the right to log on locally, and then add accounts to the group as needed.

To create the FTP group, open the Computer Management console and expand the Local Users and Groups branch. Right-click the Groups node and choose New Group to open the New Group dialog box. Specify the group name and then click Add to add local accounts to the group. After populating the group, click Create, then close the dialog box.

After you create and populate the group, you need to grant it the right to log on locally as I mentioned before. Open the Local Security Policy from the Administrative Tools folder. Expand the branch \Security Settings\Local Policies\User Rights Assignment, and then double-click the Log On Locally right to display the Log On Locally Properties dialog box. Click Add User Or Group, enter the name of the group you just created, and click OK. If you want to browse for the group, click Object Types, place a check beside Groups, and click OK. Click Advanced and search for the recently created FTP users group, then close the dialog box and the policy editor.

Now it's time to test the FTP service. You don't need to log on from another computer. Just open a command console and type **ftp localhost**. Or enter **ftp** and, at the `ftp>` prompt, type **open localhost**. Enter the necessary account credentials when prompted. If the logon fails, verify the account credentials and check that the account is included in the local ftp-users group. Also check the methods you've allowed for authentication on the FTP server, then try again.

SEE ALSO   You can use the `ftp` command from a console to perform all FTP client tasks. You can also use a web browser or one of several third-party FTP utilities. See the latter sections of this chapter for information on using Internet Explorer and third-party applications.

Although the Security Accounts tab contains an FTP Site Operators control group, you can't modify the list of operators for the site. Operators have the ability to make certain changes to a site but not to IIS general settings or settings that apply to the server as a whole. By default, IIS adds the Administrators group to the list. You must use Windows 2000 Server or Windows .NET Server platforms if you need to control operators on a more granular level.

Controlling operator access on a Windows XP Professional computer isn't really necessary anyway, because you can host only one site. Nevertheless, it would be nice to be able to designate a different user as an operator to offload some of the administrative tasks for FTP. Perhaps Microsoft will add this capability in the future.

Configuring Welcome, Exit, and Maximum Connections Messages

You can customize your FTP server to present custom messages to clients when they log on and off the FTP server, or when they attempt to log on but no more connections are available. For example, you might want to add a legal disclaimer to your welcome banner that informs the user that the site is monitored for unlawful use, violators will be prosecuted, and so on. Or maybe you just want to offer a friendly greeting to anyone connecting to the site.

Open the properties for the FTP site and click the Messages tab (Figure 39.7). In the Banner text box, type the text that you want the user to see prior to logging on. Enter in the Welcome text box the message you want displayed following successful authentication. In the Exit box, type the text the user should see when they log off. Enter in the Maximum Connections box the text the FTP server should display when there are no more available connections.

FIGURE 39.7:

Configure FTP service messages through the Messages tab.

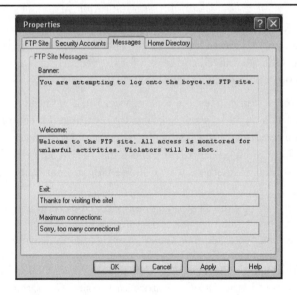

Configuring the Home Directory

The last tab in the FTP site's properties—Home Directory (Figure 39.8)—lets you specify the location of the FTP site's root folder. This is the folder in which anonymous users are placed, and the folder in which authenticated users are placed if they have no home directory (see the next section).

As Figure 39.8 illustrates, you can specify a local folder or a network share on a remote computer as the root for the FTP site. Specifying a network share lets your computer function as the entry point to the site but allows the files to actually be hosted on a different server. For example, you might place the root folder on a server that gets backed up regularly to ensure availability of your FTP files in the event your computer suffers a catastrophic failure.

FIGURE 39.8:

Use the Home Directory tab to specify the location of the site's root folder.

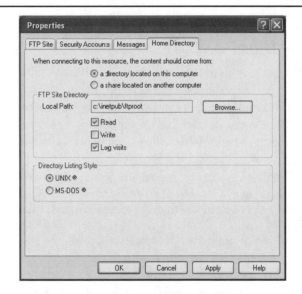

The Home Directory tab also controls the general permissions for the site. You can allow Read or Write access, or a combination of the two. Enable Read access to allow users to download files; enable Write access to allow them to upload files. Then, use NTFS permissions on individual folders to control read/write ability on a more granular basis.

The Directory Listing Style group controls how directory listings appear to remote users when they use the dir command from an ftp console or when they browse a directory using a web browser or graphical FTP client. Select the Unix option to display permissions and other directory information in Unix format, similar to what you would see when listing a directory on a Unix computer with the ls command. Select the MS-DOS option if you want the directory to look similar to the results of a dir command in a command console on a Windows-based system.

TIP   Although it won't keep persistent and skilled hackers from determining that your FTP server is running IIS, setting the directory method to Unix will at least slow down casual hackers from figuring out your server platform. The less they know about your server, the more difficult it is for them to exploit it.

Placing Users in a Specific Directory at Logon

One handy feature provided by IIS for FTP is that it checks for a folder name that matches the user's credentials during logon and, if it finds a match, places the user in that folder after authentication. For example, if I log onto the account with the user name jboyce, and the FTP server contains a folder, either physical or virtual, named jboyce, that folder becomes my initial folder after I log in.

You can use this feature in a couple of ways as it suits your needs. First, you can use it to quickly direct remote users to their own folders. Create a virtual directory for each FTP client and configure the permissions as necessary on each folder to provide the desired security. Make sure to set the alias for the directory to match the user's logon name. When the user logs on, he is automatically placed in his "home" directory.

TIP   This little trick works for the anonymous account, as well. Create a virtual directory with the alias anonymous, and when anonymous users log on, they are placed in that folder initially. This is a good way to direct anonymous users to specific content.

You can also use virtual directories to provide specific types of content. For example, you might create virtual directories with the aliases drivers, documents, tools, and so on. Users could then log on with a generic user name (assuming you've created a matching account) and immediately be directed to the associated content.

Adding Virtual Directories

The directory specified in the Home Directory tab of the FTP site's properties specifies the root directory for the FTP site's overall folder structure. If you create physical subfolders under the specified root, the remote users also see these folders as subfolders under the root. Your site isn't limited to physical folders, however. You can also create *virtual directories*.

A virtual directory is assigned an alias that serves as the client-side folder name—the folder name the user sees when connecting to the folder. When users connect to a virtual directory, IIS redirects them to the actual folder, whether it's located on the same computer or on a network share. The user, however, doesn't see the virtual directories when browsing the FTP site. For example, assume your FTP site has its root folder at c:\inetpub\ftproot. This folder has no physical subfolders. Also assume that the user connects with the anonymous account and there is no virtual directory named anonymous. So, IIS places the user in the site's root folder. But the user sees only the contents of the root folder—there are no other folders visible, because the virtual folders are not enumerated.

There are a handful of ways for the user to wind up in a virtual folder:

Alias-to-account mapping   The user logs on with a user name that matches the virtual directory's alias.

Specify the alias with the cd command   The user is working from an FTP console and uses the cd *alias* command to switch directories, where *alias* is the virtual directory alias.

Specify the alias in the URL   The user includes the virtual directory alias in the connection URL, such as ftp://ftp.boyce.ws/doorknobs. In this case, doorknobs is the virtual directory alias.

Specify the alias as the initial folder in an FTP client   Most third-party FTP clients let you specify the initial folder for the connection and automatically place you in the folder after authentication.

To create a virtual directory, open the IIS console, right-click the FTP site, and choose New ➤ Virtual Directory to start the Virtual Directory Creation Wizard. The wizard prompts for the alias, the actual path to the folder (which can be a local drive or UNC path), and the desired permissions for the folder. If you specify a UNC path, IIS prompts you for the user credentials it must use to connect to the remote share.

TIP   You can create multiple levels of virtual directories. When creating the directory, right-click the folder that will serve as the root of the virtual directory.

Providing Site Security

I've already touched a bit on site security in my discussion of authentication. Given the 10-connection limit of Windows XP Professional, I assume that you are using Windows XP to host an FTP site on an internal network rather than the public Internet. However, if you are using it to provide FTP services to the public, I then have to assume that you are providing files to friends and family rather than the public at large. Otherwise, you should be using a server platform without a connection limit.

I don't recommend that you allow anonymous access on an FTP server connected to the Internet unless you're prepared to have every nut from here to the next solar system putting files on your computer (more on this in the next section). Instead, grant access to people on an individual basis, either creating an account for each one or giving out the user name and password for a common account, but only after obtaining identifying information from each person.

Your other alternative is to give anonymous users Read access but only give Write access to users with a specific account. To accomplish this, first set up the FTP site's folders on an NTFS volume. Configure the site to allow anonymous and authenticated access as I explained earlier in this chapter. Then, configure NTFS permissions so that the IUSR account has only Read permission and the other accounts have Write permission. You can assign Write permission on an as-needed basis, or simply grant your FTP users group Write permission if everyone except anonymous users should have the ability to upload to the site.

> **TIP**   You can configure NTFS permissions on a per-folder basis, giving you lots of flexibility in the type of access each user will have.

Another important consideration is the location of your FTP root folder for the site. Make sure you place the root folder on an NTFS volume if at all possible, and don't use a folder that contains any sensitive system files. For example, *never* use the root of a system drive as the root of your FTP site. Also, avoid using the \Inetpub folder as the root, instead using the default \Inetpub\ftproot.

If you use FTP to publish your website to the server, you'll also need to set up a secure FTP virtual directory that points to the website's root folder. Make sure the site resides on an NTFS volume, and then configure the permissions on the folder and all subfolders so the publishing account has change permission in the folders.

> **TIP**   The IUSR account does not, by default, have explicit permissions in the \Inetpub folder or any of its subfolders. Instead, Windows XP grants the built-in Users group Read & Execute, List Folder Contents, and Read permissions. The IUSR account is implicitly a member of the Authenticated Users group, which is an explicit member of the Users group. This is why the IUSR account (and therefore anonymous users) can read files from the website.

One final bit of advice I offer is that you make sure to turn on logging through the FTP Site tab and select the W3C Extended Log File Format I described earlier in this chapter. Configure extended logging to include the source IP address, date and time, and user name. The date and time are as important as the IP address, because they give you a means to identify the remote user. The user's IP address could vary if he connects to the Internet through a dial-up connection, but the user's ISP can identify the user based on their connection logs. The IP address tells the ISP which port was used to log on to their service, and the date and time help them determine which user was on that port at the specified time.

Tips for Dealing with Miscreants

If you do open your FTP site to anonymous upload, I guarantee it won't be more than a few weeks at best before some joker (if not several) starts using your server to host pornography or other unwanted content. I forgot to turn off anonymous access when I set up one of my home servers, and I was the recipient of some questionable content within a matter of days. What's worse, the scum-sucking, bottom-feeding person who did it set up a corrupt folder structure that took me a few days to delete. Once I figured out the method they used, however, the solution was easy.

It's possible under certain circumstances to create folders that use reserved system names as the folder name. For example, you can create a folder called COM2 and place in it all the files you like. When you try to delete the folder, however, Windows XP will politely tell you that you can't delete the folder. That's one method that hackers and crackers use to put content on a system and prevent the average user from removing it without reformatting the volume (one reason to place your FTP site on its own disk drive or logical drive).

You can delete folders with reserved names using one of two methods. If the folder resides on an NTFS volume, open a command console and issue the command del with the folder name identified with at least one wildcard. To delete the folder LPT2, for example, use the command **del LPT?**.

If the folder or file resides on an NTFS partition, you need to take another approach. The Windows 2000 and Windows XP Resource Kits include a tool called RM.EXE. This is a POSIX application that allows you to remove folders and files, including those with reserved names. The following example would remove a file named COM1 from the c:\inetpub\ ftproot folder:

```
rm -d "//C/inetpub/ftproot/COM1"
```

As the sample illustrates, POSIX uses a path structure different from DOS / Windows. Also, POSIX commands are case sensitive, so enter the path using its actual case. In addition, the example assumes you have placed the RM.EXE executable in a folder that is on the current path.

If you need to remove an entire folder tree, use a command similar to the following, replacing the path with the appropriate path to the folder you want to delete:

```
rm -r "//C/Program Files/App"
```

Another method hackers use is to create a folder with an empty long file name. This makes it nearly impossible to delete the folder even with the rm command, because you can't use the cd command to change to a folder with an empty name. In most cases you can use the rm command to remove the entire folder tree, but in some cases you might want to preserve the tree and only delete the folder with the blank name. The trick is to use the folder's short name, not the long name, to delete the folder.

Open a command console and use the `cd` command to move to the folder that contains the blank-named subfolder. Type **dir /X** to view the short names for the items in the folder. Note the short name for the folder that has the blank long name. Then, use the `rm` command with this short name to delete the folder.

Finally, and perhaps most important, take to heart my suggestions about security in the previous section and make sure you actively monitor the FTP service's logs. If you find that someone has been abusing your FTP site, take whatever legal remedies you can against them. If nothing else, make sure to notify the remote user's ISP, if possible.

Third-Party FTP Applications

If you want to really simplify FTP, particularly for uploading and downloading multiple files and folders, consider using one of the many third-party FTP clients available on the Internet. These tools offer features such as easy file and folder handling, the ability to save a connections settings and connect to a server with a single click, the ability to restart an interrupted transfer, and much more.

A search of your favorite software download site (mine is `www.tucows.com`) will likely turn up at least a hundred FTP utilities of one kind or another, and probably more than that.

I've tried several FTP apps over the years, and while I can't say that these are necessarily the best, I have had good luck with them. We've included the following programs on the book's companion CD:

Vermillion FTP Daemon   You can use this program as an alternative to or in conjunction with IIS for FTP services. This FTP server is easy to configure and fully supports the FTP standard. It provides advanced features such as support for transfer restart, and it gives you the ability to use templates to define the time and conditions under which individual users or groups can connect and use the server. You can visit `www.arcanesoft.com` for more information.

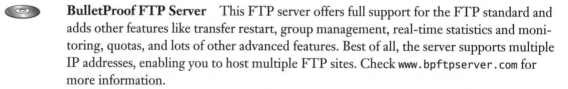

BulletProof FTP Server   This FTP server offers full support for the FTP standard and adds other features like transfer restart, group management, real-time statistics and monitoring, quotas, and lots of other advanced features. Best of all, the server supports multiple IP addresses, enabling you to host multiple FTP sites. Check `www.bpftpserver.com` for more information.

BulletProof FTP   The client version provides the typical graphical interface and adds a multiple-file download queue and the ability to restart interrupted downloads. The company's website is `www.bpftp.com`.

VShell   This server application functions as an alternative to Telnet and FTP for secure remote access and file transfer. This SSH2 server provides strong encryption and several other features to offer secure network access, remote administration, and file transfer. Because of the encryption used in the product, I couldn't include it on the CD, but you can get more information about it from www.vandyke.com/products/vshell/index.html.

Crystal FTP Pro   This FTP client includes all the usual features you would expect from an FTP client, and also lets you download up to eight files at a time while you continue to browse the FTP site. It includes a built-in Tetris game, but I could do without that. See www.casdk.com.

Internet Neighborhood   This FTP tool functions as a Windows shell addition rather than a standalone program. This means you can browse FTP sites through the standard Windows Explorer interface. The program supports transfer restart and lots of other handy features, such as the ability to save a file directly to an FTP site from an application. The company's website is in.deerfield.com.

CHAPTER 40

Setting Up a Telnet Server

Have you ever wished you could connect to a computer and manage it remotely, but didn't want to go through the expense of a third-party remote control application like pcAnywhere? Even though Windows XP now includes the ability to manage a remote computer through Remote Desktop Connection, and even though free remote control applications are available (notably VNC, covered in Chapter 31), you might desire a different method of remote access and control. Telnet can give you that ability.

Telnet is an Internet standard and offers the ability to connect to a remote computer and run a console session on that computer. Windows XP includes software necessary to turn the computer into a Telnet server, enabling remote users to connect to the computer and work from a console session.

In this chapter, I explain how to set up the Telnet service in Windows XP and configure the computer for remote Telnet access. The chapter not only covers basic configuration, but also examines security, how to run startup scripts, and third-party Telnet programs you might find useful.

TIP Windows XP Professional includes the Telnet service, but Windows XP Home Edition does not. However, you can use a third-party Telnet server under Home Edition. Also, the Windows XP Telnet service is not limited to 10 concurrent connections.

Setting Up a Telnet Server

Setup installs the Telnet service under Windows XP Professional during installation but does not configure the service for automatic startup. So, getting your computer up and running as a Telnet server is a simple matter of starting the service. You can then fine-tune the configuration to control security, change the logon banner, and other settings.

TIP Users must be members of the TelnetClients group to connect to the computer through Telnet. Simply having the right to log on locally does not provide that ability. See the section "Configuring System Security" later in this chapter for more information.

Starting the Service

To configure the service, open the Services console (Figure 40.1) from the Administrative Tools folder or the Services branch of the Computer Management console. Locate the Telnet service in the service list and click the Start button on the toolbar or the Start link if you are using the Extended tab.

FIGURE 40.1:

Start and stop the Telnet service through the Services console.

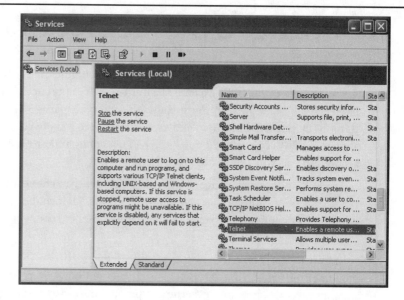

If you want to be able to connect to the computer through Telnet at any time, consider configuring the Telnet service for automatic startup. Double-click the Telnet service in the Services console and select Automatic from the Startup Type drop-down list (Figure 40.2). Before you do so, however, you should read the section "Ensuring System Security," later in this chapter, to make sure you are not exposing your system to a security risk.

Setting the Logon Banner

When a user logs onto a Windows XP Telnet server, the Telnet service opens a command console for the user and executes a default logon script. This script is located in *%systemroot%*\ System32\Login.cmd. The script by default displays the simple welcome message specified by the echo commands in the file. You can certainly use the message as-is, but I recommend you modify the message to at least warn remote users that the system is restricted to authorized users only and that access is audited. This should give you some legal recourse if someone hacks into your system through the Telnet service (assuming you catch them).

FIGURE 40.2:

Configure the service
for automatic startup
if you want access to
it all the time.

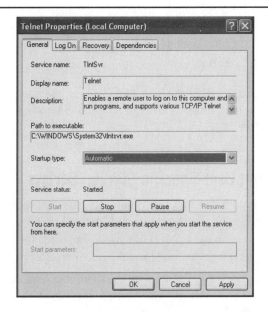

To modify the logon banner, just change the contents of the `Login.cmd` file. The following
is a sample:

```
echo *===============================================================
echo Welcome to host.boyce.ws. Access to this computer is restricted
echo to authorized personnel only! Access to this computer is audited
echo and monitored regularly. Legal action will be taken against any
echo unauthorized users. Have a nice day!
echo *===============================================================
```

Changing the Home Directory

Another function that the `Login.cmd` script performs is to change to the user's home directory. The last line of the script accomplishes this change:

```
cd /d %HOMEDRIVE%\%HOMEPATH%
```

The `cd` command is the same one you use in any command console. The `/d` switch allows a
change of drive as well as directory, in case the user's home directory is located on a different
volume from the system volume. The script replaces the *%HOMEDRIVE%* and *%HOMEPATH%* variables with the path to the user's home directory. When I log on as jboyce, for example, the
script puts me in `C:\Documents and Settings\jboyce`.

Using these variables allows the Telnet service to open the console session for the user in
his own directory, and that's the behavior that you will probably want in most cases. In some
situations, however, you might want to place the remote users in a specific folder. You can

accomplish this by simply replacing the variables with the appropriate path. For example, if you want all remote Telnet users to have their consoles open rooted in `F:\telnet`, then you would change the last line of the script to the following:

```
cd /d f:\telnet
```

NOTE   You need to create the specified folder on the specified volume first. Also keep in mind that the logon script applies to all users, so if you change the location it will apply to all Telnet users.

Running User-Specific Startup Scripts

In Windows XP, as in other Windows platforms, each user can have a script that runs when the user logs on. The logon script is defined in the user's profile and can be either a batch (BAT) or command (CMD) file. Typical uses for the logon script include mapping network drives, executing programs, and connecting printers.

To assign a logon script, open the Computer Management console and open the \Local Users And Computers\Users branch. Double-click a user account to open its properties and click the Profile tab (Figure 40.3).

SEE ALSO   I cover other profile properties in Chapter 44. This chapter focuses specifically on logon scripts for Telnet access.

FIGURE 40.3:

Specify the logon script in the Logon Script field.

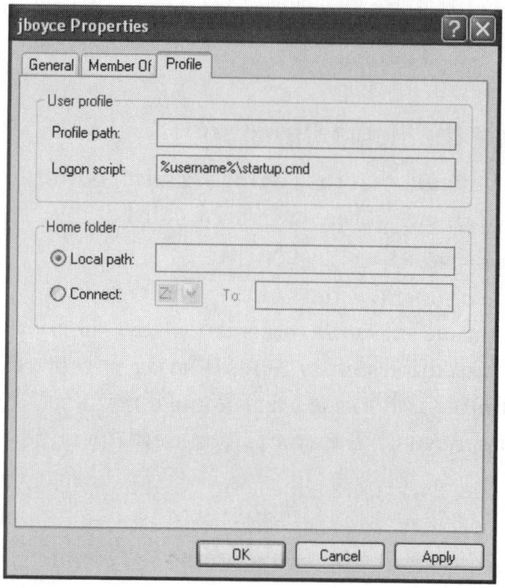

Here's where it gets a bit tricky. The Windows logon service and the Telnet service actually look in different places for the user's logon script. The Windows logon service looks in the NETLOGON share on the computer for the scripts, and the Telnet service looks in `%systemroot%\system32\repl\imports\scripts`. On a Windows NT Server platform, the NETLOGON share points to this same folder. On a Windows 2000 Server platform, however, the NETLOGON share typically points to a subfolder of the SYSVOL folder on the domain controller.

Here's the catch: the folder doesn't even exist on a Windows XP Professional computer, even though the Telnet service passes it to the client as part of the path! So, if you want a Telnet client to run a custom logon script, you need to create the folder `%systemroot%\system32\repl\import\scripts`. Then, create a folder for the user who matches the user's logon name and place the script in that folder. Then, open the user's profile and enter **%username%***scriptname* in the Logon Script field, where *scriptname* is the file name of the script.

When you're setting up the Telnet script, keep in mind that Windows logon also looks to the profile for the user's logon script, even though that script might be located in a different folder. Although you could share the `%systemroot%\system32\repl\import\scripts` folder as NETLOGON, you don't have to—you can share a different folder by that name if you like. The end result of doing so is that you will have one script for Windows logon and a different script for Telnet logon. However, you need to maintain the same folder structure for both folder locations. In other words, if you specify `%username%` as the path for the logon script in the profile, then both locations—NETLOGON and the `import\scripts` folder—must have a folder that matches the user name, and both of those folders must contain the appropriate script.

I see this behavior—two different services looking for the logon script in a different location—as a bug. There is the possibility that Microsoft will change this behavior in a future patch. Most administrators would probably prefer a consistent treatment of logon scripts to avoid having to manage two sets of scripts.

Configuring System Security

Telnet offers yet another way for remote users to access your computer. Each method of access offers certain security risks. This section examines the risks and also explains how to configure user accounts to allow Telnet access.

SEE ALSO See the later section "Using the Telnet Administrator" to learn how to specify the authentication methods supported by the Telnet service.

Protecting Your System

Providing Telnet access to your computer is, in general, more of a security risk than just sharing a folder on the network. When you share a folder, the user is restricted to that folder. However, gaining Telnet access is just like sitting in front of the computer locally. You can change drives and folders using cd and other commands. This means that unless you use NTFS and protect all folders with appropriate NTFS permissions, a remote Telnet user can gain access to all folders and files.

Before you even go to the trouble of setting up accounts for Telnet access, consider the security implications of allowing Telnet access. Convert your volume(s) to NTFS and then make sure that you review the permissions on *all* folders to make sure you restrict access as needed. I strongly recommend that you perform these tasks before allowing any access through Telnet.

Setting Up Accounts

In order for a remote user to connect to a Windows XP computer running the Telnet service, the user must be a member of a local group named TelnetClients. Windows XP does not create this group by default; you must create it to grant Telnet access to users.

To create the account, open the Computer Management console and then expand the Local Users And Computers branch. Right-click the Groups node and choose New Group. In the following dialog box (Figure 40.4), enter TelnetClients in the Group Name field. You can also add a description of your choice in the Description field.

Next, click Add, then enter the user name or browse for a user to grant Telnet access. Add any other users as needed and click OK. Close the New Group dialog box and the Computer Management console.

FIGURE 40.4:

Create a group named TelnetClients to allow Telnet access.

A Telnet user must have the right to log on locally to the computer. You don't need to grant the TelnetClients group the right to log on locally, because the members already have this right through membership in the built-in Users group. However, if you *deny* the Telnet-Clients group the right to log on locally, no one other than administrators will be able to connect through Telnet. This would defeat the whole purpose for the TelnetClients group. The bottom line is this: any user you allow Telnet access would also have the ability to log on locally. In most cases, this won't be a problem, particularly if you protect your system with NTFS permissions.

TIP   Members of the Administrators group are an exception to the requirement for membership in the TelnetClients group. These users can access the computer through Telnet without being members of the TelnetClients group.

Using the Telnet Administrator

If you have worked with the Telnet service in Windows 2000, you are probably at least somewhat familiar with the Tlntadmn program that allows you to configure and manage the Telnet service. This program has been changed considerably in Windows XP. The Windows 2000 version provided a management menu, while the Windows XP version functions as a command-line tool. This makes it handy for scripting, but makes it more difficult to manage Telnet service settings. Hopefully, Microsoft will at some point provide a GUI interface for configuring the Telnet service. In the meantime, we'll have to make do with Tlntadmn.

Managing Sessions

You can use tlntadmn to manage Telnet client connections to your computer. You can view information about sessions, kill (disconnect) a session, and send a message to a remote user.

To work with a session, you first need to know its session ID. Open a command console and type the following to see output like the lines presented here:

```
C:\>tlntadmn -s all
2

2 telnet session(s)

ID    Domain    UserName        Client           LogonDate   LogonTime    IdleTime
----------------------------------------------------------------------------------
372   VM-XPPRO  jboyce          192.168.0.11     1/25/2002   9:48:37 AM   0:04:52
920   VM-XPPRO  administrator   192.168.0.15     1/25/2002   10:22:13 AM  0:06:31
```

The session ID appears in the first column. You can then use a couple of other options with `tlntadmn` to kill the session or send a message. To kill a session, use the following syntax, replacing ID with the session ID:

```
tlntadmn -k ID
```

In some cases you might want to send a message to a remote user. For example, perhaps you need to reboot or shut down your computer. Sending a message allows the remote user to exit the session first. Use the following syntax to send a message, replacing ID with the session ID:

```
tlntadmn -m ID Type your message here, no quotes needed
```

Configuring the Server

You can also configure the Telnet service with the `tlntadmn` program using the `config` parameter and a corresponding option. The syntax for this format of the command is

```
tnltadmn config [config_option]
```

Following is a list of the actions you can perform and the associated option:

Set the default domain for user names   Set the domain against which user accounts are authenticated if different from the local computer. Example:

```
tlntadmn config dom = mydomain
```

Set the mapping of the Alt key   Map the Alt key to Ctrl+A so the Telnet server will interpret Ctrl+A as pressing the Alt key. Example:

```
tlntadmn config ctrlakeymap = yes
```

Set the idle session timeout   Specify the amount of time a session can be idle before being disconnected. This example sets the timeout to 1 hour, 30 minutes, 20 seconds:

```
tlnadmn config timeout = 1:30:20
```

Enable idle session timeout   Specify whether or not the Telnet server should disconnect idle users when the session timeout is reached. Example:

```
tlntadmn config timeoutactive = yes
```

Set the maximum number of login failure attempts disconnecting   Specify the number of failed logins allowed before the server disconnects the session. The default is three. Example:

```
tlntadmn config maxfail = 2
```

Set the maximum number of connections   Specify the maximum number of concurrent connections allows with this option. Example:

```
tlntadmn config maxconn = 20
```

Set the Telnet port   Specify the port used by the Telnet service. The default is port 23. Example:

```
tlntadmn config port = 5200
```

Set the authentication mechanism   The server can use NTLM or unencrypted authentication. If you enable both methods, the server attempts NTLM and, failing that, then attempts unencrypted authentication based on the credentials provided by the client. The following example would turn off NTLM and turn on password authentication:

```
tlntadmn config sec = -NTLM +passwd
```

Specify the name of the audit file   Set the name of the log file used by the Telnet server if other than or in addition to the event log. Example:

```
tlntadmn config fname = c:\logs\telnet.log
```

Specify the maximum size of the audit file   Set the maximum size (in MB) of the log file if using a log file in addition to or in place of the event log. Example to set the size to 4 MB:

```
tlntadmn config fsize = 4
```

Specify the mode of operation   Set the mode of operation for the Telnet server, choosing between `console` and `stream`. Console mode is most often used for screen-oriented programs, and stream mode more for dumb terminal operations (it's more efficient for command-line tasks). Example:

```
tlntadmn config mode = stream
```

Specify where to log   You can configure Telnet to log to the event log, a log file, or both. Example:

```
tlntadmn config auditlocation = eventlog
```

Specify events to audit   Specify the types of events to log. Choose among administrative logon, user logon, and failed logon. The following example would log successful logons but not failures:

```
tlntadmn config audit = +admin +user -fail
```

TIP   Issue the `tlntadmn` command without any options to view the status of current settings.

Managing a Remote Server

You can use the `tlntadmn` command to manage the Telnet service on the local computer, or use it to manage the service on a computer elsewhere on the network. However, `tlntadmn` works only for Windows XP computers. You need to use the Windows 2000 version of the program if you need to manage a Windows 2000 Telnet server.

To connect to and manage a remote Telnet server on the LAN, include the computer name in the `tlntadmn` command. The following example would set the maximum number of connections on the Telnet server named snoopy:

```
tlntadmn \\snoopy config maxconn = 20
```

You can also use `tlntadmn` from within a Telnet session to a remote Windows XP computer. Just open the Telnet session and, in the console, issue the appropriate `tlntadmn` command.

Third-Party Telnet Applications

Like FTP, Telnet is a service that developers seem to have pursued with a passion, and the result is a wide selection of Telnet applications. The vast majority of these are client applications that add support for additional terminal emulation and other features. A handful of Telnet servers are available as well. I've included a small selection of some of the most popular applications on the CD.

Absolute Telnet SSH   This Telnet client provides all the standard Telnet features and adds support for Secure Shell 1 (SSH1) and Secure Shell 2 (SSH2), which provide several compression methods, X11 forwarding, port forwarding, and other features. The program supports file transfer through xmodem, ymodem, and zmodem protocols, as well as secure file transfer. You can get a sneak preview at www.celestialsoftware.net.

SecureCRT   In addition to support for the Telnet protocol and standard features, this program also provides support for SSH, smart card–based authentication, file transfer protocols, port forwarding, font scaling, and much more. The program can work from the notification area to reduce Desktop and Taskbar clutter. Check it out at www.vandyke.com/products/securecrt/index.html.

PART VII

Managing Users

CHAPTER 41

Managing Users and Groups

If you are moving to Windows XP from Windows 9*x* or Windows Me, two topics that are probably new to you are user accounts and groups. Although these other operating systems use accounts of a sort, they are not at all like the user accounts used in Windows NT, 2000, and XP.

It's important that you understand users and groups to use Windows XP, and even more important to use them effectively and securely. They are the mechanism by which you secure your computer and its shared resources. They are also the means by which you access shared resources on other computers.

Although you can assign rights and permissions on a user-by-user basis, in most cases you should do that only when you have a very small number of accounts. Even then, using groups to assign those rights and permissions often provides a more logical method or security organization. This chapter explains the role that user accounts and groups play in Windows XP security, both locally and across the network. I explain how to create users and groups and configure group membership.

New in Windows XP is a feature called *fast user switching*, which allows you to log onto a computer and use it without logging off the current user or closing his programs. For example, your spouse might be using the computer but you need to check your e-mail before going out. You can log on, use the computer, and log off without making your spouse close any programs.

The final topics I cover in this chapter are user profiles. A user profile consists of the information that makes up a user's working environment, and includes My Documents, the Start menu, and other items, such as logon and logoff scripts. Managing user profiles might include, for example, locating a home directory on a server rather than on the local computer.

SEE ALSO Chapter 44 goes into more aspects of user accounts, especially user profiles and logon/logoff scripts.

Understanding Groups

Groups in Windows XP provide a way for you to assign rights and permissions to multiple users without having to assign those rights and permissions separately to each user. As such, groups are a tool that simplifies security administration.

For example, assume that you work in a company with a relatively small network of 50 users. You have certain files on your computer that 10 of those people need to be able to read, 10 others need to be able to modify, and the rest should have no access to at all. If you assigned the permissions without groups, you would need to assign the rights to each account. With groups, however, you simply create two groups, one for read access and the other for change access, and make the appropriate user accounts members of the required group.

If you think a bit about this example, you'll probably realize the drawback of using a workgroup in this situation rather than a domain. For each user to have individually-recognized access to the shared folder, each user must have a local account on your computer. This means creating (in this example) 20 user accounts on your computer for those 20 users.

In a domain, each user would already have an account in the domain, and these accounts would be managed by the network administrator. You would then grant access to your local share using these domain accounts, but again, the best option is to create a group and place in the group those accounts that need access. Otherwise, you need to add each account to the access control list (ACL) for the shared folder.

There is an alternative that you might consider for this situation and others like it that would otherwise require you to create multiple accounts on your computer. You could create two generic accounts, one called Read and the other called Change. Assign permissions accordingly to the shared folder using these two accounts. Then, give the account and password to the people who need access. They can connect to the share using the supplied user credentials to gain access.

The downside to this approach is the relative lack of auditing capability it offers. Although you could audit access by these two accounts, you would have no idea who was using the accounts. By creating and using individual accounts and groups, you can accurately audit which users are connecting to the shared resource.

Local and Domain Groups

You need to understand domains to really understand groups and how to use them. The exception is when your computer resides in a workgroup and you don't interact with a domain at all.

Domains act as a security boundary that serves to simplify security administration. The domain contains accounts for all users in the domain, and users can authenticate against their domain account to access resources located anywhere in the domain. This means you don't need to create an account on every computer containing a resource that a given user needs to use. Instead, you grant access to each resource using that single domain account. If you are sharing a folder on your local computer, this means that when a remote user tries to connect to the share, Windows XP communicates with the domain controller to authenticate the user based on his domain account.

Multiple domains form a *domain forest*, and domains in the forest can be grouped together hierarchically to form *domain trees*. The first domain in a domain tree is the *root domain*. Other domains in the tree are called *child domains*. The domain directly above a particular domain is that domain's *parent domain*, and the domain directly below it is called its *child domain*. Figure 41.1 illustrates domain hierarchy.

FIGURE 41.1:

A domain hierarchy begins with a forest and ends with individual members.

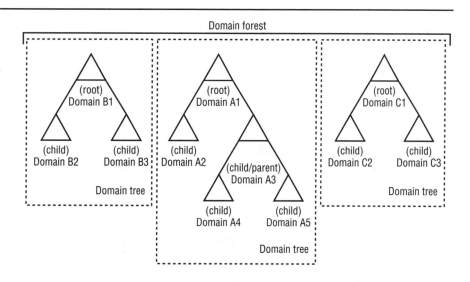

Note: Each root domain is a parent domain of those domains directly under the root.

TIP   You can't create domains on a Windows XP computer. Domains require Windows NT Server, 2000 Server, or .NET Server platforms. In addition, logical domain relationships are different from NT to the other two platforms. My discussion of domains in this chapter assumes Windows 2000 Server or later.

In Windows XP, there is only one kind of group: local. This means that the group resides on the local computer. Likewise, local user accounts also reside on the local computer.

In a domain there are three group types, each with a different scope: domain local, global, or universal. Groups with universal scope—called universal groups—can contain groups and accounts from any domain in the domain tree or forest. They can be granted permissions in any domain in the entire domain forest.

Groups with global scope—called global groups—can contain groups and accounts only from the domain in which the group is defined, but can be granted permissions in any domain in the forest.

Groups with local domain scope—called domain local groups—can contain accounts and groups only from their own domain and can be granted permissions only in the local domain.

A local group can naturally contain local user accounts. If the Windows XP computer resides in a domain, however, a local group can also include user accounts from the domain. Because this book focuses on Windows XP, I'll assume that you are creating local groups and want to add both local and domain accounts to the groups.

Creating and Managing Local Users and Groups

Windows XP provides two tools for creating user accounts and one for creating groups. In this section, I explain how to use these tools to create groups and accounts.

Creating and Managing Groups

You use the Local Users And Groups branch of the Computer Management console to create and manage groups in Windows XP. Right-click My Computer and choose Manage to open the console, and then expand the Local Users And Groups branch (Figure 41.2).

FIGURE 41.2:

Use the Local Users And Groups snap-in to create groups.

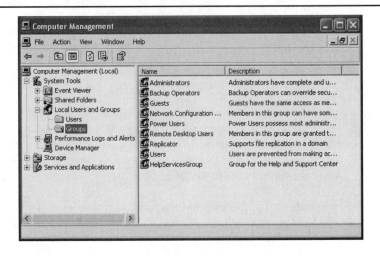

TIP   You can add the Local Users And Groups snap-in to a stand-alone MMC console or to a custom console, and then use that console instead of the Computer Management console to manage users and groups.

The Groups branch shows all of the existing groups on the local computer. There are several built-in groups:

Administrators   Members of this group have complete control over the computer and can perform all functions, including adding hardware, modifying the configuration, and managing users and groups.

Backup Operators   This group allows members to bypass certain security restrictions to perform backups. However, members of this group do not have the ability to view files for which they don't have the necessary permissions. Instead, they can only back up these files.

Guests   Members of this account, by default, have the same permissions as members of the Users group. The exception is the Guest account, which has additional restrictions.

Network Configuration Operators   This group allows members to modify certain network configuration items.

Power Users   These users have most of the same rights and permissions as administrators but lack certain rights, such as the ability to take ownership of a folder or file.

Remote Desktop Users   This group exists to support the Remote Desktop feature in Windows XP. Members of this group have the right to log on locally, giving them the ability to connect to the local computer using Remote Desktop.

Replicator   This group is used to replicate data within a domain. In most cases, you won't need to add or remove accounts from this group.

Users   Members of this group have the right to log on locally, and this group is intended to support local users of the computer. Users cannot make configuration changes to the computer (with minor exceptions), and they can run certified applications but not legacy applications.

HelpServicesGroup   This group is used by the Help and Support Center and supports the Remote Assistance feature in Windows XP.

You can add users to these groups as needed rather than create new groups. For example, when you need to give another person access to a computer, just create an account for them in the built-in Users group.

The main reason to create a new group is to assign permissions and rights to a group of users that are different from the permissions and rights assigned to an existing group. For example, perhaps you want to create a group to support remote FTP access to your computer. You would grant this group the right to log on locally but deny them access to any folders other than the FTP folders.

To create a group, right-click the Groups node in the Local Users And Groups console and click New Group to open a dialog box where you specify the name of the group and an optional description. Then click Add to open the Select Users dialog box.

You can enter the names of the accounts directly in the text box or click Advanced to expand the dialog box (Figure 41.3) to search for accounts. If you choose the latter, click Find Now in the Select Users dialog box to search the default location (typically, the local computer). You can also click Locations to open a dialog box to search the domain if the computer is a domain member.

FIGURE 41.3:

Search for and select users with the Select Users dialog box.

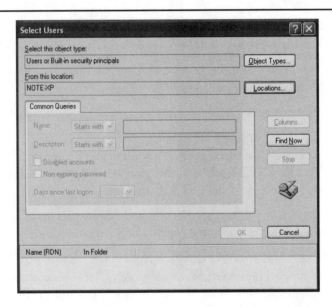

To simplify the search for accounts in a domain or on a local computer with lots of groups and accounts, click Object Types to open another dialog box. Clear the check box beside Built-In Security Principals and click OK. Windows XP will then only search for user accounts.

Repeat the process to add other users or groups to the group. When you've added all the desired accounts and/or groups, close the New Group dialog box.

You can easily add members to a group after it is created. Just open the Local Users And Groups console, then open the Groups branch. Double-click the group to open its properties, and click Add to add other users or groups.

Creating and Managing User Accounts

Creating a user account is almost as easy as creating a group. In the Local Users And Groups console, right-click Users and choose New User to display the New User dialog box (Figure 41.4). Enter the desired account name in the User Name field, the user's real name in the Full Name field, and an optional description for the account in the Description field. Enter the password for the account and verify the password.

TIP   You can also use the User Accounts object in Control Panel to create and modify user accounts. See the later section "Other User Management Tasks" for more information.

FIGURE 41.4:

Add a user account with the New User dialog box.

Next, specify the following options, click Create to create the new account, and click Close to close the dialog box:

User Must Change Password At Next Logon   Choose this option to require the user to specify a new password the next time he logs on.

User Cannot Change Password   Select this option to prevent the user from changing passwords.

Password Never Expires   Select this option if you don't want the account to be subject to password aging.

Account Is Disabled   Select this option to disable the account, which prevents it from being used.

SEE ALSO   See the section "Managing User Profiles and Scripts," later in this chapter, to learn how to configure the user's profile and logon script.

Modifying Group Membership

When you create an account, Windows XP makes it a member of the Users group. You can modify group membership afterward to add other groups or change the default membership. To change membership, open the Local Users And Groups console and double-click the user account to open its properties, and then click the Member Of tab.

To remove an existing group, select the group and click Remove. Click Add to add one or more groups with the Select Groups dialog box (Figure 41.5). You use the Select Groups dialog box in much the same way you use the Select Users dialog box.

FIGURE 41.5:

Add groups to a user's properties through the Select Groups dialog box.

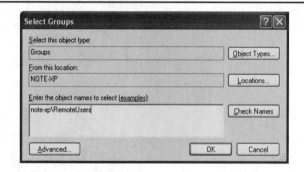

TIP   Any user can be a member of more than one group, and multiple group membership is a common means for achieving custom security settings.

Resetting an Account Password

In Windows NT, the password for an account is available within the account properties for the account. Windows 2000 and XP are a bit different, however. Right-click the account and choose Set Password if you want to change the password. Windows XP displays a warning that changing the password could prevent the user from logging on. Click Proceed to display the Set Password dialog box (Figure 41.6). Enter and confirm the password and click OK.

SEE ALSO   See "Recovering from Lost Passwords," later in this chapter, for information on changing a password with a password reset disk.

FIGURE 41.6:

Change the password
with the Set Password
dialog box.

You can use the User Accounts object in Control Panel to change the password hint that Windows XP uses to prompt you for a password when you enter the password incorrectly. The following section explains how to configure the password hint.

Other User Management Tasks

Although I prefer the Local Users And Groups console for user and group management, you can also use the User Accounts object in Control Panel to perform certain account management tasks. These include changing the password, changing the picture associated with the account, and adding a .NET password to an account.

> **TIP**   The picture for an account appears beside the account name in the Welcome screen.

Setting Password and Password Hint

You can change a password as well as the password hint that Windows XP displays to help remind you of your password. Open Control Panel and open the User Accounts link. Select an account and click Change My Password to display the window shown in Figure 41.7. Enter the current password and new password in the fields provide. Then, enter the desired password hint in the last field and click Change Password.

> **TIP**   The password hint can help you guess a forgotten password, but it also can help someone else hack into your system locally if you use a hint that is too easy to guess.

Changing Your Account Picture

The Welcome screen displays a small picture beside each user account. Windows XP chooses a picture at random from a small selection of pictures. However, you can specify the picture that you want Windows XP to use for a particular account. The image need not be a specific size—Windows XP will resize the image as needed. You can specify an image in GIF, BMP, JPG, or PNG format.

TIP   XP resizes the image so the largest side is 48 pixels, with a maximum image size of 48×48 pixels.

Click the Change My Picture link in the User Accounts window. Select one of the sample images or click Browse For More Pictures to select from a different location.

FIGURE 41.7:

You can specify a word or phrase Windows XP will display as a password hint.

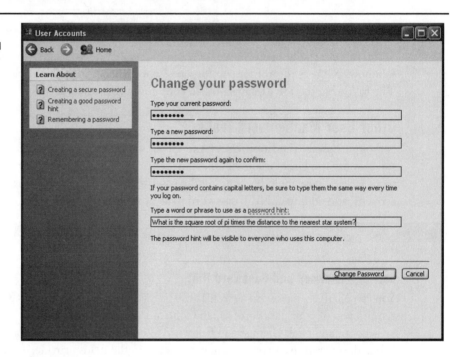

Setting Up a .NET Passport

Microsoft has created an authentication mechanism called the .NET Passport that you can use to authenticate your identity on several websites, including Microsoft's sites. Windows Messenger also uses your .NET Passport as the means by which you log onto the Messenger service and other users can contact you. Assigning a .NET Passport to your user account enables you to use the passport to authenticate on these sites and services while logged on to Windows XP.

To assign a .NET Passport to an account, open the User Accounts link in Control Panel and click Set Up My Account To Use A .NET Passport. Windows XP starts a wizard to help you through the process of assigning your existing .NET Passport or creating a new one. All you need is an e-mail account to set up a passport.

Modifying Your Network Password Cache

Windows XP can maintain the user credentials that you use to access network resources such as shared folders, secured websites, printers, and other resources. For example, if you have a membership to a particular site, you can have Windows XP save your password so you don't have to enter it each time you visit the site.

To manage your password cache, open the User Accounts link in Control Panel and then click your user account. In the left pane, click Manage My Network Passwords to open the Stored User Names And Passwords dialog box (Figure 41.8).

FIGURE 41.8:

Modify your password cache with the Stored User Names And Passwords dialog box.

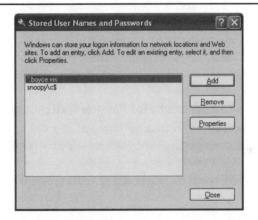

You can modify an existing password entry or add a new one. To modify one, click the item in the list and click Properties. In the dialog box for the item, specify the user name and password, and if desired, change the name of the network resource. Or click Add on the Stored User Names and Passwords dialog box to create a new password entry. Specify the URL to server or the UNC path for LAN resources, along with the user credentials to use to authenticate for the resource.

Recovering from Lost Passwords

Forgetting a password for a user account isn't a big deal as long as you know the administrator account password—just log on as an administrator and change the user's password as needed. When you lose the administrator password, however, the situation is a bit more serious. You can't make any changes to the system without the administrator account. Fortunately, there are a couple of ways to recover the administrator password, as well as a way for a user to recover his own password without help from an administrator.

Using a Password Reset Disk

Windows XP adds a new feature called a password reset disk that enables you to recover an account if you forget the password. The reset disk works for the administrator account as well as other user accounts. However, it can't recover a password unless it resets the password. You must create the recovery disk with the existing password, which means you must create the disk before you forget the password!

To create a password recovery disk, open the User Accounts link in Control Panel and click the account for which you want to create the disk. In the left pane, click Prevent A Forgotten Password. Windows XP starts a wizard that steps you through the process of creating the recovery disk. When prompted, insert a formatted diskette and provide the current password for the account.

To recover the account with the password reset disk, boot the computer and select the account at the Welcome screen. Enter any password and press Enter. Windows XP displays a warning message about your password. Insert the reset disk in the floppy drive and click Use Your Password Reset Disk. Follow the prompts provided by Windows XP to create a new password.

Recovering an Administrator Password without a Recovery Disk

If you neglected to create a password reset disk for the administrator account and have forgotten the account password, you can still recover the administrator account using one of two methods, both of which require the Recovery Console for an NTFS partition (or access to the NTFS partition where the system is stored).

Spoof the Logon Screensaver

Windows XP by default uses the Logon screensaver, displaying the screensaver after about 20 minutes. You can use this behavior to replace the Logon screensaver with the command console. When Windows XP opens the screensaver, it actually opens a command console. You can then use the net command to change the password.

You need access to the %systemroot%\system32 folder on the computer. How you get to it depends on the disk's file system or whether you've shared a folder above the system32 folder:

Folder shared   You might be able to modify the files from another computer on the network if you have shared the root of the system drive or a folder above the system32 folder. Boot the computer, then browse to the share from another computer on the network to locate the system32 folder.

FAT file system   You can boot using a DOS or Windows 9x boot disk and use cd to change to the system32 folder (which is typically located under either \WINDOWS or \WINNT).

NTFS file system   Your best bet here is to use Recovery Console, which you can run from the Windows XP CD if Recovery Console is not already installed. Check out www.winternals.com for other tools that enable you to access NTFS partitions from a bootable diskette.

After you have access to the system32 folder on the problem computer, rename the file logon.scr to logon.scr.old. Then, copy the file cmd.exe to logon.scr. The result is that there should now be a file named logon.scr in the system32 folder. However, it is actually a copy of cmd.exe, the command console processor for Windows XP.

Reboot the computer and wait until the screensaver kicks in. You should now see a command console, which fortunately is running in an administrative context. In the console, type the following command, replacing *password* with the desired password:

```
net user administrator password
```

Type **exit** to exit the command console and then log on using the administrator account and the newly assigned password.

Delete the SAM Hive File

Another, more drastic solution is to delete the file that holds the security database. I would use this method only if you can't get the screensaver method to work, or you don't care that you will lose the accounts on the computer and need to recreate them.

Boot the system using Recovery Console and change to the *%systemroot%*\system32\config folder. Rename the file sam to sam.old and reboot the computer. Your administrator account will now have a blank password, but all other accounts will be deleted. Log on using the administrator account, change the password for it, and recreate any accounts and groups as needed.

Managing Users and Groups from a Console

The net command included with Windows XP provides a console-based tool for managing users and groups. The net user command manages user accounts on the local computer, and net group manages groups.

This command, when used without any other parameters, lists the user accounts on the computer. You can use the command to add and remove accounts, change an account's active status, change password, and accomplish other tasks. You can also set several other properties, including the account expiration, home directory, profile location, and other settings.

Type **net help user** at a command prompt to view the syntax and options for this command.

TIP   The net group command only works on a domain controller, and can't be used on a Windows XP computer to manage groups.

Fast User Switching

Windows XP offers a new feature called fast user switching that allows another person to log on and use the computer without requiring that an existing user shut down all programs and log off. For example, let's say you are using the computer and your significant other wants to check e-mail, but you have several programs running. Fast user switching lets the other user log on, use the computer, and log off without affecting your running applications. When you log back on, your applications and Desktop are just like you left them.

To enable fast user switching, open Control Panel and open the User Accounts link. Click Change The Way Users Log On Or Off to display the logon and logoff options shown in Figure 41.9. Place a check beside Use Fast User Switching and then click Apply Options.

FIGURE 41.9:

Enable or disable fast user switching through the User Accounts dialog box.

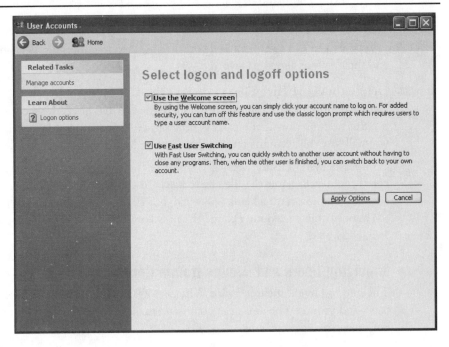

To switch users, click Start ➤ Log Off, then click Switch User. Windows XP prompts you to log on. When you're ready to switch back to the other account, just use the same procedure to switch to the previous account.

CHAPTER 42

Understanding Group and Local Policies

Microsoft introduced in Windows 2000 a new feature to take the place of the system policies in Windows NT and Windows 9*x*. This new feature—called *group policies*—makes possible a wide range of capabilities to simplify data management, system administration, and security. For example, you can use group policies to automatically install operating systems and applications to client computers, which offers an excellent method for deploying new systems and accomplishing disaster recovery.

Group policies allow for more effective user data management. You can redirect user folders from the local computer to a network server to simplify disaster recovery and to provide easier data backup and recovery.

Group policies also provide a means to apply restrictions and impose *change control* on users' working environment. Change control refers to an administrator's ability to prevent certain user-initiated changes such as changing workstation configuration, adding or removing hardware, and so on.

Windows XP, like Windows 2000, also supports local policies, which are a local implementation of group policies defined and applied at the local computer level. Group policies require a Windows 2000 Server or Windows .NET Server domain, but local policies are also available in a workgroup environment. In this chapter I explain how to use and configure group and local policies.

Overview of Group and Local Policies

Group and local policies, introduced in Windows 2000 and expanded upon in the Windows XP and Microsoft .NET platforms, provide a means of applying settings to the operating system and related environment during logon. These policies take the place of the system policies found in Windows 9*x* and Windows NT.

There are literally hundreds of policy settings that you or a network administrator can apply through group and local policies. For example, group policies can be used to automatically define aspects of the user's working environment such as Desktop settings and the location of the user's profile. Policies also control the elements that the user sees in the Windows environment, such as the volumes that are listed in My Computer, items that appear in Control Panel, and icons that appear on the Desktop.

Group and local policies are a component of Microsoft's Directory Enabled Client Management (DECM) group of technologies. Policies work in concert with other features and services such as Remote Installation Services to provide a means for deploying operating systems and applications, managing user data, and controlling the actions that a user can perform within Windows. In effect, policies provide a means to dynamically configure the operating system and working environment.

Policies can be applied at four different levels: site, domain, organizational unit (OU), and local. Policies are also separated into two categories, group and local. To use group policies, a computer must reside in a Windows 2000– or Microsoft .NET–based domain. The system administrator defines the policies in Active Directory (AD) at the appropriate level, whether site, domain, or OU, and the same policy can have different settings at different levels. For example, the administrator might deny a particular user right at the site level but grant that right at an OU. The effective policy setting would then give the members of that OU that right, because the policies are applied in a layered fashion. Local policies apply first, then site, then domain, and then OU. The last policy applied takes precedence when the same policy is defined at multiple levels.

Because this book focuses on Windows XP and not Microsoft's server platforms, I'll focus this chapter on local policies. You can configure essentially the same policies at the local level that you can apply through AD. When the computer resides in a domain, the local group policies can be overridden by policies at higher levels. So, you can configure local policy, but there is no guarantee that the policies you define won't be replaced by group policy. When the computer resides in a workgroup, however, the local policies are the only ones that apply. So local policies are a great way to automatically configure computers in a workgroup.

Many of the features made possible by group policy are not possible through local policy, however. The ability to automatically install operating systems and applications is a primary example. These capabilities require a Windows 2000– or Microsoft .NET–based domain, a Remote Installation Services server, and other resources. Even so, you can still use local policies to configure Desktop and working environment settings, apply disk quotas, and configure other Windows XP operating system settings. Local policies are particularly useful for applying restrictions and change control on computers that are shared by multiple users.

Why bother with local policies? The main reason to use local policies in a workgroup environment is to specify settings that you want applied to multiple users of the same computer. For example, you might want to configure properties for Internet Explorer different from the default settings, and have these settings applied to all users of the computer. Or, perhaps you want to remove certain items from the Start menu, turn off personalized menus, hide the system tray (now called the *notification area*), or apply other changes for the computer, either for multiple users or just for yourself. Local policies provide a one-stop-shop for changing almost all of the properties that define how your computer looks and functions.

TIP   Most of the policy settings correspond to values in the Registry. Although you can change the settings in the Registry manually, policies provide a more logical organization and safer method for settings management.

You use two very different methods to mange group policies versus local policies. You create and edit group policies through the Active Directory Users And Computers console or the Active Directory Sites And Services console, both on the server. Neither of these tools is included with Windows XP. However, you can use the Group Policy console, which is included with XP, to manage local policies.

TIP   This chapter provides an overview of local and group policies and explains how to manage them. Chapters 43 and 44 focus on specific applications of local policy, such as applying user restrictions and redirecting user data.

Working with the Group Policy Console

The Group Policy console offers the same general structure for managing local polices that the Active Directory tools offer on a server for managing group policies. The only difference is that those policies that cannot be set at the local level do not appear in the Group Policy console.

To open the console, choose Start ➢ Run and enter **MMC** in the Run dialog box. Choose File ➢ Add/Remove Snap-In to display the Add/Remove Snap-In dialog box. Click Add, select Group Policy from the snap-in list (Figure 42.1), and click Add. In the Select Group Policy Object dialog box, click Finish with Local Computer specified in the Group Policy Object field (Figure 42.2).

TIP   You can use the Local Security Policy Editor in the Administrative Tools folder to modify various security policies, which comprise a subset of the local policies.

FIGURE 42.1:

Select the Group
Policy snap-in from
the list.

FIGURE 42.2:

Select Local Computer
as the group policy
object to edit.

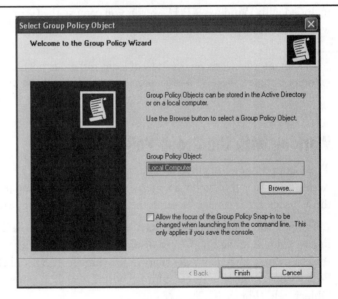

As Figure 42.3 illustrates, the Group Policy console includes two main branches: Computer Configuration and User Configuration. The Computer Configuration branch contains policies that apply to the computer, and User Configuration contains ones that apply to the user.

FIGURE 42.3:

Use the Group Policy
console to manage
local policies.

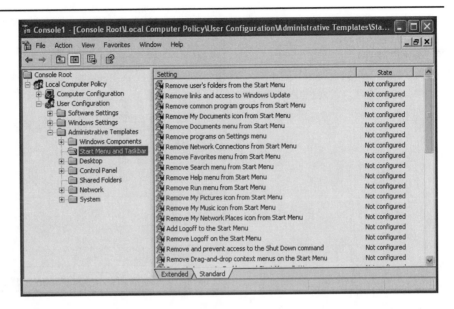

The Group Policy console works just like most other MMC consoles. To configure settings for a particular branch, just select the branch. The policies that reside in the branch appear in the right pane, as Figure 42.3 shows. To change a policy, double-click it in the right pane to open a dialog box similar to the one shown in Figure 42.4. Use the Setting tab to configure the policy, choosing Not Configured, Enabled, or Disabled.

Not Configured   This option indicates that the policy is not configured, so no change is made to the Registry to modify the policy. Use this setting when you want Windows XP to use the default behavior for the feature controlled by the policy setting.

Enabled   Apply the policy to the user or computer.

Disabled   Do not apply the policy to the user or computer.

Depending on the policy, the Setting tab might offer additional controls to set specific policy properties. For example, the Hide These Specified Drives In My Computer policy includes a drop-down list that you can use to select which drives to omit from My Computer.

Most of the settings also have an Explain tab (Figure 42.5) that provides a detailed explanation of the policy's function, how to use it, and other policies that work in conjunction with the selected policy.

FIGURE 42.4:
Use the Setting tab to
configure the policy.

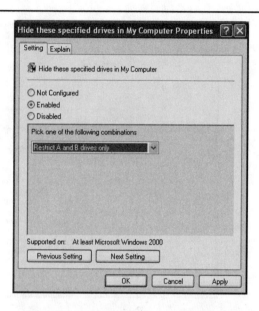

FIGURE 42.5:
Find detailed informa-
tion about a policy on
the Explain tab.

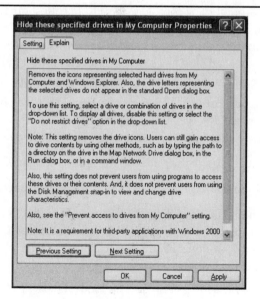

Using the Group Policy console isn't difficult, and the Explain tab generally does a good job of explaining the purpose of a given policy. For those reasons, and because there are hundreds of policies, I don't cover each policy in detail in this chapter. Instead, I offer some tips in the following sections that will help you identify the different policy branches and accomplish specific tasks.

My advice is that you spend several hours pouring through the Group Policy editor, analyzing each policy to figure out what it does and how it will help you configure your computer the way you want or impose restrictions for users as needed. Start by reading the following sections to get an idea of the things you can control through policies.

Computer Configuration

The Computer Configuration branch, as I mentioned previously, contains policy settings that apply to the computer. The following sections explain what types of settings you'll find in each branch.

Software Settings

This branch is used by group policy to install applications automatically through DECM. There are no settings you can control locally. Instead, these policies must be set through group policy at a higher level.

SEE ALSO   See Chapter 12 for more information on deploying applications with IntelliMirror and group policy.

Windows Settings

The Windows Settings branch contains several branches that control security, user rights, password policies, and related security settings.

Scripts

The Scripts branch specifies the startup and shutdown scripts for the computer. These scripts, as their names imply, execute when the system starts and when it shuts down.

SEE ALSO   For information on using startup and shutdown scripts, see Chapter 5.

Security Settings

The Security Settings branch gives you access to policies that control the way Windows XP handles logon, auditing, user rights, software restrictions, and other security-related features.

Account Policies   The Password Policy branch contains policies that control how Windows XP treats passwords. You can require that XP retain a password history to help ensure that users don't continue to reuse the same password. You can also configure other password-related settings such as password aging, minimum password length, and password complexity requirements.

The Account Lockout Policy branch specifies what actions Windows XP should take when a logon failure occurs (such as a user entering the wrong password). For example, you can configure XP to lock the account after a specified number of failed logon attempts, and also specify how and when the account is subsequently unlocked.

Local Policies   The Local Policies branch contains three sub-branches that control auditing, user rights assignment, and various security-related settings. For example, you can rename the Administrator and Guest accounts, control the users' abilities to make device changes and install device drivers, and specify what the user sees during logon.

Public Key Policies   This branch contains one setting, Enroll User And Computer Certificates Automatically, which determines whether or not Windows XP automatically installs certificates on the computer. It also determines whether Windows XP automatically renews expired certificates and performs other certificate-related tasks.

The Encrypting File System branch lets you configure data recovery agents for EFS. The recovery agents allow encrypted data to be recovered if the certificate that was used to encrypt the data is lost or removed.

SEE ALSO   See Chapter 49 to learn how to develop and implement an EFS recovery strategy.

Software Restriction Policies   Use this branch and its policies to control which applications a user can run and the paths that a user can access. For example, you might configure policies in this branch to prevent users from executing specific types of files, such as batch files or scripts. You can also specify which software publishers are trusted to determine whether applications from those publishers can be installed.

IP Security Policies   IP Security (IPSec) provides a means to encrypt and secure IP traffic between computers. The IP Security Policies branch contains the policies that determine how the local computer handles IPSec connections to other computers.

SEE ALSO   See Chapter 50 for a detailed discussion of IPSec and how to use it.

Administrative Templates

This branch contains a wealth of application and operating system settings. For example, the Windows Components branch contains policies that control NetMeeting, Internet Explorer,

Terminal Services, the Task Scheduler, Windows Installer, and Windows Messenger. The primary reason to modify these policies is to control how these applications run or to prevent users from running specific applications, even if they are installed. For example, you can prevent the user from running Windows Installer, which effectively prevents the installation of most applications.

The System branch controls system-wide settings such as the way scripts execute, how Windows XP manages user profiles, application of disk quotas, and logon. The branch contains several other branches that control other properties including Remote Assistance, the Windows Time Service, and other features.

The Network branch provides settings that control network properties and behavior for the computer. You can configure settings and behavior for DNS and offline files, prevent the use of ICS and ICF, prevent connection bridging, enable and configure QoS, and configure SNMP.

SEE ALSO   See Chapter 34 for a discussion of SNMP.

The Printers branch controls several properties for printing. For example, you can specify whether or not new printers added to the computer are published in Active Directory, enable or disable Internet-based printing to a printer on the computer, and specify a custom web page that appears in the left pane of the Printers folder to help users with printing problems.

User Configuration

The User Configuration branch contains policies that apply to users rather than to the computer.

TIP   As with the Computer Configuration branch, the Software Settings branch contains no policies that you can define at the local level.

Windows Settings

The Windows Settings branch lets you define logon and logoff scripts for users on the computer. The Public Key Policies branch contains a single policy, Autoenrollment Settings, that determines whether or not Windows XP automatically installs, updates, and renews user certificates.

The Internet Explorer Maintenance branch is the place to go to control the way IE looks and functions. You can change such properties as the animated icons that Internet Explorer displays in the toolbar, the title that appears in the browser, proxy settings, security settings, home page and other URLs, and several other settings. This branch essentially lets you customize IE without using a tool such as the Internet Explorer Administration Kit.

Administrative Templates

As in the Computer Configuration branch, the Administrative Templates branch under User Configuration contains numerous settings that control the way specific applications run and the types of actions a user can take with the application. For example, you can use the policies in the Internet Explorer branch to disable specific tabs in the Internet Explorer properties dialog box to prevent the user from changing certain types of settings.

Many of the policies under the Administrative Templates branch let you apply restrictions on the actions that a user can take within the operating system as well as in specific applications. I focus on applying restrictions separately in Chapter 43 because this is one of the main uses for modifying local policies when group policies are not available.

CHAPTER 43

Reining in Users with Policy Restrictions

Don't you just hate it when someone does something to their computer out of ignorance and you have to fix it? If you could just keep them out of Control Panel and hide all the drives in My Computer—or hide My Computer altogether—wouldn't that be great? Before it happens again and you consider homicide as an option, take a look at what group and local policies can do to prevent the problem.

In Chapter 42, I explained how group and local policies work and how you can use them to control a user's work environment. This includes the Desktop, location of My Documents, and other profile folders.

You can also use policies to restrict the actions a user can take on a computer. For example, if you don't make users a member of the Administrators group, they can't add or remove hardware or make certain other changes. But what if the computer has a FAT file system? There is nothing to prevent someone from opening a folder and deleting a bunch of critical files. Removing My Computer altogether, or at least limiting what it shows, can go a long way toward preventing this type of catastrophe.

In this chapter, I explain how you can use local and group policies to set hardware and software restrictions and to apply restrictions on the Desktop and working environment. For complete control over user settings and data, you should also go a step further, implementing folder redirection and the other suggestions I offer in Chapter 44.

> **NOTE** Windows XP Home Edition doesn't provide a means to set policies because it doesn't support them. So most of the restrictions I discuss in this chapter apply only to Windows XP Professional. Where possible, I've noted the manual method for setting these restrictions under Home Edition.

Applying System and Hardware Restrictions

Although nonadministrative users are restricted in what they can do to configure the system, there are still changes that users can make. Some of those changes present security risks, and others increase support calls. You can use group and local policies to restrict the actions that users can take within the system and for configuring hardware. The following sections explain how to implement specific restrictions, but this isn't a complete list; I've included the items most administrators and users want to control. You should take the time to scan through the policies for other possible changes that will benefit your network or the way in which you use Windows XP.

To make the changes I describe in the following sections, you need to edit group policies either at the local level or in Active Directory for domain members. I'll assume you're modifying them at the local level. Click Start ➤ Run and enter **MMC** in the Run dialog box. In the MMC, choose File ➤ Add/Remove Snap-In. Click Add in the dialog box, select the Group Policy snap-in, and click Add. Click Finish in the Select Group Policy Object dialog box. Click Close and click OK to return to the MMC console.

Disk Quotas

Disk quotas let you restrict the amount of disk space a user can consume on an NTFS volume. Quotas apply on a per-volume basis, so you don't have to worry about limiting a user's space in each folder. Quotas can help reduce wasted space taken up by MP3, AVI, and other nonessential files, and force users to more efficiently manage the space allocated to them.

NOTE FAT volumes do not support quotas. Both Windows XP Professional and Home Edition support quotas on NTFS volumes. However, Home Edition doesn't provide a means to set quotas through policies. Instead, you must configure them through the properties for the NTFS volume.

You can configure quotas manually through the Windows interface, but it's much handier to set them through policy, particularly when you need to apply the quotas to a large number of users. Setting the quota through a policy also ensures that any new users who are added to the computer or who come under the scope of the policy receive the specified quota settings.

To set quotas through a policy, open the \Computer Configuration\Administrative Templates\System\Disk Quotas branch. There are six policies that control disk quotas. I covered quotas in Chapter 20, so you can refer there if you need more details.

Remote Assistance

The Remote Assistance branch offers two policies that let you control the actions users can perform for Remote Assistance:

Solicited Remote Assistance   Use this policy to specify whether or not to permit remote control of the computer when the user requests remote assistance. If you enable the policy, you can choose between allowing remote users to control the computer or just to view it. You can also specify the maximum ticket duration, which determines how long a Remote Assistance request can be open.

Offer Remote Assistance   This policy determines whether or not Remote Assistance is allowed when the remote expert attempts to initiate the session without first receiving a request from the user. As with solicited Remote Assistance, you can choose between view-only or remote control if you enable the policy.

SEE ALSO   Remote Assistance is covered in detail in Chapter 31.

You can set Remote Assistance options on a Windows XP Home Edition computer with the Remote tab of the System properties (right-click My Computer and choose Properties).

System Restore

System Restore provides a means for Windows XP to automatically restore the system to a particular configuration. Users can create restore points that act as snapshots of the computer's configuration, and later restore the computer to one of those states, if needed. By default, System Restore is turned on. In some situations, however, you might want to prevent users from creating restore points or restoring their systems to a previous state.

There are two policies in the \Computer Configuration\Administrative Templates\System\System Restore branch that control the System Restore feature:

Turn Off System Restore   Enable this policy if you want to prevent the user from creating snapshots or performing a system restore operation. If this policy is enabled, the System Restore Wizard and configuration interface are unavailable to the user.

Turn Off Configuration   This option determines whether or not the user can configure System Restore through its configuration interface (accessed from the System Restore tab of the System properties). Enable this setting if you don't want users to be able to change System Restore configuration.

SEE ALSO   See Chapter 46 for a complete discussion of System Restore, including how to configure it, create restore points, and restore a system.

Simple Network Management Protocol (SNMP)

Security organizations recently discovered significant bugs in the public-domain code widely used by many companies to integrate Simple Network Management Protocol (SNMP) capabilities into their equipment. Although most vendors—including Microsoft—will move swiftly to address these problems, you might still want to impose some restrictions on SNMP.

The branch \Computer Configuration\Administrative Templates\Network\SNMP provides three policies that control SNMP on the client computer:

Communities   Use this policy to specify the SNMP communities for which the computer can respond to SNMP requests. With this policy enabled and the communities defined, the computer ignores requests from other communities. If the policy is not defined or is disabled, the computer responds to whatever communities are configured in its local SNMP settings.

Permitted Managers   Use this policy to specify the hosts that can submit SNMP requests to the client computer. With this policy enabled and the managers defined, the client ignores requests from other SNMP managers. If the policy is not defined or is disabled, the computer responds to the managers defined in its local SNMP settings.

Traps For Public Community   Use this policy to specify the hosts that receive SNMP traps from the local computer. If the policy is not defined or is disabled, the client sends traps to the hosts specified in its local SNMP settings.

SEE ALSO   See Chapter 34 for a complete discussion of the SNMP service and how to configure communities, managers, and traps without using policies.

Windows Explorer

The \User Configuration\Administrative Templates\Windows Components\Windows Explorer branch contains several policies that control the way the Explorer interface looks and functions. I won't cover all of these in detail, but instead just point out some of the policies you'll find most useful.

Several of the policies let you remove certain menus and functions from the Windows Explorer interface. For example, you can remove the Folder Options menu from the Tools menu, remove Map Network Drive and Disconnect Network Drive, hide the Manage item on My Computer's shortcut menu, and remove several other dialog boxes, tabs, and menu items to prevent users from accessing them.

TIP   In some cases, you can't completely prevent access to certain features. For example, although you can remove the Map Network Drive command, the user can still browse the network by entering the UNC path in the Run dialog box or in an Explorer window. They can also use the net use command to map a drive. Knowledgeable power users can get around many of these restrictions in one way or another.

One other change you might want to make is to restrict the drive icons that show up in My Computer. Use the policy Hide These Specified Drives In My Computer to specify which drives should appear.

The Common Open File Dialog sub-branch lets you specify which items show up in the Places bar, overriding the default set of paths and icons. You can specify local folders, UNC paths, and common shell folders. You can also use the remaining three policies to hide the Places bar or hide other elements.

Microsoft Management Console (MMC)

Use the \User Configuration\Administrative Templates\Windows Components\Microsoft Management Console branch to control which MMC snap-ins the user can open.

The policy Restrict The User From Entering Author Mode, if enabled, prevents the user from opening the MMC in author mode. This mode allows the user to create console files and add/remove snap-ins. Enabling this policy prevents the user from taking those actions.

The policy Restrict User To Explicitly Permitted List Of Snap-Ins lets you specify which snap-ins a user is allowed to add to a console. After you enable this setting, use the policies in the Restricted/Permitted Snap-Ins sub-branch to specify which snap-ins are allowed and which ones are denied. Enable a policy to allow the snap-in to be used; disable a policy to prevent that snap-in from being used.

If you want to give the user the ability to set some group or local policies but not others, enable the Group Policy Snap-In policy in the Group Policy sub-branch. Then, enable or disable policies in the Group Policy Snap-In Extensions and Resultant Set of Policy Snap-In Extensions branches to control which ones are allowed or denied, respectively.

Windows Update

The \User Configuration\Administrative Templates\Windows Components\Windows Update branch contains a single policy that you can use to deny access to the Windows Update site. This turns off automatic update and prevents the user from accessing the Windows Update site through the Windows Update link on the Start menu or from the Tools menu in Internet Explorer. It also prevents Device Manager from automatically installing device drivers from the Windows Update site.

Ctrl+Alt+Delete

The \User Configuration\Administrative Templates\System\Ctrl+Alt+Del Options branch contains four policies that let you control what happens when the user presses Ctrl+Alt+Delete. These policies include the following:

Remove Task Manager   Use this policy to prevent the user from running Task Manager.

Remove Lock Computer   Use this policy to remove the Lock Computer option from the Windows Security dialog box that appears when you press Ctrl+Alt+Delete.

Remove Change Password   Use this policy to remove the Change Password button from the Windows Security dialog box. The user can still change a password when prompted by the system, such as when the account password expires.

Remove Logoff   Use this policy to prevent the user from logging off of the system using any method, including scripts, console commands, or other methods.

Applying Software Restrictions

The previous sections covered policies that controlled system-wide capabilities and tasks, both hardware- and software-related. You can also use policies to control specific applications, allowing or denying the user the ability to perform certain tasks or configuration changes with the application. The following sections explore the policies you will likely find most useful for controlling applications. However, you should review all of the available policies for others that might also suit your needs.

NetMeeting

There are two places where you can set policies that control the user's ability to use specific features in NetMeeting. For example, you might want to allow video conferencing and chat but deny application sharing or remote control.

The \Computer Configuration\Administrative Templates\Windows Components\ NetMeeting branch contains one policy, Disable Remote Desktop Sharing. If enabled, this policy prevents users on the computer from using Remote Desktop Sharing, which allows another a remote user to take control of the computer.

The \User Configuration\Administrative Templates\Windows Components\NetMeeting branch contains many other policies that control NetMeeting in other ways. For example, you can configure NetMeeting, deny automatic acceptance of incoming calls, disable the Whiteboard feature, and control many other settings. You can also hide various menus and options from the user.

Internet Explorer

Use the \Computer Configuration\Administrative Templates\Windows Components\ Internet Explorer branch to control machine-wide Internet Explorer settings such as security zones, proxy settings, how Internet Explorer handles updates, and whether or not IE shows the splash screen on startup.

The \User Configuration\Administrative Templates\Windows Components\Internet Explorer branch contains several settings and sub-branches that control Internet Explorer on a per-user basis. These policies control the items that the user sees in IE's configuration interface and the actions they can take within Internet Explorer. You can also configure a handful of other application settings, including specifying whether or not Outlook Express should block attachments that could potentially contain a virus or malicious code.

Windows Installer

The \Computer Configuration\Administrative Templates\Windows Components\Windows Installer branch contains several policies that let you control whether or not the user can run the Windows Installer. Blocking the Windows Installer or limiting the user's access to it restricts the user's ability to install applications.

The \User Configuration\Administrative Templates\Windows Components\Windows Installer branch contains four additional policies that also control the Windows Installer.

Windows Messenger

Use the \Computer Configuration\Administrative Templates\Windows Components\ Windows Messenger branch to specify whether or not users on the computer can run Windows Messenger, and if so, whether or not it starts automatically. Disable this latter option to require the user to manually start Windows Messenger.

The \User Configuration\Administrative Templates\Windows Components\Windows Messenger branch contains the same settings but applies them at the user level rather than the computer level. This distinction is only applicable when imposing the policies at the OU, domain, or site level, where you can define policies so that different groups on the same computer have different policies applied.

Media Player

Use the \User Configuration\Administrative Templates\Windows Components\Windows Media Player branch to configure the appearance and behavior for Media Player. For example, you can specify the skin (appearance) of the player and lock it in that mode, preventing the user from switching views. You can prevent the user from being able to download additional codecs, and configure the ports, proxies, and protocols Media Player uses for streaming media.

Applying Desktop and Environment Restrictions

There are lots of policies you can configure to define the user's Desktop and working environment. For example, you can enable Active Desktop and set it for a particular URL, define what the user sees on the Start menu and Taskbar, and control the working environment in several other ways. The following sections provide a quick overview.

Start Menu and Taskbar

The \User Configuration\Administrative Templates\Start Menu And Taskbar branch is the place to go to control the items you want the user to see on the Start menu and Taskbar. Most of the policies in this branch let you remove specific items such as links to Windows Update, My Documents, Network Connections, Search, and other common items from the Start menu. Removing items not only streamlines the Start menu but also helps keep users out of areas where they don't belong. You can hide the system tray (a.k.a. the notification area), remove the clock from the tray, and make a handful of other tray changes.

If you prefer to give the users a classic Start menu rather than use the Windows XP Start menu, enable the policy Force Classic Start Menu. This not only forces the system to use the Windows 2000–style Start menu, but also displays My Computer, My Network Places, My Documents, My Pictures, and My Music icons on the Desktop.

Active Desktop

The \User Configuration\Administrative Templates\Desktop\Active Desktop policy branch lets you enable or disable Active Desktop, which can display dynamic data on the Desktop. In addition to displaying HTML data on the Desktop, you can also display JPEG wallpaper with Active Desktop enabled.

The policies in this branch also let you specify the wallpaper to be used and limit the wallpaper to bitmapped files only, excluding JPEG, GIF, PNG, and HTML documents. You can also add and remove URLs of data to be included or excluded from Active Desktop.

Control Panel

The \User Configuration\Administrative Templates\Control Panel branch is the place to go to restrict the user's ability to perform specific types of actions through Control Panel. For example, you might remove the Add Or Remove Programs icon from Control Panel to restrict the user's ability to modify Windows components or applications. If you are publishing applications from a server with group policys, you might want to use the policy Specify Default Category For Add New Programs to limit the display of application categories to the single specified category.

The other sub-branches in this policy branch specify other restrictions to limit the things users can do through Control Panel. For example, you can use the Display branch and its policies to prevent wallpaper changes, set the screensaver properties, and hide some or all of the tabs from the Display properties.

Use the Printers branch to prevent users from either adding or removing printers, and set the default locations for locating and adding printers. Use the Regional And Language Options branch to restrict the user to a specific language.

Offline Files

The \User Configuration\Administrative Templates\Network\Offline Files branch contains several policies that determine whether or not the user can use Offline Files and how the feature behaves. For example, you can specify synchronization settings, balloon reminders, and event logging. You can also specify that Windows XP not make redirected folders available offline by default.

Network Connections

The \User Configuration\Administrative Templates\Network\Network Connections branch is the place to go to control the tasks a user can perform in relation to the network. For example, you might use the policies in this branch to prevent the user from making changes to their network configuration, prevent them from enabling or disabling an interface, and prevent access to the New Connection Wizard. You'll also find settings here to control remote access connections and properties.

SEE ALSO   See Chapter 31 for details on configuring and using the remote access features in Windows XP.

Configuring Time

Keeping the time accurate on systems is important for a variety of reasons, but in particular for accurate backup, recovery, and event logging. To that end, Windows XP includes the Windows Time Service that lets you synchronize the time of a Windows XP computer with a time server. In a domain environment, domain members automatically synchronize their time with a domain controller at logon. In a workgroup, however, time synchronization doesn't happen by default.

You can use the \Computer Configuration\Administrative Templates\System\Windows Time Service policy branch to configure several policies that determine how the computer synchronizes its time. You can also use the Time Providers sub-branch to enable the time client and specify the time server to be used. Several time servers are freely available on the Internet, and Microsoft even provides their own at `time.microsoft.com`.

In addition, a Windows XP Professional computer can also function as a time server for other computers. Use the Enable Windows NTP Server policy to turn the computer into a time server. However, you also need to use the other policies to ensure that the computer synchronizes its time with a valid time server.

CHAPTER 44

Managing User Data and Settings

In the preceding chapter, I explained how to use group and local policies to control the changes that users can make to their Desktop and other elements of their working environment. I also explained how to apply change control to prevent users from making changes to their systems, and how to control the elements that appear on the user's Desktop, in My Computer, and in other locations in the interface.

Another aspect of good user management is ensuring that a user's documents and other data are secure and safe from system failures, or if a failure does occur, that you can recover that data quickly with minimal disruption.

In this chapter, I explain how to use local and group policies to manage user data and settings. You'll see how to redirect user data folders to a server to support roaming users and provide a higher degree of recoverability in the event of a system failure. This chapter also covers user profiles and scripts to help you understand how to create a particular working environment for a user when they log on.

Redirecting Folders

System failures are one of an IT manager's worst nightmares. If the failure happens to the CEO, it's even worse! When it happens to your own system, you know the frustration that other users feel when a critical tool suddenly goes away, taking all of their work with it.

Improving and streamlining disaster recovery is extremely important to minimizing downtime and ensuring that you can recover a system and its data quickly if the need arises. Equally important, streamlining the process reduces the pressure you will feel from users to get their systems back up and their data back in their hands.

Having been a system administrator for a long time, I can tell you that most users are notoriously bad about backing up their data, even if you give them the means to do so.

You can implement an agent-based backup mechanism to back up user data from their workstation to a server, but this approach has some potential pitfalls. For example, how can you be sure some users won't simply shut off their computers at the end of the day, preventing the server from backing them up?

A better approach is to place the users' data on a server. There are a couple of ways to achieve that, but one of the best approaches in my opinion is to use group or local policies to redirect user folders such as My Documents to a network server. With the files residing on the server it's much easier to implement a reliable backup and recovery strategy.

TIP   Folder redirection is not possible on Windows XP Home Edition because it does not support group or local policies. You can redirect folders on a Windows XP Professional system using group policies if the computer is a domain member. You cannot redirect folders using local policies, which prevents policy-based redirection for workgroup members.

Redirecting folders also considerably simplifies recovery of a failed workstation. You don't need to restore the documents; just restore the operating system or install a new system, point Windows to the server for the files, and voila! the user is back to work.

TIP   Use RIS or another automated OS deployment method to install the operating system for even better recoverability. See Chapter 3 for a discussion of using RIS for remote deployment.

Redirection Options

You can redirect five user folders: Application Data, Desktop, My Documents, My Pictures, and Start Menu. There are three policy states that control redirection of these folders. The first, No Administrative Policy Defined, takes no action on the folder. In the case of non-roaming users, the folder remains on the user's local computer. For roaming users, the folder resides in the roaming profile and is copied across the network to the user's workstation at logon.

The option Basic—Redirect Everyone's Folder To The Same Location lets you redirect folders regardless of the users' security group membership. Generally, you specify a location in the form \\server\share\%username% to cause the folder to be redirected to a folder on a network share with a name that matches the user name. For example, you might specify \\srv1\users\%username%\My Documents to redirect the My Documents folder to a network share. For the user jboyce, My Documents would be redirected to \\srv1\users\jboyce\My Documents.

You can use the Basic option to redirect a particular folder for all users to the same location to provide common content. For example, you might redirect the Start Menu folder to a common folder on a network share to ensure that all users see the same Start Menu. It's unlikely, however, that you would redirect My Documents to a common folder, unless of course you wanted the users to have a common set of documents.

The option Advanced—Specify Locations For Various User Groups lets you specify redirection based on group membership, which provides a lot more flexibility. With this policy setting, you don't specify a single location, but instead specify a location for specific security groups. For example, you might redirect Start Menu for the administrators to one folder and Start Menu for general users to a different folder. The result is that everyone in the group receives a particular folder. As with the Basic option, you can specify a common folder or use variables such as %username% to redirect based on the users' account name.

Setting Up Redirection

You configure folder redirection only at the group policy level, which requires access to the domain controller where you want the policies applied. Open the Active Directory Users And Computers console on a domain controller for the computer, open the properties for the container at which you want to apply the policies (such as an organizational unit), and edit or create a group policy object from the Group Policy tab.

With the Group Policy editor open, expand the branch \User Configuration\Windows Settings\Folder Redirection. Right-click the folder you want to redirect and choose Properties. On the Target tab (Figure 44.1), select the redirection method from the drop-down list.

FIGURE 44.1:

Use the Target tab to specify redirection method.

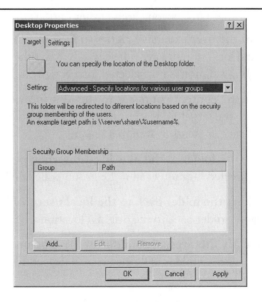

If you choose Advanced, the Security Group Membership box appears on the tab. Click Add to display the Specify Group And Location dialog box (Figure 44.2). Type the group name or click Browse to browse the Active Directory for it. Then, specify the desired folder location in the Target Folder Location field.

FIGURE 44.2:

FIGURE 44.2:

Specify the group and
its folder location.

Here's where it gets a bit tricky, regardless of the redirection option you choose. If you
specify a local path for the folder, the effect is that the user is redirected to that local path on
his computer, not on the server. So, the specified folder must exist on each system that comes
under the scope of the policy. To redirect the user to a network share, you must enter the
folder path in UNC format, such as **\\srv1\shares\%username%\My Documents**.

The Settings tab lets you choose other options that control folder redirection:

"Grant the user exclusive rights to *folder*"   Configure permissions on the folder so the
user and local system have full access, but no other users have access (including administrators). If this option is not selected, no changes are made to the folder's permissions.

"Move the contents of *folder* to the new location"   Redirect the contents of the source
folder to the target folder. For example, you would enable this option to have a user's local
My Folders contents moved to a server.

"Leave the folder in the new location when policy is removed"   Files will remain in
the redirected location even if the group policy no longer applies.

"Redirect the folder back to the local userprofile location when policy is removed"
Move the folder back to the original location when the group policy no longer applies.

"Make My Pictures a subfolder of My Documents"   The default location for My Pictures is as a subfolder of My Documents. Select this option to redirect My Pictures along
with My Documents.

"Do not specify administrative policy for My Pictures"   Leave My Pictures in its
default location as defined by the user's profile.

Working with User Profiles

In Chapter 41, I explained how to create and manage user accounts, but there were a few user account settings I opted to cover in this chapter because they relate to user profiles.

In Windows XP, each user has a user profile made up of several components, one of which is that user's set of profile folders. These include My Documents, Start Menu, and the others described in the previous section. The file ntuser.dat, a portion of the user's Registry that is stored in the user's profile folder, also becomes part of the user profile. This portion of the Registry defines the user's working environment, such as the Desktop, screensaver, and other elements.

In Windows NT, the Registry portion of the user's profile was the primary means by which administrators applied restrictions and change control. With the introduction of group policy, the need to control user settings by enforcing the use of a particular ntuser.dat became largely unnecessary. However, it can still be a useful technique for managing users, particularly those who do not fall under the scope of group policy (such as workgroup members). So, let's take a look at how you can use a profile to provide change control.

Understanding Profiles

Each user account includes several properties in addition to the user name and password. The Profile tab (Figure 44.3) shows some of these additional properties, one of which is the Profile Path setting.

FIGURE 44.3:

Use the Profile tab to configure profile location and other settings.

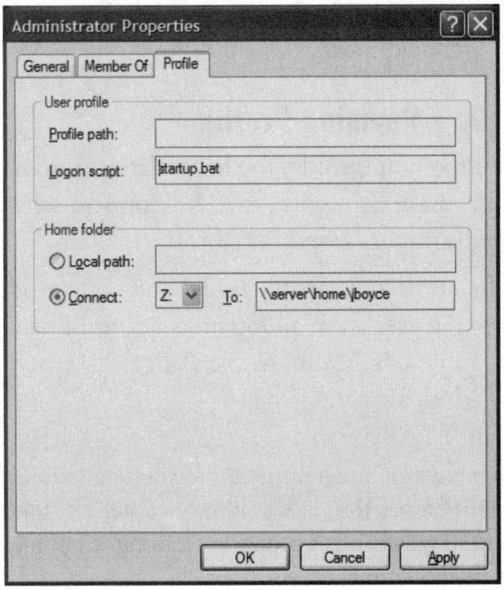

When a user logs on, Windows XP looks in the folder specified by Profile Path for the `ntuser.dat` file. If it finds one there, it applies that file as the user's portion of the Registry. The settings stored in the Registry file then define the user's work environment. The remaining profile comes from the user's profile store, located by default in `C:\Documents and Settings\`*user*, where *user* is the user's logon name. Or the profile is redirected to a network server by group policy, as I explained in the previous section.

There are three types of profiles: standard, roaming, and mandatory. With a standard profile, the user's `ntuser.dat` file is stored locally. When the user logs on to another computer, it's possible for him to have a different working environment because the profile doesn't follow him to the other computer.

With a roaming profile, however, the profile is stored on a network share and referenced in the user's Profile Path by a UNC path that is accessible from all computers where he needs to log on. When the user logs on, Windows XP copies the profile across the network from the specified location. This means that a user can have the same Desktop configuration regardless of logon location.

If you rename the `ntuser.dat` file to `ntuser.man`, it becomes a mandatory profile. The user can make changes to the working environment (such as changing Desktop schemes or colors, for example), but those changes are lost when the user logs off and the previous configuration applies when the user logs back on. So, a mandatory profile lets you control the user's initial working environment and prevent permanent changes.

If you can't use group policy to achieve the result you want, you can opt to control user settings through the profile. First decide whether you want to set up a roaming or mandatory profile. Then follow the steps outlined in the following sections to create the profile.

Setting Up a Roaming Profile

To create a roaming profile, log on as the user to one of the computers where you want the profile to be used. Configure the Desktop and other settings as needed, and then log off. Log on again, this time as administrator.

Open the user's local profile folder and copy `ntuser.dat` to a network share that will be available to the user from all logon locations. Then open the user's account properties and click the Profile tab. In the Profile Path field, enter the path to the folder where the profile is stored, in UNC format.

TIP   Keep in mind that some of the profile settings stored in `ntuser.dat` are hardware-specific, so in many cases the user will have to log on from similar workstations for the roaming profile settings to work properly. This isn't usually a major problem, but something for which you should plan.

In cases where the user logs on to a domain, you set the profile path through the domain account properties in the Active Directory Users And Groups console on a domain controller. You can set up a roaming profile for users in a workgroup, although the process becomes more complex. The user must have a logon account at each workstation they use, which means you need to set the Profile Path for each local account to point to the roaming profile path for that user. Use the Local Users And Group branch of the Computer Management console on each computer to set these properties.

Setting Up a Mandatory Profile

You use a similar method to set up a mandatory profile as when setting up a roaming profile. Log on as the user to a target workstation and configure the work environment. Log off and log back on as administrator. Open the profile folder for the account you just modified and rename `ntuser.dat` to `ntuser.man`.

If this is the user's only computer, the job is done. If you are setting up a roaming mandatory profile, however, you need to copy the `ntuser.man` file to a network share accessible to the user at logon. Then, open the user's account properties and specify the path to that folder in the Profile Path field.

Applying Logon and Logoff Scripts

Whether you are working in a workgroup or domain, you can use logon and logoff scripts to automatically perform actions when you log on or log off. As you might have guessed, the logon script executes when the user logs on and the logoff scripts executes when the user logs off. Common tasks for a logon script include mapping network drives and printers and running programs. Common logoff tasks include disconnecting resources, cleaning up local folders, sending notifications, and so on.

NOTE   Although it's most common to run batch files as logon scripts, you can actually run any executable or even launch documents through application association. However, you should use the `Startup` folder or other methods described later in this chapter instead of scripts for those purposes.

Where to Store the Scripts

When you specify a path for a script in a policy, you can enter it as a UNC path, absolute local path, or relative local path. Which particular method you use depends on how and where you assign the script.

A Windows 2000 or .NET Server maintains a script folder for each policy object. To view the location for the scripts for a particular policy, open the Active Directory Users And Computers console and open the group policy object. Open the appropriate policy, such as \User Configuration\Windows Settings\Scripts\Logon. Click Show Files on the policy's dialog box to open a folder window in the designated folder. If a script resides in this folder, you can specify only the script name in the policy and omit any other path information. Otherwise, you need to specify the path to the script. Enter a UNC path if you want to pull the script from a shared folder not local to the user's logon location. Specify an absolute path to pull the script from the user's local computer. Then, make sure you copy the script into the appropriate folder.

> **TIP**   If you're dealing with local policy–based scripts, store the scripts in the `%systemroot%\`
> `System32\GroupPolicy\User\Scripts\Logon` folder on the local computer, or a sub-
> folder of that folder.

Account-based scripts are a little different. Store account-based logon scripts in the NETLOGON share on the server, which Windows sets up by default in the \SYSVOL\ *domain*\SCRIPTS folder. The SYSVOL folder location varies depending on where you specified its location during Active Directory installation.

> **TIP**   If you're not sure where NETLOGON is located, open the Shares branch of the Computer
> Management console. The right pane lists all shares and their physical paths.

If you're specifying logon scripts for users in a workgroup, start by creating a NETLOGON share on the local computer. Place general scripts in that folder, and create user folders under the share for user-specific scripts. When you specify the path to the script in the user's properties, specify only the script name if the script resides in the NETLOGON share, or preface it with the subfolder name if it resides in a subfolder. For example, specify **special\somescript.bat** if the `somescript.bat` file resides in \NETLOGON\special.

> **TIP**   You can use the `%username%` variable to specify a script located in a folder under NETLOGON
> that matches the user's logon name.

Now, let's get down to business and assign some scripts. You can define logon and logoff scripts in two ways: with policies or through the user account properties.

Policy-Based Scripts

The \User Configuration\Windows Settings\Scripts policy branch contains two policies, Logon and Logoff, which define the scripts that execute for users who fall under the scope of the policy. You can set the scripts either locally or at the site, domain, or OU level, as needed.

To add a script, open the policy to display the properties sheet, which lists the existing scripts, if any, for the policy. Click Add to display the Add A Script dialog box. Enter the path to the script file. Usually the script is a BAT or CMD file, but you can specify other executables, as well.

You can also specify optional parameters for the script, which get passed to the script when it executes. This lets you tailor a common script that contains replaceable variables to a specific user by passing those variables to the script at execution time. Enter the optional parameters in the Script Parameters field.

Finally, make sure you copy the script to the appropriate folder depending on the default path for the particular policy object.

TIP   One advantage to using policy-based scripts is the ability to specify multiple scripts. You can only assign one account-based script (covered in the next section).

Account-Based Scripts

You can also specify logon and logoff scripts through the user's account properties. This gives you a handy means to execute scripts for members of a workgroup who don't receive policy-based scripts. What's more, you can use a combination of policy-based and account-based scripts to execute multiple scripts as needed. For example, you might use a policy-based script to perform general tasks for all users and use the account-based script to perform user-specific tasks.

To specify an account-based script for domain members, open the Active Directory Users And Computers console on the target domain controller, then open the user's account. Click the Profile tab and enter the script in the Logon Script field. Then copy the script to the appropriate location in the NETLOGON share.

To specify an account-based script for local users, open the Local Users And Groups branch of the Computer Management console. Open the properties for the account, click the Profile tab, and specify the script in the Logon Script field. Then copy the script to the appropriate location in the NETLOGON share.

Controlling Script Execution

Group and local policy offers a handful of settings that control logon and logoff script execution. The \User Configuration\Administrative Templates\System\Logon/Logoff branch of the group policy offers the following settings that affect logon and logoff scripts:

Run Logon Scripts Synchronously   Enable this policy if you want all scripts to finish processing before Windows XP displays the Explorer interface. If this policy is disabled or not set, the logon scripts need not complete before the Explorer interface appears.

Run Legacy Logon Scripts Hidden   Enable this policy if you want scripts written for Windows NT or earlier to be hidden. When the policy is disabled or not defined, the scripts appear in a console window while they execute.

Run Logon Scripts Visible   Enable this policy if you want Windows XP to display the console window for the script when it executes. When this policy is disabled or not defined, the console is hidden.

Run Logoff Scripts Visible   Enable this policy to display the console window for logoff scripts when they execute. The console is hidden if this policy is disabled or not defined.

You can also set these same policies locally. They are located in \User Configuration\ Administrative Templates\System\Scripts.

Alternatives to Logon Scripts

Logon scripts are a handy way to perform tasks during logon, but you have other methods available to you, as well. The Startup folder, for example, lets you start applications automatically at logon, making it an alternative to logon scripts. You can create a script and simply place it in your Startup folder to have it execute at startup. This is a handy technique for Home Edition, which doesn't support group or local policies.

You can also consider using the Registry to run applications at startup. To add a program for the *current* user, open the Registry Editor and expand the branch

```
\HKEY_CURRENT_USER\Software\Microsoft\Windows\CurrentVersion\Run
```

Create a new string value in this key and set as its value the program you want to execute at startup. Include the path and enclose the path in quotes. Add any optional parameters for the program outside the quotes, as in the following example:

```
"c:\program files\office\winword.exe" /a
```

TIP   If you want the program to run for *all* users at logon, create the entry in the key \HKEY_LOCAL_MACHINE\Software\Microsoft\Windows\CurrentVersion\Run.

PART VIII

Backup and Disaster Recovery

CHAPTER 45

Backup

Windows XP includes a powerful set of tools and utilities that can help you recover a failed system. These tools include the Backup Utility program and System Restore. If you use computers long enough, you'll eventually need one of these tools.

Of these, the Backup Utility is the one you should be most familiar with right from the start. You've heard it by now: if it's important, or even if you think it will be, back it up. The hard disk on your system is arguably the most important piece of your computer; without it, your computer would be little more than a calculator or a video game console. People buy computers so that they can work with a set of information day after day, and that data needs to be stored on a hard disk if it is to be available. Yet the hard disk is also one of the more fragile devices of your system, failing on average more times than any other computer component. In the event of a disk crash, your data can be impossible to retrieve without dropping the GNP of New Zealand on a data recovery service.

And, along with being at risk because of mechanical failure, your data is also vulnerable, as you may have experienced by now, to the vagaries of human error. People have been known to make typos, and they have also clicked the wrong button a time or two, sending critical data into the ether. Also, people have been known to "try out" the `format` and `fdisk` utilities for (their own) entertainment. All right, I've made my point: you are, in your lifetime as an administrator, going to lose data, and your next paycheck may depend on your ability to get it back. But you will be able to retrieve data if you are in the habit of following a regular backup strategy and have a good command of the Windows XP Backup Utility.

Backup Utility Basics

The job of the Backup Utility is to back up all selected data to a single file that is named with a file extension of `.bkf`. The Windows XP Backup Utility is an updated version of the Backup Utility included in Windows 2000, which in turn was a much more powerful version than was included with NT 4. The destination of this backup file can be any device that stores files, such as tapes, removable disks, and even network locations.

The first time you access the Backup Utility, you launch the Backup Or Restore Wizard (choose Start ➤ All Programs ➤ Accessories ➤ System Tools ➤ Backup). As Figure 45.1 shows, the Backup Utility always starts with the Welcome screen, unless you clear the Always Start In Wizard Mode check box.

FIGURE 45.1:

The Backup Or Restore Wizard opens at the Welcome screen.

You have used wizards by now, and I won't go through each and every screen of this utility. If you have backed up anything before, you'll find this tool easy to use. You simply tell the wizard which files to back up and where to store the backed-up data. When the backup is done, you can click the Report button to view a log file generated as the files were copied and verify that the backup was a success.

Instead of using the wizard, you can back up manually using Advanced Mode, as shown in Figure 45.2. When you back up manually, you can specify whether to verify the data after the backup, whether to replace the backup files or append them to existing backups, and when to run the backup.

Click the Backup tab, and select the files and folders you want to back up. At the bottom of the Backup tab, choose the location for the backup from the Backup Destination list.

You use the Restore And Manage Media tab to specify what and where you want to restore. Again, it's just a matter of a few clicks. You use the Schedule Jobs tab to schedule backups, and I'll show you how to do this later in this chapter.

What About Transferring Backups to a CD?

When you step through the Backup Or Restore Wizard, you are asked where to back up; however, backing up directly to a CD is not an option. Nevertheless, you can easily copy your backup to a CD using the CD Writing Wizard in Windows XP or your favorite burning software. In fact, this backup strategy is recommended; you can archive your backups on a medium that is effortless to store off-site and that is difficult to damage. Keep in mind that you need enough free space on your target disk to hold the backup file or files and that the backup must be small enough (650–700 MB, depending on the capacity of your CD) to fit onto a single CD-ROM. If the backup job is too big to fit on a single disk, you'll need to break up the backup so that more than one file is created.

FIGURE 45.2:

You can use Advanced Mode to back up manually.

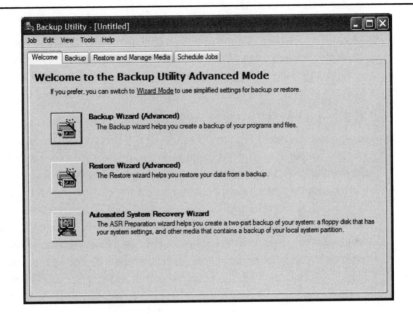

What About Backing Up Directly to a CD?

As with all things computer, you have other options if you want to back up straight to the CD, skipping the intermediary step described previously. Actually, you can attack this problem in two ways:

- Back up directly to the CD, using a third-party backup program.

- Install software, such as Roxio's Easy CD Creator, to trick the Backup Utility into thinking the CD-R device is just another hard disk on your system.

Here are a couple of great third-party programs that you can use:

Backup to CD-RW (Made Simple) 4.0   Distributed by Willow Creek Software, this is an easy-to-use program for backing up to a CD-RW or CD-R. It can even back up to a hard disk or to a network drive.

Nero Burning ROM   This program is distributed by Ahead Software, and you can download a trial version at www.nero.com.

Where Is the Backup Utility in Windows XP Home Edition?

If you are using Windows XP Professional, the Backup Utility is installed by default and is part of the System Tools. (Many think it better fits under Administrative Tools, because the backup of data is usually an administrative task, but we didn't get to write the operating system code, now did we?) If you are using the Home Edition, however, the Backup Utility isn't installed during setup. You must install it from the \Valueadd\Msft\Ntbackup folder on the Windows XP CD-ROM.

TIP   So who do you have to be to perform a backup anyway? Users with Administrator or Backup Operator privileges can back up and restore any files on the system, even files they cannot otherwise access. Individual users can back up and restore files that they own.

Creating an Automated System Recovery Disk

An automated system recovery disk (ASR) is a backup configuration whose purpose is to get your system partition up and running again quickly. It saves the entire contents of your system drive to a backup medium of your choice. Moreover, it saves information about the current location of system files, detected hardware, and partitions (or volumes) to a floppy disk. It's good administrative practice to create an ASR right after a successful installation of Windows XP and then update it any time you significantly change the system, for example, when you change or upgrade any vital device drivers. However, one of the drawbacks of the ASR is that it only backs up (and restores) data that exists on the system volume. If you want to be able to restore other disks on your computer, run the Backup Wizard and back up everything on the computer.

To create an ASR, click the Automated System Recovery Wizard option in the Welcome To The Backup Utility Advanced Mode dialog box to start the Automated System Recovery Preparation Wizard. Again, I will not walk you though each step of this wizard; it's much more important that you know the purpose of the ASR. You will be asked for the location of the system partition backup, and then when prompted, insert a floppy disk to save the system recovery information. Keep this ASR floppy disk in a safe place when you are finished.

Remember, the ASR is not a complete backup, and for this reason you should not consider your backup strategy comprehensive if all you're using is Automated System Recovery. Instead, you use the ASR to quickly repair and restart Windows XP if your computer will not start or if system files become corrupt. But remember: the ASR floppy disk is not a bootable disk. To access the ASR floppy, you must first boot the computer using either the Windows XP Professional installation CD-ROM or the setup floppies that can be created from the XP Professional CD. Follow these steps:

1. Set your computer's BIOS to boot from the CD-ROM, and then restart the computer.

2. When prompted to do so, press F2.

3. When prompted to insert the ASR floppy, do so, and follow the on-screen instructions to restore your system files.

TIP The ASR is available in Windows XP Professional, but not in Home Edition. Although the Backup Utility may appear to make an ASR disk, you can't use this disk to restore because Home Edition doesn't support setups from ASR disks.

Backing Up System State Data

The system state of a computer is generally defined as all the files that are critical to the environment. In plain English, the system state includes information about user accounts, hardware and software settings, and files required for startup. However, what exactly is included in the system state differs from operating system to operating system and depends on which services are running on a computer. In this section, I'll expand the discussion to include Windows 2000 and .NET Server products, to give you a better picture of the importance of backing up the system state. I'll then specify what constitutes the system state on an XP Professional machine, which as you will see is just a subset of system state components.

Backing up the system state is critical when many changes have been made to the computer. For example, if you have a Windows 2000 system that acts as a domain controller on a small network and the hard disk crashes, you will most likely immediately reinstall the operating system to a new disk. However, this step does not restore the contents of the Active Directory database, which is critical to recovering your network's original environment. You would have to re-create all user accounts. When you back up the system state, you ensure that the computer can be returned to its original condition.

You can back up and restore the following system state components using the Backup Utility program in Windows XP:

- The Registry
- The COM+ Class Registration database
- Boot files, including the system files
- The Certificate Services database
- The Active Directory directory service
- The SYSVOL directory
- Cluster service information

- The IIS metadirectory
- System files that are under Windows File Protection

When you choose to back up or restore the system state data, all the system state data that is relevant to your computer is backed up or restored; that is, you cannot choose to back up or restore individual components because of dependencies among the components. However, you can restore the system state data to an alternate location. If you do so, only the Registry files, the SYSVOL directory, the Cluster service information, and system boot files are restored. The Active Directory service, the Certificate Services database, and the COM+ Class Registration database are not restored.

As you can see, backing up the system state is critical for most servers on a network: domain controllers, web servers, certificate servers, and the like. It is not as quite as crucial on Windows XP Professional systems.

On XP Professional computers, the system state data comprises only the Registry, the COM+ Class Registration database, files under Windows File Protection, and boot files. In other words, unless you have tons of user accounts on your system or are using it as the network's web server, not much that can't be (relatively) quickly restored after reinstalling the operating system.

Automating Backup

Your backup strategy should include the scheduling of regular backups. You can establish a schedule using the Backup Or Restore Wizard or using the Schedule Jobs tab in the Backup Utility Advanced Mode. To use the wizard, on the final screen click the Advanced button. Now, select the backup type (discussed later in this chapter), how to back up, and what to do with the file. In the When To Backup window, choose to begin the job now or later.

To schedule a backup job from the Backup Wizard, click the Later option, and then click the Set Schedule button to open the Schedule Job dialog box, as shown in Figure 45.3. The contents of this dialog box depend on the frequency option you choose from the drop-down list box. For example, if you select Monthly, you can specify which day of the month the backup will run. You can further fine-tune the schedule by clicking the Advanced button.

You can also open the Schedule Jobs dialog box by clicking the Schedule Jobs tab on the Backup Utility Advanced Mode screen. Click the Add Job button, and you're on your way. Either way, you'll be using the interface just described. To modify an existing job, however, you will need to return to the Schedule Jobs tab in Advanced Mode. Click the Schedule Data tab, and then click the Properties button to open the Schedule Job dialog box.

You can schedule a
backup job using the
options in the Sched-
ule Job dialog box.

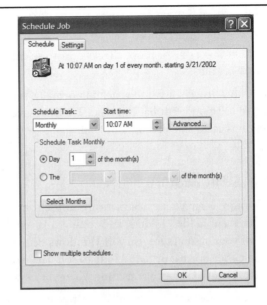

Importing Other Backup Sets

If you have previously saved a backup job, you can use these same settings to perform future
backups. The Backup Utility lets you quickly import these settings. Follow these steps:

1. From the Welcome To The Backup Utility Advanced Mode screen, click the Backup tab.

2. Choose Job ➤ Load Selections to open the Open dialog box.

3. Previously used settings are saved with the .bks extension. Select a job, and then click the Open button.

You should now see one or more checks next to selections in the Backup tab, as appropriate to the saved settings.

You can now proceed with the backup normally, setting a new schedule if you like or choosing to use a different backup type. This can save you the hassle of making several check box selections each time you back up your data.

Using System Restore

System Restore is an XP service that runs in the background, continually monitoring changes to essential files, folders, and settings. At regular intervals, System Restore takes a snapshot of your system's Registry. If Windows becomes unstable, you can use System Restore in either normal or Safe Mode to roll back your system files and Registry settings to those that were used at a previous time when your system was working properly.

Using System Restore is especially effective in the following situations:

- You install a program that conflicts with other software drivers on your system. If uninstalling the program doesn't fix the situation, you can restore to a point before the program was installed.

- You install one or more updated drivers that cause system instability. You can use System Restore to restore all previously installed derivers instead of using the Driver Rollback feature from Device Manager (a procedure that is mentioned in Chapter 22).

- Your system develops performance or stability problems for no apparent reason. This situation may not seem plausible at first glance; after all, problems always occur for a reason, right? But consider a situation in which a computer is shared by many people, family members or coworkers who may or may not document changes they make or install untested or unsupported software or devices without compatible drivers. You can restore to a point where you are reasonably sure that the system was functioning properly (that is, the last time *you* were using it).

TIP   Don't count on System Restore to replace a good antivirus program. A system can become infected and not exhibit any symptoms. Thus, files stored in restore points can be infected without your knowledge, even if the computer was functioning properly at the restore point.

System Restore keeps a log of changes to a system in the *%systemroot%*\system32\Restore folder. At regular intervals, System Restore takes snapshots of the system state, looking at the same type of information that is saved when you back up system state data.

By default, System Restore creates restore points without user intervention every 24 hours if you leave your computer on. If you shut down your system, System Restore creates a new restore point when you restart if the most recent restore point was created more than 24 hours ago.

To restore a previous system configuration, you must be logged on as a user who is a member of the Administrators group. Be sure that no other users are logged on to the machine over the network, and shut down all running programs. Then, follow these steps:

1. Choose Start ➤ Help And Support to open the Help and Support Center home page.

2. In the Pick A Task list, click Undo Changes To Your Computer With System Restore, or choose Start ➤ All Programs ➤ Accessories ➤ System Tools ➤ System Restore. Either way, you open System Restore.

3. Click Restore My Computer To An Earlier Time, and then click Next to open the Select A Restore Point screen.

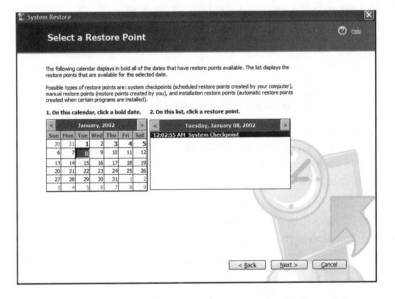

4. Select a date that represents a system restore point, and then click Next to open the Confirm Restore Point Selection screen.

5. Verify the date you selected, and then click Next.

System Restore copies the necessary files and settings from the System Restore archives. Your system then restarts automatically.

TIP   You can always run System Restore again and choose Undo My Last Restoration if the results are not what you expect.

In addition to creating restore points at 24-hour intervals, System Restore creates restore points when you do the following:

- Install an unsigned third-party driver. When you install an unsigned driver, Windows displays a warning message. If you continue anyway (who doesn't?), the system creates a restore point before completing the installation.

- Install an application using an installer that's compatible with System Restore. Applications that use the Windows Installer and InstallShield Professional 6.1 or later are included in this category.

- Install a Windows Update update or a patch. Windows creates a restore point automatically when you download and install an update using Windows Update.

- Restore a prior configuration using System Restore. Each time you run System Restore, it creates a new restore point so that you can undo the restore, as mentioned earlier.

- Restore data from a backup set created with the Windows XP Backup Utility program. If the restoration of the backed-up files creates problems, you can reverse the effects using System Restore.

Furthermore, you can customize the restore interval. Follow these steps:

1. Open the Registry Editor and locate the key

    `\HKLM\SOFTWARE\Microsoft\WindowsNT\CurrentVersion\SystemRestore`

2. Change the RPGlobalInterval value from its default setting of 86,400 (a value of seconds, which, to save you a trip to your calculator, comes out to 24 hours). Cut it in half, to 43,200 for example, to take a System Restore snapshot twice a day. Double it for snapshots every other day and so on. Automatic snapshots will still take place.

By default, restore points are deleted every 90 days. You can adjust this interval by changing the RPLifeInterval, as shown in Figure 45.4, from the default setting of 7,776,000 seconds. RPLifeInterval is also under the Registry key

   `\HKLM\SOFTWARE\Microsoft\WindowsNT\CurrentVersion\SystemRestore`

Using Third-Party Backup Applications

At `www.download.com`, you'll find many disk backup utilities, many of which are free. You'll also find several shareware and demo versions of other popular backup programs at this site. The following are only a few of your choices:

- Norton Ghost 2002, from Symantec
- EasyRecovery, published by McAffee software
- GoBack3, from Roxio

- BurnDrive 1.0, written by Burn Drive
- Second Copy 2000, from Centered Systems
- Backup to CD-RW (Make Simple) 4.0, as described earlier

FIGURE 45.4:

The RPLifeInterval value will determine how long restore points are kept.

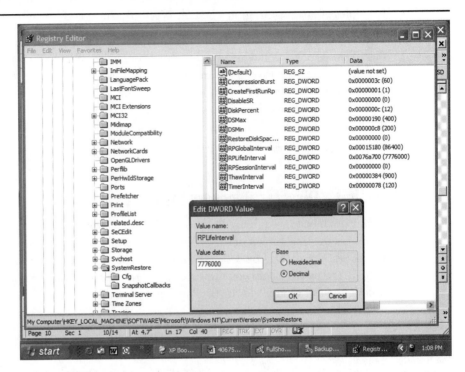

What's more, you don't even need a dedicated backup program to achieve effective backup implementation. Here are some other options:

Use the Files And Settings Transfer Wizard   Although not designed specifically for this purpose, this wizard makes a good backup tool. You can use it to move files from one system to another.

Make copies   That's right. Although not all that glamorous, and requiring little technical knowledge, just copying something to another location, whether it be a floppy disk, a Zip drive, or a CD, is an effective backup strategy. This method works as long as you can remember to make copies at regular intervals and you need a relatively simple backup. For example, keep all the data that you ever need backed up in a folder called Data, and set your Palm device to remind you every week or so to make a copy of Data.

Make a disk image   This strategy uses software not designed explicitly for backup purposes but that is very effective as such. The entire contents of the disk, operating system and all, are stored in an image file. This file represents the entire disk contents, operating system and all, and you can copy it to another blank hard disk in the event of emergency. Examples of imaging programs include Norton's Ghost and Drive Image.

Use other file-syncing utilities   These utilities are third-party versions of the File And Settings Transfer Wizard and help you set up mirror images of important data folders elsewhere, usually on a network drive. Software of this ilk was also a solution for working with offline files until Offline Files came around in Windows 2000. Using this strategy, you always have two copies of your working files, one locally and one on the network. In the event of a crash, only the most recent changes since the last sync are lost (like the last couple of paragraphs I just wrote on my laptop and which you are now enjoying immensely—see, it worked).

Planning a Disaster Recovery Strategy

Earlier, we stepped through the Backup Or Restore Wizard, telling the utility exactly what to back up. On the final screen of this wizard, you can click the Advanced Options button to open the Options dialog box. Click the Backup Type tab, which is shown in Figure 45.5, to specify what type of backup you want to make. (You can also open the Options dialog box by choosing Tools ➢ Options in the Backup Utility window.)

FIGURE 45.5:

Use the options on the Backup Type tab to select the kind of backup you want.

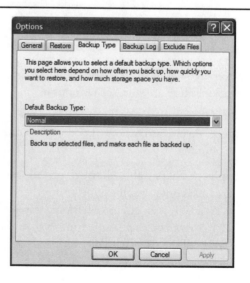

So which backup type is best? As is the case with so many computing scenarios, it all depends. The best backup type for your situation depends on how much data you are backing up, how often, how quickly you want the backup to be performed, and how many backups you are willing to apply in the event of a restore. You have the following choices:

Normal   Backs up all selected files and marks each file as having been backed up; that is, it clears the archive bit. This type of backup is often used as a benchmark that other backup types can use to determine what needs backing up. Because it backs up everything you select, the normal backup takes the longest, but is the easiest to restore. Many companies that shut down operation for the night perform a full nightly backup, because time is not a concern.

Copy   Backs up all selected files and does not mark them as being backed up. A copy is useful as a quick way to archive working data without impacting your overall backup strategy.

Differential   Backs up only the selected files that have changed since the last normal or incremental backup and does not clear the archive bit, which would mark them as having been backed up. Because it does not clear the archive bit, a differential backup always uses as a point of reference the last time the archive bit was cleared. These backups take longer, but are quicker to restore. You can restore all data using the last full backup and then apply only the most recent differential backup.

Incremental   Backs up selected files that have not been marked as archived and marks the files as having been backed up. These backup types are much more quick to back up, but take longer to restore because more backups must be applied to the last normal backup. To perform a restore, this strategy requires that the last normal backup and all the incremental backups be applied.

Daily   Backs up only the selected files that have changed on the current day and does not clear the archive bit. Each daily backup and the last normal backup are required for a successful restore. The daily backup is a way to back up a day's work without affecting the overall backup strategy.

TIP   Most of the time your backup strategies should include the normal, differential, and incremental backup types. Use the other types of backups sparingly, because it can become confusing to keep track of what files are where when its time to restore data.

How IntelliMirror Can Provide Easy Recovery

The purpose of IntelliMirror is to let many applications and operating system features share data and configuration settings. IntelliMirror works in the background and provides the engine on which many convenient features run. IntelliMirror isn't something you necessarily install. Rather, you use features that depend on IntelliMirror to function properly.

It sometimes helps to understand IntelliMirror by looking at the technologies that use IntelliMirror and at what these mechanisms do. You can use the IntelliMirror collection of technologies to do the following in a Windows environment:

- Centralize the management of user data.

- Distribute and maintain software (that is, apply Service Packs, HotFixes, updates, and so on).

- Manage user settings (so that programs and computers can easily share settings, such as your Favorites list in Windows Explorer and Internet Explorer).

When you use IntelliMirror on both the server and the client, a user's data, applications, and settings remain constant throughout the user's environment. You can mirror data from your computer to the network, which protects your critical work. In addition, you can use any Windows computer on your network and always have access to your data.

An administrator can use IntelliMirror to install Windows XP remotely.

Using Offline Files, one of the tools that rely on the IntelliMirror engine, you can work with the same data regardless of whether you are connected to the network. If you are taking your work home or on the road, you can synchronize your files with the network when you reconnect, giving you access to the latest version of your documents.

The IntelliMirror technologies provide for almost completely automated and transparent recovery of the operating system, applications, and user data. If you implement technologies that rely on IntelliMirror and a user's system fails, you can give the user a completely new computer or a blank hard drive and let IntelliMirror handle the recovery task. RIS (Remote Installation Service), for example, can install the user's operating system; group policy then installs the applications and further redirects the user to their data folders tucked away safely on a network server. You save considerable time that would otherwise be required for an administrator or the user to manually recover the system. Plus, redirecting the users' data folders to a network server that is backed up regularly can help prevent lost data.

CHAPTER 46

System Recovery Tools

For most users, recovery remains a tedious topic until the solids hit the air-conditioning, whereupon the topic becomes not only interesting but also pressing. But if you've used Windows extensively, chances are that you're aware of the dangers of system damage and data loss, and that you're therefore reading this chapter at leisure without an urgent need to solve a grisly problem immediately.

However you're approaching it, this chapter discusses how to put the backup and disaster recovery plan you created in Chapter 45 into effect recovering your system, and how to use XP's repair and recovery tools and techniques for various categories of problems.

The chapter starts with an overview of those tools and techniques, what they do, and when they're best used. The chapter then discusses the tools and techniques in approximately ascending order of seriousness of problem they're intended for, starting with recovering data from a backup set and rolling back a driver, then moving on to more serious tools such as Automated System Recovery (ASR). It discusses techniques for repairing and recovering remote systems, and finishes by discussing manual ways of recovering a system.

Which Recovery or Repair Tool Should You Use When?

Before you start using XP's various recovery and repair tools, make sure you know which tool is suited to which situation. For example, using ASR to solve a driver problem is like using a bulldozer to knock down a sand castle. Sure, it'll do the trick, but it's not the best tool for the job. And you might flatten a couple of other things in the process.

Table 46.1 lists the recovery and repair tools and techniques XP provides, roughly in order of seriousness of problem, with notes on the problems each tool or technique is best used to fix.

TABLE 46.1: Windows XP's Recovery and Repair Tools and Their Purposes

Tool	Purpose	Best Used For
Tools and Techniques Used when XP Starts Successfully		
Backup	Create and restore backups of specified files.	Protecting and restoring data files.
Device Driver Roll Back	Replace an updated device driver that seems to be causing problems with the previous driver for the device, and restore any driver settings changed during the update.	Solving problems caused by installing new device drivers.
Uninstall a program	Uninstall a program that's causing a problem.	Recovering from problems caused by installing a program.
Reinstall a program	Reinstall a program that seems to be causing problems.	Solving problems resulting from a program's files having become corrupt or been deleted.
System Restore	Create restore points containing system and application settings. Restore the system and application settings to those specified in the restore point you designate.	Recovering from installing applications or drivers that turn out to have a bad effect.
Disable a device	Take a problem device and its drivers out of the equation for solving any system instability.	Recovering from problems apparently caused by, or contributed to by, a device driver.
Clean boot	Start XP with fewer services and drivers to avoid problems caused by services that start automatically and drivers that load at startup.	Getting XP to run stably enough that you can repair its configuration manually.
Tools and Techniques Used when XP Won't Start Successfully		
Last Known Good Configuration	Restore the last control-set configuration with which XP started successfully.	Recovering from control-set problems that prevent XP from starting fully.
Automated System Recovery (ASR)	Create a backup set to which XP can be restored when it won't start.	Recovering an XP Professional installation automatically.
Recovery Console	A character-mode operating environment that provides repair-related commands.	Repairing Windows manually—for example, by replacing individual files.
Parallel installation of XP	Install XP in another directory so that you can start it and use its tools to troubleshoot and repair your installation.	Repairing your XP configuration manually when XP won't start.
Reinstall XP	Reinstall XP as an upgrade or a fresh installation.	Best *not* used until all else fails.

Recovering Data from a Backup Set

If one or more of your data files have become corrupt, run Backup Utility and restore the appropriate files as follows:

1. Launch Backup Utility from the Start menu (Start ➤ All Programs ➤ Accessories ➤ System Tools ➤ Backup) or by double-clicking the backup file from which you want to restore the files. If Backup Utility launches as a wizard, click the Advanced Mode link.

2. On the Restore And Manage Media tab, select the backup from which you want to restore. To restore from a backup file, expand the File object and select the appropriate backup file. To restore from a backup on tape, expand the Tape object and select the media name for the backup set.

3. If you want to restore only some files, select them.

4. If you haven't already done so, choose the appropriate option button on the Restore tab of the Options dialog box to specify what Backup Utility should do when a file it's restoring is already on the computer. Your choices are:

   - "Do not replace the file on my computer"
   - "Replace the file on disk only if the file on disk is older"
   - "Always replace the file on my computer"

5. In the Restore Files To drop-down list, choose whether to restore the files to their original location, an alternate location that you specify, or a single folder. If you choose an alternate location or a single folder, specify it.

6. To restore your installation of Windows XP, select the System State check box.

7. Click the Start Restore button. Backup Utility starts restoring the files.

8. If you're restoring System State files to their original locations, Backup Utility displays a Warning dialog box to make sure that you're intending to do so. Choose the OK button to proceed.

9. Backup Utility then displays the Confirm Restore dialog box, in which you can click the Advanced button to set advanced options for the restoration operation.

   "Restore security"   Controls whether Backup Utility reapplies the security settings (ownership, access permissions, and audit entries) to the restored files and folders. This option is available only for files from NTFS volumes going to NTFS volumes.

   "Restore junction points, and restore file and folder data under junction points to the original location"   Controls whether Backup Utility restores the junction points on your disk together with the data the junction points reference. If you don't select this check box (which Backup Utility selects by default), Backup Utility restores the junction points, but you may not be able to access the data they point to.

"When restoring replicated data sets, mark the restored data as the primary data for all replicas"   Controls whether any File Replication Service (FRS) data you restore is replicated to other servers after the restore operation. (Otherwise, the data you restore may appear to be older than the replicated copies of it, in which case it won't be replicated.)

"Restore the cluster registry to the quorum disk and all other nodes"   This option isn't available for Windows XP Professional or Home Edition because it applies only to server clusters.

"Preserve existing volume mount points"   Controls whether the restore operation avoids writing over volume mount points. Select this check box when you're restoring an entire drive, partition, or volume to a drive on which you don't want the volume mount points overwritten. By contrast, if you've just formatted the drive, you may want to overwrite the volume mount points with those in the backup.

10. After choosing advanced restore options, close the Advanced Restore Options dialog box. Then click the OK button in the Confirm Restore dialog box to start the restore operation.

WARNING   If you restore files from a backup created before you activated Windows XP on your computer, or from a backup created on a computer on which XP hadn't been activated, or you've made significant hardware changes since creating the backup, XP may prompt you to activate it after the backup, even though you have previously activated it. If this happens, you'll need to reactivate XP. To avoid this happening, make a full or incremental backup after making significant changes to your hardware configuration. (A full or incremental backup includes the Windows Product Activation database files, `wpa.dbl` and `wpa.bak`.)

If a restore operation doesn't give the results you want, you may be able to undo the restoration by using System Restore, which is discussed later in this chapter.

Rolling Back a Driver

If installing a new driver (or updating a driver, either manually or via Windows Update) seems to make your system unstable, use the Roll Back Driver button on the Driver tab of the Properties dialog box for the component to roll back the driver to the previous driver.

Uninstalling and Reinstalling Programs

If Windows XP becomes unstable after you install a program, use the Add Or Remove Programs feature to uninstall the program. If files for a program become corrupt and it starts crashing, reinstall it.

Using System Restore

System Restore (Start ➤ All Programs ➤ Accessories ➤ System Tools ➤ System Restore) is a powerful tool with a mostly goof-proof interface. You'll have no difficulty creating restore points manually and restoring Windows to them. But System Restore offers plenty of details and complexities—read on.

Who Can Run System Restore

Only Computer Administrator users can run System Restore. Other users receive a message telling them they don't have sufficient security privileges to restore the system if they try to run System Restore.

When Restore Points Are Created

Windows XP creates the first restore point the first time you boot it after installation. Thereafter, by default it creates a restore point every 24 hours of real time, plus restore points at these important events:

- When you install Windows Updates
- When you perform a restore operation (using System Restore itself or Backup Utility)
- When you install unsigned device drivers
- When you install or uninstall a program via the Windows Installer or InstallShield

Automatically created restore points are great as a fallback for those times when you fail to notice the disaster heading your way. But you may also want to create restore points manually when trying several different drivers for a given piece of hardware or when installing software that doesn't use the Windows Installer or InstallShield. When you create a restore point manually, you can give it a more descriptive name than Windows manages for restore points created automatically, which should help you identify the restore point later.

There's no harm in creating an extra restore point other than a) it takes a little time, and b) sooner or later, you're going to run out of restore space, at which System Restore will discard your oldest restore points.

To create more restore points automatically, use Registry Editor to change one of the following values in this key:

`\HKEY_LOCAL_MACHINE\Software\Microsoft\WindowsNT\CurrentVersion\SystemRestore`

RPGlobalInterval   A DWORD value specifying the number of seconds that System Restore waits before creating an automatic restore point based on calendar date. The default setting is 86,400 seconds (24 hours).

RPSessionInterval   A DWORD value specifying the number of seconds that System Restore waits before creating an automatic restore point based on system uptime. The default setting is 0 seconds, which switches off this function.

When Restore Points Are Deleted

By default, restore points are kept for 90 days and then deleted automatically. If System Restore grows to occupy more than 90 percent of its available storage space before that, it deletes the oldest restore points until about 25 percent of the available space is free so that it can create new restore points. (This process is known as FIFO—first in, first out.)

All restore points are deleted when you turn System Restore off on the system drive. Some restore points are deleted if you reduce the size of the data store manually.

If you run short of disk space, System Restore cedes some of its available space to help out. If necessary, it deletes the oldest restore points so that it has 25 percent or more of the remaining available space free for creating restore points.

If you select the System Restore option in Disk Cleanup, Windows XP purges all restore points but the latest.

To change the length of time that restore points are kept, adjust the RPLifeInterval value entry in the SystemRestore key. The default setting is 7,776,000 seconds (90 days).

TIP   For details of other System Restore Registry keys, see Q295659 in the Knowledge Base at support.microsoft.com.

What's Protected and What's Not

Briefly, System Restore tracks changes to program files. It doesn't protect or restore data files. (For that, you need to use Backup.) Similarly, it doesn't restore trivial user-interface settings such as your wallpaper or Desktop background image.

System Restore also doesn't protect backup files such as those created using Backup Utility. So you can't use System Restore to restore backup files you've deleted.

System Restore monitors, protects, and restores Start menu shortcuts and HTML links, because these are stored on the system drive. But if a program is installed on a non-system drive that isn't using System Restore, the program won't be restored in a restore operation, so these shortcuts or links won't start the program.

For a full list of the files, file types, and folders that System Restore doesn't protect, browse `%systemroot%\system32\Restore\filelist.xml`.

System Restore Quirks

The Select A System Restore screen shows dates in the current month that contain restore points in boldface. Dates in the previous month (at the beginning of the current month) appear grayed out even if they have restore points. To see these restore points, move back a month in the calendar control. This presentation is (to use Microsoft's phrase) "by design," but it's confusing at first, especially given that when System Restore runs out of space, it deletes old restore points to make room for new ones.

In early versions of Windows XP Professional and Home Edition, System Restore failed to update the date if you changed the date on your computer while System Restore was open. (The solution is, of course, to close System Restore before changing the date.)

System Restore is enabled by default. If you disable it temporarily, don't reenable it while installing a program. System Restore creates a restore point when you reenable it, and creating the restore point during the installation of a program can corrupt the restore point.

The only way to tell if a restore point is corrupt is to try to restore the system to it. If the restoration fails, the restore point was corrupt.

> **TIP** Close all documents before running a System Restore operation. Better, close all programs as well.

For a hard link that you've deleted, System Restore creates a new file *with the same name as the deleted link but with the same contents as the original file.*

System Restore may not fully restore printer drivers that use file extensions that are normally used by data files. If this happens, reinstall the printer drivers manually.

If the system drive has less than 200 MB of free space, or if a non-system drive has less than 50 MB of free space, XP suspends System Restore when a file that System Restore is tracking is copied, modified, or deleted. *This suspension applies to all disks, not just the disk that's short of space.* (Microsoft calls this *consistent freeze.*) To get System Restore going again, free at least 200 MB of disk space on the system disk or 50 MB on the non-system disk and either wait 15 minutes for System Restore to notice and restart itself or choose Start ➤ All Programs ➤ Accessories ➤ System Tools ➤ System Restore to start System Restore immediately.

Windows XP doesn't preserve System Restore settings if you reinstall XP or upgrade from Home Edition to Professional.

Taming the Disk Hog

You *can* turn off System Restore for all drives if you want (on the System Restore tab of the System Properties dialog box); however, for most computers, it's a better idea to run System Restore but decrease the amount of space it takes. By default, System Restore lays claim to 12 percent of each hard drive (or 400 MB for drives smaller than 4 GB), giving it the potential to move ahead of notorious disk hogs such as the Recycle Bin, Temporary Internet Files, the paging file, and the hibernation file in the Greed Stakes. That said, System Restore uses disk space only as necessary and up to this maximum setting, so the space isn't gone for good.

Because System Restore doesn't monitor, protect, or restore data files, turn it off for data-only drives. Use System Restore on your system drive (which is listed first on the System Restore tab of the System Restore tab) and on drives that contain programs.

Examining Your Restore Points

To examine your restore points, run SRDIAG.EXE, which you'll find in the *%systemroot%*systemexpr32\Restore folder. Without any parameters, SRDIAG.EXE creates a CAB file named *ComputerName_mmddyy_hhmmss*.cab in that same Restore folder. You can use the /CabLoc parameter to specify a folder for the file, and the /CabName parameter to specify the filename, as in the following example:

```
srdiag /CabName:Restore1.cab /CabLoc:c:\examples
```

Table 46.2 lists the files contained in the resulting CAB file.

The CAB file also contains, for each restore point, a restorepointsize file (named *driveletter*--RP*n*-restorepointsize—for example, C--RP3-restorepointsize) and a LOG file (named *driveletter*--RP*n*-rp.log—for example, C--RP3-rp.log).

Of the files in the System Restore cabinet, SR-RP.LOG and SR-RSTRLOG.TXT tend to be the most rewarding for human examination.

TABLE 46.2: Files Contained in a System Restore Cabinet File

File	Contents
SR-REG.TXT	Registry settings for System Restore.
MACHINEGUID.TXT	The global universal identification (GUID) of the _restore folder. The system's data store is located in \System Volume Information_restore{*GUID*}.
FILELIST.XML	A list of the files and folders included and excluded in restore operations.
DRIVETABLE.TXT	Details of the status of each drive that System Restore is monitoring. Includes the mount point path, volume GUID, volume status, and maximum size of the data store.
SR-CHGLOG.LOG	The change log containing details of the changes to files on each monitored drive for all available restore points.
SR-EVENTLOGS.TXT	A log of events for the System Restore service (for example, when System Restore is turned on and off, and when restore points are created).
SR-FILELIST.LOG	A list of the System Restore binary files, with their file information.
SR-RP.LOG	A list of the restore points, their type (for example, System Checkpoint), status, and date and time created.
SR-RSTRLOG.TXT	The restore log file for the last restore completed or attempted.
SR-FIFO.LOG	A list of FIFO restore points purged by the datastore. This file isn't created until a restore point is purged.

Locking Down System Restore

To prevent users from changing System Restore settings in Windows XP Professional, use Group Policy Editor to select the Disabled option button for the Turn Off System Restore item and the Enabled option button for the Turn Off Configuration item in the System Restore object (Computer Configuration ➢ Administrative Templates ➢ System).

Alternatively, run Registry Editor, and navigate to the following key:

    \HKEY_LOCAL_MACHINE\SOFTWARE\Policies\Microsoft\Windows NT

Create a new subkey named SystemRestore, and create under it a new DWORD value named DisableConfig with the value data 1.

Once you've taken either of these actions, the options on the System Restore tab of the System Properties dialog box then appear disabled.

"Restoration Incomplete" Error Message

The message "Restoration incomplete. Your computer cannot be restored to *date restore point*" appears when the computer is shut down improperly during restoration, interrupting the restoration. If this happens, you can try to: restore again to the same restore point, restore to another restore point, or undo the incomplete restoration.

How System Restore Handles Passwords

System Restore restores program passwords (such as those for .NET Passport or AOL Instant Messenger, which are stored on web servers), domain passwords, and computer passwords, but doesn't restore Windows XP passwords, Internet Explorer passwords, or Content Advisor passwords.

Checking that System Restore Is Running

You can check that System Restore is running by viewing the Services tab of System Configuration Utility or by issuing a `net start` command.

When Restoration Fails

If a restoration doesn't produce the effects you want, use the Undo My Last Restoration option to revert to your previous unsatisfactory state or try restoring to another restore point.

Last Known Good Configuration

System Restore is a powerful tool that can fix many configuration problems by restoring your computer to the state it was in before a problem occurred. But if your computer won't start Windows fully, or at all, System Restore can't help you. The next recovery tool to turn to is the Last Known Good Configuration feature.

Last Known Good Configuration is intended to help you recover from problems caused by installing a driver that turns out to be problematic or by a program (malware or otherwise) trashing Registry data. As its name suggests, Last Known Good Configuration starts the computer using the Registry information and driver settings used the last time Windows started successfully. This information comes from one of the ControlSet00n keys in the Registry. To see which control set key will be used, use Registry Editor to view the \HKEY_LOCAL_ MACHINE\SYSTEM\Select key. The LastKnownGood value entry identifies the control set that will be used; the Current and Default value entries are the current and default control sets; and the Failed value entry identifies the last control set with which Windows failed to start correctly. (Using Last Known Good Configuration marks the previous default control set as Failed.)

To start your computer with Last Known Good Configuration, display the Windows Advanced Options menu by pressing the F8 key at the Please Select The Operating System To Start prompt (if you have a multiboot configuration using the NT boot loader) or at the beginning of the Windows startup sequence. Then select the Last Known Good Configuration item from the menu.

Last Known Good Configuration has two disadvantages. First, you lose any configuration changes that you made since the last successful start. (Given that one of these changes may have caused the problem, this loss may not worry you too much.) Second, Last Known Good Configuration doesn't always work. It cures only certain types of problems (such as those described earlier) and can't do anything for problems that don't involve control sets (for example, problems involving passwords or policies). Even for control-set problems, if you made a change, then rebooted and logged in successfully before deciding you want to make a change, Last Known Good Configuration can't help you.

Performing a Clean Boot

If Windows XP is suffering a problem related to a startup program, a driver, or a setting that causes it to crash too soon after starting (successfully) for you to troubleshoot it, performing a *clean boot* may enable you to get XP running stably enough for you to eliminate the problem. A clean boot is one in which you disable startup programs, drivers, and settings so that they can't interfere with XP's starting. Disabling these programs, drivers, and settings of course costs you the functionality they provide until you reenable them, so a clean boot is a troubleshooting tool rather than a way of getting work done around the problem.

To perform a clean boot, run System Configuration Utility (for example, Start ➤ Run, enter **msconfig**, and click the OK button). On the General tab, select the Selective Startup option button and clear the check boxes beneath it. (XP includes four check boxes—Process SYSTEM.INI File, Process WIN.INI File, Load System Services, and Load Startup Items— but your computer may include third-party add-ins that place further check boxes here.) Click the OK button to close System Configuration Utility, and accept XP's offer to restart your computer.

When XP comes back up (minus the startup programs, drivers, and settings you've eliminated), it displays a System Configuration Utility message box telling you the computer is in Diagnostic or Selective Startup mode. You'll probably be aware of this, because XP's interface will be missing most of its visual enhancements, such as the rounded upper corners of windows, rounded buttons, and color gradation on the Taskbar and notification area.

By default, XP runs System Configuration Utility automatically in Diagnostic or Selective Startup mode. (You can select the check box in the System Configuration Utility message box to prevent it from doing so.) On the General tab, select the Selective Startup button again. Then make sure that all the check boxes you cleared are still cleared. If one of them is dimmed and unavailable, it typically means that the program's manufacturer has done something subtle to force it to load. In this case, you'll probably need to consult the manufacturer in order to disable it.

If the check boxes are clear, select the first check box and restart the computer. If XP restarts and doesn't manifest the problem you're troubleshooting, select the second check box and restart again. Continue the process until you reach the check box that reproduces the problem. Then display the tab of System Configuration Utility that corresponds to the offending check box, and follow the same process of eliminating all items, then gradually adding them back in until the problem reappears. For example, if you find that the Load Startup Items check box on the General tab of System Configuration Utility seems to be the offender, display the Startup tab and disable all the items on it. Then reenable them one by one, and see which one's giving XP grief.

Once you've finished using clean boot to troubleshoot your PC, run `msconfig`, select the Normal Startup option button on the General tab of System Configuration Utility, and reboot.

Recovery with ASR

Automated System Recovery (ASR) is designed to be used after what Microsoft delicately terms a "major failure" or (even more delicately) a "catastrophic system failure"—in other words, a failure so grim that your system isn't recoverable by conventional means such as Safe mode, System Restore, or manual recovery.

ASR is designed to be a set-and-forget process. You create a backup set that consists of a large backup file containing all your system information (your system state, your system services, and all disks that contain OS components) and a floppy disk that contains files that give access to the backup file. After your catastrophic failure, you use the floppy and the backup file to restore XP to the state it was in when you made the backup.

If all goes well and the backup set identified by your ASR disk is up to date or represents a state you're prepared to use again, ASR is very viable and far preferable to reinstalling XP from scratch. But if your ASR disk is way out of date, ASR is only marginally more appealing than reinstalling from scratch.

NOTE ASR saves only your system files. It's designed to be used in conjunction with a full backup of your data, not to supplant the backup.

Creating Your ASR Backup Set

Create your ASR disk by clicking the Automated System Recovery Wizard button on the Welcome tab of the Backup Utility window (or choosing Tools ➢ ASR Wizard) and following the wizard.

WARNING   Don't put your backup file on the boot volume or the system volume. This is because the ASR restore process partitions the C: drive as a matter of course. When the C: drive is partitioned, any backup file stored on it usually gets corrupted. The restore process then runs fine until approximately its midpoint, at which it announces that it can't find the specified backup file and invites you to produce it. You can then navigate to the directory in which the backup file was: The directory is there because the restore process has re-created it. But the file is nowhere to be found.

Using ASR

When you've determined that your system has indeed suffered a catastrophic failure and that you can't recover it by using less drastic means, use ASR:

1. Slot the floppy and your XP CD. If your backup is on removable media, make that available.

2. Boot from the CD and run Windows Setup as if you were going to install XP afresh.

3. When Windows Setup prompts you to press F2 to activate ASR, do so.

4. Sensibly enough, Windows Setup prompts you to confirm the action. When you do, Windows Setup reads the files from the floppy disk and uses that information, the XP CD, and your backup set to restore your system to the state it was in when you created the ASR set.

5. Windows then prompts you to press F3 to reboot. Remove the floppy if the computer will try to boot from it, and then press F3.

What the ASR Disk Contains

An ASR disk contains the files ASR.SIF and ASRPNP.SIF. These SIF files—*state information files*—are just text files, so you can edit them in any text editor (for example, Notepad) if necessary.

You might need to edit them to add information about files and device drivers needed during ASR Setup that the Windows XP CD-ROM doesn't contain and that you need to supply manually. For details, see Q299044 in the Microsoft Knowledge Base at support.microsoft.com.

Recreating an ASR Disk

If you've lost your ASR disk, you can re-create it as follows.

1. Open the backup file for the ASR set on the Restore And Manage Media tab of Backup Utility.

2. Expand the contents of the file.

3. Expand the second item for the drive letter containing the system files so that you can see the \Windows\Repair folder.

4. Select the check boxes for ASR.SIF and ASRPNP.SIF.

5. In the Restore Files To drop-down list, specify Single Folder and use the Alternate Location text box to specify your floppy drive (for example, **A:**). Make sure that the files go to the root of the floppy disk—if they're anywhere else, ASR won't work.

6. Click the Start Restore button. Backup Utility displays the Confirm Restore dialog box.

7. Click the OK button. If you're using NTFS on your system drive, Backup Utility displays the Continue dialog box, warning you that "the target file system does not support some [of] the features of the original file system."

8. Click the OK button. Backup Utility copies the files to the floppy disk.

Recovering Systems Remotely

So far in this chapter, we've been assuming that you have direct access to the computer that you need to recover. If it's at the other end of the wire, your options are as follows.

- If XP is functional but impaired, you can use the tools discussed in Chapter 31 to perform some of the actions discussed so far in this chapter on a remote computer. For example, if you can log on remotely to a computer that has Remote Desktop Connection (RDC) enabled, you can use RDC to run System Restore across the network. Doing so of course terminates your RDC connection as XP restarts—but you can reestablish the connection once the system comes back up.

- Likewise, if you can establish a Remote Assistance connection, you can roll back a driver, uninstall or reinstall a program, disable a device, or even use System Restore.

- If the remote system is running the Telnet service, you may be able to log in remotely to perform administration tasks if the GUI tools aren't working.

- If XP is running but has a Registry problem, you may be able to recover it by using Registry Editor to edit the Registry remotely.

- You may be able to use MMC snap-ins and extensions to access the computer remotely and to manipulate it into better health.

- If the remote computer is sick enough to be inaccessible remotely, you'll need a live body on the ground to get it going again—for example, by inserting a Remote Installation Services (RIS) client disk, restarting the PC, and getting the RIS process going, or by inserting the ASR disk (and removable media, if applicable) and starting the ASR process.

Manual Recovery Methods

This section details some manual recovery steps you may want to try when automated means of recovery don't fit your needs.

Installing a Parallel Copy of Windows XP

Earlier in this chapter, I discussed performing a clean boot to bypass and then isolate a startup problem Windows XP was having. If a clean boot doesn't get you where you want to be, install a parallel copy of XP, boot it, and work from there. The key point is to install the new copy of XP either in a different folder on the same partition or on a different partition so that you keep it separate from the previous copy.

If you're able to get the original copy of XP working again (for example, by editing the Registry from the new copy of XP), you can then revert to the original copy. If not, you'll be able to recover files or back up your data before taking further steps.

Disabling Problem Services

If using Last Known Good Configuration to restore the control set that allowed the previous boot doesn't get XP started again, you may need to disable services that you suspect of preventing XP from starting.

To do so, boot to your parallel copy of XP, fire up Registry Editor, select the HKEY_LOCAL_ MACHINE key, and use the File ➤ Load Hive command to load the \System32\Config\System file from the installation of XP that you're troubleshooting. Use the Current value entry in the \HKEY_LOCAL_MACHINE\SYSTEM\Select key to identify the current control set, then open the key for that control set and examine the Services key for services that are set to start automatically.

The Start key for each service will have the value 1 (starts during bootup), 2 (starts automatically after bootup), 3 (starts manually), or 4 (is disabled). Don't mess with the 1 values, because these services are critical to boot XP, but try changing any suspect services with the value 2 to either 3 or 4. Change a value for a suspect service (or perhaps two), then reboot with the installation of XP that you're troubleshooting and see whether things have improved. If not, boot back into your parallel copy of XP, restore the services you changed to their previous setting, and try changing another service or two. Rinse and repeat until you get results.

Reinstalling Windows XP

If the worse comes to the worst, you may need to reinstall Windows XP. Try an upgrade installation first, because then you won't need to reinstall and reconfigure all your applications as well as XP itself.

Recovering System State Information If You Don't Have a System State Backup

If you've never performed a system state backup, the repair folder will contain a backup of your original system state, not of its more recent state. But you can retrieve recent settings from the System Volume Information folder by using Recovery Console provided the option named "Recovery Console: Allow floppy copy and access to all drives and folders" is set to Enabled. This option is in the Security Options folder under Local Policies for whichever security tool you're using (for example, Local Security Policy or Domain Security Policy).

Take these steps:

1. Boot into Recovery Console.

2. Delete the current SAM, SECURITY, SOFTWARE, SYSTEM, and DEFAULT files from the %systemroot%\system32\config folder. (If you're feeling cautious, copy them to a temporary folder and then delete the originals.)

3. Issue the command **set allowallpaths = true** to enable access to all drives and paths.

4. Change directory to the System Volume Information folder. It should contain one or more folders named _restore{GUID}, where GUID is a globally unique identifier such as 49F88DFF-6A1F-4764-95C7-BE8K701B5C8C.

5. Change directory to the last folder before the one that has the current time. It should contain one or more restore-point folders named RP0, RP1, and so on.

7. Change directory to the latest RP folder and then to the snapshot folder it contains.

6. Copy these files to the %systemroot%\system32\config folder and rename them as indicated:

   - _REGISTRY_MACHINE_SAM: rename to SAM
   - _REGISTRY_MACHINE_SECURITY: rename to SECURITY
   - _REGISTRY_MACHINE_SOFTWARE: rename to SOFTWARE
   - _REGISTRY_MACHINE_SYSTEM: rename to SYSTEM
   - _REGISTRY_USER_DEFAULT: rename to DEFAULT

8. Exit Recovery Console and restart XP.

If your Windows drive uses FAT32 rather than NTFS, you can retrieve recent settings files from the System Volume Information folder using Windows Explorer and copy them to a temporary folder, then boot into Recovery Console and copy them to the %systemroot%\system32\ config folder. If you want to do this, make sure XP is displaying protected operating system files. (If not, choose Tools ➤ Folder Options, clear the Hide Protected Operating System Files check box on the View tab of the Folder Options dialog box, click the Yes button in the resulting warning dialog box, and close the Folder Options dialog box.)

Restoring Files with the Recovery Console

Another tool you can use for recovering your system when XP won't start is the Recovery Console. The next chapter discusses the Recovery Console in detail. Recovery tasks you can perform with the Recovery Console include restoring your Registry from backup and restoring critical files, as discussed in the following sections.

Using the Recovery Console to Restore the Registry from a Backup Copy

To restore the Registry from a backup copy by using Recovery Console, install the Recovery Console and boot to it (as discussed in Chapter 47). Then use the copy command to copy, to the *%systemroot%*\system32\config folder, either XP's default backups of the Registry files from the *%systemroot%*\repair folder or your manual backups of the Registry files from another location. Issue the exit command to exit Recovery Console, restart your computer, and then use System Restore to restore your computer to an earlier restore point.

Using the Recovery Console to Restore Critical Files

You may also need to restore critical files other than Registry files after a program has damaged a Windows file in such as way that Windows can't recover it. Use the copy command to copy files from a local drive or a network drive. (Use the net use command to map to a network drive in order to copy backups of files from it.)

CHAPTER 47

Recovery Console

Sometimes, your Windows get broken, leaving you in great pane. OK, enough bad humor since this is a serious subject.

If you've been with PCs for more than a few years, you know that repair solutions for the operating system weren't always easy to come by. When you could find them (such as with PC manufacturers who would pack a recovery CD with their systems), these solutions usually weren't too elegant or customizable. Often, such methods resulted in almost as much work to restore a system to operating capacity as it would take to reformat the disk and reinstall the OS and all the applications.

For most of us, the first step in coming back meant having a boot disk handy. But you had to remember to add various commands and utilities (not to mention drivers, scanners, and so on) to the boot disk so that you had everything you needed in the event that Windows or the PC wouldn't boot. Just to assemble what you needed and to reach the point where you could troubleshoot required more than an ounce of skill and perseverance.

But this is a new millennium, and it's time for a somewhat updated approach. To that end, I present you with Recovery Console, the command-line console interface you're going to use with Windows XP to try to restore it to operation when lesser methods fail.

Let's get started because there is a good deal to learn.

Overview of Recovery Console

Recovery Console (RC) is a command-line console troubleshooting tool included with Windows XP.

Do think of Recovery Console as a tool in your arsenal to combat problems encountered in getting Windows XP to load and behave properly.

Don't think of it as a panacea for resolving all that may be wrong.

Later, in "Recovery Console Commands," you'll see many similarities in XP's Recovery Console to what many of us know as a DOS troubleshooting environment. By this, I mean that you execute commands at the command line to try to fix a disk, load or unload a service or driver, or copy/delete a file.

But if you approach Recovery Console as just another DOS program, you'll be frustrated, because RC is deliberately more limited than DOS. You don't have access to every file and folder, for example, but you do have access to strategic files and to the folders that are most likely to contain the files you need to access, change, or restore from a fresh copy, such as may be found in your root directory or your Windows installation folder. Table 47.1 provides basic information on your capabilities and disabilities when using Recovery Console.

TABLE 47.1: Recovery Console System Access Capabilities and Disabilities

Capability	Disability
Access to root directory for all volumes.	Attempts to access anything beyond items in Capability list result in an "Access Denied" message.
Access to Windows installation folder and subfolders (`%systemroot%`).	Cannot use any text-editing tools within RC.
Access to `Recovery Console` folder and subfolders (available only when installed to `Startup` folder, not from CD execution).	Cannot change local administrator password from RC.
Can read files and folders stored on supported removable media types (CD, floppy, etc.).	Cannot write to supported removable media types such as floppy or CD.
	Documents and Settings folder files are unavailable.
	Restrictions apply across both FAT32 and NTFS volumes.

SEE ALSO   For exceptions to the access disabilities, see the section "Administering Recovery Console through Policy Setting" later in this chapter.

By default, you need Administrator-level access to use Recovery Console. While other levels of users can be given rights to use RC, that should be done only with care because, despite Recovery Console's limitations, it can do things that can result in problems such as data destruction and loss of system integrity. For this reason, I advise you take the time to familiarize yourself with the commands and their options so you can use Recovery Console most effectively and with reduced chance of mishap.

Launching Recovery Console

Before we get into details, I would strongly recommend that you take some time both while reading this chapter and beyond, to become hands-on acquainted with Recovery Console, its powers, and its limitations. The more experience you have with RC before you hit a problem, the better prepared you will be to work through the console to fix it. You'll also better understand the types of issues you really can't resolve with it. For example, if an operation requires editing several files to restore the system, Recovery Console won't allow you to do this.

Don't overlook the need for a full backup before you do much experimentation. We learn some of our best lessons through making mistakes—sometimes, catastrophic ones. The backup ensures you can restore your work and operations in the unlikely event this occurs.

Before You Use Recovery Console

Under most circumstances, you should always try to restart your Windows XP system in safe mode or by using the Last Known Good Configuration option from Startup before you use Recovery Console.

If you can get into Windows XP at all, there are some additional things you should do, including:

- Reverse the last operation performed—think about what you did just before the problem developed; try to reverse it.

- Perform a backup of essential data (just in case).

- Pare down your Startup Menu so that you're not loading unessential services, utilities, and programs, which may be affecting a successful boot.

The Two Ways to Launch Recovery Console

There are two different ways you can make Recovery Console available for your use:

- Run it from your Windows XP CD.

- Install it as a startup option.

Which option you choose to use depends on your preference and, to some degree, the situation at hand. In some situations, one means of launching Recovery Console may succeed when the other fails. An example of this can be seen when the boot disk is damaged or somehow misconfigured, as might happen with a computer virus infection. In this case, the installed version of Recovery Console probably won't load, but you can still access it from the CD.

Running Recovery Console from CD

When used from the Windows XP compact disk, Recovery Console behaves very much like a boot disk or CD, permitting you to try to boot the system enough to get into the command console.

Follow these steps to run Recovery Console from the CD:

1. Restart the PC with the Windows XP CD already inserted into the CD drive.

2. You may be prompted to load certain options to make the system boot from the CD; choose any required.

3. When Setup loads, follow on-screen prompts until you reach the point where you can select **R** for repair/recovery.

4. Choose the Windows installation you want to recover. (This option will only be available on systems running more than one operating system.)

5. When prompted, provide your Administrator password.

6. When Recovery Console appears, you can begin typing commands, or type **help** for a list of them.

7. Type **exit** to quit Recovery Console and restart the PC.

NOTE If you need to load special SCSI or RAID drivers for using Recovery Console, press F6 when prompted during the launch process.

NOTE If you choose to run Recovery Console from CD, please be sure to keep your Windows XP setup CD in a safe location where you can find it when you need it (as you should in any event). This should go without saying, but I talk to a dozen experienced users every day (not to mention the number of novices) who can't find their setup CD when they need it most.

Adding Recovery Console as a Startup Option

For expediency with troubleshooting, you have the option of making Recovery Console a Startup option for Windows XP. By doing this, when you subsequently reboot your system, you'll be presented with a list of options, much as you see if you run additional operating systems on separate partitions on your XP system. You would then select Recovery Console to try to start the system.

TIP You must be logged on as an administrator to do this.

To enable this option, perform these steps:

1. With Windows XP loaded, insert your Windows XP CD into your CD-ROM drive.

2. Click Start ➢ Run.

3. From the Run dialog box, type *CD_drive_letter*:\i386\winnt32.exe /cmdcons.

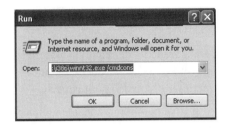

4. Follow the on-screen instructions.

You'll find that, as part of the install and setup process for Recovery Console, the module automatically connects to the Internet and downloads and installs dynamic updates before it reports that it has been successfully installed to your system.

To launch the installed Recovery Console, do this:

1. Shut down and restart the PC.

2. When prompted by the Startup menu, select Recovery Console.

3. Enter your Administrator password, when prompted.

WARNING After three failed attempted to supply the Administrator password, you'll be prompted to press Enter to restart the system.

4. Whether or not you have just one operating system installed, you will need to select the Windows installation for which you want to use RC.

5. When Recovery Console loads, you're ready to type your commands.

6. When your work is complete, type **exit** to quit Recovery Console and restart the PC.

TIP There are situations in which this installed version of Recovery Console will not work. In this event, try running Recovery Console from the CD; that method may work when the other does not.

NOTE The installed Recovery Console takes approximately 7 MB of disk space.

Using Recovery Console

You now know how to launch and exit Recovery Console. Next, you need to know the basic tools you have available to you within this environment, and that these tools are entirely command line–driven.

For those of you who haven't worked much with a command line or commands, here are some tips:

- Command-line environments demand absolutely correct syntax and are literal in their execution of commands, so double-check them before you press Enter. You may not be able to undo something if you do it improperly.

- Anything deleted from a command console will *not* be available for recovery under Windows Recycle Bin.

- Do not try to introduce commands from other operating systems; Recovery Console works with a fixed, limited list of commands and their options.

In the next section, we'll turn our eye to the major commands available for use in Recovery Console, and then provide some examples of how they may be used.

Recovery Console Commands

If you're familiar with standard DOS commands such as dir, you'll see that many of these are available under Recovery Console, with some updates and new commands to reflect that this is a command-line console running within a powerful 32-bit operating environment.

However, if you've done troubleshooting through a DOS environment in the past, you need to realize that Recovery Console behaves quite a bit differently, despite the similarity of commands and execution. You don't have the free range of access to virtually everything contained on the disk that you have with DOS. The idea here is to get in, try to recover (a service, a bad boot sector, etc.), get out, and not allow a huge window of opportunity for foul-ups and security breaches, intentional or unintentional.

NOTE   I've heard it asked several times, "Why are we sitting at a command line to fix Windows?" A graphical user environment with massive integration and multiple components and services, as you find with Windows XP, requires a phenomenal amount of power—and variables—to load. A command line doesn't demand that overhead, and reduces the variables to make troubleshooting a bit saner.

In Table 47.2, the Recovery Console commands are listed along with the function each performs. The switches and parameters for each are too numerous to list here. Please consult Help and Support under Windows XP and search on **Recovery Console**. You can click each command in the Help and Support Center window to expand it to see its options, as shown in Figure 47.1.

TABLE 47.2: Recovery Console Commands

Command	Function
attrib	Changes the attributes (Hidden, System, etc.) of a file.
batch	Loads a batch file to run one or more batch commands.
bootcfg	Launches a utility for boot file configuration and recovery.
cd or chdir	Changes to a different directory.
chkdsk	Runs the CHKDSK file system utility and reports results.
cls	Clears the console screen.
copy	Copies a file.
del or delete	Erases a file.
dir	Lists the contents of a directory.
disable	Stops either a specified system service or a device driver.
diskpart	Loads the disk partition manager.
enable	Starts a system service or loads a device driver.
exit	Quits Recovery Console and attempts to restart the PC.
expand	Extracts a file from a Microsoft-compressed file store, such as a cabinet (.cab) file.
fixboot	Overwrites (and hopefully repairs) the partition boot sector of a specified partition.
fixmbr	Overwrites (and repairs) the specified drive's Master Boot Record (MBR).
format	(Re)formats a drive to prepare it for use or the installation of an operating system.
help	Presents a list of available Recovery Console commands.
listsvc	Presents a list of services and drivers in use.
logon	Initiates a logon.
map	Shows the drive letters mapped to each drive connected to and recognized by the system.
md or mkdir	Creates a directory whose label you specify.
more	Pauses between screens when reading a text file.
net use	Establishes a connection between a particular drive letter and a network share.
rd or rmdir	Removes a specified directory.
ren or rename	Changes the name of a file from its current name to a different one.
set	Displays and/or sets the current environment variables.
systemroot	Establishes the current directory (*systemroot*) as that of the root directory of the system you're working from.
type	Displays the contents of a text file; often used in conjunction with the |more option.

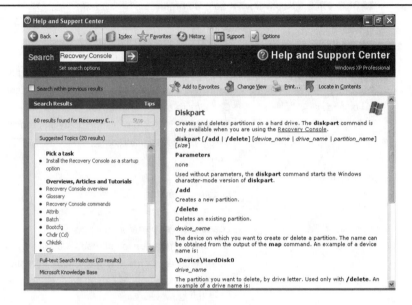

Examples of Recovery Console Command Usage

Table 47.3 presents some examples of Recovery Console commands, their switches and parameters, and situations they might be used in.

TABLE 47.3: Recovery Command Examples

Sample Command	What the Example Does
attrib -r -h crit.cfg	Removes the Read-Only and Hidden attributes from the file crit.cfg.
batch e:\fixit.txt e:\fixed.txt	Runs the commands stored as a text batch file (fixit.txt) and reports the results in another file (fixed.txt).
bootcfg /scan	Checks all Windows installations for boot information and reports results to screen.
chkdsk /f D:	Checks the D: drive for error and fixes any it finds.
disable eventlog	Disables the event-logging service in Windows.
diskpart /add \device\HardDisk1 100	Adds a 100 MB disk partition to the hard disk designated as 1.
diskpart /delete \device\HardDisk0\Partition3	Removes the designated disk partition from the hard disk identified as 0.
enable eventlog service_auto_start	Turns on event logging automatically on startup.

Continued on next page

TABLE 47.3 CONTINUED: Recovery Command Examples

Sample Command	What the Example Does
`fixboot E:`	Repairs the boot record for the partition of drive E: by overwriting it.
`fixmbr /device/HardDisk0`	Rewrites the Master Boot Record when corruption or a virus may have caused a problem.
`format f: /fs:FAT32`	Formats the F: drive and makes it a system drive using FAT32.
`logon`	Checks the system for all Windows installations, displays options, and prompts you to provide the administrator's password for the Windows installation you want to work with.
`md c:\logs`	Creates a new directory called `logs`.
`net use \\pax\\sam /sam /q9e7h F: /d`	Connects the system specified as \\pax\sam, using the user name sam and a password of q9e7h to the D: drive.
`set allowwildcards=true`	Establishes the ability to use wildcards with supporting Recovery Console commands.
`rd d:\logs`	Removes a directory called `logs` from the D: drive.

Administering Recovery Console through Policy Setting

Two settings under \Local Policy\Security Options affect options for Recovery Console. Both are disabled by default. These are:

- "Automatic administrative logon"
- "Allow access to floppy copy and access to all drives and all folders"

Let's take a moment to understand the functionality and implications for each.

Enabling the automatic administrative logon option allows an administrator to log onto the system without having to provide a password. This is convenient but can be an unwise choice for better security, because anyone with enough knowledge to try to run Recovery Console could do so.

Now here, there is a big difference between Windows XP Home Edition and Professional. Out of the box, no administrator password is required (or assigned) for Home Edition. Users must force an administrator's password onto this edition if they want to use one. I certainly wouldn't feel comfortable running a system where anyone who happens by the keyboard can get instant access, let alone administrator-level access.

The second setting ("Allow access to floppy…"), when enabled, permits the use of the set command under Recovery Console (see the preceding two sections) to show or modify environment variables. Within the set command are a limited number of variables you can act upon. These can be set to either =true or =false (example: AllowWildCards=true) and include:

AllowAllPaths   Using this opens up access to all files and folders on the system on which Recovery Console is being used.

AllowRemovableMedia   Using this grants the right of the administrative user logged onto Recovery Console to copy files to recognized removable media drives, such as floppies.

AllowWildCards   Using this turns on support for the use of wildcards (* or !) for commands that support them, such as dir and del.

Follow these steps to enable one or both of these policy settings:

1. From Control Panel, double-click Administrative Tools, then click Local Security Policy.

2. Under Security Settings from the left pane, open the Local Policies node, then click to select Security Options, which opens the options list in the right pane.

3. Locate the two listings that begin with Recovery Console.

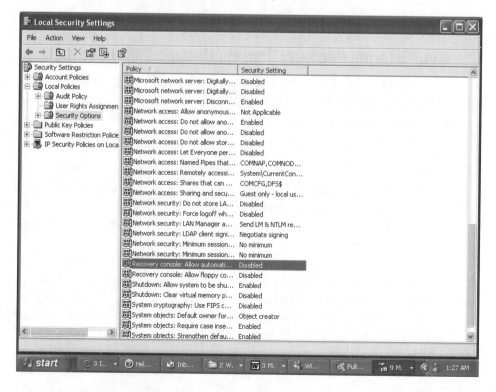

4. Double-click to select "Allow automatic administrative logon," which produces the Local Security Setting window for that option. Click Enabled, then click OK.

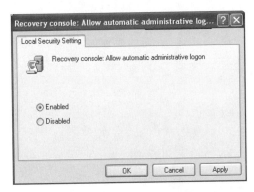

5. Double-click to select "Allow access to floppy copy and access to all drives and all folders." Click Enabled, then click OK.

PART IX

Security

CHAPTER 48

Managing Certificates

This chapter discusses what digital certificates are, what they're used for, and how to use them on Windows XP. It shows you how and where to get certificates that meet your needs; how to manage certificates with the Certificates console and with Internet Explorer's Certificates dialog box; and how to update the root certificates to keep XP current.

Understanding Certificates

Before you get a certificate and start using it, you need to understand what certificates are, what they're for, and what problems and weaknesses they have.

What Is a Certificate?

A *certificate* is a relatively small amount of encrypted code intended to identify its holder and to secure communications and documents coming from and going to the holder. To these ends, a certificate contains information about the certificate holder, the purposes for which the certificate has been issued, the keys used, and the certification path from the certification authority (CA) ultimately responsible for the certificate through any intermediate CAs involved in issuing it. Depending on its packaging, the certificate may also contain details of the certificates held by the authorities involved in the certification path.

What Is a Certification Authority?

A *certification authority (CA)* is an organization that issues certificates to individuals or organizations—preferably after verifying their identity thoroughly. CAs can be government organizations, but at this writing, most of the major public CAs are public companies.

A public key infrastructure (PKI) typically consists of a hierarchy of CAs. At the top of the certification hierarchy are the *root certification authorities* (root CAs) or *root authorities*. Root CAs issue themselves their own certificates—in effect, stating that everyone can trust them. (More on this in a moment.) Because root CAs in a PKI trust each other, the intermediate CAs in the different branches of the certification hierarchy trust each other too. This trust cascades down to the holders of the certificates issued by the CAs, who should therefore be able to trust each other as well.

How Do Certificates Work?

Certificates use a *key pair*—a public key and a private key—to secure data. Data encrypted with the public key can be decrypted only with the private key, and data encrypted with the private key can be decrypted only with the public key. The public key and private key are related to each other mathematically, but in such a way that the private key can't be derived from the public key.

Therefore, you (as a key holder) can safely distribute your public key worldwide so that it's available to whomever needs it. When someone wants to send you an encrypted message, they encrypt it using your public key; you decrypt it with your private key. When you want to prove that a message or document comes from you, you sign it with your private key, and the recipient uses the public key to verify that the message or document was signed by you.

How do you distribute your public key? You can of course send it to people, but you'd need to be omniprescient to get the key to everyone who needed it. So public key cryptography requires a PKI to make the keys available. For protection, the public key isn't distributed on its own: Instead, a CA produces a digital certificate that binds the public key to the key holder's identity. The digital certificate is then distributed.

What Does a Certificate Prove?

Most CAs issue a variety of certificates for different purposes, including the following widely-used types of certificates:

Personal certificates   For signing and encrypting e-mail and proving one's identity to a remote computer.

Developer certificates   For signing macros and software you develop so that other people can be sure that they come from you, that your identity has been verified, and that the software hasn't been tampered with in transit.

SSL server certificates   For certifying that a server belongs to the company or organization specified and securing the connection between the browser and the server. (I'll discuss SSL server certificates more later in this chapter.)

As you'd imagine, certificates held by intermediate CAs and root CAs have a wide range of other purposes—for example, verifying Windows system components and recovering keys.

Weaknesses of Digital Certificates

Digital certificates have three main weaknesses:

- First, you need to trust the CA to be trustworthy and to have verified the identity of the individual or organization in question.

- Second, you need to trust that the person or organization that has applied the digital certificate to whatever item it's securing was the person or organization they're supposed to be.

- Third, problems with the validity of a certificate aren't necessarily apparent immediately.

Let's look at these problems in detail, because you should understand them if you use digital certificates.

Trusting the CA

The first part of trusting a CA is the old question *sed quis custodiet ipsos custodes*—"but who guards the guards themselves?" In this case, the question is, "but who certifies the CA?"

In a PKI, each intermediate CA is certified by a root CA. So far, so good. But each root CA certifies itself, issuing its own root public key and binding it to its root certificate—a cornerstone of the PKI edifice of trust. In other words, you're required to trust the root CAs in order to use the PKI, and to trust the root CAs because everybody else in the PKI trusts them and the root CAs trust each other. In *Secrets and Lies*, Bruce Schneier, a leading cryptographer, points out that while CAs may be authorities on making certificates, they're almost never authorities on what the certificates they make contain. For example, most CAs who issue SSL server certificates aren't authorities on the DNS name assignments bound into the server certificates. Schneier comments, "Basically, certificates only protect you from those that the PKI vendor refuses to do business with."

> **NOTE** Trust may be less of an issue for certificates issued within a company. For example, you may feel that you can trust HR and IT between them to ensure that the holder of any certificate is who they claim to be.

Then you need to trust the CA to verify the identity of the certificate holder enough for the purposes of the transaction. For example, if you're using certificates to verify the sender of an e-mail message, you might settle for a modest level of certainty, whereas if you were buying software from them, you'd probably want a high level of certainty.

But most verification takes place at one or more removes, with the CA leveraging an existing means of identification (such as a credit-card or credit-agency listing for an individual or a Dun & Bradstreet listing for a company) instead of performing direct identification themselves. Few, if any, certification authorities interface directly with national or even state agencies—bodies widely trusted to identify people and companies with a great degree of accuracy.

(Consider how many people have problems with inaccurate credit reports and how few have problems with passport mix-ups. Which would you rather have issuing digital certificates that you needed to trust—a credit agency or the passport guys?)

Trusting the Certificate Holder

Even if you feel you can trust the CA or the PKI, you're not out of the woods yet: You also need to trust the certificate holder to keep their certificate to themselves (or to the appropriate group of people), not lose the private key (certainly not let the private key get stolen), and apply it only voluntarily, consciously, and after due consideration to the appropriate documents or communication sessions.

Linking Digital ID to Physical ID

What would it take to make CAs truly trustworthy? Some commentators envision a national (or better, international) identity scheme that would work both in the physical world and the digital world. Each individual would apply to a national (or international) agency for identity documentation that would cover the areas currently covered by passports, driver's licenses, and digital certificates. Digital certificates could be derived from the information supplied by the individual—information that would probably include biometric data such as digital fingerprints, a facial scan, and a DNA profile—and could be verified by using a scanner attached to the computer (for example, a fingerprint scanner built into the keyboard or a facial scanner mounted on the monitor). Then we'd need to create a similar structure for businesses... Given such technology, you could be pretty sure who was at the other end of the wire.

Depending on the nature of the certificate and the information it contains, you may also not be able to identify the certificate holder conclusively. With most personal digital certificates, the only pieces of information you get about the holder are their name and their e-mail address. Unless you know already that the e-mail address belongs to the person you know by this name, you won't be able to use the e-mail address to distinguish that person from another with the same name or a similar name.

In any case, many of the personal certificates issued by CAs don't verify the holder's identity. For example, you can get a personal certificate from VeriSign for signing e-mail without proving anything more than that you know a credit card number and its billing details and that the e-mail address works.

Making Sure the Certificate Is Still Valid

Each certificate has its validity period encoded into it, so when a certificate is past its expiration data, applications that use the certificate automatically warn you of the problem and refuse to use the certificate. But if a certificate or its private key is lost or stolen, problems arise. Each user of the public key essentially needs to check that the certificate hasn't been reported lost (or stolen) and isn't on the certificate revocation list (CRL) before each use. There isn't a good mechanism for doing this.

Similarly, a certificate issued by a company's CA might prove that the certificate holder worked for the company in a certain capacity and had authority to take certain actions (for example, making purchases). If the person moves to a different role, they'll need a new certificate. If they're fired, the certificate needs to be removed from them before they can use it when they shouldn't. Any communications encrypted with the certificate's public key (for example, messages sent to the newly unemployed person) will then be unreadable.

What Are Certificates Good For?

As you've seen, at this writing, digital certificates are an unsatisfactory means of proving identity. But once you're clear on their limitations and know why you must keep your wits about you when using certificates, certificates can be very useful.

Certificates are particularly useful in closed systems, such as military or government organizations, in which a competent authority vets each applicant in depth before issuing a certificate limited to their needs and probably with a short validity period.

Where Are Certificates Stored?

Windows XP stores certificates in certificate stores that you can view using the Certificates console, discussed later in this chapter. By using the Certificates console and by using Internet Explorer's Certificates dialog box, you can export a certificate to a file—for example, to back it up or to copy or move it to another computer.

Windows XP can also work with certificates stored on smart cards, provided that you have a smart-card reader installed on or attached to your computer.

To use a smart card or a certificate to secure a network connection, select the Use Extensible Authentication Protocol (EAP) option button in the Logon Security group box in the Advanced Security Settings dialog box for the connection, then click the Properties button and use the Smart Card Or Other Certificate Properties dialog box to specify whether to use a smart card or certificate, whether to validate the server certificate (and if so, how), and whether to use a different user name for the connection.

Using the Certificates Console

Windows XP provides two tools for working with certificates: the Certificates console, which is a snap-in for the MMC and which we'll examine in this section, and the Certificates dialog box, which we'll examine in the next section.

To open the Certificates console, open the MMC (Start ➢ Run, **mmc /a**, OK) and add the Certificates snap-in by using the Add/Remove Snap-in dialog box (File ➢ Add/Remove Snap-in; see Chapter 15 for more details).

If you have permission to manage certificates for the services account and the computer account, the Certificates snap-in displays the Certificates Snap-in dialog box. Select the My User Account option button, the Service Account option button, or the Computer Account option button to specify which certificates you want to manage with the Certificates console.

If you want to use this MMC console for managing certificates in the future, save the console. Alternatively, open an existing console and add the Certificates snap-in to it.

Viewing the Certificate Stores

The Certificates console lets you view the certificates listed by their purposes or by the logical stores in which they're kept. Listing certificates by their purposes helps you find certificates for a particular purpose. (Bear in mind that many certificates fulfill multiple purposes and so appear in multiple categories.) Viewing the logical stores lets you see which certificates are in each store.

To change the view, choose View ➢ Options to display the View Options dialog box (see Figure 48.1) and choose the Certificate Purpose option button or the Logical Certificate Stores option button as appropriate.

FIGURE 48.1:

Use the View Options dialog box to specify how the Certificates console should display the certificates.

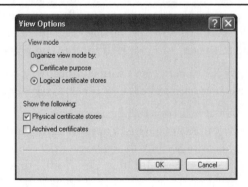

You can display the physical certificate stores by selecting the Physical Certificate Stores check box in the View Options dialog box. Doing so can be useful for exporting an entire store.

You can also display archived certificates by selecting the Archived Certificates check box. XP archives a certificate when you replace it with a new certificate. Under normal circumstances, you'll seldom need to view archived certificates.

Finding a Certificate

To find a certificate matching certain criteria, choose Action ➤ Find Certificates to display the dialog box shown in Figure 48.2. Specify the certificate store or stores to search, specify the information in the Contains text box, select the appropriate item in the Look In Field list box (Issued By, Issued To, MD5 Hash, Serial Number, or SHA1 Hash), and click Find Now.

Once you've found a certificate, you can take assorted actions with it (such as exporting it, requesting it, or renewing it) by using the commands on the File menu or the shortcut menu for the certificate. The sections after the next section discuss actions you'll commonly want to take with certificates.

FIGURE 48.2:

If you can't find a certificate, use the Find Certificates dialog box to search for certificates matching specified criteria.

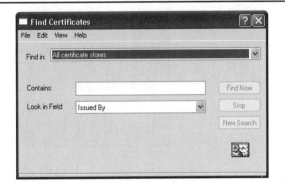

Managing Certificates with Internet Explorer

To manage certificates with Internet Explorer, display the Certificates dialog box by choosing Tools ➤ Internet Options and, on the Content page of the resulting dialog, clicking the Certificates button. Figure 48.3 shows the Certificates dialog box.

As you can see in the figure, the Certificates dialog box breaks up the certificates into different categories—Personal, Other People, Intermediate Certification Authorities, Trusted Root Certification Authorities, and Trusted Publishers—each of which appears on a separate tab. You can narrow the display further by selecting a certificate purpose in the Intended Purpose drop-down list.

Once you've selected a certificate, Internet Explorer makes the View, Export, Remove, and Advanced buttons available. The Import button (which starts the Certificate Import Wizard) is always available. The following sections discuss the tasks you can perform with these buttons: viewing a certificate, exporting and importing a certificate, removing a certificate, and changing the properties of a certificate.

FIGURE 48.3:

Use the Certificates dialog box to manage certificates from Internet Explorer.

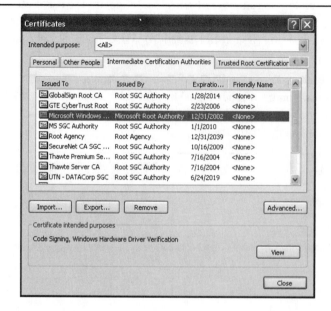

Viewing a Certificate

To view a certificate, double-click it in the Certificates dialog box or in Certificates console. Windows XP displays the Certificate dialog box with its General tab selected (see Figure 48.4). This tab lists the certificate's purpose, the person to whom the certificate was issued, the issuer, and the certificate's validity information. If the Issuer Statement button is available, you can click it to display information about the issuer of the certificate or to connect to the issuer's website.

The Details tab (see Figure 48.5) gives you access to all the fields of data contained in the certificate. You can limit the set of fields displayed by choosing Version 1 Fields Only, Extensions Only, Critical Extensions Only, or Properties Only in the Show drop-down list. To display the full contents of a field in the lower text box, select it in the list box.

The Certification Path tab (see Figure 48.6) shows the certification path for the certificate—the chain of certificates from the current certificate to the CA ultimately responsible for it. Use the View Certificate button to display the certificate for one of the other entities in the certification chain.

The General tab of the Certificate dialog box includes the certificate's purpose and validity period.

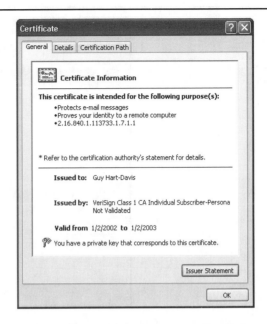

You can examine all the fields in the certificate on the Details tab of the Certificate dialog box.

Editing a Certificate

From the Details tab of the Certificate dialog box for a certificate, you can click the Edit Properties button to display the Certificate Properties dialog box (see Figure 48.7), in which you can use the controls in the Certificate Purposes group box to enable all purposes for the certificate, disable all purposes, or enable only the purposes you specify. If the certificate and the issuing CA support adding purposes to the certificate, you can do so by clicking the Add button.

In most cases, you won't be able to add purposes to a certificate, and you'll seldom want to disable any of the purposes a certificate has. However, you may well want to edit the "friendly name" (the descriptive name) and description for the certificate to make it easier to identify.

Obtaining a Certificate

Depending on your circumstances, you can get a digital certificate either from a public CA or from a CA hosted by your company. Public CAs supply certificates that you can use for authentication and security with anyone who trusts the CA through the PKI, whereas CAs run by companies supply certificates mostly for internal use within the company or group. (In some cases, company CAs are part of the PKI, but most are not.)

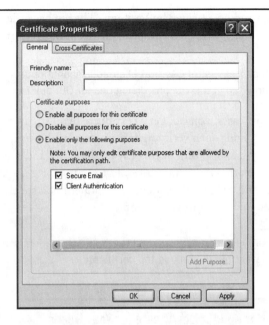

You can change the
purposes for which
the certificate can
be used.

TIP   If you want to practice importing, exporting, and deleting certificates, look for an applet that lets you create your own certificates for testing. The CDs of most versions of Microsoft Office include an applet named SELFCERT.EXE that creates a sample digital certificate with the name you specify and installs it on your computer. The certificates are limited to signing VBA projects, but you can export, import, and delete them.

Obtaining a Certificate from a Public CA

At this writing, leading public CAs include the following:

VeriSign, Inc.   (www.verisign.com) Provides a wide variety of digital certificates, from individual certificates to SSL server certificates. VeriSign owns Network Solutions, the original Internet registrars, and Thawte (discussed below).

GlobalSign NV   (www.globalsign.net) Provides certificates to individual users and companies, including 56-bit SSL server certificates. Headquartered in Brussels, GlobalSign is developing a Europe-based network that extends to 20 countries at this writing.

Thawte Consulting (Pty) Ltd.   (www.thawte.com) Provides certificates to individual users, developers, and companies. Thawte's server certificates include SSL server certificates and SuperCerts, SSL server certificates that let browsers with weak encryption (for example, 40-bit encryption) communicate with servers using 128-bit encryption. Based in South

Africa and now owned by VeriSign, Thawte has offices in the U.S. and representatives in most First World countries, and claims to have certified 30 percent of the world's servers.

TIP   For the latest list of CAs that Microsoft recommends, click the Get Digital ID button on the Security tab in the Options dialog box for Outlook Express (Tools ➢ Options).

In most cases, you can get a certificate by filling in an application form on a public CA's website, giving such verifying information as they require (name, address, phone number, credit card, and so on), paying (by credit card), and supplying via snail mail any supporting documents that the CA requires. For example, for a personal certificate, GlobalSign requires you to send a copy of the identity document you specified in your application, together with a signed membership agreement.

WARNING   Usually you need to carry out the whole application from the same computer on which you ultimately install and use the certificate.

Getting the Right Certificate for Your Needs

Before you start filling out any application form for a certificate, assess your needs and make sure the type of certificate you're getting fills them. Some CAs offer free personal certificates that you can use for purposes such as e-mail and proving your identity to a remote computer, but they don't cover heavier-duty uses such as software development or SSL (Secure Sockets Layer—a protocol that enables a web browser and a web server to communicate securely with each other across the Internet).

If you develop software or macros and need to apply a digital signature to them, you'll need a developer certificate. The digital signature assures the people who download your code that it came from you (rather than from anyone else), that your identity has been verified, and that the code hasn't been tampered with since you signed it.

If you need to support SSL on a server, you'll need a SSL server certificate. A SSL server certificate essentially guarantees to the browser connecting to it that the site belongs to the company or organization specified. SSL is vital for any transaction in which the customer needs to trust the company in question.

When you've connected to an Internet server via SSL, Internet Explorer displays the lock icon in the status bar, indicating that the connection is secured via SSL. This authentication is handled seamlessly by the browser, but the user can view the SSL server certificate if they want to verify its details.

For some types of certificates, however, you may need to visit an office or representative of the CA in person to demonstrate that you match your identity documents. For example, the primary way to become a member of Thawte's Web of Trust is to meet enough existing members (and prove your identity to them) to accumulate 50 points. Each member makes an assertion to Thawte confirming the identity of the person they've met. Meeting a member gets you a number of points corresponding to the number of people they've authenticated. Once you meet enough members to get 100 points, you can start making assertions yourself.

Once the CA has verified your identity to the degree required for the type of certificate you're requesting, it provides the certificate. A typical mechanism is for the CA to e-mail you a custom URL at which you can pick up the certificate and install it on your computer via an automated process.

Obtaining a Certificate from a Company CA

Companies can get certificates from public CAs, of course, and many do so, particularly SSL certificates for web servers that need to offer secure connections to visitors. But many companies also run their own CA, because doing so gives them far greater flexibility in their use of certificates.

If your company has a stand-alone Windows 2000 Server computer running the Certification Authority service, you can request a certificate from it by using Internet Explorer. Open `http://servername/certsrv`, where *servername* is the name or IP address of the server. The page displayed provides options for requesting a certificate, retrieving the CA certificate or certificate revocation list, and checking on a pending certificate.

In the example, you'd select the Request A Certificate option button and click the Next button to access the procedure for requesting a certificate. Once you've submitted the request, it's held in the `Pending Requests` folder in the Certification Authority until an administrator reviews it and issues the certificate (or denies the request). So normally you'd return to the Certification Services page after an interval dictated by the speed of your administrator's reactions and use the Check On A Pending Certificate procedure to see whether the certificate has been issued. If it has, the procedure installs it automatically for you.

If your company's CA is integrated into Active Directory, you can request a certificate by using the Certificate Request Wizard. To run the wizard, right-click the appropriate certificate store in Certificates console and choose All Tasks ➢ Request New Certificate from the shortcut menu. (Alternatively, select the store and choose Action ➢ All Tasks ➢ Request New Certificate.)

Exporting and Importing Certificates

Unless you confine your use of certificates those that are automatically installed on your computer or computers, you'll sometimes need to export a certificate to a file or import a certificate from a file.

Reasons for exporting a certificate include backing up the certificate (with or without its private key), and copying or moving the certificate to another computer so that you can use it on that computer as well as or instead of the computer it's currently installed on.

Reasons for importing a certificate include installing the certificate on the computer in the first place (if it wasn't installed automatically) and restoring from backup a certificate that's been damaged or deleted.

Certificate File Formats

XP supports the following standard file formats for certificates:

Personal Information Exchange (PFX or PKCS #12)   You can use this format to transfer a certificate with its corresponding private key from one computer to another, or to copy the certificate and its private key to removable media. *PKCS #12* stands for Public Key Cryptography Standard number 12, an industry standard for backing up, restoring, and transferring certificates. PKCS #12 files use the .pfx extension.

Cryptographic Message Syntax Standard (PKCS #7)   Use this format to transfer a certificate, together with all the certificates in its certificate path, from one computer to another or to copy the certificate to removable media. PKCS #7 files use the .p7b extension. If you don't need to transfer the private key with the certificate, PKCS #7 is usually the best format to use.

DER-encoded binary X.509   Use this binary encoding format to transfer certificates to other Windows applications (for example, other browsers) that don't support PKCS #12. DER-encoded files use the .cer extension.

Base64-encoded X.509   Use this ASCII-based format to transfer certificates to and from operating systems other than Windows. For example, if your CA is running on Linux, you may receive a certificate in a Base64-encoded X.509 file. These files use the .cer extension.

NOTE   Depending on the type of certificate you're exporting and on whether the certificate's issuer marked its private key as exportable, the Certificate Export Wizard may not offer you all these formats.

Exporting a Certificate

To export a certificate, start the Certificate Export Wizard by taking either of these actions:

- In the Certificates console, right-click the certificate and choose All Tasks ➤ Export from the shortcut menu. Alternatively, select the certificate and choose Action ➤ All Tasks ➤ Export.

- In the Certificates dialog box, select the certificate and click the Export button.

The Certificate Export Wizard makes the export process easy, but you have two key decisions to make. The first is whether to export the private key with the certificate. This choice applies only if you hold the private key to the certificate *and* the private key is marked as exportable. If you don't hold the private key, the wizard doesn't display the Export Private Key page. If you hold the private key but it's not marked as exportable, the wizard displays the page but makes the Yes, Export The Private Key option button unavailable.

The second choice is which file format to use for the certificate. This choice comes on the Export File Format page of the Certificate Export Wizard (see Figure 48.8).

FIGURE 48.8:

Choose the file format to use for the certificate—if you have any choice.

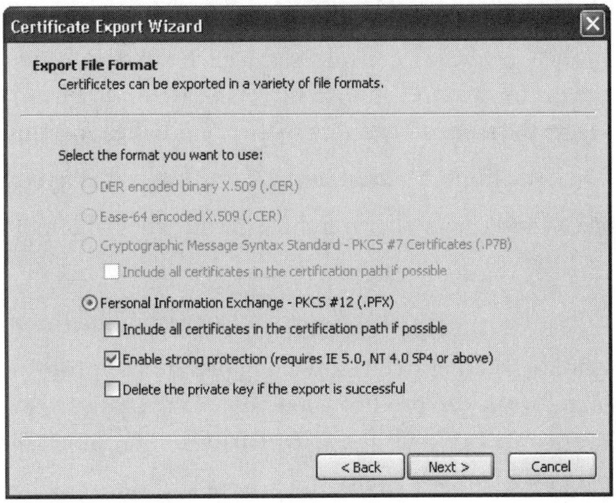

If you chose to export the private key with the certificate, you can use only the Personal Information Exchange – PKCS #12 format. You can then choose the following options:

"Include all certificates in the certification path if possible"   Select this check box if you want to include in the exported certificate file all the certificates in the certification path. Doing so is usually a good idea.

"Enable strong protection"   Select this check box if you want to use strong encryption on the exported certificate file. Using strong encryption is usually a good idea, and the wizard checks this box by default.

"Delete the private key if the export is successful"   Select this check box only if you're moving the certificate from one computer to another.

If you chose not to export the private key (or if you didn't have the choice), you can choose among DER Encoded Binary X.509 format, Base-64 Encoded X.509 format, and Cryptographic Message Syntax Standard – PKCS #7 format.

If you choose the PKCS #7 format, you can select the "Include all certificates in the certification path if possible" check box to include all the certificates in the certificate's certification path.

If you chose to export the private key, you then get to enter a password for it. If not, or after you do so, you specify the name for the certificate file, check the details on the Completing The Certificate Export Wizard page, and click the Finish button. The wizard then exports the certificate file and notifies you when it has done so.

Importing a Certificate

To import a certificate, start the Certificate Import Wizard by taking any of these steps:

- Double-click a certificate file.
- In the Certificates console, right-click the certificate store into which you want to import the certificate and choose All Tasks ➤ Import from the context menu. Alternatively, select the store and choose Action ➤ All Tasks ➤ Import.
- Click the Import button in the Certificates dialog box.

The wizard then walks you through the steps of importing the file:

1. Identify the certificate file to import.

2. Enter the password for the private key (if it's included in the certificate).

3. Choose whether to enable strong private key protection. Use this option if you want Windows XP to prompt you to enter the password every time an application needs to use the private key. This is good security, but it can get old fast.

4. Choose whether to mark the private key as exportable, so that you can back up or export the private key with the certificate. (For security, you may choose to mark the private key as not being exportable.)

Updating the Root Certificates

As you'll recall from earlier in the chapter, root certificates are the certificates that are held by the highest-level CAs and that underpin the PKI. To make sure that your root certificates are current, you need to update them periodically. Given that different certificates last for different periods, and that they're issued at different times, updating them manually would be a miserable job. So it'll be no surprise that Windows XP can update the certificates for you. In fact, XP is configured to update the root certificates automatically by using its Update Root Certificates component, which is installed by default.

To prevent XP from updating its root certificates, you need to remove the Update Root Certificates component. To do so, launch the Windows Components Wizard by choosing Start ➤ Control Panel ➤ Add Or Remove Programs and clicking the Add/Remove Windows Components button. Clear the Update Root Certificates check box, and click the Next button.

To re-enable updating of root certificates, reinstall the Update Root Certificates component by selecting the Update Root Certificates check box in the Windows Components Wizard and clicking the Next button.

CHAPTER 49

Encrypting File System

If your files contain sensitive or confidential information, consider encrypting them with Encrypting File System (EFS) to prevent other people from being able to read the files if they're able to access them or steal them.

The chapter begins by providing an overview of EFS: what it is, why you might use it, and things you should consider before you start using it. It then discusses how to implement EFS and encrypt and decrypt files and folders using both the GUI and the `cipher` command. It shows you how to share encrypted data, and ends by discussing how to plan and implement a recovery policy for EFS.

Overview of EFS

EFS—Encrypting File System—is a security feature of Windows XP Professional (Home Edition doesn't include EFS) that lets you encrypt specified files or folders on your computer to protect them from intrusion.

Windows XP handles encryption transparently, as it does compression on NTFS volumes, so you perform file operations (creating, saving, deleting, copying, and so on) as usual—you don't have to decrypt a file before you can work with it.

> **WARNING** EFS is a powerful feature with strong appeal to many users, but you need to approach it with caution, because if you get things wrong, you can end up with encrypted files that you'll never be able to decrypt. This danger is eminently avoidable, but you need to understand how EFS works before you start using it. So please read the whole of this chapter before experimenting with EFS.

How Does EFS Work?

EFS encrypts data using a key linked to the public key based on the security identifier (SID) for your user account. The data can be decrypted only by using the key for that SID, so someone using another user account can't decrypt it, because other accounts have different SIDs. If you designate another user as a recovery agent, that user can also recover files.

As you'd imagine, encrypting and decrypting files takes more processor cycles than does handling unencrypted files. Generally speaking, a computer that can run Windows XP Professional comfortably should be able to handle EFS without breaking a sweat; if the computer is struggling to run Professional, EFS will diminish the computer's performance further. EFS is more likely to create problems for a server that's serving encrypted files to many clients than the clients themselves.

What You Can and Can't Encrypt

EFS can encrypt files and folders stored on NTFS volumes. (You can't use EFS on FAT or FAT32 volumes unless you convert them to NTFS.) You can encrypt either folders or individual files. In most cases, it's much better to encrypt folders. (More on this in a moment.)

Even on NTFS volumes, you can't encrypt files in the *%systemroot%* folder, nor can you encrypt any files marked with the System attribute.

You also can't encrypt compressed files or folders. If you mark a compressed file or folder for encryption, XP decompresses it before applying the encryption.

Similarly, if you tell XP to compress an encrypted file or folder, XP needs to decrypt it first. Before doing so, it warns you in the Confirm Attribute Change dialog box that it will decrypt the file, so you have a chance to cancel the action.

How Encrypted Files and Folders Behave

You can apply encryption to files and folders (with the constraints discussed in the previous section). When you encrypt a folder, you can choose whether to encrypt all its contents (all files and subfolders) or just the folder itself.

Once you've encrypted a file or folder, only you or a designated recovery agent can decrypt it, unless you explicitly choose to share an encrypted file (not a folder) with other specified users.

Once you've encrypted a file or folder, you can access it transparently from your user account. Other users can't access the file or folder. If they try to do so, XP stops them with an "Access denied" message. (The wording of the message depends on the application from which the user is trying to access the file or folder.)

Here's how XP handles encryption for files you move or copy:

- When you move or copy unencrypted files into an encrypted folder, XP encrypts them without comment.

- When you move encrypted files from an encrypted folder to an unencrypted folder on an NTFS volume, they stay encrypted: If you want them decrypted, you need to decrypt them manually.

- If you copy or move encrypted files from an encrypted folder to a volume that doesn't use NTFS (for example, a FAT volume), XP decrypts them. Before doing so, it displays the Encrypted File dialog box to let you decide whether to carry out the operation for this file (click the Ignore button), for all files you're copying or moving (the Ignore All button), or whether to cancel it.

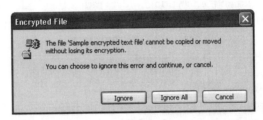

- XP's Backup Utility supports EFS, so files and folders that you back up using Backup Utility remain encrypted.

(Why) Should You Use EFS?

The usual reason for using EFS is to protect your files from being read by unauthorized persons. (A less usual reason is curiosity.) While you can use Windows XP Professional's user accounts and NTFS permissions to keep other users out of your files, these features don't protect your computer against direct physical attacks, such as theft of a laptop, CPU, or hard disk, or against someone accessing your files by booting with a different operating system or from a utility that lets you mount NTFS volumes from a floppy disk.

EFS isn't a substitute for using XP's user accounts and permissions to keep people out of your files, because anyone with permission to read a folder can view the list of its contents (even though they can't read the contents of files). Worse, anyone with permission to delete files or folders can delete encrypted files or folders.

Why Must You Be Careful with EFS?

You need to be careful with EFS because if you lose your private key for decrypting data and haven't designated a recovery agent, you'll never be able to decrypt the data. That means in effect that you lose access to the contents of the encrypted files or folders forever.

Even if you don't lose your private key, system problems can effectively lose it for you. In particular, be aware that reinstalling Windows prevents you from accessing encrypted files.

Because reinstalling Windows creates accounts with different SIDs, you won't be able to access encrypted files directly, even if the account names are the same. Instead, you'll need to import your EFS certificate in order to be able to access encrypted files.

Tips for Implementing EFS for Maximum Protection

This section provides tips on implementing EFS for maximum protection of your files.

Encrypt Folders Rather Than Individual Files

Microsoft recommends encrypting folders rather than individual files, but you can encrypt individual files if necessary. The reason for encrypting folders is that doing so makes sure that the temporary files that many programs create while working are encrypted as well as the files themselves. Because many programs (particularly older programs) place their temporary files in folders other than the folder containing the file they're working with, you may need to encrypt your temporary folders as well.

Create Files in Already-Encrypted Folders

To keep a file as secure as possible, create it in an already encrypted folder so that it's never saved to disk in an unencrypted file.

If you use the My Documents folder for your personal documents, encrypt it.

Encrypt Your Temporary Folders

Encrypt your temporary folders (the %temp% and %tmp% folders) so that temporary files created by programs that don't use the current folder are encrypted as well.

Turn Off Print Spooling or Encrypt Your Print Spool Folder

If possible, turn off print spooling—writing print files to disk before printing them. If this isn't possible, encrypt the folder in which print spool files are stored.

Export Your EFS Certificate and Keep It Safe

To implement its encryption, EFS uses a key bound to a certificate. Because you won't be able to decrypt your encrypted files without this key, it's vital to back up the certificate and keep the backup in a safe place.

Set Up a Recovery Agent

If you use your computer in a stand-alone configuration or in a workgroup (in other words, it's not part of a domain), create a recovery agent as described in "Planning and Implementing an EFS Recovery Policy" later in this chapter. Then back up the recovery agent's certificate.

Keep Your Old Recovery Agent Certificates

If you update your recovery agent certificates, keep your old certificates so that you can recover previously encrypted files if necessary.

Secure Encrypted Data in Transit Across Your Network

If you're connecting to a computer on which remote encryption has been enabled, you can encrypt or decrypt files and folders from across the network. But be aware that when you open an encrypted file over the network, the data that's transmitted back and forth isn't encrypted. To encrypt the data in transit, you need to use another protocol, such as IPSec or PPTP.

Before you can encrypt on a remote computer in a domain, the administrator has to designate the remote computer as trusted for delegation in Active Directory Users And Computers. However, if the remote computer is running WebDAV, it doesn't need to be designated as trusted for delegation. WebDAV can encrypt the file at the local computer and transmit encrypted data.

> **NOTE** In order to use EFS on remote folders, your computer and the remote computer need to be in the same domain. If the remote computer is in another domain, XP displays the error message "Key not valid for use in specified state" when you try to encrypt a file on the remote computer.

Clear Your Paging File at Shutdown

Because your paging file may contain sensitive information that was temporarily stored in virtual memory by a program, you may want to clear it when you shut down your computer so that nobody can glean data from it.

To clear the paging file at shutdown, run Registry Editor, navigate to the key

```
\HKEY_LOCAL_MACHINE\SYSTEM\CurrentControlSet\Control\Session Manager\Memory
Management
```

and change the value of the value entry ClearPageFileAtShutdown to 1. Then restart XP to make the change take effect.

Beware of System Restore

If you encrypt only file types that aren't monitored by System Restore, you don't need to worry about someone being able to use System Restore to restore the files to their unencrypted state. For example, if you encrypt only data files, System Restore won't pose a threat to the encryption.

But if you need to encrypt files of types that are being monitored by System Restore, you have two choices. Either store the encrypted files on a drive on which you're not using System Restore—for example, a data-only drive. Or turn off System Restore (as discussed in Chapter 45) before encrypting the files, then turn it back on once they're encrypted.

Encrypting Files and Folders

To encrypt a folder, you set the Encryption property for it. The easiest way to do so is as follows:

1. Display the Properties dialog box for the file or folder by right-clicking the item in an Explorer window and choosing Properties from the context menu.

2. Display the Advanced Attributes dialog box by clicking the Advanced button on the General tab.

3. Select the Encrypt Contents To Secure Data check box in the Compress Or Encrypt Attributes group box.

4. Click the OK button to close the Advanced Attributes dialog box.

5. Click the OK button or the Apply button in the Properties dialog box for the file or folder.

6. If you're encrypting a folder, XP displays the Confirm Attribute Change dialog box. Select the Apply Changes To This Folder Only option or the Apply Changes To This Folder, Subfolders And Files option as appropriate, and click the OK button.

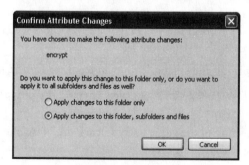

7. XP applies encryption to the file or folder. Depending on the size of the file or the folder's contents, applying the encryption may take a while.

To decrypt a file or folder, you repeat the above process but clear the Encrypt Contents To Secure Data check box. If you're decrypting a folder, XP displays the Confirm Attribute Change dialog box so that you can indicate whether to decrypt only the folder or the folder and all its contents.

NOTE   By default, encrypted files and folders appear in a green font in Explorer windows. To display them in the same color as unencrypted files and folders, clear the Show Encrypted Or Compressed NTFS Files In Color check box on the View tab of the Folder Options dialog box (Tools ➤ Folder Options).

Encrypting and Decrypting with the Cipher Command

XP provides GUI tools for performing most encryption and decryption operations, but it also provides the cipher command for working from the command prompt. As you'll see in a moment, there are a couple of operations for which you *must* use cipher; the rest of the time, it's there as an option.

If you're prepared to put in a little work with the switches shown in Table 49.1, cipher gives you greater flexibility than the GUI tools for encrypting and decrypting files and folders.

TABLE 49.1: Switches for the Cipher Command

Switch	Explanation
[no switch]	Display the encryption state (E for encrypted, U for unencrypted) for the current folder and the files and subfolders it contains.
/D	Decrypt the specified folders.
/E	Encrypt the specified folders.
/A	Encrypt or decrypt both files and folders.
/F	Force the encryption on all the objects specified, even if they're already encrypted. (By default, cipher skips objects that are already encrypted.)
/H	Include files with the Hidden attribute or System attribute in the listing. (By default, cipher doesn't list files that have these attributes.)
/I	Ignore any errors encountered and continue encrypting or decrypting files. (By default, cipher stops when it encounters an error.)
/K	Create a new encryption key for the current user.
/U	Examine all the encrypted files on local drives, updating the user's file encryption key or the recovery agent's key.
/U /N	Examine all the encrypted files on local drives, but without updating keys.
/Q	Report a minimal set of information.
/R	Create an EFS recovery agent key and certificate. (More on this switch in a moment.)
/S	Perform the specified operation on the specified folder and its subfolders, but not on files in that folder and those subfolders.
/W	Remove data from available unused disk space on the volume.

A word of explanation about the `cipher /K` command, which you'll see from the table creates a new encryption key for the user currently logged on. This encryption key isn't a replacement for a lost key, and you can't use it to decrypt data encrypted with the original key—you can use it only to encrypt new data.

Sharing Encrypted Data

Once you've encrypted a file, you can't blithely share it with other people the way you can an unencrypted file, because they won't be able to decrypt it. Instead, you need to take the actions discussed in this section.

Sharing an Encrypted File with Other Users

Windows XP lets you share an encrypted file (but not a folder) with specified other users who each have an EFS certificate. Other users of your computer can create EFS certificates by encrypting one or more files under their accounts. Remote users will need to export their EFS certificates and supply them to you so that you can import them on your computer.

To share an encrypted file, display the Advanced Attributes dialog box for the file. Then click the Details button to display the Encryption Details For dialog box (Figure 49.1). Click the Add button to display the Select User dialog box and use it to add the appropriate people to the Users Who Can Transparently Access This File list.

FIGURE 49.1:

To share an encrypted file with another user, add them to the list in the Encryption Details For dialog box for the file.

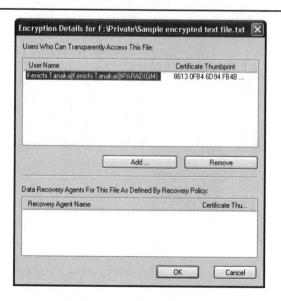

Using Your Encrypted Files from Another Computer

To use your encrypted files from another computer, you need to have your encryption certificate on that computer. If your network administrator has set you up with a roaming profile, Windows XP automatically makes the encryption certificate available to any computer at which you log on successfully. If you don't have a roaming profile, import your certificate manually on the computer by using the techniques described in Chapter 48.

Disabling and Enabling EFS

You can disable EFS on a computer attached to a domain by creating a domain policy that denies the use of EFS and applying that policy to the computer (or, more likely, to the appropriate group of computers).

If the computer isn't part of a domain, run the Registry Editor and create a new DWORD value entry named EfsConfiguration in the key

```
\HKEY_LOCAL_MACHINE\SOFTWARE\Microsoft\Windows NT\CurrentVersion\EFS
```

Assign the value 1 to the value entry, then restart the computer.

To reenable EFS, assign the EfsConfiguration value entry the value 0.

WARNING   If you're going to disable EFS, do so before any user of the computer has had the chance to encrypt any of their files. Otherwise, any user who has encrypted files or folders will no longer be able to access them.

Planning and Implementing an EFS Recovery Policy

As discussed earlier in this chapter, EFS provides strong encryption, but that encryption necessarily comes with some major gotchas against which you need to protect yourself so that you can recover encrypted files if anything goes wrong.

If your computer is part of a domain, Windows XP automatically sets up the domain administrator as the recovery agent. The administrator can set up other recovery agents as necessary by using the domain's enterprise certification authority (CA) to create recovery agent certificates and then adding them to the domain security policy—but even if the administrator doesn't add any recovery agents, the domain's users are automatically covered for data recovery.

If your computer stands alone or is part of a workgroup, however, XP doesn't automatically create a recovery agent, leaving you with the potential of losing all access to your encrypted files.

So if you're not part of a domain, you need to designate one or more recovery agents who can recover encrypted files if your certificate goes AWOL.

Creating a Recovery Agent Certificate

Before you designate a recovery agent, you need to create a recovery agent certificate by using the cipher command. Take these steps:

1. Log on to your computer as Administrator and open a Command Prompt window.

2. Enter **cipher /r:filename**, where *filename* is the name (and, if necessary, path) of the files in which you want the certificate files stored. (File*s*? Yes—the cipher command creates certificate files in both the CER format and the PFX format.)

3. When cipher prompts you for a password, enter an unguessable password and press the Enter key. cipher creates the certificate files.

4. Copy the certificate files to a safe location *away from your computer* (for example, on a floppy disk, another removable medium, or a secure online drive) and delete the original files.

Designating a Recovery Agent

Once you've created the recovery agent certificate, you can designate your recovery agent. You can use any account other than the account with which you're creating the encrypted files. In most cases, the Administrator account provides the best solution.

To designate your recovery agent, log on to the account you'll use as the data recovery agent. Then use the Certificates console (or an MMC console with the Certificates snap-in) to import the recovery certificate's PFX file to the Personal branch under Certificates – Current User. On the Password page of the Certificate Import Wizard, select the Mark This Key As Exportable check box. On the Certificate Store page, select the "Automatically select the certificate store based on the type of certificate" option.

Then run the Local Security Settings console (for example, Start ➤ Run, **secpol.msc**, OK) and take the following actions:

1. Under Security Settings, expand the Public Key Policies item.

2. Right-click the Encrypting File System item and choose Add Data Recovery Agent from the context menu to start the Add Recovery Agent Wizard.

3. On the Select Recovery Agents page of the wizard, click the Browse Folders button.

4. Use the resulting Open dialog box to select and open the recovery certificate's CER file. The wizard adds the contents of the certificate to the Recovery Agents list, listing the user as USER_UNKNOWN.

5. Finish the wizard.

You've now set up the current user as recovery agent, so any files encrypted from now on will be encrypted with both the user's public key and the recovery agent's public key, so they can be recovered by either the user or the recovery agent. But it's a good idea to add another level of protection by removing the recovery agent's key from the account you just designated as recovery agent so that nobody can log on under that account and easily decrypt the encrypted files.

To remove the recovery agent's key, log on to the recovery agent account (if you're not still logged on) and use Certificates console to export the certificate. On the Export Private Key screen of the wizard, select the "Yes, export the private key" option button. On the Export File Format screen, select the "Enable strong protection" and "Delete the private key if the export is successful" check boxes.

Keeping Your Encryption and Recovery Certificates Safe

When the wizard has finished the export, store the certificate in a secure location away from your computer. In order to use the recovery agent to decrypt files, you'll need to import the certificate again to the recovery agent account—but that's the price of security.

If you lose your encryption certificate and the recovery agent certificate, there's not much you can do to recover your encrypted files. As mentioned earlier, you can create a new encryption certificate by using the cipher command (cipher /K), but this certificate will work only for new files you encrypt—you won't be able to use it to decrypt the files you encrypted using the previous certificate. So it's vital to keep a backup of your encryption certificate and the recovery agent certificate.

Recovering Encrypted Data

Once you've designated your recovery agent, you can recover encrypted data by logging onto the recovery agent account and importing the recovery agent certificate (if you removed it for security).

Finding and Examining Encrypted Files and Folders

Of course, recovering the encrypted files and folders presupposes that you can find them in the first place and decrypt only those for the user who has lost their private key. Even if you've designated a central location for all your encrypted files, working out which belong to whom can be a daunting task.

As you saw earlier in the chapter, you can use the cipher /u /n command to produce a list of the encrypted files on your system (without updating the encryption key). But this list doesn't tell you who encrypted the files. You can use the Encryption Details dialog box for a file to see who encrypted it, but this means plugging through file by file, which could take you halfway till eternity for a system with many encrypted files.

Before you ask—yes, Microsoft is aware of the problem. Load your Windows XP Professional CD and install EFSINFO.EXE from the \SUPPORT\TOOLS folder, either by extracting it from the SUPPORT.CAB cabinet file or by running SUPTOOLS.MSI from the \SUPPORT\TOOLS folder and using the Windows Support Tools Setup Wizard to install either the Typical set of tools or the Complete set of tools.

Examining Encrypted Files with efsinfo

Once you've installed EFSINFO.EXE, open a Command Prompt window and run the program from the location to which you installed it (XP doesn't add it to your path). Table 49.2 lists the switches for efsinfo.

TABLE 49.2: Switches for the efsinfo Command

Switch	Explanation
[no switch]	Display the encryption state (Encrypted or Not Encrypted) for the current folder and the files and subfolders it contains.
/U	Display the user information for the file. (This is the default option.)
/R	Display the recovery agent information for the file.
/C	Display the thumbnail information for the certificate.
/I	Ignore any errors encountered and continue listing. (By default, efsinfo stops when it encounters an error.)
/Y	Display the thumbnail information for the current EFS certificate on the local PC.
/S	Perform the specified operation on the directories and subdirectories in the current directory.

For example, you could use the efsinfo /r /u command to return user information and recovery agent information for all the files in the current folder.

> **TIP**   Another tool for examining encrypted files is EFSDump (for information dumper), a free utility that you can download from the Systems Internals website (www.sysinternals.com/ntw2k/source/misc.shtml).

CHAPTER 50

IPSec

As you'll know only too well if you surf the Web and read the news, Internet Protocol (IP) is a truly wonderful invention, but it suffers from having been designed with flexibility and robustness rather than security in mind. The result is that networks running on IP (such as the Internet) are vulnerable to a wide range of attacks, from the undetectable sniffing of unencrypted data through to distributed denial-of-service attacks launched by "zombie" computers commandeered by malicious hackers.

Chances are that you don't want any attacks happening to your IP traffic. To secure your IP traffic on computers running Windows XP Professional, you can use IP Security (IPSec), as discussed in this chapter. (Windows XP Home Edition doesn't include IPSec.)

You can also apply TCP/IP filtering to your network connections on either Professional or Home Edition to limit the traffic that passes across them. I discuss this topic briefly at the end of the chapter.

Understanding IPSec

This section discusses the basics of IPSec: what it is, how you use it, when to use it, and the requirements for using it.

What IPSec Is

IPSec is a suite of protocols and services for securing IP traffic across a network connection. By establishing trust from a source IP address to a destination IP address, IPSec aims to provide end-to-end security combined with ease of use. IPSec includes mechanisms for encrypting data, authenticating the computers connected, securing the transmission and receipt of data, and filtering IP traffic.

Windows XP Professional implements IPSec through policies. IPSec policies can be stored either in Active Directory or in a local computer's Registry. Usually, global IPSec policies are stored in Active Directory and apply to computers that connect to the domain. If a computer gets disconnected from the domain, the domain's IPSec policy information is cached in the computer's Registry. For computers that don't connect to a domain, local IPSec policies are stored in the computer's Registry.

This chapter discusses how to configure local IPSec policies on computers running Windows XP Professional.

How to Use IPSec

You can use IPSec when establishing VPN connections using Layer 2 Tunneling Protocol (L2TP), as discussed in the next chapter, for either remote-access connections or for ultra-secure communications on an internal network. You can also use IPSec by itself (which is referred to as *IPSec tunnel mode* or *IPSec pure tunnel*) to secure communications on an internal network or intranet.

As mentioned a moment ago, Windows XP Professional can use global or local IPSec policies. Global IPSec policies (which are set on the domain using Domain Security Policy) override local IPSec policies (which are set on the local computer by using Local Security Policy).

When to Use IPSec

Use IPSec when you need to secure communications between two computers. But don't use it unthinkingly on all network connections just because you can. Evaluate your need for IPSec by assessing the following considerations:

- How vulnerable is your network to attacks from outside? If your network isn't connected to the Internet or other external networks, its vulnerability will be low.

- How vulnerable is your network to attacks from inside? In most cases, this consideration boils down to the question, Does your network carry sensitive data that you need to protect from the rest of the company? For example, you might need to protect financial data or patent information from the regular users of the network. But if such data is already cordoned off in secure systems, you shouldn't need to use IPSec to secure it.

- Do you need to secure traffic on the LAN or just data on remote-access connections?

- Will your IPSec policies work for all the computers that need to access the data in question? You may need to upgrade some of the computers in order to use IPSec effectively.

If you decide you need IPSec, bear the following in mind:

- If your network uses a domain, you'll almost always do best to manage your IPSec policies at the domain level. In other cases, you may want to let server administrators apply IPSec policies on an as-needed basis. Only rarely will you do well to apply IPSec policies at the local computer level in a domain.

- IPSec encryption—like any other strong encryption—involves considerable processor overhead. Now that gigahertz-plus chips are so widely used as to be hard to avoid, this is less of an issue than it used to be; but even so, don't run IPSec unless you need it, because it will slow your computer down. However, if you're using a legacy computer that's struggling to run XP Professional, adding IPSec to its burden may hamstring it entirely. Check to see whether your network adapter can handle encryption duties, and if so, offload them onto it.

- Because misconfigured IPSec policies can cripple communications between vital computers rather than securing communications, test your IPSec policies thoroughly in the lab or on test workstations and servers before deploying them for real.

Requirements for Using IPSec

In order to use IPSec, your computers need a means of authentication and the capability for encryption. Your firewall or other filtering devices need to apply filters that allow IPSec traffic to pass. The following sections contain details on these requirements.

Kerberos V5 or Certificates for Authentication

Windows XP Professional systems that are part of a domain can use Kerberos V5 for authentication, so they don't need certificates for authentication on an intranet. Windows XP Home Edition systems (which can't connect to a domain), and Windows XP Professional systems that don't connect to a domain, need certificates for authentication.

DES or 3DES Encryption

To use IPSec, your systems need to be capable of at least Data Encryption Standard (DES) encryption, and preferably Triple DES (3DES) strong encryption. DES uses a 56-bit key, while Triple DES uses two 56-bit keys.

For Windows XP Professional systems, this isn't an issue. But if you want to apply 3DES to your IPSec-secured connections, make sure you've applied Service Pack 2 (or later) or the High Encryption Pack to your Windows 2000 computers. Otherwise, the Windows 2000 machines will knock the encryption back to DES.

Packet Filtering

In order for IPSec to be implemented, the source computer and the destination computer need to know about the traffic that's being secured. The computers through which the traffic is routed don't need to know about the traffic—unless they're filtering IP traffic.

If you use a device that filters packets between your Internet connection and computers in a DMZ or perimeter network, you'll need to apply filtering to make sure that IPSec-secured packets can pass through the device. Table 50.1 lists a basic set of filters that the device will need to permit to pass.

TABLE 50.1: Basic Filters for a Firewall Device to Allow IPSec Traffic to Pass

Purpose	Item	Value (Decimal)	Value (Hex)
IPSec Encapsulating Security Protocol (ESP) traffic	IP protocol ID	50	0x32
IPSec Authentication Header (AH) traffic	IP protocol ID	51	0x33
Internet Key Exchange (IKE) traffic	UDP port	500	0x1F4

Depending on the packet-filtering software you're using, you may be able to improve on the basic set of filters shown in Table 50.1 by defining separate input filters and output filters for each network interface involved and by specifying IP addresses for the computers in the DMZ. Table 50.2 lists restrictive filters for IPSec traffic based on a computer secured with IPSec communicating through a dedicated interface with a firewall device in a DMZ.

TABLE 50.2: Restrictive Filters for a Firewall Device to Allow IPSec Traffic to Pass

Purpose	Source/Destination IP Address	Port/Protocol	Value (Decimal)	Value (Hex)
Input Packet Filters for Computer's DMZ Interface				
Incoming IKE traffic	Destination	UDP destination port	500	0x1F4
Incoming IPSec ESP traffic	Destination	IP protocol	50	0x32
Incoming IPSec AH traffic	Destination	IP protocol	51	0x33
Output Packet Filters for Computer's DMZ Interface				
Outgoing IKE traffic	Source	UDP source port	500	0x1F4
Incoming IPSec ESP traffic	Source	IP protocol	50	0x32
Outgoing IPSec AH traffic	Source	IP protocol	51	0x33
Input Packet Filters on DMZ Interface of Firewall				
Outgoing IKE traffic	Source	UDP source port	500	0x1F4
Outgoing IPSec ESP traffic	Source	IP protocol	50	0x32
Outgoing IPSec AH traffic	Source	IP protocol	51	0x33
Output Packet Filters on DMZ Interface of Firewall				
Incoming IKE traffic	Destination	UDP port	500	0x1F4
Incoming IPSec ESP traffic	Destination	IP protocol	50	0x32
Incoming IPSec AH traffic	Destination	IP protocol	51	0x33

Overview of Preconfigured Policies

Windows XP Professional provides three standard IPSec policies that you can use as they are or edit to suit your needs:

Client (Respond Only)   Usually used on a client, this policy uses unsecured communication unless a server requests security. When one does, the client uses security only for the protocol and the port requested by the server. Other traffic remains unsecured.

Secure Server (Require Security)   Usually used on a secure server, this policy requires security using Kerberos trust for all IP traffic. This policy doesn't allow any unsecured communication.

Server (Request Security)   Usually used on a server, this policy requests security using Kerberos trust for IP traffic but allows unsecured IP traffic from clients that don't respond to the request for secured traffic.

To use one of these policies as it stands, assign it as described in "Assigning IPSec Policies," later in this chapter. To modify a policy before assigning it, follow the steps in the next section.

Modifying Existing IPSec Policies

In many cases, the best way to start working with IPSec policies is to modify one of the existing policies, because they're already fully enough formed to need little further configuration. To work with IPSec policies using Local Security Policy, take the following steps:

1. Open Local Security Policy (choose Start ➢ Control Panel ➢ Performance and Maintenance ➢ Administrative Tools ➢ Local Security Policy).

2. Click the IP Security Policies branch to display its contents.

3. To view the description of a policy, double-click it to display its Properties dialog box with the Rules tab foremost, then click the General tab.

4. On the General tab, you can change the following items:

   - The name of the rule. (This appears in the IP Security Policy snap-in.)

   - The description of the rule. For example, clarify the changes you're making and their intended effects.

   - The interval at which Windows XP Professional should poll Active Directory for policy changes. This setting applies only if the computer is part of a domain.

5. Also on the General tab, you can click the Advanced button to display the Key Exchange Settings dialog box (shown on the left in Figure 50.1), in which you can choose the following settings:

- Select the Master Key Perfect Forward Secrecy check box if you want to force Windows XP Professional to reauthenticate and negotiate a new master key each time it needs a new session key.

- Reduce the "Authenticate and generate a new key after every *nn* minutes" setting to tighten security by changing keys more frequently.

- To force Windows XP Professional to get a new key after a specific number of sessions, enter the number in the "Authenticate and generate a new key after every *nn* settings" box. The default setting, 0, doesn't force a change. If you select the Master Key Perfect Forward Secrecy check box, Windows XP Professional applies a value of 1 to this option and doesn't let you change it.

- To specify your preferred security methods, click the Methods button and work in the resulting Key Exchange Security Methods dialog box (shown on the right in Figure 50.1).

FIGURE 50.1:

Use the Key Exchange Settings dialog box (left) to tighten IPSec authentication and key security. If necessary, click the Methods button and use the Key Exchange Security Methods dialog box (right) to specify these methods.

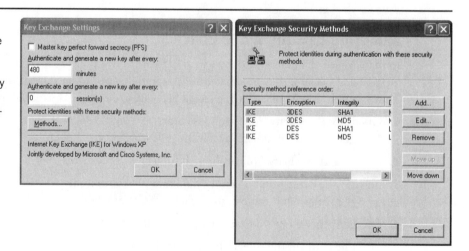

6. On the Rules tab, you can select or clear the check boxes for the existing rules in the IP Security Rules list box to apply them to the policy or turn them off. You can edit a rule by double-clicking it and working with the options on the tabs of the resulting Edit Rule Properties dialog box; Figure 50.2 shows an example of this dialog box. (Note that the selection of tabs in the Edit Rule Properties dialog box varies depending on the rule you're editing.)

FIGURE 50.2:

Use the Edit Rule
Properties dialog box
to edit an existing
IPSec policy to meet
your needs.

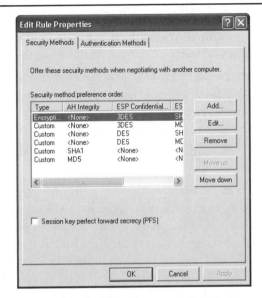

7. On the Security Methods tab of the Edit Rule Properties dialog box, you can make changes such as the following:

   • Use the Move Up and Move Down buttons to change the preference order of the security methods.

   • Add a new security method by clicking the Add button and choosing the appropriate option in the New Security Method dialog box: Encryption And Integrity (which uses ESP), Integrity Only (which uses AH), or Custom. If you select the Custom option button, click the Settings button and use the resulting dialog box to define the custom settings.

   • Edit an existing security method by selecting it, clicking the Edit button, and working in the Modify Security Method dialog box and the Custom Security Method Settings dialog box as necessary.

   • Remove a security method by selecting it, clicking the Remove button, and then clicking the Yes button in the IP Security Policy Management confirmation dialog box.

   • Tighten security by selecting the Session Key Perfect Forward Secrecy check box. This option forces Windows XP Professional to renegotiate a new master key each time it needs a new session key.

8. On the Authentication Methods tab of the Edit Rule Properties dialog box, you can change the types of authentication used by the rule and the order in which to apply them. The default for Windows XP Professional in a domain is Kerberos V5. The alternatives are to use a specified certificate or a preshared key.

Creating New IPSec Policies

If the preconfigured IPSec policies don't suit you, and you don't want to change them, you can create new IPSec policies from scratch from the Local Security Settings snap-in.

To create a new IPSec policy, you can either use the IP Security Policy Wizard to create the basic details of your new policy and then edit some settings manually, or create the whole policy manually. For your first policies, you may prefer to use the wizard. Subsequently, you'll probably want to graduate to creating your policies manually.

To run the wizard, right-click the IP Security Policies item and choose Create IP Security Policy from the shortcut menu.

To create an IP security policy manually, you need to turn off the IP Security Policy Wizard. To do so, right-click an existing IPSec policy and choose Properties to display the Properties dialog box for the policy. On the Rules tab, clear the Use Add Wizard check box, then click the Add button to display the New Rule Properties dialog box. This dialog box contains most of the same tabs and controls as the Edit Rule Properties dialog box, shown in Figure 50.2 earlier in this chapter. (Like that dialog box, the New Rule Properties dialog box contains different sets of tabs depending on the type of rule you're working with.)

Should You Use ESP or AH?

As you've seen, Windows XP Professional lets you choose between using Encapsulating Security Protocol (ESP) or Authentication Header (AH) for protecting your IP traffic. What's the difference, and which should you use?

Briefly, AH computes a keyed hash for each IP packet and header being transferred. It then includes this hash with the packet, thus providing data authentication and integrity. Each packet includes a sequence number for packet replay services.

ESP also computes a keyed hash for each IP packet and includes it with the packet. But with ESP, the hash doesn't protect the IP header—the hash calculation includes the ESP header, trailer, and payload, but not the IP header. ESP encrypts the payload using DES or (better) 3DES, and includes a sequence number with each packet for packet replay services.

AH offers better performance than ESP, while ESP offers better protection than AH. Consider using AH for securing LAN traffic and ESP for more vulnerable traffic, such as traffic that crosses the Internet. If you have network adapters on which you can offload IPSec encryption, you may want to use ESP for internal traffic as well.

Assigning IPSec Policies

Once you've chosen or modified an IPSec policy, you need to assign it in order to put it into effect. To assign a policy in Windows XP Professional, run the IP Security Policy snap-in, right-click the policy, and choose Assign from the shortcut menu.

Only one IPSec policy can be assigned at a time, so assigning a policy unassigns any currently assigned policy. You can also unassign the currently assigned policy without assigning another by right-clicking the policy and choosing Un-assign.

Managing Global Filters

Instead of creating IP filters as necessary when you need them while creating a policy, you can define global filters ahead of time so that you can apply them to policies easily.

To manage global IPSec filters, right-click the IP Security Policies item in Local Security Settings and choose Manage IP Filter Lists And Filter Actions from the context menu to display that option's dialog box, whose two tabs are shown in Figure 50.3.

To add an IPSec filter, click the Add button on the Manage IP Filter Lists tab. In the resulting IP Filter List dialog box, enter the name and description for the new filter list. Then click the Add button and follow the steps of the IP Filter Wizard as it walks you through specifying the source address of the IP traffic, the traffic's destination, the protocol, and other details. To edit the resulting filter, select the Edit Properties check box on the final page of the wizard before clicking the Finish button.

FIGURE 50.3:

Use the Manage IP Filter Lists And Filter Actions dialog box to manage global IP filters.

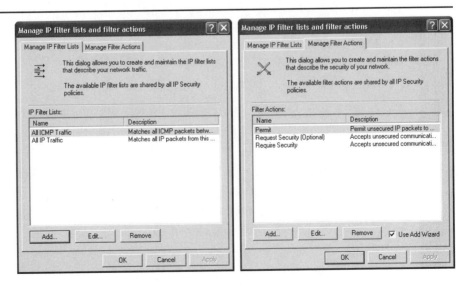

To edit an IPSec filter, double-click it on the Manage IP Filter Lists tab. In the resulting dialog box, change the name or description as appropriate; use the Edit button to edit an existing filter, the Remove button to remove an existing filter, or the Add button to add a new filter.

To create a new filter action, click the Add button on the Manage Filter Actions tab and follow the Filter Action Wizard through the steps of creating a new filter action. These steps involve supplying the name and description for the filter; choosing whether to permit, block, or negotiate security; and (if you chose to negotiate), specifying whether to refuse to communicate with computers that don't support IPSec or to fall back to unsecured communication; and specifying which methods of IP traffic security to use.

To edit an existing filter action, double-click it on the Manage Filter Actions tab and work in the resulting Properties dialog box. For example, you might choose to apply Session Key Perfect Forward Secrecy to a filter action.

Using TCP/IP Filtering

Another tool for restricting the IP traffic that your Windows XP computer receives is TCP/IP filtering. You can filter TCP ports, UDP ports, and IP protocols on a port-by-port basis. Filtering applies to *all* the network adapters that your computer is using: You can't apply filtering to one adapter but not to the others.

By default, XP doesn't apply filtering. This means that it allows all the IP traffic to pass across the network adapters. You can tighten up your security considerably by filtering ports and protocols, but it's a ticklish business, because filtering the wrong ports can cripple your network. So before you start applying filters, you need to know which ports are used for which purpose. Visit www.iana.org/assignments/port-numbers for the latest list of TCP/IP port assignments.

To configure and apply TCP/IP filtering, take the following steps:

1. Choose Start ➤ Connect To, right-click any network interface, and choose Properties.

2. Double-click the Internet Protocol (TCP/IP) item on the General tab to display the Internet Protocol (TCP/IP) Properties dialog box.

3. Click the Advanced button to display the Advanced TCP/IP Settings dialog box.

4. On the Options tab, double-click the TCP/IP Filtering item in the Optional Settings list box to display the TCP/IP Filtering dialog box.

5. Select the Enable TCP/IP Filtering (All Adapters) check box.

6. For each type of filter (TCP Ports, UDP Ports, and IP Protocols) that you need to apply, select the Permit Only option instead of Permit All, then use the Add button and the resulting dialog box to add the port or protocol number you want to add. Use the Remove buttons to remove a selected filter that has outlived its usefulness.

7. Click the OK buttons to close the TCP/IP Filtering dialog box, the Advanced TCP/IP Settings dialog box, the Internet Protocol (TCP/IP) Properties dialog box, and the network interface's Properties dialog box.

8. Make sure that your network is functioning as it ought to. If it's not, chances are that you'll need to tweak the filters you applied.

Once you apply TCP/IP filtering, Windows XP accepts only TCP packets destined for the TCP ports you've added, UDP packets for the UDP ports you've added, IP protocols matching the list of protocols you've specified, and all ICMP packets. TCP/IP filtering doesn't filter ICMP traffic—for ICMP filtering, use RRAS to configure IP packet filters.

CHAPTER 51

VPN Connections

This chapter discusses how to create and manage virtual private network (VPN) connections for connecting securely to remote networks via a shared or public network, such as the Internet.

VPNs are popular with corporations for allowing secure remote connectivity at low cost, but individual users can also use them to good effect. Windows XP provides both VPN client and VPN server capabilities.

Understanding Virtual Private Network Connections

This section provides an overview of what VPN connections are, how they work, and what they're used for.

What VPN Connections Are

Virtual private network (VPN) connections let you establish a secure connection across an unsecured network (such as the Internet) so that your computer becomes a node on the remote network. The computer connecting to the network is the VPN client, and the computer to which it connects is the VPN server.

You're most likely to need to use XP (Professional or Home Edition) as a VPN client, but both versions of XP also include a minimal VPN server that can accept a single incoming connection. This chapter shows you how to use both the VPN client and the VPN server components, starting with the client.

How VPN Connections Work

A VPN connection establishes a secure connection by *tunneling* under the protocols of the unsecured network (for example, TCP/IP in the case of an Internet connection) to create a virtual direct connection between the VPN client and the VPN server. This connection operates as a dedicated WAN link on a logical level and is secured by encrypting each packet or frame to be transmitted and enveloping it in another packet or frame with a new header for transmission. This process is called *encapsulation*. When the packet or frame reaches its destination, the header is removed, the envelope (as it were) is opened, and the packet or frame inside it is decrypted *(unencapsulation)*.

As a VPN client, Windows XP can use the Point-to-Point Tunneling Protocol (PPTP) or the Layer 2 Tunneling Protocol (L2TP). As a VPN server, XP can use only PPTP, while Windows 2000 Server can use either PPTP or L2TP. Both PPTP and L2TP are based on the Point-to-Point Protocol (PPP), the suite of standard protocols commonly used for connecting to an ISP.

If your configuration allows you the choice, use L2TP rather than PPTP for your VPN connection, because it offers greater security. (I'll discuss VPN security in detail later in this chapter.) To use L2TP VPN connections, you'll need to install a certificate on the VPN client or use a smart card.

SEE ALSO   See Chapter 48 for a discussion of certificates.

NOTE   Another option for creating VPN connections is to use IPSec tunnel mode (also known as "IPSec pure tunnel"). You may need to do this when working with routers or gateways that don't support PPTP tunneling or L2TP tunneling. If you're using a Windows XP/2000 solution for your VPN, use L2TP or PPTP rather than IPSec tunnel mode. (See the previous chapter for details on IPSec.)

What VPN Connections Are Used For

VPN connections are typically used to enable remote users to access a corporate network securely across the Internet. In this scenario, the remote user connects to their ISP for Internet access as usual, then establishes an encrypted connection across the Internet to a VPN server attached to the corporate network. By connecting to their ISP using their usual Internet connection rather than establishing a dial-up connection to the corporate server, a user with a broadband Internet connection can connect at broadband speeds rather than being limited to modem speeds. If the user has a dial-up Internet connection, there's no speed advantage to a VPN connection, but the Internet connection should at least be a local call rather than a long-distance call.

VPN connections benefit the company as well by reducing costs in two ways. First, the company can offload the burden of supporting dial-up connections to the remote users' ISPs, so its remote access servers don't need to be stuffed with modems and connected to a large number of phone lines. Second, instead of users dialing long-distance (presumably at company expense) to connect, they can connect with a local call to their ISP, greatly reducing the cost of remote access.

VPN connections can also be used within secure networks to cordon off ultra-sensitive data from areas where users who are authorized to use the network but not to see that data could otherwise access it. Authorized users can establish VPN connections across the network to the VPN server containing the protected data, while unauthorized users can't even see the VPN server.

Creating Outgoing VPN Connections

To create an outgoing VPN connection, take the following steps, clicking the Next button to drive each screen of the wizard:

1. Start the New Connection Wizard (for example, choose Start ➤ All Programs ➤ Accessories ➤ Communications ➤ New Connection Wizard).

2. Select the Connect To The Network At My Workplace option on the Network Connection Type page of the wizard.

3. Select the Virtual Private Network Connection option on the Network Connection page of the wizard.

4. Enter the name for the connection on the Connection Name page. The wizard names the text box Company Name, but you can call the connection anything you want.

5. If the wizard displays the Public Network page offering to dial an initial connection to the Internet before establishing the VPN connection, select the Do Not Dial The Initial Connection button or the Automatically Dial This Initial Connection button, as appropriate. If you choose the latter, select the appropriate connection in the drop-down list.

6. Enter the VPN server's host name or IP address on the VPN Server Selection page of the wizard. (If your VPN server has a dynamic IP address rather than a static IP address, leave this page blank. You'll need to fill in the information when you use the connection.)

7. Click the Finish button on the completion page. The wizard creates the connection, assigns it the name you specified, and closes.

If necessary, display the Properties dialog box for the connection and choose further options, such as the following:

General tab options   In the Host Name Or IP Address Of Destination text box, enter the IP address or host name of the VPN server. You shouldn't need to change this entry unless the VPN server has a dynamic IP address that you need to update each time you connect. If you need to change your setting for dialing an Internet connection before connecting to the VPN server, select the Dial Another Connection First check box and choose the connection in the drop-down list.

Security tab options   Use the Typical option button or the Advanced option button to specify how to authenticate your identity. If you choose Typical and your VPN requires encryption, select the Require Data Encryption (Disconnect If None) check box.

Networking tab options   By default, Windows XP automatically negotiates the VPN type—L2TP with IPSec (which XP tries first, because it's more secure) or PPTP. To override this, choose the PPTP VPN item or the L2TP IPSec VPN item instead of Automatic, in the Type Of VPN drop-down list. To specify an IP address for the VPN instead of having the VPN server assign an IP address automatically, double-click the Internet Protocol (TCP/IP) item to display the Internet Protocol (TCP/IP) dialog box, select the Use The Following IP Address option button, and enter the address.

Advanced tab options   You can share a VPN connection with other computers on your network by selecting the "Allow other network users to connect through this computer's connection" check box. You can use ICF on the connection by selecting the "Protect my computer and network by limiting or preventing access to this computer from the Internet" check box.

Connecting to a VPN Connection

To connect to a VPN connection, choose Start ➤ Connect To and select the connection's name from the submenu to display the Connect dialog box for the VPN.

If you need to tweak any of the parameters for the connection, click the Properties button to display the connection's Properties dialog box and make the changes, as discussed in the previous section.

Enter your user name and password, choose whether to save them and for whose use (if applicable), and then click the Connect button.

Once XP has established the connection, you'll be able to connect to resources on the VPN server or its LAN (if you're permitted to do so) as if you were connected directly to the network. The big difference is that the connection happens at the speed of your Internet connection rather than at LAN speeds, and the overhead of encrypting the packets or frames slows down the connection a little further. If you have a slow connection, running programs across the wire will take a long time.

To disconnect the VPN connection, right-click its icon in the notification area and choose Disconnect from the context menu.

Configuring Incoming VPN Connections

As mentioned earlier in this chapter, Windows XP includes a minimal VPN server that can accept one incoming connection. You might want to implement a VPN server so that other people can connect to it across the Internet to access files you're sharing or upload files—for example, to work together on a project.

This section describes how to configure an incoming connection on an XP computer that connects directly to the Internet, on an XP computer that connects to the Internet through ICS, and on a Windows 2000 Server computer.

Incoming Connection on an XP Computer with an Internet Connection

To configure Windows XP to accept incoming VPN connections, log on as an administrator and take the following steps:

1. Start the New Connection Wizard (for example, click the Create A New Connection link in the Network Tasks list on the Network Connections screen).

    - If you haven't set up a modem and specified your location, XP displays the Location Information dialog box. Enter your country and area code, and any other information needed for a modem connection. (Even if you don't have a modem, enter your area code.) When you dismiss the Location Information dialog box, XP displays the Phone And Modem Options dialog box, in which you can rename your default location and create new locations and dialing rules as necessary.

2. Select the Set Up An Advanced Connection option on the Network Connection Type page of the wizard.

4. Select the Accept Incoming Connections option on the Advanced Connection Options page of the wizard.

5. If your computer has a modem, parallel port, or IrDA port, the wizard displays the Devices For Incoming Connections page, which lists those devices installed on your computer and invites you to select the check box for each device you want to use for incoming connections. You *can* select one or more check boxes (for example, select the check box for your modem), but you don't have to.

6. Select the Allow Virtual Private Connections option on the Incoming Virtual Private Network (VPN) Connection page of the wizard.

7. Select the check boxes for the users you want to be able to use the VPN connection on the User Permissions page. Use the Add button and the resulting New User dialog box to add a user *to the computer* (not just to the connection). Use the Remove button to remove a user account *from the computer*. Use the Properties button and the resulting Properties dialog box to change the full name for a user, to specify a password for them, or to set callback options if necessary.

8. Select the networking software to use for the connection on the Networking Software page of the wizard. If necessary, use the Install button to install an additional protocol, service, or client.

9. In most cases, it's a good idea to check the TCP/IP settings for the incoming VPN connection. Double-click the Internet Protocol (TCP/IP) item on the Networking Software page to display the Incoming TCP/IP Properties dialog box (shown in Figure 51.1) and choose settings as appropriate:

FIGURE 51.1:

Use the Incoming TCP/IP Properties dialog box to specify whether to allow callers access to your LAN and whether to assign TCP/IP addresses automatically or manually.

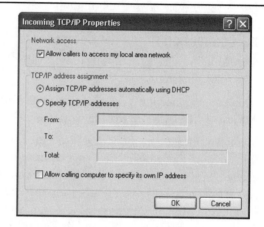

- Select or clear the Allow Callers To Access My Local Area Network check box to allow or deny access to your LAN. (Callers will be able to access shared folders and other resources on your computer either way.)

- Designate how to assign TCP/IP addresses—automatically or manually—in the TCP/IP Address Assignment group box. If you select the Specify TCP/IP Addresses option button, use the From and To text boxes to specify the range of addresses, and check the readout shown in the Total text box. Note that selecting the "Allow calling computer to specify its own IP address" check box could cause an address conflict with a computer already connected to the network.

10. Click the Finish button on the completion page. The wizard creates the connection, names it Incoming Connections, and closes.

You can turn off the VPN connection by clearing the "Allow others to make private connections to my computer by tunneling through the Internet or another network" check box on the General tab of the Incoming Connections Properties dialog box.

If your computer's Internet connection has a dynamic IP address rather than a static IP address, you'll need to communicate the current IP address to anyone who wants to connect. (To get the IP address, run an `ipconfig` command and look at the appropriate line of the readout—for example, the PPP Adapter line for a dial-up connection.)

Incoming PPTP Connection via ICS

If your VPN server connects to the Internet via Internet Connection Sharing (ICS), configure the ICS host to pass PPTP traffic on TCP port 1723 to the VPN server as follows:

1. On the ICS host, display the Properties dialog box for the shared Internet connection.

2. Click the Settings button on the Advanced tab to display the Advanced Settings dialog box.

3. On the Services tab, select the Incoming Connection VPN (PPTP) item and click the Edit button to display the Service Settings dialog box for the service.

NOTE   If you want to change the name of the incoming connection to make clear that it's being redirected to the internal VPN server, use the Delete button to delete the Incoming Connection VPN (PPTP) connection and the Add button to create a new entry. Use 1723 for the external port number and the internal port number, and select the TCP option button.

4. Change the contents of the "Name or IP address of the computer hosting this service on the network" text box to the IP address (for example, 192.168.0.145) or qualified name (for example, VPNServer.MSHOME.NET) of the VPN server.

5. Click the OK buttons to close the Service Settings dialog box, the Advanced Settings dialog box, and the Properties dialog box.

Incoming Connection on a Windows 2000 Server

To configure an incoming VPN connection on a Windows 2000 Server, enable Routing and Remote Access Service as follows:

1. Choose Start ➢ Programs ➢ Administrative Tools ➢ Routing And Remote Access to display the RRAS console.

2. Right-click the server and choose Configure And Enable Routing And Remote Access from the shortcut menu to run the RRAS setup wizard. The wizard walks you through the setup process, in which these are the key decisions:

3. On the Common Configurations page, select the Virtual Private Network (VPN) Server option.

4. On the Remote Client Protocols page, make sure that the appropriate protocols are listed. If not, select the No, I Need To Add Protocols option and add them on the next page.

5. On the Internet Connection page, select the Internet connection through which the VPN clients will access the server.

6. On the IP Address Assignment page, choose whether to assign IP addresses to VPN clients automatically or whether to use a range of addresses that you specify.

7. On the Managing Multiple Remote Access Servers page, choose whether you want to use RADIUS for managing your remote access servers. If you use RADIUS, provide the necessary information.

Implementing Optimum Security on Your VPN Connections

To implement optimum security on your VPN connections, follow the suggestions in the following sections.

Restrict VPN Users to a Minimum

Allow VPN use only to those users who need it. Deny access by default to each user on the Dial-In tab of the user's Properties dialog box or through your remote access policy.

Prefer L2TP to PPTP

Use L2TP rather than PPTP if possible, because L2TP is more secure. If your VPN clients are running Windows XP or 2000, the only reason to use PPTP is if your VPN *server* is running XP—which it shouldn't be, as XP limits the server to a single incoming connection at a time—or if you haven't installed a certificate on the clients.

Close All Unnecessary VPN Ports

By default, Windows 2000 Server sets up five ports for PPTP connections and five ports for L2TP connections when you enable RRAS. Reduce these numbers of ports to the minimum practicable for the degree of connectivity you want to provide. For example, if your server will never need to support more than three simultaneous VPN connections, and all the clients will be using Windows 2000 or XP, disable the PPTP ports and reduce the number of L2TP ports to three.

To change the ports open, right-click the Ports item for the server in the Routing And Remote Access Console and choose Properties from the shortcut menu to display the Ports Properties dialog box, then double-click the relevant WAN Miniport entry and work in the Configure Device dialog box:

- To disable ports, clear the Remote Access Connections (Inbound Only) check box.

- To reduce the number of ports, change the setting in the Maximum Ports box.

As mentioned earlier, XP provides only a single port for VPN connections. When you don't need the VPN, turn off access to it by clearing the "Allow others to make private connections to my computer by tunneling through the Internet or other network" check box on the General tab of the Incoming Connections Properties dialog box.

Require Encryption on Passwords and Data

Require encryption on passwords and data for all clients that connect. For example:

- In Windows 2000 Server, define a group profile that requires users who connect via the VPN to authenticate using EAP and use 128-bit encryption to encrypt their data.
- On a Windows XP VPN server, select the "Require all users to secure their passwords and data" check box on the Users tab of the Incoming Connections Properties dialog box.

   The VPN clients will then need to select the Require Data Encryption (Disconnect If None) check box on the Security tab of the Properties dialog box for the VPN connection in order to connect.

Use Strong Authentication–Preferably EAP

Make sure that your VPN server requires authentication for each user who connects. If possible, use Extensible Authentication Protocol (EAP) with a certificate or a smart card.

   If you can't use EAP, use encrypted authentication such as Microsoft Challenge Handshake Authentication Protocol version 2 (MS-CHAP v2). Using MS-CHAP v2 rather than MS-CHAP may require you to update NT4, Windows 95, and Windows 98 clients with MS-CHAP v2, but v2 provides stronger authentication. (You can download the MS-CHAP v2 updates from the Microsoft website.)

Use DHCP or Configure a Static IP Address Pool

Configure your VPN server to use Dynamic Host Configuration Protocol (DHCP) to assign IP addresses to VPN clients rather than letting VPN clients specify their own addresses. If you can't use DHCP:

- If your network has a single subnet, configure a static IP address pool consisting of a subset of the IP addresses for the subnet that contains the VPN server.
- If your network has multiple subnets and a routed infrastructure, configure a static IP address pool with a range of addresses in a different subnet from the subnet that contains the VPN server. Enable the routing protocol for your infrastructure on the VPN server, or add static routes for the address ranges to the routing tables of your routers.

Create Input and Output Filters

Create input filters and output filters for your VPN connections to restrict the packets that can pass through the connections.

In the Routing And Remote Access console, expand the IP Routing branch and select the General item. Display the Properties dialog box for the interface on which you want to edit the IPSec filters.

To create an input filter, click the Input Filters button on the General tab of the Properties dialog box to display the Input Filters dialog box. To create an output filter, click the Output Filters button on the General tab to display the Output Filters dialog box. From either dialog box (as appropriate), click the Add button to display the Add IP Filter dialog box.

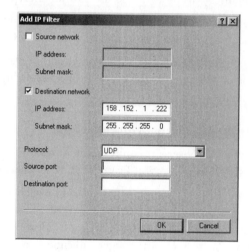

L2TP/IPSec Input and Output Filters

For an L2TP VPN connection, set the following filters:

- An input filter with the Destination Network check box selected, the IP address of the network interface, the subnet mask 255.255.255.255, the protocol UDP, the source port 500, and the destination port 500.

- An input filter with the Destination Network check box selected, the IP address of the network interface, the subnet mask 255.255.255.255, the protocol UDP, the source port 1701, and the destination port 1701.

In the Input Filters dialog box, select the "Drop all packets except those that meet the criteria below" option.

Then set the following output filters from the Output Filters dialog box:

- An output filter with the Source Network check box selected, the IP address of the network interface, the subnet mask 255.255.255.255, the protocol UDP, the source port 500, and the destination port 500.

- An output filter with the Source Network check box selected, the IP address of the network interface, the subnet mask 255.255.255.255, the protocol UDP, the source port 1701, and the destination port 1701.

In the Output Filters dialog box, select the "Drop all packets except those that meet the criteria below" option button.

PPTP Input and Output Filters

For a PPTP VPN connection, set the following input filters:

- An input filter with the Destination Network check box selected, the IP address of the network interface, the subnet mask 255.255.255.255, the protocol Other, and the value 47 in the Protocol Number box. (This box appears when you choose Other in the Protocol drop-down list.)

- An input filter with the Destination Network check box selected, the IP address of the network interface, the subnet mask 255.255.255.255, the protocol TCP, the source port 0, and the destination port 1723.

- If your PPTP VPN server also acts as a PPTP VPN client, add a third input filter with the Destination Network check box selected, the IP address of the network interface, the subnet mask 255.255.255.255, the protocol TCP (Established), the source port 1723, and the destination port 0.

In the Input Filters dialog box, select the "Drop all packets except those that meet the criteria below" option button.

Then set the following output filters from the Output Filters dialog box:

- An output filter with the Source Network check box selected, the IP address of the network interface, the subnet mask 255.255.255.255, the protocol Other, and the value 47 in the Protocol Number box.

- An output filter with the Source Network check box selected, the IP address of the network interface, the subnet mask 255.255.255.255, the protocol TCP, the source port 1723, and the destination port 0.

- If your PPTP VPN server also acts as a PPTP VPN client, add a third output filter with the Source Network check box selected, the IP address of the network interface, the subnet mask 255.255.255.255, the protocol TCP (Established), the source port 0, and the destination port 1723.

In the Output Filters dialog box, select the "Drop all packets except those that meet the criteria below" option button.

Using Internal VPN Connections for Sensitive Data

As mentioned earlier in the chapter, while VPN connections are typically used for remote access, they can be used on an internal network as well—for example, to cordon off servers that contain ultra-sensitive data from the casual depredations of regular users. Issue the appropriate permissions to the authorized users so that they can establish VPN connections to the hidden servers across the LAN. You then get the full security that VPN connections offer together with full LAN speeds (minus the overhead of encryption).

Index

Note to the Reader: Throughout this index **boldfaced** page numbers indicate primary discussions of a topic. *Italicized* page numbers indicate illustrations.

F

G

H

Q

U

TELL US WHAT YOU THINK!

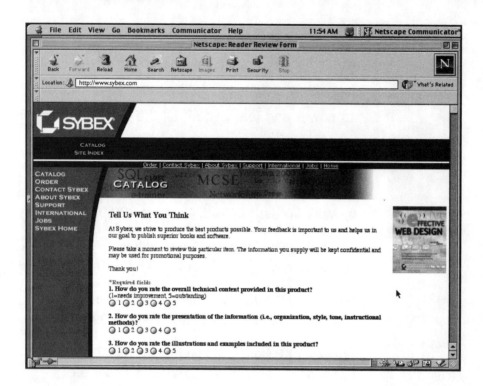

Your feedback is critical to our efforts to provide you with the best books and software on the market. Tell us what you think about the products you've purchased. It's simple:

1. Visit the Sybex website
2. Go to the product page
3. Click on **Submit a Review**
4. Fill out the questionnaire and comments
5. Click **Submit**

With your feedback, we can continue to publish the highest quality computer books and software products that today's busy IT professionals deserve.

www.sybex.com

SYBEX Inc. • 1151 Marina Village Parkway, Alameda, CA 94501 • 510-523-8233

About the CD

The CD included with this book contains three additional chapters and over thirty freeware and evaluation versions of commercial software that will help you get the most from Windows XP.

Additional Chapters

Three bonus chapters on the CD cover the following topics:

Scheduling Applications and Events   This chapter discusses how to use the Scheduled Tasks folder, the at and schtasks commands, the WinAT program, and third-party tools to schedule applications and events.

Command History and Doskey   This chapter covers some of the tools behind the command line in Windows XP, including command history and its options, as well as Doskey, used for creating and running macros both from the command console and within supporting applications.

Batch Programming   This chapter explains the basic steps and rules of batch file programming, how to create and run your own batch files (and why you might find that helpful to do), and some advanced techniques for running more than one or a collection of commands from your batch files.

Security Configuration Tools   This chapter covers the Windows XP tools and templates that allow you to easily tweak settings to fit the particular security needs of your setup.

Software Utilities

The CD includes over thirty utilities in a variety of categories:

FTP Utilities   Internet Neighborhood, Crystal FTP Pro, BulletProof FTP, BulletProof FTP Server

Security Utilities   ZoneAlarm, WinRoute, Personal Firewall

System Tuning Utilities   Registry Toolkit, X-Setup, Tweak-XP

System Diagnostic Utilities   TechFacts, VBSys, BlueSave

Data Management and Recovery Utilities   Drive Image, DeployCenter, NFTS for Win98, PartitionMagic

Cross-Platform and Connectivity Utilities   Visual Route, Absolute Telnet SSH, Exceed, Virtual Network Computing, Virtual PC

Servers and Mail Utilities   EFS, Mail Server Pro, Blat, VPOP3 Email Server, Sambar Server Pro, MailServer

Help and Authoring Utilities   Windows Help Designer/HTML Edition, RoboHelp, Help and Manual, HelpKit, Help Development Studio